2006

Song Writer's Market

Ian Bessler, Editor
Michael Schweer, Assistant Editor

WRITER'S DIGEST BOOKS
CINCINNATI, OH

If you would like to be considered for a listing in the next edition of *Songwriter's Market*, send a SASE (or SAE and IRC) with your request for a questionnaire to *Songwriter's Market—QR*, 4700 East Galbraith Road, Cincinnati OH 45236. Please indicate in which section you would like to be included.

Managing Editor, Writer's Digest Annual Books: Alice Pope
Supervisory Editor, Writer's Digest Market Books: Donna Poehner

Writer's Digest Books website: www.writersdigest.com
Writer's Market website: www.writersmarket.com

International Standard Serial Number 0161-5971
International Standard Book Number 1-58297-398-9

Cover design by Kelly Kofron
Interior design by Clare Finney
Production coordinated by Robin Richie

Attention Booksellers: This is an annual directory of F + W Publications. Return deadline for this edition is December 31, 2006.

Contents

ADVANCED ARTICLES

MARKETS

RESOURCES

INDEXES

From the Editor

In today's songwriting world, the "pure" songwriters—those who only write and do not perform their own songs—are an increasingly rare breed. Many songwriters have realized the importance of being able to sing and perform their own material (or ally with a skilled performer) to "diversify" their career prospects.

On the other hand, many bands and singer-songwriters may write their own material, but they may not have "songwriter" at the top of the list when they describe themselves. They may think of record deals and album sales first, and not pay attention to music publishing.

If this sounds like you, then it's time to start thinking of yourself as a songwriter, *because the real money is made in songwriting and publishing*. Songwriters long ago organized and pushed for their rights, and there is a system in place to benefit songwriters financially. Performers who write can take advantage of this to diversify *their* careers.

To begin, turn to **Getting Started** on page 2, and **Music Biz Basics** on page 28. These sections give you the essential basics on music publishing and how to use this book.

If you're interested in chasing down a label contract, **Music Publishing Tips for Recording Artists**, by producer Scott Mathews (page 49) shows how music publishing knowledge can help you negotiate a good contract. **The Power of the Re-Mix**, by producer Blake Althen (with Paula Bellenoit) of Human Factor Productions (page 56), shows independent musicians how dance re-mixes can bring extra exposure.

For inspiration and advice, we have interviews with Woodstock legend **Richie Havens (page 40)** and singer-songwriter Jonatha Brooke (page 44). Also take a look at the **Editor's Report on the Mid-Atlantic Song Contest** winners on page 79 for inspirational profiles of working songwriters building their careers one step at a time.

So, step in, take a look around, absorb as much information as you can, and use it to chart your course. Bon voyage!

Ian C. Bessler
songmarket@fwpubs.com
www.writersdigest.com

P.S. Be on the lookout in fall 2006 for *Instant Songwriting with the Piano*, by Charles and Colleen Segal, a new songwriting book from Writer's Digest Books.

Quick-Start

New to Songwriter's Market?

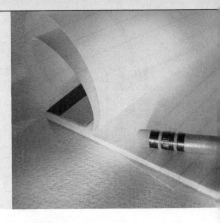

This "Quick-Start" guide is designed to lay it out for you step by step. Each step shows you where to find the information you need in *Songwriter's Market*, from basic to more advanced.

Use this as guide to launch your songwriting career. Look over the whole list once, then go back and read each article completely. They will show you new facets of the music industry and reinforce what you already know. Good luck!

1. Join a songwriting organization. Connecting with other songwriters and learning from their experience will save you a lot of trouble starting out. Organizations help you learn about the music business, polish your songwriting and help you make contacts who can take you to the next level.

- Organizations, page 323

2. Learn about the music business. Protect yourself with knowledge. Learn how money is really made in the music business and avoid scams. Go to songwriting workshops and music conferences.

- How Do I Avoid the Rip-Offs?, page 19
- Royalties: Where Does the Money Come From?, page 28
- What About Copyright?, page 32
- What About Contracts?, page 36
- Career Songwriting: What Should I Know?, page 34
- Music Publishing Tips for Recording Artists, page 49
- Please Play This Song on the Radio, page 75
- Workshops & Conferences, page 346
- Publications of Interest, page 365

3. Develop your songwriting skill. Get letterhead, have your songs critiqued, make contacts and subscribe to songwriting/music magazines. Start building your catalog of songs. If you also perform, start developing your performance skills and build a following.

- Commercial Songwriting: Creative Secrets for Success, page 66
- Organizations, page 323
- Workshops & Conferences, page 346
- Publications of Interest, page 365
- Websites of Interest, page 372

4. Choose your best three songs and make a demo recording.

- Demo Recordings: What Should I Know?, page 13
- What About Copyright?, page 32

5. Learn how to spot rip-offs.
- How Do I Avoid the Rip-Offs?, page 19
- What About Copyright?, page 32
- What About Contracts?, page 36

6. Decide which arm(s) of the music business you will submit your songs to.
- Where Should I Send My Songs?, page 9
- Submission Strategies, page 23
- Music Publishers Section Introduction, page 84
- Record Companies Section Introduction, page 141
- Record Producers Section Introduction, page 194
- Managers & Booking Agents Section Introduction, page 224
- Advertising, Audiovisual & Commercial Music Firms Section Introduction, page 262
- Contests & Awards Section Introduction, page 310

7. Find companies open to your style of music and level of experience or use your contacts at Organizations and Performing Rights Organizations (ASCAP, BMI, SESAC) to get a referral and permission to submit. Be picky about where you send your material. Do not waste your time and effort submitting to every company listed in this book without regard to whether they want your style of music.
- Where Should I Send My Songs, page 9
- Openness to Submissions Index, page 411
- Category Indexes, page 383

8. Locate companies in your area.
- Geographic Index, page 421

9. Read the listings and decide which companies to submit to and whether they are appropriate for you (pay special attention to the **Music** subhead and also the royalty percentage they pay). Do additional research through trade publications, the Internet and other songwriters.
- Markets, beginning on page 84
- Publications of Interest, page 365
- Websites of Interest, page 372

10. Find out how to submit. Read information under the How to Contact subhead of each listing. Learn the etiquette involved in contacting companies. Learn how to package your demo in a professional way. Learn how to avoid getting ripped off.
- *Songwriter's Market*: How Do I Use It?, page 7
- How Do I Submit My Demo?, page 15
- Quiz: Are You Professional?, page 26
- How Do I Avoid the Rip-Offs?, page 19

11. Call the companies and verify their submission policy has not changed. Also check to make sure the contact person is still there.

12. Send your submission package according to each company's directions. Read the information under the How to Contact subhead in each listing again.
- Quiz: Are You Professional?, page 26
- How Do I Submit My Demo?, page 15
- What About Copyright?, page 32

13. Decide whether to sign with a company.
- Royalties: Where Does the Money Come From?, page 28
- How Do I Avoid the Rip-Offs?, page 19

14. Have an entertainment attorney look over any contract before you sign.
- What About Contracts?, page 36
- How Do I Avoid the Rip-Offs?, page 19

Getting Started

15. After signing, how do you get paid?

Songwriter's Market

How Is It Put Together?

The following articles are for songwriters who have never used this book before and are new to the music industry. This is all important information so don't skip straight to the listings. There's a lot to learn, but it's been rewritten for clarity and simplicity. Taking a little time now to educate yourself can save you from having to learn a lot of things the hard way.

How do I use *Songwriter's Market*?

First, take a minute to get to know the book and how it's put together. Here's a rundown of *what* is in the book:

What you'll find inside this book

Songwriter's Market is a big book and can seem overwhelming at first. But don't worry, it's not that tough to find your way around the book. Here's a quick look at how it's put together.

The book has six basic parts:

1. Articles about the music business and songwriting craft
2. Introductions to each section of listings
3. Listings of music companies and organizations
4. Insider Reports
5. Indexes
6. Lists of websites, magazines, books, and other useful extras

Music biz and songwriting articles

These range from articles on the basics of how the music business works—the essentials, laid out in plain English, of how songwriters and artists make money and advance their careers—to articles with more detail and depth on business and creativity, written by music industry insiders with many years of experience in the trenches.

Section intros and listings—the "meat" of the book

There are 11 sections in the book, from Music Publishers and Record Companies to Contests & Awards. Each section begins with an introduction detailing how the different types of companies function—what part of the music industry they work in, how they make money, and what you need to think about when approaching them with your music.

The listings are the heart of *Songwriter's Market*. They are the names, addresses and contact information of music biz companies looking for songs and artists, as well as descriptions of the types of music they are looking for.

What are Insider Reports?

Insider Reports are interviews with songwriters, performers and music industry honchos working at all levels in the music business. By showing how others have achieved success, you learn by example. By peeking behind the curtain of record labels, music publishers and others, you understand more about how the industry works. You learn how the businessmen think, and how to work that to your advantage. Reading them gives you an important edge over songwriters and performers who don't. Insider Reports are scattered throughout the listings and are listed in the Table of Contents.

Songwriter's Market

How Do I Use It?

The quick answer is that you should use the indexes to find companies who are interested in your type of music, then read the listings for details on how they want the music submitted. For support and help of all sorts, join a songwriting or other music industry association. Become a student of the music industry. (Also see the Quick-Start guide on page 2.)

How does *Songwriter's Market* "work"?

The listings in *Songwriter's Market* are packed with a lot of information. It can be intimidating at first, but they are put together in a structured way to make them easy to work with. Take a few minutes to get used to how the listings are organized, and you'll have it down in no time. For more detailed information about how the listings are put together, skip ahead to Where Should I Send My Songs? on page 9.

What are the general rules for working with listings?

Look at A Sample Listing Decoded on page 11 for an example of how a typical listing is put together. The following are general rules about how to use the listings.

1. **Read the entire listing** to decide whether to submit your music! Do not use this book as a mass mailing list! If you blindly mail out demos by the hundreds, you'll waste a lot of money on postage, annoy a lot of people, and your demos will wind up in the trash.
2. **Pay close attention to the "Music" section in each listing.** This will tell you what kind of music the company is looking for. If they want rockabilly only and you write heavy metal, don't submit.
3. **Pay close attention to submission instructions** shown under "How to Contact" and follow them to the letter. A lot of listings are very particular about how they want submissions packaged. Pay close attention. If you do not follow their instructions, they will probably throw your submission in the garbage. You have been warned! If you are confused about their directions, call, e-mail or write to the company for clarification.
4. **If in doubt, contact the company for permission to submit.** This is a good general rule. Many companies don't mind if you send an unsolicited submission, but some will want you to get special prior permission from them. Contacting a company first is also a good way to find out their latest music needs. This is also a chance to briefly make contact on a personal level.
5. **Be courteous, be efficient** and always have a purpose to your personal contact—

DO NOT WASTE THEIR TIME! If you call, always have a reason for making contact—permission to submit, checking on guidelines, following up on a demo, etc. These are solid reasons to make personal contact, but once you have their attention do not wear out your welcome! Always be polite! Always have an upbeat, pleasant attitude when you call (even if you are feeling frustrated or uptight at that particular moment)!

6. **Check for a preferred contact.** A lot of listings have a designated contact person shown after a bolded "**Contact**" in the heading. This is the person you should contact with questions or address you're submission to.

7. **Read the "Tips" section.** This part of the listing provides extra information on how to submit or what it might be like to work with the company.

This is just the beginning. For more detailed information about the listings, see Where Should I Send My Songs? on page 9 and the sidebar with the sample listing called A Sample Listing Decoded on page 11. Also see Quiz: Are You Professional? on page 26.

Frequently Asked Questions

1 **How do these companies get listed in the book anyway?** No company pays to be included—all listings are free. The listings come from a combination of research the editor does on the music industry and questionnaires requested by companies who want to be listed (many of them contact us to be included). All questionnaires are screened for known sharks and to make sure they meet our requirements (see How Do I Avoid the Rip-Offs? on page 19 for details of what makes us reject or remove a listing).

2 **Why aren't other companies I know about listed in the book?** We may have sent them a questionnaire, but they did not return it, were removed for complaints, went out of business, specifically asked not to be listed, could not be contacted for an update, etc.

3 **What's the deal with companies that don't take unsolicited submissions?** In the interest of completeness, the editor will sometimes include listings of crucial music companies he thinks you should be aware of. Major labels such as Capitol Records and Warner Bros. fall under this category. You want to at least have some idea of what their policies are, don't you? If a company is closed to unsolicited submissions, you can do either of two things: 1) don't submit to them; or 2) find a way around the roadblock by establishing a relationship or finding a backdoor of some kind (charming them on the phone, through managers, producers, artists, entertainment attorneys, or the fabled Seven Degrees of Separation—i.e. networking like crazy).

4 **A company said in their listing they take unsolicited submissions. My demo came back unopened. What happened?** Some companies needs change rapidly and may have changed since we contacted them for this edition of the book. This is another reason why it's often a good idea to contact a company before submitting.

Where Should I Send My Songs?

It depends a lot on whether you write mainly for yourself as a performer, or if you only write and want someone else to pick up your song for their recording (usually the case in country music, for example). *Are you mainly a performing songwriter or a non-performing songwriter?* This is important is figuring out what kind of companies to contact, as well as how you contact them. (For more detail, skip to Submission Strategies on page 23.)

What if I'm a non-performing songwriter?

Many well-known songwriters are not performers in their own right. Some are not skilled instrumentalists or singers, but they understand melody, lyrics and harmony and how they go together. They can write great songs, but they need someone else to bring it to life through skilled musicianship. A non-performing songwriter will usually approach music publishers first for access to artists looking for songs, as well as artists' managers, their producers and their record companies. On the flip side, many incredibly talented musicians can't write to save their lives and need someone else to provide them with good songs to perform. (For more details on the different types of companies and the roles they play for performing songwriters, see the section introductions for Music Publishers on page 84, Record companies on page 141, Record Producers on page 194, and Managers & Booking Agents on page 262. Also see Submission Strategies on page 23.)

What if I am a performing songwriter?

Many famous songwriters are also famous as performers. They are skilled interpreters of their own material, and they also know how to write to their own particular talents as musicians (which can often be quirky and unique to them). In this case, their intention is also usually to sell themselves as a performer in hopes of recording and releasing an album, or they have an album and want to find gigs and people who can help guide their careers. They will usually approach record companies or record producers first, on the basis of recording an album. For gigs and career guidance, they talk to booking agents and managers.

A smaller number also approach publishers in hopes of getting others to perform their songs, much like non-performing songwriters. Some music publishers in recent years have also taken on the role of developing artists as both songwriters and performers, or are connected to a major record label, so performing songwriters might go to them for these reasons. (For more details on the different types of companies and the roles they play for performing songwriters, see the section introductions for Music Publishers on page 84, Record companies on page 141, Record Producers on page 194, and Managers & Booking Agents on page 262. Also see Submission Strategies on page 23.)

Getting Started

Types of Music Companies

- **Music Publishers**—evaluate songs for commercial potential, find artists to record them, finds other uses for the songs such as film or TV, collects income from songs, protects copyrights from infringement

- **Record Companies**—sign artists to their labels, finance recordings, promotion and touring, releases songs/albums to radio and TV

- **Record Producers**—works in the studio and records songs (independently or for a record company), may be affiliated with a particular artist, sometimes develop artists for record labels, locates or co-writes songs if an artist does not write their own

- **Managers & Booking Agents**—works with artists to manage their careers, finds gigs, locates songs to record if the artist does not write their own

How do I use *Songwriter's Market* to narrow my search?

Once you've identified whether you are primarily interested in getting others to perform your songs (non-performing songwriter) or you perform your own songs and want a record deal, etc., there are several steps you can then take:

1. **Identify what kind of music company you wish to approach.** Based on whether you're a performing or non-performing songwriter, do you want to approach a music publisher for a publishing deal? Do you want to approach a record producer because you need somone to help you record an album in the studio? Maybe you want to approach a producer in hopes that an act he's producing needs songs to complete their album. Also see Submission Strategies on page 23 and the Section Introductions for Music Publishers on page 84, Record companies on page 141, Record Producers on page 194, and Managers & Booking Agents on page 224.

2. **Check for companies based on location.** Maybe you need a manager located close by. Maybe you need to find as many Nashville-based companies as you can because you write country and most country publishers are in Nashville. In this case start with the Geographic Index on page 421. You can also tell Canadian and Foreign listings by the icons in the listing (see A Sample Listing Decoded below and on page 11).

3. **Look for companies based on the type of music they want.** Some companies want country. Some record labels want only punk rock. Check the Category Indexes on page 383 for a list of music companies broken down by the type of music they are interested in.

4. **Look for companies based on how open they are to beginners.** Some companies are more open than others to beginning artists and songwriters. Maybe you are a beginner and it would help to approach these companies first. Some music publishers are hoping to find that wild card hit song and don't care if it comes from an unknown writer. Maybe you are just starting out looking for gigs or record deals, and you need a manager willing to help build your band's career from the ground up. Check the Openness to Submissions Index on page 411.

For more information on how to read the listings, see A Sample Listing Decoded on page 11.

Getting Started

A SAMPLE LISTING DECODED
What do the little symbols at the beginning of the listing mean?

Those are called "icons," and they give you quick information about a listing with one glance. Here is a list of the icons and what they mean:

Openness to submissions

means the company is open to beginners' submissions, regardless of past success

means the company is mostly interested in previously published songwriters/well-established acts*, but will consider beginners

these companies do not want submissions from beginners, only from previously published songwriters/well-established* acts

companies with this icon only accept material referred by a reputable industry source**

*   Well-established acts are those with a following, permanent gigs or previous record deal

** Reputable industry sources include managers, entertainment attorneys, performing rights organizations, etc.

Other icons

means the listing is Canadian

means the listing is based overseas (Europe, Britain, Australia, etc.)

indicates a listing is new to this edition

means there has been a change in the contact information: contact name, phone number, fax, e-mail or website

is for companies who have won an industry award of some sort

shows a company places songs in films or television shows (excluding commercials)

EASY-TO-USE
REFERENCE
ICONS

DETAILED
SUBMISSION
GUIDELINES

INSIDER
ADVICE

TERMS OF
AGREEMENT

WHAT THEY'RE
LOOKING FOR

METAL BLADE RECORDS
2828 Cochran St., Suite 302, Simi Valley CA 93065. (805)522-9111. Fax: (805)522-9380. E-mail: metalblade@metalblade.com. Website: www.metalblade.com. Record company. Estab. 1982. Releases 20 LPs, 2 EPs and 20 CDs/year. Pays negotiable royalty to artists on contract. **How to Contact** Submit demo CD by mail. Unsolicited submissions are OK. CD with 3 songs. Does not return material. Responds in 3 months.
Music Mostly **heavy metal** and **industrial**; also **hardcore, gothic** and **noise.** Released "Gallery of Suicide," recorded by Cannibal Corpse; "Voo Doo," recorded by King Diamond; and "A Pleasant Shade of Gray," recorded by Fates Warning, all on Metal Blade Records. Other artists include As I Lay Dying, The Red Chord, The Black Dahlia Murder, and Unearth.
Tips "Metal Blade is known throughout the underground for quality metal-oriented acts."

Getting Started

Additional Resources

For More Info

Songwriter's Market lists music publishers, record companies, producers and managers (as well as advertising firms, play producers and classical performing arts organizations) along with specifications on how to submit your material to each. If you can't find a certain person or company you're interested in, there are other sources of information you can try.

The Recording Industry Sourcebook, an annual directory published by Norris-Whitney Communications, lists record companies, music publishers, producers and managers, as well as attorneys, publicity firms, media, manufacturers, distributors and recording studios around the U.S. Trade publications such as *Billboard* or *Variety*, available at most local libraries and bookstores, are great sources for up-to-date information. These periodicals list new companies as well as the artists, labels, producers and publishers for each song on the charts.

CD booklets and cassette j-cards can also be valuable sources of information, providing the name of the record company, publisher, producer and usually the manager of an artist or group. Use your imagination in your research and be creative—any contacts you make in the industry can only help your career as a songwriter. See Publications of Interest on page 365.

Demo Recordings

What Should I Know?

What is a "demo"?

The demo, shorthand for *demonstration recording*, is the most important part of your submission package. They are meant to give music industry professionals a way to hear all the elements of your song as clearly as possible so they can decide if it has commercial potential.

Should I send a cassette or a CD?

More and more music industry people want CDs, although the cassette is still commonly accepted. A few companies want demos sent on CD only. It's getting cheaper and easier all the time to burn recordings onto CDR ("CD-Recordable"), so it is worth the investment to buy a burner or borrow one. Other formats such as DAT ("Digital Audio Tape") are rarely requested.

What should I send if I'm seeking management?

Some companies want a video of an act performing their songs. Most want VHS format videocassettes. A few ask for video on DVD. Check with the companies for specific requirements.

How many songs should I send, and in what order and length?

Most music industry people agree that three songs is enough. Most music professionals are short on time, and if you can't catch their attention in three songs, your songs probably don't have hit potential. Also, put three *complete songs* on your demo, not just snippets. Make sure to put your best, most commercial song first. An up-tempo number is usually best. If you send a cassette, *put all the songs on one side of the cassette and cue the tape to the beginning of the first song so no time is wasted fast-forwarding or rewinding.*

Should I sing my own songs on my demo?

If you can't sing well, you may want to find someone who can. There are many places to check for singers and musicians, including songwriters organizations, music stores and songwriting magazines. Some aspiring professional singers will sing on demos in exchange for a copy they can use as a demo to showcase their singing.

Should I use a professional demo service?

Many songwriters find professional demo services convenient if they don't have time or the resources to put together musicians on their own. For a fee, a demo service will produce your songs in their studio using in-house singers and musicians (this is pretty common in

Nashville). Many of these advertise in music magazines, songwriting newsletters and bulletin boards at music stores. Make sure to hear samples of work they've done in the past. Some are mail-order businesses—you send a rough tape of your song or the sheet music, and they produce and record a demo within a month or two. Be sure you find a service that will let you have some control over how the demo is produced, and tell them exactly how you want your song to sound. As with studios, shop around for a service that fits your needs and budget. (Some will charge as low as $300 for three songs, while others may go as high as $3,000 and boast a high-quality sound—shop around and use your best judgment!)

Should I buy equipment and record demos myself?

If you have the drive and focus to learn good recording technique, yes. If not, it might be easier to have someone else do it. Digital multi-track recorders are now easily available and within reasonable financial reach of many people. For performing songwriters in search of record deals, the actual sound of their recordings can often be an important part of their artistic concept. Having the "means of production" within their grasp can be crucial to artists pursuing the independent route. But, if you don't know how to use the equipment, it may be better to go into a professional studio.

How elaborate and full should the demo production be if I'm a non-performing songwriter?

Many companies in *Songwriter's Market* tell you what they prefer. If in doubt, contact them and ask. In general, country songs and pop ballads can often be demoed with just a vocal plus guitar or piano, although many songwriters in those genres still prefer to get a more complete recording with drums, guitars and other backing instruments. Up-tempo pop, rock and dance demos usually need a more full production.

What kind of production do I need if I'm a performing songwriter?

If you are a band or artist looking for a record deal, you will need a demo that is as fully produced as possible. Many singer/songwriters record their demos as if they were going to be released as an album. That way, if they don't get a deal, they can still release it on their own. Professionally pressed CDs are also now easily within reach of performing songwriters, and many companies offer graphic design services for a professional-looking product.

How Do I Submit My Demo?

Y ou have three basic options for submitting your songs: submitting by mail, submitting in person and submitting over the Internet (the newest and least widely accepted option at this time).

SUBMITTING BY MAIL

Should I call, write or e-mail first to ask for permission or submission requirements?

This is always a good idea, and many companies ask you to contact them first. If you call, be polite, brief and specific. If you send a letter, make sure it is typed and to the point. Include a typed SASE they can use to reply. If you send an e-mail, again be professional and to the point. Proofread your message before you send it, and then be patient. Give them some time to reply. Do not send out mass e-mails or otherwise spam their e-mail account.

What do I send with my demo?

Most companies have specific requirements, but here are some general pointers:

- Read the listing carefully and submit *exactly* what they ask for, in the exact way they describe. It's also a good idea to call first, just in case they've changed their submission policies.
- Listen to each demo to make sure they sound right and are in the right order (see Demo Recordings: What Should I Know? on page 13).
- If you use cassettes, make sure they are cued up to the beginning of the first song.
- Enclose a *brief*, typed cover letter to introduce yourself. Tell them what songs you are sending and why you are sending them. If you are pitching your songs to a particular artist, say so in the letter. I you are an artist/songwriter looking for a record deal, you should say so. Be specific.
- Include *typed* lyric sheets or lead sheets, if requested. Make sure your name, address and phone number are on each sheet.
- Neatly label each tape with your name, address and phone number, along with the names of the songs in the order they appear on the tape.
- Include a SASE with sufficient postage and large enough to return all your materials. **Warning: Many companies do not return materials, so read each listing carefully!**
- If you submit to companies in other countries, include a self-addressed envelope (SAE) and International Reply Coupon (IRC), available at most post offices. Make sure the envelope is large enough to return all of your materials.
- Pack everything neatly. Neatly type or write the company's address and your return

Submission Mailing Pointers

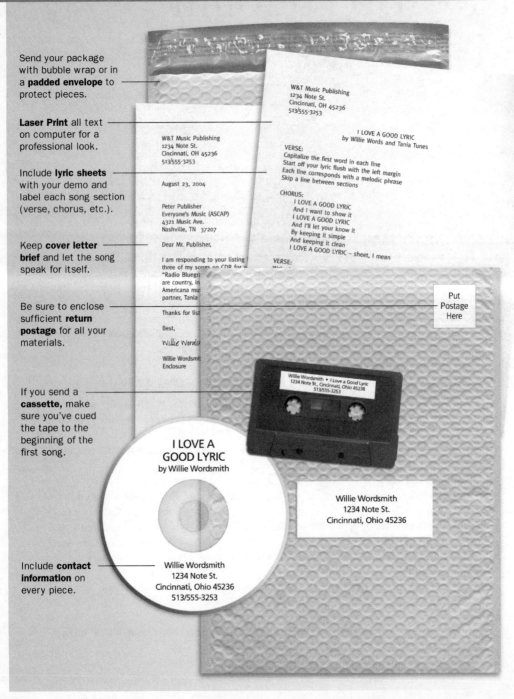

Send your package with bubble wrap or in a **padded envelope** to protect pieces.

Laser Print all text on computer for a professional look.

Include **lyric sheets** with your demo and label each song section (verse, chorus, etc.).

Keep **cover letter brief** and let the song speak for itself.

Be sure to enclose sufficient **return postage** for all your materials.

If you send a **cassette,** make sure you've cued the tape to the beginning of the first song.

Include **contact information** on every piece.

W&T Music Publishing
1234 Note St.
Cincinnati, OH 45236
513/555-3253

August 23, 2004

Peter Publisher
Everyone's Music (ASCAP)
4321 Music Ave.
Nashville, TN 37207

Dear Mr. Publisher,

I am responding to your listing
three of my songs on CDR for
"Radio Bluegra
are country, in
Americana mu
partner, Tania

Thanks for list

Best,

Willie Words

Willie Wordsmit
Enclosure

W&T Music Publishing
1234 Note St.
Cincinnati, OH 45236
513/555-3253

I LOVE A GOOD LYRIC
by Willie Words and Tania Tunes

VERSE:
Capitalize the first word in each line
Start off your lyric flush with the left margin
Each line corresponds with a melodic phrase
Skip a line between sections

CHORUS:
I LOVE A GOOD LYRIC
And I want to show it
I LOVE A GOOD LYRIC
And I'll let your know it
By keeping it simple
And keeping it clean
I LOVE A GOOD LYRIC – sheet, I mean

VERSE:

Put
Postage
Here

Willie Wordsmith • I Love a Good Lyric
1234 Note St., Cincinnati, Ohio 45236
513/555-3253

I LOVE A
GOOD LYRIC
by Willie Wordsmith

Willie Wordsmith
1234 Note St.
Cincinnati, Ohio 45236
513/555-3253

Willie Wordsmith
1234 Note St.
Cincinnati, Ohio 45236

address so they are clearly visible. Your package is the first impression a company has of you and your songs, so neatness counts!

- Mail first class. Stamp or write "First Class Mail" on the package and the SASE you enclose.
- **Do not use registered or certified mail unless requested!** Most companies will not accept or open demos sent by registered or certified mail for fear of lawsuits.
- Keep records of the dates, songs and companies you submit to.

Is it OK to send demos to more than one person or company at a time?

It is usually acceptable to make simultaneous submissions. One exception is when a publisher, artist or other industry professional asks to put your song "on hold."

What does it mean when a song is "on hold"?

This means they intend to record the song and don't want you to give the song to anyone else. This is not a guarantee, though. Your song may eventually be returned to you, even if it's been on hold for months. Or it may be recorded and included on the album. If either of these happens, you are free to pitch your song to other people again.

How can I protect myself from my song being put "on hold" indefinitely?

You can, and should, protect yourself. Establish a deadline for the person who asks for the hold (for example, "You can put my song on hold for [number of] months."), or modify the hold to specify you will still pitch the song to others but won't sign another deal without allowing the person with the song on hold to make you an offer. Once you sign a contract with a publisher, they have exclusive rights to your song and you may not pitch it to other would-be publishers.

SUBMITTING IN PERSON

Is a visit to New York, Nashville or Los Angeles to submit in person a good idea?

A trip to one of the major music hubs can be valuable if you are organized and prepared to make the most of it. You should have specific goals and set up appointments before you go. Some industry professionals are difficult to see and may not feel meeting out-of-town writers is a high priority. Others are more open and even encourage face-to-face meetings. By taking the time to travel, organize and schedule meetings, you can appear more professional than songwriters who submit blindly through the mail.

What should I take?

Take several copies of your demo and typed lyric sheets of each of your songs. More than one company you visit may ask you to leave a copy for them to review. You can expect occasionally to find a person has cancelled an appointment, but want you to leave a copy of your songs so they may listen and contact you later. (Never give someone the only or last copy of your demo if you absolutely want it returned, though.)

Where should I network while visiting?

Coordinate your trip with a music conference or make plans to visit ASCAP, BMI or SESAC offices while you are there. For example, the South by Southwest Music Conference in Austin and the NSAI Spring Symposium often feature demo listening sessions, where industry professionals listen to demos submitted by songwriters attending the seminar. ASCAP, BMI and SESAC also sometimes sponsor seminars or allow aspiring songwriters to make appointments with counselors who can give them solid advice.

How do I deal with rejection?

Many good songs have been rejected simply because they were not what the publisher or record company was looking for at that particular point. Do not take it personally. If few people like your songs, it does not mean they are not good. On the other hand, if you have a clear vision for what your particular songs are trying to get across, specific comments can also teach you a lot about whether your concept is coming across as you intended. If you hear the same criticisms of your songs over and over—for instance, the feel of the melody isn't right or the lyrics need work—give the advice serious thought. Listen carefully and use what the reviewers say constructively to improve your songs.

SUBMITTING OVER THE INTERNET
Is it OK to submit over the Internet?

It can be done, but it's not yet widely accepted. There can still be problems with audio file formats. Although e-mail is more common now if you look through the listings in *Songwriter's Market*, not all music companies are necessarily equipped with computers or Internet access sufficient to make the process easy. But it shows a lot of promise for the future. Web-based companies like Tonos.com or TAXI, among many others are making an effort to connect songwriters and industry professionals over the Internet. The Internet is proving important for networking. Tunesmith.net has extensive bulletin boards and allow members to post audio files of songs for critique. Stay tuned for future developments.

If I want to try submitting over the Internet, what should I do?

First, send an e-mail to confirm whether a music company is equipped to stream or download audio files properly (whether mp3 or real audio, etc.). If they do accept demos online, one strategy becoming common is build a website with audio files that can be streamed or down-loaded. Then, when you have permission, send an e-mail with links to that website or to particular songs. All they have to do is click on the link and it launches their web browser to the appropriate page. Do not try to send mp3s or other files as attachments. They are often too large for the free online e-mail accounts people commonly use, and they may be mistakenly erased as potential viruses.

How Do I Avoid the Rip-Offs?

The music industry has its share of dishonest, greedy people who will try to rip you off by appealing to your ambition, by stroking your ego or by claiming special powers to make you successful—for a price, of course. Most of them use similar methods, and you can prevent a lot of heartbreak by learning to spot them and stay away.

What is a "song shark"?

"Song sharks," as they're called, prey on beginners—songwriters unfamiliar with how the music industry works and what the ethical standards are. Two general signs of a song shark are:

- Song sharks will take *any* songs—quality doesn't count.
- They're not concerned with future royalties, since they get their money up front from songwriters who think they're getting a great deal.

What are some of the more blatant rip-offs?

A request for money up front is the most common element. Song sharks may ask for money in the form of submission fees, an outright offer to publish your song for a fee or an offer to re-record your demo for a sometimes hefty price (with the implication that they will make your song wildly successful if you only pay to have it re-demoed in *their studio*). There are many variations on this theme.

If You Write Lyrics, But Not Music

- **You must find a collaborator.** The music business is looking for the complete package: music plus lyrics. If you don't write music, find a collaborator who does. The best way to find a collaborator is through songwriting organizations. Check the Organizations section (page 323) for songwriting groups near you.

- **Don't get ripped-off.** "Music mills" advertise in the back of magazines or solicit you through the mail. For a fee they will set your lyrics or poems to music. The rip-off is that they may use the same melody for hundreds of lyrics and poems, whether it sounds good or not. Publishers recognize one of these melodies as soon as they hear it.

Here is a list of rules that can help you avoid a lot of scams:

- **DO NOT SELL YOUR SONGS OUTRIGHT!** It's unethical for anyone to offer such a proposition. If your song becomes successful after you've sold it outright, you will never get royalties for it.
- **Never pay any sort of "submission fees," "review fees," "service fees," "filing fees," etc.** Reputable companies review material free of charge. If you encounter a company in this book who charges to submit, report them to the editor. If a company charges "only" $15 to submit your song, consider this: *if "only" 100 songwriters pay the $15, this company has made an extra $1,500 just for opening the mail!*
- **Never pay to have your songs published.** A reputable company interested in your songs assumes the responsibility and cost of promoting them, in hopes of realizing a profit once the songs are recorded and released. If they truly believe in your song, they will accept the costs involved.
- **Do not pay a company to pair you with a collaborator.** It's much better to contact a songwriting organization that offers collaboration services to their members.
- **Never pay to have your lyrics or poems set to music.** This is a classic rip-off. "Music mills"—for a price—may use the same melody for hundreds of lyrics and poems, whether it sounds good or not. Publishers recognize one of these melodies as soon as they hear it.
- **Avoid "pay-to-play" CD compilation deals.** It's totally unrealistic to expect this will open doors for you. These are mainly a money-maker for the music company. CDs are cheap to manufacture, so a company that charges $100 to include your recording on a CD is making a killing. They claim they send these CDs to radio stations, producers, etc., but they usually wind up in the trash or as drink coasters. Music industry professionals have no incentive to listen to them. Everybody on the CD paid to be included, so it's not like they were carefully screened for quality.
- **Avoid "songpluggers" who offer to "shop" your song for an upfront fee or retainer.** This practice is not appropriate for *Songwriter's Market* readers, many of whom are beginners and live away from major music centers like Nashville. Professional, established songwriters in Nashville are sometimes known to work on a fee basis with songpluggers they have gotten to know over many years, *but the practice is controversial even for professionals.* Also, the songpluggers used by established professionals are very selective about their clients and have their own reputation to uphold. Companies who offer you these services but barely know you or your work are to be avoided. Also, contracting a songplugger by long distance offers little or no accountability—they take your money and then you have no real way of knowing what they're doing on your behalf, if anything.
- **Avoid paying a fee up front to have a publisher make a demo of your song.** Some publishers may take demo expenses out of your future royalties (a negotiable contract point usually meant to avoid endless demo sessions), but avoid paying up front for demo costs for a song signed to a publisher.
- **No record company should ask you to pay them or an associated company to make a demo.** The job of a record company is to make records and decide which artists to sign *after* listening to demo submissions.
- **Read all contracts carefully before signing.** And don't sign any contract you're unsure about or that you don't fully understand. It is well worth paying an attorney for the time it takes him to review a contract if you can avoid a bad situation that may cost you thousands of dollars.
- **Before entering a songwriting contest, read the rules carefully.** Be sure what you're giving up in the way of entry fees, etc., is not more than what you stand to gain by

winning the contest. See the Contests & Awards section on page 310.

- **Verify any situation about an individual or company if you have any doubts at all.** Contact the company's Performing Rights Society—ASCAP, BMI, SESAC or SOCAN (in Canada). Check with the Better Business Bureau in the company's town, or contact the state attorney general's office. Contact professional organizations you're a member of and inquire about the reputation of the company.
- **If a record company or other company asks you to pay expenses up front, be careful.** Record producers commonly charge up front to produce an artist's album. Small indie labels sometimes ask a band to help with recording costs (but seek less control than a major label might). It's up to you to decide to whether or not it is a good idea. Talk to other artists who have signed similar contracts before you sign one yourself. Research companies to find out if they can deliver on their claims, and what kind of distribution they have. Visit their website, if they have one. Beware of any company that won't let you know what it has done in the past. If a company has had successes and good working relationships with artists, it should be happy to brag about them.

I noticed record producers charge to produce albums. Is this bad?

No. Just remember what your goals are. If you write songs, but do not sing or perform, you are looking for publishing opportunities with the producer instead of someone who can help you record an album or CD. If you are a performing artist or band, then you might be in the market to hire a producer, in which case you will most likely pay them up front (and possibly give them a share in royalties or publishing, depending on the specific deal you negotiate). For more information see the Record Producers section introduction on page 194 and Royalties: Where Does the Money Come From? on page 28.

How Do I File a Complaint?

Write to the *Songwriter's Market* editor at: 4700 E. Galbraith Rd., Cincinnati OH 45236. Include:

- A complete description of the situation, as best you can describe it.

- Copies of any materials a company may have sent you that we may keep on file.

If you encounter situations similar to any of the "song shark" scenarios described above, let us know about it.

Will it help me avoid rip-offs if I join a songwriting organization?

Yes. You will have access to a lot of good advice from a lot of experienced people. You will be able to research and compare notes, which will help you avoid a lot of pitfalls.

What should I know about contracts?

Negotiating a fair contract is important. You must protect yourself, and there are specific things you should look for in a contract (see What About Contracts? on page 36).

Are companies that offer demo services automatically bad?

No, but you are not obligated to make use of their services. Many music companies have their own or related recording studios, and with good recording equipment becoming so cheap and easy to use in recent years, a lot of them are struggling to stay afloat. This doesn't mean a company is necessarily trying to rip you off, but use your best judgment. In some cases, a company will submit a listing to *Songwriter's Market* for the wrong reasons—to pitch their demo services instead of finding songs to sign—in which case you should report them to the *Songwriter's Market* editor.

Submission Strategies

NON-PERFORMING SONGWRITERS

Here's a short list of avenues non-performing songwriters can pursue when submitting songs:

1. Submit to a music publisher. This is the obvious one. Look at the information under "Music" in the listing to see examples of a publisher's songs and the artists they've found cuts with. Do you recognize the songs? Have you heard of the artists? Who are the writers? Do they have cuts with artists you would like to get a song to?

2. Submit to a record company. Are the bands and artists on the record company's roster familiar? Do they tend to use outside songs on their albums? When pursuing this angle, it often helps to contact the record company first. Ask if they have a group or artist in development who needs material.

3. Submit to a record producer. Do the producer's credits in the listings show songs written by songwriters other than the artist? Does he produce name artists known for using outside material? Be aware that producers themselves often write with the artists, so your song might also be competing against the producer's songwriting.

4. Submit to an artist's manager. If an artist needs songs, their manager is a prime gateway for your song. Contact the manager and ask if he has an act in need of material.

5. Join a songwriting organization. Songwriting organizations are a good way to make contacts. You'll discover opportunities through the contacts you make that others might not hear about. Some organizations can put you in direct contact with publishers for song critique sessions. You can increase your chances of a hit by co-writing with other songwriters. Your songs will get better because of the feedback from other members.

6. Approach Performing Rights Organizations (PROs). PROs like ASCAP and BMI have songwriter counselors who can sometimes (if they think you're ready) give you a reference to a music company. This is one of the favored routes to success in the Nashville music scene.

PERFORMING SONGWRITERS

This is a bit more complicated, because there are a lot of different avenues available.

Finding a record deal.

This is often a performing songwriter's primary goal—to get a record deal and release an album. Here are some possible ways to approach it:

1. Approach a record company for a record deal. This is another obvious one. Independent labels will be a lot more approachable than major labels, who are usually deluged with demos. Independent labels give you more artistic freedom, while major labels will demand more compromise, especially if you do not have a previous track record. A compromise between the two is to approach one of the "fake indie" labels owned a major. You'll get more of the benefits of an indie, but with more of the resources and connections of a major label.

2. Approach a record producer for a development deal. Some producers sign artists, produce their album and develop them like a record company and then approach major labels for distribution deals. This has advantages and drawbacks. For example, the producer gives you guidance and connections, but it can also be harder to get paid because you are signed to the producer and not the label.

3. Get a manager with connections. The right manager with the right connections can make all the difference in getting a record deal.

4. Ask a music publisher. Publishers are taking on more and more of a role of developing performing songwriters as artists. Many major publishers are sister companies to record labels and can shop you for a deal when they think you're ready.

5. Approach an entertainment attorney. Entertainment attorneys are a must when it comes to negotiating record contracts, and some moonlight by helping artists make connections for record deals (they will get their cut, of course).

6. Approach PROs. ASCAP and BMI can counsel you on your career and possibly make a referral. They also commonly put on performance showcases where A&R ("artist and repertoire") people from record labels attend to check out new artists.

Finding a producer to help with your album

Independently minded performing songwriters often find they need help navigating the studio when it comes time to produce their own album. In this case, the producer often works for an upfront fee from the artist, for a percentage of the royalty when the album is released and sold, or a combination of both.

Things to keep in mind when submitting a demo to a producer on this basis:

1. Is the producer known for a particular genre or "sound"? Many producers have a signature sound to their studio productions and are often connected to specific genres. Phil Spector had the "Wall of Sound." Bob Rock pioneered a glossy metal sound for Metallica and The Cult. Daniel Lanois and Brian Eno are famous for the atmospheres they created on albums by U2. Look at your favorite CDs to see who produced. Use these as touchstones when approaching producers to see if they are on your wavelength.

2. What role does a particular producer like to take in the studio? The "Tips" section of *Songwriter's Market* Record Producers listings often have notes from the producer about how they like to work with performing songwriters in the studio. Some work closely as a partner with the artist on developing arrangements and coaching performances. Some prefer final authority on creative decisions. Think carefully about what kind of working relationship you want.

Finding a manager

Many performing songwriters eventually find it necessary to find a manager to help with developing their careers and finding gigs. Some things to keep in mind when looking:

1. Does the manager work with artists in my genre of music? A manager who typically works with punk rock bands may not have as many connections useful to an aspiring country singer-songwriter. A manager who mainly works with gospel artists might not know what to do with a hedonistic rock band.

2. How big is the manager's agency? If a manager is working with multiple acts, but has a small (or no) staff, you might not get the attention you want. Some of the listings have information in the heading about the agency's staff size.

3. Does the manager work with acts from my region? You can check the Geographic

Index on page 421 to check for management agencies located near your area. Many of the listings also have information in their headings provided by the companies describing whether they work with regional acts only or artists from any region.

4. Does the manager work with name acts? A manager with famous clients could work wonders for your career. Or you could get lost in the shuffle. Use your best judgment when sizing up a potential manager and be clear with yourself about the kind of relationship you would like to have and the level of attention you want for your career.

5. If I'm a beginner, will the manager work with me? Look in the Openness to Submissions Index on page 411 to find companies open to beginners. Some may suggest extensive changes to your music or image. On the other hand, you may have a strong vision of what you want to do and need a manager who will work with you to achieve that vision instead of changing you around. Decide for yourself how much you are willing to compromise in good faith.

Remember that a relationship between you and a manager is a two-way street. You will have to earn each other's trust and be clear about your goals for mutual success.

Quiz: Are You Professional?

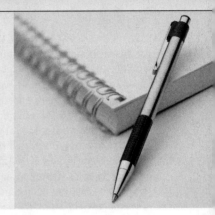

Okay, everybody! Take out your submission package and let's take a look. Hmm . . . very interesting. I think you're well on your way, but you should probably change a few things.

We asked record companies, music publishers and record producers, "What do songwriters do in correspondence with your company (by phone, mail or demo) that screams 'amateur'?" Take this quiz and find out how professional you appear to those on the receiving end of your submission. The following are common mistakes songwriters make all the time. They may seem petty, but, really, do you want to give someone an excuse not to listen to your demo? Check off the transgressions you have committed.

BY MAIL YOU SENT:

☑ anything handwritten (lyrics, cover letters, labels for cassettes). Today there is no excuse for handwritten materials. Take advantage of your local library's typewriters or businesses that charge by the hour to use a computer. And don't even think about using notebook paper.

☑ materials without a contact name *and* phone number. Put this information on *everything*.

☑ lyrics only. Music companies want music and words. See the If You Write Lyrics, But Not Music sidebar on page 19.

☑ insufficient return postage, an envelope too small to return materials, no SASE at all, or a "certified mail" package. If you want materials returned, don't expect the company to send it back on their dime with their envelope—give them what they need. Certified mail is unnecessary and annoying; first class will suffice.

☑ long-winded, over-hyped cover letters, or no cover letter at all. Companies don't need (or want) to hear your life story, how many instruments you play, how many songs you've written, how talented you are or how all your songs are sure-fire hits. Briefly explain why you are sending the songs (e.g., your desire to have them published) and let the songs speak for themselves. Double check your spelling too.

☑ over-packaged materials. Do not use paper towels, napkins, foil or a mountain of tape to package your submission. Make the investment in bubble wrap or padded envelopes.

☑ photos of your parents or children. As much as you love them, your family's pictures or letters of recommendation won't increase your chances of success (unless your family is employed by a major music company).

☑ songs in the style the company doesn't want. Do not "shotgun" your submissions. Read the listings carefully to see if they want your style of music.

YOU CALLED THE CONTACT PERSON:

☑ to check on the submission only a couple days after it was received. Read the listings to see how soon (or if) they report back on submissions. Call them only after that time has elapsed. If they are interested, they will find a way to contact you.

☑ excessively. It's important to be proactive, but check yourself. Make sure you have given them enough time to respond before you call again. Calling every week is inappropriate.

☑ armed with an angry or aggressive tone of voice. A bad attitude will get you nowhere.

WITH THE DEMO YOU PROVIDED:

☑ no lyric sheet. A typed sheet of lyrics for each song is required.

☑ poor vocals and instrumentation. Spending a little extra for professionals can make all the difference.

☑ a poor-quality cassette. The tape should be new and have a brand name.

☑ long intros. Don't waste time—get to the heart of the song.

☑ buried vocals. Those vocals should be out front and clear as a bell.

☑ recordings of sneezes or coughs. Yuck.

SCORING

If you checked 1-3: Congratulations! You're well within the professional parameters. Remedy the unprofessional deeds you're guilty of and send out more packages.

If you checked 4 or more: Whoa! Overhaul your package, let someone check it over, and then fire away with those impeccably professional submissions!

Royalties

Where Does the Money Come From?

NON-PERFORMING SONGWRITERS

How do songwriters make money?

The quick answer is that songwriters make money through rights available to them through the copyright laws. For more detail, keep reading and see the article What About Copyright? on page 32.

What specific rights make money for songwriters?

There are two primary ways songwriters earn money on their songs. Performance Royalties and Mechanical Royalties.

What is a performance royalty?

When you hear a song on the radio, on television, in the elevator, in a restaurant, etc. the songwriter receives royalties, called "Performance Royalties." Performing Rights Organizations (ASCAP, BMI and SESAC in the U.S.A.) collect payment from radio stations, television, etc. and distribute those payments to songwriters (see below).

What is a mechanical royalty?

When a record company puts a song onto a CD, cassette, etc. and distributes copies for sale, they owe a royalty payment to the songwriter for each copy they press of the album. It is called a "mechanical royalty" because of the mechanical process used to mass produce a copy of a CD, cassette or sheet music. The payment is small per song (see the "Royalty Provisions" subhead of the Basic Song Contract Pointers sidebar on page 38), but the earnings can add up and reach massive proportions for songs appearing on successful major label albums. ****Note: This royalty is totally different from the artist royalty on the retail price of the album.****

Who collects the money for performance and mechanical royalties?

Performing Rights Organizations collect performance royalties. There are three organizations that collect performance royalties: ASCAP, BMI and SESAC. These organizations arose many years ago when songwriters and music publishers gathered together to press for their rights and improve their ability to collect fees for the use of their songs. ASCAP, BMI and SESAC collect fees for the use of songs and then pass along the money to their member songwriters and music publishers.

Mechanical rights organizations collect mechanical royalties. There are three organizations that collect mechanical royalties: The Harry Fox Agency (HFA), The American Mechanical Rights Agency (AMRA) and The Songwriters Guild of America (SGA). These three organizations collect mechanical royalties from record companies of all sizes—major labels, mid-size and independents—and pass the royalties along to member music publishers and songwriters.

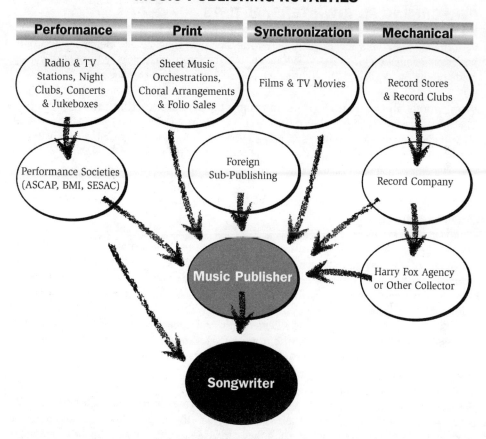

MUSIC PUBLISHING ROYALTIES

How do songwriters hook up with this system to earn royalties?

For **Performance Royalties**, individual songwriters **affiliate** with a Performing Rights Organization of their choice, and register their songs in the PRO database. Each PRO has a slightly different method of calculating payment, different ownership, and different membership structure, so choosing a PRO is an individual choice. Once a songwriter is affiliated and has registered their songs, the PROs then collect fees as described above and issue a check to the songwriter.

For **Mechanical Royalties**, three different things can happen:

1. The songwriter is signed to a publisher that is affiliated with The Harry Fox Agency. The Harry Fox Agency collects the mechanical royalties and passes them along to the publisher. The publisher then passes these along to the songwriter within 30 days. This case usually happens when a songwriter is signed to a major publisher and has a song on a major label album release.

2. The songwriter is not signed to a publisher and owns exclusive rights to his songs, and so works with AMRA or The Songwriters Guild of America, who cut a check directly to the songwriter instead of passing them to the publisher first.

3. They are signed to a publisher, but the songs are being released on albums by independent labels. In this case, the songwriter often works with AMRA since they have a focus on the independent music publishing market.

PERFORMING SONGWRITERS/ARTISTS
How do performing songwriters make money?
Performing songwriters and artists (if they write their own songs) make money just like non-performing songwriters, as described above, but they also make money through royalties made on the retail price of an album when it is sold online, in a store, etc.

What about all the stories of performing songwriters getting into bad deals?
The stories are generally true, but if they're smart, performing songwriters usually can hold on to the money they would be owed as songwriters (performing and mechanical royalties). But when it comes to retail sale royalties, all they will usually see is an "advance"—essentially a loan—which must then be paid off from record sales. You will not see a royalty check on retail sales until you're advance is paid off. If you are given a $600,000 advance, you will have to pay back the record company $600,000 out of your sales royalties before you see any more money.

Do performing songwriters and artists get to keep the advance?
Not really. If you have a manager who has gotten you a record deal, he will take his cut. You will probably be required in the contract to pay for the producer and studio time to make the album. Often the producer will take a percentage of subsequent royalties from album sales, which comes out of your pocket. Then there are also music video costs, promotion to radio stations, tour support, paying sidemen, etc. Just about anything you can think of is eventually paid for out of your advance or out of sales royalties. There are also deductions to royalties usually built in to record company contracts that make it harder to earn out an advance.

What should a performing songwriter wanting to sign with a major label do?
Their best option is to negotiate a fair contract, get as big of an advance as possible, and then manage that advance money the best they can. A good contract will keep the songwriting royalties described above completely separate from the flow of sales royalties, and will also cut down on the number of royalty deductions the record company builds into the contract. And because of the difficulty in earning out any size advance or auditing the record company, it makes sense to get as much cash up front as you can, then to manage that as best you can. You will need a good lawyer.

RECORD COMPANIES, PRODUCERS AND MANAGERS & BOOKING AGENTS
How do music publishers make money?
A publisher works as a songwriter's agent, looks for profitable commercial uses for the songs he represents, and then takes a percentage of the profits. This is typically 50% of all earning from a particular song—often referred to as the *publisher's share*. A successful publisher stays in contact with several A&R reps, finding out what upcoming projects are in need of new material, and whether any songs he represents will be appropriate.

How do record companies make money?

Record companies primarily make their money from profits made selling CDs, cassettes, DVDs, etc. Record companies keep most of the profit after subtracting manufacturing costs, royalties to recording artists, distribution fees and the costs of promoting songs to radio (which for major labels can reach up to $300,000 per song). Record companies also usually have music publishing divisions that make money performing all the functions of publishers.

How do record producers make money?

Producers mostly make their money by charging a flat fee up front to helm a recording project, by sharing in the royalties from album sales, or both. A small independent producer might charge $10,000 (or sometimes less) up front to produce a small indie band, while a "name" producer such as Bob Rock, who regularly works with major label bands, might charge $300,000. Either of these might also take a share in sales royalties, referred to as "points"— as in "percentage points." A producer might say, "I'll produce you for $10,000 and 2 points." If an artist is getting a 15% royalty an album sales, then two of those percentage points will go to the producer instead. Producers also make money by co-writing with the artists to get publishing royalties, or they may ask for part of the publishing from songs written by outside songwriters.

How do managers make money?

Most managers make money by taking a percentage commission of their clients' income, usually 10-25%. If a touring band finishes a show and makes a $2,000 profit, a manager on 15% commission would get $300. If an artist gets a $40,000 advance from a mid-size label, the manager would get $6,000. Whether an artist's songwriting income is included in the manager's commission comes down to negotiation. *The commission should give the manager incentive to make things happen for your career, so avoid paying flat fees up front.*

What About Copyright?

How am I protected by the copyright laws?

Copyright protection applies to your song the instant you it them down in fixed form—a recording, sheet music, lead sheet, etc. This protection lasts for your lifetime plus 70 years (or the lifetime of the last surviving writer, if you co-wrote the song with somebody else). When you prepare demos, place notification of copyright on all copies of your song—the lyric sheets, lead sheets and labels for cassettes, CDs, etc. The notice is simply the word "copyright" or the symbol © followed by the year the song was created (or published) and your name: © 2006 by John Q. Songwriter.

What parts of a song are protected by copyright?

Traditionally, the melody line and the lyrics are eligible for copyright. Period. Chords and rhythm are virtually never protected. An incredibly original arrangement can sometimes qualify, but the original copyright owner of the song must agree to it (and they usually don't). Sound recordings can also be copyrighted, but this applies strictly to the actual sounds on the recording, not the song itself (this copyright is usually owned by record companies).

What songs are not protected?

Song titles or mere ideas for music and lyrics cannot be copyrighted. Very old songs in the "public domain" are not protected. You could quote a melody from a Bach piece, but you could not then stop someone else from quoting the same melody in their song.

When would I lose or have to share the copyright?

If you *collaborate* with other writers, they are assumed to have equal interests unless you state some other arrangement, in writing. If you write under a *work-for-hire* arrangement, the company or person who hired you to write the song then owns the copyright. Sometimes your spouse may automatically be granted an interest in your copyright as part of their *spousal rights*, which might then become important if you got divorced.

Should I register my copyright?

Registering your copyright with the Library of Congress gives the best possible protection. Registration establishes a public record of your copyright—even though a song is legally protected whether or not it is registered—and could prove useful in any future court cases involving the song. Registration also entitles you to a potentially greater settlement in a copyright infringement lawsuit.

How do I register my song?

To register your song, request government form PA from the Copyright Office. Call the 24-hour hotline at (202)707-9100 and leave your name and address on the messaging system. Once you receive the PA form, you must return it, along with a registration fee and a CD (or tape) and lead sheet of your song. Send these to the Register of Copyrights, Copyright Office, Library of Congress, Washington DC 20559. It may take several months to receive your certificate of registration from the Copyright Office, but your songs are protected from the date of creation (the date of registration will reflect the date you applied). For more information, call the Copyright Office's Public Information Office at (202)707-3000 or visit their website at http://lcweb.loc.gov/copyright.

Government Resources

For More Info

The Library of Congress's copyright website is your best source for current, complete information on the subject of copyright. Not only can you learn all you could possibly wish to know about intellectual property rights and U.S. copyright law (the section of the U.S. Code dealing with copyright is reprinted there in its entirety), but you can also download copyright forms directly from the site. The site also includes links to other copyright-related web pages, many of which will be of interest to songwriters, including ASCAP, BMI, SESAC, and the Harry Fox Agency. Check it out at **http://www.copyright.gov**.

How likely is it that someone will try to steal my song?

Copyright infringement is very rare. But, if you ever feel that one of your songs has been stolen—that someone has unlawfully infringed on your copyright—you must prove that you created the work and that the person you are suing had access to your song. Copyright registration is the best proof of a date of creation. You *must* have your copyright registered in order to file a lawsuit. Also, it's helpful if you keep your rough drafts and revisions of songs, either on paper or on tape.

Why did song sharks start soliciting me after I registered my song?

This is one potential, unintended consequence of registering your song with the Library of Congress. The copyright indexes are a public record of your songwriting, and song sharks often search the copyright indexes and mail solicitations to songwriters who live out away from major music centers such as Nashville. They figure these songwriters don't know any better and are easy prey. *Do not allow this possibility to stop you from registering your songs!* Just be aware, educate yourself, and then throw the song sharks' mailings in the trash.

What if I mail a tape to myself to get a postmark date on a sealed envelope?

The "poor man's copyright" has not stood up in court, and is not an acceptable substitute for registering your song. If you feel it's important to shore up your copyright, register it with the Library of Congress.

Career Songwriting

What Should I Know?

What career options are open to songwriters who do not perform?

The possibilities range from a beginning songwriter living away from a music center like Nashville who lands an occasional single-song publishing deal, to a staff songwriter signed to a major publishing company. And then there are songwriters like Desmond Child who operate independently, have developed a lot of connections, work with numerous artists and set up their own independent publishing operations.

What is "single-song" songwriting about?

In this case, a songwriter submits songs to many different companies. One or two songs gain interest from different publishers, and the songwriter signs separate contracts for each song with each publisher. The songwriter can then pitch other songs to other publishers. In Nashville, for instance, a single-song contract is usually the first taste of success for an aspiring songwriter on his way up the ladder. Success of this sort can induce a songwriter to move to a music center like Nashville (if they haven't already), and is a big boost for a struggling songwriter already living there. A series of single-song contracts often signals a songwriters' maturing skill and marketability.

What is a "staff songwriter"?

A staff songwriter usually works for a major publisher and receives a monthly stipend as an advance against the royalties he is likely to earn for the publisher. The music publisher has exclusive rights to everything the songwriter writes while signed to the company. The publisher also works actively on the writer's behalf to hook him or her up with co-writers and other opportunities. A staff songwriting position is highly treasured by many because it offers a steady income, and in Nashville is a sign the songwriter has "arrived."

What comes after the staff songwriting position?

Songwriters who go to the next level have a significant reputation for their ability to write hit songs. Famous artists seek them out, and they often write actively in several markets at once. They often write on assignment for film and television, and commonly keep their own publishing companies to maximize their income.

As my career grows what should I do about keeping track of expenses, etc.?

You should keep a ledger or notebook with records on all financial transactions related to your songwriting—royalty checks, demo costs, office supplies, postage, travel expenses, dues to organizations, class and workshop fees, plus any publications you purchase pertaining to songwriting. You may also want a separate checking account devoted to your songwriting activities. This will make record keeping easier and help to establish your identity as a business for tax purposes.

What should I know about taxes related to songwriting income?

Any royalties you receive will not reflect taxes or any other mandatory deductions. It is your responsibility to keep track of income and file the correct tax forms. For specific information, contact the IRS or talk to an accountant who serves music industry clients.

Music Biz Basics

What About Contracts?

CO-WRITING
What kind of agreements do I need with co-writers?

You may need to sign a legal agreement between you and a co-writer to establish percentages you will each receive of the writer's royalties. You will also have to iron out what you will do if another person, such as an artist, wants to change your song and receive credit as a co-writer. For example, in the event, a major artist wants to cut your song for her album—but also wants to rewrite some lyrics and take a share of the publishing—you and your co-writer need to agree whether it is better to get a song on an album that might sell millions (and make a lot of money) or pass on it because you don't want to give up credit. The situation could be uncomfortable if you are not in sync on the issue.

When do I need a lawyer to look over agreements?

When it comes to doing business with a publisher, producer or record company, you should always have the contract reviewed by a knowledgeable entertainment attorney. As long as the issues at stake are simple, the co-writers respect each other, and they discuss their business philosophies before writing a song together, they can probably write up an agreement without the aid of a lawyer.

SINGLE-SONG CONTRACTS
What is a single-song contract?

A music publisher offers a single-song contract when he wants to sign one or more of your songs, but doesn't want to hire you as a staff songwriter. You assign your rights to a particular song to the publisher for an agreed-upon number of years, so that he may represent the song and find uses profitable for both of you. This is a common contract and will probably be the first you encounter in your songwriting career.

What basic elements should every single-song contract contain?

Every contract should have the publisher's name, the writer's name, the song's title, the date and the purpose of the agreement. The songwriter also declares the song is a original work and he is creator of the work. The contract *must* specify the royalties the songwriter will earn from various uses of the song, including performance, mechanical, print and synchronization royalties.

How should the royalties usually be divided in the contract?

The songwriter should receive no less than 50% of the income his song generates. That means the songwriter and publisher split the total royalties 50/50. The songwriter's half is

When Does 50% Equal 100%?

Tip

NOTE: the publisher's and songwriter's share of the income are sometimes referred to as each being 100%—for 200% total! You might hear someone say, "I'll take 100% of the publisher's share." **Do not be needlessly confused!** If the numbers confuse you, ask for the terms to be clarified.

called the "writer's share" and the publisher's half is called the "publisher's share." If there is more than one songwriter, the songwriters split the writer's share. Sometimes, successful songwriters will bargain for a percentage of the publisher's share, negotiating what is basically a co-publishing agreement. For a visual explanation of how royalties are collected and flow to the songwriter, see the chart called Music Publishing Royalties on page 29.

What should the contract say about a "reversion clause"?

Songwriters should always negotiate for a "reversion clause," which returns all rights back to the songwriter if some provision of the contract is not met. Most reversion clauses give a publisher a set amount of time (usually one or two years) to work the song and make money with it. If the publisher can't get the song recorded and released during the agreed-upon time period, the songwriter can then take his song to another publisher. The danger of *not* getting some sort of reversion clause is that you could wind up with a publisher sitting on your song for the entire life-plus-70-years term of the copyright—which may as well be forever.

Is a reversion clause difficult to get?

Some publishers agree to it, and figure if they can't get any action with the song in the first year or two, they're not likely to ever have much luck with it. Other publishers may be reluctant to agree to a reversion clause. They may invest a lot of time and money in demoing and pitching a song to artists and want to keep working at it for a longer period of time. Or, for example, a producer might put a song on hold for a while and then go into a lengthy recording project. A year can easily go by before the artist or producer decides which songs to release as singles. This means you may have to agree to a longer time period, be flexible and trust the publisher has your best mutual interests in mind. Use your best judgment.

What other basic issues should be covered by a single-song contract?

The contract should also address these issues:

- will an advance be paid, and if so, how much will the advance be?
- when will royalties be paid (annually or semiannually)?
- who will pay for demos—the publisher, songwriter or both?
- how will lawsuits against copyright infringement be handled, including the cost of lawsuits?
- will the publisher have the right to sell its interest in the song to another publisher without the songwriter's consent?
- does the publisher have the right to make changes in a song, or approve changes by someone else, without the songwriter's consent?
- the songwriter should have the right to audit the publisher's books if he feels it is necessary and gives the publisher reasonable notice.

Music Biz Basics

Basic Song Contract Pointers

Tips

The following list, taken from a Songwriters Guild of America publication, enumerates the basic features of an acceptable songwriting contract:

1 **Work for Hire.** When you receive a contract covering just one composition, you should make sure the phrases "employment for hire" and "exclusive writer agreement" are *not* included. Also, there should be no options for future songs.

2 **Performing Rights Affiliation.** If you previously signed publishing contracts, you should be affiliated with either ASCAP, BMI or SESAC. All performance royalties must be received directly by you from your performing rights organization and this should be written into your contract.

3 **Reversion Clause.** The contract should include a provision that if the publisher does not secure a release of a commercial sound recording within a specified time (one year, two years, etc.), the contract can be terminated by you.

4 **Changes in the Composition.** If the contract includes a provision that the publisher can change the title, lyrics or music, this should be amended so that only with your consent can such changes be made.

5 **Royalty Provisions.** You should receive fifty percent (50%) of all publisher's income on all licenses issued. If the publisher prints and sells his own sheet music, your royalty should be ten percent (10%) of the wholesale selling price. The royalty should not be stated in the contract as a flat rate ($.05, $.07, etc.).

6 **Negotiable Deductions.** Ideally, demos and all other expenses of publication should be paid 100% by the publisher. The only allowable fee is for the Harry Fox Agency collection fee, whereby the writer pays one half of the amount charged to the publisher for mechanical rights. The current mechanical royalty collected by the Harry Fox Agency is 8.5 cents per cut for songs under 5 minutes; and 1.65 cents per minute for songs over 5 minutes.

7 **Royalty Statements and Audit Provision.** Once the song is recorded, you are entitled to receive royalty statements at least once every six months. In addition, an audit provision with no time restriction should be included in every contract.

8 **Writer's Credit.** The publisher should make sure that you receive proper credit on all uses of the composition.

9 **Arbitration.** In order to avoid large legal fees in case of a dispute with your publisher, the contract should include an arbitration clause.

10 **Future Uses.** Any use not specifically covered by the contract should be retained by the writer to be negotiated as it comes up.

Where else can I go for advice on contracts?

The Songwriters Guild of America has drawn up a Popular Songwriter's Contract which it believes to be the best minimum songwriter contract available (see the Ten Basic Points Your Contract Should Include sidebar above). The Guild will send a copy of the contract at no charge to any interested songwriter upon request (see the Songwriters Guild of America listing in the Organizations section on page 323). SGA will also review—free of charge—any contract offered to its members, and will check it for fairness and completeness. Also see these two books published by Writer's Digest Books: *The Craft and Business of Songwriting*, by John Braheny and *Music Publishing: A Songwriter's Guide*, by Randy Poe.

Music Biz Basics

Richie Havens

Touch the Planet with Honesty, Optimism, and DIY

by Robin Renée

J udging from much mainstream music today, many would think that the hour of protest songs and the music of social struggle have long passed. Not so, says veteran singer/songwriter Richie Havens. Deeply dedicated to both music and message, he says the times still are a-changin', perhaps now more than ever.

Before striking the opening chords that began Woodstock in August 1969, the Brooklyn-born Havens had turned from his early days in street-corner doo-wop to the emerging folk scene in Greenwich Village, New York City, where he encountered the styles and ideas that changed him profoundly. From there, he gained the confidence to develop his signature warm, earnest vocals and fiery guitar. The title of his 1967 debut album, *Mixed Bag*, refers to Havens' ease of movement between cutting-edge original material and traditional folk, and his blending of acoustic sounds with the attitude of rock, jazz, and more. It was his next release in 1968, *Something Else Again*, that first hit the Billboard Chart, rekindling interest in *Mixed Bag*. He continued to develop as a timelessly relevant songwriter and a compelling interpreter of the best of his contemporaries. In 1970, it was a cover of The Beatles' "Here Comes The Sun" that lifted his *Alarm Clock* album into the Top 30.

Now more than 20 albums later, Havens' latest, *Grace of the Sun*, carries through it all of the passion for humanity, love, and justice that continue to be hallmarks of this classic career-in-progress. The CD, out on his own Stormy Forest Records, presents new original material such as "By The Grace of the Sun" and "Way Down Deep," and includes classics like Joni Mitchell's "Woodstock" and Dylan's "All Along the Watchtower."

Havens continues to open the eyes of many an aspiring songwriter and activist. His do-it-yourself attitude inspires confidence for all new performers and established artists who wish to make their way as creative beings and approach the music business on their own terms.

"Grace of the Sun" is a great title. The words themselves evoke a kind of natural optimism. What do the title and the song mean for you?

It's basically my recognition that there is definitely something we can look at from every part of the world and know, or learn, that if it wasn't there we wouldn't be here. And basically,

---

ROBIN RENÉE is an independent performing songwriter and freelance writer. She has interviewed music greats such as Ani DiFranco, Janis Ian, and B.B. King, and contributed to *Curve Magazine*, *PanGaia*, and *Elmore Magazine*. Her independent CD releases include *In Progress* and *All Six Senses*. Visit www.robinrenee.com.

the sun is a big battery in the sky for me. When it comes out, I wake up, I don't care what time I went to sleep. So it's definitely part of my connection with life.

Do you have an overall message or vibe to this CD?

I think "Grace of the Sun" is the platform for all of the other songs. It's like the sun is there, and then we have strands of the sun, whether they be rays or whether they be direct connections to things here on the planet. And it spans relationships. I think every album I've ever done was really about relationships. Relationships man to man, man to woman, woman to man, children to parents, parents to children, man to God—you know, all of the dimensions we actually have.

What was your songwriting process like for this album?

Well, you know, I only have one process since I left doo-wop. In doo-wop, I used to sit down and write 20 songs a day. But when I got to The Village and heard these songs that changed my life, I realized there was a deeper song to be sung. I didn't think I was gonna be doing it, but I realized that there were songs much deeper than "I love you and the sky is blue" or what kind of car you want to drive. And it changed me personally. It took a couple years of me singing along with the guys on stage from the audience. But one of my friends who was there when I got there—Freddy Neil—came to me one day after he got offstage and said, "Hey Richie, I need to tell you something. You've been sittin' here for two years singing these songs with me onstage. Here's a guitar. You borrow it, you learn the darn songs and sing 'em yourself!"

What are some of those songs that changed your life?

One was called "Tear Down The Walls" to show you where their heads were at. One was called "To Be A Man." One of the first traditional folk songs I learned was "The Drinking Gourd." It's a true song about a man who was a troubadour back when slavery was happening and he basically traveled around. But he sang these songs that were teaching people how to locate the Underground Railroad. It's a wonderful metaphor—he says, "Follow the drinking gourd." Well, the drinking gourd represents the Big Dipper. So if you follow that to the river he talks about, there'll be someone there. The captain will be waiting to take you from that point. There was also a song called "The Klan"—which is a very heavy song—and I learned that one as well. So it was kind of eclectic from the beginning.

Many people revere you as having been the opening performer at Woodstock. From your perspective, what has made you a legend in music?

Well, you know in actuality, I had been to Europe twice and was about to go back there when Woodstock happened. I was working on my third album. So I had been around the planet a couple of times before that, and I think that the song ["Freedom"] sort of became an anthem of kids who couldn't make it [to Woodstock], whose mothers wouldn't let them go. So if we can imagine the seven million people that might have shown up there, that's the way it would have really been. I think that it had an effect especially from the movie 'cause there were a lot of people who didn't make it. And the fact that ["Freedom"] was made up on the stage, in essence, I think that people still go "Wow! You made it up on the stage?" Yeah, I had been there for 2 hours and 45 minutes and I didn't have any more songs to sing. I sang everything I knew and I wasn't about to revert to doo-wop! So, it came out that way and I even had to go see the movie to see what I did.

Advanced Articles

Is there anything else about your work that you feel has really captivated people?

I have this other privilege that's been given to me. You know, when I was in The Village, everybody called me a folksinger even though I didn't do a heck of a lot of traditional folk songs. When I made my first album in 1967 and went out on the road, they sent me to Johnny's Jazz Joint. I freaked out completely. I said "I don't do jazz! They're gonna throw me outta here on the second song!" So I walked up and on the window was a little bill and it said "Richie Havens—folk-jazz singer." The next place I'd go to would be, like, Billy's Blues Club and I'd have the same freak out. I'd walk up to the window and it would say "Richie Havens—folk-blues singer." So I was really fortunate enough to play any kind of venue when I first started. There isn't anybody that I came up with that crossed those lines like that. They were folk, or blues, or jazz, which gives me great feelings for those who are still there doing it. You know, it wasn't easy to keep going. A lot of those places and a lot of those people dropped out.

What else stands out for you about your Woodstock experience?

I get to tell these young guys who ask about it the real history, because it wasn't just the biggest music festival in the world at the time. It had a deeper purpose. We had Civil Rights going, we had Vietnam going, we had all of these things that people were concerned about and becoming more aware of. And at the time, we didn't know any of the West Coast bands that played. Santana hadn't been this way yet, Big Brother and the Holding Company hadn't been to the East yet; it was their first time here. Sly and the Family Stone—first time in New York. And so there was a lot of discovery going on, between musicians as well as by the audience. We got to see each other and realize what was really out there. Those who were there became a part of everything that happened.

You still can go and see the movie. So every year, I gain new people who've never seen me play those songs from the movie. For all the years I've been doing it, it's been constantly growing. And I get to sing, you know, songs that I've been singing for 25 years or 30 years, which mean more today than they did then, even, which is very interesting.

In the past you've said that on the surface, the music of protest and social change seems like it's not often heard in music today, but at the same time you feel like its influence is everywhere. Would you talk about that a little bit?

I think it's a saturation situation. You know, during the early '70s when we went out on the road, we knew maybe we shouldn't sing half of these songs—they might chase us out of town, anyway. But we did anyhow. I think it took the whole '70s to actually saturate the country with some consciousness that we were going through in the '60s. [There have been] massive changes, which nobody advertises because they were actually natural things that should have been in the first place. I find that there are so many more of us, and I say "us" in terms of anybody looking to get some justice or freedom. There are so many more of us now that we just may possibly pull it off. Years ago, when they said grassroots, they really *meant* grassroots. It was one or two people in the whole city trying to do something. Today, grassroots is the actual turf that's keeping it going. So it's about us being able to organize to a degree that we do affect a change, and we have affected a lot of change. I started out at 13 years old realizing that America didn't exist yet. It was a long way we had to go. I think that we've covered at least two-thirds of that territory at this point. So, we're on the verge of a new wave of new people with new music that basically carries on from what started back then. It's amazing. I mean, I do get to see a lot of opening acts that are local who really are serious about what they're doing. People use the word "hope." I don't. I use the word "realism." If it's real, I'll get to see it somewhere. And I get to see it everywhere. And that to me sort of reinforces me staying out there doing what I do as well, because that's how it happens. We affect each other. I do believe we're really on the verge of a whole different world, and better than it's been.

What do you think about the music business these days? How has it changed since you started and do you have advice for emerging singers today?

Well, I think there are two things going on. [Record companies] have had to merge to stay alive, and so there's fewer now than when I started. It was coming for a long time that it would have its problems, but I think the best that has come along is the net. Young performers who want to get their music out there can go directly to the world. I think that is a real platform that appeared for every talented person to find their own talent, define it themselves, and to get it out to people. So I think the music business now is 80% net and the rest divvied up with the whole world's record companies. I do think that the young people have an affinity with the technology. It's made for them. They forgot all about us. They went, "We ain't makin' vinyl no more!" [laughter] But it is their technology and it's there for them to actually touch the whole planet. I would advise them to start there. Go to the Net. Go to some of these download things, you know. [Upload] clips of your music. If people like it, they will ask you where they can buy it. It's that simple. It really is.

What is the most important thing to which songwriters could aspire today?

I think the most important thing they could aspire to is to actually get their music around. If they've got a job and they get some free money, then they should get on a train, go as far as it will take them, get off and look around, and if there's an opportunity to play your music there, you do it. Even if you're not getting paid, because it's that audience that passes by, that stops, that's teaching you what you're doing. Their response is your ammunition to keep going. Even if it's in your own town. If there's a place, a corner to stand on to do it, you should be out there doing it. Don't wait for anybody to come and do anything for you—do it yourself.

You think that works for unknown artists as well?

Oh yeah. A friend of mine from the Midwest writes me one day and says, "Richie, I sold 15,000 albums. I'm the #1 on the Top Ten list of this MP3 thing." I said, "What MP3 thing?" So I go and start listening to these people. A lot of it was really bad, but it was honest, you know. You find yourself even listening to that, because it's honest. But I think that's the opportunity we still have with the Web. You do something artistic, and people will come back to it. That to me is the best thing that's happened to us. We do have access to the world and we should really be taking advantage of it.

Advanced Articles

Jonatha Brooke

*Indie Singer-Songwriter Feels the
Steady Pull of Success*

by Lauren Mosko

W hen Jonatha Brooke begins the opening chords to her song "I'll Take It From Here," originally written as the theme for the television show "Felicity," it's not unusual for young women in the audience to squeal, "that's *my* song!" But with lyrics like

*You can take your love and keep your money but
Not my will and not my way
At least every mistake will be my own
And I'll take it from here
I'll succeed or I will fail but I will decide*

The track is as much a declaration of her own independence as it is that of Felicity or Brooke's fans.

Going her own way is not a decision Brooke has made lightly. She began her career in music as one half of the Boston-based folk group The Story and produced albums under both Elektra Records and MCA Records before fate and circumstance led her to create her own publishing entity, Dog Dream Music, and her own independent label, Bad Dog Records. Since then, she's produced four albums and a DVD-audio recording, established her own Web site (www.jonathabrooke.com), and has taken her music across Europe. Here, the indomitable Brooke reflects on her experiences.

What was your experience with MCA? What did you learn from the whole affair?

Plumb. Plumbing the depths. (Laughs) You know, it was actually a really good experience while it lasted. I have to credit MCA with spending a lot of money on me. I mean, the record was not a cheap record to make, and they invested in me and my band, traveling back and forth to Europe three times. They helped with tour support in the States. I was playing with great musicians who are not cheap. I don't really have any complaints.

I think when you sign with a major label, you have to go in with your eyes wide open and know the pitfalls. You have this little window of opportunity and if you don't sell two million records, the odds are they won't stick with you because it's a lot of money on their part and they need big cash. So I was very lucky to have the stretches of support that I did. I kind of knew that if the records didn't explode, who knew if I'd get to do it again. So I just worked my butt off and took what I could, and I think I've definitely benefited from it.

LAUREN MOSKO is editor of *Novel & Short Story Writer's Market* and a devoted Jonatha Brooke fan.

How did you guys part company? Did you kick and scream?

No. (Laughs) I've been the victim of bad timing again and again with these labels. I think the reason I was dropped from Elektra was not just that [the Story] had split. There was a huge regime change. And all of the guys who had been my staunch believers were gone. So there was no one there to say, "Wait a minute; we believe in her as a solo artist." I didn't know anyone there all of the sudden and it didn't make any sense to stay. Same thing with MCA. There was kind of a regime change going on right at the tail end of working the second single for *Plumb*. Blue Thumb was folding; Tommy LiPuma was going elsewhere and he was my champion there—as he was at Elektra—and it was just crummy timing.

The beauty of it was that Tommy funded the next record, *10¢ Wings*. He actually said, "Look. I don't know what's going to happen with this deal, but I want you to make another record. I will fund it." And so I did at least get to go into the studio and make *10¢ Wings*. But then I had to find a home for it.

What made you decide to start Bad Dog Records?

Necessity is the mother of invention. After *10¢ Wings* came out and we had searched for someone who would help us with it and found this little boutique label on MCA, Refuge Records, again big regime change. We had no idea the two guys who were running Refuge were battling each other in court and not doing really a thing to help their label. In the middle of my tour they basically dropped me. This is right as "Secrets and Lies" was starting to chart at radio.

It's a very long story, but basically my option for the next record came up and they wanted me to compromise on my budget. I said wait a minute, let's talk in six months, let's just work on *this* record first. They never got back to me on my proposal and so I was dropped. They actually put a notice on every single person's desk at MCA saying that I no longer existed there and not to work my record. They called the radio and told them to stop playing "Secrets and Lies" and that was that.

So I was in the middle of this tour thinking, "This really sucks." I had come home for a week to deal with all this business stuff, but I had to get right back out there. I cried for two days and sat on the couch thinking, "Again! Why me?" and then threw a party and drank a lot of great wine and had Michelle N'degeocello come over and Wendy and Lisa from Prince's old band and we commiserated about the major labels and realized we'd all been dropped at least twice and that must be some kind of badge of honor we should be proud of.

That's when I decided I had to go back out on the road anyway, so why didn't I record some shows and make a live record in this interim time while I gathered my thoughts for a new studio record? It was something the fans had been asking for forever. Why not try it out, build the Web site up, figure out how to sell it on the Web site, see what the vibe was, maybe then get distribution, and see if I could do it myself? So that's how the live record happened. And Bad Dog was born.

What frustrates you most about running your own label?

Money. You have all these great ideas and cool things that you want to do and you don't have the 50 thousand bucks it takes. Like this DVD: We somehow figured out how to tape all this footage. We had five cameras at the Anspacher's show in New York last Spring, and all these people worked for nothing. They'd all helped us with the video for "Better After All"—just the sweetest, coolest, young, hip film-making people, and they agreed to come do it because they were fans.

So we have all this footage, we have ProTools recordings of all the shows, but we just ran out of cash. I can't wait to make that DVD. I think it's going to be really beautiful. That's why we're doing a fundraiser now on the Web site. People have been so lovely and generous but we need a lot more. But it's coming along.

What's the most rewarding aspect?

It's making decisions because you believe in them—deciding "Hey, let's go to Europe because that's somewhere we can actually see progress quickly." And the audiences are so beautiful over there. In Denmark, I did a songwriting seminar, and all these people showed up from the Danish Conservatory of Music to take my little songwriting class. And then two months later I came and did a gig, and 250 people showed up. And then three months after that we did another gig and I brought the band and 600 people showed up. And then a year and a half later, we had 1,200 people. So Europe is this place where there's still word of mouth and deejays can still play what they want and you don't have to pay them for it. You can have a sort of organic build in the course of a year and a half or two years and really see it come back to you. That's the beauty of doing it myself. I can experiment and try stuff like that. You lose your shirt but it's so exciting to see there's still the possibility of the little dog winning.

How do you balance business and creativity? Do you feel there's a danger in one overwhelming the other?

This week the business is overwhelming the creativity; I'll tell you that! But for the most part, I'd rather be crazed and busy and overwhelmed because somehow that tends to inspire music. I don't know why, but the less time you have the more stuff sort of seeps out into the spaces and into the notebooks. It's like that old adage: If you want something done, call a busy person to do it because they'll actually get it done. So I sort of feel like it doesn't necessarily hurt me to have all this other responsibility; it's in my nature to want to be involved in it. I'm lucky that way.

What (besides money) must a musician have or know in order to start her own label?

I was lucky enough that I had the fan base. I had these little stretches of major label money and that was the ideal situation because people knew I was out there and they knew to look on my Web site and just check out what was happening and come to the gigs. I have to say I can't imagine starting a label from nothing and figuring out a way to translate it into record sales and/or tour dates and getting to an audience. Radio airplay costs money, and radio is still one of the most powerful ways to sell records and get your name out there. And television as well. But just hiring a publicist is prohibitive.

Everyone thought that the Internet would be such a great leveler, but I still feel like people need to know that you're there first. How will they know to go look for you on the Internet unless you have some lucky break or you get some sort of groundswell word-of-mouth thing because you write some catchy song that gets onto some . . . *something*. How are you going to get through? It's overwhelming to me. I can't even imagine trying now.

When did you join ASCAP? Why do you feel it's important?

I first joined because that's what you did. I didn't know anything else except that when you start making records you're supposed to join ASCAP or BMI. And I think most of my friends were ASCAP, so that's where I went.

Now, they've become really good friends, incredible supporters. They've helped me with entrées into the London publishing scene, with entrées into Nashville. It feels like they sort of have my back in a way. If you're not making a ton of airplay money, they have special awards programs you can sign up for. You say, "Look, I wrote these 20 songs this year.

They're not getting airplay, but I wrote this for Fox Film and Television, I wrote this for Walt Disney." Then this panel decides, "Okay, let's give her some extra money because she's working her butt off and not making a ton on airplay. Let's help her out a little." I've definitely gotten extra money from those things, which is awesome. It saves my life four times a year. Every time it happens I'm like, "Thank God! I can pay for groceries this month" or "I can pay off that credit card that I've been living on."

Your latest effort, *Back in the Circus*, saw the introduction of co-writing. What made you decide to try it?

It was mostly because I ran into Eric Bazillion [of the Hooters]. We had been talking about getting together and writing a song because we're goober fans of each other and that was really how it started. I went down to Philadelphia and we just hung out for a couple of days and we wrote "Less Than Love is Nothing" and then we produced "Better After All" together. It was so much fun that it finally broke my very strong resistance to co-writing. [laughs] I think I'd tried it a couple times before and it was just a disaster. Just sitting in a room going "Uh, I don't know? What do you think? I don't know. What do you think?" and getting nothing done.

You've said on several occasions that *Back in the Circus* was inspired by your revisitation of an old carnie girl character, whom you call Charmaine. Was there also some sort of distinct muse for *Steady Pull*? *10¢ Wings*? *Plumb*? What sparked those albums?

Usually I figure it out after the fact. The record will be finished and mastered and artwork all done and then I'll sort of realize, "Oh, so this is what it was about." [laughs] After the fact, I realized *10¢ Wings* was really about the end of a marriage. And *Steady Pull* was all about new love and meeting my husband and being thrown wide open. *Plumb* was, in a way, about the end of The Story, and in some ways the end of my parents' marriage. With *Back in the Circus*, I moved to New York, I got remarried—it was all those things in one.

I revisited this carnie girl [from The Story's song "Damn Everything But The Circus"] because in some ways she's me—though I don't feel as downtrodden and cynical as the character in the song. You know, I've been doing this a while, going town to town for 10 or 15 years now, and there are nights when I feel like Charmaine and I feel a little tattered and world-weary and every town is the same and like "is this all?" Like that Peggy Lee song.

You mentioned in your interview with the San Francisco Chronicle that you keep five or six journals going all the time. Do you still write this much? Can you talk a little bit about your songwriting process?

Right now I'm looking at about four notebooks strewn around my floor. I always have to have four or five at a time and I just keep buying them on the road. I'll always get an idea when I'm on a bus or in a café or walking through an airport, and I won't have the notebook that I need.

Each one has its own particular magic. But they have to have graph paper inside; that's the one constant. Graph paper makes better songs. And there's a particular kind of notebook I find most inspiring. It's French, of course. Claire Fontaine is the brand; they make these great little school notebooks with graph paper inside.

There's mostly stream of consciousness in a lot of them, but then I try to keep only songs going [in one or two]. I'm not allowed to put bullshit. These notebooks will have the most complete poetic ideas.

So I'll sort of be fudging between the stream of consciousness ones and the journally ones and try to correlate those with the songs ones and figure out what it was about because they'll be in code. [laughs] Half the time I'm on a plane or a train or something and I'm terrified that someone is looking over my shoulder, so I'll write in code to myself and try to figure out later what it was I was really thinking. Or I'll call my cell phone and I'll leave melodies and little lyric blips on my cell phone. So at any given time there are like 20 different cell phone messages of me sort of going [hums tune]. It's almost indecipherable except that somehow I'll remember what the melody I meant was.

I do have my Minidisc recorder, with its little stereo microphone, and that's here too. On really good days I'll be organized enough and I'll have that with me when I get an idea. I'm trying to cover all the bases. Not to let anything slip through. It's a wonder that I ever get a song written. It's just torture every time. It doesn't get any easier; you think it would, but it's a battle and you just keep chipping away at it. It's like sculpting out of marble. You just have to keep sanding it down and chipping away and trying to figure out what it's trying to say, what it's trying to mean, and how to get to that crystal of truth at the core of it.

What's the one piece of songwriting advice you wish you would have known before you started your career?

I think I wouldn't have listened anyway. [laughs] When I first started writing, it was such a revelation. I was like, "I can do this! Oh my God, or I can do *this*!" I was just so excited to be doing it and working with Jennifer who had this great voice and ear for harmony. It was just heaven. It was like Christmas everyday. We were like, 'Oh, God, okay, sing this. And then we'll hold this dissonance for 10 minutes and then you can do this sort of trilly arpeggio thing and that would be *so cool*.' It was like throwing every possible seasoning and herb and the kitchen sink into every song because we could and because it was exciting and fun and weird and different. I think the advice I probably wouldn't have listened to but would have been good was simple: Less is more. Get to the kernel of it, the diamond part. You don't have to say every possible thing at every possible moment.

What about business advice?

Get a sugar daddy. [laughs] You know, I'd say—and I'm kind of a gambler—just go for it. If you really believe in it and believe in yourself then take the risks. Okay, so you lose your shirt a few times, but you can always buy another one.

Music Publishing

Tips for Recording Artists

by Scott Mathews

If you are a would-be recording artist, by now you have certainly heard all the horror stories of artists left high and dry, with not a penny to show for years of hard work. Well, I'm here to tell you it doesn't have to be this way. *The key is to understand songwriting royalties and music publishing.*

It is important to follow the money in the music business. There are so many areas in which one can see a positive cash flow from music. Some areas where an artist can generate money, to name just a few, are:

- publishing royalties
- royalty advances from publishers
- record sale royalties
- royalty advances from record companies
- touring revenues
- merchandise revenues (think "KISS")

We are going to focus on publishing income, and how recording artists can use publishing to protect and build their income, mainly in the context of recording contracts. (Even if you plan to go the independent route, you may at some point wind up licensing to a label a master you produced and recorded yourself, so pay attention, because this information could help you.)

WHY YOU SHOULD CARE ABOUT PUBLISHING

Music publishing should matter to recording artists because if you control your own publishing, you will be paid:

a. every time that song is sold in any form (record sales, download sales, ringtone sales, etc.); or

b. publicly played in any form (radio, TV, movies, clubs, live performances).

And nothing has to be recouped! (More on this in a minute.) That means from the first

---

SCOTT MATHEWS of Hit or Myth Productions has produced, recorded, or performed with a range of artists including John Hiatt, Van Morrison, Keith Richards and John Lee Hooker. His songs have been cut by artists such as Barbra Streisand and Dave Edmunds. See his listing in the Record Producers section. "Not affiliated with scottmathewsmusic.com or scottmathewsproductions.com. Beware of these and other impostors using the name 'Scott Mathews.'" E-mail him at hitormyth@aol.com.

sale or performance of the song, there is money flowing into the till. Not bad. That's the way it should be!

In fact, artists who retired from performing decades ago have made huge fortunes from the ownership of their songs. So besides the fact that it may be the first actual amount of money flowing into the artist's pockets (outside of possible advances, sometimes called "bonuses") publishing revenue may very well end up being the greatest amount of money an artist earns during his or her career, and beyond.

So, if you are a songwriter (and I know you are) understand that unless you sign away your rights to an outside music publisher, you own your songs and *you are the publisher*. (Don't forget, you also have your songwriting portion as well. If your song were a pie, the revenues would be split equally right down the middle; 50% goes to the songwriter(s) and 50% goes to the publisher.) The flow of money from these rights is completely separate from the artist's royalty for record sales, and you can use this to your advantage.

PUBLISHING IN RECORDING CONTRACTS

To understand how much music publishing can do for you as a recording artist, let's look at how record company royalties work in a label contract.

The record label royalty vortex

When artists sign record deals, they usually receive a royalty advance against their share of the money generated when the record is sold at retail. (Artist royalty rates can range from 10-12% for new artists to 17-25% for successful artists.) This money is basically a loan from the label, and the artist will see nothing else until this money is paid back ("recouped") from subsequent royalties flowing in as the record sells (or doesn't).

To repeat, *no royalties will be paid to the artist until every penny of the record company's investment is paid back/recouped.* Labels will make this repayment difficult by adding every possible expense to the artist's account, by restricting the uses of the advance money, and by choking the positive flow of sales royalties down to a trickle using a series of deductions.

Among the things artists will see added to their accounts are:

• video costs
• recording/studio costs
• tour support
• radio promotion
• catering for the big album launch party
• distribution and store display costs
• remastering

In short, anything and everything will be charged back to your account and ultimately paid for by the artist. It's amazing to view all the extras that can be charged against one's royalty statement, and as you might guess, an artist can deliver a record to a label, see it sell millions of copies, but still end up owing that label quite a chunk of change.

Major labels in particular may also restrict the artist's use of the advance money. The artist may be required to use the advance to fund recording costs and force the artist to use the most expensive studio possible. They may also specify an expensive producer. If the artist had hoped to use some of that money to live on, he may be in trouble.

Some of the ways record companies will reduce the flow of sales royalties into an artist's account include (but are not limited to):

• **Packaging/Container Deduction:** Sometimes as high as 25%, the cost of packaging CDs and cassettes is commonly deducted before calculating the royalty.

- **Breakage Deduction:** This deduction is around 10% and created in the days when vinyl records commonly broke in shipping.
- **Free Goods Deduction:** This is for freebie copies of your album given to stores, reviewers, etc.
- **Reduced Royalty Scheme:** Your 12% royalty may drop to 10% if it is sold anywhere except a major chain record store. Read the fine print.
- **3/4 Royalty Rate:** If your album is released on new formats such as SACD or DVD-A, the royalty is reduced by $\frac{1}{4}$. (Regular CD is sometimes still designated a "new" format.)
- **"Double Dips":** Record contracts may contain confusing clauses applying any of the above deductions *twice or more*!
- **"Cross-Collateralization":** If your first three albums cross-collateralized, you will have to earn out their combined recording and promotion debt before you get a royalty check, even if your first two albums, looked at separately, have paid for themselves.

In addition, if you are like me suspicious of the record companies' accounting practices, know that auditing their books costs tens of thousands of dollars and brings unfortunate relations between the artist and label. Consequently, it is rarely done, although in certain situations where one has sold a bazillion units, it is indeed worth it. A famous friend of mine audits the same company every year without even bothering to look at his statements first. It's just a matter of course, and he finds huge sums each and every year that otherwise would go unpaid to him.

So, back to publishing (maybe it will cheer you up!)

Publishing in record contracts

Unlike recording artists (who have maybe been too competitive or ego-driven), songwriters long ago organized and pushed for their interests as a group. This led to a system of royalties under law exclusively for songwriters, and this system operates in parallel with record sales, but also must be accounted for in record contracts. As both artist *and songwriter*, you can benefit from this.

Under the copyright laws, any time a record label presses and *distributes* a copy of a song on a CD, vinyl, tape, whatever, the label is required to pay the songwriter and publisher of the song a small royalty of a few cents per song per copy—also known as a *mechanical royalty*. The amount of the royalty, known as the statutory rate, is adjusted upward every year to account for inflation (as of this printing the *statutory rate* for 2006 is 9.1 cents per song under 5 minutes and 1.75 cents per song over 5 minutes).

Note that the royalty is paid anytime a record is *distributed*, not sold. This means the songwriter is paid *before* any copies have been sold, which means this publishing revenue is paid to you as the songwriter even if the retail royalty from the record label does not come through for you as an artist. *This publishing income is a completely separate revenue stream from the sales royalty.*

Record labels naturally do not like to pay these royalties, and when they offer a contract they may engage in a variety of schemes to hold on to as much of this money as possible. The most common ones to watch for are these:

Cross-Collateralization: You may find a record company intends to hold publishing royalties owed to you as a songwriter against your artist account. *In no case would I ever allow my publishing royalties to be cross-collateralized.* Your label (or distributor, if you are independent and have licensed your master recording) should make or lose money on the sales of your records, not your publishing. Keep those income streams separate.

Sister Publishing Agreements: Many record labels have "sister" publishing companies and may push hard for an artist to sign to that company as well as the record division. Publishers know that hit songs never die, and it's unreal what the annual revenues are for the major companies. But, the selling of records is not the same field of endeavor as exploiting songs ("exploit" understood as "to find revenue sources"—a good thing). By taking control of your publishing in this way, they can sit back and keep half of the publishing money generated by the album, including performance royalties.

Reduced Mechanical Rates: Record labels may try to reduce what is owed to you under the statutory rate (usually to a ³⁄₄ rate), or try to freeze your mechanical rate at a certain level. This means in 20 years, if your records are still being pressed and distributed, you could be stuck with a mechanical royalty rate that hasn't kept up with inflation.

I always suggest that writers have at least a piece of their publishing if for no other reason than to afford them the opportunity to watch their distributors and be able monitor sales/royalty statements. *Also, if you are the writer in a band, you will need to decide whether to keep the publishing for yourself or share it with the members of the group.*

Possible negotiating strategies for record contracts

So, what we've learned about publishing income vs. record sale royalties suggests several prime strategies in pursuing a recording contract:

- **Protect your publishing first, then negotiate other areas.** Never let record companies cross-collateralize your publishing and tie it up with other income streams.
- **Go for the full adjustable statutory mechanical rate.** You may or may not be able to get rid of the ³⁄₄ rate, but at least make sure your rate will adjust upward every year as it's supposed to. Plan for the future.
- **Form your own publishing company to collect mechanicals.** Keep it all! Since songwriting royalties are divided in halves, one for the publisher and one for the songwriter, you will have to form a company to collect the publisher's half for yourself. It's not that hard.

After your publishing is secure, then work on getting rid of unfavorable clauses for your sales royalty arrangement—and ask for the biggest advance possible. Your advance against sales royalties may well be the only money you ever get from that income stream, so get as much as you can upfront with as few restrictions on its use as possible.

Exceptions to the rule

My publishing company is called "Hang On To Your Publishing Company"—really!—so you might guess how I feel about sharing the rights to your songs—but there are always exceptions. I can think of one or two occasions in my own career where it probably would have made fiscal sense to do so, and there are specific situations when this might be advantageous:

- **Publishing Advance:** I have always viewed publishing companies as banks. If a writer needs money, it is a place to go and collect funds in return for future royalties that may be more or less than what they were advanced. Large publishing companies may float an advance to the writers just for the chance ride along with a record. If it's a hit, it was a great investment and if it's not, they write it off.
- **Administration Deal:** In return for a 15-25% cut of your publishing income, you can still form your own company but allow the big company to take care of the paperwork for you.
- **Co-Writing/Film & TV Placement/Additional Uses:** Greater use of your music in other areas, and additional co-written songs being plugged and cut, could potentially bring in more royalties over the long run than you might have gotten from just your

Starting Your Own Publishing Company

You can set up a publishing company right in your bedroom on a shoestring budget and accomplish everything established publishing companies do. It's easy. Here are the steps:

- **Choose a name:** Establish the professional name you want for your company. Brainstorm a list and pick something unique.

- **Affiliate:** Once you have established a short list of your favorite names, affiliate with a Performing Rights Society (in America, it's usually BMI or ASCAP). Contact them both, describe your situation, find answers to any burning questions you may have, and then go where you feel most comfortable.

- **Clear your name:** Once you choose a PRO, they will check their database for the proposed company name to make sure you don't use someone else's. (In the future, they will protect your name from others as well.)

- **Affiliate again:** Songwriters also need to affiliate with these agencies. If you have not already done so, ask them to assist you in that process at the same time.

- **Legalize it:** Now that you own a company, you need a business license to legally do business under that name. Go to your local county recorder, fill out some simple paperwork, and then publish a report in a newspaper. Any small local newspaper will do.

- **Take it to the bank:** To set up a bank account for this new business, you will need your official business registration document stating your new business name belongs to you. Show it to your banker and then file it.

- **Update your copyrights:** Alert the U.S. Copyright Office that any songs currently be copyrighted in your personal name should be reassigned under your publishing company's name. Yes, you will fill out yet another form to transfer these rights. (Go to http://www.copyright.gov for details.)

- **The final hoop:** Register your mighty song catalogue with your Performing Arts Society. You need only register your songs under either your business name (as publisher) or yourself (as songwriter).

These are the basics. Sure there will be situations not addressed in this rather stripped down "how to" column but you now know the nuts and bolts of how to get it done. It doesn't cost an arm and a leg to do this—only the few finger nails you probably chewed off before realizing how easy it truly is.

own album release. However, you most likely will have to take the initiative in building relationships with people inside the publishing company.

So, there are cases where you may want to sign with a label's sister publishing company, but make sure it is to your advantage. If they're going to keep half of the publishing royalties for themselves, make sure you're getting something you want in return.

Warning: Most publishing companies claim to work, exploit and promote their writers' material. Indeed some do this very well and both parties benefit, but be careful. It has been my experience that companies often make these claims to potential clients, sign said clients, but then do not follow through on the promises.

It happened to me early in my career. I was told by one of the largest publishing companies in the world that I would be a priority writer, but after I signed I could not get them to return my call regarding paying me my advance! It took several months to collect. I had already begun the construction of a recording studio in San Francisco and I needed that dough! They signed me on the basis of a record that sold in the millions so they coasted on that and never bothered to work the material to any other possible forms of revenue (i.e. movies, TV, commercials, etc.).

I also have a platinum record on my wall that I earned early in my career when I was willing to sign away my publishing. ("Platinum record" means sales have reached beyond the one million units mark.) Off the top, I'd estimate the publisher has actually paid less than half the actual amount owed to me. Just like record companies report to the artist on how much or little the artist is owed (usually in biannual statements), so do publishers report to songwriters on this information.

This is important information folks! If you sign away your songs, you are trusting that party with control of your songs to report to you fairly and therefore pay you fairly. The problem here is that money from mechanical royalties finds it's way to the writer(s) *through the publishers*. Trickle down economics . . .

TAKE ADVANTAGE OF PERFORMANCE ROYALTIES

But record contracts are not the only ways you can benefit from the system of songwriting royalties. There is also the whole issue of performance royalties from radio play, television, etc. Performance royalties flow in a separate stream from mechanical royalties, so if you never recoup your artist's advance, and the mechanicals are not forthcoming, you can still benefit from this third income stream. (In fact, if you're on a big label and they're charging all of the radio promotion back to your account, you can still earn money from that radio play, and it is yours free and clear.)

Join a PRO

No matter whether you have a record contract or are releasing your music independently, you will need to affiliate with a Performing Rights Organization (PRO). Once your music makes its way out into the world, it could wind up being performed somewhere (Internet or community radio, or maybe over the stereo in a small shop or restaurant—who knows?). The PRO's track this stuff, and if it shows up in their tracking system, you need to be affiliated with them as a songwriter and register your songs to receive the royalties. (If you've kept your own publishing, you will need to affiliate twice, once as a songwriter, and once again as a publisher—remember the 50/50 split I mentioned before between songwriter and publisher?—and you will definitely want to collect royalties for the whole pie.)

BMI and ASCAP are the two major collectors of publishing royalties in the United States. Both are non-profit and have enormous catalogues of songs in all genres of music registered for royalty collection on behalf of songwriters and publishers. Both organizations run on similar principles and formulas (that are forever changing and adapting to the times) to the extent that there is no significant difference between them in my opinion. (There is also a third organization, SESAC, but they're a more exclusive for-profit operation started by a coven of lawyers.)

The quick history lesson is that ASCAP was formed in the '20s, the Tin Pan Alley days, for primarily white songwriters and publishers (Jelly Roll Morton never saw a penny). BMI got its start as an answer to the more segregated approach and published music by blacks (and everyone else). Noticing the amount of money flowing into BMI funds, ASCAP soon changed its ways and included all races. But the race was on from that point as to who was #1 and #2 in the world of song royalties.

I am often asked which organization to go with and if one company is better than the other and my answer is always to "go where you are loved." Both organizations set up showcases and sponsor songwriting events and contests so I think it is wise to attend these gatherings and see what feels best to you individually. You may find a supporter of your music among the staff, and any level of personal care is a good sign.

Mind the details

I have been with one of the two organizations for quite a while and have been relatively happy with their service with only one rather large problem in the past 20-plus years. The problem was my last name was erroneously spelled with two Ts in the songwriting credits, a common error and burr in my saddle throughout my career in all areas. But if it happens that one's name is misspelled in the songwriter's credits, it is virtually impossible for BMI or ASCAP to properly account to and pay that person.

Unfortunately for me, this particular song was released as a single and was a big record all over the world. So, on the first (and biggest) pay period, my co-writers and I were talking about the song and the other two guys were ecstatic about the windfall they had received, whereas I was confused as to why my statement read and paid a much lesser figure. I contacted the fine folks that administer my publishing company who in turn contacted the collection agency I was signed to (and still am today) to find out if any compensation could be made.

So, I learned the hard way about the importance of details such as spelling of credits when I was informed that no royalties are collectible or due in retrospect to the initial pay period. Yowza! I wrote a hit song and did not collect my royalties during the critical time it paid. That has not happened since due to the diligent work of maintaining a watchful eye on such credits. Still, record companies continue to spell my last name with two Ts (the saintly spelling) in other areas of credits but that doesn't usually interfere with my royalties.

Knowledge is power

The fact is a lot of the big money in the music industry is in songwriting. This has been sort of an open secret, but now you can see how the royalty system for songwriters can benefit you as a recording artist. Given the resources a major label can put behind you to get your songs onto albums and the radio (and create publishing income for you), it's easier to make a case for that path, but remember that you will have to give up some control. It's a very personal choice.

Many of you may still choose to remain independent, and more and more independents are making an honorable living. This is great. Music publishing and songwriting provides other opportunities such as film and television licensing that could benefit you. Plus, given enough independent success, you may find the majors courting you because of your track record. If that happens, you will be in a much better position to retain control over your career, and you will know how play the music publishing card to your best benefit.

The Power of the Re-Mix

by Blake Althen with Paula Bellenoit

Artists pay thousands of dollars to promoters, consultants, managers, and producers to help them get airplay, distribution, and of course make their music sound great. They spend hundreds of hours on strategy planning, photo shoots, follow-up phone calls, rehearsals, websites, and traveling. Naturally enough, having spent money, time, and energy creating and marketing a song, the artists are fixed on their version of the song. Too often they don't realize that, for relatively little money and virtually no effort on their part, they can have their song re-mixed multiple times so it will be heard by diverse new audiences that otherwise would never have been exposed to it. I am frequently perplexed. As I have said many times in my production workshops, why don't artists maximize their song's potential?

Most music projects (even entry level projects) start with some kind of plan. Of course, major and independent labels will have more detailed plans than individual artists, but the basic plan is usually something like this:

1. Write songs
2. Hire a producer and get the songs recorded
3. Get the CDs manufactured
4. Make a music video (if budget allows)
5. Hire a radio promoter/publicist to get airplay, set up interviews, and get press
6. Go on tour to promote and sell the record

Simple and to the point, right? If only executing it was so easy. But it misses a simple and potentially lucrative step—the re-mix of the song into multiple genres. There should be a step added between steps 2 and 3:

2½. Get the a cappella vocal tracks off to the re-mixer(s).

I think this is a crucial step and is often overlooked by even the major labels. In the words of one of the country's top DJs Twisted Dee, ''Don't underestimate the power of the re-mix.''

BLAKE ALTHEN and **PAULA BELLENOIT** are also the record production duo known as Human Factor. They've worked with Michael Manring and DJ Logic, and have produced artists such as Pale Beneath the Blue, Michelangelo, and Abby SomeOne. They are also known for their interactive production seminars and clinics both at music conferences and independently. Visit www.hfproductions.com.

WHY RE-MIX?

Most people have heard stories of major artists getting their original productions re-mixed by some very expensive and big named DJ. Labels will sometimes "leak" a re-mixed song that has not yet been released into the DJ record pools in order to get the buzz going about the track. Then the songs turn into dance sensations and explode into the club circuit helping to launch the artist into the pop world. Of course, that is a great goal, but I prefer to give examples of smaller success stories to illustrate how to get a dance mix done for under $10,000.

Create "buzz" at your own shows

Human Factor (my production company) produced a Midwest rock band called Abby Some-One. They recorded a catchy up-beat track at around 100 BPM (beats per minute) with an adult contemporary/rock feel. Human Factor did a re-mix for them at 120 BPM that began subtly and gradually built up in intensity.

Abby SomeOne played their re-mix on the PA between sets and after their gigs. They figured every band plays music at intermission, so why shouldn't the music be theirs? But they didn't want to play the same tunes people were about to hear or had just heard, so they got re-mixes. An interesting phenomenon occurred in the audience as the re-mixes played. The audience had just heard the songs, and were hearing them again, but people just stood around dancing or listening with big smiles on their faces. People in the audience asked, "What is this?" or "Is this on the CD I just bought?" The band members replied "Nope, but we'll give you a copy if you sign up for our mailing list." Dance tracks that designed to be filler between sets became a vehicle for getting more fans signed up on their mailing list.

Increase your exposure even when you're not playing

I find that many artists tend to record a song and put it in the proverbial "can." I think now more than ever that mentality needs to be changed. While I agree that an artist should always be developing new material, I think the "can" should be replaced with "Tupperware." You may want to come back and re-open the song for future mixes. The more versions of a song you have the more chances you have of it being a success. I don't mean you should just make club or dance mixes. Acoustic versions are powerful as well. Have you ever been in a dentist's office and heard the elevator music version of a rock song? Major recording artists didn't have those recordings done just for fun. The more versions, the more chances for royalties. They are trying to maximize their song's potential.

For example, at one of Abby SomeOne's shows there was a DJ between the sets. After the show, the DJ played club tracks, and the band's manager convinced the DJ to spin the band's re-mixes. It turned out the DJ loved the mixes. After the band's next set he immediately played the re-mixes and the audience continued to sing along with the songs. He told the band that their tracks were going to be in his set from now on.

Think about it like this: artists are performing every night, but an artist can only be in one place at one time . . . or can they? What if you are rocking a live gig in Spokane, while at the same time, your dance tracks are being played in Miami, and your down beat mixes are thumping in Cincinnati? Your exposure just tripled. Likewise, there is no way a rock band is going to be able to play a gig in a dance club. But through re-mixing, the possibilities for a band are nearly endless.

These examples are just a few of the creative ways independent artists generated "buzz" about their group and songs. But there are many more ways that solo artists, indie labels, and major labels use re-mixes to create buzz.

HOW TO RE-MIX?

Much like when you first start your music project, the first thing you may want to do is set a budget and some goals. Some artists may attempt to hire the biggest name re-mixer they can get. Others may attempt to develop an entire record of different mixes of the same one or two songs (tribal, dub, etc.) to send out to a DJ pool (I will talk about DJ pools in a moment). The important thing here is keeping in mind why you're going for it, and do what makes the most sense toward that goal.

Decide what kind of re-mix

I mentioned a moment ago that some artists get an entire record of different mixes of the same song. Just as the rock scene has metal, alternative, emo, hair bands, nu-metal, classic rock, and many more sub-genres, the club scene also has its own sub-genres: trance, tribal, house, dub, drum & bass, etc. A re-mix in each sub-genre will increase your chances of exposure. A DJ who plays a trance set will not play a house re-mix and vice-versa. It may ruin the mood of his set. If you have a mix for many sub-genres, you have a chance with each DJ.

Here's a typical track list for a record of this type:

Track Listing
1. Keepers of our Souls (Original Edit) 3:20
2. Keepers of our Souls (DJ Blake's Filter Edit) 5:23
3. Keepers of our Souls (BA's Dub Mix) 7:75
4. Keepers of our Souls (BA's Tribal Mix) 9:23
5. Keepers of our Souls (DJ MRX Trance Mix) 9:54
6. Keepers of our Souls (DJ MRX Early Lounge Mix) 7:56
7. Keepers of our Souls (PMB's Anthem Mix) 8:59
8. Keepers of our Souls (BA's Soul Mix Extended) 10:32
9. Keepers of our Souls (BA's Soul Mix) 4:20

You may be thinking, "Wow, how can I distinguish between the different club sub-genres when all I listen to is rock (or country, or pop, etc)?" At first they may all sound the same to you. They certainly did to me in my early days of exposure to dance music. Before I got into the whole re-mix craze, I talked to an acquaintance who was very much into re-mixing. I told him club music all sounded the same to me—THUMP THUMP THUMP THUMP! He smiled (knowing I had a résumé full of rock music) said some people think all rock music sounds the same—some dude yelling and too much guitar! That made me curious and I began to familiarize myself with many different sub genres. Of course, the only way to do that is to take the time to listen to the music. (Since I can't include a CD in this article, I posted up a few examples at my company's website. http://humanfactor.net/remix.)

Pick a DJ or re-mixer

Once you have your project goals and budget set down, it's time to find your re-mixer. You can find DJ's willing to re-mix your track in just about every metropolitan city. Prices range from free to $10,000.00 (or more) for a re-mix.

Why would anyone do it for free? The first reason is probably the simplest. They love your song. The next is that they are new at re-mixing and they want to get their feet wet and build a résumé. You can go this route for an initial experience, but as in most things, you get what you pay for.

The process for selecting re-mixers is similar to that of finding a producer for the "main" mix. Unfortunately there is no Bureau of Producer Licensing. To become a re-mixer all you really need is a computer, speakers and a business card that says "John Doe: Re-mixer." This means there are many re-mixers out there today. You will have to do your own research to find some good ones. Ask them for a sample of their work, credits, and maybe even references.

Many re-mixers are also DJ's. They probably play a fair share of their own re-mixes, so go check out their set in a club. Certain DJs report their club playlists to charts (such as *Billboard*). This may be of interest if you want to get on the charts, but call the chart the DJ reports to and ask them if they have ever heard of him or her. Above all, remember—when the truth is told, the music does the talking!

So, the first thing you do to pick your re-mixer is decide whose music you like the most. Or try to get the biggest "brand name" DJ you can afford. If you care about getting on the charts, ask the DJ if he reports to any of them. Do your homework. Do some research by going out to a few different clubs—you don't have to stay long.

You will find that different clubs attract a different audience and a different audience may attract a different sound. Try to experience the music the way the audience will. Don't stand in the corner with a notepad. Go the club with friends. Remember that the people on the dance floor may be celebrating something or they may just be out for a night on the town. (They may have even had a couple of drinks. You may want to join them—just to understand the music more).

Re-mix tips

When it comes to how to make a re-mix there is no set of rules. However I can tell you what some of the elements of a successful re-mix are:

- **As in pop, catchy and big hooks are always a plus.** The more the audience can recognize the chorus the better.
- **The track's energy climaxes and then comes down.** Good dance music ebbs and flows like the cycles in nature. Remember, people are dancing to it. You need to give them a break to catch their breath so they can go full speed again.
- **The re-mix targets the right audience.** What may go over very well in NYC may not do so well in Madrid. Again, do your research.
- **The re-mix is designed to sync and segue with other tracks.** A DJ must be able to cross-fade into and out of your re-mix. So, a good re-mix will have a few measures of naked beat (little or no pitch) at the beginning and the ending. The DJ uses those measures to sync it up with the outro of the previous track and have a smooth and seamless transition from one song to the next.

AFTER THE RE-MIX IS DONE

OK. Now you have a screaming re-mix of your current favorite song. What do you do with it? I mentioned DJ record pools as a possibility. In a nutshell, record pools are companies that provide music to club DJs, and in return, the DJs report results back to them. Record labels use them as a source of information on what is working in the clubs. Obviously, record pools can be a crucial part of making a dance mix a success.

One of the quality companies is Starfleet Record Pool run by Ronnie Matthews. In writing this article, I had an extensive conversation with him, and he has several tips:

- **Go to the record pools.** Matthews told me that labels are tightening their belts and not servicing as many record pools, and this creates opportunities for your re-mixes. (What is "servicing" a record pool? That means providing them multiple copies of your re-mix so they can make it available to the DJs in their pool.)
- **Don't forget vinyl.** Matthews also illustrated the importance of vinyl. There is still widespread opinion that vinyl "just sounds better."
- **Don't forget intros and outros.** He made sure to remind me that songs had to have a nice intro and outro, like I discussed above.
- **Make sure to have a "clean" mix.** This last tip was for hip-hop. He seemed to think that having a clean edit (no profanity) was a good idea. I happen to agree.

Some artists have a fear of the unknown when it comes to re-mixing. I have had singer/songwriter clients do every thing from giggle to look at me like I am speaking Chinese when I ask, "Are you planning on having this re-mixed"? It may be surprising at first, but believe me, once you hear your song in a club and see 2000 happy people jumping around to your beat, your mind will be changed. So take a chance, try something new—just go for it. Maximize your song's potential!

Instrumental Work

A Professional Roundtable

by Anne Leighton

Musicians often seek to expand their career prospects by branching out into composition for commercial uses (film, TV, videogames, etc.) or by building a name as an instrumentalist, most often as session musician. But, the competition is fierce. This article brings together four composers and instrumentalists who have built diverse careers to share their experience and advice with *Songwriter's Market* readers.

Beyond the Academy Award for his compositions in the film, *The Red Violin*, **John Corigliano** earns money through compositions for orchestra and films. **Carl Strommen** creates band charts, and just about anyone who has gone thru the public school music education system the last 30 years has played one of Strommen's charts. **Steve Horowitz** supplies video game music for Nickonline; he created score for the critically acclaimed movie, *Supersize Me*; and he has his own band, The Code International. Rock/fusion violinist **Joe Deninzon** has his own band, Stratospheerius, but also finds session and sideman work for established acts ranging from Smokey Robinson to Ritchie Blackmore.

All of these musicians also have taught. Strommen and Corigliano teach part time at New York colleges—Strommen at LIU and Corigliano at Julliard and Lehman. Horowitz taught at summer camp, while Deninzon teaches both privately and at various schools.

Growing up, what were your career visualizations? Did you have to make compromises?

Carl Strommen: When I entered high school, I was very impressed by the sound of the jazz band. I wanted to play piano and write for the group, which I did.

Joe Deninzon: I wanted to be a musician since I was seven. In high school, I wanted to be a rock star—playing guitar and singing. When it came time for college, my parents nudged me to major in violin—I was stronger as a violinist. I earned a double major at Indiana University in violin performance and jazz. I saw all the possibilities as a violinist from the Mahavishnu Orchestra to classical. I could be the demented *Fiddler on the Roof*. Also there were so many guitarists who played at such a high level, that I would have had to give up the violin to kick ass on guitar. I still jam on guitar and get a great feeling from it.

Steve Horowitz: I started with guitar lessons from my neighbor. Our high school in Berkley, California had an amazing jazz program; we went to festivals, and the teacher gave me

ANNE LEIGHTON is a working music publicist, whose clients include Joe Deninzon & Stratospheerius, plus a variety of classic rockers including Tower of Power (several members started their careers in military bands). She is the author of the book, *Using Your Art & The Media To Comfort People*, and her website is www.anneleighton.com.

a stand up bass. I was always interested in recording and studio technology, and we had a four track in high school. It was a compromise that I did sessions to make money, but then again I could have flipped burgers.

My big crisis was in high school—our lead singer was a great musician who was 30 and always bitter about not making it.

Deninzon: I wanted to be a famous musician by the time I was 30, too. But at a certain point I realized the real goal is to be a working musician. It's not about fame but about making music with friends and enjoying the process.

Joe Deninzon

John Corigliano: I wanted to be a cartoonist. My father was a violinist. I became interested in music with the LP and hi-fi set. I always thought I had to do something else than write scores. I've done many things as most composers have. I teach at Lehman and Julliard now. I ran a music festival in Greece, handled theatre music rental, programmed television shows and music for radio stations—WQXR and WBAI in New York City.

How necessary is education to finding music work?

Deninzon: It gives you a foundation for music history and technique. Every music style has its snobbery—rock looks down on any musical training, but how can any knowledge be bad? I don't believe in overintellectualizing music, because music is music. Nowadays I don't have time for lessons but my wife [Yulia Ziskel, violinist with New York City Philharmonic] teaches me stuff.

Corigliano: Writing music is difficult technically. You have to know the orchestra, and education is part of that learning. It's good to get into the world of Academia but you can get trapped in it, going after doctoral degrees. Get into the real world because they listen differently to music [than academics].

John Corigliano

Musicians and composers need a public space, and college can supply that. Professional orchestras have to rehearse a mammoth amount of music in a small amount of time. There are financial realities in the real world of orchestras: payrolls, union rehearsal hours when you can't go any further. I earned my bachelors degree from Columbia and have nine honorary doctorates. I teach because of my success as a musician . . . it's because I've gotten out into the world.

Strommen: Here the question is "will college help you as a composer or an arranger?" The answer is "Who are the people teaching in that college?" If they are actively involved in writing and arranging and it's what you're going for, then you'll want to learn from them. Find the teacher first, then the college. Usually, working players and writers will be teaching part time as adjuncts, making a living as professional composers and arrangers. Students often don't know that many of the finest musicians come out of the military bands, particularly those based in Washington, D.C. These are select bands, the auditions are rigorous, and the quality is outstanding. Many of the education publishers use the D.C.-based military bands for their promotional recordings. There are also permanent-party bands at West Point, Annapolis, and the Air Force Academy.

Carl, what's the best way to break into arranging?

Strommen: I'm involved in the print end of the music business. It's important to get to know people in the print industry. And, there's always the first piece that you submit. If it's accepted and does well, the publishers will look at whatever you send. However, you're only as good as your last piece.

In the print industry, when you create arrangements and compositions designed for schools, you have to be aware of the abilities of students at different grade levels. There are very strict technical limitations for younger players. The parameters get wider for high school and college players.

Steve, how did you break into working in a studio and into interactive music composition?

Steve Horowitz

Horowitz: A friend of mine had an eight track recording studio and let me do whatever I wanted. I took out an ad that I was available to do sessions. And right now I'd like to apologize to the first few people I worked for—it took me a few years to get good.

I was always doing composition, and when I was in San Francisco, my cousin asked if I wanted to write music for interactive media and video games for companies like Sega, Sony and Crystal Dynamics. So now I'm with Nickonline. Back in the '90s I was part of the staff—an in-house composer. Now I'm a freelancer. When you're in-house, there is more stability but you're also doing administrative stuff.

It's hard to define me as "just" a commercial writer. I write chamber music and just recently had a piece played in Holland in 2004. I did variations of David Shire's original score of *The Taking of Pelham 1-2-3* for a 14-piece ensemble at the Kitchen in New York City; I found grants and also self-financed that performance.

Joe, how did you break into work as a sideman?

Deninzon: When I first came to New York City, I went to the Musician's Union (Local 802) and posted signs. I also had a friend from Indiana who gave me a few breaks. I met people, one thing led to another.

John, what is the best way nowadays to make connections in classical composition field?

Corigliano: Most composers have a long road ahead of them. There isn't one way of doing it. Composers have to get out there and make friends with musicians, conductors and more. People can create connections by making friends in school with young performers. Carry that out of the school and get involved with competitions and conductors.

What mental, emotional, physical qualities are needed in your field?

Strommen: You have to be completely focused and it has to be a part of your life. All the musicians I know who are successful writers and arrangers, are constantly studying the compositions, arrangements and orchestrations of others. They are always looking for new combinations of sounds and learning how to use instruments more effectively. They're always listening to other players, and seeking information from other writers.

Horowitz: Insanity! A sense of humor is the best thing, because there are a lot of messed up situations. You also need friends. Also don't believe the hype. So many people are doing what we're doing and going around saying, "Everything's great."

Deninzon: I agree about the insanity. You can't be too sensitive because you have to be able to take rejection. But you have to be sensitive when you're making the music.

Corigliano: My friend Bill Hoffman, the playwright [collaborator with Corigliano on the opera *Ghost Of Versailles*], doesn't understand why it takes so long to write a 25-minute piece for a full orchestra. But everybody's gotta play a note, and it takes forever to write one minute of music. I'm writing vertically and horizontally. So it's a slow language and quite intensive. The orchestra has no time to fix mistakes. A few errors are okay, but it really has to be all gone over before they play it.

Strommen: I have strict editors who check all scores and parts. I use the computer program Finale. I can see the full score on the screen and it gives me playback capability.

Corigliano: The main thing is composers have delayed gratification. It takes a year to write; you continue working month after month just amassing great quantities of music. Some people need instant gratification.

How do you stay up-to-date with trends—both technical and musical?

Horowitz: In video and interactive media it helps if you like games. You need to keep in touch with studio technology and the industry—the tools people are using, how things are done and how they are delivered. There is a big technology side for interactive music.

Deninzon: I have to keep up with music trends but I don't like following trends. I listen to a lot of pop music for the songwriting structure but I can't try to imitate a particular style because I'm still a fusion guy at heart.

Strommen: I tune into VH1 and MTV to see what's current that's related to the music business even though I'm not scoring for contemporary pop groups. The type of arrangements I do are usually for orchestras, wind ensembles, and jazz bands.

Carl Strommen

Corigliano: Listen and look selectively. Focus in on what you find interesting. If something's not interesting, don't go any further. Orchestral concert music seems to be having a pop influence. Maybe [the composer is] going for minimalism. Different composers do things differently. There's electronics with orchestra. Right now we should be concerned about the economics of classical music.

What do you think of this line: "Those who can't do, teach"?

Corigliano: I do teach. Some people teach for financial reasons while they're waiting for their music career to happen. I went the other way, became a composer and then later became a teacher part time.

There are devoted teachers whose creative energy is directed to their students and the music. They can offer practical world experience. There are people like Mr. Holland (from the movie *Mr. Holland's Opus*) who love teaching. I don't think you have to be one or the other when it comes to "doing" or teaching—you can do it all.

Strommen: Most of the music teachers I know are doing their craft professionally. They bring that experience to the classroom. Mr. Holland's story is interesting because, once he became a teacher, he spent 30 years trying to finish a piece. It was never published, but he was an incredibly successful teacher, as witnessed in the last scene of the movie.

Deninzon: Teaching requires a certain commitment, I had a Mr. Holland in school, who spent all night working on arrangements. When you're a working performer it's tough to balance it. You have to be straight up with your students and schools.

Horowitz: I did teach at music camp—the best place on earth. I taught six-year-olds how to play guitar and bass. When I was living in Europe I taught audio production, music theory and interactive music at an audio engineering school. That's how I moved to New York and continued to teach there.

As musicians we're constantly learning our whole lives. Some people have to teach; back when Charles Ives was composing there were 500 registered composers in the United States. Now there are 50,000.

How do you adapt for survival in your field?

Horowitz: Frank Zappa's biggest message was figure out what you want to do. Do not worry about how much money you want to make but go where the music takes you.

Do cold-calling. Figure out what's going on and make sure it's what you want to do. It is a business. Musicians are chumps—business people live to make money.

There are going to be bigger trends with video games because more games are being sold. There are 500 cable channels and some will be licensing music. Maybe you can start a music library or submit your songs to one.

Strommen: I agree with Mr. Horowitz; you must go where the music takes you. But know that talent and ability by themselves do not guarantee success. It takes hard work and perseverance to arrive at whatever musical goals you set for yourself. And you need to understand that music is business; you need to be able to develop good relationships with people in the industry.

Corigliano: I can survive because I've done it for years. I have a big repertoire—80-90 pieces and they're all out there, they've been played again and again. The economy is making the orchestra a stagnant art form. So young classical composers create their own groups.

My assistant Mark Baechle is an up-and-coming composer and into all kinds of things— electronics and television. He has a very healthy approach. Mark creates compositions for smaller ensembles, student and short films, jingles and live shows. He has a great quote: "It's a matter of doing everything till you get choices, and then you can make decisions for the work you really want to do."

Deninzon: Wayne Shorter said, "You've gotta pollinate people's consciousness." How do musicians survive? Hover around people and let them know you're there. I make most of my living playing with other people and teaching. Musicians should adapt but in the proper context. I can always be a musician if there's work.

Commercial Songwriting

Creative Secrets for Success

by H. Rusty Gordon

I teach a college level course in the Business of Music and the Crafting of Commercially Viable Songs. My first seminar was in the Fall of 1970. Since that time, my primary commitment has always been to provide songwriters with the songwriting techniques and skills necessary to compete successfully in the commercial marketplace.

One thing I've found again and again is that aspiring pro songwriters consistently create songs publishers and record producers turn down time after time. They become lost in the competitive shuffle without knowing why their songs are non-commercial. Also, many would-be professionals do not know how to write on demand like the established track record songwriters. To compete, aspiring professionals must better utilize both the conscious and subliminal aspects of creativity, inspiration and craft to boost their songwriting skills.

For example, writer's block is the nemesis of the songwriting industry, and there are a number of things that cause or lead to this enemy of creativity. The pressure and stress of performing can eat into the time a songwriter might otherwise use for writing new songs. The songwriter's personal life can become stressful, make them feel pressured, frustrated, and anxious, and lead to a loss of concentration. Since most songwriters believe that song ideas should come to them naturally and spontaneously, when the ideas stop coming easily, they are at a loss over what to do.

Many successful songwriter/performers also find themselves in this trap. If artists are on deadline to write songs for their next album, panic can set in. They get in this bind due to a conflict between their creative selves and their business commitment to market their current record and exploit themselves with a grueling performing schedule. The time, mood, and necessary inspiration for writing songs doesn't arrive when these obstacles are present.

Inconsistent creativity results in an uneven playing field, and demands techniques for triggering ideas with reliability and shaping those song ideas along competitive lines. Let's level that playing field!

TRIGGERING INSPIRATION

A songwriter's mind should be a fertile field of ideas and language flexibility, and a songwriter should be able to generate a wide range of variations on common themes. This is often easier

H. RUSTY GORDON has been an artist's consultant and manager, record producer, song publisher, lyricist, even producer/promoter, and the creator of a college course entitled ''The Business of Music.'' She has been presenting music business seminars and songwriter's workshops since 1970. Her company, Rustron-Whimsong Music Productions specializes in the production of benefits, music festivals, and special events.

Consider Collaboration

Tip

The great majority of songwriters are "lyric dominant." This means they find lyric writing easier than composing the melody or note pattern for a song. Maybe 10% of songwriters are "melody dominant" and find lyrics don't come easily or at all. In both cases, a songwriter who is very strong in either lyrics or music, may seek a collaborating partner to write songs with. Finding a collaboration that works well between two or more people isn't easy, but when it works, the results can be exceptional. About 30% of songwriters can balance the relationship between words and music, where lyric dominance or melody dominance is hardly noticeable. Songwriters who can identify their strengths and weaknesses can work to improve the balance.

Wherever the story or circumstances of a song take the listener, it's imperative the listener be willing to go. Both the melody and the lyrics working together provide the elements that entice the listener to make the song their own, so be realistic about your strengths and weaknesses and find collaborators who can complement your abilities.

said than done. But, there is room for conscious choice. Writing lyrics is part inspiration with a lot of method thrown in. If we can't control inspiration, then let us concentrate on method and approach inspiration by the back door.

Learn to activate your "creative space"

Pay attention and see if you can identify circumstances or activities that tend to trigger songs for you. Every writer has patterns of behavior and external experiences that lead to the songwriting mode. Consider what you are doing and how you are doing it when a song seems to write itself and the ideas are flowing naturally. Have you suddenly come up with ideas while driving your car? Are you just sitting calmly and strumming your guitar in a rhythm pattern when a song idea, a title, or an interesting riff pops into your head? Have ideas come to you when you were relaxing in the great outdoors, watching the flow of water in a river, a lake or the ocean? Does Mother Nature act as a catalyst when you enjoy a forest, hike trails or admire a beautiful vista?

You may notice many activities conducive to your creativity are rhythmic, feed an ever-changing flow of visual stimuli, or engage your linear, task-oriented left brain so that your right brain is free to create associations and slip into something resembling a dream state. When in need of inspiration, seek out these activities and trigger that state of consciousness.

So when song ideas dry up, take the time to put yourself in a conducive stimulating or calming environment, whatever your preference. Get away from the "same old" routines. Take something to write on, your instrument and a tape recorder. Taking other people or your pets with you will be a distraction. Create your own space, your own rhythm and free your imagination. The key to unlock a writer's block is always there and within reach.

Expand your focus

When looking for ideas, songwriters tend to focus in one of two ways—internal or external. Most songwriters naturally create from the internal and focus on their own personal emotional experiences. This exclusive focus can limit the possible viewpoints and themes for the listener to identify with, and therefore limit the songwriter's potential audience. A limited audience equals limited commercial possibilities. (This doesn't mean every individual song you write must cover all possible bases of theme and viewpoint and be all things to all people. As I discuss below, it's very important for songwriters to write many varied songs and cover as much ground as possible in the selection of topics, themes or concepts.)

Externally sourced, or "method" songwriting, takes its concepts from the real life experiences of people the songwriter knows or from the imagination of the songwriter who creates a lyrical work of fiction and tells a story in song. Writing for musical theater, motion pictures, children's music, television theme songs, topical, socio-political, historical, or patriotic themes are examples of songs created externally by choice, or as a result of a contracted request for songs on a specific theme. Music industry contract songwriters can become very successful at creating theme-identified songs upon request by their employer. For many songwriters, this requires the conscious cultivation of observation skills and a willingness to consciously shift their focus from internal concerns to the world around them.

Fill the well using lists

A songwriter's mind must be fertile and nourished by words, phrases, titles and raw ideas that can blossom into songs, and the "song concept list" is a useful tool for bringing song concept ideas to the surface. Create one for yourself in a handy notebook and use it to collect concepts you think will be great for future songs. Carry it around with you. Wherever you are and whatever you're doing, when you get an idea that could make a great song, waste no time in writing it down. Refer to this list to trigger your creative process when nothing seems to be coming into focus naturally.

When you have an experience that is remarkable, or find you can identify with someone else's experience, consider it a possible song concept and write it down. When you see something on television or in a film and it inspires you, create a song concept from it. If something said on a radio talk show or a news program grabs your attention and makes you angry, sad, happy or determined to take action, write it down. Concepts for songs are everywhere around you, all the time, and if you take the time to notice and look a little past the obvious, you will find a potpourri of choices and ideas you might otherwise miss.

Review the songs you have already written

When you look back over your catalog isolate the concepts and themes you were exploring at the time you wrote each song. Do any of these concepts still apply to newer songs you are writing today? You may discover all the songs written over a specific period of time mainly addressed personal issues from that time frame of your life as a songwriter, but ignored other topics, concepts, or viewpoints. You may find you write mainly from your own innermost emotions and that these familiar patterns are hard to break.

Even if the most-repeated theme is "love won and/or lost" the songwriter must consciously try to approach the issue from different directions. Otherwise, the songwriter in search of a good concept for a new song may easily become caught up in personal experience and issues and inadvertently stifle their commercial potential. A songwriter's catalog needs variety to be commercially competitive. Their body of work should cover many different themes and include a variety of viewpoints on common themes the listener may identify with.

Why is listener identification so important? When a song absorbs the listener through the magic of good storytelling and clever manipulation of theme, the listener feels disappointed when the song is over. They want to hear the song and have that experience again and again and again. This reaction translates to money in the bank. Once a new song on the radio hooks a customer, a consumer has been born. The next step is the purchase of the record product and an appreciation for the artist as a performer. Like any other business winning loyal customers (a "fan base" for performing artists) and new consumers builds success.

You may find this simple act of analyzing your song catalog and brainstorming new angles and viewpoints on old themes triggers the excitement and inspiration you have been looking for.

SHAPING INSPIRATION WITH CRAFT

Once you've found your inspiration, it's time to shape that inspiration with effective craft techniques. Since your aim is to be competitive in the marketplace, these tried and true techniques for shaping inspired raw ideas into commercial songs will put you ahead of the game while inspiration is fresh, and you will waste less time.

Build "definitive melody"

A "definitive melody" repeats the same notes exactly from section to section while the lyrics change each time. Verses need definitive melody and once the songwriter has picked the melody (note pattern) for the first verse, the lyrics for the remaining verses should be edited to that note pattern. Good definitive melody means a song is flexible and can be easily covered by other artists and produced with many different arrangements. (A commercially viable chorus keeps the same set of lyrics each time the chorus is repeated. A chorus and a bridge also require one definitive note pattern *different* from the verse melody.)

Songwriters who write verse lyrics to meter and rhythm instead of to a specific note pattern, create verses that each have a slightly different melody. The phrases in the first verse will be different in the subsequent verses because of this. Doing this creates the problem of run-away lyric, wandering phrasing, and rambling melody. These are very common problems found in the songs of songwriters who do not pay much attention to note patterns. Loosely structured verses make a song less commercially viable for single-song marketing. They could be adequate album cuts for the singer-songwriter's own album product, but they would be too eclectic and loosely crafted for the serious marketing of an individual song.

Spot weak melody and recompose/rewrite

Weak melody is easy to detect. If a songwriter knows they tend to be lyric dominant, they should pay special attention to their melodies. One way to review a melody without the words is to sing it into a tape recorder using sounds, not words. Sing *la la la* or *dum dum dum*, or whatever sound you are partial to and record the entire song that way. Listen to it many times and try to evaluate if this melody can stand on its own without words. If it falls on its face without the words, the melody will require a revamping or a complete replacement. With this in mind, songwriters should check through their song catalog for songs they think are worth the time to workshop and rebuild with definitive melody. Sometimes a song you've almost forgotten can be given a second life (and renewed commercial viability) with a dose of careful crafting.

Focus on titles, primary phrases, hooks, and tags

Titles should be selected from a phrase in the song that stands out lyrically and melodically, and these will usually be spotlighted in strategic areas at the beginning or end of a song section. Careful planning of a chorus should render at least one phrase that stands out well enough to be the title of the song. An average song title usually has no more than eight syllables. In selecting your title, try to avoid titles that have already been successfully exploited in the commercial music industry. Titles are important, especially for selling songs to the public. Make them memorable!

Hooks can be a catchy part of the melody or they can be a section of words and music (usually a phrase) often found in the chorus. Publishers and record producers are always on the lookout for strong hooks. If you have created a phrase that is catchy, hard to forget, and really puts something special into a song, you have created a hook!

Tags are short phrases of words and melody that are repeated to emphasize a thought. They are used most often at the end of a song. Tags wind the song down, repeating over and over until the sound gets lower and fades away. Commercial producers often use this technique in the studio as part of the arrangement. Songs that have a tag phrase in their chorus or at the end of the last verse are prepared for tag arrangements.

Watch out for verse redundancy

Give special attention and take your time with your verse lyrics. Your chorus is the attention getter, but the verses explain your reasons for writing. Don't shortchange your verses. Apply your wordsmith skills to present them in a logical and sensible sequence, as in a story. If the verses tell a story, the chorus can elaborate on the primary point the song is trying to make.

Redundancy occurs when verse after verse is saying the same thing over and over, just using different words. When this happens, the songwriter stifles the song's ability to hold the listener's interest and to evolve to reach conclusion. If any verse in a song can fall in any sequence, the song's concept will not progress.

Develop your rhyming skills

How the songwriter works with rhyming is a crucial song element publishers look at when they review a song. Rhyming helps to unify the end of lyrical lines with one another. Rhyming makes a song easier to sing and easier to remember. When careful attention is not paid to rhyming, it is easy to fall into a very predictable pattern. If a listener who has never heard a song before is asked to guess what the rhyme word will be at the end of a line and they guess correctly, that's a problem. All songwriters should have a rhyming dictionary'. Don't settle for the easy rhyming patterns. Craft your lyrical lines so they can end in rhymes that are not easily second-guessed. The old ''moon/ june/ spoon'' rhyming patterns have become over-used and predictable. Don't take the easy way out!

Focus on who, what, where, when, why and how

A good lyric should reveal bits and pieces of what is realistically happening within the song's storyline by carefully intermingling details of who, what, where, when, and why.

- **WHO** Who are the people in a lyric's storyline? What about them is significant, interesting, poignant, special, troublesome, or difficult? Bring out the individual characteristics, behavior, personality, style, or attitude that makes them come alive in the song.
- **WHAT** What is the song trying to reveal, explain, express or amplify? Like a short story, a song is focusing on a storyline revealing a small segment of life experience. But the song has only three or four minutes of communication time between the songwriter and the listening potential consumer. Clearly develop and identify the reasons for writing the song and don't wander off into confusion.
- **WHERE** Where, if the song is not just emotional expression, does the song describe things happening—places, atmosphere, weather, colors, inside or outside, venues and seasons? Using descriptive phrases and words usually enhances song lyrics and makes them more interesting.
- **WHEN** When is functional to time—past, present or future. When does the song's theme or concept take place? Is the song reminiscing, or reviewing the past? Is what's happening in the song occurring in the here and now or is the song's focus on the future? This includes combinations of all three, moving backward and forward in time.
- **WHY** Why is personal to the songwriter and contains the reasons and motivations for

the creation of the song. It is good creative expression and direction for the songwriter to explore his reasons for writing a song, but only after he allows all his creative ideas to flow as naturally as possible. Don't second-guess your inspirations while they are in progress. When the song reaches completion in the songwriter's mind, then the review of why the song was written may be revealing and empowering.

- **HOW** How is about the specifics of using the techniques of songwriting craft to the best advantage of each song a songwriter creates. Songcraft guides the songwriter through the many variables that are tried and kept or discarded during the song's creative evolution. It comprises the songwriter's skills and personal confidence in himself. It guides the song from the first to the last syllable and note.

TAKING IT TO THE MARKET

Creativity and craft obviously have to happen before you can even think about marketing your songs. But, if you've incorporated the suggestions I've outlined above, then you are already on track to build the sort of songs that achieve success in the marketplace, and you have saved yourself time, effort and frustration.

Building "standards"

If a songwriter creates one song that becomes a "standard," they will be fixed for life, and a focus on melody and lyrics early in the writing process, rather than arrangement and production style, widens the "standard potential" for any song. For example, in certain styles of commercial music, the words of a song are secondary to the arrangement and production techniques used to record the song. Studio production techniques can sometimes cover for significant lyric and melodic weaknesses, and become a trendy "hit" sound for its time, but this type of song often doesn't translate into other styles or arrangements and has a short shelf life. Once this trend in recording style runs its course, the song almost never becomes a standard. The song has its run, slips from consumer interest, and does not generate further royalties from other recording artists who could have cut the song on their own records with new arrangements and production. It doesn't generate royalties from translation into foreign languages and release in foreign countries.

On the other hand, if a song is strong on the basic level—lyrics and melody—and is of the caliber to be a standard, and the songwriters are lucky, the song may in time be picked up by the "golden-oldie" radio stations, be cut by other artists over many years, be translated into foreign languages, etc. This is how standards are born, and if you've developed accessible song concepts and crafted these with strong definitive melody and strong lyrics from the beginning, you already have the focus and elements in place that could lead to a standard.

Effective demos and copyright

If you are not a performing songwriter looking for both a publishing and a record label combination deal, the demos you present do not require the depth of arrangement a performing artist's original song does. As a freelance songwriter, your demo can be arranged simply with just a vocal and piano or guitar. The vocal will make or break the demo so get someone who can sing well. Have the song clearly reflect the style of music you believe it fits best. Don't get suckered by sound studios who want to charge you lots of money for more complicated arrangements. If a song is selected by a publisher, it's the publisher's responsibility to produce a demo. Remember, if you have written a song with definitive melody that can be arranged in different styles, keeping the demo simple makes it easier for industry professionals to take notice of that fact. They will not become lost in an overpowering arrangement or lose interest from one that does not do the song justice.

Advanced Articles

Lawyer Alert

Important

Twenty-five years ago, a music industry attorney was just that—an experienced music industry attorney, representing music industry operatives in both the administrative end of the business and the creative/entertainment end of the industry. They represented music corporations, and small businesses working with musical performing artists, bands and songwriters. These attorneys were specialized industry "legal eagles" and knew the music business inside and out. They are still out there using their professional expertise to make money for and not take money from their clients, but another breed of lawyers has cropped up.

A new breed
In the past 15 years, there has been a ground swell of licensed lawyers who represent naïve, unpublished songwriters of all ages, and they laugh all the way to the bank while their clients wait and nothing legitimate happens. They are real lawyers, but they have discovered that working the fringes of the music industry can be lucrative. You will not find these con-artist lawyers listed in the *Billboard International Buyers Guide*, which lists credible attorneys in the United States, state by state, and city by city. This new breed of lawyers advertise in music entertainment magazines, but not the respected industry guides, resources, or directories, like the *Billboard* directories. They attend music conferences, conventions, and music festivals. They attend these events as "vendors" and peddle their wares.

If you are an innocent songwriter who really doesn't know much about the music industry, they are looking for you. You may be impressed because a music business lawyer listened to your demo, wants to represent you, and convinces you that he or she can make your path to success easier. They allude to contacts and friends they have throughout the music industry. If they are successful, they get you to become their client. They offer to help with your marketing and all of the administrative paperwork that crops up around publishing contracts and Library of Congress copyright registrations.

Service for a fee
Since you're paying a service fee for all the things they do for you, be prepared to pay the legal administrative standard fee for having this lawyer fill out and file your copyright forms. He or she will tell you they are preventing you from making mistakes on the federal forms and he or she is also registering your songs one at a time for a $20 or more service fee and of course the $30 songwriter fee for the Library of Congress. That's $50 per song! (These lawyers also neglect to tell you that you can copyright *collections* of your songs as long as you are the primary or co-writer of all the songs in the collection—that's a $30 [no service charge] fee for the registration of 50 songs.)

The LOC forms are not complicated as each one has complete directions explaining every question and how to answer those questions. You can contact the LOC Monday thru Friday, 9 a.m. to 4 p.m. and speak to a copyright registration professional on their 1-800 number. If a songwriter can read at a fifth grade level, they can easily fill out their own LOC forms. Unfortunately, if you are caught in the pay-as-you-go, service-for-a-fee scam, you take the loss, and free enterprise revolves around charging fees for services provided.

Improve your knowledge
In the past eight years, I have personally alerted over 200 songwriters who had no clue they were retaining the services of this type of lawyer and that there would never be a light at the end of that tunnel. I also recommend the book *This Business of Music* published by Billboard Books in New York. This book is valuable to someone starting out in the music industry could own. It provides a complete education on the music business. The book comes with a CD containing copies of every legitimate, fair and equitable contract used in the music business. Empower yourself with real knowledge, close the door to con artists and be your own best representative.

I also sincerely encourage songwriters to invest in their own home recording studio. Pick the price range you can afford. A 2-track or 4-track set-up will suffice to record a clear, clean demo that allows a reviewer to hear a dominant vocal and simple instrumentation in the background. Remember, *a song with strong lyrics and definitive melody can be sung a cappella*. The addition of instruments and arrangements should only help the song sound better. Note: the actual basic song you copyright with the Library of Congress is comprised strictly of melody (note pattern) and the words that are sung with those notes. Chord progressions and arrangement ideas are not copyrightable. Even when you send the library of Congress a completely arranged version of a song, the words and melody are the focus of the song, and are carried by the singer's voice (which should then be the focus of the demo arrangement). The instrumental arrangement is superfluous when it comes to copyright. It is also advisable that songwriters copyright all songs they plan to market to the music industry before they begin distributing them. If you plan to record, manufacture, and sell your original songs to the public, *copyright them first*!

Expand your catalog or "body of work"
A word of caution! In today's music market, the singer-songwriter with less than 100 songs in their catalog may be steering themselves into a corner, allowing little latitude for rescue. The songs chosen by a record label for a debut CD will be the 10 most commercially viable songs as selected by A&R, producers, and arrangers. The songs that remain are the second stage selections for a subsequent album that will also require newer songs not available for selection the first time around. The more songs a songwriter has when they contract with a label, the less stressful their career will be. Publishers also appreciate a songwriter who has a sizable song catalog/body of work.

Advanced Articles

Copyright Notes

For More Info

Songwriters should Copyright their songs individually or in collections. Using the Library of Congress form PA to register for copyright gives the songwriter ownership of the exclusive rights to their songs, covering any future arrangement created for the songs by others. Form PA gives the songwriter world-wide protection for any and all uses of each song registered.

The Library of Congress form SR is used to register sound recordings for copyright. The owner of the exclusive rights to a sound recording captures the rights to only the specific arrangements of the songs on that specific sound recording. Record labels, independent record producers and songwriters with demos to distribute or sell, use form SR.

FINDING THE BALANCE

The serious songwriter is pursuing the kind of creative lifestyle and success only the music industry can provide. That success can be incalculable in today's world. By presenting these techniques and insights, it's my hope songwriters can take their creativity to the limit and open their minds to new options, new creative directions and a self confidence that will carry them past the inevitable failures and rejections to the breakthrough.

I especially want songwriters to keep writing and turning out wonderful songs. I want them to write songs people will treasure and remember and songs that will make a difference in people's lives. Hopefully, the elements of inspiration and songcraft I've discussed will help you take control of your creativity and build a career that is both artistically and commercially satisfying.

Please Play This Song on the Radio

by Michael Schweer

Getting your music played on the radio is not easy. You must have a song people want to listen to; you must be able to promote yourself and your music; and most importantly you must be able to convince the people at the radio station that they should play your song. There is no exact science to getting on the radio, but there are steps that you can take that will increase your chances of getting your music played. Here are a few tips to get you started and on your way to a successful radio campaign.

WHY DO I WANT TO BE ON THE RADIO?

This is the first question you must ask yourself before sending anything to a radio station. Do you want to be on the air because hearing your song played on the radio will be a great accomplishment for you as a musician? Or do you want to be on the radio so you can sell records, increase your fan base, and gain press in the music scene? Answering this question will tell you which radio stations to send your music to, how many stations to send to, where you want to sell records and just how much in the way of promoting you must do.

If you are satisfied with just getting on the radio, then having your song on a local station's specialty show should suit your needs. This level of radio play is more than sufficient to support CD sales at local performances and music shops.

On the other hand, if you want radio play to build your music career to the next level, it has to be done as part of a coordinated plan. You will need a professionally manufactured CD, regional distribution into stores, plans for a tour, and a radio promotion campaign focused on the area in which you plan to tour.

HOW DOES RADIO WORK?

There are a few misconceptions about radio. The first is the dream. You know the one—you press your CD, send it to the radio station and then voila! A disk jockey will listen to it, say, "This song is great," and put your song into heavy rotation. Record sales will go through the roof. Headlining tours ensue, and Gold records adorn the walls of your posh new pad.

I hate to be the bearer of bad news but this is not how it works. *The key to getting your song on the radio, in particular on commercial radio, is promotion.* No matter how good the

---

MICHAEL SCHWEER is assistant editor for *Songwriter's Market* and *Novel & Short Story Writer's Market*. In his spare time he studies metalsmithing and interpretive dance.

song is, commercial radio won't play it unless you give them a good reason, beyond "this song is great." You need to approach them as an investor in your music. They are going to play your music only if it generates listeners.

The bottom line is that commercial radio is not about the music, it's about the money. And this money comes from advertisers, which in turn is derived from the size of the listening audience that in the end is determined by which and how many people are tuning into the radio station to listen to.

So it only makes sense for a radio station to play a commercially viable song with the backing of a label and a slew of promotional power as opposed to a song from an unknown band on no label or a small label with little exposure. You need to be able to come to them with a strategy that shows them you mean business.

The other misconception people have about radio is that once you get a song accepted at one station the other stations will just naturally begin playing it. This is not the case. In order to get your music played at a station you need to send it to them, pitch it to them and then constantly call the station with news about your band/record. It is also important to find out the status of your record on their station: how often it is being played, when it is being played, and how the listening audience is responding to it.

DO I NEED A RADIO PROMOTER?

It is possible to get your record on non-commercial radio without a promoter. But once again you have to ask yourself what are your reasons for getting on the radio. If you are running a small campaign in order to drum up some buzz then you can probably go at it on your on own. *If you do it on your own, it's important to make sure you are sending your music to the right stations and the right people.*

You will probably need to hire a radio promoter if you are running a medium-to-large radio campaign. This person makes the much-needed calls to the radio station to make sure your song is being played. They also track the progress of your song so it can be posted on the radio airplay charts. Of course in return for that dirty work you will have to pay the promoter. And remember you are hiring a radio airplay promoter, not a booking promoter.

Intensive phone calling is the key to successful radio promotion, and it takes a lot of time, so make sure your promoter has the time and staff to make the calls. *You need your promoter and his staff in constant contact with the stations.* A promoter who is hard to contact or has a very little staff will have a hard time accomplishing this.

Choose your promoter carefully. If you pick the wrong one you could sabotage your music career. If the promoter leaves a bad taste in the mouths of the program directors at the radio stations then you will have a hard time working with these radio stations in the future. So take your time and make the right choice.

ARE INDEPENDENT PROMOTERS EXPENSIVE?

The major labels routinely spend hundreds of thousands of dollars *per song* getting singles onto commercial radio across the nation. If you are an independent artist or on a small label, you will not be able to compete at this level. You may instead wind up spending a few thousand for promotion to college radio or specialty show, or you may spend a few tens of thousands for a smaller regional campaign.

WHICH RADIO STATIONS ARE RIGHT FOR ME?

There are two forms of radio scaling the FM Dial in the U.S: commercial radio and non-commercial radio.

I Only Write—Do I Need a Promoter?

For More Info

The quick answer is that you should be looking for cuts, not spending money on radio promotion. If a company pitches promotion services to you, be realistic—a generic songwriter's genre demo (perhaps with an anonymous demo singer) will not be able to compete with expensive major label studio productions for airplay on national commercial radio. If you absolutely must try for radio play, go to Internet radio or local public access radio-and save money by doing it yourself. Otherwise, stick to your goal of finding cuts and gaining success as a behind-the-scenes player.

Non-commercial radio

Non-commercial radio encompasses college, community and National Public Radio (NPR) stations and are those stations hiding at the bottom of the dial. There are about 2,500 non-comercial radio stations in the U.S. Non-commercial radio tends to play an eclectic range of music and has looser programming guidelines. They mostly play Alternative, Metal, Rap, Hip Hop, Jazz (non-smooth), New Age, World, and Electronic music. It is not uncommon for a station to have a range of music from Metal to Rap during the same day since most of the music formats are hour long specialty shows ran by various DJs.

For a musician just starting out and looking to start a buzz or possibly land on a label, non-commercial radio may be the perfect fit. While you can sell records as a result of the airplay, non-commercial radio stations are better suited to increase your number of gigs and overall exposure. *Using non-commercial radio successfully will give you a strong track record to show commercial radio stations if you choose to go that route in the future.*

Commercial radio

Commercial radio includes all the major music stations on the dial. There are about 10,000 commercial stations in the U.S. They are the established stations with a strict play list and a well-defined music format. Commercial radio usually sticks to Alternative, Modern Rock, Rap, R&B, Smooth Jazz, Pop, Adult Contemporary, Country and Americana music. The downside to commercial radio is that it is very difficult to break into; the upside is that once you do break into it your exposure will increase dramatically.

If you are an established act or on a label, commercial radio may be a right for you. A single on commercial radio can open doors to increased record sales, increased attendance at shows, and increased merchandise sales. It is simple—the more people that listen to your music the better publicity you will receive.

However, it is almost impossible to get on commercial radio without a promoter. But remember in order to run a successful radio campaign for commercial radio it will cost a large amount of money and time. If you don't have a promoter, you will be wasting your time—time you would probably rather devote to your creativity.

HOW DO I SEND MY MUSIC TO STATIONS?

If you are just starting out, focus on non-commercial stations and smaller commercial stations. This will be your best chance of getting airplay. Look for stations that play your genre of music. If you find that a radio station only plays established acts, find out if they have a specialty show or mix show that showcases music from lesser-known artists. You might be able to get a few spins a week on one of these shows. It also is a good way for you to get your foot in the door at a larger station. Getting played on one of these smaller shows is most likely your best and only chance of being played on commercial radio if you are an unknown musician.

Promotion to commercial radio

Press your music onto a CD. Once you have decided which radio stations you want to send your music to you must have a CD to give to the station. If you are sending to a commercial station make sure your CD has a professional look. Here a few further pointers for submitting music to commercial radio:

- No CD-Rs!
- Make sure that you send them a single and not an album.
- On the CD itself, be sure to state artist, title, label, song length, contact info, and what album the single is from.
- Use a standard jewel case. No slim cases or cardboard cases. Make sure that your name, song title, song length and label are on the case.

If you are sending music to a non-commercial station, CDRs are acceptable, but CDs are preferred. If you are sending your music to a college radio station, go ahead and send them your entire album with a note highlighting the songs you think would work best on the radio. The DJs may take your advice or they may decide to play the CD themselves and hand-select various tracks off the album. It is common in college radio for more than one of your songs to be played off an album since the DJs have more freedom over what they play.

Making the call

So now that your CD pressed it is time to make contact. *First try to get a hold of a program director at a commercial station or a DJ at a non-commercial station.* Over the phone tell them about your music/single and why it would be a perfect fit for their programming. Or if you are lucky attempt to set up a meeting with the program director or DJ so you can personally hand them your CD.

Meeting a program director at a commercial station is a long shot, but it is worth a call on the rare chance they agree to listen to you. If you do get a chance to meet a program director make sure you are ready to seize the opportunity. Tell the program director about your fan base. Convince him that you have fans who listen to your music who also listen to their radio station. Inform them of any live performances you have planned or have played and tell them about release parties you have in the works. Make sure they know that you are going to do your part to get your record off the ground. It's important that they feel you will bring more listeners to the station.

If you do not get a chance to meet a program director follow through with sending your CD to the station by mail. *Send the CD out using first-class postage.* This way you won't have to worry about the delays that arise using third-class postage.

It's important that you make follow up phone calls a few days after you send your single to the stations. This call is to remind the radio stations that they have your CD and to encourage them once again to play your music. If you are not able to contact the station, make sure you leave a message and then try calling again.

Keeping constant contact with the radio station is what will put your CD/single on the radio. Remember nobody at the station will listen to your CD and say "this is good, let's put it on the air." You must promote your music and convince them that your music is a good fit for their station.

The Mid-Atlantic Song Contest

Editor's Report from the 2004 Awards Gala

by Ian Bessler

On Sunday, November 21, 2004, the Songwriters Association of Washington (SAW) once again held their awards gala at the Hard Rock Café in the heart of Washington, D.C. The gala mixed the presentation of awards with performances of the winning songs. The winning songwriters and performers wrote in styles ranging from folk to hip-hop and came from all across the country to share their music with an appreciative audience.

Will Hopkins and Mersaidee Soules, Grand Prize Winners

Songwriter Will Hopkins and co-writer/artist Mersaidee Soules won the Grand Prize (as well as Gold in the Country category) for "He Knew," a moving and immaculate love song that was actually a last-minute entry by the co-writers after they had already submitted several other songs. "We had just recorded this song," says Hopkins, "and literally finished mixing it at 10:45 the night of the deadline. I raced it to the post office and got it postmarked 6 minutes before the contest deadline. I had just submitted a *bunch* of songs, but I loved this song and decided I had to enter it."

Mersaidee Soules & Will Hopkins

The Grand Prize consists of $1,000 cash, a free three-year SAW membership, a free one-year TAXI membership, and a copy of *Songwriter's Market*, but the credibility gained from a song contest win like this was also an incentive. "I'm in Nashville right now," says Soules, "and I'm actually going for an artist deal—artist-slash-writer—so how can this be bad? Out of 900 songs to actually win the grand prize. I can definitely say this will get us notice and open a few more doors where we might not otherwise have had the opportunity."

Hopkins splits his time between Washington, D.C. and Nashville, and agrees that success in a song contest can help make a bigger splash in a big pond like Nashville and help them stand out from the hordes of songwriters thronging Music City. "The hard part in Nashville," he says, "is that there are so many writers who have moved to Nashville to make it as writers, and a lot of them are really talented, but a lot of them are only OK. And if a publisher spent all their time listening to every tape or CD presented to them, they wouldn't have time to do anything else. What happens is they don't listen to *anything* unless they hear about it from some other source. So being able to say this song was the *grand prize winner* will immediately

---

IAN BESSLER has been editor of *Songwriter's Market* since the 2001 edition.

give us credibility we wouldn't otherwise have. Otherwise, it's like, 'Oh, yeah, well I've got a thousand songs that were submitted today.' "

Hopkins and Soules had recently begun writing together after meeting at a Tuesday night song critique workshop in Nashville. They respected what they heard of each other's work at these gatherings, and hit it off as co-writers. They are optimistic at the success they've achieved at this early stage in their collaboration, but also recognize major challenges remain, and they encourage other writers to keep working and to persist "I think the most important thing to do is write, write, write, write," says Hopkins. "You gotta just keep on writing, and while you have to work on songs you've finished—and I think it's important to get feedback and revise—at some point move on and write another song. And eventually you learn so much that your first drafts become better, and to me one of the most inspiring things I've heard at a songwriter workshop was a very big writer in Nashville who said that his first 300 songs were never recorded—and most people give up before 300 songs! But if you believe, you've got to keep on writing. Just like any other profession, you get better with time and with practice. You may not recognize it immediately, but six months later, a year later, two years later, you say, 'Well I'm writing at a higher level than I used to.' "

Kyler England, Second Place Overall

Singer-songwriter Kyler England returned for another Second Place Overall win of $500 cash and free memberships to SAW and TAXI for the soaring ballad, "If You Want Me To." Since her win in the 2003 Mid-Atlantic Song Contest, England has been busy touring behind her album, *A Flower Grows In Stone*, including opening slots for Sting, Annie Lennox, and Melissa Etheridge. She has also landed airplay on Hot AC radio stations for "Something So Beautiful," her winning song from 2003, and has continued co-writing sessions in Nashville on the side. "I think they take me more seriously because I've won some songwriting awards," she says, "which is really great. I've really enjoyed the writing in Nash-

Kyler England

ville, and I continue to do that every 3-4 months. Hopefully one day I'll write a hit song in Nashville. I'm [also] getting ready to do a demo deal with a label, so we're going to be recording three songs with the label. I'm looking for a record deal right now, so hopefully that will lead to something and help me take everything to the next level."

As a previous winner, England agrees that a song contest win brings extra validation to a songwriter's efforts to break through. "When someone is just reading about you before they've heard your music, a contest win has a chance to make an impact," she says. "Things like that definitely add validity to what you're doing, and make people more interested in checking out the music and getting them to take that extra step and listen to a file on your website or get the CD and check it out."

With success as both performer and writer coming her way, England has focused ideas about what she wants in the long term. "I definitely intend to be an artist," she says. "The cool thing is I'm already doing everything I want to do—I'm writing songs, I'm performing them for people, and I'm recording them and getting them out to people in the form of CDs. I feel really lucky because I'm already doing what I want to do. I just want to take it up a notch. I want to have more radio airplay and more exposure so more people can hear my music."

Daniel Lee, Third Place Overall

This year's Third Place Overall prize of $250 cash and free SAW and TAXI memberships went to singer-songwriter Daniel Lee for "Starboard," a song featuring a funky rock/alternative groove and a surreal lyric Lee describes as: "A New York song about furious love spouting over the fringes of modern worklife."

Daniel Lee

When asked about the benefits of a song contest win, Lee says, "It's a really good thing for press and promo. We try to put things out there like samplers—a disc with three songs, and stuff like that—and it's helpful if people see this recognition. I also won the Eddie's Attic Shootout, which is really big at least down in the area where I'm from [in Atlanta], and we've been using that a lot, because people recognize it and relate to it. John Mayer won that along with other very recognized people. So this is another one of those things that helps people get a picture of the music actually being a real and professional thing, and I'm excited about that."

When asked how he chose "Starboard" for submission to the contest, Lee describes it as an intuition based on audience feedback. "I get a feel from people, in terms of direct appeal—appeal in that 'first listen' kind of sense," he says. "And so all those things draw me to say 'hey, maybe this is noteworthy.' But it's weird. You never know what somebody is going to like. It has as much to do with what they ate for breakfast that morning as with truly breaking it down to a science."

According to Lee, this intuitive sense also guides his songwriting process and informs his lyrics and themes. "I try to write from experience," he says, "but I do try to attempt some sort of fictional process, more like short story writers and novelists and people in other genres of art. I think it's a construct we've invented where the common perception is 'Write about you. Write about something that's happened to you.' But I like to write about things that maybe I dream about or things that involve a sense of me or diagram my own passion, something like that. It's much more a visceral process than a cerebral one."

Jason Samson and Chris Rusin, Gold in Hip-Hop/Dance/Urban

This year's Gold winners in Hip-Hop/Dance/Urban, rapper Jason Samson and singer-songwriter Chris Rusin describe their winning song, "Can You Hear Me," as an exploration of "the universal desire . . . to not only be heard, but to be understood." The song features Samson rapping in the guise of a man longing for his girl, with melodic falsetto vocals in the background courtesy of Rusin.

Jason Samson

Samson and Rusin met through Samson's uncle three years ago and began collaborating shortly thereafter when they found their co-writing relationship offered a refreshing combination of creative sensibilities. "What I like about the whole co-writing process with Jason," says Rusin, "is that I've worked with rock and other forms a lot, but the urban hip-hop stuff is just so wide open and so free-flowing that you can say whatever you want and use as many words as you want to say it. It's a really freeing type of music."

From the other side of the equation, Samson found a sense of structure in Rusin's background that he had been looking for. "There were some things in my writing that flow-wise weren't all there," says Samson, "and Chris helped me rearrange that to get the same point

Advanced Articles

across but do it in a way that was a little bit smoother. It was a good balance.''

Like other winners, Samson enjoys the recognition of his contest win. ''It's a great experience for me to let my music finally be heard,'' he says, ''because Chris and I work very hard at doing it. It's a good way to get our music across. When we submitted this song I wasn't expecting to get the feedback I did. Even people who don't listen to rap have told me they like this song, so it must mean I'm doing something right if it touches somebody.''

Chris Rusin

Julie Clark, Gold Winner in Folk

Folk singer-songwriter Julie Clark had previously won in the Kerrville New Folk Competition and heard about the Mid-Atlantic Song Contest from a fellow Kerrville and former MASC winner Ron Fetner. ''He told me about it on the very last day I could enter,'' says Clark, ''and I threw an entry together and had some good luck. It was kind of a last minute thing.''

As a recent Kerrville winner, Clark agrees that a song contest win can be a big help to music industry newcomers. ''[The Kerrville win] has been opening up a lot of doors for me in the industry. It's given me a chance to perform at some of the premiere clubs on the acoustic circuit, like Jammin' Java and the Tin Angel and places like that. That award only came my way in late May, so I'm still getting my feet wet with putting the word out about it. But, people notice, they look twice and listen. They'll give you a chance, and that's really all I want. With so much music out there, as you know, the competition to have someone just listen and give you the benefit of the doubt that you are worth listening to, that makes all the difference.''

After writing for seven years, Clark didn't feel ready to submit until she had released her first CD, *Feel Free*, and had professionally produced tracks available. Now, she feels like her success in song contests has validated her songwriting ability, and she no longer feels fully-produced recordings are absolutely necessary to submit if the songwriting holds up. ''As a songwriter it's hard to be objective about whether your songs are good or not,'' she says. ''For me it's been hard to dare to hope they are good. It has taken consistent wins and good responses for me to feel like I'm getting where I want to go. I now have a sense that this is something I'm capable of doing well, and I want to learn more and get stronger.''

Julie Clark

Clark also hopes her contest win, and the validation it brings to her skill as a songwriter, could help open doors to a wider range of songwriting opportunities. ''I'm very interested in doing collaborative songwriting,'' she says, ''and I think that would be an interesting opportunity, and an interesting challenge. My process has been very solitary so it's hard to imagine what that would be like-just as an experience, to have that goal to walk in and produce something so personal as a song with someone else. And as far as writing for others, I have hopes that if I keep writing and keep writing well, when I get to that level with my craft, my songs will get covered.''

Donna Lisa, Gold and Silver in Children's

Donna Lisa, winner of Gold and Silver in the Children's category for, respectively, ''My Pockets'' and ''Toucan You Can,'' has a multi-pronged artistic approach encompassing books and other media beside music. She has won several other awards including an iParenting

Media Award and a Children's Music Web Award (for Best Preschool Album) for her children's album, *Toucan You Can*, an Honorable Mention in the John Lennon Songwriting Contest (for "Cheeribye"), and an Honorable Mention in the 2004 USA Songwriting Contest Children's Category (for "Oliver Otter"). "[Winning contests] has actually been helpful for me in other areas related to this," she says. "For example, I acquired a literary agent who's going to represent my stories, in conjunction with my songs for book/CD publishing. Winning this contest, and other contests, makes me more credible as a songwriter/writer. I am also working on two family film/ animation projects that have garnered some interest from an

Photo by Cindy Gold

Donna Lisa

established entertainment company. Being an award winner definitely helped me to connect with this company. For me, the synergy between song, story and screenwriting is very exciting."

The idea for "My Pockets" came from an actual experience with her niece. "I was spending time with my niece, Madeline, who was four at the time. She was wearing overalls and a shirt with many, many pockets. Madeline also had on a pair of sneakers with little Velcro pockets on the sides. I loved watching her open and close her pockets, as she put in tiny treasures—such as rocks, feathers, and shells—and pulled them out again. I thought that this would be a great idea for a song."

Greg Alan, Silver in Adult Contemporary/Soft Rock

Singer-songwriter Greg Alan, Silver winner in Adult Contemporary/Soft Rock for "Amazing," heard about the Mid-Atlantic Song Contest through the listing in *Songwriter's Market*. He submitted in 2003 and didn't win anything, but by 2004 he had accumulated some Honorable Mentions in other contests and felt ready to try the Mid-Atlantic song contest again using those songs. The previous good showing was the confidence booster he needed. "It's one thing when your friends and family tell you your song is great," says Alan, "and sometimes they're obliged to say that, but when you have third party recognition, it makes you feel you're doing something correctly and it's being appreciated by more than just your family and friends. I'm hoping that if anything it's a resume builder, so when you're out there performing people would notice."

Photo by Ian Bessler

Greg Alan

When asked if he would recommend contests to other songwriters, Alan answers affirmatively. "I definitely would encourage them to do it," he says, "even if they have doubts about themselves, because it's very easy to doubt yourself. If you really love doing it, you have absolutely nothing to lose and everything to gain, so I would definitely suggest it."

Positive exposure

Contest Director Jean Bayou is a big believer in the ability of a song contest to open doors, but she also believes it's up to songwriters to take the risk and put their songs on the line. "The Mid-Atlantic Song Contest is a great vehicle for recognition and exposure for aspiring songwriters," she says. "One of the favorite parts of my job as contest director is promoting and spreading the word about these fantastic songwriters. But as they say, 'If you want to win, you gotta buy a ticket.' You've got to just get out there and do it."

Advanced Articles

Music Publishers

Music publishers find songs and then get them recorded. In return for a share of the money made from your songs, they work as an agent for you by plugging your songs to recording artists, taking care of paperwork and accounting, setting you up with co-writers (recording artists or other songwriters), and so on.

HOW DO MUSIC PUBLISHERS MAKE MONEY FROM SONGS?

Music publishers make money by getting songs recorded onto albums, Film and TV soundtracks, commericals, etc.and other areas. While this is their primary function, music publishers also handle administrative tasks such as copyrighting songs; collecting royalties for the songwriter; negotiating and issuing synchronization licenses for use of music in films, television programs and commercials; arranging and administering foreign rights; auditing record companies and other music users; suing infringers; and producing new demos of new songs. In a small, independent publishing company, one or two people may handle all these jobs. Larger publishing companies are more likely to be divided into the following departments: creative (or professional), copyright, licensing, legal affairs, business affairs, royalty, accounting and foreign.

HOW DO MUSIC PUBLISHERS FIND SONGS?

The *creative department* is responsible for finding talented writers and signing them to the company. Once a writer is signed, it is up to the creative department to develop and nurture the writer so he will write songs that create income for the company. Staff members often put writers together to form collaborative teams. And, perhaps most important, the creative department is responsible for securing commercial recordings of songs and pitching them for use in film and other media. The head of the creative department—usually called the "professional manager"—is charged with locating talented writers for the company.

HOW DO MUSIC PUBLISHERS GET SONGS RECORDED?

Once a writer is signed, the professional manager arranges for a demo to be made of the writer's songs. Even though a writer may already have recorded his own demo, the publisher will often re-demo the songs using established studio musicians in an effort to produce the highest-quality demo possible.

Once a demo is produced, the professional manager begins shopping the song to various outlets. He may try to get the song recorded by a top artist on his or her next album or get the song used in an upcoming film. The professional manager uses all the contacts and leads he has to get the writer's songs recorded by as many artists as possible. Therefore, he must be able to deal efficiently and effectively with people in other segments of the music industry, including A&R personnel, recording artists, producers, distributors, managers and lawyers. Through these contacts, he can find out what artists are looking for new material, and who may be interested in recording one of the writer's songs.

HOW IS A PUBLISHING COMPANY ORGANIZED?

After a writer's songs are recorded, the other departments at the publishing company come into play.

- The *licensing and copyright departments* are responsible for issuing any licenses for use of the writer's songs in film or TV and for filing various forms with the copyright office.
- The *legal affairs department and business affairs department* works with the professional department in negotiating contracts with its writers.
- The *royalty and accounting departments* are responsible for making sure that users of music are paying correct royalties to the publisher and ensuring the writer is receiving the proper royalty rate as specified in the contract and that statements are mailed to the writer promptly.
- Finally, the *foreign department*'s role is to oversee any publishing activities outside of the United States, to notify sub-publishers of the proper writer and ownership information of songs in the catalogue and update all activity and new releases, and to make sure a writer is being paid for any uses of his material in foreign countries.

LOCATING A MUSIC PUBLISHER

How do you go about finding a music publisher that will work well for you? First, you must find a publisher suited to the type of music you write. If a particular publisher works mostly with alternative music and you're a country songwriter, the contacts he has within the industry will hardly be beneficial to you.

Each listing in this section details, in order of importance, the type of music that publisher is most interested in; the music types appear in **boldface** to make them easier to locate. It's also very important to submit only to companies interested in your level of experience (see A Sample Listing Decoded on page 11). You will also want to refer to the Category Indexes on page 11, which list companies by the type of music they work with. Publishers placing music in film or TV will be proceded by a ⊠ (see the Film & TV Index on page 419 for a complete list of these companies).

Do your research!

It's important to study the market and do research to identify which companies to submit to.

- Many record producers have publishing companies or have joint ventures with major publishers who fund the signing of songwriters and who provide administration services. Since producers have an influence over what is recorded in a session, targeting the producer/publisher can be a useful avenue.
- Since most publishers don't open unsolicited material, try to meet the publishing representative in person (at conferences, speaking engagements, etc.) or try to have an intermediary intercede on your behalf (for example, an entertainment attorney; a manager, an agent, etc.).
- As to demos, submit no more than 3 songs.
- As to publishing deals, co-publishing deals (where a writer owns part of the publishing share through his or her own company) are relatively common if the writer has a well-established track record.

- Are you targeting a specific artist to sing your songs? If so, find out if that artist even considers outside material. Get a copy of the artist's latest album, and see who wrote most of the songs. If they were all written by the artist, he's probably not interested in hearing material from outside writers. If the songs were written by a variety of different writers, however, he may be open to hearing new songs.
- Check the album liner notes, which will list the names of the publishers of each writer. These publishers obviously have had luck pitching songs to the artist, and they may be able to get your songs to that artist as well.
- If the artist you're interested in has a recent hit on the *Billboard* charts, the publisher of that song will be listed in the "Hot 100 A-Z" index. Carefully choosing which publishers will work best for the material you write may take time, but it will only increase your chances of getting your songs heard. "Shotgunning" your demo packages (sending out many packages without regard for music preference or submission policy) is a waste of time and money and will hurt, rather than help, your songwriting career.

Once you've found some companies that may be interested in your work, learn what songs have been successfully handled by those publishers. Most publishers are happy to provide you with this information in order to attract high-quality material. As you're researching music publishers, keep in mind how you get along with them personally. If you can't work with a publisher on a personal level, chances are your material won't be represented as you would like it to be. A publisher can become your most valuable connection to all other segments of the music industry, so it's important to find someone you can trust and feel comfortable with.

Independent or major company?

Also consider the size of the publishing company. The publishing affiliates of the major music conglomerates are huge, handling catalogs of thousands of songs by hundreds of songwriters. Unless you are an established songwriter, your songs probably won't receive enough attention from such large companies. Smaller, independent publishers offer several advantages. First, independent music publishers are located all over the country, making it easier for you to work face-to-face rather than by mail or phone. Smaller companies usually aren't affiliated with a particular record company and are therefore able to pitch your songs to many different labels and acts. Independent music publishers are usually interested in a smaller range of music, allowing you to target your submissions more accurately. The most obvious advantage to working with a smaller publisher is the personal attention they can bring to you and your songs. With a smaller roster of artists to work with, the independent music publisher is able to concentrate more time and effort on each particular project.

SUBMITTING MATERIAL TO PUBLISHERS

When submitting material to a publisher, always keep in mind that a professional, courteous manner goes a long way in making a good impression. When you submit a demo through the mail, make sure your package is neat and meets the particular needs of the publisher. Review each publisher's submission policy carefully, and follow it to the letter. Disregarding this information will only make you look like an amateur in the eyes of the company you're submitting to.

Listings of companies in Canada are preceded by a ◼ , and international markets are designated with a ◼ . You will find an alphabetical list of these companies at the back of the book, along with an index of publishers by state in the Geographic Index (see page 421).

Icons

For More Info

For more instructional information on the listings in this book, including explanations of symbols (![symbols]), read the article *Songwriter's Market: How Do I Use It?* on page 5.

PUBLISHING CONTRACTS

Once you've located a publisher you like and he's interested in shopping your work, it's time to consider the publishing contract—an agreement in which a songwriter grants certain rights to a publisher for one or more songs. The contract specifies any advances offered to the writer, the rights that will be transferred to the publisher, the royalties a songwriter is to receive and the length of time the contract is valid.

- When a contract is signed, a publisher will ask for a 50-50 split with the writer. *This is standard industry practice*; the publisher is taking that 50% to cover the overhead costs of running his business and for the work he's doing to get your songs recorded.
- It is always a good idea to have a publishing contract (or any music business contract) reviewed by a competent entertainment lawyer.
- There is no "standard" publishing contract, and each company offers different provisions for their writers.

Make sure you ask questions about anything you don't understand, especially if you're new in the business. Songwriter organizations such as the Songwriters Guild of America (SGA) provide contract review services, and can help you learn about music business language and what constitutes a fair music publishing contract. Be sure to read What About Contracts? on page 36 for more information on contracts. See the Organizations section, beginning on page 323 of this book, for more information on the SGA and other songwriting groups.

When signing a contract, it's important to be aware of the music industry's unethical practitioners. The "song shark," as he's called, makes his living by asking a songwriter to pay to have a song published. The shark will ask for money to demo a song and promote it to radio stations; he may also ask for more than the standard 50% publisher's share or ask you to give up all rights to a song in order to have it published. Although none of these practices is illegal, it's certainly not ethical, and no successful publisher uses these methods. *Songwriter's Market* works to list only honest companies interested in hearing new material. (For more on "song sharks," see How Do I Avoid the Rip-Offs? on page 19.)

ADDITIONAL PUBLISHERS

There are **more publishers** located in other sections of the book! On page 139 use the list of Additional Publishers to find listings within other sections who are also music publishers.

Music Publishers

☑ ABALORN MUSIC (ASCAP)

P.O. Box 5537, Kreole Station, Moss Point MS 39563-1537. (228)475-0059. "No collect calls." Estab. 1974. **Contact:** Joe F. Mitchell, executive vice president/general manager. First Vice President: Justin F. Mitchell. Second Vice President: Jonita F. Mitchell. Music publisher and record company (Missile Records).

> • Also see the listing for Bay Ridge Publishing in this section and the listing for Missile Records in the Record Companies section.

Affiliate(s) Bay Ridge Publishing Co. (BMI).

How to Contact *"Please don't send us anything until you contact us by phone or in writing and receive submission instructions. You must present your songs the correct way to get a reply.* Always whenever you write to us, be sure you include a #10 business-size envelope addressed back to you with a first class USA postage stamp on the envelope. We reply back to you from the SASE you send to us. All songs sent for review must include sufficient return postage. No reply made back to you without SASE or return of material without sufficient return postage. **Absolutely no reply postcards—only SASE.** If you only write lyrics, do not submit. We only accept completed songs, so you must find a collaborator. We are not interested in reviewing homemade recordings." Prefers CD (first choice) or cassette with 3-8 songs and lyrics to songs submitted. Responds in 2 months. "A good quality demo recording will always get preference over a poor recording."

Music All types and styles of songs. "Mississippi, Mississippi" (single by Kadish Millett) and "Innocent Little One" (single by Bob Levy) from *If It Takes All Night* (album), recorded by Christian Ramsey (modern pop country), released on Missile Records.

Tips "Our doors are always open to young recording artists who are exceptional talented and want to make a name for themselves in the music business. Your success is our success. We will work with you to reach your goal. We also are in the business of getting your professionally-recorded album of 10-12 well-produced and well-written, radio-ready songs placed with record companies in the USA and foreign countries for the possibility of record deals. Here is what we have gotten for some artists: $850,000 record deal for Charity (religious singing group) on Big Easy (USA) in 2001; $500,000 record deal for Vance Greek on Dime-A-Dozen (Germany) in 2002; and a $150,000 record deal for Randell Ruthledge (country) on Dime-A-Dozen (Germany) in 2003. Two more artists are under consideration as of 2004, and others may be considered. Missile Records, Abalorn Music (ASCAP) and Bay Ridge Publishing Co. (BMI) are listed in some well-known publications such as the *Billboard International Buyer's Guide, Mix Master Directory, Industrial Source Book, Pollstar, Yellow Pages of Rock* and other publications. Some well-known recording artists born and raised in Mississippi include Elvis Presley, Conway Twitty, B.B. King and Faith Hill. The Moss Point, MS area music scene is also home to nationally-known rock group Three Doors Down, who sold more than 10 million of their CD albums and singles. Singers and songwriters thinking about doing professional recording, give us a call before you make that move. We can save you money, time, headaches, heartaches and troubles you may run into. We know what to do and how to do it to benefit you and get the best results."

☐ ABEAR PUBLISHING (BMI)/SONGTOWN PUBLISHING (ASCAP)

323 N. Walnut St., Murfreesboro TN 37130. (615)890-1878. Fax: (615)890-3771. E-mail: ron@icofm .com. **Contact:** Ron Hebert.

☑ ACUFF-ROSE MUSIC (BMI)

65 Music Square W., Nashville TN 37203. (615)321-5000. Fax: (615)321-5655. **Contact:** Jerry Bradley, president. Vice President: Troy Tomlinson. Vice President Creative: Jim Vienneau, Clay Bradley.

☒☐ ALEXANDER SR. MUSIC (BMI)

PMB 364, 7100 Lockwood Blvd., Boardman OH 44512. (330)726-8737. Fax: (330)726-8747. E-mail: dap@netdotcom.com. Website: www.dapentertainment.com. **Contact:** LaVerne Chambers, promotions. Owner: Darryl Alexander. Music publisher, record company (DAP Entertainment), music consulting, distribution and promotional services and record producer. Estab. 1992. Publishes 12-22 songs/year; publishes 2-4 new songwriters/year. Staff size: 3. Pays standard royalty.

• Also see the listing for DAP Entertainment in the Record Producers section of this book.

How to Contact *Write first and obtain permission to submit.* Prefers cassette with 4 songs and lyric sheet. "We will accept finished masters (CD) for review." Include SASE. Responds in 2 months. "No phone calls or faxes please."

Film & TV Places 2 songs in TV/year. Music Supervisor: Darryl Alexander. Recently published "Love Never Fails in Saturday Night Live" (through DSM); "Feel Your Love" and "You Are So Beautiful" for the film *The Doctor Is Upstairs*, both written and recorded by Darryl Alexander.

Music Mostly **contemporary jazz** and **urban gospel**; also **R&B**. Does not want rock, gangsta rap, heavy metal or country. Published "Plumb Line" (single by Herb McMullan/Darryl Alexander) from *Diamond In The Sky* (album), recorded by Darryl Alexander (contemporary jazz); "3rd Eye" and "Too Late For Love" (singles) from *Diamond In The Sky* (album), written and recorded by Darryl Alexander (contemporary jazz), all released 2004 on DAP Entertainment.

Tips "Send only music in styles that we review. Submit your best songs and follow submission guidelines. Finished masters open up additional possibilities. Lead sheets may be requested for material we are interested in. Must have SASE if you wish to have CD returned. No phone calls, please."

☐ ALIAS JOHN HENRY TUNES (BMI)

11 Music Square E., Suite 607, Nashville TN 37203. (615)255-4437. E-mail: bobbyjohnhenry@bellso uth.net. **Contact:** Bobby John Henry, owner. Music publisher and record producer. Publishes 3 songs/year; publishes 1 new songwriter/year. Staff size: 3. Pays standard royalty.

How to Contact Send by mail. Prefers cassette or CD with 3 songs and lyric sheet. Does not return material. Responds in 6 months only if interested.

Music Mostly **country**, **rock** and **alternative**. Does not want rap. Published *Mr. Right Now* (album by Kari Jorgensen), recorded by "Hieke" on Warner Bros. (rock); and *Nothing to Me* (album by B.J. Henry), recorded by Millie Jackson on Spring.

Tips "Focus and rewrite, rewrite, rewrite."

⊕ ☐ ALL ROCK MUSIC

31-186-604266. Fax: 32-0186-604366. Website: www.collectorrecords.nl. **Contact:** Cees Klop, president. Music publisher, record company (Collector Records) and record producer. Estab. 1967. Publishes 40 songs/year; publishes several new songwriters/year. Staff size: 3. Pays standard royalty.

Affiliate(s) All Rock Music (United Kingdom).

• Also see the listings for Collector Records in the Record Companies and Record Producers sections of this book.

How to Contact Submit demo tape by mail. Unsolicited submissions are OK. Prefers cassette. SAE and IRC. Responds in 2 months.

Music Mostly **'50s rock**, **rockabilly** and **country rock**; also **piano boogie woogie**. Published *Rock Crazy Baby* (album), written and recorded by Art Adams (1950s rockabilly), released 2001; *Bobby Crain-Rock-A-Sock-A-Hop* (album), written and recorded by Bobby Crain (1950s rocker), released 2003; and *Marvin Jackson* (album), written and recorded by Marvin Jackson (1950s rockers), released 2004, all on Collector Records.

Tips "Send only the kind of material we issue/produce as listed."

☐ ALLEGHENY MUSIC WORKS (ASCAP, BMI)

1611 Menoher Blvd., Johnstown PA 15905. (814)255-4007. E-mail: TunedOnMusic@aol.com. Website: www.alleghenymusicworks.com. **Contact:** Al Rita, managing director. Music publisher and record company (Allegheny Records). Estab. 1991. Staff size: 2. Pays standard royalty.

Affiliate(s) Allegheny Music Works Publishing (ASCAP) and Tuned on Music (BMI).

• Also see the listings for Allegheny Music Works in the Record Companies section and The Leads Sheet in Publications of Interest section of this book.

How to Contact *Does not accept unsolicited submissions.* "E-mail queries are acceptable. Do not include attachments or pictures. NO Phone Calls! We will not reply to voice mail requests. We will respond ASAP to e-mail queries. We sometimes offer suggestions on other markets to try.''

Music Mostly **country**; also **pop**, **A/C**, **R&B**, **novelty**, **Halloween** and **inspirational**. Does not want rap, metal or x-rated lyrics. Published ''Flying In the Sky'' (single by Penny Towers Wilber) from *Halloween Bash* (album), recorded by Victor R. Vampire (pop/novelty/Halloween), released 2000 on Allegheny.

Tips ''Bookmark our website and check it regularly, clicking on *Songwriter Opportunities*. Each month, as a free service to songwriters, we list a new artist or company looking for songs. Complete contact information is included.''

☑ ☑ ALLISONGS INC. (ASCAP, BMI)

2132 Elm Hill Pike, Nashville TN 37214. (615)313-8764. E-mail: jim@allisongs.com. Website: www .allisongs.com. President: Jim Allison. Professional Manager: Stacy Hogan. Music publisher, record company (ARIA Records) and record producer (Jim Allison). Estab. 1985. Publishes 50 songs/year. Staff size: 4. Pays standard royalty.

Affiliate(s) Jim's Allisongs (BMI), Songs of Jim Allison (BMI) and Annie Green Eyes Music (BMI).
  • Reba McEntire's ''What Am I Gonna Do About You,'' published by AlliSongs, Inc., was included on her triple-platinum album, *Greatest Hits*.

How to Contact Submit demo tape by mail. Unsolicited submissions are OK. Send CD and lyric sheet. Does not return material. Responds in 6 weeks only if interested.

Music Mostly **country** and **pop**. Published ''Beautiful World'' (single by Anne Delana Reeves/Billy Montana/Jim Allison) from *Beautiful World* (album), recorded by Sheri Porter (alternative country), released 2001 on ARIA Records; and ''Montgomery to Memphis'' (single by Anne Delana Reeves/ Billy Montana) from *Lee Ann Womack* (album), recorded by Lee Ann Womack (country), released 1997 on Decca Records.

Tips ''Send your best—we will contact you if interested. No need to call us. It will be listened to.''

☑ ☑ ALPHA MUSIC INC. (BMI)

747 Chestnut Ridge Rd., Chestnut Ridge NY 10977. (845)356-0800. Fax: (845)356-0895. E-mail: alpha@trfmusic.com. Website: www.trfmusic.com. **Contact:** Michael Nurko. Music publisher. Estab. 1931. Pays standard royalty.

Affiliate(s) Dorian Music Publishers, Inc. (ASCAP) and TRF Music Inc.
  • Also see listing for TRF Production Music Libraries in the Advertising, Audiovisual & Commercial Music Firms section of this book.

How to Contact ''We accept submissions of new compositions. Submissions are not returnable.''

Music All **categories**, mainly **instrumental** and **acoustic suitable for use as production music**, including **theme and background music** for television and film. ''Have published over 50,000 titles since 1931.''

☑ AMERICATONE INTERNATIONAL (ASCAP)

1817 Loch Lomond Way, Las Vegas NV 89102-4437. (702)384-0030. Fax: (702)382-1926. E-mail: jjj@americatone.com. Website: www.americatone.com. President: Joe Jan Jaros. Estab. 1975. Publishes 25 songs/year. Pays variable royalty.

Affiliate(s) Americatone Records International, Christy Records International USA, Rambolt Music International (ASCAP).
  • Also see the listing for Americatone Records International in the Record Companies section of this book.

How to Contact Submit demo tape by mail. Unsolicited submissions OK. Prefers CDs, ''studio production with top sound recordings.'' Include SASE. Responds in 1 month.

Music Mostly **country**, **R&B**, **Spanish** and **classic ballads**. Published *Explosion* (album), recorded by Sam Trippe; *A New Life Start* (album), by Gabriel Oscar Rosati; *Many Ways to Go*, by Bill Perkins; and *Jazz in the Rain* (album), by the Rain Jazz Band; all on Americatone International Records.

❑ ANTELOPE PUBLISHING INC. (BMI)

P.O. Box 55, Rowayton CT 06853. **Contact:** Tony LaVorgna, owner/president. Music publisher. Estab. 1982. Publishes 5-10 new songs/year; publishes 3-5 new songwriters/year. Pays standard royalty.

How to Contact Submit demo tape by mail. Unsolicited submissions are OK. Prefers cassette with lead sheet. Does not return material. Responds in 1 month "only if interested."

Music Only **bebop** and **1940s swing**. Does not want anything electronic. Published *Inspiration* (album), written and recorded by T. LaVorgna (jazz); *Please Stay* (album by Nicole Pasternak), recorded by Cathy Gale (1940s swing), both on Antelope; *Nightcrawler* (album by Tommy Dean), recorded by Swing Fever on Alto Sound (jazz); and "Latin Blues," recorded by David Budway.

Tips "Put your best song first with a short intro."

❑ AUDIO MUSIC PUBLISHERS (ASCAP)

449 N. Vista St., Los Angeles CA 90036. (818)362-9853. Fax: (323)653-7670. E-mail: parlirec@aol.com. Website: www.parliamentrecords.com. **Contact:** Len Weisman, professional manager. Owner: Ben Weisman. Music publisher, record company and record producer (The Weisman Production Group). Estab. 1962. Publishes 25 songs/year; publishes 10-15 new songwriters/year. Staff size: 10. Pays standard royalty.

- Also see the listings for Queen Esther Music Publishers in the Music Publishers section of this book; the Weisman Production Group in the Record Producers section of this book and Parliament Records in the Record Companies section of this book.

How to Contact Submit demo tape by mail. Unsolicited submissions are OK. "No permission needed." Prefers cassette with 3-10 songs and lyric sheet. "We do not return unsolicited material without SASE. Don't query first; just send tape." Responds in 6 weeks. "We listen, we don't write back. If we like your material we will telephone you."

Music Mostly **pop, R&B** and **rap**; also **dance, funk, soul** and **gospel**. Does not want heavy metal. "Crazy About You" (single) and *Where Is Love* (album), both written by Curtis Womack; and *Don't Make Me Walk Away* (album by Debe Gunn), all recorded by Valerie (R&B) on Kon Kord.

❑ BAGATELLE MUSIC PUBLISHING CO. (BMI)

P.O. Box 925929, Houston TX 77292. (713)680-2160 or (800)845-6865. **Contact:** Byron Benton, president. Music publisher, record company and record producer. Publishes 40 songs/year; publishes 2 new songwriters/year. Pays standard royalty.

Affiliate(s) Floyd Tillman Publishing Co.

- Also see the listing for Bagatelle Record Company in the Record Companies section of this book.

How to Contact Submit demo tape by mail. Unsolicited submissions are OK. Prefers cassette (or videocassette) with any number of songs and lyric sheet. Include SASE.

Music Mostly **country**; also **gospel** and **blues**. Published "Everything You Touch" (single), written and recorded by Johnny Nelms; "This Is Real" and "Mona from Daytona" (singles), written and recorded by Floyd Tillman, all on Bagatelle Records.

❑ BARKIN' FOE THE MASTER'S BONE (ASCAP)

405 Broadway St. Suite 900, Cincinnati OH 45202-3329. (513)241-6489. Fax: (513)241-9226. E-mail: autoredcurtis@aol.com. Website: www.1stbook.com. Company Owner (rock, R&B): Kevin Curtis. Professional Managers: Shonda Barr (country, jazz, pop, rap); Betty Barr (gospel, soul, soft rock). Music publisher. Estab. 1989. Publishes 4 songs/year; publishes 1 new songwriter/year. Staff size: 4. Pays standard royalty.

Affiliate(s) Beat Box Music (ASCAP) and Feltstar (BMI).

How to Contact Submit demo tape by mail. Unsolicited submissions are OK. Prefers CD (or VHS videocassette) with 3 songs. Include SASE. Responds in 2 weeks.

Music Mostly **top 40** and **pop**; also **soul, gospel, rap** and **jazz**. Does not want classical. Published "Lover, Lover" (single by J Tea/Jay B./Skylar) from *The Time Has Come* (album), recorded by J-Trey (rap), released 2003 on East Side Records; "Been A Long Time" (single by J Tea/Jay B./

Skylar), from *The Time Has Come* (album), recorded by J-Trey (rap), released 2003 on East Side Records; "No Worries" (single by Mejestic/7-Starr/D-Smooy/Hardhead), from *Home Grown* (album), recorded by Low Down Boyz (rap), released 2002 on Untamed Records.

☑ BAY RIDGE PUBLISHING CO. (BMI)

P.O. Box 5537, Kreole Station, Moss Point MS 39563-1537. (228)475-0059. "No collect calls." Estab. 1974. **Contact:** Joe F. Mitchell, executive vice president/general manager. First Vice President: Justin F. Mitchell. Second Vice President: Jonita F. Mitchell. Music publisher and record company (Missile Records).

> • Also see the listing for Abalorn Music in this section and the listing for Missile Records in the Record Companies section of this book.

Affiliate(s) Abalorn Music (ASCAP).

How to Contact *"Please don't send us anything until you contact us by phone or in writing and receive submission instructions. You must present your songs the correct way to get a reply.* No registered mail—no exceptions! Always whenever you write to us, be sure you include a #10 business-size envelope addressed back to you with a first class USA postage stamp on the envelope. We reply back to you from the SASE you send to us. All songs sent for review must include sufficient return postage. No reply made back to you without SASE or return of material without sufficient return postage. **Absolutely no reply postcards—only SASE**. If you only write lyrics, do not submit. We only accept completed songs, so you must find a collaborator. We are not interested in reviewing homemade recordings." Prefers CD (first choice) or cassette with 3-8 songs and lyrics to songs submitted. Responds in 2 months. "A good quality demo recording will always get preference over a poor recording."

Music All types and styles of songs. "Mississippi, Mississippi" (single by Kadish Millett) and "Innocent Little One" (single by Bob Levy) from *If It Takes All Night* (album), recorded by Christian Ramsey (modern pop country), released on Missile Records.

Tips "Our doors are always open to young recording artists who are exceptional talented and want to make a name for themselves in the music business. Your success is our success. We will work with you to reach your goal. We also are in the business of getting your professionally-recorded album of 10-12 well-produced and well-written, radio-ready songs placed with record companies in the USA and foreign countries for the possibility of record deals. Here is what we have gotten for some artists: $850,000 record deal for Charity (religious singing group) on Big Easy (USA) in 2001; $500,000 record deal for Vance Greek on Dime-A-Dozen (Germany) in 2002; and a $150,000 record deal for Randell Ruthledge (country) on Dime-A-Dozen (Germany) in 2003. Two more artists are under consideration as of 2004, and others may be considered. Missile Records, Abalorn Music (ASCAP) and Bay Ridge Publishing Co. (BMI) are listed in some well-known publications such as the *Billboard International Buyer's Guide*, *Mix Master Directory*, *Industrial Source Book*, *Pollstar*, *Yellow Pages of Rock* and other publications. Some well-known recording artists born and raised in Mississippi include Elvis Presley, Conway Twitty, B.B. King and Faith Hill. The Moss Point, MS area music scene is also home to nationally-known rock group Three Doors Down, who sold more than 10 million of their CD albums and singles. Singers and songwriters thinking about doing professional recording, give us a call before you make that move. We can save you money, time, headaches, heartaches and troubles you may run into. We know what to do and how to do it to benefit you and get the best results."

🌐 ☑ BEARSONGS (PRS)

Box 944, Birmingham B16 8UT United Kingdom. 44-121-454-7020. E-mail: jim@bigbearmusic.com. Website: www.bigbearmusic.com. Managing Director: Jim Simpson. Professional Manager: Juliet Kenny. Music publisher and record company (Big Bear Records). Member PRS, MCPS. Publishes 25 songs/year; publishes 15-20 new songwriters/year. Pays standard royalty.

> • Also see the listings for Big Bear Records in the Record Companies section and Big Bear in the Record Producers section of this book.

How to Contact Submit demo tape by mail. Unsolicited submissions are OK. Prefers CD. Does not return material. Responds in 3 months.

Music Mostly **blues, swing** and **jazz**. Published *Blowing With Bruce* and *Cool Heights* (by Alan Barnes), recorded by Bruce Adams/Alan Barnes Quintet; and *Blues For My Baby* (by Charles Brown), recorded by King Pleasure & The Biscuit Boys, all on Big Bear Records.

Tips "Have a real interest in jazz, blues, swing."

⊠ BEAVERWOOD AUDIO-VIDEO (BMI)

133 Walton Ferry, Hendersonville TN 37075. (615)824-2820. Fax: (615)824-2833. E-mail: beaverwd @bellsouth.net. Website: www.beaverwoodaudiovideo.com. **Owner:** Clyde Beavers. Music publisher, record company (Kash Records, JCL Records), record producer, 32 track studio, audio-video duplication. Estab. 1976. Pays standard royalty.

Affiliate(s) Jackpot Music (BMI).

How to Contact Submit demo tape by mail. Unsolicited submissions are OK. Prefers CD, DAT or videocassette with 1-5 songs. Does not return material.

Music Mostly **gospel** and **country**. Published "Mary Had a Little Lamb," "Listen to My Story" and "I Heard His Call," all written and recorded by Lawrence Davis on JCL Records (gospel).

⊠ ⊘ BIG FISH MUSIC PUBLISHING GROUP (ASCAP, BMI)

11927 Magnolia Blvd., Suite 3, N. Hollywood CA 91607. (818)984-0377. President, CEO and Music Publisher: Chuck Tennin. Producer: Gary Black (country, pop, adult contemporary, rock, crossover songs, other styles). Professional Music Manager: Lora Sprague (jazz, New Age, instrumental, pop rock, R&B). Professional Music Manager: B.J. (pop, TV, film and special projects). Professional Music & Vocal Consultant: Zell Black (country, pop, gospel, rock, blues). Producer Independent Artists: Darryl Harrelson—Major Label Entertainment (country, pop and other genres). Music publisher, record company (California Sun Records) and production company. Estab. 1971. Publishes 10-20 songs/year; publishes 5-10 new songwriters/year. Staff size: 7. Pays standard royalty. "We also license songs and music copyrights to users of music, especially TV and film."

Affiliate(s) Big Fish Music (BMI) and California Sun Music (ASCAP).

How to Contact *Write first and obtain permission to submit.* Include SASE for reply. "*Please do not call.* After permission to submit is confirmed, we will assign and forward to you a submission code number allowing you to submit up to 4 songs maximum, preferably on CD or cassette. Include a properly addressed cover letter, signed and dated, with your source of referral (*Songwriter's Market*) with your assigned submission code number and SASE for reply and/or return of material. Include lyrics. *Unsolicited material will not be accepted.* That is our Submission Policy to review outside and new material." Responds in 2 weeks.

Film & TV Places 6 songs in TV/year. Recently published "Even the Angels Knew" (by Cathy Carlson/Craig Lackey/Marty Axelrod); "Stop Before We Start" (by J.D. Grieco); "Oh Santa" (by Christine Bridges/John Deaver), all recorded by The Black River Girls in *Passions* (NBC); licensed "A Christmas Wish" (by Ed Fry/Eddie Max), used in *Passions* (NBC); "Girls Will Be Girls" (by Cathy Carlson/John LeGrande), recorded by The Black River Girls, used in *All My Children* (ABC); "The Way You're Drivin' Me" and "Ain't No Love 'Round Here' " (by Jerry Zanandrea), both recorded by The Black River Girls, used in *Passions* (NBC).

Music Country, including **country pop**, **country A/C** and **country crossover** with a cutting edge; also **pop**, **pop ballads**, **adult contemporary**, **uplifting**, **praise**, **worship**, **spiritual**, and **inspirational adult contemporary gospel** with a powerful message, **instrumental background and theme music** for TV & films, **New Age/instrumental jazz** and **novelty, orchestral classical, R&B** and **Children's music** for all kinds of commercial use. Published "If Wishes Were Horses" (single by Billy O'Hara); "Purple Bunny Honey" (single by Robert Lloyd/Jim Love); "Leavin' You For Me" (single by J.D. Grieco); "Move That Train" (single by Robert Porter); "Happy Landing" (by T. Brawley/B. Woodrich); "Girls Will Be Girls" (single by Cathy Carlson/John LeGrande); "You Should Be Here With Me" (single by Ken McMeans); "Stop Before We Start" (single by J.D. Grieco); "The Way You're Drivin' Me" and "Ain't No Love 'Round Here' " (singles by Jerry Zanandrea), all recorded by Black River Girls on California Sun Records; "Let Go and Let God" and "There's A Power in Prayer" (singles by Corinne Porter/Molly Finkle), recorded by Molly Pasutti, released on California Sun Records.

Tips "Demo should be professional, high quality, clean, simple, dynamic, and must get the song across on the first listen. Good clear vocals, a nice melody, a good musical feel, good musical arrangement, strong lyrics and chorus—a unique, catchy, clever song that sticks with you. Looking for unique country and pop songs with a different edge that can crossover to the mainstream market for ongoing Nashville music projects and songs for a hot female country trio that crosses over to adult contemporary and pop with great lush, warm harmonies that reach out to middle America and baby boomers and their grown up children (25 to 65). Also, catchy up-tempo songs with an attitude, meaningful lyrics (Shania Twain style), and unique pop songs (Celine Dion style) for upcoming album projects and song pitches. Also, soundtrack music of all types (melodic, uplifting, moody, mystique, orchestral, mind soothing, pretty, action packed, etc.) for new film production company and upcoming film and TV projects. Demo should be broadcast quality."

BIXIO MUSIC GROUP & ASSOCIATES/IDM MUSIC (ASCAP)

111 E. 14th St., Suite 140, New York NY 10003. (212)695-3911. Fax: (212)967-6284. E-mail: dusl@ idmusic.com. Website: www.bixio.com and www.idmmusic.com. General Manager: Johannes in der Muhlen. Administrator: Miriam Westercappel (all styles). A&R Director: Office Manager: Courtney Stack-Slutsky. Administrative Assistant: Karlene Evans (soundtracks). Creative Director: Robert Draghi (all styles). Senior Creative Director/Producer: Tomo. A&R: Claudene Neysmith (world/ New Age). Music publisher, record company and rights clearances. Estab. 1985. Publishes a few hundred songs/year; publishes 2 new songwriters/year. Staff size: 6. Pays standard royalty.

How to Contact *Does not accept unsolicited material.*

Music Mostly **soundtracks**. Published "La Strada Nel Bosco," included in the TV show *Ed* (NBC); "La Beguine Du Mac," included in the TV show *The Chris Isaac Show* (Showtime); and "Alfonsina Delle Camelie," included in the TV show *UC: Undercover* (NBC).

BLACK MARKET ENTERTAINMENT RECORDINGS (ASCAP, BMI)

2144 Hills Ave. Suite D-2, Atlanta GA 30318. (404)367-8130. Fax: (404)367-8630. E-mail: bmeinc @bellsouth.net. **Contact:** D. Searcy, A&R. Music publisher and record company (B.M.E. Records). Estab. 1992. Staff size: 10.

Affiliate(s) SWOLE Music (ASCAP).

How to Contact Submit demo tape by mail at P.O. Box 20084, Atlanta GA 30325. Unsolicited submissions are OK. Prefers CD/CDR with cover letter. "Please do not call; enclose mailing and e-mail address." Does not return material. Responds in 1 month.

Film & TV Places 3 songs in film and 1 song in TV/year. Music Supervisor: Vincent Phillips. Recently published "I Like Dem" (by J. Smith/S. Norris), recorded by Li'l Jon and the Eastside Boyz; "Kissable Spot" (by Jonathan Smith), recorded by Devon, both placed in *Big Momma's House*; and "Trick Busta" (by Hardnett/Anderson/Bryon), recorded by Lyrical Giants, placed in *Sex and the City*.

Music Mostly **rap** and **R&B**; also **rock** and **alternative**. Published "Bia, Bia" (single by J. Smith/ S. Norris/T. Shaw/S. Martin) from *Put Yo Hood Up* (album), recorded by Lil Jon and the Eastside Boyz (rap), released 2001 on BME/TVT; "Shut Up" (single by R. McDowell/J. Jones/D. Green/R. Lewis) from *Right Quick* (album), recorded by Jim Crow (rap), released 2001 on Noontime/Interscope; and "I Like Dem" (single by J. Smith/S. Norris) from *We Still Crunk* (album), recorded by Lil Jon and the Eastside Boyz (rap), released 2000 on BME Recordings.

Tips "Put your best foot forward. Submit only the best stuff you have. First impressions are important."

BLACK STALLION COUNTRY PUBLISHING (BMI)

P.O. Box 368, Tujunga CA 91043. E-mail: bscmgmt@aol.com. **Contact:** Kenn Kingsbury, president. Music publisher, management firm and book publisher (*Who's Who in Country & Western Music*). Member CMA, CMF. Publishes 2 songs/year; publishes 1 new songwriter/year. Pays standard royalty.

How to Contact Submit demo tape by mail. Unsolicited submissions are OK. Prefers cassette with 3 songs and lyric sheet. Include SASE. Responds in 1 month.

Music Mostly **jazz** and **country**.

☑ ⊘ BMG MUSIC PUBLISHING (ASCAP)

245 5th Ave. 8th Floor, New York NY 10016. (212)287-1300. Fax: (212)930-4263. Website: www.bm gmusicsearch.com. Beverly Hills office: 8750 Wilshire Blvd., Beverly Hills CA 90211. (310)358-4700. Fax: (310)358-4727. **Contact:** Scott Francis, president BMG songs. Nashville office: 1600 Division St. Suite 225, Nashville TN 37203. (615)687-5800. Fax: (615)687-5839. Music publisher.
How to Contact BMG Music Publishing does not accept unsolicited submissions.
Music Published works by Maroon 5, Christina Aguilera, Coldplay, Nelly, Britney Spears, Keane and R. Kelly.

⊘ BOURNE CO. MUSIC PUBLISHERS (ASCAP)

5 W. 37th St., New York NY 10018. (212)391-4300. Fax: (212)391-4306. E-mail: bourne@bournemu sic.com. Website: www.bournemusic.com. **Contact:** Professional Manager. Music publisher. Estab. 1919. Publishes educational material and popular music.
Affiliate(s) ABC Music, Ben Bloom, Better Half, Bogat, Burke & Van Heusen, Goldmine, Harborn, Lady Mac and Murbo Music.
How to Contact *Does not accept unsolicited submissions.*
Music Piano/vocal, band pieces and **choral pieces**. Published "Amen" and "Mary's Little Boy Child" (singles by Hairston); "When You Wish Upon a Star" (single by Washington/Harline); and "Unforgettable" (single by Irving Gordon).

☑ ◻ ALLAN BRADLEY MUSIC (BMI)

835 E. Buckeyewood Ave., Orange CA 92865. (626)441-4453. E-mail: melodi4ever@earthlink.net. Website: www.ablmusic.com. **Contact:** Allan Licht, owner. Music publisher, record company (ABL Records) and record producer. Estab. 1993. Publishes 10 songs/year; publishes 5 new songwriters/year. Staff size: 2. Pays standard royalty.
Affiliate(s) Holly Ellen Music (ASCAP).
• Also see the listing for ABL Records in the Record Companies section of this book.
How to Contact Submit demo by mail. Unsolicited submissions are OK. Prefers CD with 3 songs and lyric sheet. "Send only unpublished works." Does not return material. Responds in 2 weeks only if interested.
Music Mostly **A/C, pop** and **R&B**; also **country** and **Christian contemporary**. Does not want hard rock. Published *Time to Go* (album), written and recorded by Alan Douglass; *The Sun that Follows the Rain* (album by R.K. Holler/Rob Driggers), recorded by Michael Cavanaugh (pop), released 1999; and *Only In My Mind* (album by Jonathon Hansen), recorded by Allan Licht, all on ABL Records.
Tips "Be open to suggestions from well-established publishers. Please send only songs that have Top 10 potential. Only serious writers are encouraged to submit."

ℕ ◻ BRANDON HILLS MUSIC, LLC (BMI)

N 3425 Searle County Line Rd., Brandon WI 53919. (920)398-3729 or (cell) (920)570-1076. E-mail: marta@dotnet.com. **Contact:** Marsha Brown, president. Music publisher. Estab. 2005. Publishes 4 new songwriters/year. Staff size: 2. Pays standard royalty of 50%.
How to Contact Submit demo tape by mail. Unsolicited submissions are OK. Prefers CD with 1-4 songs and cover letter. Does not return submissions. Responds in 5 weeks.
Music Mostly **country (traditional, modern, country rock)**, **contemporary Christian**, **blues**; also **children's** and **bluegrass**. Does not want rap or hip-hop.
Tips "We prefer studio-produced CDs. The lyrics and the CD must match. Cover letter, lyrics, and CD should have a professional look. Demos should have vocals up front and every word should be distinguishable. Submit only your best. The better the demo, the better of chance of getting your music published and recorded."

ℕ ◖ BRIAN SONG MUSIC CORP. (BMI)

P.O. Box 1376, Pickens SC 29671. (864)878-7217. Fax: (864)878-6274. E-mail: braines105@aol.c om. **Contact:** Brian E. Raines, president. Music publisher, record company (Palmetto Records), record producer and artist management. Estab. 1985. Publishes 5 songs/year; publishes 2-3 new songwriters/year. Staff size: 3. Pays standard royalty.

How to Contact *Write first and obtain permission to submit.* Prefers CD or VHS videocassette with 3 songs and lyric sheet. "Unsolicited material not accepted, and will be returned. Demo must be good quality, lyrics typed. Send photo if an artist; send bio on writer or artist." Does not return material. Responds in 1 month.

Music Mostly **country, gospel** and **country/gospel**; also **country/blues**. Published *I Wasn't There* (album), written and recorded by Dale Cassell on Mark V (gospel); and *From the Heart* (album), written and recorded by Jim Hubbard on Hubbitt (gospel).

☒ ☒ ◯ BSW RECORDS (BMI)

P.O. Box 2297, Universal City TX 7814. (210)599-0022. E-mail: bswr18@txdirect.net. **Contact:** Frank Willson, president. Music publisher, record company and record producer (Frank Willson). Estab. 1987. Publishes 26 songs/year; publishes 14 new songwriters/year. Staff size: 5. Pays standard royalty.

Affiliate(s) WillTex Music and Universal Music Marketing (BMI).

- This company has been named Record Label of the Year ('94-'01) by the Country Music Association of America. Also see the listings for BSW Records in the Record Companies section, Frank Wilson in the Record Producers section, and Universal Music Marketing in the Managers & Booking Agents section of this book.

How to Contact Submit demo tape or CD by mail. Unsolicited submissions are OK. Prefers cassette or CD with 3 songs, lyric sheet and cover letter. Include SASE. Responds in 2 months.

Film & TV Places 2 songs in film/year.

Music Mostly **country, blues** and **soft rock**. Does not want rap. Published *These Four Walls* (album), written and recorded by Dan Kimmel (country); and *I Cried My Last Tear* (album by T. Toliver), recorded by Candeeland (country), both released 1999 on BSW Records.

☑ ◯ BUG MUSIC, INC. (ASCAP, BMI)

7750 Sunset Blvd, Los Angeles CA 90046. (323)969-0988. Fax: (323)969-0968. E-mail: buginfo@bug music.com. Website: www.bugmusic.com. Vice President of Creative: Eddie Gomez. Creative Manager: Sasha Ross. Creative Assistant: Nissa Pedraza. **Nashville:** 1910 Acklen Ave., Nashville TN 37212. (615)279-0180. Fax: (615)279-0184. Creative Director: John Allen; Creative Manager: Drew Hale. **New York:** 347 W. 36th St., Suite 1203, New York NY 10018. (212)643-0925. Fax: (212)643-0897. Senior Vice President: Garry Valletri. Music publisher. Estab. 1975. "We handle administration."

Affiliate(s) Bughouse (ASCAP).

How to Contact *Does not accept unsolicited submissions.*

Music All genres. Published "You Were Mine" (by E. Erwin/M. Seidel), recorded by Dixie Chicks on Monument.

☒ ◯ BUGLE PUBLISHING GROUP (ASCAP, BMI)

14724 Ventura Blvd., Penthouse Suite, Sherman Oaks CA 91403. (818)461-1706. Fax: (818)461-1739. Senior Vice President: Stevo Glendining. Music publisher. Estab. 1992. Publishes 5 songs/year. Staff size: 1. Hires staff songwriters. Pays standard royalty.

Affiliate(s) I.R.S. Songs/Firstars Music (ASCAP) and I.R.S. Music, Inc./Illegal Songs, Inc. (BMI).

How to Contact *Does not accept unsolicited submissions.*

Music Mostly **country** and **pop/rock**. Published *Love Or the Lack Of* (by Rich Wayland), recorded by Daryle Singletary; and *Then There's You* (by Pat MacDonald), recorded by The Wilkinsons (country), both on Giant; and *The Reason* (by Greg Wells), recorded by Celine Dion on Sony (pop).

Tips "Research the market and make sure your songs have a credible lyric; songs impact the listener and must be moving enough to cause excitement!"

◯ BURIED TREASURE MUSIC (ASCAP)

524 Doral Country Dr., Nashville TN 37221. **Contact:** Scott Turner, owner/manager. Music publisher and record producer (Aberdeen Productions). Estab. 1972. Publishes 30-50 songs/year; publishes 3-10 new songwriters/year. Pays standard royalty.

Affiliate(s) Captain Kidd Music (BMI).
• Also see the listing for Aberdeen Productions in the Record Producers section of this book.
How to Contact Submit demo tape by mail. Unsolicited submissions are OK. Prefers cassette or VHS videocassette with 1-4 songs and lyric sheet. Responds in 2 weeks. "Always enclose SASE if answer is expected."
Music Mostly **country**, **country/pop** and **MOR**. Does not want rap, hard rock, metal, hip-hop or alternative. Published "It Just Ain't Right" (single by Scott Turner/John Marascalco), recorded by Tina Turner (R&B/pop), released 2004 on E.M.I.; and "I Still Can't Say Goodbye" (single by Bob Blinn/Jimmy Moore) from a *C.B.S./Sony Compilation*, recorded by Chet Atkins, released 2004 on C.B.S.
Tips *"Don't* send songs in envelopes that are 15″×20″, or by registered mail. The post office will not accept tapes in regular business-size envelopes. Also, always enclose a SASE. Submission without same aren't answered because of the wealth of tapes that come in."

CALIFORNIA COUNTRY MUSIC (BMI)
112 Widmar Pl., Clayton CA 94517. (925)833-4680. **Contact:** Edgar J. Brincat, owner. Music publisher and record company (Roll On Records). Estab. 1985. Staff size: 1. Pays standard royalty.
Affiliate(s) Sweet Inspirations Music (ASCAP).
• Also see the listing for Roll On Records in the Record Companies section of this book.
How to Contact Submit demo by mail. Unsolicited submissions are OK. Do not call or write. Prefers CD or cassette with 3 songs and lyric sheet. Any calls will be returned collect to caller. Include SASE. Responds in 6 weeks.
Music Mostly **MOR**, **contemporary country** and **pop**; also **R&B**, **gospel** and **light rock**. Does not want rap, metal or rock. Published *For Realities Sake* (album by F.L. Pittman/R. Barretta) and *Maddy* (album by F.L. Pittman/M. Weeks), both recorded by Ron Banks & L.J. Reynolds on Life & Bellmark Records; and *Quarter Past Love* (album by Irwin Rubinsky/Janet Fisher), recorded by Darcy Dawson on NNP Records.

CHRISTMAS & HOLIDAY MUSIC (BMI)
24351 Grass St., Lake Forest CA 92630. (949)859-1615. E-mail: justinwilde@christmassongs.com. Website: www.christmassongs.com. **Contact:** Justin Wilde, president. Music publisher. Estab. 1980. Publishes 8-12 songs/year; publishes 8-12 new songwriters/year. Staff size: 1. "All submissions must be complete songs (i.e., music and lyrics)." Pays standard royalty.
Affiliate(s) Songcastle Music (ASCAP).
How to Contact Submit demo CD or cassette by mail. Unsolicited submissions are OK. *Do not call.* See website for submission guidelines. "First class mail only. Registered or certified mail not accepted." Prefers CD or cassette with no more than 3 songs with lyric sheets. Do not send lead sheets or promotional material, bios, etc." Include SASE but does not return material out of the US. Responds only if interested.
Film & TV Places 4-5 songs in TV/year. Published "Mr. Santa Claus" in *Casper's Haunted Christmas*.
Music Strictly **Christmas**, **Halloween**, **Hanukkah**, **Mother's Day**, **Thanksgiving**, **Father's Day** and **New Year's Eve music** in every style imaginable: easy listening, rock, R&B, pop, blues, jazz, country, reggae, rap, children's secular or religious. *Please do not send anything that isn't a holiday song.* Published "It Must Have Been the Mistletoe" (single by Justin Wilde/Doug Konecky) from *Christmas Memories* (album), recorded by Barbra Streisand (pop Christmas), released 2001 by Columbia; "What Made the Baby Cry?" (single by Toby Keith) and "You've Just Missed Christmas" (single by Penny Lea/Buzz Smith/Bonnie Miller) from *The Vikki Carr Christmas Album* (album), recorded by Vikki Carr (holiday/Christmas), released 2000 on Delta; and "Mr. Santa Claus" (single by James Golseth) from *Casper's Haunted Christmas* soundtrack (album), recorded by Scotty Blevins (Christmas), released 2000 on Koch International.
Tips "We only sign one out of every 100 submissions. Please be selective. If a stranger can hum your melody back to you after hearing it twice, it has 'standard' potential. Couple that with a lyric filled with unique, inventive imagery, that stands on its own, even without music. Combine the two elements, and workshop the finished result thoroughly to identify weak points. Submit to us

only when the song is polished to perfection. Submit positive lyrics only. Avoid negative themes like 'Blue Christmas'.''

☑ ☑ SONNY CHRISTOPHER PUBLISHING (BMI)

P.O. Box 9144, Ft. Worth TX 76147-2144. (817)685-8343. E-mail: ebbycondra@aol.com. **Contact:** Sonny Christopher, CEO. Music publisher, record company and record producer. Estab. 1974. Publishes 20-25 new songs/year; publishes 3-5 new songwriters/year. Staff size: 1. Pays standard royalty.

How to Contact *Write first, then call and obtain permission to submit.* Prefers cassette with lyric sheet. Include SASE (#10 or larger). Responds in 3 months.

Music Mostly **country**, **rock** and **blues**. Published *Did They Judge Too Hard* (album by Sonny Christopher), recorded by Ronny Collins (collins@abilene.com) on Sonshine Records.

Tips "Be patient. I will respond as soon as I can. A songwriter should have a studio-cut demo with a super vocal. I am one who can hear a song with just acoustic guitar. Don't be hesitant to do a rewrite. To the young songwriter: *never, never* quit.''

☑ CHRYSALIS MUSIC GROUP (ASCAP, BMI)

8500 Melrose Ave., Suite 207, Los Angeles CA 90069. (310)652-0066. Fax: (310)652-2024. Website: www.chrysalismusic.com. **Contact:** Mark Friedman, vice president of creative services. Music publisher. Estab. 1968.

How to Contact *Chrysalis Music does not accept any submissions.*

Music Published "Sum 41" (single), recorded by Outcast; "Light Ladder" (single), recorded by David Gray. Administer, David Lee Roth; Andrea Boccelli; Velvet Revolver.

☑ CLEARWIND PUBLISHING (SESAC)/LADY MARION PUBLISHING (ASCAP)/SUNSCAPE PUBLISHING (BMI)

256 S. Robertson Blvd., Suite 6100, Beverly Hills CA 90211. (310)629-6420. E-mail: clearwindpub@ earthlink.net. **Contact:** A&R Director. Music publisher, sub-publisher, music licensing and personal management company (Sapphire Management). Estab. 1983. Publishes 12-15 songs/year; sub-publishes over 25. Staff size: 2. Pays standard royalty and collects standard fees for administration of sub-publishing and licensing deals.

• "Our main focus is international, specifically the Asia/Pan-Pacific Region and Europe.''

How to Contact *"Write to obtain permission to submit.* Do NOT call! Unsolicited submissions will be returned unopened." Prefers CD, DVD with no more than 3 songs and typed lyric sheet (with promo pack and photo if applicable). Does not return material. Will respond before 3 months after receipt.

Music Mostly **pop**, **rock**, **metal**, **R&B**, **jazz**, **smooth jazz**, **rap** and **hip-hop**. Recently sub-published "Somewhere Tonight" and "Too Late" (singles by Peter Roberts/Scott Cross); and "OOH Yea" (single by Peter Roberts/Dorothy Sea Gazely) all from *Heart of Gold* (album), recorded by Lisa Frazier (R&B/dance), released 2000 on Universal Discopui (Italy), Imperial Teichiku (Japan) and AVEX.

☑ COAL HARBOR MUSIC (BMI)

P.O. Box 148027, Nashville TN 37214-8027. (616)883-2020. E-mail: info@coalharbmusic.com. Website: www.coalharbormusic.com. **Contact:** Jerry Ray Wells, president. Music publisher, Record company (Coal Harbor Music), Record producer (Jerry Ray Wells), also recording studio, demo services, sheet music, number charts, management and booking services, artist development. Estab. 1990. Publishes 28 songs/year; publishes 3 new songwriters/year. Staff size: 2. Pays standard royalty.

• Also see the listing for Coal Harbor Music in the Record Companies Record section of this book.

How to Contact *Contact first via e-mail to obtain permission to submit a demo.* Send CD and SASE with lyric sheet and cover letter. Does not return submissions. Only responds if interested.

Music Mostly **country**, **gospel** and **bluegrass**; also **contemporary Christian**, **Christmas, patriotic,**

comedyand **pop/rock**. Does not want heavy metal, rap, hard rock/grunge. Released ''Forever True'' (single) written by Ogie De Guzman, recorded by Back on Track (contemporary Christian) released 2005 on Tribute Family Corporation label; ''So Good to Know'' (single) from *All I Need* (album), written and recorded by Damon Westfaul (country Gospel), released 2004 on Coal Harbor/ Shoreline Music; ''You'' (single) from *Unraveled* (album), written and recorded by Anne Borgen (contemporary Christian), released 2004 on Coal Harbor.

Tips ''Write from the heart—the listener knows. Join songwriter organizations, go to seminars, co-write, etc. When submitting material send everything on one cassette or CD. Don't send two CDs and one cassette and tell us what song or track numbers to listen to. We don't have time. Put your best song first, even if it is a ballad. Keep writing; we ARE looking for GREAT songs!''

COME ALIVE COMMUNICATIONS, INC. (ASCAP)

348 Valley Rd., Suite 1, West Grove PA 19390-0436. (610)869-3660. Fax: (610)869-3660. E-mail: info@comealivemusic.com. Website: www.comealivemusic.com. Professional Managers: Joseph L. Hooker (pop, rock, jazz); Bridget G. Hylak (spiritual, country, classical). Music publisher, record producer and record company. Estab. 1985. Publishes 4 singles/year. Staff: 7. Pays standard royalty of 50%.

• Come Alive Communications received a HIS Ministries Award in 1996.

How to Contact *Call first to obtain permission to submit a demo.* For song publishing submissions, prefers CD/CDR with 3 songs, lyric sheet, and cover letter. Does not return submissions. Responds only if interested.

Music Mostly **pop**, **easy listening**, **contemporary Christian**, and **patriotic**; also **country** and **spiritual**. Does not want obscene, suggestive, violent, or morally offensive lyrics. Produced ''In Search of America'' (single) from *Long Road to Freedom* (album), written and recorded by J. Hooker (patriotic), released 2003 on ComeAliveMusic.com.

CORELLI MUSIC GROUP (BMI/ASCAP)

P.O. Box 2314, Tacoma WA 98401-2314. (253)798-5281. E-mail: corellismusicgroup@yahoo.com. Website: www.CorelliMusicGroup.com. **Contact:** Jerry Corelli, owner. Music publisher, record company (Omega III Records), record producer (Jerry Corelli/Angels Dance Studio) and booking agency (Tone Deaf Booking). Estab. 1996. Publishes 12 songs/year; publishes 6 new songwriters/ year. Staff size: 3. Pays standard royalty.

Affiliate(s) My Angel's Songs (ASCAP); Corelli's Music Box (BMI).

How to Contact Submit demo by mail. Unsolicited submissions are OK. ''No phone calls or letters asking to submit.'' Prefers CD with 3 songs, lyric sheet and cover letter. ''We want songs with a message and overtly Christian. Make sure all material is copyrighted.'' Include SASE. Responds in 2 months.

Music Mostly **contemporary Christian**, **soft rock Christian** and **Christmas**; also **love songs**, **ballads** and **new country**. Does not want rap, hip-hop, southern gospel or songs without lyrics. Published ''God Bless the Wise Men'' (single by Angie Richter), ''Peace At Christmas'' (single by Nina Bolin) and ''Cowboy Christmas'' (single by Rosalie Glenmann) released 2004 on Omega III Records.

Tips ''Success is obtained when opportunity meets preparation! If a SASE is not sent with demo, we don't even listen to the demo. Be willing to do a rewrite. Don't send matrial expecting us to place it with a Top Ten artist. Be practical. Do your songs say what's always been said, except differently? Don't take rejection personally.''

THE CORNELIUS COMPANIES (BMI, ASCAP, SESAC)

Dept. SM, 1719 West End Ave., Suite 805-E, Nashville TN 37203. (615)321-5333. E-mail: corneliusco mps@aol.com. Website: www.corneliuscompanies.com. **Contact:** Ron Cornelius, owner/manager. Music publisher and record producer (Ron Cornelius). Estab. 1986. Publishes 60-80 songs/year; publishes 2-3 new songwriters/year. Occasionally hires staff writers. Pays standard royalty.

Affiliate(s) RobinSparrow Music (BMI), Strummin' Bird Music (ASCAP) and Bridgeway Music (SESAC).

How to Contact *Write or call first and obtain permission to submit.* Submit demo tape by mail. Unsolicited submissions are OK. Prefers CD, DAT or cassette with 2-3 songs. Include SASE. Responds in 2 months.
Music Mostly **country** and **pop**; also **positive country**, **gospel** and **alternative**. Published songs by Confederate Railroad, Faith Hill, David Allen Coe, Alabama and over 50 radio singles in the positive Christian/country format.
Tips "Looking for material suitable for film."

⊕ ☑ CRINGE MUSIC (PRS,MCPS)
The Cedars, Elvington Lane, Folkestone Kent CT18 7AD. (01) (303) 893-472. Fax: (01) (303) 893-833. E-mail: info@cringemusic.co.uk. Website: www.cringemusic.co.uk. **Contact:** Christopher Ashman, CEO. Music publisher and record company (Red Admiral Records). Estab. 1979. Staff size: 2.
How to Contact Submit demo tape by mail. Unsolicited submissions are OK. Prefers CD with unlimited number of songs and lyric sheet, lead sheet. Include SASE or SAE and IRC for outside United States. Responds in approximately 3 months.
Music All styles.

⊕ ▣ ○ CTV MUSIC (GREAT BRITAIN)
Television Centre, St. Helier, Jersey JE1 3ZD Channel Islands Great Britain. (1534)816816. Fax: (1534)816817. E-mail: gordon.destecroix@channeltv.co.uk. Website: www.channeltv.co.uk. **Contact:** Gordon De Ste. Croix, director of special projects. Music publisher of music for TV commercials, TV programs and corporate video productions. Estab. 1986. Staff size: 1. Pays standard royalty.
How to Contact *Does not accept unsolicited submissions.*
Music Mostly **instrumental**, for TV commercials and programs.

▣ ○ CUPIT MUSIC GROUP (ASCAP, BMI)
P.O. Box 121904, Nashville TN 37212. (615)731-0100. Fax: (615)731-3005. E-mail: info@cupitmusic.com. Website: www.cupitmusic.com. **Contact:** Publishing Division. Music publisher, record producer, record company, entertainment division and recording studio. Estab. 1986. Staff size: 8. Pays standard royalty.
Affiliate(s) Cupit Memaries (ASCAP) and Cupit Music (BMI).
- Also see the listing for Jerry Cupit Productions in the Record Producers section. Cupit Music's "What If He's Right" was number 1 on the CCRB Chart for ten consecutive weeks, and was named Song of the Year.
How to Contact *Please visit cupitmusic.com for our submission policy.* Prefers CD with lyric sheet. "We will return a response card." Include SASE. Usually responds in 2 months.
Music Mostly **country**, **bluegrass**, **blues**, **pop**, **gospel** and **instrumental**. Does not want rap, hard rock or metal. Published "What If He's Right" (single by Jerry Cupit) from *Memarie* (album), recorded by Memarie, released 2000 on HotSong Records; and "I'm Not Homeless" (single by Jerry Cupit/Ken Mellons/Randy Roberts) from *Wings of a Dove* (album), recorded by Ken Mellons, released 2000 on Curb Records.

☑ CURB MUSIC (ASCAP)
48 Music Square East, Nashville TN 37203. (615)321-5080. Fax: (615)742-3152. Website: www.curb.com. **Contact:** Porpis Tanner, creative manager of the publishing dept.

◖ JOF DAVE MUSIC (ASCAP)
1055 Kimball Ave., Kansas City KS 66104. (913)593-3180. **Contact:** David Johnson, CEO. Music publisher, record company (Cymbal Records). Estab. 1984. Publishes 30 songs/year; publishes 12 new songwriters/year. Pays standard royalty.
How to Contact *Contact first and obtain permission to submit.* Prefers cassette or CD. Include SASE. Responds in 1 month.

Music Mostly **gospel** and **R&B**. Published "The Woman I Love" (single) from *Sugar Bowl* (album), written and recorded by King Alex, released 2001 on Cymbal Records.

⊠ ⊘ THE EDWARD DE MILES MUSIC COMPANY (BMI)

28 E. Jackson Bldg., 10th Floor, #S627, Chicago IL 60604-2263. (773)509-6381. Fax: (312)922-6964. Website: www.edmsahara.com. **Contact:** Professional Manager. Music publisher, record company (Sahara Records), record producer, management, bookings and promotions. Estab. 1984. Publishes 50-75 songs/year; publishes 5 new songwriters/year. Hires staff songwriters. Pays standard royalty.
- • Also see the listings for Edward De Miles in the Record Producers and Managers & Booking Agents sections, and Sahara Records And Filmworks Entertainment in the Record Companies section of this book.

How to Contact *Write first and obtain permission to submit.* Prefers cassette with 1-3 songs and lyric sheet. Does not return material. Reponds in 1 month.

Music Mostly **top 40 pop/rock**, **R&B/dance** and **country**; also **musical scores for TV, radio, films** and **jingles**. Published "Dance Wit Me" and "Moments" (singles), written and recorded by Steve Lynn on Sahara Records (R&B).

Tips "Copyright all songs before submitting to us."

⊘ DELEV MUSIC COMPANY (ASCAP, BMI)

7231 Mansfield Ave., Philadelphia PA 19138-1620. (215)276-8861. Fax: (215)276-4509. E-mail: delevmusic@msn.com. President/CEO: W. Lloyd Lucas. A&R: Darryl Lucas. Music publisher. Publishes 6-10 songs/year; publishes 6-10 new songwriters/year. Pays standard royalty.

Affiliate(s) Sign of the Ram Music (ASCAP) and Delev Music (BMI).

How to Contact *Does not accept unsolicited material. Write or call first to obtain permission to submit.* Prefers CD with 1-8 songs and lyric sheet. "We will not accept certified mail or SASE." Does not return material. Responds in 1-2 months.

Music Mostly **R&B ballads** and **dance-oriented**; also **pop ballads**, **christian/gospel**, **crossover** and **country/western**. No gangsta rap. Published "Angel Love" (single by Barbara Heston/Geraldine Fernandez) from *The Silky Sounds of Debbie G* (album), recorded by Debbie G (light R&B/easy listening), released 2000 on Blizzard Records; *Variety* (album), produced by Barbara Heston and Carment Lindsay, released on Luvya Records; and "Ever Again" by Bernie Williams, released 2003 on SunDazed Records.

Tips "Persevere regardless if it is sent to our company or any other company. Most of all, no matter what happens, believe in yourself."

⊘ DISNEY MUSIC PUBLISHING (ASCAP, BMI)

500 S. Buena Vista St., Burbank CA 91521-6182. (818)569-3228. **Contact:** Brian Rawlings, vice president of music publishing.

Affiliate(s) Seven Peaks Music and Seven Summits Music.

How to Contact *Call first and obtain permission to submit.* Does not return material.

◻ DREAM SEEKERS PUBLISHING (BMI)

21 Coachlight Dr., Danville IL 61832-8240. (615)822-1160. **Contact:** Jerry Webb, professional manager. President: Sally Sidman. Music publisher. Estab. 1993. Publishes 25-50 songs/year; publishes 15-20 new songwriters/year. Pays standard royalty.

Affiliate(s) Dream Builders Publishing (ASCAP).

How to Contact Submit demo tape by mail. Unsolicited submissions are OK. "Please do not call to request permission—just submit your material. There are no code words. We listen to everything." Prefers cassette or CD with 2 songs and lyric sheet. "If one of your songs is selected for publishing, we prefer to have it available on CD for dubbing off copies to pitch to artist." Include SASE. Responds in 6 weeks.

Music Mostly **country**. "All types of **country** material, but mostly in need of up-tempo songs, preferably with positive lyrics." Does not want rap, jazz, classical, children's, hard rock, instrumental or blues. Published "Not Done Yet" (single by Coley McCabe/Mark Collie) from *Alabama Love*

Story (album), recorded by Mark Collie (country), released 2004; "A Dad Like That" (single by Jamie Champa) from *Ken Mahon* (album), recorded by Ken Mahon (country), released 2003; and "City Lights" (single by Kim Caudill) from *So Far So Good* (album), recorded by Avery Lovey (country), released 2004.

Tips "Be willing to work hard to learn the craft of songwriting. Be persistent. Nobody is born a hit songwriter. It often takes years to achieve that status."

⊘ DREAMWORKS SKG MUSIC PUBLISHING

331 N. Maple Dr., Suite 300, Beverly Hills CA 90210. Website: www.dreamworkspublishing.com. Music publisher and record company (DreamWorks Records).

  • Dreamworks SKG Music Publishing has been bought out by Universal Music Publishing.

⊌ DUANE MUSIC, INC. (BMI)

382 Clarence Ave., Sunnyvale CA 94086. (408)739-6133. **Contact:** Garrie Thompson, President. Music publisher and record producer. Publishes 10-20 songs/year; publishes 1 new songwriter/year. Pays standard royalty.

Affiliate(s) Morhits Publishing (BMI).

How to Contact Submit demo CD by mail. Unsolicited submissions are OK. Prefers CD with 1-2 songs. Include SASE. Responds in 2 months.

Music Mostly **blues**, **country**, **disco** and **easy listening**; also **rock**, **soul** and **top 40/pop**. Published "Little Girl" (single), recorded by The Syndicate of Sound & Ban (rock); "Warm Tender Love" (single), recorded by Percy Sledge (soul); and "My Adorable One" (single), recorded by Joe Simon (blues).

⊙ EARITATING MUSIC PUBLISHING (BMI)

P.O. Box 1101, Gresham OR 97030. Website: www.earitating.com. Music publisher. Estab. 1979. Pays individual per song contract, usually greater than 50% to writer.

How to Contact Submit demo by mail. Unsolicited submissions are OK. Prefers CD or CD-R with lyric sheet. "Submissions should be copyrighted by the author. We will deal for rights if interested." Does not return material. Responds only if interested.

Music Mostly **rock**, **country** and **folk**. Does not want rap.

Tips "Melody is most important, lyrics second. Style and performance take a back seat to these. A good song will stand with just one voice and one instrument. Also, don't use staples on your mailers."

◻ EGYPTIANMAN PRODUCTIONS (ASCAP)

(formerly May Peace Be Upon You Music), 4855 E. Warner Rd., Suite 24-169, Phoenix AZ 85044. (602)212-6735. Fax: (775)942-0589. E-mail: info@egyptianmanproductions.net. Website: www.eg yptianmanproductions.net. CEO/Writer/Publisher/President: Carlos C. Muhammad. Music publisher. Estab. 1996.

Affiliate(s) May Peace Be Upon You Music (ASCAP).

How to Contact Submit demo CD by mail. Unsolicited submissions are OK. Prefers CD with 3-4 songs, lyric sheet, 8×10 b&w glossy and bio on a floppy disk. "Do not call. In cover letter say whether you are seeking a publishing or record deal." Include SASE. Responds in 3 weeks.

Music Mostly **pop/R&B** and **hip-hop**. "Deep into the Night" and "Seasons of Your Love" (singles by Carlos Muhammad/Brendan Woodward/Alex Hamilton); and "Risk Taker" (single by Brendan Woodward/Alex Hamilton) from *Aren B* (album), recorded by Aren B (R&B), released April 2003 on Egyptianman Productions.

⊘ ELECTRIC MULE PUBLISHING COMPANY (BMI)/NEON MULE MUSIC (ASCAP)

1500 Clifton Ln., Nashville TN 37215. E-mail: emuleme@aol.com. **Contact:** Jeff Moseley, president.

◻ EMANDELL TUNES

10220 Glade Ave., Chatsworth CA 91311. (818)341-2264. Fax: (818)341-1008. **Contact:** Leroy C. Lovett, Jr., president/administrator. Music Publisher. Estab. 1979. Publishes 6-12 songs/year; publishes 3-4 new songwriters/year. Pays standard royalty.

Affiliate(s) Ben-Lee Music (BMI), Birthright Music (ASCAP), Em-Jay Music (ASCAP), Northworth Songs, Chinwah Songs, Gertrude Music (all SESAC), Andrask Music, Australia (BMI), Nadine Music, Switzerland.

How to Contact *Write first and obtain permission to submit.* Prefers cassette, videocassette or CD with 4-5 songs and lead or lyric sheet. Include bio of writer, singer or group. Include SASE. Responds in 6 weeks.

Music Mostly **inspirational**, **contemporary gospel** and **choral**; also **strong country** and **light top 40**. Published "Under My Skin" and "Colorada River" (singles by Diana/Kim Fowley), recorded by Diana, released 2001 on WFL Records; and "Runaway Love" (single by Gil Askey), recorded by Linda Clifford (new gospel), released 2001 on Sony Records.

Tips "We suggest you listen to current songs. Imagine how that song would sound if done by some other artist. Keep your ear tuned to new groups, bands, singers. Try to analyze what made them different, was it the sound? Was it the song? Was it the production? Ask yourself these questions: Do they have that 'hit' feeling? Do you like what they are doing?"

⊿ EMF PRODUCTIONS (ASCAP)

1000 E. Prien Lake Rd., Suite D, Lake Charles LA 70601. E-mail: emfprod@aol.com. Website: www.emfproductions.com. President: Ed Fruge. Music publisher and record producer. Estab. 1984. Pays standard royalty.

• Also see the listing for EMF Productions in the Record Companies section of this book.

How to Contact Submit demo tape by mail. Unsolicited submissions are OK. Prefers CD or VHS videocassette with 4 songs and lyric sheet. Does not return material. Responds in 6 weeks.

Music Mostly **R&B**, **pop** and **rock**; also **country** and **gospel**.

⊿ EMI CHRISTIAN MUSIC PUBLISHING (ASCAP, BMI, SESAC)

P.O. Box 5085, Brentwood TN 37024. (615)371-6800. Website: www.emicmg.com. Music publisher. Publishes 100 songs/year; publishes 2 new songwriters/year. Hires staff songwriters. Pays standard royalty.

Affiliate(s) Birdwing Music (ASCAP), Sparrow Song (BMI), His Eye Music (SESAC), Ariose Music (ASCAP), Straightway Music (ASCAP), Shepherd's Fold Music (BMI), Songs of Promise (SESAC), Dawn Treader Music (SESAC), Meadowgreen Music Company (ASCAP), River Oaks Music Company (BMI), Stonebrook Music Company (SESAC), Bud John Songs, Inc. (ASCAP), Bud John Music, Inc. (BMI), Bud John Tunes, Inc. (SESAC).

How to Contact *"We do not accept unsolicited submissions."*

Music Published "Concert of the Age" (by Jeffrey Benward), recorded by Phillips, Craig & Dean; "God Is In Control," written and recorded by Twila Paris, both on StarSong Records; and "Faith, Hope and Love" (by Ty Lacy), recorded by Point of Grace on Word Records.

Tips "Come to Nashville and be a part of the fastest growing industry. It's nearly impossible to get a publisher's attention unless you know someone in the industry that is willing to help you."

⊿ EMI MUSIC PUBLISHING

1290 Avenue of the Americas, 42nd Floor, New York NY 10104. (212)492-1200. Website: www.emimusic.com. Contact: Jodi Gerson; Big Jon. Music publisher.

How to Contact *EMI does not accept unsolicited material.*

Music Published "All Night Long" (by F. Evans/R. Lawrence/S. Combs), recorded by Faith Evans featuring Puff Daddy on Bad Boy; "You" (by C. Roland/J. Powell), recorded by Jesse Powell on Silas; and "I Was" (by C. Black/P. Vassar), recorded by Neal McCoy on Atlantic.

Tips "Don't bury your songs. Less is more—we will ask for more if we need it. Put your strongest song first."

⊿ EMSTONE MUSIC PUBLISHING (BMI)

Box 398, Hallandale FL 33008. (305)936-0412. E-mail: webmaster@emstonemusicpublishing.com. **Contact:** Michael Gary, Creative Director. President: Mitchell Stone. Vice President: Madeline Stone. Music publisher. Estab. 1997. Pays standard royalty.

How to Contact Submit demo CD by mail with any number of songs. Unsolicited submissions are OK. Does not return material. Responds only if interested.

Music Everything except classical and opera. Published "www.history" (single by Tim Eatman) and "Gonna Recall My Heart" (single by Dan Jury) from *No Tears* (album), recorded by Cole Seaver and Tammie Darlene, released on CountryStock Records; and "I Love What I've Got" (single by Heather and Paul Turner) from *The Best of Talented Kids* (compilation album) recorded by Gypsy.

Tips "We only offer publishing contracts to writers whose songs exhibit a spark of genius. Anything less can't compete in the music industry."

FAMOUS MUSIC PUBLISHING COMPANIES (ASCAP, BMI)

10635 Santa Monica Blvd., Suite 300, Los Angeles CA 90025. (310)441-1300. Fax: (310)441-4722. Website: www.syncsite.com. President: Ira Jaffe. Vice President, Film and TV: Stacey Palm. Senior Creative Director: Carol Spencer (rock/pop/alternative). Senior Creative Director/Latin: Claribell Cuevas. New York office: 1633 Broadway, 11th Floor, New York NY 10019. (212)654-7433. Fax: (212)654-4748. Chairman and CEO: Irwin Z. Robinson. Executive Vice President, Finance and Administration: Margaret Johnson. Vice President Catalogue Development: Mary Beth Roberts. Creative Director: Tanya Brown. Nashville office: 65 Music Square East, Nashville TN 37212. (615)329-0500. Fax: (615)321-4121. Senior Creative Director: Curtis Green. Music Publisher. Estab. 1929.

Affiliate(s) Famous Music (ASCAP) and Ensign Music (BMI).

How to Contact Famous Music does not accept unsolicited submissions.

Film & TV Famous Music is a Paramount Pictures' company. Music Supervisor: Stacey Palm.

FIFTH AVENUE MEDIA, LTD. (ASCAP)

1208 W. Broadway, Hewlett NY 11557. (212)691-5630. Fax: (212)645-5038. E-mail: thefirm@thefirm.com. Website: www.thefirm.com. Professional Managers: Bruce E. Colfin(rootsy bluesy rock/reggae, Jam Bands/alternative rock/heavy metal); Jeffrey E. Jacobson (hip-hop/R&B/dance). Music publisher and record company (Fifth Avenue Media, Ltd.). Estab. 1995. Publishes 2 songs/year. Staff size: 4. Pays standard royalty.

Music Published "Analog" (single by Paul Byrne) from *Paul Byrne & the Bleeders* (album), recorded by Paul Byrne (pop rock), released 2001 on Independent.

FIRST TIME MUSIC (PUBLISHING) U.K. (PRS, MCPS)

Sovereign House, 12 Trewartha Road, Praa Sands, Penzance, Cornwall TR20 9ST United Kingdom. (01736)762826. Fax: (01736)763328. E-mail: panamus@aol.com. Website: www.songwriters-guild .com. **Contact:** Roderick G. Jones, managing director. Music publisher, record company (Rainy Day Records, Mohock Records, HepCat Records). Estab. 1986. Publishes 500-750 songs/year; 20-50 new songwriters/year. Staff size: 6. Hires staff writers. Pays standard royalty; "50-60% to established and up-and-coming writers with the right attitude."

Affiliate(s) Scamp Music Publishing, Panama Music Library, Musik Image Library, Caribbean Music Library, Psi Music Library, ADN Creation Music Library, Heraldic Production Music Library, Promo Sonor International, Eventide Music, Melody First Music Library, Piano Bar Music Library, Corelia Music Library, Panama Music Ltd.

How to Contact Submit demo tape by mail. Unsolicited submissions are OK. Submit on CD only, "of professional quality" with unlimited number of songs and lyric or lead sheets. Responds in 1 month. SAE and IRC required for reply.

Film & TV Places 200 songs in film and TV/year. "Copyrights and phonographic rights of Panama Music Limited and its associated catalogue idents have been used and subsist in various productions broadcasts and adverts produced by major and independent production companies, television, film/video companies, radio broadcasters (not just in the UK, but in various countries world-wide) and by commercial record companies for general release and sale. In the UK & Republic of Ireland they include the BBC networks of national/regional television and radio, ITV network programs and promotions (Channel 4, Border TV, Granada TV, Tyne Tees TV, Scottish TV, Yorkshire TV, HTV, Central TV, Channel TV, LWT, Meridian TV, Grampian TV, GMTV, Ulster TV, Westcountry

TV, Channel TV, Carlton TV, Anglia TV, TV3, RTE (Ireland), Planet TV, Rapido TV, VT4 TV, BBC Worldwide, etc.), independent radio stations, satellite Sky Television (BskyB), Discovery Channel, Learning Channel, National Geographic, Living Channel, Sony, Trouble TV, UK Style Channel, Hon Cyf, CSI, etc., and cable companies, GWR Creative, Premier, Spectrum FM, Local Radio Partnership, Fox, Manx, Swansea Sound, Mercury, 2CRFM, Broadland, BBC Radio Collection, etc. Some credits include copyrights in programs, films/videos, broadcasts, trailers and promotions such as Desmond's, One Foot in the Grave, EastEnders, Hale and Pace, Holidays from Hell, A Touch of Frost, 999 International, and Get Away.''

Music All styles. Published ''Innocence'' (single) from *Innocence* (album), recorded by Rik Waller (soul music), released 2005 on Red Admiral Records; ''Fast Decay'' (single) from *Heavy Rock Spectacular* (album), recorded by Bram Stoker (Gothic rock music), released 2004 on Windmill Records, Arkama Records, Black Widow Records, Comet Records; and ''Horsehead Nebula'' (single) from *Light From Orion* (album), recorded by Kevin Kendle (New Age instrumental), released 2004 on Eventide Records.

Tips ''Have a professional approach—present well produced demos. First impressions are important and may be the only chance you get. Writers are advised to join the Guild of International Songwriters and Composers in the United Kingdom.''

⌨ ◯ FRESH ENTERTAINMENT (ASCAP)

1315 Simpson Rd., Atlanta GA 30314. E-mail: whunter1122@yahoo.com. **Contact:** Willie W. Hunter, managing director. Music publisher and record company. Publishes 5 songs/year. Staff size: 4. Hires staff songwriters. Pays standard royalty.

Affiliate(s) !Hserf Music (ASCAP), Blair Vizzion Music (BMI) and Santron Music (BMI).

How to Contact Submit demo tape by mail. Unsolicited submissions are OK. Prefers cassette or videocassette with 3 songs and lyric sheet. ''Send photo if available.'' Include SASE. Responds in 6 weeks.

Film & TV Places 1 song in TV/year. Published the theme song for BET's *Comic Vue* (by Charles E. Jones), recorded by Cirocco.

Music Mostly **rap**, **R&B** and **pop/dance**. Published *Ancestral Spirits* (album), written and recorded by Robert Miles (jazz), released 2004 on Sheets of Sound/Fresh Entertainment; and *My Life My Hustle* (album), written and recorded by Jamal Smith (rap/hip-hop), released 2004 on Vision Vibe/ Fresh Entertainment.

◪ FRICON MUSIC COMPANY (BMI)

1048 S. Ogden Dr., Los Angeles CA 90019. (323)931-7323. Fax: (323)938-2030. E-mail: fricon@com cast.net. President: Terri Fricon. **Contact:** Madge Benson, professional manager. Music publisher. Estab. 1981. Publishes 25 songs/year; publishes 1-2 new songwriters/year. Staff size: 6. Pays standard royalty.

Affiliate(s) Fricout Music Company (ASCAP) and Now and Forever Songs (SESAC).

How to Contact *Contact first and obtain permission to submit.* Prefers CD with 3- 4 songs and lyric or lead sheet. ''Prior permission must be obtained or packages will be returned.'' Include SASE. Responds in 2 months.

Music Mostly **country**.

◯ FURROW MUSIC (BMI)

P.O. Box 4121, Edmond OK 73083-4121. E-mail: furromusic@sbcglobal.net. **Contact:** G.H. Derrick, owner/publisher. Music publisher, record company (Gusher Records) and record producer. Estab. 1984. Publishes 10-15 songs/year. Staff size: 1. Pays standard royalty.

How to Contact Submit demo tape by mail. Unsolicited submissions are OK. Prefers CD with no more than 5 songs or cassette with 1 song and lyric sheet. ''One instrument and vocal is OK for demo.'' Include SASE. Responds in 2 weeks.

Music Mostly **country** and **cowboy**. Prefer up-tempo; no drinking or cheating songs.

Tips ''Have your song critiqued by other writers (or songwriter organizations) prior to making the demo. Only make and send demos of songs that have a universal appeal. Make sure the vocal is out front of the music. Never be so attached to a lyric or tune that you can't rewrite it. Don't forget to include your SASE and lyric sheet with all submissions."

✅ G MAJOR MUSIC (BMI)

P.O. Box 3331, Fort Smith AR 72913-3331. E-mail: JerryGlidewell@juno.com. **Owner:** Jerry Glidewell. Professional Managers: Alex Hoover. Music publisher. Estab. 1992. Publishes 10 songs/year; publishes 2 new songwriters/year. Staff size: 2. Pays standard royalty.

How to Contact Submit inquiry by mail. No unsolicited submissions. Prefers CD. Submit up to 3 songs. Include SASE. Responds in 3 weeks.

Music Mostly **country** and **contemporary Christian**. Published *Set The Captives Free* (album by Chad Little, Jeff Pitzer, Ben Storie), recorded by Sweeter Rain for Cornerstone Television (contemporary Christian); "Don't Talk About Love" (single by Chad Little and Jerry Glidewell), recorded by Carrie Underwood (country); and "Competition with a Track" (by Elaine Wooslsey), recorded by Libby Benson (Christian contemporary), all on MBS.

Tips "We are looking for 'smash hits' to pitch to the Country and Christian markets."

☐ ALAN GARY MUSIC (ASCAP, BMI)

P.O. Box 179, Palisades Park NJ 07650. President: Alan Gary. Creative Director: Fran Levine. Creative Assistant: Harold Green. Music publisher. Estab. 1987. Publishes a varying number of songs/year. Staff size: 3. Pays standard royalty.

How to Contact Submit demo tape by mail. Unsolicited submissions are OK. Prefers cassette or VHS videocassette with lyric sheet. Include SASE.

Music Mostly **pop**, **R&B** and **dance**, also **rock**, **A/C** and **country**. Published "Liberation" (single by Gary/Julian), recorded by Les Julian on Music Tree Records (A/C); "Love Your Way Out of This One" (single by Gary/Rosen), recorded by Deborah Steel on Bad Cat Records (contemporary country); and "Dueling Rappers" (single by Gary/Free), recorded by Prophets of Boom on You Dirty Rap! Records (rap/R&B).

☐ GLAD MUSIC CO. (ASCAP, BMI, SESAC)

14340 Torrey Chase, Suite 380, Houston TX 77014. (281)397-7300. Fax: (281)397-6206. E-mail: hwesdaily@gladmusicco.com. Website: www.gladmusicco.com. **Contact:** Wes Daily, A&R Director (country). Music publisher, record company and record producer. Estab. 1958. Publishes 10 songs/year; publishes 10 new songwriters/year. Staff size: 4. Pays standard royalty.

Affiliate(s) Bud-Don (ASCAP) and Rayde (SESAC).

How to Contact *Write first and obtain permission to submit or to arrange personal interview.* Prefers CD with 3 songs, lyric sheet and cover letter. Does not return material. Responds in 6 weeks. SASE or e-mail address for reply.

Music Mostly **country**. Does not want weak songs. Published *Love Bug* (album by C. Wayne/W. Kemp), recorded by George Strait, released 1995 on MCA; *Walk Through This World With Me* (album), written and recorded by George Jones and *Race Is On* (album by D. Rollins), recorded by George Jones, both released 1999 on Asylum.

☑ ☐ THE GOODLAND MUSIC GROUP INC. (ASCAP, BMI, SESAC)

P.O. Box 24454, Nashville TN 37202. (615)269-7071. Fax: (615)269-0131. E-mail: rachel@aristomedia.com. Website: www.thegoodlandgroup.com. **Contact:** Rachel Barnhard, publishing coordinator. Estab. 1988. Publishes 50 songs/year; 5-10 new songwriters/year. Pays standard royalty.

Affiliate(s) Goodland Publishing Company (ASCAP), Marc Isle Music (BMI) and Gulf Bay Publishing (SESAC).

How to Contact Submit demo tape by mail. Unsolicited submissions are OK. Include SASE with first class postage.

Music Mostly **country/Christian**, but open to **all styles**. "We are now listening to **pop, hip-hop, rock, dance** for publishing consideration."

GOODNIGHT KISS MUSIC (BMI)

10153½ Riverside Dr. #239, Toluca Lake CA 91602. (831)479-9993. Website: www.goodnightkiss.c om. **Contact:** Janet Fisher, managing director. Music publisher, record company and record producer. Estab. 1986. Publishes 6-8 songs/year; publishes 4-5 new songwriters/year. Pays standard royalty.

• Goodnight Kiss Music specializes in placing music in movies and TV.

Affiliate(s) Scene Stealer Music (ASCAP).

How to Contact "Check our website or subscribe to free newsletter (wwww.goodnightkiss.com) to see what we are looking for and to obtain codes. Packages must have proper submission codes, or they are discarded." Only accepts material that is requested on the website. Prefers CD or cassette with 1-3 songs and lyric sheet. Send SASE for reply. Does not return material. Responds in 6 months.

Film & TV Places 3-5 songs in film/year. Published "I Do, I Do, Love You" (by Joe David Curtis), recorded by Ricky Kershaw in *Road Ends*; "Bee Charmer's Charmer" (by Marc Tilson) for the MTV movie *Love Song*; "Right When I Left" (by B. Turner/J. Fisher) in the movie *Knight Club*.

Music All modern styles. Published and produced *Addiction: Highs & Lows* (CD), written and recorded by various artists (all styles), released 2004; *Tall Tales of Osama Bin Laden* (CD), written and recorded by various artists (all styles parody), released 2004; and *Rythm of Honor* (CD), written and recorded by various artists (all styles), slated release 2005, all on Goodnight Kiss Records.

Tips "The absolute best way to keep apprised of the company's needs is to subscribe to the online newsletter. Only specifically requested material is accepted, as listed in the newsletter (what the industry calls us for is what we request from writers). We basically use an SGA contract, and there are never fees to be considered for specific projects or albums. However, we are a real music company, and the competition is just as fierce as with the majors."

HAPPY MELODY

VZW, Paul Gilsonstraat 31, St-Andries 8200 Belgium. 00 32 50-316380. Fax: 00 32 50-315235. E-mail: happymelody@skynet.be. **Contact:** Eddy Van Mouffaert, general manager. Music publisher, record company (Jump Records) and record producer (Jump Productions). Member SABAM S.V., Brussels. Publishes 100 songs/year; publishes 8 new songwriters/year. Staff size: 2. Pays standard royalty via SABAM S.V.

How to Contact Submit demo CD or tape by mail. Unsolicited submissions are OK. Prefers CD. Does not return material. Responds in 2 weeks.

Music Mostly **easy listening**, **disco** and **light pop**; also **instrumentals**. Published "Football Mania" (single by R. Mondes/J. Towers/D. Winters), recorded by Le Grand Julot (accordion), released 2005 on Scorpion; *Don't Give Up Your Dream* (album), written and recorded by Chris Clark (pop), released 2004 on 5 Stars; and *Instrumental Delight* (album), written and recorded by various artists (pop), released 2005 on Belstar.

Tips "Music wanted with easy, catchy melodies (very commercial songs)."

HICKORY LANE PUBLISHING AND RECORDING (ASCAP, SOCAN)

19854 Butternut Lane, Pitt Meadows BC V3Y 2S7 Canada. (604)465-1258. **Contact:** Chris Urbanski, president. Music publisher, record company and record producer. Estab. 1988. Hires staff writers. Publishes 30 songs/year; publishes 5 new songwriters/year. Pays standard royalty.

How to Contact *Does not accept unsolicited submissions.*

Music Mostly **country** and **country rock**. Published "Just Living For Today" (single by Chris Urbanski), recorded by Chris Michaels (country), released 2005 on Hickory Lane Records; "This is My Sons" (single by Tyson Avery/Chris Urbanski/Alex Bradshaw) recorded by Chris Michaels (country), released 2005 on Hickory Lane Records; "Stubborn Love" (single by Owen Davies/Chris Urbanski/John Middleton), recorded by Chris Michaels (country), released 2005 on Hickory Lane Records.

Tips "Send us a professional quality demo with the vocals upfront. We are looking for hits, and so are the major record labels we deal with. Be original in your approach, don't send us a cover tune."

⚅ ◪ HIGH-MINDED MOMA PUBLISHING & PRODUCTIONS (BMI)

P.O. Box 487, Myrtle Point OR 97458. **Contact:** Kai Moore Snyder, president. Music publisher and production company. Pays standard royalty.

How to Contact Prefers 7$\frac{1}{2}$ ips reel-to-reel, CD or cassette with 4-8 songs and lyric sheet. Include SASE. Responds in 1 month.

Music Mostly **country**, **MOR**, **rock (country)**, **New Age** and **top 40/pop**.

⚁ ◯ HIS POWER PRODUCTIONS AND PUBLISHING (ASCAP, BMI)

1304 Canyon, Plainview TX 79072-4740. (806)296-7073. Fax: (806)296-7111. E-mail: dcarter@texas online.net. Professional Managers: T.D. (Darryl) Carter (R&B, gospel, country rock, jazz, pop, new rock, classic rock) Music publisher, record company (Lion and Lamb), record producer and management and booking agency (End-Time Management & Booking Agency). Estab. 1995. Publishes 0-3 songs/year; publishes 3 new songwriters/year. Staff size: 4. May hire staff songwriters. Pays negotiable royalty.

Affiliate(s) Love Story Publishing (BMI).

  • The song "Heal Me," published by His Power, was awarded ASCAP Popular Award from 1998-2005.

How to Contact *Write or call first and obtain permission to submit.* Prefers cassette, CD or DAT with 1- 4 songs and lyric sheet. Include SASE. "No material returned without SASE." Responds if interested.

Music Mostly **power gospel**, **pop**, **new rock**, **classic rock**, **country rock gospel** and **adult contemporary gospel**; also **R&B**, **jazz**, **Christ-oriented Christmas music**, **pro-life and family**. Looking for unconventional styles and structure. Does not want negative-based lyrics of any kind. Published "She Used to Be Me" (single), written and recorded by Crystal Cartier on Love Story (blues); "It's His Life" (single), written and recorded by Mike Burchfield (country gospel), released on Lion and Lamb Records.

Tips "Be serious. We are only interested in those who have meaning and substance behind what is created. Music is an avenue to change the world. Submit what comes from the heart. Don't be in a hurry. Good music has no time limits. And yet, time will reward the desire you put into it. Be willing to embark on newly designed challenges that will meet a new century of opportunity and needs never before obtainable through conventional music companies."

◯ HITSBURGH MUSIC CO. (BMI)

P.O. Box 1431, 233 N. Electra, Gallatin TN 37066. (615)452-0324. Promotional Director: Kimolin Crutcher. A&R Director: K'leetha Gilbert. Executive Vice President: Kenneth Gilbert. **Contact:** Harold Gilbert, president/general manager. Music publisher. Estab. 1964. Publishes 12 songs/year. Staff size: 4. Pays standard royalty.

Affiliate(s) 7th Day Music (BMI).

How to Contact Submit demo tape by mail. Unsolicited submissions are OK. Prefers cassette or quality videocassette with 2-4 songs and lead sheet. Prefers studio produced demos. Include SASE. Responds in 6 weeks.

Music Mostly **country gospel** and **MOR**. Published "That Kind'a Love" (single by Kimolin Crutchet and Dan Serafini), from *Here's Cissy* (album), recorded by Cissy Crutcher (MOR), released 2005 on Vivaton; and "Disorder at the Border" (single), written and recorded by Donald Layne, released 2001 on Southern City.

⚅ ◯ HOME TOWN HERO'S PUBLISHING (BMI)

112 West Houston, Leonard TX 75452. (903)587-2767. **Contact:** Tammy Wood, owner. Music publisher. Estab. 2003. Staff size: 2. Pays standard royalty of 50%.

How to Contact Submit demo by mail. Unsolicited submissions are OK. Prefers cassette or CD with 3-6 songs, lyric sheet and cover letter. Does not return submissions. Responds only if interested.

Music Mostly **country (all styles)**, **pop**, **Southern rock**; also **ballads**, **gospel**, and **blues**. Does not want heavy metal and rap.

Tips "Most of all, believe in yourself. The best songs come from the heart. Don't get discouraged, be tough, keep writing, and always think positive."

ISLAND CULTURE MUSIC PUBLISHERS (BMI)

Chateau Bordeaux, St. John 00830. U.S. Virgin Islands. E-mail: L_monsanto@hotmail.com. **Contact:** Liston Monsanto, Jr., president. Music publisher and record company (Island King Records). Estab. 1996. Publishes 10 songs/year; publishes 3 new songwriters/year. Hires staff songwriters. Staff size: 3. Pays standard royalty.

How to Contact Submit demo tape by mail. Unsolicited submissions are OK. Prefers cassette with 8 songs and lyric sheet. Send bio and 8×10 glossy. Does not return material. Responds in 1 month.

Music Mostly **reggae**, **calypso** and **zouk**; also **house**. Published "Jah Give Me Life" (single by Chubby) from *Best of Island King* (album), recorded by Chubby (reggae), released 2003 on Island King Records; "When People Mix Up" (single by Lady Lex/L. Monsanto/Chubby) from *Best of Island King* (album), recorded by Lady Lex (reggae), released 2003 on Island King Records; "I Am Real" (single by L. Monsanto) from *Best of Island King* (album), recorded by Lady Lex (reggae), released 2003 on Island King Records.

IVORY PEN ENTERTAINMENT (ASCAP)

P.O. Box 1097, Laurel MD 20725. (301)490-4418. Fax: (301)490-4635. E-mail: ivorypen@comcast.n et. Website: www.uwritethehit.com. Professional Managers: Steven Lewis (hip-hop/rap, R&B, inspirational); Sonya Lewis (pop, jazz, A/C). Music publisher. Estab. 2003. Publishes 10 songs/year. Staff size: 4. Pays standard royalty.

How to Contact Submit demo by mail. Unsolicited submissions are OK. Prefers CD/CDR with 3-5 songs and cover letter. Include SASE. Does not return material without SASE. Responds in 1 month. "Don't forget contact info! Always be professional when you submit your work to any company."

Music Mostly **R&B**, **hip-hop**, and **inspirational/gospel**; also **jazz**, **adult contemporary**, and **pop/rock**. Published One Dose (album), written and recorded by Jeremy Wills Project (hip-hop), released on Ivory Pen Entertainment.

Tips "Learn your craft and don't steal from other musicians. Be original. Ivory Pen Entertainment is a music publishing company with distribution that caters to the producer and aspiring artist. We release CDs of music tracks (no vocals) for aspiring singers and songwriters to use for their demos. This enables you, the aspiring recording artist or songwriter to cut your recording costs in half, if not more. Ivory Pen also allows you to send your completed demo to record companies if you are an artist or to publishing companies if you are a songwriter, meanwhile, the producer gets paid every time his/her tracks are used. All CDs are licensed under Ivory Pen Entertainment (ASCAP) and sell for $15.99."

JA/NEIN MUSIKVERLAG GMBH

Oberstr. 14 A, D-20144, Hamburg Germany. Fax: (+49)40 448850. E-mail: janeinmv@aol.com. General Manager: Mary Dostal. Music publisher, record company and record producer. GEMA. Publishes 50 songs/year; publishes 5 new songwriters/year. Staff size: 3. Pays 60% royalty.

Affiliate(s) Pinorrekk Mv., Star-Club Mv. and Wunderbar Mv. (GEMA).

How to Contact Submit audio (visual) carrier by mail. Unsolicited submissions are OK. Prefers CDR or VHS videocassette. Enclose e-mail address. Responds in 2 months.

Music Mostly **jazz**, **klezmer**, **pop**, **rap** and **rock**. Published *Groovology* (album) written and recorded by Axel Zwingenberger and Gottfried Boettger (boogie woogie & blues), released 2004 on Vagabond; *Horizons* (album) written and recorded by Gottfried Boettger (ragtime/jazz), released 2004 on Vagabond.

Tips "We do not return submitted material. Send A-Side songs or extraordinary works/ideas only, please. Write what you expect from collaboration. If artist, enclose photo. If CS, leave three seconds between tracks. Enclose lyrics. Be fantastic!"

JANA JAE MUSIC (BMI)

P.O. Box 35726, Tulsa OK 74153. (918)786-8896. Fax: (918)786-8897. E-mail: janajae@janajae.com. Website: www.janajae.com. **Contact:** Kathleen Pixley, secretary. Music publisher, record company

(Lark Record Productions, Inc.) and record producer (Lark Talent and Advertising). Estab. 1980. Publishes 5-10 songs/year; publishes 1-2 new songwriters/year. Staff size: 8. Pays standard royalty.
How to Contact Submit demo tape by mail. Unsolicted submissions are OK. Prefers CD or VHS videocassette with 3-4 songs and typed lyric and lead sheet if possible. Does not return material. Responds only if accepted for use.
Music Mostly **country, bluegrass**, **jazz** and **instrumentals** (**classical** or **country**). Published *Mayonnaise* (album by Steve Upfold), recorded by Jana Jae; and *Let the Bible Be Your Roadmap* (album by Irene Elliot) recorded by Jana Jae, both on Lark Records.

JAELIUS ENTERPRISES (ASCAP, BMI)
P.O. Box 459, Royse City TX 75189. (972)636-9230. Fax: (972)636-0036. E-mail: jaelius@flash.net. Website: www.jaelius.com. **Contact:** James Cornelius, managing director. Music publisher. Staff size: 2. Pays standard royalty.
Affiliate(s) Jaelius Music (ASCAP), Hitzgalore Music (BMI), Air Rifle Music (ASCAP) and Bee Bee Gun Music (BMI).
How to Contact *Write or call first and obtain permission to submit.* Prefers CD. Include SASE. Responds in 6 weeks.
Film & TV Places 2 songs in film/year. Recently published "Night Has a Thousand Eyes" (by Wayne/Weisman/Garrett), recorded by Anita Kelsey in *Dark City*; and "Feeling in Love," written and recorded by J.J. Cale in *Lawn Dogs*.
Music Mostly **gospel**. Published "Make a Joyful Noise" and "I Know" (singles), recorded by Olivia Mojica (gospel); "Where Would I Be Without Your Love" (single), recorded by Lee Mays (gospel); "God Gives His Love International" (single), recorded by Michelle Deck (gospel).
Tips "Today's market requires good demos. Strong lyrics are a must."

JODA MUSIC (BMI)
P.O. Box 100, Spirit Lake IA 51360. (712)336-2859. President: John Senn. Music publisher and record company. Estab. 1970. Publishes 10 songs/year. Pays standard royalty.
Affiliate(s) Okoboji Music (BMI).
How to Contact Prefers CD with no more than 4 songs and lyric sheet. "Keep demos short." Include SASE. Responds in 3 weeks.
Music Mostly **light rock**, **country** and **gospel**. Published "Beer & Popcorn" (by Dave Peterson), recorded by Ralph Lundquist (country); "Change is Going to Come" (by Roger Hughes), recorded by Silver $ Band (pop); and *Ain't Like it Used to Be*, (by Dave Petersen and John Senn), recorded by Brent (pop), all on IGL Records.

QUINCY JONES MUSIC (ASCAP)
6671 Sunset Blvd., #1574A, Los Angeles CA 90028. (323)957-6601. E-mail: info@quincyjonesmusic. com. Music publisher.
How to Contact *Quincy Jones Music does not accept unsolicited submissions.*

JPMC MUSIC INC. (BMI)
P.O. Box 526, Burlington VT 05402. (802)860-7110. Fax: (802)860-7112. E-mail: music@jpmc.com. Website: www.jpmc.com. **Contact:** Jane Peterer, president. Music publisher, record company (JPMC Records) and book publisher. Estab. 1989. Publishes 20 songs/year; publishes 10 new songwriters/year. Pays standard royalty.
Affiliate(s) GlobeSound Publishing (ASCAP) and GlobeArt Publishing Inc. (BMI).
How to Contact Submit a demo tape by mail. Unsolicited submissions are OK. Prefers "professional" DAT, CD or cassette with 3 songs and lyric sheet. "If submitting a CD, indicate which three tracks to consider, otherwise only the first three will be considered." Include SASE. Responds in 2 months. See website for complete guidelines.
Music Mostly **pop/R&B**, **jazz** and **gospel**; also **country** and **instrumental**. Published "Ode to Ireland" (single by Breschi), recorded by Breschi/Cassidy on Pick Records (instrumental); and "Ici Paris" (single), written and recorded by Michael Ganian.

Tips "We are in constant communication with record and film producers and will administer your work on a worldwide basis. We also publish songbooks for musicians and fans, as well as educational and method books for students and teachers."

⃞ ⃞ JUKE MUSIC (BMI)

P.O. Box 120277, Nashville TN 37212. **Contact:** Becky Gibson, songwriter coordinator. Music publisher. Estab. 1987. Publishes 60-150 songs/year; publishes 3-25 new songwriters/year. Pays standard royalty.

How to Contact Submit demo tape by mail. Unsolicited submissions are OK. Prefers CD with 3 songs and lyric sheet. "Send only radio-friendly material." Does not return material. Responds only if interested.

Music Mostly **country/pop** and **rock**; also **alternative adult** and **Christian**. Does *not* want theatrical, improperly structured, change tempo and feel, poor or no hook. Published "Cross on the Highway" (single) from *Sumner Country Drive Inn* (album), written and recorded by Ronnie Mc-Dowell, released 2001 on Portland; "April Fool" (single by Phil Delberg) from *Georgia Rockitt* (album), recorded by Tuscaloosa (southern rock/country), released 2000 on Blackstone; and "King & Queen of Love" (single by Ralph Lake) from *Running Scared 2001* (album), recorded by Michael Sheahan (pop/rock), released 2001 on Daydreamer.

Tips "Do your homework, craft the song, be sure you're willing to gamble your songwriting integrity on this song or songs you're sending. We recommend songwriters attend workshops or conferences before submitting material. Help us cut through the junk. Send *positive, up-tempo, new country* for best results. It seems most of our submitters read what we *do not* want and send that! *Please* listen to country radio."

⃞ KAUPPS & ROBERT PUBLISHING CO. (BMI)

P.O. Box 5474, Stockton CA 95205. (209)948-8186. Fax: (209)942-2163. Website: www.makingmusic4u.com. **Contact:** Melissa Glenn, A&R coordinator (all styles). Production Manager (country, pop, rock): Rick Webb. Professional Manager (country, pop, rock): Bruce Boun. President: Nancy L. Merrihew. Music publisher, record company (Kaupp Records), manager and booking agent (Merri-Webb Productions and Most Wanted Bookings). Estab. 1990. Publishes 15-20 songs/year; publishes 5 new songwriters/year. Pays standard royalty.

How to Contact *Write first and obtain permission to submit.* Prefers cassette or VHS videocassette (if available) with 3 songs maximum and lyric sheet. "If artist, send PR package." Include SASE. Responds in 6 months.

Music Mostly **country**, **R&B** and **A/C rock**; also **pop**, **rock** and **gospel**. Published "Prisoner of Love" (single by N. Merrihew/Rick Webb), recorded by Nanci Lynn (country/rock/pop); "Excuse Me, But That Ain't Country"; "I Thank You Father" and "On the Other Side" (singles by N. Merrihew/B. Bolin), recorded by Bruce Bolin (country/rock/pop); and "Did You Think That I Thought That You Liked Me" (single by N. Merrihew/B. Bolin), recorded by Nanci Lynn (country/rock/pop) and Cheryl (country/rock/pop), all released on Kaupp Records.

Tips "Know what you want, set a goal, focus in on your goals, be open to constructive criticism, polish tunes and keep polishing."

⃞ KAYSARAH MUSIC (ASCAP)

P.O. Box 1264, 6020 W. Pottstown Rd., Peoria IL 61654-1264. (309)673-5755. Fax: (309)673-7636. E-mail: uarltd@A5.com. Website: www.unitedcyber.com. **Contact:** Jerry Hanlon, owner/producer. Music Publisher, record company, and record producer. Estab. 2000. Publishes 2 new songwriters/year. Staff size: 3. Pays standard royalty.

Affiliate(s) Jerjoy Music (BMI); Abilite Music (BMI).

• Also see the listing for Jerjoy Music in this section and UAR Records in the Record Companies section of this book.

How to Contact Submit demo tape by mail. Unsolicited submissions are OK. Prefers cassette or CD with 4 songs and lyric sheet and cover letter. Include SASE. Responds in 2 weeks.

Music Mostly **traditional country**, **modern country** and **country gospel**; also **Irish country**, **Irish**

ballads and **Irish folk/traditional**. Recently published "It's Too Late For Goodbye" (single by Dorothy Wallace) and "A World Without You" (single by Sue Rapp) from *Candlelight and Wine* (album), recorded by Jackie Nelson (modern country), released 2001 on Irish Records.

Tips "Be honest and extremely critical of your work. Make every word in a song count. Attempt to create work that is not over 2:50 minutes in length. Compare your work to the songs that seem to be what you hear on radio. Have your work evaluated by 2 or 3 industry music professionals before spending a lot of money on expensive demos. Remember, a good A&R person or professional recording artist with a creative mind can determine the potential value of a song simply by hearing a melody line (guitar or keyboard) and the lyrics. DON'T convince yourself that your work is outstanding if you feel that it will not be able to compete with the tough competition of today's market."

☑ LAKE TRANSFER PRODUCTIONS & MUSIC (ASCAP, BMI)

11300 Hartland St., North Hollywood CA 91605. (818)508-7158. **Contact:** Jim Holvay, professional manager (pop, R&B, soul); Tina Antoine (hip-hop, rap); Steve Barri Cohen (alternative rock, R&B). Music publisher and record producer (Steve Barri Cohen). Estab. 1989. Publishes 11 songs/year; publishes 3 new songwriters/year. Staff size: 6. Pay "depends on agreement, usually 50% split."

Affiliate(s) Lake Transfer Music (ASCAP) and Transfer Lake Music (BMI).

How to Contact *Does not accept unsolicited submissions.*

Music Mostly **alternative pop, R&B/hip-hop** and **dance**. Does not want country & western, classical, New Age, jazz or swing. Published "Tu Sabes Que Te Amo (Will You Still Be There)" (single by Steve Barri Cohen/Rico) from *Rico: The Movement II* (album), recorded by Rico (rap/hip-hop), released 2004 on Lost Empire/Epic-Sony; "When Water Flows" (single by Steve Barri Cohen/Sheree Brown/Terry Dennis) from *Sheree Brown "83"* (album), recorded by Sheree Brown (urban pop), released 2004 on BBEG Records (a division of Saravels, LLC); and "Fair Game" (single by LaTocha Scott/Steve Barri Cohen) soundtrack from the movie *Fair Game* (album), recorded by LaTocha Scott (R&B/hip-hop), released 2004 on Raw Deal Records, College Park, Georgia. "All our staff are songwriters/producers. Jim Holvay has written hits like 'Kind of a Drag' and 'Hey Baby They're Playin our Song' for the Buckinghams. Steve Barri Cohen has worked with every one from Evelyn 'Champagne' King (RCA), Phantom Planets (Epic), Meredith Brooks (Capitol) and Dre (Aftermath/Interscope)."

Tips "Trends change, but it's still about the song. Make sure your music and lyrics have a strong (POV) point of view."

☑ LARI-JON PUBLISHING (BMI)

P.O. Box 216, Rising City NE 68658. (402)542-2336. **Contact:** Larry Good, owner. Music publisher, record company (Lari-Jon Records), management firm (Lari-Jon Promotions) and record producer (Lari-Jon Productions). Estab. 1967. Publishes 20 songs/year; publishes 2-3 new songwriters/year. Staff size: 1. Pays standard royalty.

How to Contact Submit demo CD by mail. Unsolicited submissions are OK. Prefers CD with 5 songs and lyric sheet. "Be professional." Include SASE. Responds in 2 months.

Music Mostly **country, Southern gospel** and **'50s rock**. Does not want rock, hip-hop, pop or heavy metal. Published "Bluegrass Blues" and "Carolina Morning" (singles by Larry Good) from *Carolina Morning* (album), recorded by Blue Persuasion (country), released 2002 by Bullseye; "Those Rolling Hills of Glenwood" (single by Tom Campbell) from *Single* (album), recorded by Tom Campbell (country), released 2001 by Jeffs-Room-Productions.

☑ ▢ LCS MUSIC GROUP (ASCAP, BMI, SESAC)

P.O. Box 7809, Dallas TX 75209. E-mail: chris@dallastexas.cc. Website: www.ccentertainment.com. Professional Managers: Chris Christian(pop/Christian); Gina Madrigal. Music publisher, record company and record producer. Estab. 1981. Publishes 2,000 songs/year. Staff size: 3. Hires staff songwriters. Pays standard royalty.

Affiliate(s) Home Sweet Home Music/Bug and Bear Music (ASCAP), Chris Christian Music (BMI) and Monk and Tid (SESAC).

How to Contact Submit demo tape by mail. Unsolicited submissions are OK. Prefers CD, DAT or videocassette. Include name, phone number and e-mail on CD or tape. Does not return material. Responds if interested.

Music Does not want quartet music.

Tips "Keep writing until you get good at your craft. Co-write with the best you can—always put phone number on tape or CD's."

⚡ ✉ ◯ LILLY MUSIC PUBLISHING (SOCAN)

61 Euphrasia Dr., Toronto ON M6B 3V8 Canada. (416)782-5768. Fax: (416)782-7170. E-mail: panfilo @sympatico.c. **Contact:** Panfilo Di Matteo, president. Music publisher and record company (P. & N. Records). Estab. 1992. Publishes 20 songs/year; publishes 8 new songwriters/year. Staff size: 3. Pays standard royalty.

Affiliate(s) San Martino Music Publishing and Paglieta Music Publishing (CMRRA).

How to Contact Submit demo tape by mail. Unsolicited submissions are OK. Prefers cassette (or videocassette if available) with 3 songs and lyric and lead sheets. "We will contact you only if we are interested in the material." Responds in 1 month.

Film & TV Places 12 songs in film/year.

Music Mostly **dance**, **ballads** and **rock**; also **country**. Published "This Broken Heart Will Kill Me A Day Soon" (single by Glenna J. Sparkes), recorded by Suzanne Michelle (country crossover), released 2005 on Lilly Records.

◯ LINEAGE PUBLISHING CO. (BMI)

P.O. Box 211, East Prairie MO 63845. (573)649-2211. **Contact:** Tommy Loomas, professional manager. Staff: Alan Carter and Joe Silver. Music publisher, record producer, management firm (Staircase Promotions) and record company (Capstan Record Production). Pays standard royalty.

How to Contact Submit demo tape by mail. Unsolicited submissions are OK. Prefers cassette with 2-4 songs and lyric sheet; include bio and photo if possible. Include SASE. Responds in 2 months.

Music Mostly **country**, **easy listening**, **MOR**, **country rock** and **top 40/pop**. Published "Let It Rain" (single by Roberta Boyle), recorded by Vicarie Arcoleo on Treasure Coast Records; "Country Boy" (single), written and recorded by Roger Lambert; and "Boot Jack Shuffle" (single by Zachary Taylor), recorded by Skid Row Joe, both on Capstan Records.

◯ LITA MUSIC, (ASCAP)

2831 Dogwood Place, Nashville TN 37204. (615)269-8682. Fax: (615)269-8929. Website: http://songsfortheplanet.com. **Contact:** Justin Peters, president. Music publisher. Estab. 1980.

Affiliate(s) Justin Peters Music, Platinum Planet Music and Tourmaline (BMI).

How to Contact Submit demo by mail. Unsolicited submissions are OK. Prefers CD with 5 songs and lyric sheet. Does not return material. "Place code '2006' on each envelope submission."

Music Mostly **Southern gospel/Christian**, **country** and **classic rock**. Published "No Less Than Faithful" (single by Don Pardoe/Joel Lyndsey), recorded by Ann Downing on Daywind Records, Jim Bullard on Genesis Records and Melody Beizer (#1 song) on Covenant Records; "No Other Like You" (single by Mark Comden/Paula Carpenter), recorded by Twila Paris and Tony Melendez (#5 song) on Starsong Records; "Making A New Start" and "Invincible Faith" (singles by Gayle Cox), recorded by Kingdom Heirs on Sonlite Records; and "I Don't Want To Go Back" (single by Gayle Cox), recorded by Greater Vision on Benson Records; "Lost In The Shadow of the Cross" (single by James Elliott and Steven Curtis Chapman) recorded by Steven Curtis Chapman on Spawn Records.

◯ M & T WALDOCH PUBLISHING, INC. (BMI)

4803 S. Seventh St., Milwaukee WI 53221. (414)482-2194. VP, Creative Management (rockabilly, pop, country): Timothy J. Waldoch. Professional Manager (country, top 40): Mark T. Waldoch. Music publisher. Estab. 1990. Publishes 2-3 songs/year; publishes 2-3 new songwriters/year. Staff size: 2. Pays standard royalty.

How to Contact Submit demo tape by mail. Unsolicited submissions are OK. Prefers cassette with

3-6 songs and lyric or lead sheet. "We prefer a studio produced demo tape." Include SASE. Responds in 3 months.

Music Mostly **country/pop**, **rock**, **top 40 pop**; also **melodic metal**, **dance**, **R&B**. Does not want rap. Published "It's Only Me" and "Let Peace Rule the World" (by Kenny LePrix), recorded by Brigade on SBD Records (rock).

Tips "Study the classic pop songs from the 1950s through the present time. There is a reason why good songs stand the test of time. Today's hits will be tomorrow's classics. Send your *best* well-crafted, polished song material."

◪ MAGIC MESSAGE MUSIC (ASCAP)

P.O. Box 9117, Truckee CA 96162. E-mail: alanred@telis.org. Website: www.alanredstone.com. **Owner:** Alan Redstone. Music publisher and record company (Sureshot Records). Estab. 1979.

How to Contact *Write or call first and obtain permission to submit or submit demo tape by mail.* Include SASE. Responds in 1 week. Currently inactive and not looking for material. Do not send any material without permission.

☑ ☒ ◪ MANUITI L.A. (ASCAP)

% Rosen Music Corp., 717 El Medio, Pacific Palisades CA 90272 . (310)230-6040. Fax: (310)230-4074. E-mail: assistant@rosenmusiccorp.com. **Contact:** Steven Rosen, president. Music publisher and record producer. "The exclusive music publishing company for writer/producer Guy Roche."

How to Contact *Does not accept unsolicited material.*

Film & TV Recently published "As If," recorded by Blaque in *Bring It On* ; "Turn the Page," recorded by Aaliyah in *Music of the Heart*; and "While You Were Gone," recorded by Kelly Price in *Blue Streak*.

Music Mostly **pop** and **R&B**. Published "What A Girl Wants" (single), recorded by Christina Aguilera (pop); "Almost Doesn't Count" (single), recorded by Brandy (R&B) on Atlantic; "Beauty" (single), recorded by Dru Hill (R&B) on Island; and "Under My Tree" (single), recorded by *NSync on RCA.

Tips "Do your homework on who you are contacting and what they do. Don't waste yours or their time by not having that information."

◪ ◪ MANY LIVES MUSIC PUBLISHERS (SOCAN)

RR #1, Kensington PE COB 1MO Canada. (902)836-1051. E-mail: paul.milner@summerside.ca. **Contact:** Paul C. Milner, publisher. Music publisher. Estab. 1997. Pays standard royalty.

How to Contact Submit song demo by mail. Unsolicited submissions are OK. Prefers CD and lyric sheet (lead sheet if available). Does not return material. Responds in 3 months if interested.

Music All styles. Released *Your Friend Phil* (album), written and recorded by Phil Morris (Christian), released 2002 on Healing Heart; *Temptation* (album), various writers, arrangement by Paul Milner, Patrizia, Dan Cutrona (rock/opera), will be released in 2003 on United One Records.

☒ ◪ MARKEA MUSIC/GINA PIE MUSIC/SI QUE MUSIC (BMI, SESAC, ASCAP)

P.O. Box 121396, Nashville TN 37212. (615)242-2424. Fax: (615)242-2211. E-mail: keatonmusic@mindspring.com. Professional Managers: Kent Martin(folk/pop). Music publisher. Estab. 1995. Publishes 19 songs/year; publishes 1 new songwriter/year. Staff size: 2. Hires staff songwriters. Pays standard royalty.

Affiliate(s) Markea Music (BMI) and Gina Pie Music (SESAC).

How to Contact *Call first and obtain permission to submit.* Prefers cassette or CD with 3 songs and lyric sheet. Does not return material. Responds in 6 weeks.

Film & TV Places 1 song in film and 1 song in TV/year. Published "Keep Coming Back," written and recorded by Mike Younger in *Time of Your Life*; and "If By Chance...," written and recorded by Mike Younger in *A Galaxy, Far, Far Away*.

Music Mostly **country, folk** and **pop**; also **R&B**. Published "I'm Happy" (single by Ronna Reeves/ Tom McHugh) from *Ronna Reeves* (album), recorded by Ronna Reeves (pop/country), released 2000 on Hello.

Tips "Send your best."

☑ JOHN WELLER MARVIN PUBLISHING (ASCAP)

P.O. Box 99232, Cleveland OH 44199. (330)733-8585. Fax: (330)733-8595. E-mail: stephanie.arble@ jwmpublishing.net. Website: www.jwmpublishing.net. **Contact:** Stephanie Arble, president. Music Publisher. Estab. 1996. Pays standard royalty.

How to Contact Submit demo tape by mail. Unsolicited submissions are OK. Prefers cassette, CD or VHS and lyric or lead sheet. Responds in 6 weeks.

Music All genres, mostly **pop**, **R&B**, **rap**; also **rock**, and **country**. Published "Downloading Files" (single by S. Arble/R. Scott), recorded by Ameritech Celebration Choir (corporate promotional). "We work with a promoter, booking major label artists, and we're also involved in television and corporate promotional recordings."

☑ MAVERICK MUSIC (ASCAP)

9348 Civic Center Dr., Beverly Hills CA 90210. (310)385-7800. Website: www.maverick.com. Music publisher and record company (Maverick).

How to Contact *Maverick Music does not accept unsolicited submissions.*

☑ MCA MUSIC PUBLISHING

12 Music Circle S., Nashville TN 37203.

- MCA music has been taken over by Universal, now functions only as a catalog of past music, and does not publish new material any longer.

🅽 ☐ MCCLURE & TROWBRIDGE PUBLISHING, LTD. (ASCAP,BMI)

P.O. Box 70403, Nashville TN 37207. (615)902-0509. E-mail: manager@trowbridgeplanetearth.c om. Website: www.jiprecords.com. **Contact:** George McClure, president/CEO. Music publisher. Record company (JIP Records/Artist Choice CD) and record production company (George McClure, producer). Estab. 1983. Publishes 25 songs/year. Publishes 3 new songwriters/year. Staff size: 8. Pays standard royalty of 50%.

How to Contact *Contact first and obtain permission to submit a demo.* Prefers cassette or CD with 2-5 songs, lyric sheet and cover letter. Does not return submissions. Responds in 3 weeks.

Music Mostly **country**, **Americana/alt**, **gospel**; also **rock**, **hip-hop**, and **latin**. "We are very open-minded as far as genres. If it's good music, we like it!" Published "What A Country" (single) and "Sis Boom Bah" (single) from *Sis Boom Bah* (album), written and recorded by Gus Rhein (country), released 2005 on JIP Records; "My Way or Hit the Highway" (single), written and recorded by Jacqui Watson (Americana), released 2005 on Artist Choice CD.

☐ JIM MCCOY MUSIC (BMI)

25 Troubadour Lane, Berkeley Springs WV 25411. (304)258-9381. E-mail: mccoytroubadour@aol.c om. Website: www.troubadourlounge.com. **Contact:** Bertha and Jim McCoy, owners. Music pub-lisher, record company (Winchester Records) and record producer (Jim McCoy Productions). Estab. 1973. Publishes 20 songs/year; publishes 3-5 new songwriters/year. Pays standard royalty.

Affiliate(s) New Edition Music (BMI).

How to Contact Submit demo tape by mail with lyric sheet. Unsolicited submissions are OK. Prefers cassette or CD with 6 songs. Include SASE. Responds in 1 month.

Music Mostly **country**, **country/rock** and **rock**; also **bluegrass** and **gospel**. Published "Stand By Lover" (single by Earl Howard/Jim McCoy) from *Earl Howard Sings His Heart Out* (album), re-corded by Earl Howard (country), released 2002 on Winchester; "Let Her" and "Same ole Town" (singles by Tommy Hill), recorded by R. Lee Gray (country), released 2002 on Winchester.

📧 ☑ MCJAMES MUSIC INC. (BMI)

1724 Stanford St., Suite B, Santa Monica CA 90404. (310) 712- 1916. Fax: (419)781-6644. E-mail: info@mcjamesmusic.com. Website: www.mcjamesmusic.com. Also: 701 Hollow Rd., Nashville TN 37205. Professional Managers: Tim James(country/pop); Steven McClintock (pop/country). Music publisher, record company (37 Records) and record producer (Steven McClintock). Estab.

1977. Publishes 10 songs/year. Staff size: 3. Pays standard royalty. Does administration and collection for all foreign markets for smaller publishers and writers.

Affiliate(s) 37 Records (ASCAP) and McJames Music, Inc. (BMI).

How to Contact *Only accepts material referred by a reputable industry source.* Prefers cassette with 2 songs and cover letter. Does not return material. Responds in 6 months.

Film & TV Places 2 songs in film and 3 songs in TV/year. Music Supervisor: Tim James. Recently published "Look At Me Now" recorded by SIXWIRE for Warner Brothers Records, "Three Songs in a Little Inside" written and recorded by Matt and Gunnar Nelson and Cathy Anne.

Music Mostly **country**, **pop** and **dance**; also **bluegrass** and **alternative**. Does not want rap or classical. Published *That's What Love Is* (by S. McClintock/T. Douglas), recorded by Mark Vance (country) on Sony; *Keeps Bringing Me Back* (by S. McClintock/V. Shaw), recorded by Victoria Shaw (easy listening) on Taffita; and *Don't Let This Plan* (by S. McClintock/R. Irving), recorded by Steven McClintock (country) on 37 Records. Recent cover by ATC on BMG/Universal with "If Love is Blind," selling over 300,000 CDs in less than 6 months; single by new Warner Bros. act Six Wire called "Look At Me Now," recent duet by Victoria Shaw and Richard Schneider on Universal Holland with the song "Loved By You." Place three songs in the new Sony Play Station with the writer/artist Chad Petry.

Tips "Write a song we don't have in our catalog or write an undeniable hit. We will know it when we hear it."

🌐 🎵 MENTO MUSIC GROUP

Symphony House, Eppendorfer Weg 7, D-20259 Hamburg Germany. (040)22716552+53. Fax: (040)22716554. E-mail: mento_music@t-online.de. **Contact:** Arno H. Van Vught, general manager. Professional Manager: Michael Frommhold. Music publisher and record company (Playbones Records). Estab. 1970. Pays standard royalty.

Affiliate(s) Auteursunie, Edition Lamplight, Edition Melodisc, Massimo Jauch Music Productions and Marathon Music.

How to Contact Submit demo CD by mail. Unsolicited submissions are OK. Prefers cassette with 3-4 songs. "Put your strongest/best song first. Put your name and address on the inlay card of the CD. Tell us in a typed cover letter what you want/what you are looking for." Does not return material. Responds in 3 weeks.

Music Mostly **instrumental**, **pop**, **MOR**, **country**, **background music** and **film music**. Does not want classical. Published "Vergessen wir die Mark" (single by DP/Volker Frank), recorded by Volker Frank (pop), released 2001; *Paradise* (album), written and recorded by Anna C. Nova (pop), released 2001 on Playbones Records; *Lord of the Dance* (album), written and recorded by Wolfgang Bauer (world music), released 2001 on Playbones Records.

🎵 🎵 MIDI TRACK PUBLISHING (BMI)/ALLRS MUSIC PUBLISHING CO. (ASCAP)

P.O. Box 1545, Smithtown NY 11787. (718)767-8995. E-mail: allrsmusic@aol.com. Website: www.g eocities.com/allrsmusic. **Contact:** Renee Silvestri, president. Music publisher, record company (MIDI Track Records), music consultant, artist management. Voting member of NARAS (The Grammy Awards), CMA, SGMA, SGA. Estab. 1994. Staff size: 5. Publishes 3 songs/year; publishes 2 new songwriters/year. Pays standard royalty.

Affiliate(s) Midi-Track Publishing Co. (BMI).

How to Contact *Write or e-mail first to obtain permission to submit. "We do not accept unsolicited submissions."* Prefers CD or cassette with 3 songs, lyric sheet and cover letter. "Make sure your CD or cassette tape is labeled with your name, mailing address, telephone number, and e-mail address. We do not return material." Responds via e-mail in 3 months.

Film & TV Places 1 song in film/year. Published "Why Can't You Hear My Prayer" (single by F. John Silvestri/Leslie Silvestri), recorded by Iliana Medina in a documentary by Silvermine Films.

Music Mostly **country**, **gospel**, **top 40**, **R&B**, **MOR** and **pop**. Does not want showtunes, jazz, classical or rap. Published "Why Can't You Hear My Prayer" (single by F. John Silvestri/Leslie Silvestri), recorded by five-time Grammy nominee Huey Dunbar of the group DLG (Dark Latin Groove), released on Trend Records (other multiple releases, also recorded by Iliana Medina and released 2002 on MIDI Track Records); "Chasing Rainbows" (single by F. John Silvestri/Leslie Silvestri), recorded by Tommy Cash (country), released on MMT Records (including other multiple releases); "Because of You" (single by F. John Silvestri/Leslie Silvestri), recorded by Iliana Medina, released 2002 on MIDI Track Records, also recorded by three-time Grammy nominee Terri Williams, released on KMA Records; also recorded by Grand Ole Opry member Ernie Ashworth, released 2004 on KMA Records; "My Coney Island" (single by F. John Silvestri/Leslie Silvestri), recorded by eight-time Grammy nominee Huey Dunbar, released 2005 on MIDI Track Records.

Tips "Attend workshops, seminars, join songwriters organizations and keep writing, you will achieve your goal."

⅗ ⊘ MONK FAMILY MUSIC GROUP (ASCAP, BMI, SESAC)

P.O. Box 150768, Nashville TN 37215-0768. (615)292-6811. Fax: (615)292-7266. **Contact:** Irving Telder or McKenna Monk, professional managers. Music publisher. Estab. 1983. Hires staff songwriters. Pays standard royalty.

Affiliate(s) Charlie Monk Music (ASCAP), Monk Family Music (BMI), and Monkids Music (SESAC).

• Received the 1998 "Publisher of the Year" Award from SESAC and the 2001 Performance Award from ASCAP.

How to Contact *Contact first and obtain permission to submit.* "We only accept material referred to us by a reputable industry source (manager, entertainment attorney, etc.)" Does not return submissions.

Music Mostly **country**. Published "Kiss This" (single by Philip Douglas/Thea Tippin/Aaron Tippin) from *People Like Us* (album), recorded by Aaron Tippin (country), released 2000 on Lyric Street; "Commitment" (single by Tony Martin/Bubby Wood/Tony Colton) from *Sittin' On Top Of The World* (album), recorded by Leann Rimes (country), released 1998 on Curb Records; and "Until We Fall Back In Love Again" (single by Philip Douglas/Jim Weatherly/Jeff Carson) from *Real Life* (album), recorded by Jeff Carson (country), released 2001 on Curb Records.

⅗ ⊘ MONTINA MUSIC (SOCAN)

Box 702, Snowdon Station, Montreal QC H3X 3X8 Canada. **Contact:** David P. Leonard, professional manager. Music publisher and record company (Monticana Records). Estab. 1963. Pays negotiable royalty.

Affiliate(s) Saber-T Music (SOCAN).

How to Contact Unsolicited submissions are OK. Prefers CD. SAE and IRC. Responds in 3 months.

Music Mostly **top 40**; also **bluegrass**, **blues**, **country**, **dance-oriented**, **easy listening**, **folk**, **gospel**, **jazz**, **MOR**, **progressive**, **R&B**, **rock** and **soul**. Does not want heavy metal, hard rock, jazz, classical or New Age.

Tips "Maintain awareness of styles and trends of your peers who have succeeded professionally. Understand the markets to which you are pitching your material. Persevere at marketing your talents. Develop a network of industry contacts, first locally, then regionally, nationally and internationally."

☐ MOON JUNE MUSIC (BMI)

4233 SW Marigold, Portland OR 97219. (507)777-4621. Fax: (503)277-4622. **Contact:** Bob Stoutenburg, president. Music publisher. Estab. 1971. Staff size: 1. Pays standard royalty.

How to Contact Submit demo tape by mail. Unsolicited submissions are OK. Prefers cassette or CD with 2-10 songs.

Music Country.

⊘ THE MUSIC ROOM PUBLISHING GROUP (BMI)

P.O. Box 219, Redondo Beach CA 90277. (310)316-4551. E-mail: mrp@aol.com. **Contact:** John Reed, president/owner. Music publisher and record producer. Estab. 1982. Pays standard royalty.

Affiliate(s) MRP (BMI).

How to Contact *Not accepting unsolicited material.*

Music Mostly **pop/rock/R&B** and **crossover**. Published "That Little Tattoo," "Mona Lisa" and

"Sleepin' with an Angel" (singles by John E. Reed) from *Rock With An Attitude* (album), recorded by Rawk Dawg (rock), released 2002 on Music Room Productions®.

☑ MUST HAVE MUSIC (ASCAP/BMI)

P.O. Box 801181, Santa Clarita CA 91380-1181. (661)645-7618. Fax: (661)799-3732. E-mail: info@m usthavemusic.com. Website: www.musthavemusic.com. **Contact:** Kenneth R. Klar, managing director. Music publisher and music library. Estab. 1990. Pays standard royalty.

Affiliate(s) Must Have More Music (ASCAP); Must Have Music (BMI).

How to contact Submit demo by mail with your personal e-mail address included for directors response. Unsolicited submissions are OK. Prefers CD with lyric sheet and cover letter. Does not return submissions. Responds in 2 months.

Film & TV Music supervisor: Ken Klar, managing director.

Music Mostly **pop/R&B**, **pop/country** and **rock**; also **AAA**, **adult contemporary**, and **contemporary Christian/gospel**. Does not want instrumental music. "We only work with completed songs with lyric and vocal." Published "Come to the Table" (single by Ken Klar/Steve Massey) from *Worship Leader Magazine's Song Discovery, Vol. 26* (album), recorded by various artists, released 2002 on Worship Leader; "Fool" (single by Ken Klar) from *If You Want My Love* (album), recorded by Jennifer Young (pop/R&B), released 2002 on Independent; and "Blame It On My Heart" (single by Ken Klar/Steve Kir wan) fom *Blame It On My Heart* (album), recorded by Steve Kirwan (adult contemporary), released 2001 on Independent.

Tips "Write what you know and what you believe. Then re-write it!"

☒ ☑ NAKED JAIN RECORDS (ASCAP)

P.O. Box 4132, Palm Springs CA 92263-4132. (760)325-8663. Fax: (760)320-4305. E-mail: info@nak edjainrecords.com. Website: www.nakedjainrecords.com. **Contact:** Dena Banes, vice president/ A&R. Music publisher, record company and record producer (Dey Martin). Estab. 1991. Publishes 40 songs/year; publishes 2 new songwriters/year. Staff size: 5. Pays standard royalty.

Affiliate(s) Aven Deja Music (ASCAP).

How to Contact Does not accept unsolicited material.

Film & TV Places 10 songs in TV/year. Music Supervisors: Dey Martin (alternative). Recently published "Yea Right" (single), written and recorded by Lung Cookie in Fox Sports TV; "Just Ain't Me" (single), written and recorded by Lung Cookie in ESPN-TV; and "Speak Easy" (single), written and recorded by Lung Cookie in ESPN-TV.

Music Mostly **alternative rock**. Does not want country.

Tips "Write a good song."

⊕ ◻ NERVOUS PUBLISHING

5 Sussex Crescent, Northolt, Middlesex UB5 4DL. United Kingdom. +44(020) 8423 7373. Fax: +44(020) 8423 7773. E-mail: nervous@compuserve.com. Website: www.nervous.co.uk. **Contact:** Roy Williams, owner. Music publisher, record company (Nervous Records) and record producer. MCPS, PRS and Phonographic Performance Ltd. Estab. 1979. Publishes 100 songs/year; publishes 25 new songwriters/year. Pays standard royalty; royalties paid directly to US songwriters.

• Nervous Publishing's record label, Nervous Records, is listed in the Record Companies section.

How to Contact Submit demo tape by mail. Unsolicited submissions are OK. Prefers cassette with 3-10 songs and lyric sheet. "Include letter giving your age and mentioning any previously published material." SAE and IRC. Responds in 3 weeks.

Music Mostly **psychobilly**, **rockabilly** and **rock** (impossibly fast music—e.g.: Stray Cats but twice as fast); also **blues**, **country**, **R&B** and **rock** ('50s style). Published *Trouble* (album), recorded by Dido Bonneville (rockabilly); *Rockabilly Comp* (album), recorded by various artists; and *Nervous Singles Collection* (album), recorded by various artists, all on Nervous Records.

Tips "Submit *no* rap, soul, funk—we want *rockabilly*."

☑ A NEW RAP JAM PUBLISHING (BMI)

P.O. Box 683, Lima OH 45802. E-mail: st_chilling_2002@yahoo.com. Professional Managers: William Roach (rap, clean); James Milligan (country, 70s music, pop). **Contact:** A&R Dept. Music publisher and record company (New Experience/Grand Slam Records, Pump It Up Records, and Rough Edge Records). Estab. 1989. Publishes 30 songs/year; publishes 2-3 new songwriters/year. Hires staff songwriters. Staff size: 6. Pays standard royalty.

Affiliate(s) Party House Publishing (BMI), Creative Star Management, and Rough Edge Records.

How to Contact *Write first to arrange personal interview or submit demo tape by mail.* Unsolicited submissions are OK. Prefers cassette with 3-5 songs and lyric or lead sheet. Include SASE. Responds in up to weeks.

Music Mostly **R&B**, **pop**, **blues** and **rock/rap**; also **contemporary**, **gospel**, **country** and **soul**. Published "Can't Play a Playa" and "Get Your Own" (singles by David Fawcett) from *Enter the Mind* (album), recorded by Devious 01 (rap), released 2002 on Pump It Up Records; "The Broken Hearted" (single by Carl Milligan/James Milligan) from *The Final Chapter* (album), recorded by T.M.C. the milligan conection (R&B gospel), released 2003/2004 on New Experience/Pump It Up Records.

Tips "We are seeking hit artists of the 1970s and 1980s who would like to be resigned, as well as new talent and female solo artists. Send any available information supporting the group or act. We are a label that does not promote violence, drugs or anything that we feel is a bad example for our youth. Establish music industry contacts, write and keep writing and most of all believe in yourself. Use a good recording studio but be very professional. Just take your time and produce the best music possible. Sometimes you only get one listen. Make sure you place your best song on your demo first. This will increase your chances greatly. If you're the owner of your own small label and have a finished product, please send it. And if there is interest we will contact you. Also be on the lookout for our new blues label Rough Edge Records and Rough Edge Entertainment now reviewing material. Please be aware of the new sampling laws and laws for digital downloading. It is against the law. People are being jailed and fined for this act. Do your homework. Read the new digital downloading contracts carefully or seek legal help if need be. Good luck and thanks for considering our company."

◪ NEWBRAUGH BROTHERS MUSIC (ASCAP, BMI)

228 Morgan Lane, Berkeley Springs WV 25411-3475. (304)258-3656. E-mail: Nbtoys@verizon.net. **Contact:** John S. Newbraugh, owner. Music publisher, record company (NBT Records BMI/ASCAP). Estab. 1967. Publishes 124 songs/year. Publishes 14 new songwriters/year. Staff size: 1. Pays standard royalty.

Affiliates NBT Music (ASCAP) and Newbraugh Brothers Music (BMI).

How to Contact Submit demo tape by mail. Unsolicited submissions are OK. Prefers cassette or CD with any amount of songs, a lyric sheet and a cover letter. Include SASE. Responds in 6 weeks.

Music Mostly **rockabilly**, **hillbilly**, **folk** and **bluegrass**; also **rock**, **country**, and **gospel**. "We will accept all genres of music except songs with vulgar language." Published "Moonshine Stomp" (single by Del Clark) from *Hot Rod Daddy* (album), recorded by The Rhythmatics (rockabilly), released 2003; "Messin Around" (single by Nic Nilsson) from *Don't Wear Me Out* (album), recorded by Uncle Nic and the Alternators (rock), released 2003; and "Trainman" (single by John Modaff) from *Ride The Train—Volume Three* (album), recorded by Good Enough (folk), released in 2004, all on NBT Records.

Tips "Find out if a publisher/record company has any special interest. NBT, for instance, is always hunting 'original' train songs. Our 'registered' trademark is a train and from time to time we release a compilation album of all train songs. We welcome all genres of music for this project."

☐ NEWCREATURE MUSIC (BMI)

P.O. Box 1444, Hendersonville TN 37077-1444. (615)452-3234. E-mail: lmarkcom@bellsouth.net. **Contact:** Bill Anderson, Jr., president. Professional Manager: G.L. Score. Music publisher, record company, record producer (Landmark Communications Group) and radio and TV syndicator. Publishes 25 songs/year; publishes 2 new songwriters/year. Pays standard royalty.

Affiliate(s) Mary Megan Music (ASCAP).

How to Contact *Contact first and obtain permission to submit.* Prefers CD or videocassette with 4-10 songs and lyric sheet. Include SASE. Responds in 6 weeks.

Music Mostly **country**, **gospel**, **jazz**, **R&B**, **rock** and **top 40/pop**. Published *Glory* and *Popcorn, Peanuts and Jesus* (albums by Harry Yates), both recorded by Joanne Cash Yates on Angel Too Records (gospel); and *Were You Thinkin' Of Me* (album), written and recorded by Jack Mosley on Landmark Records (country).

OLD SLOWPOKE MUSIC (BMI)

P.O. Box 526 26, Tulsa OK 74152. (918)742-8087. E-mail: ryoung@cherrystreetrecords.com. Website: www.cherrystreetrecords.com. **Contact:** Steve Hickerson, professional manager. President: Rodney Young. Music publisher and record producer. Estab. 1977. Publishes 10- 20 songs/year; publishes 2 new songwriters/year. Staff size: 2. Pays standard royalty.

How to Contact *Does not accept unsolicited submissions.*

Film & TV Places 1 song in film/year. Recently published "Samantha," written and recorded by George W. Carroll in *Samantha*. Placed two songs for Tim Drummond in movies "Hound Dog Man" in *loving Lu Lu* and "Fur Slippers" in a CBS movie *Shake, Rattle & Roll*.

Music Mostly **rock**, **country** and **R&B**; also **jazz**. Published *Promise Land* (album), written and recorded by Richard Neville on Cherry Street Records (rock).

Tips "Write great songs. We sign only artists who play an instrument, sing and write songs."

ORCHID PUBLISHING (BMI)

Bouquet-Orchid Enterprises, P.O. Box 1335, Norcross GA 30091. Phone/fax: (770)339-9088. **Contact:** Bill Bohannon, president. Music publisher, record company, record producer (Bouquet-Orchid Enterprises) and artist management. Member: CMA, AFM. Publishes 10-12 songs/year; publishes 3 new songwriters/year. Pays standard royalty.

How to Contact Submit demo tape by mail. Unsolicited submissions are OK. Prefers cassette or CD with 3-5 songs and lyric sheet. "Send biographical information if possible—even a photo helps." Include SASE. Responds in 1 month.

Music Mostly **religious** ("Amy Grant, etc., contemporary gospel"); **country** ("Garth Brooks, Trisha Yearwood-type material"); and **top 100/pop** ("Bryan Adams, Whitney Houston-type material"). Published "Blue As Your Eyes" (single), written and recorded by Adam Day; "Spare My Feelings" (single by Clayton Russ), recorded by Terri Palmer; and "Trying to Get By" (single by Tom Sparks), recorded by Bandoleers, all on Bouquet Records.

PEERMUSIC (ASCAP, BMI)

5358 Melrose Ave., Suite 400, Los Angeles CA 90038. (323)960-3400. Fax: (323)960-3410. Website: www.peermusic.com. Music publisher and artist development promotional label. Estab. 1928. Publishes 600 songs/year (worldwide); publishes 1-2 new songwriters/year. Hires staff songwriters. Royalty standard, but negotiable.

Affiliate(s) Peer Southern Organization (ASCAP) and Peer International Corporation (BMI).

How to Contact *"We do NOT accept unsolicited submissions. We only accept material through agents, attorneys and managers."* Prefers CD and lyric sheet. Does not return material. Responds in 6 weeks.

Music Mostly **pop**, **rock** and **R&B**. Published music by David Foster (writer/producer, pop); Andrew Williams (writer/producer, pop), Shelly Peiken (writer, pop); Christopher "Tricky" Stewart (R&B writer/producer); and the Coma Boyz (R&B writers/producers). Also published music by the bands Over It and Bleed the Dream.

JUSTIN PETERS MUSIC, (BMI)

P.O. Box 40251, Nashville TN 37204. (615)269-8682. Fax: (615)269-8929. Website: http://songsfort heplanet.com. **Contact:** Justin Peters, president. Music publisher. Estab. 1981.

Affiliate(s) Platinum Planet Music, Tourmaline (BMI) and LITA Music (ASCAP).

How to Contact Submit demo by mail. Unsolicited submissions are OK. Prefers CD with 5 songs and lyric sheet. Does not return material. "Place code '2006' on each envelope submission."

Music Mostly **pop**, **reggae**, **country** and **comedy**. Published "Saved By Love" (single), recorded by Amy Grant on A&M Records; "Nothing Can Separate Us", recorded by Al Denson; "A Gift That

She Don't Want" (single), recorded by Bill Engvall on Warner Brother Records; and "I Wanna Be That Man" (single), recorded by McKameys on Pamplin Records, all written by Justin Peters.

⬦ PHOEBOB MUSIC (BMI)
5181 Regent Dr., Nashville TN 37220. (615)832-4199. **Contact:** Phoebe Binkley.
How to Contact We do not want unsolicited submissions.
Music Country **Christian**, and **theatre**.

⬦ PIANO PRESS (ASCAP)
P.O. Box 85, Del Mar CA 92014-0085. (619)884-1401. Fax: (858)755- 1104. E-mail: pianopress@aol.com. Website: www.pianopress.com. **Contact:** Elizabeth C. Axford, M.A., owner. Music publisher. Publishes songbooks & CD's for music students and teachers. Estab. 1998. Licenses 32-100 songs/year; publishes 1-24 new songwriters/year. Staff size: 5. Pays standard print music and/or mechanical royalty; composer retains rights to songs.
How to Contact *Write or call first and obtain permission to submit.* Prefers cassette or CD with 1-3 songs, lyric and lead sheet, cover letter and sheet music/piano arrangements. "Looking for children's songs for young piano students and arrangements of public domain folk songs of any nationality." Currently accepting submissions for *Kidtunes II*. Include SASE. Responds in 2-3 months.
Music Mostly **children's**, **folk songs** and **funny songs**; also **teaching pieces**, **piano arrangements**, **lead sheets with melody, chords and lyrics** and **songbooks**. Does not want commercial pop, R&B, etc. Published "I Can" (single by Tom Gardner) from *Kidtunes* (album), recorded by The Uncle Brothers (children's), released 2002 by Piano Press; "Rock & Roll Teachers" (single by Bob King) from *Kidtunes* (album), recorded by Bob King & Friends (children's), released 2002 by Piano Press; and "It Really Isn't Garbage" (single by Danny Einbender) from *Kidtunes* (album), recorded by Danny Eibende/Pete Seeger/et al. (children's), released 2002 by Piano Press.
Tips "Songs should be simple, melodic and memorable. Lyrics should be for a juvenile audience and well-crafted."

▢ PLATINUM PLANET MUSIC, INC., (BMI)
2831 Dogwood Place, Nashville TN 37204. (615)269-8682. Fax: (615)269-8929. Website: http://songsfortheplanet.com. **Contact:** Justin Peters, president. Music publisher. Estab. 1997.
Affiliate(s) Justin Peters Music, Tourmaline (BMI) and LITA Music (ASCAP).
How to Contact Submit demo by mail. Unsolicited submissions are OK. Prefers CD with 5 songs and lyric sheet. Does not return material. "Place code '2006' on each envelope submission."
Music Mostly **R&B, dance** and **country**; also represents many Christian artists/writers. Published "Happy Face" (single by Dez Dickerson/Jordan Dickerson), recorded by Squirt on Absolute Records; "Welcome To My Love" (single by Mike Hunter), recorded by Kyndl on PPMI; "Love's Not A Game" (single), written and recorded by Kashief Lindo on Heavybeat Rewards; "Dancing Singing" (single by A. Craig/Justin Peters) recorded by Dan Burda on Independent; and "Loud" (single), written and recorded by These Five Down on Absolute Records.

⬦ POLLYBYRD PUBLICATIONS LIMITED (ASCAP, BMI, SESAC)
P.O. Box 261488, Encino CA 91426. (818)506-8533. Fax: (818)506-8534. E-mail: pplzmi@aol.com. Website: www.pplzmi.com. Branch office: 468 N. Camden Drive Suite 200, Beverly Hills CA 90210. **Contact:** Dakota Hawk, vice president. Professional Managers: Cisco Blue (country, pop, rock); Tedford Steele (hip-hop, R&B). Music publisher, record company (PPL Entertainment) and Management firm (Sa'mall Management). Estab. 1979. Publishes 100 songs/year; publishes 25-40 new songwriters/year. Hires staff writers. Pays standard royalty.
Affiliate(s) Kellijai Music (ASCAP), Pollyann Music (ASCAP), Ja'Nikki Songs (BMI), Velma Songs International (BMI), Lonnvanness Songs (SESAC), PPL Music (ASCAP), Zettitalia Music, Butternut Music (BMI), Zett Two Music (ASCAP), Plus Publishing and Zett One Songs (BMI).
How to Contact *Write first and obtain permission to submit.* No phone calls. Prefers cassette or CD videocassette with 4 songs and lyric and lead sheet. Include SASE. Responds in 2 months.
Music Published "Return of the Players" (album) by Juz-Cuz 2004 on PPL; "Believe" (single by

J. Jarrett/S. Cuseo) from *Time* (album), recorded by Lejenz (pop), released 2001 on PRL/Credence; *Rainbow Gypsy Child* (album), written and recorded by Riki Hendrix (rock), released 2001 on PRL/Sony; and "What's Up With That" (single by Brandon James/Patrick Bouvier) from *Outcast* (album), recorded by Condottieré; (hip-hop), released 2001 on Bouvier.

Tips "Make those decisions—are you really a songwriter? Are you prepared to starve for your craft? Do you believe in delayed gratification? Are you commercial or do you write only for yourself? Can you take rejection? Do you want to be the best? If so, contact us—if not, keep your day job."

☑ PORTAGE MUSIC (BMI)

16634 Gannon W., Rosemount MN 55068. (952)432-5737. E-mail: lmlp34@juno.com. President: Larry LaPole. Music publisher. Publishes 5-20 songs/year. Pays standard royalty.

How to Contact *Does not accept unsolicited submissions.*

Music Mostly **country** and **country rock**. Published "Lost Angel," "Think It Over" and "Congratulations to Me" (by L. Lapole), all recorded by Trashmen on Sundazed.

Tips "Keep songs short, simple and upbeat with positive theme."

◻ PREJIPPIE MUSIC GROUP (BMI)

P.O. Box 816, Van Buren Twp. MI 48152. E-mail: prejippie@comcast.net. Website: www.prejippie.com. **Contact:** Bruce Henderson, president. Music publisher, record company (PMG Records) and record producer (PMG Productions). Estab. 1990. Publishes 50-75 songs/year; publishes 2-3 new songwriters/year. Hires staff writers. Staff size: 3. Pays standard royalty.

How to Contact Submit demo tape by mail. Unsolicited submissions are OK. Prefers cassette or CD with 3-4 songs and lyric sheet. "No phone calls please." Include SASE. Responds in 6 weeks.

Music Mostly **alternative R&B**, **alternative rock**, **techno/house** and **experimental**. Does not want country, gospel, show tunes or lyrics only. Published "Do What I Can Do Right" (single), written and recorded by Bourgeoisie Paper Jam (funk/rock); and "2001 Bass Blizzard" (single), written and recorded by Tony Webb (jazz) all on PMG Records.

Tips "We're always looking for new approaches to traditional genres. We want to hear vocals, lyrics and music that is passionate and takes a chance, but still keeps hooks that are solid."

◻ PRESCRIPTION COMPANY (BMI)

Box 222249, Great Neck NY 11021. (415)553-8540. Fax: (415)553-8541. E-mail: hasf525@ sbcglobal .net. President: David F. Gasman. Vice President of Sales: Bruce Brennan. Vice President of Finance: Robert Murphy. Music publisher and record producer. Staff size: 7. Pays standard royalty.

● Also see the listing for The Prescription Co. in the Record Producers section of this book.

How to Contact *Write or call first and obtain permission to submit.* Prefers cassette with any number of songs and lyric sheet. "Send all submissions with SASE (or no returns)." Responds in 1 month.

Music Mostly **bluegrass**, **blues**, **children's** and **country**, **dance-oriented**; also **easy listening**, **folk**, **jazz**, **MOR**, **progressive**, **R&B**, **rock**, **soul** and **top 40/pop**. Published "The World's Most Dangerous Man," "Here Comes Trouble" and "Automated People" (singles by D.F. Gasman) from *Special EP No. 1* (album), all recorded by Medicine Mike (rock), released 2003 on Prescription.

Tips "Songs should be good and written to last. Forget fads—we want songs that'll sound as good in ten years as they do today. Organization, communication and exploration of form are as essential as message (and sincerity matters, too)."

▣ ☑ THEODORE PRESSER CO. (ASCAP, BMI, SESAC)

588 N. Gulph Rd., King of Prussia PA 19406. (610)592-1222. Fax: (610)592-1229. E-mail: presser@p resser.com. Website: www.presser.com. **Contact:** Laurie Albert, editorial assistant. Music publisher. Estab. 1783. Publishes 200 songs/year; publishes 3 new songwriters/year. Staff size: 51. Pays standard royalty; 10% on print.

Affiliate(s) Theodore Presser, Beekman, Oliver Ditson, John Church, Elkan-Vogel (ASCAP), Merion Music (BMI) and Mercury Music (SESAC).

How to Contact Submit music ms by mail. Tape or CD can supplement score but are not accepted by themselves. Unsolicited submissions are OK. Prefers cassette and score. Include SASE. Responds in 3 months.

Film & TV Places 12 songs in film and 14 songs in TV/year.

Music Mostly **serious concert music**, **sacred and secular choral** and **educational music**. Does not want popular music.

Tips "Write honest, high quality music and send it to us, following our submission guidelines which you can receive via e-mail or on our website."

☑ QUEEN ESTHER MUSIC PUBLISHERS (ASCAP)

449 N. Vista St., Los Angeles CA 90036. (323)653-0693. E-mail: unclelenny@aol.com. **Contact:** Len Weisman, owner. Record producer, personal manager, music publisher. Estab. 1980. Publishes 30-50 songs/year.

    • Also see the listings for Audio Music Publishers in the Music Publishers section of this book; Parliament Records in the Record Companies section and The Weisman Production Group in this section of this book.

How to Contact Send demo CD or cassette with 3-10 songs. Include SASE. We only return in prepaid large envelopes.

Music Mostly **R&B**, **soul**, **rap**, **blues** and **2nd gospel**. Just finished "E'morey" CD; "Jus van" CD; and "Jewel With Love" CD.

Ⓝ ⊕ ☑ R.J. MUSIC

'The Return', 10A Margaret Rd., Barnet, Herts EN4 9NP United Kingdom. (020)440-9788. **Contact:** Roger James and Susana Boyle, managing directors. Music publisher and management firm (Roger James Management). PRS. Pays negotiable royalty (up to 50%).

How to Contact Submit demo tape by mail. Unsolicited submissions are OK. Prefers cassette with 1 song and lyric or lead sheet. "Will return cassettes, but only with correct *full* postage!"

Music Mostly **MOR**, **blues**, **country** and **rock**; also **chart material**. Does not want disco or rap.

⊕ ◖ R.T.L. MUSIC

White House Farm, Shropshire TF9 4HA United Kingdom. (01630)647374. Fax: (01630)647612. **Contact:** Tanya Woof, international A&R manager. Professional Managers: Ron Dickson (rock/rock 'n roll); Katrine LeMatt (MOR/dance); Xavier Lee (heavy metal); Tanya Lee (classical/other types). Music publisher, record company (Le Matt Music) and record producer. Estab. 1971. Publishes approximately 30 songs/year. Pays standard royalty.

Affiliate(s) Lee Music (publishing), Swoop Records, Grenouille Records, Check Records, Zarg Records, Pogo Records, R.T.F.M. (all independent companies).

How to Contact Submit demo tape or CD by mail. Unsolicited submissions are OK. Prefers CD, cassette, MDisc or DVD (also VHS 625/PAL system videocassette) with 1-3 songs and lyric and lead sheets; include still photos and bios. "Make sure name and address are on CD or cassette." Send IRC. Responds in 6 weeks.

Music All types. Published *Orphan in The Storm* (album), recorded by Emmitt Till; *The Chromatic* (album) recorded by Chromatics; *One Night* (album), recorded by Hush.

▣ ☑ RAINBOW MUSIC CORP. (ASCAP)

45 E. 66 St., New York NY 10021. (212)988-4619. Fax: (212)861-9079. E-mail: fscam45@aol.com. **Contact:** Fred Stuart, vice president. Music publisher. Estab. 1990. Publishes 25 songs/year. Staff size: 2. Pays standard royalty.

Affiliate(s) Tri-Circle (ASCAP).

How to Contact *Only accepts material referred by a reputable industry source.* Prefers CD with 2 songs and lyric sheet. Include SASE. Responds in 1 week.

Film & TV Published "You Wouldn't Lie To An Angel, Would Ya?" (single by Diane Lampert/Paul Overstreet) from *Lady of the Evening* (album), recorded by Ben te Boe (country), released 2003 on Mega International Records; "Gonna Give Lovin' A Try" (single by Cannonball Adderley/Diane Lampert/Nat Adderley) from *The Axelrod Chronicles* (album), recorded by Randy Crawford (jazz), released 2003 on Fantasy Records; "Breaking Bread" (single by Diane Lampert/Paul Overstreet) from *Unearthed* (album), recorded by Johnny Cash (country), released 2003 on Lost Highway Records and "Gonna Give Lovin' A Try" (single by Cannonball Adderley/Diane Lampert/Nat Adderley) from *Day Dreamin'* (album), recorded by Laverne Butler (jazz), released 2002 on Chesky Records.

Music Mostly **pop**, **R&B** and **country**; also **jazz**.

◻ RED SUNDOWN MUSIC (BMI)

P.O. Box 609, Pleasant View TN 37212. (615)746-0844. E-mail: rsdr@bellsouth.net. Website: www. redsundown.com. **Contact:** Ruby Perry.

How to Contact Does not accept unsolicited submissions. Submit CD and cover letter. Does not return submissions.

Music Country, **rock**, and **pop**. Does not want rap or hip-hop. Published "Take A Heart" (single by Kyle Pierce) from *Take Me With You* (album), recorded by Tammy Lee (country) released in 1998 on Red Sundown Records.

⚡ ⊘ REN ZONE MUSIC (ASCAP)

P.O. Box 3153, Huntington Beach CA 92605. (714)596-6582. Fax: (714)596-6577. E-mail: renzone@ socal.rr.com. **Contact:** Keith Wolzinger, president. Music publisher. Estab. 1998. Publishes 14 songs/year; publishes 2 new songwriters/year. Staff size: 2. Pays standard royalty.

• This company won a Parents Choice 1998 Silver Honor Shield.

How to Contact *Does not accept unsolicited submissions.*

Music Mostly **klezmer** and **children's**. Does not want rap, punk or holiday music. Published "Walk Like the Animals" (single by Dayle Lusk) from *Tumble 'n' Tunes* (album), recorded by Dayle Lusk/ Danielle Ganya (children's); "Surf Town" (single by Dayle Lusk) from *City Song at Huntington Beach* (album), recorded by Lisa Worshaw (pop); and "Snowboardin' (single by Stephanie Dona- toni) from *Sea Cliff Tunes* (album), recorded by Lisa Worshaw (children's), all released 2000 on Ren Zone. Recent klezmer releases include *Glazele Wine,Classic American Klezmer* and *Klezmer Coast to Coast.*

Tips "Submit well-written lyrics that convey important concepts to kids on good quality demos with easy to understand vocals."

✓ ⊘ RHINESTONE COWBOY MUSIC (ASCAP)

P.O. Box 22971, Nashville TN 37202. (615)554-3400.

Affiliate(s) ASCAP.

How to Contact Contact first and obtain permission to submit a demo. Submit demo CD with 5 songs. Responds only if interested.

◗ RHYTHMS PRODUCTIONS (ASCAP)

P.O. Box 34485, Los Angeles CA 90034. **Contact:** Ruth White, president. Music and multimedia publisher. Member NARAS. Publishes 4 titles/year. Pays negotiable royalty.

Affiliate(s) Tom Thumb Music.

How to Contact Submit tape with letter outlining background in educational children's music. Include SASE. Responds in 2 months.

Music "We're only interested in **children's songs** and interactive programs that have educational value. Our materials are sold in schools and homes, so artists/writers with an 'edutainment' back- ground would be most likely to understand our requirements." Published "Professor Whatzit®" series including "Adventures of Professor Whatzit & Carmine Cat" (cassette series for children); "Musical Math," "Musical Reading" and "Theme Songs."

ℕ ◻ RIDGE MUSIC CORP. (ASCAP, BMI)

38 Laurel Ledge Court, Stamford CT 06903. E-mail: pmtannen@optonline.net. President/General Manager: Paul Tannen. Music publisher. Estab. 1961. Member CMA. Publishes 6 songs/year. Pays standard royalty.

Affiliate(s) Tannen Music Inc. and Deshufflin, Inc.
How to Contact Submit demo tape by mail. Unsolicited submissions OK. Prefers CD or cassette with 3 songs and lyric sheet. Include SASE. Responds in 2 months.
Music Mostly **country**, **rock**, **top 40/pop** and **jazz**.

ℕ ⧉ ROCKFORD MUSIC CO. (ASCAP, BMI)
150 West End Ave., Suite 6-D, New York NY 10023. **Contact:** Danny Darrow, manager. Music publisher, record company (Mighty Records), record and video tape producer (Danny Darrow). Publishes 1-3 songs/year; publishes 1-3 new songwriters/year. Staff size: 3. Pays standard royalty.
Affiliate(s) Corporate Music Publishing Company (ASCAP) and Stateside Music Company (BMI).
How to Contact Submit demo tape by mail. Unsolicited submissions are OK. "No phone calls and do not write for permission to submit." Prefers cassette with 3 songs and lyric sheet. Does not return material. Responds in 2 weeks.
Music Mostly **MOR** and **top 40/pop**; also **adult pop**, **country**, **adult rock**, **dance-oriented**, **easy listening**, **folk** and **jazz**. Does not want rap. Published "Carnival Nights" (single by Vincent C. Delucia and Raymond Squillacote) from *Falling In Love* (album), recorded by Danny Darrow (country); "Motherless Child" (single by Danny Darrow/Robert Lee Lowery) from *Great Folk Songs* (album), recorded by Danny Darrow (folk); and "Impulse" (single by Danny Darrow) from *Impulse* (album), recorded by Danny Darrow (Euro jazz), all released 2004 on Mighty Records.
Tips "Listen to Top 40 and write current lyrics and music."

⧉ RONDOR MUSIC INTERNATIONAL/ALMO/IRVING MUSIC, A UNIVERSAL MUSIC GROUP COMPANY (ASCAP, BMI)
2440 Sepulveda Blvd., Suite 119, Los Angeles CA 90064. (310)235-4800. Fax: (310)235-4801. Website: www.universalmusicpublishing.com. **Contact:** Creative Staff Assistant. Nashville office: 1904 Adelicia St., Nashville TN 37212. (615)321-0820. Fax: (615)329-1018. Music publisher. Estab. 1965.
Affiliates Almo Music Corp. (ASCAP) and Irving Music, Inc. (BMI).
How to Contact *Does not accept unsolicited submissions.*

☑ ◻ RUSTIC RECORDS, INC. PUBLISHING (ASCAP, BMI, SESAC)
6337 Murray Lane, Brentwood TN 37027. (615)371-0646. Fax: (615)370-0353. E-mail: info@countryalbums.com. Website: www.countryalbums.com. **Contact:** Jack Schneider, president. Vice President: Claude Southall. Office Manager: Nell Tolson. Music publisher, record company (Rustic Records Inc.) and record producer. Estab. 1984. Publishes 20 songs/year. Pays standard royalty.
Affiliate(s) Covered Bridge Music (BMI), Town Square Music (SESAC), Iron Skillet Music (ASCAP).
How to Contact Submit demo tape or CD by mail. Unsolicited submissions are OK. Prefers CD with 3-4 songs and lyric sheet. Include SASE. Responds in 3 months.
Music Mostly **country**. Published "In Their Eyes" (single by Jamie Champa); "Take Me As I Am" (single by Bambi Barrett/Paul Huffman); and "Yesterday's Memories" (single by Jack Schneider), recorded by Colte Bradley (country), to be released 2003.
Tips "Send three or four traditional country songs, novelty songs 'foot-tapping, hand-clapping' gospel songs with strong hook for male or female artist of duet. Enclose SASE (manilla envelope)."

◻ RUSTRON MUSIC PUBLISHERS (BMI)
1156 Park Lane, West Palm Beach FL 33417-5957. (561)686-1354. E-mail: rmp_wmp@bellsouth.net. **Contact:** Sheelah Adams, office administrator. Professional Managers: Rusty Gordon (adult contemporary, acoustic, electric, New Age fusions, children's, cabaret); Ron Caruso (all styles); Davilyn Whims (folk fusions, country, blues). Music publisher, record company, management firm and record producer (Rustron Music Productions). Estab. 1972. Publishes 100-150 songs/year; publishes 10-20 new songwriters/year. Staff size: 9. Pays standard royalty.
Affiliate(s) Whimsong Publishing (ASCAP).
How to Contact Submit demo tape or CD by mail. Cover letter should explain reason for submitting and what songwriter needs from Rustron-Whimsong. Unsolicited submissions are OK. For freelance songwriters we prefer CD with up to 10 songs or cassette with 1-3 songs and typed lyric sheets.

For performing songwriters we prefer CD with up to 15 songs. A typed lyric sheet for each song submitted is required. "Clearly label your tape container or jewel box. We don't review songs on websites." SASE required for all correspondence. No exceptions. Responds in 4 months.

Music Mostly **pop** (ballads, blues, theatrical, cabaret), **progressive country** and **folk/rock**; also **R&B** and **New Age** (instrumental fusions with classical, jazz or pop themes) and **women's music**, **children's music** and **Yankee Reggae**. Does not publish rap, hip-hop, new wave, youth music, hard rock, heavy metal or punk. Published "Yankee Reggae All The Rave" (single) from *Yankee Reggae All The Rave* (album), written and recorded by Jeremy White & Kalliope (Yankee Reggae), released 2005 on Whimsong; "A Trimaran on The Gulf of Mexico" (single) from *A Trimaran on The Gulf of Mexico* (album), written and recorded by Song On A Whim (folk fusions), released 2005 on Rustron Records; and "Solstice in The Big Cypress" (single) from *Solstice in The Big Cypress* (album), written and recorded by The Dinner Key Boys (folk-rock blues), released 2005 on Whimsong Records.

Tips "Accepting performing songwriter's CD for full product review of all songs on CD. Write strong hooks. Keep song length 3½ minutes or less. Avoid predictability—create original lyric themes. Tell a story. Compose definitive melody. Tune in to the trends and fusions indicative of commercially viable new music for the new millennium. Songs reviewed for single-song marketing must be very carefully crafted."

⬛ ⬛ ⬛ ⊘ S.M.C.L. PRODUCTIONS, INC.

P.O. Box 84, Boucherville QC J4B 5E6 Canada. (450)641-2266. **Contact:** Christian Lefort, president. Music publisher and record company. SOCAN. Estab. 1968. Publishes 25 songs/year. Pays standard royalty.

Affiliate(s) A.Q.E.M. Ltee, Bag Music, C.F. Music, Big Bazaar Music, Sunrise Music, Stage One Music, L.M.S. Music, ITT Music, Machine Music, Dynamite Music, Cimafilm, Coincidence Music, Music and Music, Cinemusic Inc., Cinafilm, Editions La Fete Inc., Groupe Concept Musique, Editions Dorimen, C.C.H. Music (PRO/SDE) and Lavagot Music.

How to Contact *Write first and obtain permission to submit.* Prefers CD with 4-12 songs and lead sheet. SAE and IRC. Responds in 3 months.

Film & TV Places songs in film and TV. Recently published songs in French-Canadian TV series and films, including *Young Ivanhoe, Twist of Terror, More Tales of the City, Art of War, Lance & Comte (Nouvelle Generation), Turtle Island* (TV series), *Being Dorothy,* and *The Hidden Fortress.*

Music Mostly **dance, easy listening** and **MOR**; also **top 40/pop** and **TV and movie soundtracks**. Published *Always and Forever* (album by Maurice Jarre/Nathalie Carien), recorded by N. Carsen on BMG Records (ballad); *Au Nom De La Passion* (album), written and recorded by Alex Stanke on Select Records.

⬛ ▢ SABTECA MUSIC CO. (ASCAP)

P.O. Box 10286, Oakland CA 94610. (510)465-2805. Fax: (510)832-0464. Professional Managers: Sean Herring (pop, R&B, jazz); Lois Shayne (pop, R&B, soul, country). **Contact:** Duane Herring, president. Music publisher and record company (Sabteca Record Co., Andre Romare). Estab. 1980. Publishes 8-10 songs/year; 1-2 new songwriters/year. Pays standard royalty.

Affiliate(s) Toyiabe Publishing (BMI).

How to Contact *Write first and obtain permission to submit.* Prefers cassette with 2 songs and lyric sheet. Include SASE. Responds in 1 month.

Music Mostly **R&B, pop** and **country**. Published "Walking My Baby Home" (single by Reggie Walker) from *Reggie Walker* (album), recorded by Reggie Walker (pop), 2002 on Andre Romare Records/Sabteca; "Treat Me Like a Dog" (single by Duane Herring/Thomas Roller), recorded by John Butterworth (pop), released 2004 Sabteca Music Co.

Tips "Listen to music daily, if possible. Keep improving writing skills."

⬛ ⬛ ▢ SADDLESTONE PUBLISHING (BMI, SOCAN)

556 Amess St., New Westminster BC V3L 4A9 Canada. (604)930-9309. Fax: (604)523 -9310. E-mail: saddles@telus.net. Website: http://saddlestone.ontheweb.nu. **Contact:** Candice James (country),

CEO. President: Grant Lucas (rock). Professional Manager: Sharla Cuthbertson (pop, R&B). Music publisher, record company (Saddlestone) and record producer (Silver Bow Productions). Estab. 1988. Publishes 100 songs/year; publishes 12-30 new songwriters/year. Pays standard royalty.

Affiliate(s) Silver Bow Publishing (SOCAN, ASCAP).

How to Contact Submit demo CD by mail. Unsolicited submissions are OK. Prefers CD with any amount of songs and lyric sheet. ''Make sure vocal is clear.'' Does not return material. Responds in 3 months.

Film & TV Places 1 song in film and 2 songs in TV/year. Music Supervisors: Janet York; John McCullough. Recently published ''Midnite Ride'' (by Cam Wagner), recorded by 5 Star Hillbillies in *North of Pittsburgh*.

Music Mostly **country**, **rock** and **pop**; also **gospel** and **R&B**. Published *That's Real Love* (album), written and recorded by Darrell Meyers (country), released 2000; *Silent River* (single by John Reilly), album recorded by Wolfe Milestone.

Tips ''Submit clear demos, good hooks and avoid long intros or instrumentals. Have a great singer do vocals.''

▥ ☐ SANDALPHON MUSIC PUBLISHING (BMI)

P.O. Box 29110, Portland OR 97296. (503) 957-3929. E-mail: jackrabbit01@sprintpcs.com. **Contact:** Ruth Otey, president. Music publisher, record company (Sandalphon Records), and management agency (Sandalphon Management). Estab. 2005. Staff size: 2. Pays standard royalty of 50%.

How to Contact Submit demo tape by mail. Unsolicited submissions are OK. Prefers cassette or CD with 1-5 songs, lyric sheet and cover letter. Include SASE or SAE and IRC for outside United States. Responds in 1 month.

Music Mostly **rock**, **country**, and **alternative**; also **pop**, **blues**, and **gospel**.

▥ ☑ SDB MUSIC GROUP

P.O. Box 158507, Nashville TN 37215. **Contact:** Sherrill Blackman.

Music Mostly **country**. Published ''Sinners And Saints'' (single), recorded by George Jones (country); ''I Need You All The Time'' (single), recorded by Blackhawk (country); and ''Journey On Believer'' (single), recorded by Melody Bieser (Christian country). SDB has had cuts with other artists, including John Michael Montgomery, Leann Rimes, Don Williams, Steve Holy, and Trace Adkins.

☑ SEGAL'S PUBLICATIONS (BMI)

P.O. Box 507, Newton MA 02459. (617)969-6196. Website: www.charlessegal.com **Contact:** Charles Segal. Music publisher and record producer (Segal's Productions). Estab. 1963. Publishes 80 songs/year; publishes 6 new songwriters/year. Pays standard royalty.

• Look for *Instant Songwriting With the Piano*, by Charles and Colleen Segal, available from Writer's Digest Books in Spring 2006.

Affilate(s) Charles Segal's Publications (BMI) and Charles Segal's Music (SESAC).

How to Contact Submit demo tape by mail. Unsolicited submissions are OK. Prefers CD or VHS videocassette with 3 songs and lyric or lead sheet. Does not return material. Responds only if interested.

Music Mostly **rock**, **pop** and **country**; also **R&B**, **MOR** and **children's songs.** ''Go to Bed'' (by Colleen Segal), recorded Susan Stark (MOR); and ''Only In Dreams'' (by Chas. Segal), recorded by Melanie Reeve (MOR), all on Spin Records.

Tips ''Besides making a good demo cassette, include a lead sheet of music—words, melody line and chords. Put your name and phone number on CD.''

☑ ☑ SHAWNEE PRESS, INC. (ASCAP)

P.O. Box 1250, Marshalls Creek PA 18335. (570)476-0550. Fax: (570)476-5247. E-mail: shawnee-info@shawneepress.com. Website: www.ShawneePress.com. **Contact:** Director of Church Music Publications (sacred choral music): Joseph M. Martin. Director of School Music Publications (secular choral music): Greg Gilpin. Music publisher. Estab. 1917. Publishes 150 songs/year. Staff size: 35. Pays negotiable royalty.

Affiliate(s) GlorySound, Harold Flammer Music, Mark Foster Music, Wide World Music, Concert Works.

How to Contact Submit manuscript. Unsolicited submissions are OK. See website for guidelines. Prefers manuscript; recording required for instrumental submissions; recordings optional for choral submissions. Include SASE. Responds in 4 months. "No unsolicited musicals or cantatas."

Music Mostly **church/liturgical**, **educational choral** and **instrumental**. No musicals or contatas.

Tips "Submission guidelines appear on our website."

☐ SILICON MUSIC PUBLISHING CO. (BMI)

222 Tulane St., Garland TX 75043-2239. President: Gene Summers. Vice President: Deanna L. Summers. Public Relations: Steve Summers. Music publisher and record company (Front Row Records). Estab. 1965. Publishes 10-20 songs/year; publishes 2-3 new songwriters/year. Pays standard royalty.

• Also see the listing for Front Row Records in the Record Companies section of this book.

How to Contact Submit demo tape by mail. Unsolicited submissions are OK. Prefers cassette with 1-2 songs. Does not return material. Responds ASAP.

Music Mostly **rockabilly** and **'50s material**; also **old-time blues/country** and **MOR**. Published "Almost Persuaded," "Someone Somewhere," and "Who Stole The Marker" (singles) all recorded by Gene Summers on Crystal Clear Records (rockabilly). Also publishing "I'm Gonna Find Me Some Neon" (b/w); and "Mr. Radio Face" (singles), written and recorded by Joe Hardin Brown, released 2002 on Mister Rock Records. New CD to be released in 2002 with 10 newly published Silicon songs.

Tips "Hear our latest published songs by clicking on to: mp3.com/shawnsummers. We are very interested in '50s rock and rockabilly *original masters* for release through overseas affiliates. If you are the owner of any '50s masters, contact us first! We have releases in Holland, Switzerland, United Kingdom, Belgium, France, Sweden, Norway and Australia. We have the market if you have the tapes! Our staff writers include James McClung, Gary Mears (original Casuals), Robert Clark, Dea Summers, Shawn Summers, Joe Hardin Brown, Bill Becker and Dan Edwards."

⊕ ☑ SINUS MUSIK PRODUKTION, ULLI WEIGEL

Geitnerweg 30a, D-12209, Berlin Germany. +49-30-7159050. Fax: +49-30-71590522. E-mail: ulli.w eigel@arcor.de. Website: www.ulli-weigel.de. **Contact:** Ulli Weigel, owner. Music publisher, record producer and screenwriter. Wrote German lyrics for more than 500 records. Member: GEMA, GVL. Estab. 1976. Publishes 20 songs/year; publishes 6 new songwriters/year. Staff size: 3. Pays standard royalty.

Affiliate(s) Sinus Musikverlag H.U. Weigel GmbH.

How to Contact Submit demo tape or CD by mail. Unsolicited submissions are OK. Prefers cassette or CD-R with up to 10 songs and lyric sheets. Responds in 2 months. "If material should be returned, please send 2 International Reply Coupons (IRC) for cassettes and 3 for a CD. No stamps."

Music Mostly **rock, pop** and **New Age**; also **background music for movies**. Published "Simple Story" (single), recorded by MAANAM on RCA (Polish rock); *Die Musik Maschine* (album by Klaus Lage), recorded by CWN Productions on Hansa Records (pop/German), "Villa Woodstock" (film music/comedy) Gebrüder Blattschuss, Jürgen Von Der Lippe, Hans Werner Olm (2005).

Tips "Take more time working on the melody than on the instrumentation. I am also looking for master-quality recordings for non-exclusive release on my label (and to use them as soundtracks for TV and movie scripts I am working on)."

☑ SIZEMORE MUSIC (BMI)

P.O. Box 210314, Nashville TN 37221. (615)356-3453. E-mail: gary@sizemoremusic.com. Website: www.sizemoremusic.com. **Contact:** Gary Sizemore. Music publisher, record company (The Gas Co.) and record producer (G.L. Rhine). Estab. 1960. Publishes 5 songs/year; 1 new songwriter/year. Pays standard royalty.

How to Contact Submit demo tape by mail. Unsolicited submissions are OK. Prefers CD, cassette or VHS videocassette with lyric sheets. Does not return material. Responds in 2 weeks.
Music Mostly **soul** and **R&B**; also **blues**, **pop** and **country**. Published "Liquor and Wine" and "The Wind," written and recorded by K. Shackleford on Heart Records (country); and "She's Tuff" (by Jerry McCain), recorded by The Fabulous Thunderbirds on Chrysalis Records (blues).

☑ SME PUBLISHING GROUP (ASCAP/BMI)
2375 County Rd. 1211, Blanchard OK 73010. (405)392-3421. Fax: (405)392-3421. E-mail: smemusic @juno.com. Website: www.smepublishinggroup.com. Professional Managers: Cliff Shelder (southern gospel); Sharon Kinard (country gospel). Music publisher. Estab. 1994. Publishes 6 songs/year; publishes 2 new songwriters/year. Staff size: 2. Pays standard royalty.
Affiliates Touch of Heaven Music (ASCAP) and SME Music (BMI).
How to Contact Submit demo tape by mail. Unsolicited submissions are OK. Prefers cassette or CD/CDR with 3 songs and lyric sheet. Make sure tapes and CDs are labeled and include song title, writer's name and phone number. Does not return material. Responds only if interested.
Music Mostly **Southern gospel**, **country gospel** and **Christian country**. Does not want Christian rap, rock and roll, and hard-core country. Released "Come See A Man" (single by Mike Spanhanks) from *God Writes Our Story* (album), recorded by The Jody Brown Indian Family (southern gospel) on Crossroads Records; and "I Love You Son" (single by Quint Randle, Patricia Smith and Jeff Hinton) from *Here I Come Again* (album) recorded by Jackie Cox (Christian country), released 2005 on Stonghouse Records.
Tips "Always submit good quality demos. Never give up."

☐ SONGTOWN PUBLISHING (ASCAP)/ABNEAR PUBLISHING (BMI)
323 North Walnut St., Mufreesboro TN 37310. (615)890-1878. Fax: (615)890-3771. E-mail: ron@ico fm.com. **Contact:** Ron Herbert.

☑ SONY/ATV MUSIC PUBLISHING (ASCAP, BMI, SESAC)
(formerly Sony Tree International), 8 Music Square W., Nashville TN 37203. (615)726-8300. Fax: (615)242-3441. Website: www.sonyatv.com. **Santa Monica:** 2100 Colorado Ave., Santa Monica CA 90404. (310)449-2100. **New York:** 550 Madison Ave., 18th Floor, New York NY 10022. (212)833-8000.
How to Contact *Sony/ATV Music does not accept unsolicited submissions.*

☑ SOUND CELLAR MUSIC (BMI)
703 N. Brinton Ave., Dixon IL 61021. (815)288-2900. E-mail: president@cellarrecords.com. Website: www.cellarrecords.com. **Contact:** Todd Joos (country, pop, Christian), president. Professional Managers: James Miller (folk, adult contemporary); Mike Thompson (metal, hard rock, alternative). Music publisher, record company (Sound Cellar Records), record producer and recording studio. Estab. 1987. Publishes 15-25 songs/year. Publishes 5 or 6 new songwriters/year. Staff size: 7. Pays standard royalty.
How to Contact Submit demo CD by mail. Unsolicited submissions are OK. Prefers CD with 3 or 4 songs and lyric sheet. Does not return material. "We contact by phone in 3-4 weeks only if we want to work with the artist."
Music Mostly **metal**, **country** and **rock**; also **pop** and **blues**. Published "Problem of Pain" (single by Shane Sowers) from *Before the Machine* (album), recorded by Junker Jorg (alternative metal/rock), released 2000; "Vaya Baby" (single by Joel Ramirez) from *It's About Time* (album), recorded by Joel Ramirez and the All-Stars (latin/R&B), released 2000; and "X" (single by Jon Pomplin) from *Project 814* (album), recorded by Project 814 (progressive rock), released 2001, all on Cellar Records.

🌐 🖼 ☐ STANDARD MUSIC PUBLISHING (BMI)
Lennox House, 229 Lennox St., Richmond Vic 3121. Australia. (61-3)9428-4862. Fax: (61-3)9429-9137. E-mail: music@std.com.an. Managers: Ralph Carr; Adrian Marchesoni. Record Label man-

agement company (RCM International). Estab. 1994. Publishes a variable number of songs/year; publishes a variable number of new songwriters/year. Staff size: 5. Pays negotiable royalty.

How to Contact *Write first and obtain permission to submit.* Prefers CD with 6 songs and lyric sheet. Does not return material. Responds in 1 month.

Film & TV Places 1 song in TV/year. Recently published "Burn" (by Reswick/Werfel/Arena), recorded by Tina Arena in *Baywatch*.

Music Mostly **rock** and **pop**; also **country** and **dance** music. Published "Chains" (pop) and "Wasn't It Good" (pop); by Reswick/Werfel/Arena, all recorded by Tina Arena on Epic. Alson "Shine" by Vanessa Amorosi on Universal Records and "Burn by Jo Dee Messina on Curb (country).

◩ STARBOUND PUBLISHING CO. (BMI)

Dept. SM, 207 Winding Rd., Friendswood TX 77546. E-mail: bb207@msn.com. **Contact:** Buz Hart, partner; Lonnie Wright, partner; Jack Duncan, partner. Music publisher, record company (Juke Box Records, Quasar Records and Eden Records) and record producers (Lonnie Wright, Buz Hart, Jack Duncan). Estab. 1970. Publishes 15-30 songs/year; publishes 5-10 new songwriters/year. Pays standard royalty.

How to Contact *Write or call first and obtain permission to submit.* Prefers CD with 3 songs and lyric sheet. Include SASE. Responds in 2 months.

Music Mostly **country**, **R&B** and **gospel**. Does not want rap. Published "If I Had Another Heart" (single by Larry Wheeler/Buz Hart) from *Day One* (album), recorded by Waylon Adams (country), released 1999 on Jukebox Records; "My Biggest Thrill" and "Old Fashioned Girl" (singles by Phil Hamm/Buz Hart) from *This and That* (album), recorded by Raiders of the Lost Heart (country), released 2000 on MP3.com.

◪ ◩ STILL WORKING MUSIC GROUP (ASCAP, BMI, SESAC)

1625 Broadway, Nashville TN 37203. (615)242-4201. Fax: (615)242-4202. Website: www.royorbiso n.com. **Owner:** Barbara Orbison. Music publisher and record company (Orby Records, Inc.). Estab. 1994.

Affiliate(s) Still Working for the Woman Music (ASCAP), Still Working for the Man Music (BMI) and Still Working for All Music (SESAC).

How to Contact *Does not accept unsolicited submissions.*

Film & TV Published "First Noel," recorded by The Kelions in *Felicity*.

Music Mostly **rock**, **country** and **pop**; also **dance** and **R&B**. Published "If You See Him/If You See Her" (by Tommy Lee James), recorded by Reba McIntire/Brooks & Dunn; "Round About Way" (by Wil Nance), recorded by George Strait on MCA; and "Wrong Again" (by Tommy Lee James), recorded by Martina McBride on RCA (country).

Tips "If you want to be a country songwriter you need to be in Nashville where the business is. Write what is in your heart."

◩ JEB STUART MUSIC CO. (BMI)

P.O. Box 6032, Station B, Miami FL 33101-6032. (305)547-1424. **Contact:** Jeb Stuart, president. Music publisher, record producer (Esquire International) and management firm. Estab. 1975. Publishes 4-6 songs/year. Pays standard royalty.

   ● Also see the listing for Esquire International in the Record Producers section of this book.

How to Contact Submit demo tape by mail. Unsolicited submissions are OK. Prefers cassette or CD with 2-4 songs and lead sheet. Include SASE. Responds in 1 month.

Music Mostly **gospel**, **jazz/rock**, **pop**, **R&B** and **rap**; also **blues**, **church/religious**, **country**, **disco** and **soul**. Published "Peer Pressure" and "So All Alone," both written and recorded by Jeb Stuart and Cafidia Stuart (R&B), released 2004 on Esquire International.

⊕ ◪ ◻ SUCCES

Pijnderslaan 84, Dendermonde 9200 Belgium. (052)21 89 87. Fax: (052)22 52 60. E-mail: deschuyten eer@hotmail.com. **Contact:** Deschuyteneer Hendrik, director. Music publisher, record company and record producer. Estab. 1978. Publishes 400 songs/year. Hires staff songwriters. Staff size: 4. Pays standard royalty.

How to Contact Submit demo tape by mail. Unsolicited submissions are OK. Prefers cassette or VHS videocassette with 3 songs. SAE and IRC. Responds in 2 months.

Film & TV Places songs in TV. Recently released "Werkloos" (by Deschuyteneer), recorded by Jacques Vermeire in *Jacques Vermeire Show*.

Music Mostly **pop**, **dance** and **variety**; also **instrumental** and **rock**. Published "Hoe Moet Dat Nou" (single by Henry Spider), recorded by Monja (ballad), released 2001 on MN; "Liefde" (single by H. Spider), recorded by Rudy Silvester (rock), released 2001 on Scorpion; and "Bel Me Gauw" (single by H. Spider), recorded by Guy Dumon (ballad), released 2001 on BM Records.

SUPREME ENTERPRISES INT'L CORP. (ASCAP, BMI)

12304 Santa Monica Blvd., 3rd Floor, Los Angeles CA 90025. (818)707-3481. Fax: (818)707-3482. E-mail: supreme2@earthlink.net. **Contact:** Lisa Lew, general manager copyrights. Music publisher, record company and record producer. Estab. 1979. Publishes 20-30 songs/year; publishes 2-6 new songwriters/year. Pays standard royalty.

Affiliate(s) Fuerte Suerte Music (BMI), Bigh Daddy G. Music (ASCAP).

How to Contact Submit demo tape by mail. Unsolicited submissions are OK. Prefers CD. Does not return material. **Mail Demos To:** P.O. Box 1373, Agoura Hills CA 91376. "Please copyright material before submitting and include e-mail." Responds in 12-16 weeks if interested.

Music Mostly **reggae**, **rap** and **dance**. Published "Paso La Vida Pensando," recorded by Jose Feliciano on Motown Records; "Cucu Bam Bam" (by David Choy), recorded by Kathy on Polydor Records (reggae/pop); and "Mineaita," recorded by Gaby on SEI Records.

Tips "A good melody is a hit in any language."

T.C. PRODUCTIONS/ETUDE PUBLISHING CO. (BMI)

121 Meadowbrook Dr., Hillsborough, NJ 088 44. (908)359-5110. Fax: (908)359-1962. E-mail: tcproductions@rcn.com. Website: www.vmgmusic.com. President: Tony Camillo. Music publisher and record producer. Estab. 1992. Publishes 25-50 songs/year; publishes 3-6 new songwriters/year. Pays negotiable royalty.

Affiliate(s) We Iz It Music Publishing (ASCAP) and Etude/Barcam (BMI).

How to Contact *Write or call first and obtain permission to submit.* Prefers CD or cassette with 3-4 songs and lyric sheet. Include SASE. Responds in 1 month.

Music Mostly **R&B** and **dance**; also **country** and **outstanding pop ballads**. Published "What the World Needs Now" (single) from *I Take A Stand For Women* (album), recorded by Michelle Parto (pop); *God Loves You* (album), recorded by Faith (spiritual), released 2001 on Faith Records.

TALBOT MUSIC GROUP (ASCAP, BMI)

810 Bellevue Rd. #151, Nashville TN 37221. (615)244-6200. Fax: (615)646-4335. E-mail: talbotmusicgroup@earthlink.net. Music publisher. Estab. 1984. Publishes 40 songs/year. Hires staff songwriters. Pays standard royalty.

Affiliate(s) Talbot Music Publishing, Inc. (BMI), Plainspoken Music Publishing, Inc. (ASCAP) and Harbot (SESAC).

How to Contact *Talbot Music Group does not accept unsolicited submissions.*

Music Published "Austin" (single by David Kent/Kirsti Manna) from *Blake Shelton* (album), recorded by Blake Shelton (country), released 2001 on Giant/Warner Bros.

THISTLE HILL (BMI)

P.O. Box 707, Hermitage TN 37076. (615)320-6071. E-mail: wendy@greyhousestudio.com. **Contact:** Wendy Mazur.

How to Contact Submit demo tape by mail. Unsolicited submissions OK. Submit CD with 3-10 songs. Responds only if interested.

Music Country, **pop**, and **rock**; also **songs for film/TV**. Published "Angry Heart" (single) from *See What You Wanna See* (album), recorded by Radney Foster (Americana); and "I Wanna be

Free'' (single by Jordon Mycoskie) from *I Wanna be Free* (album), recorded by Jordon MyCoskie (Americana), released 2003 on Ah! Records.

▢ TIKI ENTERPRISES, INC. (ASCAP, BMI)
195 S. 26th St., San Jose CA 95116. (408)286-9840. Fax: (408)286-9845. **Contact:** Gradie O'Neal, president. Professional Manager: Jeannine O'Neil. Music publisher, record company (Rowena Records) and record producer (Jeannine O'Neal and Gradie O'Neal). Estab. 1967. Publishes 40 songs/year; publishes 12 new songwriters/year. Staff size: 3. Pays standard royalty.
Affiliate(s) Tooter Scooter Music (BMI), Janell Music (BMI) and O'Neal & Friend (ASCAP).
How to Contact Submit demo tape by mail. Unsolicited submissions are OK. Prefers cassette with 3 songs and lyric or lead sheets. Include SASE. Responds in 2 weeks.
Music Mostly **country**, **Mexican**, **rock/pop gospel**, **R&B** and **New Age**. Does not want atonal music. Published "You're Looking Good To Me" (single) from *A Rock 'N' Roll Love Story* (album), written and recorded by Warren R. Spalding (rock 'n' roll), released 2003-2004; "I Am Healed" (single) from *Faith On The Front Lines* (album), written and recorded by Jeannine O'Neal (praise music), released 2003-2004; and "It Amazes Me" (single by David Davis/Jeannine O'Neal) from *The Forgiven Project* (album), recorded by David Davis and Amber Littlefield, released 2003, all on Rowena Records.
Tips "Keep writing and sending songs in. Never give up—the next hit may be just around the bend."

▣ TOUCABACA MUSIC (BMI)
P.O. Box 727, Goodlettsville TN 37070. (615)851-7126. E-mail: razzy_bailey@hotmail.com. **Contact:** Razzy Bailey.

▢ TOURMALINE MUSIC, INC., (BMI)
2831 Dogwood Place, Nashville TN 37204. (615)269-8682. Fax: (615)269-8929. Website: http://songsfortheplanet.com. **Contact:** Justin Peters, president. Music publisher. Estab. 1980.
Affiliate(s) Justin Peters Music (BMI), LITA Music (ASCAP) and Platinum Planet Music.
How to Contact Submit demo by mail. Unsolicited submissions are OK. Prefers CD with 5 songs and lyric sheet. Does not return material. "Place code '2006' on each envelope submissions."
Music Mostly **rock and roll, classy alternative, adult contemporary, classic rock, country** and some **Christmas music**. Published "Santa Can You Bring My Daddy Home" (single by D. Mattarosa); "The Hurt Is Worth The Chance" (single by Justin Peters/Billy Simon), recorded by Gary Chapman on RCA/BMG Records; and "For So Long" (single by Monroe Jones/Chris McCollum), recorded by GLAD on Benson Records (also recorded by DMB Band, Connie Scot).

☑ ▨ ▣ TOWER MUSIC GROUP (ASCAP, BMI)
30 Music Square W., Suite 102, Nashville TN 37203. (615)320-7003. Fax: (615)320-7006. E-mail: castlerecords@castlerecords.com. Website: www.castlerecords.com. **Contact:** Dave Sullivan, A&R Director. Professional Managers: Ed Russell; Eddie Bishop. Music publisher, record company (Castle Records) and record producer. Estab. 1969. Publishes 50 songs/year; publishes 10 new songwriters/year. Staff size: 15. Pays standard royalty.
Affiliate(s) Cat's Alley Music (ASCAP) and Alley Roads Music (BMI).
How to Contact *See submission policy on website.* Prefers cassette with 3 songs and lyric sheet. Does not return material. "You may follow up via e-mail." Responds in 3 months only if interested.
Film & TV Places 2 songs in film and 26 songs in TV/year. Published "Run Little Girl" (by J.R. Jones/Eddie Ray), recorded by J.R. Jones in *Roadside Prey*.
Music Mostly **country** and **R&B**; also **blues**, **pop** and **gospel**. Published "If You Broke My Heart" (single by Condrone) from *If You Broke My Heart* (album), recorded by Kimberly Simon (country); "I Wonder Who's Holding My Angel Tonight" (single) from *Up Above* (album), recorded by Carl Butler (country); and "Psychedelic Fantasy" (single by Paul Sullivan/Priege) from *The Hip Hoods* (album), recorded by The Hip Hoods (power/metal/y2k), all released 2001 on Castle Records.
Tips "Please contact us via e-mail with any other demo submission questions."

🌐 ⬛ ✅ TRANSAMERIKA MUSIKVERLAG KG
Wilhelmstrasse 10, Bad Schwartau 23611. Germany. 0049-451-21530. E-mail: transamerika@online
.de. Website: www.TRANSAMERIKAmusik.de. General Manager: Pia Kaminsky. **Hamburg**: Ises-
trasse 77, 20149 Hamburg, Germany. Phone: 0049-40-46961527 E-mail: transamerika@t-online.de.
Professional Manager: Kirsten Jung. Member: GEMA, PRS, KODA, NCB, APRA. Music publisher
and administrator. Estab. 1978. Staff size: 3. Pays 50% royalty if releasing a record; 85% if only
administrating.
Affiliate(s) German Fried Music, Screen Music Services Ltd. (London), Cors Ltd. (London), MCI
Ltd. (London), Leosong Music Australia Rty. Ltd. (Sydney), MCS Music Ltd. (USA, London), Pacific
Electric Music Publishing.
How to Contact "We accept only released materials—no demos!" Submit CD or VHS videocassette.
Does not return material. Responds only if interested.
Film & TV Places several songs in film and 2 songs in TV/year.
Music Mostly **pop**; also **rock**, **country**, **film music** and **reggae**.
Tips "We are specializing in administering (filing, registering, licensing and finding unclaimed
royalties, and dealing with counter-claims) publishers worldwide."

⬜ TRANSITION MUSIC CORPORATION (ASCAP, BMI, SESAC)
11288 Ventura Blvd., #709, Studio City CA 91604. (323)860-7074. Fax: (323)860-7986. E-mail:
info@transitionmusic.com. Website: www.transitionmusic.com. Director of Film and Television
Music: Jennifer Brown. President: Donna Ross-Jones. Vice President: David Jones. Administration:
Mike Dobson. Music publisher. Estab. 1988. Publishes 250 songs/year; publishes 20 new songwrit-
ers/year. Variable royalty based on song placement and writer.
Affiliate(s) Pushy Publishing (ASCAP), Creative Entertainment Music (BMI) and One Stop Shop
Music (SESAC).
How to Contact Address submissions to: New Submissions Dept. Submit demo tape by mail. Unso-
licited submissions are OK. Prefers cassette, DAT or CD with 3 songs. Include SASE. Responds in
5 weeks.
Film & TV "TMC provides music for film, TV and commercials."
Music All styles.
Tips "Supply master quality material with great songs."

✅ ✅ TRIO PRODUCTIONS (BMI, ASCAP)
1026 15th Ave. S., Nashville TN 37212. (615)726-5810. Fax: (615)254-0519. E-mail: info@trioprodu
ctions.com. Website: www.trioproductions.com. **Contact:** Robyn Taylor-Drake.
Affiliate(s) Birdseye Ranch Music (ASCAP), Unframed Music (ASCAP) and Whiskey Gap Music
(BMI).
How to Contact *Contact first by e-mail to obtain permission to submit demo.* Submit CD with 3-4
songs and lyric sheet. We do not return submissions.
Music Country, **Americana** and **bluegrass**.

✅ ✅ TWIN TOWERS PUBLISHING CO. (ASCAP)
8455 Beverly Blvd., Suite 400, Los Angeles CA 90048. (323)655-5007. President: Michael Dixon.
Music publisher and booking agency (Harmony Artists, Inc.). Publishes 24 songs/year. Pays stan-
dard royalty.
How to Contact *Call first and get permission to submit.* Prefers CD's with 3 songs and lyric sheet.
Include SASE. Responds only if interested.
Music Mostly **pop**, **rock** and **R&B**. Published "Magic," from *Ghostbusters* soundtrack on Arista
Records; and "Kiss Me Deadly" (by Lita Ford) on RCA Records.

✅ UNIVERSAL MUSIC PUBLISHING (ASCAP, BMI, SESAC)
2440 Sepulveda Blvd., Suite 100, Los Angeles CA 90064. (310)235-470012 **New York:** 1755 Broadway, 8th Floor, New York NY 10019. (212)841-8000 **Tennessee:** 1904 Adelicia St., Nashville TN
37221. (615)340-5400. Website: www.umusicpub.com.

• In 1999, MCA Music Publishing and PolyGram Music Publishing merged into Universal Music Publishing.

How to Contact *Does not accept unsolicited submissions.*

N ☑ UNKNOWN SOURCE MUSIC (ASCAP)

120-4d Carver Loop, Bronx NY 10475. E-mail: unknownsourcemusic@hotmail.com. **Contact:** James Johnson, A&R. Music publisher, record company (Smokin Ya Productions) and record producer. Estab. 1993. Publishes 5-10 songs/year; publishes 5-10 new songwriters/year. Hires staff songwriters. Staff size: 10. Pays standard royalty.

Affiliate(s) Sundance Records (ASCAP), Critique Records.

• Also see the listing for SunDance Records in the Record Companies section of this book.

How to Contact Send e-mail first then mail. Unsolicited submissions are OK. Prefers CD with 3 songs. Responds within 7 weeks.

Music Mostly **rap/hip-hop**, **R&B** and **alternative**. Published "Tha Streets" recorded by Lord Jayz; "Pickett Fence" recorded by Harrie Bit'em.

Tips "Keep working with us, be patient, be willing to work hard. Send your very best work."

☑ ☑ VAAM MUSIC GROUP (BMI)

P.O. Box 29550, Hollywood CA 90029-0550. E-mail: pmarti3636@aol.com. Website: www.vaammusic.com. **Contact:** Pete Martin, president. Music publisher and record producer (Pete Martin/Vaam Productions). Estab. 1967. Publishes 9-24 new songs/year. Pays standard royalty.

Affiliate(s) Pete Martin Music (ASCAP).

• Also see the listings for Blue Gem Records in the Record Companies section of this book and Pete Martin/Vaam Music Productions in the record Producers section of this book.

How to Contact Send CDs or cassette with 2 songs and lyric sheet. Include SASE. Responds in 1 month. "Small packages only."

Music Mostly **top 40/pop, country** and **R&B**. "Submitted material must have potential of reaching top 5 on charts."

Tips "Study the top 10 charts in the style you write. Stay current and up-to-date with today's market."

☐ VALIANT RECORDS & MANAGEMENT (ASCAP, SESAC)

P.O. Box 1, Waveland MS 39576. (228)467-5323. Fax: (228)467-5347. Website: www.vincevance.com and www.vincevance.net. **President:** Andy Stone. Music Publisher. Estab. 1971. Publishes 20 songs/year; publishes 1 new songwriter/year. Staff size: 5. Pays standard royalty of 50%.

Affiliate(s) Brightstone Publishing (ASCAP) and Brightstone Music Publishing (SESAC).

How to Contact Submit demo tape by mail. Unsolicited submissions are OK. Prefers cassette, CD, videocassette with a maximum of 4 songs and lyric sheet, lead sheet, and cover letter. SASE. "No guarantees!" Does not return submissions. Responds only if interested.

Music Mostly **novelty, parodies, Top 40 country**; also **adult contemporary**, **top 40** and **children's**. No rap or X-rated material. Published "Cruising the Coast" (single by Terry Houle/Troy Powers/Andy Stone) and "Contents Under Pressure" (single by Troy Powers) from *Cruising the Coast* (album), recorded by Vince Vance (rock), released 2001 on Valiant Records; and "My Valentine" (single by Troy Powers/Ed Loftus/Andy Stone), from a single release, recorded by Vince Vance (AC), released 2002 on Valiant Records.

Tips "Submit clear recordings where we can hear the lyrics, melody, chord structure. Your expertise as an arranger is appreciated, but we find that producers have their own ideas. We have had the best luck with novelty, parodies, holiday songs and mainstream country, but we are looking for hits!"

☑ VINE CREEK MUSIC (ASCAP)

P.O. Box 171143, Nashville TN 37217. (615)366-1326. Fax: (615)367-1073. E-mail: vinecreek@aol.com. **Contact:** Darlene Austin, Brenda Madden. Administration: Jayne Negri. Creative Director: Brenda Madden. Song Plugger: Markham Brown.

How to Contact "Only send material of good competitive quality. We do not return tapes/CDs unless SASE is enclosed."

☑ WALKER PUBLISHING CO. L.L.C. (ASCAP/BMI)

P.O. Box 11084, Birmingham AL 35202-1084. (205)601-4420. Fax: (775)514-8462. E-mail: superior_marketing@msn.com. Website: www.walkerpublishingco.com. **Contact:** Gary Walker, owner. Professional Managers: Gary Walker (pop/R&B/ country), Charlie Craig (country/new country). Music Publisher, record producer (Charlie Craig Productions). Estab. 2000. Publishes 10 new songs/year; publishes 3 new songwriters/year. Staff size: 3. Hires staff songwriters. Pays standard royalty.

• Also see the listing for Charlie Craig Productions in the Record Producers section of this book.
Affiliates Cryptogram Music (ASCAP) and Star Alliance Music (BMI).
How to Contact Submit demo tape by mail. Unsolicited submissions are OK. Prefers CD with 3 songs, lyric sheet and writer's e-mail address. Does not return material. Responds in 6 weeks, via e-mail only. "Submit only professional studio quality demos."
Music Mostly **country** and **new country**. Does not want rap, hard rock or metal. Published "Dallas Didn't Do It" (single by Craig/Wilkinson/Crosby) from a yet-unnamed album recorded by The Wilkinsons (country); "Tin Can" (single by Charlie Craig/Jerry Cupid) from debut album recorded by Brad & Shelly (country), released on Cupid Records.
Tips "Walker Publishing Co. L.L.C. has partnered with Charlie Craig Productions, owned by legendary writer/producer Charlie Craig—his writing credits include Alan Jackson's 'Wanted'; Travis Tritt's 'Between an Old Memory and Me'; Dolly Parton's 'Chicken Every Sunday'; and Johnny Cash's 'I Would Like to See You Again.' See www.charliecraig.com."

☒ ☑ WARNER/CHAPPELL MUSIC, INC.

10585 Santa Monica Blvd., Third Floor, Los Angeles CA 90025. (310)441-8600. Fax: (310)470-3232. **New York:** 1290 Avenue of the Americas, 23rd floor, New York NY 10104. (212)707-2600. Fax: (212)405-5428. **Nashville:** 20 Music Square E., Nashville TN 37203. (615)733-1880. Fax: (615)733-1885. Website: www.warnerchappell.com. Music publisher.
How to Contact *Warner/Chappell does not accept unsolicited material.*

☒ ☐ ANGELA BAKER WELLS MUSIC (ASCAP)

P.O. Box 148027, Nashville TN 37214-8027. (615) 883-2020. E-mail: angie@coalharbormusic.com. Website: www.coalharbormusic.com. **Contact:** Angela Baker Wells, president/owner. Music publisher. Estab. 2004. Publishes 25 songs/year. Publishes 2 new songwriters/year. Staff size: 2. Pays standard royalty of 50%.
How to Contact *Contact first and obtain permission to submit a demo.* Prefers CD with 3-5 songs and cover letter. "Include SASE or stamped reply card for reply to submission." Does not return submissions. Responds only if interested.
Music Mostly **Christian country**, **contemporary Christian**, **Southern gospel**; also **gospel (all forms)**, **country**, **bluegrass**. Does not want heavy metal, hard rock, rap, grunge, or punk. Published "They Never Had You" (single) from *Coal Harbor Gospel, Vol. 2*, written and recorded by Don Freeman (country/Christian country/AC); "Storms of Life" (single by Angela Renee Wells) from *Coal Harbor Gospel, Vol. 2*, recorded by Angela Baker Wells (Christian country/Southern gospel); "The Anointing" (single), written and recorded by Ray Holland (Southern gospel/inspirational), all released 2004 on Coal Harbor Music.
Tips "We are actively seeking great songs to pitch to Christian and country artists. We are also interested in Christmas, patriotic, and children's songs. Please put all contact info on your cover letter, and include your name, phone, and e-mail on your CD. Do not send certified or registered mail! Put 'Attn: Publ.' on submissions."

☐ WEMAR MUSIC CORP. (BMI)

836 N. La Cienega Blvd., #276, W. Hollywood CA 90069. Phone/fax: (323)692-1037. **Contact:** Stuart Wiener, president. Music publisher. Estab. 1940. Publishes 30 songs/year; publishes 30 new songwriters/year. Pays standard royalty.

Affiliate(s) Grand Music Corp. (ASCAP).

How to Contact Submit demo tape by mail. Unsolicited submissions are OK. "No phone calls." Include SASE. Responds in 2 months.

Music Mostly **pop**, **country**, **R&B** and **dance**. Published "Dick's Boogie" (single by Johnny Brandon), recorded by Dick Vance (jazz), released 2002 on Direct Source; "Your Old Lady" (single by The Isley Bros.), recorded by The Isley Bros. (R&B), released 2002 on Rhino; "The Wonder of You" (single) from multiple albums, written and recorded by Duke Ellington, released on Columbia Records.

🌐 ○ BERTHOLD WENGERT (MUSIKVERLAG)

Hauptstrasse 36, Pfinztal-Sollingen, D-76327 Germany. **Contact:** Berthold Wengert. Music publisher. Pays standard GEMA royalty.

How to Contact Prefers cassette and complete score for piano. SAE and IRC. Responds in 1 month. "No cassette returns!"

Music Mostly **light music** and **pop**.

○ WHITE CAT MUSIC (ASCAP, BMI)

P.O. Box 19720, Fountain Hills AZ 85269. (480)951-3115. Fax: (480)951-3074. Professional Manager: Frank Fara. Producer: Patty Parker. Music publisher, record company and record producer. Member CMA, CCMA, BCCMA and BBB. Estab. 1978. Staff size: 2. "50% of our published songs are from non-charted and developing writers." Pays standard royalty.

Affiliate(s) Rocky Bell Music (BMI), How The West Was Sung Music (BMI) and Crystal Canyon Music (ASCAP).

> • Fara and Parker are authors of the book *How to Open Doors in the Music Industry—the Independent Way*. Also see the listing for Comstock Records in the Music Publishers section and Patty Parker in the Record Producers section of this book.

How to Contact "Submit demo by postal mail only. We do not accept audiofiles online." Unsolicited submissions are OK. "Song submission by CD only (no cassettes) with 2-4 songs and lyric sheet. Include SASE if demo is to be returned." Responds in 2 weeks.

Music All styles of **country**—traditional to crossover. Published "Great American Country" (single by Paula Mengarelli/Tom Mengarelli/Jaff Hansel), recorded by Paula Mengarelli (country), released on Comstock; "She's Bad News" (single by Roy G. Ownbey/Alexandria Sheraton), recorded by Jentille (country), released 2001 on Comstock; and "Give Your Love to Me" (single by Michael Ray) from *Reason to Believe* (album), recorded by Derek Carle (country), released on Comstock.

Tips "Have an out front vocal presentation so lyric can be heard. Go easy on long instrumental intros and breaks which distract. Send only two to four songs—medium to up-tempo are always in demand. This helps stack the odds in your favor for getting heard."

☑ ○ WILCOM PUBLISHING, (ASCAP)

Box 913, Cherokee Village AR 72525. (870)847-1721. Fax: (870)847-1721. E-mail: william@wilcom publishing.com. **Contact:** William Clark, owner. Music publisher. Estab. 1989. Publishes 10-15 songs/year; publishes 1-2 new songwriters/year. Staff size: 2. Pays standard royalty.

How to Contact *Write or call first and obtain permission to submit.* Prefers cassette with 1-2 songs and lyric sheet. Include SASE. Responds in 3 weeks.

Music Mostly **R&B**, **pop** and **rock**; also **country**. Does not want rap. Published "Girl Can't Help It" (single by W. Clark/D. Walsh/P. Oland), recorded by Stage 1 on Rockit Records (top 40).

○ SHANE WILDER MUSIC (BMI)

P.O. Box 335687, North Las Vegas NV 89033. (701)395-5624. **Contact:** Shane Wilder, president. Music publisher, record producer (Shane Wilder Productions) and Management firm (Shane Wilder Artists' Management). Publishes 20-40 songs/year.

Affiliate(s) Shane Wilder Artist's Management.

How to Contact Send demo by mail. Unsolicited submissions are OK. "Submit with no more than 5 songs per submission and include lyric sheet." Responds within 30 days.

Music Country songs only.

☑ WINDSWEPT MUSIC (BMI)

33 Music Square W., #104B, Nashville TN 37203. (615)313-7676. Fax: (615)313-7670. Website: www.windsweptpacific.com. **Contact:** Lisa Gamerts Selder.

▣ ☐ WINSTON & HOFFMAN HOUSE MUSIC PUBLISHERS (ASCAP, BMI)

P.O. Box 1415, Burbank CA 91507-1415. E-mail: sixties1@aol.com. **Contact:** Lynne Robin Green, president. Music publisher. Estab. 1958. Publishes 25 songs/year. Staff size: 2. Pays standard royalty.

Affiliate(s) Lansdowne Music Publishers (ASCAP), Bloor Music (BMI) and Ben Ross Music (ASCAP), "also administers 26 other firms."

How to Contact Submit demo tape by mail. Unsolicited submissions are OK. "*Do not query first.* Do not call. Do not send lyrics without completed music." Prefers cassette or CD with 3 songs maximum and lyric sheet. "*Must* include SASE or e-mail, or *no* reply!" Responds in 1 month.

Film & TV Places 45 songs in film and 25 songs in TV/year. Recently published "Dooley" (by Dillard/Jayne) in *Baby Blues*; "Closer Walk With Thee" (by Craver/Henderson) in *Smiling Fish and Goat on Fire*; and "Born to Jump" (by Larry Dunn) in *Olympics 2000*. And songs placed in *Alias*, *Six Feet Under*, and MTV.

Music Mostly **R&B pop, ballads, hip-hop, vocal jazz, alternative rock** and **R&B**; also **bluegrass, Spanish pop** and **pop ballads**.

Tips "Be very selective in what you send. 'A' side hit quality single songs only. For film or T.V. submissions you must specify you own all the master rights! Be interesting lyrically and strikingly original melodically. No metal or hard rock, vague lyric alternative, New Age, violent or sexist lyrics, novelty or holiday songs. We don't work with lyricis only. No instrumental score type synthy music, please. Independent artist's album material most welcome."

▣ ☑ YOUR BEST SONGS PUBLISHING (ASCAP)

1402 Auburn Way N, Suite 396, Auburn WA 98002. (877)672-2520. General Manager: John Markovich. Music publisher. Estab. 1988. Publishes 1-5 songs/year; publishes 1-3 new songwriters/year. Query for royalty terms.

How to Contact *Write first and obtain permission to submit.* Prefers CD or cassette with 1-3 songs and lyric sheet. "Submit your 1-3 best songs per type of music. Use separate CDs or cassettes per music type and indicate music type on each CD or cassette." Include SASE. Responds in 3 months.

Music Mostly **country, rock/blues** and **pop/rock**; also **progressive, A/C**, some **heavy metal** and **New Age**. Published "Sea of Dreams," written and recorded by J.C. Mark on Cybervoc Productions, Inc. (New Age).

Tips "We just require good lyrics, good melodies and good rhythm in a song. We absolutely do not want music without a decent melodic structure. We do not want lyrics with foul language or lyrics that do not inspire some form of imaginative thought."

▣ ☑ ZETTITALIA MUSIC INTERNATIONAL (ASCAP, BMI)

P.O. Box 261488, Encino CA 91426. (818)506-8533. Fax: (818)506-8534. E-mail: zettworks@aol.com. Website: www.pplzmi.com. **Contact:** Cheyenne Phoenix, A&R. Assistant, A&R: Kaitland Diamond. Music publisher. Estab. 1995. Publishes 40 songs/year; publishes 2 new songwriters/year. Staff size: 2. Hires staff songwriters. Pays standard royalty.

Affiliate(s) Zett One Songs (ASCAP) and Zett Two Music (BMI).

How to Contact *E-mail or write to obtain permission to submit. No phone calls.* "Include SASE or e-mail." Prefers cassette or CD with 3 songs. Include SASE. Responds in 6 weeks.

Film & TV Places 2 songs in film and 4 songs in TV/year.

Music Mostly **pop, film music, country, instrumental** and **R&B**.

Tips "In art, be a good student and stay true to your instincts. In business, be thorough, realistic, flexible and straightforward. Finally, The Golden Rule rules."

☑ ZOMBA MUSIC PUBLISHING (ASCAP, BMI)

137-139 W. 25th St., 8th Floor, New York NY 10001. (212)727-0016. Website: www.zomba.com. **Beverly Hills:** 8750 Wilshire Blvd., Beverly Hills CA 90211. (310)358-4200. Music publisher. Publishes 5,000 songs/year.

Affiliate(s) Zomba Enterprises, Inc. (ASCAP); Zomba Songs, Inc. (BMI).

How to Contact *Zomba Music Publishing does not accept unsolicited material.* "Contact us through management or an attorney."

Music Mostly **R&B**, **pop** and **rap**; also **rock** and **alternative**. Published "Baby One More Time" (single by M. Martin), recorded by Britney Spears on Jive; "Home Alone" (single by R. Kelly/K. Price/K. Murray), recorded by R. Kelly featuring Keith Murray on Jive; and "Taking Everything" (single by G. Levert/D. Allamby/L. Browder/A. Roberson), recorded by Gerald Levert on EastWest.

ADDITIONAL MUSIC PUBLISHERS

The following companies are also music publishers, but their listings are found in other sections of the book. Read the listings for submission information.

Record Companies

R ecord companies release and distribute records, cassettes and CDs—the tangible products of the music industry. They sign artists to recording contracts, decide what songs those artists will record, and determine which songs to release. They are also responsible for providing recording facilities, securing producers and musicians, and overseeing the manufacture, distribution and promotion of new releases.

MAJOR LABELS & INDEPENDENT LABELS

Major labels and independent labels—what's the difference between the two?

The majors

Major labels are defined as those record companies distributed by one of the "Big 5" distribution companies: BMG Distribution, EMI Music Distribution (EMD), Sony Music Distribution, Warner/Elektra/Atlantic Distribution (WEA) and Universal Music and Video Distribution (UMVD). Distribution companies are wholesalers that sell records to retail outlets. If a label is distributed by one of these major companies, you can be assured any release coming out on that label has a large distribution network behind it. It will most likely be sent to most major retail stores in the United States.

The independents

Independent labels go through smaller distribution companies to distribute their product. They usually don't have the ability to deliver records in massive quantities as the major distributors do. However, that doesn't mean independent labels aren't able to have hit records just like their major counterparts. A record label's distributors are found in the listings after the **Distributed by** heading.

Which do I submit to?

Many of the companies listed in this section are independent labels. They are usually the most receptive to receiving material from new artists. Major labels spend more money than most other segments of the music industry; the music publisher, for instance, pays only for items such as salaries and the costs of making demos. Record companies, at great financial risk, pay for many more services, including production, manufacturing and promotion. Therefore, they must be very selective when signing new talent. Also, the continuing fear of copyright infringement suits has closed avenues to getting new material heard by the majors. Most don't listen to unsolicited submissions, period. Only songs recommended by attorneys, managers and producers who record company employees trust and respect are being heard

The Case for Independents

Tip

If you're interested in getting a major label deal, it makes sense to look to independent record labels to get your start. Independent labels are seen by many as a stepping stone to a major recording contract. Very few artists are signed to a major label at the start of their careers; usually, they've had a few independent releases that helped build their reputation in the industry. Major labels watch independent labels closely to locate up-and-coming bands and new trends. In the current economic atmosphere at major labels—with extremely high overhead costs for developing new bands and the fact that only 10% of acts on major labels actually make any profit—they're not willing to risk everything on an unknown act. Most major labels won't even consider signing a new act that hasn't had some indie success.

But independents aren't just farming grounds for future major label acts; many bands have long term relationships with indies, and prefer it that way. While they may not be able to provide the extensive distribution and promotion that a major label can (though there are exceptions), indie labels can help an artist become a regional success, and may even help the performer to see a profit as well. With the lower overhead and smaller production costs an independent label operates on, it's much easier to ''succeed'' on an indie label than on a major.

by A&R people at major labels (companies with a referral policy have a Ø preceding their listing). But that doesn't mean all major labels are closed to new artists. With a combination of a strong local following, success on an independent label (or strong sales of an independently produced and released album) and the right connections, you could conceivably get an attentive audience at a major label.

But the competition is fierce at the majors, so you shouldn't overlook independent labels. Since they're located all over the country, indie labels are easier to contact and can be important in building a local base of support for your music (consult the Geographic Index at the back of the book to find out which companies are located near you). Independent labels usually concentrate on a specific type of music, which will help you target those companies your submissions should be sent to. And since the staff at an indie label is smaller, there are fewer channels to go through to get your music heard by the decision makers in the company.

HOW RECORD COMPANIES WORK

Independent record labels can run on a small staff, with only a handful of people running the day-to-day business. Major record labels are more likely to be divided into the following departments: A&R, sales, marketing, promotion, product management, artist development, production, finance, business/legal and international.

- The *A&R department* is staffed with A&R representatives who search out new talent. They go out and see new bands, listen to demo tapes, and decide which artists to sign. They also look for new material for already signed acts, match producers with artists and oversee recording projects. Once an artist is signed by an A&R rep and a record is recorded, the rest of the departments at the company come into play.

- The *sales department* is responsible for getting a record into stores. They make sure record stores and other outlets receive enough copies of a record to meet consumer demand.
- The *marketing department* is in charge of publicity, advertising in magazines and other media, promotional videos, album cover artwork, in-store displays, and any other means of getting the name and image of an artist to the public.
- The *promotion department*'s main objective is to get songs from a new album played on the radio. They work with radio programmers to make sure a product gets airplay.
- The *product management department* is the ringmaster of the sales, marketing and promotion departments, assuring that they're all going in the same direction when promoting a new release.
- The *artist development department* is responsible for taking care of things while an artist is on tour, such as setting up promotional opportunities in cities where an act is performing.
- The *production department* handles the actual manufacturing and pressing of the record and makes sure it gets shipped to distributors in a timely manner.
- People in the *finance department* compute and distribute royalties, as well as keep track of expenses and income at the company.
- The *business/legal department* takes care of contracts, not only between the record company and artists but with foreign distributors, record clubs, etc.
- And finally, the *international department* is responsible for working with international companies for the release of records in other countries.

LOCATING A RECORD LABEL

With the abundance of record labels out there, how do you go about finding one that's right for the music you create? First, it helps to know exactly what kind of music a record label releases. Become familiar with the records a company has released, and see if they fit in with what you're doing. Each listing in this section details the type of music a particular record company is interested in releasing. You will want to refer to the Category Index on page 383 to help you find those companies most receptive to the type of music you write. You should only approach companies open to your level of experience (see A Sample Listing Decoded on page 11). Visiting a company's website can also provide valuable information about a company's philosophy, the artists on the label and the music they work with.

Networking

Recommendations by key music industry people are an important part of making contacts with record companies. Songwriters must remember that talent alone does not guarantee success in the music business. You must be recognized through contacts, and the only way to make contacts is through networking. Networking is the process of building an intercon-

Icons

For More Info

For more instructional information on the listings in this book, including explanations of symbols (N ✔ Y 🍀 🌐 ○ ◐ ◒ ◌), read the article *Songwriter's Market: How Do I Use It?* on page 5.

necting web of acquaintances within the music business. The more industry people you meet, the larger your contact base becomes, and the better are your chances of meeting someone with the clout to get your demo into the hands of the right people. If you want to get your music heard by key A&R representatives, networking is imperative.

Networking opportunities can be found anywhere industry people gather. A good place to meet key industry people is at regional and national music conferences and workshops. There are many held all over the country for all types of music (see the Workshops and Conferences section for more information). You should try to attend at least one or two of these events each year; it's a great way to increase the number and quality of your music industry contacts.

Creating a buzz

Another good way to attract A&R people is to make a name for yourself as an artist. By starting your career on a local level and building it from there, you can start to cultivate a following and prove to labels that you can be a success. A&R people figure if an act can be successful locally, there's a good chance they could be successful nationally. Start getting booked at local clubs, and start a mailing list of fans and local media. Once you gain some success on a local level, branch out. All this attention you're slowly gathering, this "buzz" you're generating, will not only get to your fans but to influential people in the music industry as well.

SUBMITTING TO RECORD COMPANIES

When submitting to a record company, major or independent, a professional attitude is imperative. Be specific about what you are submitting and what your goals are. If you are strictly a songwriter and the label carries a band you believe would properly present your song, state that in your cover letter. If you are an artist looking for a contract, showcase your strong points as a performer. Whatever your goals are, follow submission guidelines closely, be as neat as possible and include a top-notch demo. If you need more information concerning a company's requirements, write or call for more details. (For more information on submitting your material, see the article Where Should I Send My Songs? on page 9, Demo Recordings: What Should I Know? on page 13 and Quiz: Are You Professional? on page 26.)

RECORD COMPANY CONTRACTS

Once you've found a record company that is interested in your work, the next step is signing a contract. Independent label contracts are usually not as long and complicated as major label ones, but they are still binding, legal contracts. Make sure the terms are in the best interest of both you and the label. Avoid anything in your contract that you feel is too restrictive. It's important to have your contract reviewed by a competent entertainment lawyer. A basic recording contract can run from 40-100 pages, and you need a lawyer to help you understand it. A lawyer will also be essential in helping you negotiate a deal that is in your best interest.

Recording contracts cover many areas, and just a few of the things you will be asked to consider will be: What royalty rate is the record label willing to pay you? What kind of advance are they offering? How many records will the company commit to? Will they offer tour support? Will they provide a budget for video? What sort of a recording budget are they offering? Are they asking you to give up any publishing rights? Are they offering you a publishing advance? These are only a few of the complex issues raised by a recording contract, so it's vital to have an entertainment lawyer at your side as you negotiate.

ADDITIONAL RECORD COMPANIES

There are **more record companies** located in other sections of the book! On page 192 use the list of Additional Record Companies to find listings within other sections who are also record companies.

🔊 ◯ ⊿ A.A.M.I. MUSIC GROUP

Maarschalklaan 47, 3417 SE Montfoort, The Netherlands. Fax: 31-384-471214. E-mail: aamimus@w xs.nl. Release Manager: Joop Gerrits; manager (dance, rap): Carlo Bonti. Labels include Associated Artists, Disco-Dance Records and Italo. Record company, music publisher (Hilversum Happy Music/BUMA-STEMRA, Intermedlodie/BUMA-STEMRA and Hollands Glorie Productions), record producer (Associated Artists Productions) and TV promotions. Estab. 1975. Releases 10 singles, 25 12″ singles, 6 LPs and 6 CDs/year. Pays 14% royalty to artists on contract; variable amount to publishers.

How to Contact Submit demo tape by mail. Unsolicited submissions are OK. Prefers CD or DVD with any number of songs and lyric or lead sheets. Records also accepted. SAE and IRC. Responds in 6 weeks.

Music Mostly **dance, pop, house, hip-hop** and **rock**. Released "Black Is Black" (single by Gibbons/ Hayes), recorded by Belle Epoque (dance); *Pocket Full of Whishes* (single by Robert Jones), recorded by Assault Team (dance), both on Movin' Novelties; and "Let Me Be Free" (single), written and recorded by Samantha Fox on LLP (pop). Other artists include Robert Ward, Yemisi, F.R. David and Black Nuss.

Tips "We invite producers and independent record labels to send us their material for their entry on the European market. Mark all parcels as 'no commercial value—for demonstration only.' We license productions to record companies in all countries of Europe and South Africa. Submit good demos or masters."

◯ ABL RECORDS

835 E. Buckeywood Ave., Orange CA 92865. (714)685-9958. E-mail: melodi4ever@earthlink.net. Website: www.ABLmusic.com. **Contact:** Allan Licht, owner. Record company and music publisher (Allan Bradley Music/BMI and Holly Ellen Music/ASCAP). Estab. 1993. Staff size: 2. Releases 10 singles/year. Pays 50% royalty to artists on contract; statutory rate to publisher per song on record.

● Also see the listing for Allan Bradley Music in the Music Publishers section of this book.

How to Contact Submit demo tape by mail. Unsolicited submissions are OK. Prefers cassette with 3 songs and lyric sheet. Does not return material. Responds in 1 month.

Music Mostly **A/C, pop** and **R&B**; also **country** and **Christian contemporary**. Released *I'll Keep the Change* (by Betty Kay Miller/Marcia McCaslin), recorded by Dakota Brad (country), released 1999 on ABL Records. Other artists include Tracy Todd, Sam Morrison, Donna West, Jill J. Switzer and Michael Cavanaugh.

Tips "Submit top-notch material with great demos."

◯ ALLEGHENY MUSIC WORKS

1611 Menoher Blvd., Johnstown PA 15905. (814)255-4007. E-mail: TunedOnMusic@aol.com. Website: www.alleghenymusicworks.com. **Contact:** Al Rita, managing director. Labels include Allegheny Records. Record company and music publisher (Allegheny Music Works Publishing/ASCAP and Tuned on Music/BMI). Estab. 1991. Pays 10-12% royalty to artists on contract; statutory rate to publisher per song on record.

How to Contact *Does not accept unsolicited submissions.* "E-mail queries are acceptable; responds ASAP to e-mail queries. We will not open e-mails containing attachments or pictures. NO PHONE CALLS! We sometimes offer suggestions on other markets to try."

Music Mostly **country (all styles)**; also **pop, A/C, R&B, inspirational, novelty** and **Halloween**. Does not want rap, metal, or x-rated lyrics. Released "That's My Jack O'Lantern" (single), written and recorded by Neil Hartenburg) from *Halloween Bash* (album) (country), released 2000 on Allegheny.

Tips "Bookmark our website and check it regularly, clicking on *Songwriter Opportunities.* Each month, as a free service to songwriters, we list a new artist or company looking for songs. Complete contact information is included."

☑ ⬛ AMERICAN RECORDINGS

8920 Sunset Blvd., 2nd Floor, W. Hollywood CA 90069. (310)288-5300. Website: www.americanrec ordings.com. A&R: Dino Paredes, George Drakoulias, Antony Bland, Brendon Mendoza. Labels include Too Pure, Infinite Zero, UBL, Venture and Onion. Record company.

Distributed by Sony.

How to Contact Submit demo tape by mail. Unsolicited submissions are OK. Prefers CD, cassette or videocassette with lyric and lead sheet.

Music Released *Unchained*, recorded by Johnny Cash on American Recordings. Other artists include Slayer, System of a Down, The Jayhawks, Rahat Feteh Ali Khan, Paloalto, Noise Ratchet, and The (International) Noise Conspiracy.

☑ ⬛ AMERICATONE RECORDS INTERNATIONAL USA

1817 Loch Lomond Way, Las Vegas NV 89102-4437. (702)384-0030. Fax: (702)382-1926. E-mail: jjjamericatone@aol.com. Website: www.americatone.com. Estab. 1985. **Contact:** A&R Director. Labels include The Rambolt Music International (ASCAP), Americatone Publishers (BMI) and Christy Records International. Record company, producer and music publisher. Releases 4-5 CDs and cassettes/year. Pays 10% royalty.

Distributed by Big Band Dist., Otter Music, North County, General, Harbor Export, International Dist., Twinbrook Dist., Gibson Dist.

How to Contact Submit demo CD by mail. Unsolicited submissions are OK. Prefers cassette or CD. Include SASE. Responds in 1 month.

Music Jazz and **Spanish jazz** only. Artists include Raoul Romero and His Jazz Stars Orchestra, Mark Masters and His Jazz Orchestra, Dick Shearer and His Stan Kenton Spirits, Sam Trippe and His Jazz Orchestra, Ladd McIntosh and His Orchestra, Caribbean Jazz, Jazz in the Rain Quintet, Brad Saunders and His Quintet, Bill Perkins and His Jazz Quintet, and the Eugene Shapiro Jazz Quintet. Americatone International USA is also a publisher of piano music and orchestrations.

☑ ⬛ ANGEL RECORDS

(formerly Angel/EMI Records), 150 Fifth Ave., 6th Floor, New York NY 10011. (212)786-8600. Website: www.angelrecords.com. Record company. Labels include EMI Classics, Manhattan Records, and Virgin Classics.

Distributed by EMI Music Distribution.

How to Contact *Angel/EMI Records does not accept unsolicited submissions.*

Music Artists include Sarah Brightman, Paul McCartney and Bernadette Peters.

⬛ ARIANA RECORDS

1312 S. Avenida Polar, Tucson AZ 85710. E-mail: jgasper1596@earthlink.net. Website: www.cdbab y.com/all/myko. **Contact:** James M. Gasper, president. Vice President (pop, rock): Tom Dukes. Partners: Tom Privett (funk, experimental, rock); Scott Smith (pop, rock, AOR). Labels include Egg White Records. Record company, music publisher (Myko Music/BMI) and record producer. Estab. 1980. Staff size: 4. Releases 5 CDs a year and 1 compilation/year. Pays negotiable royalty to artists on contract; negotiable rate to publisher per song on record.

Distributed by Impact Music Distributors and Care Free Music.

How to Contact "We are only interested in finished CD projects. *No tapes. No demos.* Unsolicited submissions are OK. Include SASE. Responds in 6 months.

Music Mostly **rock**, **funk**, **jazz**, **anything weird**, **strange** or **lo-fi** (must be mastered to CD). Released "Bloated Floater" (single by Mr. Jimi/Trece Broline/Larry's Fault) from *Bloated Floater* (album), recorded by Bloated Floater (space funk), released 2004 on Ariana Records; "Feel My Face" (single by James Gasper) from *Soledad* (album), recorded by Scuba Tails (electro rock), released 2004 on Ariana Records; and "Smak You Up" (single by Trece Broline/Mr. Jimi/Larry's Fault) from *Headphones Plez*, recorded by Beatnik Grip (trash euro funk), released 2004 on Ariana Records. Other artists include Tom P., Big White Teeth, J. Tiom, Slim Taco Explosion, and The Miller Boys.

Tips "We're a small company, but working your material is our job. If we like it, we'll sell it! It's a tough business. Keep trying."

☑ ⊘ ARISTA RECORDS
888 7th Ave., New York NY 10019. (212)489-7400. Fax: (212)977-9843. Website: www.arista.com. Beverly Hills office: 8750 Wilshire Blvd., 3rd Floor, Beverly Hills CA 90211. (310)358-4600. Nashville office: 7 Music Circle North, Nashville TN 37203. (615)846-9100. Fax: (615)846-9192. Labels include Bad Boy Records, Arista Nashville and Time Bomb Recordings. Record company.
Distributed by BMG.
How to Contact *Does not accept unsolicited material.*
Music Artists include Outkast, Dido, Pink, Usher, Avril Lavigne, Babyface, and Sarah McLachlan.

☑ ⊙ ARKADIA ENTERTAINMENT CORP.
34 E. 23rd St., New York NY 10010. (212)533-0007. Fax: (212)979-0266. E-mail: info@arkadiarecords.com. Website: www.arkadiarecords.com. **Contact:** A&R Song Submissions. Labels include Arkadia Jazz, Arkadia Classical, Arkadia Now and Arkadia Allworld. Record company, music publisher (Arkadia Music), record producer (Arkadia Productions) and Arkadia Video. Estab. 1995.
How to Contact *Write or call first and obtain permission to submit.*
Music Mostly **jazz**, **classical** and **pop/R&B**; also **world**.

☑ ⊙ ASTRALWERKS
104 W. 29th St., 4th Floor, New York NY 10001. Website: www.astralwerks.com/demo.html. **Contact:** A&R. Record company. Estab. 1979. Releases 10-12 12″ singles and 100 CDs/year. Pays varying royalty to artists on contract; statutory rate to publisher per song.
How to Contact Send submissions to "Alt. A&R" to address above. No unsolicited phone calls please.
Music Mostly **alternative/indie/electronic**. Artists include VHS or BETA, Badly Drawn Boy, The Beta Band, Chemical Brothers, Turin Breaks and Fatboy Slim.
Tips "We are open to artists of unique quality and enjoy developing artists from the ground up. We listen to all types of 'alternative' music regardless of genre. It's about the aesthetic and artistic quality first. We send out rejection letters so do not call to find out what's happening with your demo."

☐ ATLAN-DEC/GROOVELINE RECORDS
2529 Green Forest Court, Snellville GA 30078-4183. (770)985-1686. Fax: (877)751-5169. E-mail: atlandecc@prodigy.net. Website: www.ATLAN-DEC.com. President/Senior A&R Rep: James Hatcher. A&R Rep: Wiletta J. Hatcher. Record company, music publisher and record producer. Estab. 1994. Staff size: 2. Releases 3-4 singles, 3-4 LPs and 3-4 CDs/year. Pays 10-25% royalty to artists on contract; statutory rate to publisher per song on record.
Distributed by ATLAN-DEC Records.
How to Contact Submit demo tape by mail. Unsolicited submissions are OK. Prefers CDR and lyric sheet. Does not return material. Responds in 3 months.
Music Mostly **R&B/urban**, **hip-hop/rap** and **contemporary jazz**; also **soft rock**, **gospel**, **dance** and **new country**. Released "Temptation" by Shawree, released 2004 on Atlan-Dec/Grooveline Records. Other artists include Furious D (rap/hip-hop), Tobias (rap/hip-hop) single due in 2005, and Mark Cocker (new country).

☑ ⊘ ATLANTIC RECORDS
1290 Avenue of the Americas, New York NY 10104. (212)707-2000. Fax: (212)581-6414. Website: www.atlanticrecords.com. **New York:** 1290 Avenue of the Americas, New York, NY 10104. **Los Angeles:** 3400 W. Olive Ave., 3rd Floor, Burbank CA 91505. (818)238-6800. Fax: (310)205-7411. **Nashville:** 20 Music Square East, Nashville TN 37203. (615)272-7990. Labels include Big Beat Records, LAVA, Nonesuch Records, Atlantic Classics and Rhino Records. Record company. Pays negotiable royalty to artists on contract; negotiable rate to publisher per song on record.

Distributed by WEA.
How to Contact *Does not accept unsolicited material.* "No phone calls please."
Music Artists include Matchbox Twenty, Jewel, Sugar Ray, Kid Rock, Luna, P.O.D., The Darkness, and The Corrs.

⊕ ☑ AUDIO-VISUAL MEDIA PRODUCTIONS

(formerly First Time Records), Sovereign House, 12 Trewartha Rd., Praa Sands, Penzance, Cornwall TR20 9ST England. (01736)762826. Fax: (01736)763328. E-mail: panamus@aol.com. Website: www.songwriters-guild.co.uk. **Contact:** Roderick G. Jones, managing director A&R. Labels include Pure Gold Records, Panama Music Library, Rainy Day Records, HepCat Records, Panama Records, Mohock Records. Registered members of Phonographic Performance Ltd. (PPL). Record company, music publisher (First Time Music Publishing U.K./MCPS/PRS), management firm and record producer (First Time Management & Production Co.). Estab. 1986. Staff size: 6. Pays variable royalty to artists on contract; statutory rate to publisher per song on record subject to deal.
Distributed by Media U.K. Distributors.
How to Contact Submit demo tape by mail. Unsolicited submissions are OK. Prefers CD with unlimited number of songs and lyric or lead sheets, but not necessary. SAE and IRC. Responds in 3 months.
Music All styles. Released "Topaz" (single) from *Acid Jazz* (album), recorded by David Jones (urban jazz music), released 2005 on Panama Music Library; "Star Cloud" (single) from *Deep Skies* (album), recorded by Kevin Kendle (New Age), released 2005 on Panama Music Library; and "Ancient Hedgerows" (single) from *Distant Horizons* (album), recorded by Kevin Kendle, released 2004 on Eventide/Panama Records.

☑ AVITA RECORDS

P.O. Box 764, Hendersonville TN 37077-0764. (615)824-9313. Fax: (615)824-0797. E-mail: Tachoir @bellsouth.net. Website: www.tachoir.com. **Contact:** Robert Kayre, manager. Record company, music publisher (Riohcat Music, BMI) and record producer (Jerry Tachoir). Estab. 1976. Staff size: 8. Releases 2 LPs and 2 CDs/year. Pays negotiable royalty to artists on contract; statutory rate to publisher per song on record.
   • Also see the listing for Riohcat Music in the Managers & Booking Agents section of this book.
How to Contact *Contact first and obtain permission to submit.* We only accept material referred to us by a reputable industry source. Prefers cassette, CD or DAT. Does not return materials. Responds only if interested.
Music Mostly **jazz**. Released *Improvised Thoughts* (album by Marlene Tachoir/Jerry Tachoir/Van Manakas), recorded by Jerry Tachoir and Van Manakas (jazz), released 2001 on Avita Records. Other artists include Van Manakas.

☑ ☑ AVITOR MUSIC

(formerly Seague International Records), P.O. Box 5537 Kreole Station, Moss Point MS 39563-1537. (228)475-0059. "No collect calls, please." **Contact:** Jemiah F. Mitchell, president/owner. Estab. 2003. Releases 10 singles and 5 LPs/year. Pays negotable royalty to artists on contract; statutory rate to publisher per song on record. "Avitor Music has National and International distribution."
Distributed by Select-O-Hits, CD Baby, and Amazon.Com.
How to Contact *Write or call first for submission instructions.* "Always whenever you write, be sure you include a #10 business-size envelope addressed back to yourself with a first-class USA postage stamp on the envelope. A reply will come back to you using the SASE you include in your mailing when you write. *Absolutely no reply postcards—only SASE.* If you only write lyrics, do not submit; only complete songs reviewed, so you must find a collaborator. Not interested in reviewing homemade recordings." Prefers CD (first choice) or cassette with 3-10 songs along with lyrics to songs submitted. Responds in 2 months.
Music All types and styles of songs. "Recording artists with 10-12 professionally recorded and finished songs ready for release can contact Seague International Records for release and National Distribution. Songs and artist must be outstanding in all respects."

Tips "We are reaching out to find undiscovered, talented writers and singers who deserve a chance to be heard, accepted, and appreciated. We are looking for serious-minded people who are hungry for success and filled with ambition. Singers and songwriters wanting to record professionally, contact Avitor Music before you make a move. Save time and money and problems you could run into. For the best results to benefit you, call Avitor Music to get the job done right from the start."

☑ AWAL.COM

P.O. Box 879, Ojai CA 93024. (805)640-7399. Fax: (805)646-6077. E-mail: info@awal.com. Website: www.awal.com. **Contact:** A&R Department. President: Denzyl Feigelson. Record company. Estab. 1996. Staff size: 3.

Distributed by Primarily distributes via digital downloads but physical distribution available.

How to Contact Submit demo by mail. Unsolicited submissions are OK. Prefers CD with 5 songs, lyric sheet, cover letter and press clippings. Does not return materials.

Music Mostly **pop**, **world** and **jazz**; also **techno**, **teen** and **children's**. Released *Go Cat Go* (album by various), recorded by Carl Perkins on ArtistOne.com; *Bliss* (album), written and recorded by Donna Delory (pop); and *Shake A Little* (album), written and recorded by Michael Ruff, both on Awal Records.

☑ ☑ AWARE RECORDS

2336 W. Belmont Ave., Chicago IL 60618. (773)248-4210. E-mail: info@awarerecords.com. Website: www.awarerecords.com. A&R: Steve Smith. President: Gregg Latterman. Record company. Distributed by Sony and Redeye. Estab. 1993. Staff size: 8. Releases 5 LPs, 1 EP and 3 CD/year. Pays negotiable royalty to artists on contract; statutory rate to publisher per song on record.

Distributed by Sony and RED.

How to Contact *Does not accept unsolicited submissions.*

Music Mostly **rock/pop**. Released *Aware 9* (album), written and recorded by various artists (pop/rock); and *More Sounds from Spaghetti Westerns* (album), recorded by Red Elephant, both on Aware Records. Other artists include John Mayer, Five for Fighting, Riddlin Kid, Alice Peacock and Bleu.

☑ ☑ BELMONT RECORDS

484 Lexington St., Waltham MA 02452. (781)891-7800. Fax: (781)893-1771. E-mail: jpennycw@rcn.com. **Contact:** John Penny, president. Labels include Waverly Records. Record company and record producer. Pays standard royalty to artists on contract; statutory rate to publisher per song on record.

How to Contact *Write first and obtain permission to submit.* Prefers cassette with 3 songs and lyric sheet. Include SASE. Responds in 3 weeks.

Music Mostly **country**. Released *Barbara Lawrence* (album), recorded by Barbara Lawrence (c&w), released 1999; and *Listen To Me* (album), recorded by Barbara Lawrence (c&w), released 2000, both on Belmont Records. Other artists include Stan Jr., Tim Barrett, Jackie Lee Williams, Robin Right, Mike Walker and Dwain Hathaway.

⊕ ☑ BIG BEAR RECORDS

Box 944, Birmingham B16 8UT United Kingdom. 44-121-454-7020. Fax: 44-121-454-9996. E-mail: jim@bigbearmusic.com. Website: www.bigbearmusic.com. A&R Director: Jim Simpson. Labels include Truckers Delight and Grandstand Records. Record company, record producer and music publisher (Bearsongs). Releases 6 LPs/year. Pays 8-10% royalty to artists on contract; $8\frac{1}{4}$% to publishers for each record sold. Royalties paid directly to songwriters and artists or through US publishing or recording affiliate.

- Big Bear's publishing affiliate, Bearsongs, is listed in the Music Publishers section, and Big Bear is listed in the Record Producers section of this book.

How to Contact Submit demo tape by mail. Unsolicited submissions are OK. Prefers CD. Does not return material. Responds in 3 weeks.

Music **Blues** and **jazz**. Released *I've Finished with the Blues* and *Blues for Pleasure* (by Skirving/

Nicholls), both recorded by King Pleasure and the Biscuit Boys (jazz); and *Side-Steppin'* (by Barnes), recorded by Alan Barnes/Bruce Adams Quintet (jazz), all on Big Bear Records. Other artists include Lady Sings the Blues, Drummin' Man and Kenny Baker's Dozen.

☑ 🎵 🛇 BIG HEAVY WORLD

P.O. Box 428, Burlington VT 05402-0428. (802)865-1140. E-mail: redshift@bigheavyworld.com. Website: www.bigheavyworld.com. **Contact:** James Lockridge, founder/A&R director. Record company. Estab. 1996. Staff size: 12. Releases 3 CDs/year. Pays negotiable royalty to artists on contract; pay varies by project to publisher per song on record.

- This company was given the 1998 Visionary Award by the Women's Rape Crisis Center. Big Heavy World promotes the music of Burlington, Vermont, and its region. Their compilation CDs vary in genre and theme and often benefit humanitarian services.

How to Contact *Big Heavy World does not accept unsolicited submissions.*

Music Compilation projects vary in genre. Released *Pop Pie* (pop); *Pulsecuts Vol II* (alternative); *No Secrets* and *Tonic Two: Core Breach Burlington* (rock/alternative), *242.01 The Bands of Burlington Vermont* (hardcore/punk/alternative); *Hop 3 An Independent Collection of Rhythms and Melodies from the North Upper Most* (downtempo urban); *Hop 4 A Bumpnthump Electronic Loopngroove Compilation from the Green Mountains* (uptempo hip-hop); *Sullivan Square The Contemporary Folk Collection; The 10th Annual Los Angeles Music Awards Sonic Sampler* (eclectic).

Tips "Vermont-based artists are welcome to contact us, both as a record label and online music retail venue."

🛇 BLUE GEM RECORDS

P.O. Box 29550, Hollywood CA 90029. (323)664-7765. E-mail: pmarti3636@aol.com. Website: www.VaamMusic.com. **Contact:** Pete Martin. Record company, music publisher (Vaam Music Group) and record producer (Pete Martin/Vaam Productions). Estab. 1981. Pays 6-15% royalty to artists on contract; statutory rate to publisher per song on record.

- Also see the listings for Vaam Music Group in the Music Publishers section of this book and Pete Martin/Vaam Music Productions in the Record Producers section of this book.

How to Contact Submit demo tape by mail. Unsolicited submissions are OK. Prefers CD or cassette with 2 songs. Include SASE. Responds in 3 weeks.

Music Mostly **country** and **R&B**; also **pop/top 40** and **rock**.

🛇 BLUE WAVE

3221 Perryville Rd., Baldwinsville NY 13027. (315)638-4286. Fax: (315)635-4757. E-mail: bluewave@localnet.com. Website: www.bluewaverecords.com. **Contact:** Greg Spencer, president/producer. Labels include Blue Wave/Horizon. Record company, music publisher (G.W. Spencer Music/AS-CAP) and record producer (Blue Wave Productions). Estab. 1985. Staff size: 1. Releases 3 LPs and 3 CDs/year. Pays variable royalty to artists on contract; statutory rate to publisher per song on record.

Distributed by Select-O-Hits, Action Music, Burnside Dist.

- Also see the listing for Blue Wave Productions in the Managers & Booking Agents section of this book.

How to Contact Submit demo tape by mail. Unsolicited submissions are OK. Prefers cassette or videocassette (live performance only) and as many songs as you like. Include SASE. Responds in 1 month only if interested. "Do not call."

Music Mostly **blues/blues rock**, **roots rock** and **roots R&B/soul**; also **roots country/rockabilly** or **anything with "soul."** Released "Leave Married Women Alone" (single by Jimmy Cavallo) from *The House Rocker* (album), recorded by Jimmy Cavallo (jump blues), released 2002 on Blue Wave; "Sometimes You Gamble" (single by Kim Simmonds) from *Blues Like Midnight* (album), recorded by Kim Simmonds (blues), released 2001 on Blue Wave; and "Motherless World" (single by Pete McMahon) from *Trouble on the Run* (album), recorded by The Kingsnakes (blues), released 2001 on Blue Wave.

Tips "Be able to put the song across vocally."

☐ BMX ENTERTAINMENT

P.O. Box 10857, Stamford CT 06904. Fax: (203)329-1639. E-mail: info@bmxentertainment.com. Website: www.bmxentertainment.com. **Contact:** Mauris Griffin, CEO. Labels include Red Tape Records. Record company. Estab. 1984. Releases 7 singles, 7 12″ singles, 7 LPs, 7 EPs and 7 CDs/year. Pays 10-12% royalty to artists on contract.

How to Contact Submit demo tape by mail. Unsolicited submissions are OK. Prefers cassette, CD or VHS videocassette with 4 songs or more. "Send bio, résumé, 8×10 photo, contact information." Include SASE. Responds in 3 weeks.

Music Mostly **top 40**, **country**, **R&B** and **rock**; also **hip-hop**, **pop**, **jazz**, **classical**, **children's**, **New Age**, **gospel** and **salsa**.

⊕ ☐ BOULEVARD MUSIC & PUBLISHING

16 Limetrees, Llangattock, Crickhowell NP8 1IL Wales. (0044)(0)1873 810142. Fax: (0044)(0)1873 811557. E-mail: boulmusic@aol.com. A&R Director: Kevin Holland-King (MOR/jazz). Labels include Silverword, Associate, Mirabeau. Record company and music publisher (Boulevard Publishing). Estab. 1987. Staff size: 2. Releases 8 singles and 25 CDs/year. Pays negotiable royalty to artists on contract; statutory rate to publisher per song on record.

Distributed by SMG/T.H.E.

How to Contact Submit demo tape by mail. Unsolicited submissions are OK. Prefers cassette, CD or VHS videocassette with 3 songs, lead sheet and cover letter. SAE and IRC. Responds in 1 month.

Music Mostly **MOR**, **rock** and **R&B**; also **country** and **jazz**. Released "I Say Strawberry Fields Forever" (single by P. Eaton/R. Brook), recorded by Ronnie Brock (pop), released 2002 on Wizard; *Every Word* (album), recorded by Mike Doyle (pop ballads), released 2002 on Silverword; and *Neopolitan Love Songs* (album), recorded by Dewi Wyn (classical), released 2002 on Chateau. Other artists include Jeff Hooper, Southlanders, Screemer, Modern Romance, Ashmore, Poe-Alley and Richard Beavis.

Tips "A well-written song is like any masterpiece: hard to find—easy to recognize."

☑ ◐ BOUQUET RECORDS

Bouquet-Orchid Enterprises, P.O. Box 1335, Norcross GA 30091. (770)814-2420. Fax: (770)339-9088. **Contact:** Bill Bohannon, president. Record company, music publisher (Orchid Publishing/BMI), record producer (Bouquet-Orchid Enterprises) and management firm (Bouquet-Orchid Enterprises). Releases 3-4 singles and 2 LPs/year. Pays 5-8% royalty to artists on contract; pays statutory rate to publishers for each record sold.

How to Contact Submit demo tape by mail. Unsolicited submissions are OK. Prefers cassette or CD with 3-5 songs and lyric sheet. Include SASE. Responds in 1 month.

Music Mostly **religious** (contemporary or country-gospel, Amy Grant, etc.), **country** ("the type suitable for Clint Black, George Strait, Patty Loveless, etc.") and **top 100** ("the type suitable for Billy Joel, Whitney Houston, R.E.M., etc."); also **rock** and **MOR**. Released *Blue As Your Eyes* (by Bill Bohannon), recorded by Adam Day (country); *Take Care of My World* (by Bob Freeman), recorded by Bandoleers (top 40); and *Making Plans* (by John Harris), recorded by Susan Spencer (country), all on Bouquet Records.

Tips "Submit 3-5 songs on a cassette tape with lyric sheets. Include a short biography and perhaps a photo. Enclose SASE."

☑ ◐ BSW RECORDS

P.O. Box 2297, Universal City TX 78148. E-mail: bswr18@wmconnect.com. Website: www.bswrec ords.com. President: Frank Willson. Vice Presidents: Frank Weatherly (country, jazz); Regina Willson (blues). Record company, music publisher (BSW Records/BMI), management firm (Universal Music Marketing) and record producer (Frank Willson). Estab. 1987. Staff size: 5. Releases 18 albums/year. Pays standard royalty to artists on contract; statutory rate to publisher per song on record.

● Also see the listings for BSW Records in the Music Publishers section, Frank Wilson in the Record Producers section and Universal Music Marketing in the Managers & Booking Agents section of this book.

How to Contact Submit demo CD by mail. Unsolicited submissions are OK. Prefers CD (or ¾"
videocassette) with 3 songs and lyric sheet. Include SASE. Responds in 6 weeks.
Music Mostly **country**, **rock** and **blues**. Released *Memories of Hank Williams, Sr.* (album), recorded
by Larry Butler and Willie Nelson. Other artists include Candee Land, Crea Beal, John Wayne,
Sonny Marshall and Bobby Mountain.

◉ CAMBRIA RECORDS & PUBLISHING

P.O. Box 374, Lomita CA 90717. (310)831-1322. Fax: (310)833-7442. E-mail: cambriamus@aol.c
om. **Contact:** Lance Bowling, director of recording operations. Labels include Charade Records.
Record company and music publisher. Estab. 1979. Staff size: 3. Pays 5-8% royalty to artists on
contract; statutory rate to publisher for each record sold.
Distributed by Albany Distribution.
How to Contact *Write first and obtain permission to submit.* Prefers cassette. Include SASE. Re-
sponds in 1 month.
Music Mostly **classical**. Released *Songs of Elinor Remick Warren* (album) on Cambria Records.
Other artists include Marie Gibson (soprano), Leonard Pennario (piano), Thomas Hampson (voice),
Mischa Leftkowitz (violin), Leigh Kaplan (piano), North Wind Quintet and Sierra Wind Quintet.

◉ CANDYSPITEFUL PRODUCTIONS

2051 E. Cedar St., #8, Tempe AZ 85281. (480)968-7017. E-mail: mandrakerocks@yahoo.com. Website: www.candyspiteful.com. President: William Ferraro. Professional Managers: Maxwell Frye
(jazz, rock). Record company, music publisher (Candyspiteful Productions), record producer (William Ferraro). Estab. 2000. Staff size: 2. Produces 20 demo projects, 12 albums per year. Charges
producer/engineer fee's, other fees are negotiable.

   • Also see the listings for Candyspiteful Productions in the Record Producers section and Major
   Entertainment (formerly Majestic Control) in the Music Publishers section of this book.

How to Contact Submit CD by mail. Unsolicited submissions are OK. Prefers CD/CDR with 3 songs,
lyric sheet and cover letter. "Please include a fact sheet, bio, current play dates, etc." Does not
return material. Responds only if interested.
Music Mostly **progressive rock**, **rock/pop**. Released *Cloud Nine* (album by Richard Farnsworth),
recorded by Thunderhead (hard rock); and "Seven Opus" (single by Sharon Barlow) from *Seven
Opus* (album), recorded by Sharon Barlow (pop), both released 2001 on Candyspiteful Productions.
Tips "We are out in the trenches with our artists and fight hard for them. Often in N.Y. and L.A.
and we just may be that person standing in the back checking you out."

◉ CAPITOL RECORDS

1750 N. Vine St., Hollywood CA 90028-5274. (323)462-6252. Fax: (323)469-4542. Website: www.ho
llywoodandvine.com. **Nashville:** 3322 West End Ave., 11th Floor, Nashville TN 37203. (615)269-
2000. Labels include Blue Note Records, Grand Royal Records, Pangaea Records, The Right Stuff
Records and Capitol Nashville Records. Record company.
Distributed by EMD.
How to Contact *Capitol Records does not accept unsolicited submissions.*
Music Artists include Coldplay, Beastie Boys, Liz Phair, and Auf der Maur.

☑ ▣ ◉ CAPP RECORDS

P.O. Box 150871, San Rafael CA 94915-0871. (415)457-8617. Fax: (415)453-6990. E-mail: submissio
ns@capcompany.com. Website: www.capprecords.com. CEO/International Manager: Dominique
Toulon (pop, dance, New Age); Creative Manager/A&R: Manus Buchart (dance, techno). President:
Rudolf Stember. Vice President/Publisher: Marc Oshry (pop, rock, dance). Music publisher (Lapps-
ter music/ASCAP and CIDC Music/BMI) and record company. Member: NARAS, NCSA, Songwrit-
er's Guild of America. Estab. 1993. Publishes 100 songs/year; publishes 25 new songwriters/year.
Staff size: 8. Pays standard royalty.
Affiliate(s) Cary August Publishing Co./CAPP Company (Germany)/Capp Company (Japan).
How to Contact Submit demo by mail. Unsolicited submissions are OK. Prefers CD, NTSC videocas-

sette or CD-R with 3 songs and cover letter. "E-mail us in advance for submissions, if possible." Include SASE. Only responds if interested.

Film & TV Places 20 songs in film and 7 songs in TV/year. Music Supervisors: Dominique Toulon (pop, dance, New Age); Mark D. D'Elicio (dance, techno). Published "Wish You Were Here" (by Cary August/Marc Oshry/Brian Wood/Tom Finch), recorded by Cary August for "Cafe Froth" TV/ ad; "Indian Dream" and "Song For the Earth," both written and recorded by Steven Buckner in "Deep Encounters."

Music Mostly **pop**, **dance** and **techno**; also **New Age**. Does not want country. Released "It's Not a Dream" (single by Cary August/Andre Pessis), recorded by Cary August on CAPP Records (dance).

☑ CAPSTAN RECORD PRODUCTION
P.O. Box 211, East Prairie MO 63845. (575)649-2211. **Contact:** Joe Silver or Tommy Loomas. Labels include Octagon and Capstan Records. Record company, music publisher (Lineage Publishing Co.), management firm (Staircase Promotion) and record producer (Silver-Loomas Productions). Pays 3-5% royalty to artists on contract.

How to Contact Unsolicited submissions are OK. Prefers cassette or VHS videocassette with 2-4 songs and lyric sheet. "Send photo and bio." Include SASE. Responds in 1 month.

Music Mostly **country**, **easy listening**, **MOR**, **country rock** and **top 40/pop**. Released "Country Boy" (single by Alden Lambert); and "Yesterday's Teardrops" and "Round & Round" (single), written and recorded by The Burchetts. Other artists include Bobby Lee Morgan, Skidrow Joe, Vicarie Arcole, Fleming and Scarlett Britoni.

☑ CASE ENTERTAINMENT GROUP/C.E.G. RECORDS, INC.
102 E. Pikes Peak Ave., #200, Colorado Springs CO 80903. (719)632-0227. Fax: (719)634-2274. E-mail: rac@hpi.net. Website: www.newpants.com. and www.oldpants.com. **Contact:** Robert A. Case, president. Record company and music publisher (New Pants Publishing/ASCAP, Old Pants Publishing/BMI). Estab. 1989. Releases 3-4 LPs and 3-4 CDs/year. Pays negotiable royalty to artists on contract.

How to Contact Submit demo tape by mail. Unsolicited submissions are OK. Prefers CD with 3-5 songs and lyric sheet. "Include a brief history of songwriter's career. Songs submitted must be copywritten or pending with copyright office." Does not return material. "Our representative will contact you if interested in material."

Music Mostly **pop**, **rock** and **country**. Released *James Becker* (album), recorded by James Becker (folk), released 2001 on New Pants; *Romancing the Blues* (album), by Kathy Watson (pop), released 2001 on New Pants; and *Stephanie Aramburo* (album), recorded by Stephanie Aramburo (pop), released 2001 on Old Pants.

Tips "Think of the music business as a job interview. You must be able to sell yourself and the music is your baby. You have to be strong and not deal with rejection as a personal thing. It is not a rejection of you, it's a rejection of the music. Most songwriters don't know how to communicate with labels. The best way is to start a friendship with people at the label."

☑ ☑ CELLAR RECORDS
703 N. Brinton Ave., Dixon IL 61021. (866)287-4997. E-mail: president@cellarrecords.com. Website: www.cellarrecords.com. **Contact:** Todd Joos, president. A&R Department: Bob Brady, Albert Hurst, Jim Miller, Mark Summers, Jon Pomplin. Record company, music publisher (Sound Cellar Music/BMI) and record producer (Todd Joos). Estab. 1987. Staff size: 6. Releases 6-8 CDs/year. Pays 15-100% royalty to artists on contract; statutory rate to publisher per song on record. Charges in advance "if you use our studio to record."

Distributed by Harvest Media (www.harvest-mg.com).

How to Contact Submit demo CD by mail. Unsolicited submissions are OK. Prefers CD with 3-4 songs and lyric sheet. Does not return material. Responds in 1 month only if interested. "If we like it we will call you."

Music Mostly **metal**, **country**, **rock**, **pop** and **blues**. *"No rap."* Released "With Any Luck at All" (single by Tony Stampley/Randy Boudreaux/Joe Stampley) from *With Any Luck At All* (album), recorded by Cal Stage (pop/country); "Sleeping With a Smile" (single by Tony Stampley/Melissa Lyons/Tommy Barnes) from *With Any Luck At All* (album), recorded by Cal Stage (pop/country); and "Speed of My Life" (single by Jon Pomplin/Todd Joss) from *Declassified* (album), recorded by Project 814 (rock), all released 2001 on Cellar Records. Other artists include Eric Topper, Snap Judgment, Ballistic, Dago Red, Sea of Monsters, Rogue, Kings, James Miller, Vehement, Noopy Wilson, Dual Exhaust, Junker Jorg, The Unknown, Joel Ramirez & the Allstars, Tracylyn, Junk Poet, Cajun Anger, Roman, Flesh Pilgrims, LYZ, and Justice4.

Tips "Make sure that you understand your band is a business and you must be willing to self-invest time, effort and money just like any other new business. We can help you, but you must also be willing to help yourself."

◯ CHATTAHOOCHEE RECORDS

2544 Roscomare Rd., Los Angeles CA 90077. (818)788-6863. Fax: (310)471-2089. E-mail: cyardum @prodigy.net. **Contact:** Robyn Meyers, Music Director/A&R. Music Director: Chris Yardum. Record company and music publisher (Etnoc/Conte). Member NARAS. Releases 4 singles/year. Pays negotiable royalty to artists on contract.

How to Contact Submit demo tape by mail. Unsolicited submissions are OK. Prefers CD with 2-6 songs and lyric sheet. *Does not return material.* Responds in 2 months only if interested.

Music Mostly **rock**. Released *Don't Touch It Let It Drip* (album), recorded by Cream House (hard rock), released 2000 on Chattahoochee Records. Artists include DNA, Noctrnl and Vator.

◯ CHERRY STREET RECORDS

P.O. Box 52626, Tulsa OK 74152. (918)742-8087. Fax: (918)742-8003. E-mail: info@cherrystreetmu sic.com. Website: www.cherrystreetrecords.com. President: Rodney Young. Vice President: Steve Hickerson. Record company and music publisher. Estab. 1990. Staff size: 2. Releases 2 CD/year. Pays 50% royalty to artists on contract; statutory rate to publisher per song on record.

Distributed by Internet.

How to Contact *Write first and obtain permission to submit.* Prefers cassette or videocassette with 4 songs and lyric sheet. Include SASE. Responds in 4 months.

Music Rock, **country** and **R&B**; also **jazz**. Released *Promise Land* (album), written and recorded by Richard Neville on Cherry Street (rock). Other artists include George W. Carroll and Chris Blevins.

Tips "We sign only artists who play an instrument, sing and write songs. Send only your best four songs."

◯ CHIAROSCURO RECORDS

830 Broadway, New York NY 10003. (212)473-0479. Fax: (845)279-5025. E-mail: jon@chiaroscuroj azz.com. Website: www.ChiaroscuroJazz.com. **Contact:** Jon Bates, A&R/operations manager. Labels include Downtown Sound. Record company and record producer (Hank O'Neal, Andrew Sordoni, Jon Bates). Estab. 1973. Releases 12 CDs/year. Pays negotiable royalty to artists on contract; statutory rate to publisher per song on record.

Distributed by Allegro.

How to Contact Submit demo tape by mail. Unsolicited submissions are OK. Prefers cassette, CD, DAT or videocassette with 1-3 songs. Include SASE. Responds in 6 weeks.

Music Mostly **jazz** and **blues**. "A full catalog listing is available on the web at www.chiarascurojazz .com or by calling (800)528-2582. Reissues and new recordings for 2003 by the following artists: Earl Hines, Junior Nance & Joe Temperly, Abdullah Ibrahim and Bobby Hackett."

Tips "We are not a pop label. Our average release sells between 3,000-5,000 copies in the first three years. We do not give cash advances or tour support, and our average budget per release is about $15,000 including all production, printing and manufacturing costs."

◯ CKB RECORDS/HELAPHAT ENTERTAINMENT

527 Larry Court, Irving TX 75060. (214)223-5181. E-mail: spoonfedmusik@juno.com. **Contact:** Tony Briggs, CEO. Record company and production company. Estab. 1999. Staff size: 5. Pays negotiable royalty to artists on contract.

Distributed by Crystal Clear Distribution.

How to Contact Submit demo by mail. Unsolicited submissions are OK. Prefers CD with 4 songs, cover letter and press clippings. Does not return materials. Responds only if interested.

Music Mostly **rap**, **hip-hop** and **R&B**. Released "Body, Body" (single), recorded by T-Spoon (hip-hop), released 2002 on CKB Records; and "We Can't Be Stopped" (single) from *Ouncified* (album), written and recorded by Tha 40 Clique (hip-hop), released 2002 on CKB. Other artists include Baby Tek, Lil' Droop, Shampoo, Deuce Loc, Tre and Laticia Love.

Tips "Be confident, honest and open to ideas."

✔ ☑ COAL HARBOR MUSIC

P.O. Box 148027, Nashville TN 37214-8027. (615)883-2020. E-mail: info@coalharborbmusic.com. Website: www.coalharbormusic.com. President/Owner: Jerry R. Wells (country/pop/rock). Vice President: Angela R. Wells (gospel/contemporary Christian). Labels include Coal Harbor. Record company, music publisher (Coal Harbor Music/BMI), record producer (Jerry R. Wells), radio promotion agency, management firm, booking agency, demo services, recording studio, artist development. Estab. 1990. Staff size: 2. Releases 16 singles/year and 4 CDs/year. Pays negotiable royalty to artists on contract; statutory royalty to publisher per song on record.

• Also see the listing for Coal Harbor Music in the Music Publishers section of this book.

Distributed by Self distribution.

How to Contact Contact first by e-mail to obtain permission to submit a demo. Send CD with 3-5 songs, lyric sheet, and cover letter. Does not return submissions. Responds only if interested.

Music Mostly **country**, **gospel** and **contemporary Christian**; also **pop**, **rock** and **jazz/bluegrass instrumental**. Does not want hard rock, rap, heavy metal or grunge.

✔ ☑ COLUMBIA RECORDS

550 Madison Ave., 24th Floor, New York NY 10022. (212)833-4000. Fax: (212)833-4389. E-mail: sonymusiconline@sonymusic.com. Website: www.columbiarecords.com. **Santa Monica:** 2100 Colorado Ave., Santa Monica CA 90404. (310)449-2100. Fax: (310)449-2743. **Nashville:** 34 Music Square E., Nashville TN 37203. (615)742-4321. Fax: (615)244-2549. Labels include So So Def Records and Ruffhouse Records. Record company.

Distributed by Sony.

How to Contact *Columbia Records does not accept unsolicited submissions.*

Music Artists include Aerosmith, Marc Anthony, Beyonce, Bob Dylan, and Patti Smith.

☑ COMPADRE RECORDS

708 Main St, Suite 720, Houston TX 77002. (713)228-3847. Fax: (713)228-3843. E-mail: info@compadrerecords.com. Website: www.compadrerecords.com. **Contact:** Brad Turcotte, president. **Tennessee Office:** 806 Centeroak Dr., Knoxville TN 37920. (615)423-2038. Fax: (615)726-8601. Record company. Estab. 2001.

Distributed by RED/Sony Music.

How to Contact "We can't promise that we will listen to every demo that is sent to us, but we welcome any submission. We enjoy listening to new material and support the creative process. Keep writing, sing loud and keep the spirit alive."

Music Mostly **Americana**. Released *Billy and the Kid* (album), recorded by Billy Joe Shaver; and *James McMurtry—Live* (album), recorded by James McMurtry, both released 2004 on Compadre. Other artists include Suzy Bogguss, Flaco Jimenez, Kate Campbell, and Kevin Kinney.

✔ ☑ COMPENDIA MUSIC

210 25th Ave. N., Suite 1200, Nashville TN 37203. (615)277-1800. Fax: (615)277-1801. Website: www.compendiamusic.com. Vice President/General Manager, Compendia Label & Intersound: Ric Pepin (country/rock; contemporary jazz); Vice President/General Manager, Light Records: Phillip White (black gospel). Record company. Labels include Compendia, Light Records, Life², Intersound. Pays negotiable royalty to artists on contract; negotiable rate to publisher per song on record.

How to Contact *Write or call first and obtain permission to submit.* Prefers CD with 3 songs. "We will contact the songwriter when we are interested in the material.'' Does not return material. Responds only if interested.

Music Mostly **country**, **rock**, **gospel** and **classical**. Artists include Joan Osborne, Robert Palmer, Mighty Clouds of Joy.

☑ ☐ COMSTOCK RECORDS LTD.

P.O. Box 19720, Fountain Hills AZ 85269. (480)951-3115. Fax: (480)951-3074. E-mail: fara@comstockrecords.com. Website: www.comstockrecords.com. Production Manager/Producer: Patty Parker. President: Frank Fara. Record company, music publisher (White Cat Music/ASCAP, Rocky Bell Music/BMI, How the West Was Sung Music/BMI), record producer (Patty Parker) and radio promotion. Member CMA, BBB, CCMA, BCCMA, British CMA and AF of M. ''Comstock Records, Ltd. has three primary divisions: Production, Promotion and Publishing. We distribute and promote both our own Nashville productions, as well as already completed country or pop/rock CDs. We also offer CD design and mastering and manufacturing for products we promote. We can master from a copy of your DAT master or CD.'' Staff size: 2. Releases 10-12 CD singles, 10-12 albums/year and 5-6 international sampler CDs. Pays 10% royalty to artists on contract; statutory rate to publishers for each record sold. ''Artists pay distribution and promotion fee to press and release their masters.''

- Comstock Records was named indie Label of the Year at ECMA of Europe's Country Music Awards for 1998 and 1999. Fara & Parker are also authors of the book *How To Open Doors in the Music Industry—The Independent Way* (available through amazon.com).

How to Contact Submit CD by postal mail only. ''We do not accept audio files online.'' Unsolicited submissions are OK. ''Submission by CD only (no cassette).'' Include SASE. ''Enclose stamped return envelope if demo is to be returned.'' Responds in 2 weeks.

Music Released *Weed and Water* (album by Paul Marshall and various co-writers), recorded by Paul Marshall (country), released on Comstock/Scostepa Music; *Britt Hammond* (album), recorded by Britt Hammond (country). Other artists include Kevin Atwater, Mahoney Brothers, Lorena Prater, Crissy Cummings and Kelli Lidell.

Tips ''Go global—good songs and good singers are universal. Country acts from North America will find a great response in the overseas radio market. Likewise U.S. Radio is open to the fresh new sounds that foreign artists bring to the airwaves.''

☑ COSMOTONE RECORDS

PMB 412, 3350-A Highway 6 S., Sugar Land TX 77478. E-mail: marianland@earthlink.net. Website: www.marianland.com/music.html. Record company, music publisher (Cosmotone Music, ASCAP) and record producer (Rafael Brom). Estab. 1984.

Distributed by marianland.com.

How to Contact ''We do not accept material at this time.'' Does not return materials.

Music All types. Released *Angelophany, The True Measure of Love, All My Love to You Jesus* (albums), and *Rafael Brom Unplugged* (live concert DVD), by Rafael Brom.

☑ CPA RECORDS

15104 Golden Eagle Way, Tampa FL 33625-1545. (813)920-4605. Fax: (813)926-0846. E-mail: al@cparecords.com. Website: www.cparecords.com. **Contact:** Al McDaniel, president. Labels include Coffee's Productions and Associates. Record company and music publisher (CPA Music Publishing). Estab. 1999. Staff size: 5. Releases 3 singles and 2 albums/year. Pays negotiable royalty to artists on contract; negotiable royalty to publisher per song on record.

How to Contact *Write or call first and obtain permission to submit a demo.* Prefers CD/CDR and VHS videocassette with 3 songs, lyric sheet, lead sheet and cover letter. Include SASE. Responds in 2 weeks.

Music Mostly **gospel/Christian**, **rhythm**, **blues** and **jazz**; also **pop** and **rap**. Does not want country. Released ''Somewhere'' (single by Al McDaniel) from *''Coffee'' Greatest Oldies* (album), recorded by Al ''Coffee'' McDaniel (jazz), released 2002 on CPA Records; and ''The Last Dance'' (single by Al McDaniel) from *''Coffee'' Greatest Oldies* (album), recorded by Al ''Coffee'' McDaniel (R&B),

released 2002 on CPS Records. Other artists include Sax Kari, Anthony "Big Lou" McDaniel, and Mike and Anita.

Tips "Be marketable, creative, committed to achieving success, and willing to work hard to accomplish your goals."

☑ ☐ CRANK! A RECORD COMPANY

Attn: New Rock, 1223 Wilshire Blvd. #823, Santa Monica CA 90403. (310)392-8985. E-mail: fan@crankthis.com. Website: www.crankthis.com. **Contact:** Jeff Matlow. Record company. Estab. 1994. Releases 6 singles, 5 LPs, 2 EPs and 5 CDs/year. Pays negotiable royalty to artists on contract.

Distributed by Southern, Revolver, Lumberjack and Nail.

How to Contact Submit demo by mail. Unsolicited submissions are OK. Prefers CD. "Send whatever best represents your abilities." Does not return material. Responds in 6 weeks.

Music Mostly **indie/alternative rock** and **pop**. Released *Neva Dinova* (album), written and recorded by Neva Dinova; *Mono* (album), written and recorded by The Icarus Line (rock/punk); *Down Marriott Lane!* (album), written and recorded by the Get Set (rock/pop); *The Power of Failing*, written and recorded by Mineral (rock); *Boys Life*, written and recorded by Boys Life (rock); and *Such Blinding Stars for Starving Eyes*, written and recorded by Cursive (rock), all on Crank! Other artists include Fireside, Errortype:11, Onelinedrawing, The Regrets, Sunday's Best and Gloria Record.

☐ CREATIVE IMPROVISED MUSIC PROJECTS (CIMP) RECORDS

Cadence Building, Redwood NY 13679. (315)287-2852. Fax: (315)287-2860. Website: www.cadencebuilding.com. **Contact:** Bob Rusch, producer. Labels include Cadence Jazz Records. Record company and record producer (Robert D. Rusch). Estab. 1980. Releases 25-30 CDs/year. Pays negotiable royalty to artists on contract; pays statutory rate to publisher per song on record.

Distributed by North Country Distributors.

  ● CIMP specializes in jazz and creative improvised music.

How to Contact Submit demo tape or CD by mail. Unsolicited submissions are OK. Prefers cassette or CD. "We are not looking for songwriters but recording artists." Include SASE. Responds in 1 week.

Music Mostly **jazz** and **creative improvised music**. Released *The Redwood Session* (album), recorded by Evan Parker, Barry Guy, Paul Lytton and Joe McPhee; *Sarah's Theme* (album), recorded by the Ernie Krivda Trio, Bob Fraser and Jeff Halsey; and *Human Flowers* (album), recorded by the Bobby Zankel Trio, Marily Crispell and Newman Baker, all released on CIMP (improvised jazz). Other artists include Arthur Blyme, John McPhee, David Prentice, Anthony Braxton, Roswell Rudd, Paul Smoker, Khan Jamal, Odean Pope, etc.

Tips "CIMP Records are produced to provide music to reward repeated and in-depth listenings. They are recorded live to two-track which captures the full dynamic range one would experience in a live concert. There is no compression, homogenization, eq-ing, post-recording splicing, mixing, or electronic fiddling with the performance. Digital recording allows for a vanishingly low noise floor and tremendous dynamic range. This compression of the dynamic range is what limits the 'air' and life of many recordings. Our recordings capture the dynamic intended by the musicians. In this regard these recordings are demanding. Treat the recording as your private concert. Give it your undivided attention and it will reward you. CIMP Records are not intended to be background music. This method is demanding not only on the listener but on the performer as well. Musicians must be able to play together in real time. They must understand the dynamics of their instrument and how it relates to the others around them. There is no fix-it-in-the-mix safety; either it works or it doesn't. What you hear is exactly what was played. Our main concern is music not marketing."

☑ ⊘ CURB RECORDS

47 Music Square E., Nashville TN 37203. (615)321-5080. Fax: (615)327-1964. Website: www.curb.com. **Contact:** John Ozler, A&R coordinator. Record company.

How to Contact Curb Records does not accept unsolicited submissions; accepts previously published material only. *Do not submit without permission.*

Music Released *Everywhere* (album), recorded by Tim McGraw; *Sittin' On Top of the World* (album), recorded by LeAnn Rimes; and *I'm Alright* (album), recorded by Jo Dee Messina, all on Curb Records. Other artists include Mary Black, Merle Haggard, Kal Ketchum, David Kersh, Lyle Lovett, Tim McGraw, Wynonna and Sawyer Brown.

◻ ALAN DALE PRODUCTIONS
1630 Judith Lane, Indianapolis IN 46227. (317)786-1630. E-mail: AlanDale2211@aol.com. **Contact:** Alan D. Heshelman, president. Labels include ALTO Records. Record company. Estab. 1990. Pays 10% royalty to artists on contract.
How to Contact *Write or call first and obtain permission to submit or to arrange personal interview.* Prefers cassette with 3 songs. Does not return material. Responds in 10 weeks.
Music Mostly **A/C**, **country**, **jazz**, **gospel** and **New Age**.
Tips "At the present time, we are only looking for vocalists to promote as we promote the songs we write and produce."

☑ ☑ DEARY ME RECORDS
P.O. Box 19315, Cincinnati OH 45219. (859)442-0477. E-mail: jim@dearymerecords.com. Website: www.dearymerecords.com. **Contact:** Jim Farmer, director of business & A&R. Record company. Estab. 1995. Staff size: 2. Releases 3 CDs/year. Pays 50% royalty "after we break even."
How to Contact Unsolicited submissions are OK. "Please check our website for submission policy."
Music Mostly **garage rock**, **country punk** and **rockabilly**. Released *This Is Our ~ Music* (album by Matt Hart/Darren Callahan), recorded by Travel (off-beat punk), released 2000 on Deary Me Records; *Tender Trap* (album), recorded by Fairmount Girls (indie rock), released 2001 on Deary Me Records; and *Black Box Broken* (album), recorded by Chalk (indie rock), released 2001 on Deary Me Records. Also released singles by the Greenhornes and Thee Shams (garage rock), and rereleased the Wolverton Brothers first album (country punk).
Tips "We can't do it all. So be absolutely willing to push your release by playing as many shows as possible."

◻ DEEP SOUTH ENTERTAINMENT
P.O. Box 17737, Raleigh NC 27619-7737. (919)844-1515. Fax: (919)847-5922. E-mail: info@deepsou thentertainment.com. Website: www.deepsouthentertainment.com. Director of Artist Relations: Amy Cox, manager. Record company and management company. Estab. 1996. Staff size: 10. Pays negotiable royalty to artists on contract; statutory rate to publisher per song on record.
Distributed by Redeye Distribution, Valley, Select-O-Hits, City Hall, AEC/Bassin, Northeast One Stop, Pollstar and Koch International.
How to Contact Submit demo tape by mail. Unsolicited submissions are OK. Prefers cassette or CD with 3 songs, cover letter and press clippings. Does not return material. Responds only if interested.
Music Mostly **pop**, **modern rock** and **alternative**; also **swing**, **rockabilly** and **heavy rock**. Does not want rap or R&B. Artists include Bruce Hornsby, Little Feat, Mike Daly, SR-71, Stretch Princess, Darden Smith and many more.

☑ DEL-FI RECORDS, INC.
8271 Melrose Ave., Suite 103, Los Angeles CA 90046. (800)993-3534. Fax: (323)966-4805. E-mail: info@del-fi.com. Website: www.del-fi.com. **Contact:** Bob Keane, owner and president. Labels include Del-Fi, Del-Fi Nashville, Donna, Mustang, Bronco and others. Record company. Estab. 1957. Releases 5-10 LPs and 40 CDs/year. Pays negotiable royalty to artists on contract; statutory rate to publisher per song on record.
Distributed by Bayside, Burnside, Action Music, Hep Cat and Get Hip.
   ● Del-Fi's open door policy is legendary.
How to Contact Submit demo tape by mail. Unsolicited submissions are OK. Prefers cassette or CD. "Please enclose bio information and photo if possible. Send a résumé via fax." Does not return material "unless specified. Allow several weeks." Responds in 1 month.

Music Mostly **rock, surf/drag** and **exotica**. Recently released *Out There in the Dark* (album), written and recorded by Outrageous Cherry (rock); and *Cloud Eleven* (album), written and recorded by Cloud Eleven (rock/pop), *Be Pretty, Be Naked, Be Quiet* (album), recorded by the Rumble Bees (comedy). Other artists include The El Caminos.

Tips "Be sure you are making/writing music that specifically meets your own artistic/creative demands, and not someone else's. Write/play music from the heart and soul and you will always succeed on a personal rewarding level first. We are *the* surf label . . . home of the 'Delphonic' sound. We've also released many of the music world's best known artists, including Ritchie Valens and the Bobby Fuller Four."

☐ DENTAL RECORDS

P.O. Box 20058 DHCC, New York NY 10017. (212)486-4513. Fax: (212)832-6370. E-mail: rsanford@ dentalrecords.com. Website: www.dentalrecords.com. **Contact:** Rick Sanford, owner. Record company. Estab. 1981. Staff size: 2. Releases 1-2 CDs/year. Pays negotiable royalty to artists on contract; statutory rate to publisher per song on record.

Distributed by Dutch East India Trading.

How to Contact Submit demo tape by mail. Unsolicited submissions are OK. Prefers CD with any number of songs, lyric sheet and cover letter. "Check our website to see if your material is appropriate." Include SASE. Responds only if interested.

Music Pop **derived structures, jazz derived harmonies** and **neo-classic-wannabee-pretenses**. Does not want urban, heavy metal or hard core. Released *Perspectivism*, written and recorded by Rick Sanford (instrumental), released 2003 on Dental Records. Other artists include Les Izmor.

☐ DISCMEDIA

2134 Newport Blvd., Costa Mesa CA 92627. (949)631-8597. Fax: (949)515-7499. E-mail: irmavideo @hotmail.com. Website: www.discmedia.com. **Contact:** Irma Moller, manager. Producers: Glenn Moller (rock, dance) and Henry Moller (pop). Record company, music publisher (Discmedia) and record producer (Moller Digital Studios). Estab. 1989.

How to Contact Submit demo tape by mail. Unsolicited submissions are OK. Prefers cassette, CD or VHS with 1 or more songs, lyric sheet and cover letter. "Do not call after submitting." Does not return materials. Responds only if interested.

Music Mostly **rock, pop** and **dance**; also **bilingual Spanish material** (dance, pop-merengue, rock ballads).

☐ DISCOS FUENTES/MIAMI RECORDS & EDIMUSICA USA

(formerly Miami Records), % Arc Music Group, 254 W. 54th St., 13th Floor, New York NY 10019. (212)246-3333. E-mail: info@arcmusic.com. Website: www.arcmusic.com. **Contact:** Juan Carlos Barguil. Vice President: Jorge Fuentes. President: Alejandro Fuentes. Labels include Discos Fuentes. Record company, music publisher (Edimusica-USA). Estab. 1936. Staff size: 14. Releases 13 singles and 89 CDs/year. Pays negotiable royalty to artists on contract; statutory rate to publisher per song on record.

  • Edimusica-USA, Discos Fuentes/Miami Publishing Division entered into an administration deal effective August 18, 2000 with Arc Music Group.

Distributed by Miami Records.

How to Contact Submit demo CD/CDR by mail. Unsolicited submissions are OK. Prefers CD/CDR with lyric sheet. Does not return material. Responds only if interested.

Music Mostly **salsa, cumbia** and **vallenato**; also **grupera, merengue** and **tropical**. Released *Que Lindo Cu* (album) by Rafael Benitez), recorded by Sonora Dinamita (cumbia); *Mi Libertad* (album by Saulo Sanchez), recorded by Fruko y Sostesos (salsa); and *El Majedro (El Viagra)* (album by Elkin Garcia), recorded by Embajadores Vallenatos (vallenato). Other artists include Sonora Carruseles, The Latin Brothers, Los Chiches Vallenatos, Latinos En La Casa, Chambacu, Pastor Lopez, Grupo Mayoral, Los Titanes and Frank La P & Anthony.

Tips "Please keep sending us material. Don't give up if we do not use your first demo."

☑ ☑ DM RECORDS GROUP

(formerly DM/Bellmark/Critique Records), 301 Yamato Rd., Suite 1250, Boca Raton FL 33431. (561)988-1820. Fax: (561)988-1821. E-mail: brian@studio561.com. Website: www.dmrecords.c om. President: Mark Watson. Contact: Brian Fleniken. Record company, music publisher (Bass Tracks & Ashley Watson Publishing) and record producer (Bass 305). Estab. 1992. Releases 16-20 CDs/year. Pays negotiable royalty to artists on contract; 75% statutory rate to publisher per song on record. Labels include Ichiban, Belmark, Wrap Records, Sky Records, Wild Dog Blues, and Altered.

Distributed by Ryko/WEA.

How to Contact Submit CD/CDR by mail. Unsolicited submissions are OK. Prefers CD/CDR. Does not return material. Responds in 2 weeks, if interested.

Music Mostly **southern rap**, **R&B** and **gospel**; also **dance**.

☑ ☑ ☑ DREAMWORKS RECORDS

2220 Colorado Ave., Santa Monica CA 90404. (310)365-1000. Fax: (310)865-8059. Website: www.dr eamworksrecords.com. **Nashville:** 60 Music Sq. E., Nashville TN 37203. (615)463-4600 Fax: (615)463-4601. Record company and music publisher (DreamWorks SKG Music Publishing). Labels include Interscope, Geffen, and A&M.

How to Contact Material must be submitted through an agent or attorney. *Does not accept unsolicited submissions.*

☑ DWELL RECORDS

Attn: A&R, P.O. Box 39439, Los Angeles CA 90039. (323)663-8073. Website: www.dwellrecords.c om. Label Managers: Rex Quick. Record company. Estab. 1991. Staff size: 11. Releases 15 CDs/ year.

Distributed by DNA, Navarre, Handleman, BMG and Columbia House.

How to Contact Submit demo tape by mail. Unsolicited submissions are OK. Prefers CD, bio and photo with press clippings. Does not return materials. Responds only if interested.

Music Mostly **extreme heavy music**. Released *Procession to the Infraworld* (album), written and recorded by The Chasm (dark metal); and *Gods of Creation, Death, and Afterlife* (album).

Tips "Submit quality music."

☑ ELEKTRA RECORDS

75 Rockefeller Plaza, 17th Floor, New York NY 10019. Website: www.elektra.com. Labels include Elektra Records, Eastwest Records and Asylum Records. Record company.

Distributed by WEA.

How to Contact *Elektra does not accept unsolicited submissions.*

Music Mostly **alternative/modern rock**. Artists include Phish, Jason Mraz, Bjork, Busta Rhymes, and Metallica.

☐ ENTERPRIZE RECORDS-TAPES

1507 Scenic Dr., Longview TX 75604-2319. (903)759-0300. Fax: (903)234-2944. **Contact:** Johnny Patterson, studio manager/A&R (country, gospel). Owner: Jerry Haymes (all styles). Record company and music publisher (Enterprize Entertainment). Estab. 1974. Staff size: 3. Pays negotiable royalty to artists on contract.

Distributed by Warner Bros Europe.

How to Contact *Write or call first and obtain permission to submit.* Prefers cassette, CD or videocassette with lyric and lead sheet, cover letter and press clippings. Does not return material. Responds in 1 month.

Music Mostly **pop (AC)**, **country** and **gospel**; also **rock**. Does not want rap.

☑ ☐ ENTOURAGE MUSIC GROUP

11115 Magnolia Blvd., N. Hollywood CA 91601. (818)505-0001. Fax: (818)761-7956. E-mail: guy@E 51.biz. Website: www.entouragestudios.com. **Contact:** Guy Paonessa, president. Record company and recording studio. Estab. 1986 (studio); 1995 (label). Releases 4 CDs/year. Pays negotiable royalty to artists on contract; statutory rate to publisher per song on record.

Distributed by Touchwood Distribution.

How to Contact Submit demo tape by mail. Unsolicited submissions are OK. Prefers cassette, CD, DAT or ½″ videocassette with 3-10 songs. "No phone calls please." Include SASE. Responds in 3 months.

Music Mostly **rock**, **alternative** and **contemporary jazz**; also **alternative country**. Released *The Mustard Seeds*, written and recorded by The Mustard Seeds (alternative rock); *MacAnanys*, written and recorded by MacAnanys (alternative country); and *P.O.L. Sprockett*, recorded by P.O.L. (rock), all on Entourage Records.

☑ ☑ EPIC RECORDS

550 Madison Ave., 21st Floor, New York NY 10022. (212)833-8000. Fax: (212)833-4054. Website: www.epicrecords.com. Senior Vice Presidents A&R: Ben Goldman, Rose Noone. **Santa Monica:** 2100 Colorado Ave., Santa Monica CA 90404. (310)449-2100. Fax: (310)449-2848. A&R: Pete Giberga, Mike Flynn. Labels include Epic Soundtrax, LV Records, Immortal Records and Word Records. Record company.

Distributed by Sony Music Distribution.

How to Contact *Write or call first and obtain permission to submit* (New York office only). Does not return material. Responds only if interested. *Santa Monica and Nashville offices do not accept unsolicited submissions.*

Music Artists include Celine Dion, Macy Gray, Modest Mouse, Audioslave, Fuel, Jennifer Lopez, B2K, Incubus, Ben Folds.

Tips "Do an internship if you don't have experience or work as someone's assistant. Learn the business and work hard while you figure out what your talents are and where you fit in. Once you figure out which area of the record company you're suited for, focus on that, work hard at it and it shall be yours."

☑ FIREANT

2009 Ashland Ave., Charlotte NC 28205. E-mail: lewh@fireantmusic.com. Website: www.fireantmusic.com. **Contact:** Lew Herman, owner. Record company, music publisher (Fireant Music) and record producer (Lew Herman). Estab. 1990. Releases several CDs/year. Pays negotiable royalty to artists on contract; statutory royalty to publisher per song on record.

Distributed by City Hall and North Country.

How to Contact Submit demo tape by mail. Unsolicited submissions are OK. Prefers cassette, DAT or videocassette. Does not return material.

Music Mostly **progressive**, **traditional** and **musical hybrids**. "Anything except New Age and MOR." Released *Loving the Alien: Athens Georgia Salutes David Bowie* (album), recorded by various artists (rock/alternative/electronic), released 2000 on Fireant; and *Good Enough* (album), recorded by Zen Frisbee. Other artists include Mr. Peters' Belizean Boom and Chime Band.

☑ ☐ FLYING HEART RECORDS

Dept. SM, 4015 NE 12th Ave., Portland OR 97212. E-mail: flyheart@teleport.com. Website: http://home.teleport.com/~flyheart. **Contact:** Jan Celt, owner. Record company and record producer (Jan Celt). Estab. 1982. Releases 2 CDs/year. Pays variable royalty to artists on contract; negotiable rate to publisher per song on record.

Distributed by Burnside Distribution Co.

How to Contact Submit demo tape by mail. Unsolicited submissions are OK. Prefers cassette with 1-10 songs and lyric sheets. Does not return material. "SASE required for *any* response." Responds in 3 months.

Music Mostly **R&B**, **blues** and **jazz**; also **rock**. Released *Vexatious Progr.* (album), written and recorded by Eddie Harris (jazz); *Juke Music* (album), written and recorded by Thara Memory (jazz); and *Lookie Tookie* (album), written and recorded by Jan Celt (blues), all on Flying Heart Records.

Other artists include Janice Scroggins, Tom McFarland, Obo Addy, Snow Bud and The Flower People.

☐ FRONT ROW RECORDS

Ridgewood Park Estates, 222 Tulane St., Garland TX 75043. **Contact:** Gene or Dea Summers. Public Relations/Artist and Fan Club Coordinator: Steve Summers. A&R: Shawn Summers. Labels include Juan Records. Record company and music publisher (Silicon Music/BMI). Estab. 1968. Releases 5-6 singles and 2-3 LPs/year. Pays negotiable royalty to artists on contract; standard royalty to songwriters on contract.

Distributed by Crystal Clear Records.

 • Also see the listing for Silicon Music Publishing Co. in the Music Publishers section of this book.

How to Contact Submit demo tape by mail. Unsolicited submissions are OK. Prefers cassette or VHS videocassette with 1-3 songs. *"We request a photo and bio with material submission."* Does not return material. Responds ASAP.

Music Mostly '50s rock/rockabilly; also **country, bluegrass, old-time blues** and **R&B**. Released "Domino" (single), recorded by Gene Summers on Pollytone Records (rockabilly); "Goodbye Priscilla" and "Cool Baby" (singles), both recorded by Gene Summers on Collectables Records.

Tips "If you own masters of 1950s rock and rockabilly, contact us first! We will work with you on a percentage basis for overseas release. We have active releases in Holland, Switzerland, Belgium, Australia, England, France, Sweden, Norway and the US at the present. We need original masters. You must be able to prove ownership of tapes before we can accept a deal. We're looking for little-known, obscure recordings. We have the market if you have the tapes! We are also interested in country and rockabilly *artists* who have not recorded for awhile but still have the voice and appeal to sell overseas."

☑ ◙ MARTY GARRETT ENTERTAINMENT

320 West Utica Place, Broken Arrow OK 74011. (888)HE4-GAVE. E-mail: musicbusiness@telepath.com. Website: www.breakingintothemusicbiz.com. Marty R. Garrett, president. Labels include MGE Records Lonesome Wind Records. Record company, record producer, music publisher and entertainment consultant. Estab. 1988. Releases 1-2 EPs and 1 CD/year. Pays negotiable royalty to artists on contract; statutory rate to publisher per song on record.

How to Contact *Call or check Internet site first and obtain permission to submit.* Prefers CD or cassette with 4-5 songs and lyric or lead sheet with chord progressions listed. Does not return material. No press packs or bios, unless requested. Responds in 4-6 weeks.

Music Mostly **honky tonk, progressive/traditional country** or **scripturally-based gospel**. Most recent release, *He Bought Me Back Again* (album) by Marty Garrett on MGE Records.

Tips "We help artists secure funding to record and release major label quality CD products to the public for sale through 1-800 television and radio advertising and on the Internet. Although we do submit finished products to major record companies for review, our main focus is to establish and surround the artist with their own long-term production, promotion and distribution organization. Professional studio demos are not required, but make sure vocals are distinct, up-front and up-to-date. I personally listen and respond to each submission received, so check website to see if we are reviewing for an upcoming project."

☐ GENERIC RECORDS, INC.

433 Limestone Rd., Ridgefield CT 06877. (203)438-9811. Fax: (203)431-3204. E-mail: hifiadd@aol.com. President (pop, alternative, rock): Gary Lefkowith. A&R (pop, dance, adult contemporary): Bill Jerome. Labels include Outback, GLYN. Record company, music publisher (Sotto Music/BMI) and record producer. Estab. 1976. Staff size: 2. Releases 6 singles and 2 CDs/year. Pays 15% royalty to artists on contract; statutory rate to publisher per song on record.

Distributed by Dutch East India.

How to Contact Submit demo tape by mail. Unsolicited submissions are OK. Prefers cassette with 2-3 songs. Include SASE. Responds in 2 weeks.

Music Mostly **alternative rock**, **rock** and **pop**; also **country** and **rap**. Released "Young Girls" (by Eric Della Penna/Dean Sharenow), recorded by Henry Sugar (alternative/pop); "Rock It," written and recorded by David Ruskay (rock/pop); and *Tyrus*, written and recorded by Tyris (alternative), all on Generic Records, Inc. Other artists include Hifi, Honest, Loose Change and John Fantasia.
Tips "Love what you're doing. The music comes first."

⊘ GIG RECORDS

520 Butler Ave., Point Pleasant NJ 08742. (732)701-9044. Fax: (732)701-9777. E-mail: Indian@gigre cords.com. Website: www.gigrecords.com. **Contact:** Lenny Hip, A&R. Labels include AMPED. Record company and music publisher (Gig Music). Estab. 1998. Staff size: 8. Releases 2 singles, 2 EPs and 15 CDs/year. Pays negotiable royalty to artists on contract; statutory rate to publisher per song on record.
Distributed by Amazon, E-Music, CD Now, Nail and Sumthing.
How to Contact Submit demo tape by mail. Unsolicited submissions are OK. Prefers cassette, CD or VHS videocassette with lyric sheet and cover letter. Does not return materials. Responds ASAP if interested.
Music Mostly **rock** and **electronic**; also **drum & bass**, **trip-hop** and **hip-hop**. Does not want country. Released *Hungry* (album), recorded by Gum Parker (electronico), released 2003 on Gig Records; *Waiting For You* (album), recorded by Nick Clemons Band (alternative rock/pop), released 2003 on Groove Entertainment; and 3 new releases to come from Michael Ferentino, Amazing Meet Project, Love in Reverse. Other artists include Ned's Atomic Dustbin, Virginia, The Vibrators, Groundswell UK, Nebula Nine, The Youth Ahead, Dryer and Red Engine Nine.
Tips "No egos."

☑ ◯ GOTHAM RECORDS

Attn: A&R, P.O. Box 237067, New York NY 10023. E-mail: ar@gothamrecords.com. Website: www. gothamrecords.com. **Contact:** John Cross, vice president A&R/retail. Record company. Estab. 1994. Staff size: 3. Releases 8 LPs and 8 CDs/year. Pays negotiable royalty to artists on contract; statutory rate to publisher per song on record.
Distributed by Dutch East India and MS Distributing.
How to Contact Submit demo tape by mail "in a padded mailer or similar package." Unsolicited submissions are OK. Prefers cassette or CD and bios, pictures and touring information. Does not return material. Responds in 6 weeks.
Music Mostly **rock**, **pop**, **alternative** and **AAA**. Released *Nineteenth Soul*, recorded by Liquid Gang (rock); *Supafuzz*, written and recorded by Supafuzz (rock); and *Oh God! Help Our Fans!*, written and recorded by The Loose Nuts (ska), all on Gotham Records. Other artists include Love Huskies.
Tips "Send all submissions in regular packaging. Spend your money on production and basics, not on fancy packaging and gift wrap."

☑ ⊘ GROOVE MAKERS' RECORDINGS

P.O. Box 271170, Houston TX 77227-1170. E-mail: mistamadd@paidnphull.com. Website: www.pa idnphull.com. **Contact:** Ben Thompson (R&B, rap), CEO. Labels include Paid In Full Entertainment. Record company, music publisher and record producer (Crazy C). Estab. 1994. Staff size: 4. Releases 3 singles, 2 LPs and 2 CDs/year. Pays negotiable royalty to artists on contract; statutory rate to publisher per song on record.
Distributed by S.O.H.
How to Contact *Write first and obtain permission to submit.* Prefers cassette or CD. Does not return material.
Music Mostly **rap** and **R&B**. Released "They Don't Know" (single by Paul Wall/Mike Jones) from *Chick Magnet* (album), recorded by Paul Wall (rap), released 2004 on Paid In Full; "Down South Pt. II" (single by Ben Thompson III) from *Supa Thugz Pt. II* (album), recorded by Mista MADD (rap), released 2004 on Paid In Full; and "Ballin Is A Habit" (single) from *Grown Man Style* (album), recorded by 50/50 Twin (rap), released 2004 on Paid in Full. Other artists include S.O.U.L., Yung Ro, and Shei Atkins.

☑ ◯ GUESTSTAR RECORDS, INC.

17321 Ritchie Ave. NE, Sand Lake MI 49343-9475. (616)636-5068. Fax: (775)743-4169. E-mail: gueststarww@wingsisp.com. Website: www.mountainmanww.com. **Contact:** Marilyn Dietz, office manager. Record company, management firm (Gueststar Entertainment Agency), record producer and music publisher (Sandlake Music/BMI). Estab. 1967. Staff size: 3. Releases 8 singles, 2 LPs and 2 CDs/year. Pays variable royalty to artist on contract, "depending on number of selections on product; 3½¢ per record sold; statutory rate to publisher per song on record."

Distributed by Guestar Worldwide Music Distributors.

How to Contact Submit demo by mail. "Include contact information." Unsolicited submissions are OK. Prefers CD, cassette or VHS videocassette with lyric and lead sheet. Returns submissions after 1 year if SASE and correct postage are included. Responds in 6 months if contact information is added in kit.

Music Mostly **traditional country**. Released "I'm in Love with a Stranger" (single by Raymond Dietz); and "When Jesus Comes" (single by Raymond Dietz), both from *Best of Mountain Man* (album), recorded by Mountain Man (country), released 2001 on GuestStar. Other artists include Jamie "K" and Sweetgrass Band.

Tips "Songwriters: send songs like you hear on the radio. Keep updating your music to keep up with the latest trends. Artists: send VHS video and press kit with shoulder shot only. E-mail and return address is very important."

◯ HACIENDA RECORDS & RECORDING STUDIO

1236 S. Staples St., Corpus Christi TX 78404. (361)882-7066. Fax: (361)882-3943. E-mail: info@haci endarecords.com. Website: www.haciendarecords.com. **Contact:** Rick Garcia, executive vice president. Founder/CEO: Roland Garcia. Record company, music publisher, record producer. Estab. 1979. Staff size: 10. Releases 12 singles and 15 CDs/year. Pays negotiable royalty to artists on contract; negotiable rate to publisher per song on record.

How to Contact Submit demo by mail. Unsolicited submissions are OK. Prefers CD or cassette with cover letter. Does not return material. Responds in 6 weeks.

Music Mostly **tejano**, **regional Mexican**, **country** (Spanish or English) and **pop**. Released "Chica Bonita" (single), recorded by Albert Zamora and D.J. Cubanito, released 2001 on Hacienda Records; "Si Quieres Verme Llorar" (single) from *Lisa Lopez con Mariachi* (album), recorded by Lisa Lopez (mariachi), released 2002 on Hacienda; "Tartamudo" (single) from *Una Vez Mas* (album), recorded by Peligro (norteno); and "Miento" (single) from *Si Tu Te Vas* (album), recorded by Traizion (tejano), both released 2001 on Hacienda. Other artists include Ricky Naramzo, Gary Hobbs, Steve Jordan, Grammy Award nominees Mingo Saldivar and David Lee Garza, Michelle, Victoria Y Sus Chikos, La Traizion.

◙ HEADS UP INT., LTD.

23309 Commerce Park Dr., Cleveland OH 44122. (216)765-7381. Fax: (216)464-6037. E-mail: dave @headsup.com. Website: www.headsup.com. **Contact:** Dave Love, president. Record company, music publisher (Heads Up Int., Buntz Music, Musica de Amor) and record producer (Dave Love). Estab. 1980. Staff size: 57. Releases 10 LPs/year. Pays negotiable royalty to artists on contract.

Distributed by Telarc Int. Corp.

How to Contact Submit demo tape by mail. Unsolicited submissions are OK. Prefers CD. Does not return material. Responds in one month.

Music Mostly **jazz**, **R&B** and **pop**. Does not want anything else. Released *Keeping Cool* (album), written and recorded by Joyce Cooling (jazz); *Another Side of Midnight* (album), written and recorded by Marion Meadows (jazz); and *Love Letters* (album), written and recorded by Gerald Veasley (jazz). Other artists include Philip Bailey, Joe McBride, Richard Smith, Robert Perera, Spyro Gyra and Pieces of a Dream.

☑ ∅ HEART MUSIC, INC.

P.O. Box 160326, Austin TX 78716-0326. (512)795-2375. E-mail: info@heartmusic.com. Website: www.heartmusic.com. **Contact:** Tab Bartling, president. Record company and music publisher

(Coolhot Music). Estab. 1989. Staff size: 2. Releases 1-2 CDs/year. Pays statutory rate to publisher per song on record.

How to Contact *Not interested in new material at this time.* Does not return material. Responds only if interested.

Music Mostly **rock**, **pop** and **jazz**; also **blues** and **contemporary folk**. Released *Mirror* (album), recorded by Monte Montgomery (pop/rock), released June 1999; *Goodnight Venus* (album), recorded by Libby Kirkpatrick, released in 2003, and *Be Cool Be Kind* (album), recorded by Carla Helmbrecht (jazz), released January 2001.

⬛ ☑ ◻ HI-BIAS RECORDS INC.

Attn: A&R Dept., 20 Hudson Dr. (side entrance), Maple ON L6A 1X3 Canada. (905)303-9611. Fax: (905)303-6611. E-mail: info@hibias.ca. Website: www.hibias.ca. **Contact:** Nick Fiorucci, director. Labels include Tilt, Riff, Toronto Underground, Remedy and Club Culture. Record company, music publisher (Bend 60 Music/SOCAN) and record producer (Nick Fiorucci). Estab. 1990. Staff size: 5. Releases 20-30 singles and 2-5 CDs/year. Pays negotiable royalty to artists on contract; statutory rate to publisher per song on record.

Distributed by EMI.

How to Contact Submit demo tape by mail. Unsolicited submissions are OK. Prefers cassette or DAT with 3 songs and lyric sheet. Does not return material. Responds in 6 weeks.

Music Mostly **dance**, **house**, **club**, **pop** and **R&B**. Released "Hands of Time" (single by N. Fiorucci/B. Cosgrove), recorded by Temperance; "Now That I Found You" (single by B. Farrinco/Cleopatra), recorded by YBZ; and "Lift Me Up" (single), written and recorded by Red 5, all on Hi-Bias (dance/pop). Other artists include DJ's Rule.

◙ HOLLYWOOD RECORDS

500 S. Buena Vista St., Old Team Bldg., Burbank CA 91521-1840. (818)560-5670. Fax: (818)563-3551. Website: www.hollywoodrecords.com. Senior Vice President of A&R: Geoffrey Weiss. Senior Vice President of A&R (soundtracks): Mitchell Leib. Vice Presidents: Jon Lind, Eric Clinger. **New York:** 320 7th Ave., Brooklyn NY 11215. (718)832-0860. Fax: (718)832-0869. Website: www.hollywoodrec.com. Executive Director: Jason Jordan. Labels include Acid Jazz Records, Mountain Division Records and Bar/None Records. Record company.

How to Contact *Hollywood Records does not accept unsolicited submissions.* Queries accepted only from a manager or lawyer.

Music Artists include Hilary Duff, Jess McCartney, Breaking Benjamin, and Los Lobos.

◻ HOTTRAX RECORDS

1957 Kilburn Dr., Atlanta GA 30324. (770)662-6661. E-mail: hotwax@hottrax.com. Website: www.hottrax.com. **Contact:** George Burdell, vice president, A&R. Labels include Dance-A-Thon and Hardkor. Record company and music publisher (Starfox Publishing). Staff size: 6. Releases 8 singles and 3-4 CDs/year. Pays 5-15% royalty to artists on contract.

Distributed by Get Hip Inc.

• Also see the listing for Alexander Janoulis Productions/Big Al Jano Productions in the Record Producers section of this book.

How to Contact *Write first and obtain permission to submit.* Prefers CDR with 3 songs and lyric sheet. Does not return material. Responds in 6 months. "When submissions get extremely heavy, we do not have the time to respond/return material we pass on. We do notify those sending the most promising work we review, however."

Music Mostly **blues/blues rock**, some **top 40/pop**, **rock** and **country**; also **hardcore punk** and **jazz-fusion**. Released *Starfoxx* (album), written and recorded by Starfoxx (rock); *Lady That Digs The Blues* (album), recorded by Big Al Jano's Blues Mafia Show (blues rock); and *Vol. III, Psychedelic Era. 1967-1969* (album), released 2002 on Hottrax. Other artists include Big Al Jano, Sammy Blue and Sheffield & Webb.

☑ IDOL RECORDS PUBLISHING

P.O. Box 720043, Dallas TX 75372. (214)826-4365. Fax: (214)370-5417. E-mail: info@idolrecords.c om. Website: www.Idol-Records.com. **Contact:** Erv Karwelis, president. Record company. Estab. 1992. Releases 2-3 singles, 30 LPs, 2-3 EPs and 15-20 CDs/year. Pays negotiable royalty to artists on contract; negotiable rate to publisher per song on record.

Distributed by Cargo and Hepcat Dist.

How to Contact See website at www.idolrecords.com for submission policy. No phone calls or e-mail follow-ups.

Music Mostly **rock**, **pop** and **alternative**. Released *Onward Quirky Soldiers* (album), recorded by Chomsky (alternative); *Distance and Clime* (album), recorded by Centro-Matic (alternative); and *Falling Hard in the Key of E* (album), recorded by Macavity (alternative), all released 2001 on Idol Records. Other artists include Pervis, Billyclub, Old 97's, Hoarse, Feisty Cadavers, The American Fuse and Watershed.

☐ IMAGINARY RECORDS

P.O. Box 66, Whites Creek TN 37189-0066. E-mail: jazz@imaginaryrecords.com. Website: www.im aginaryrecords.com. **Contact:** Lloyd Townsend, proprietor. Labels include Imaginary Records, Imaginary Jazz Records. Record company. Estab. 1981. Staff size: 1. Releases 1-3 CDs/year. Pays negotiable royalty to artists on contract; statutory rate to publisher per song on record.

Distributed by North Country, Harbor Record Export and Imaginary Distribution.

How to Contact *Write first to obtain permission to submit.* "We do not act as a publisher placing songs with artists." Prefers CD with 3-5 songs, cover letter and press clippings. Include SASE. Responds in 4 months if interested.

Music Mostly **mainstream jazz**, **swing jazz** and **classical**. Does not want country, rap, hip-hop or metal. Released *Fifth House* (album), recorded by New York Trio Project (mainstream jazz), released 2001; *Triologue* (album), recorded by Stevens, Siegel, and Ferguson (mainstream jazz), released 2001; and *Perspectives* (album), written and recorded by the Tom Dempsey/Tim Ferguson Quartet (jazz), released 2003.

Tips "Be patient, I'm slow. I'm primarily considering mainstream jazz or classical—other genre submissions are much less likely to get a response."

☑ ☒ ☑ INTERSCOPE/GEFFEN/A&M RECORDS

2220 Colorado Ave., Santa Monica CA 90404. (310)865-1000. Fax: (310)865-7908. Website: www.in terscoperecords.com. Labels include Death Row Records, Nothing Records, Rock Land, Almo Sounds, Aftermath Records and Trauma Records. Record company.

- As a result of the PolyGram and Universal merger, Geffen and A&M Records have been folded into Interscope Records.

How to Contact *Does not accept unsolicited submissions.*

Music Released *Worlds Apart*, recorded by . . . And You Will Know Us By The Trail Of Dead; and *Guero*, recorded by Beck. Other artists include U2, M.I.A, Keane, and Marilyn Manson.

☑ ☑ ISLAND/DEF JAM MUSIC GROUP

825 Eighth Ave., 29th Floor, New York NY 10019. (212)333-8000. Fax: (212)603-7654. Website: www.islanddefjam.com. **Los Angeles:** 8920 Sunset Blvd, 2nd Floor, Los Angeles CA 90069. (310)276-4500. Fax: (310)242-7023. Executive A&R: Paul Pontius. Labels include Mouth Almighty Records, Worldly/Triloka Records, Blackheart Records, Private Records, Slipdisc Records, Thirsty Ear, Blue Gorilla, Dubbly, Little Dog Records, Rounder and Capricorn Records. Record company.

How to Contact *Island/Def Jam Music Group* does not accept unsolicited submissions. Do not send material unless requested.

Music Artists include Bon Jovi, Ja Rule, Jay-Z and Ludacris.

☑ J RECORDS

745 Fifth Ave., 6th Floor, New York NY 10151. (646)840-5600. Website: www.jrecords.com.

How to Contact *J Records does not accept unsolicited submissions.*

Music Artists include Faithless, Alicia Keys, and Annie Lennox.

⊕ ◙ JUPITER RECORDS

Rinkermarkt 16, 80331 Munchen Germany. E-mail: contact@jupiter-records.de. Website: www.jup iter-records.de. **Owner:** Ralph Siegel. Record company and record producer.

How to Contact Submit demo tape or CD by mail. Unsolicited submissions are OK. SAE and IRC. Responds in 2 months.

Music Mostly **pop**, **rock** and **dance**; also **soul** and **Black music**.

Tips "If you believe that your song could be No. 1 on the charts, please submit it!"

☑ ◙ KAUPP RECORDS

P.O. Box 5474, Stockton CA 95205. (209)948-8186. **Contact:** Melissa Glenn. Record company, music publisher (Kaupps and Robert Publishing Co./BMI), management firm (Merri-Webb Productions) and record producer (Merri-Webb Productions). Estab. 1990. Releases 1 single and 4 LPs/year. Pays standard royalty to artists on contract; statutory rate to publisher per song on record.

Distributed by Merri-Webb Productions and Cal-Centron Distributing Co.

How to Contact *Write first and obtain permission to submit or to arrange personal interview.* Prefers cassette or VHS videocassette with 3 songs. Include SASE. Responds in 3 months.

Music Mostly **country**, **R&B** and **A/C rock**; also **pop**, **rock** and **gospel**. Released "I Thank You Father" and "On the Other Side" (singles by N. Merrihew/B. Bolin), recorded by Bruce Bolen; and "Did You Think That I Thought That You Liked Me" (single by N. Merrihew/B. Bolin), recorded by Cheryl, all on Kaupp Records.

◙ KILL ROCK STARS

120 N.E. State #418, Olympia WA 98501. E-mail: krs@killrockstars.com. Website: www.killrockstar s.com. **Contact:** Slim Moon, CEO. Record company. Estab. 1991. Releases 6-8 singles, 6 LPs, 4-6 EPs and 18 CDs/year. Pays 50% of net profit to artists on contract; negotiated rate to publisher per song on record.

Distributed by Mordam, Caroline, Dutch East India, Revolver, Bayside, Valley, Rotz, Pacific Coast One Stop and AEC.

How to Contact *Write first and obtain permission to submit.* Prefers CD. Does not return material.

Music Mostly **punk rock**, **neo-folk or anti-folk** and **spoken word**. Artists include Sleater-Kinney, Phranc, and Bikini Kill (pop guitar punk); *Julie Ruin*, written and recorded by Kathleen Hanna (punk); and *Frumpies One Piece*, written and recorded by Frumpies (punk), all on Kill Rock Stars. Other artists include Thrones, Emily's Sassy Lime, Long Hind Legs, Mocket and Free Kitten.

Tips "Send a self-released CD. Prefer working with touring acts, so let us know if you are playing Olympia, Seattle or Portland. Particularly interested in young artists with indie-rock background."

◙ KINGSTON RECORDS

15 Exeter Rd., Kingston NH 03848. (603)642-8493. E-mail: kingstonrecords@adelphia.net. Website: www.kingstonrecords.com. **Contact:** Harry Mann, coordinator. Record company, record producer and music publisher (Strawberry Soda Publishing/ASCAP). Estab. 1988. Releases 3-4 singles, 2-3 12″ singles, 3 LPs and 2 CDs/year. Pays 3-5% royalty to artists on contract; statutory rate to publisher per song.

How to Contact *Write first and obtain permission to submit.* Prefers cassette, DAT, 15 ips reel-to-reel or videocassette with 3 songs and lyric sheet. Does not return material. Responds in 2 months.

Music Mostly **rock**, **country** and **pop**; "no heavy metal." Released *Two Lane Highway* and *Armand's Way* (albums), written and recorded by Armand Learay (rock); and *Count the Stars* (album), written and recorded by Doug Mitchell, released 1999, all on Kingston Records.

Tips "Working only with N.E. and local talent."

◙ LARI-JON RECORDS

P.O. Box 216, Rising City NE 68658. (402)542-2336. **Contact:** Larry Good, owner. Record company, management firm (Lari-Jon Promotions), music publisher (Lari-Jon Publishing/BMI) and record producer (Lari-Jon Productions). Estab. 1967. Staff size: 1. Releases 15 singles and 5 LPs/year. Pays varying royalty to artists on contract.

How to Contact Submit demo tape by mail. Unsolicited submissions are OK. Prefers CD's with 5 songs and lyric sheet. Include SASE. Responds in 2 months.

Music Mostly **country**, **gospel-Southern** and **'50s rock**. Released "Glory Bound Train" (single), written and recorded by Tom Campbell; *The Best of Larry Good* (album), written and recorded by Larry Good (country); and *Her Favorite Songs* (album), written and recorded by Johnny Nace (country), all on Lari-Jon Records. Other artists include Kent Thompson and Brenda Allen.

⬛ LARK RECORD PRODUCTIONS, INC.

P.O. Box 35726, Tulsa OK 74153. (918)786-8896. Fax: (918)786-8897. E-mail: janajae@janajae.com. Website: www.janajae.com. **Contact:** Kathleen Pixley, vice president. Record company, music publisher (Jana Jae Music/BMI), management firm (Jana Jae Enterprises) and record producer (Lark Talent and Advertising). Estab. 1980. Staff size: 8. Pays negotiable royalty to artists on contract; statutory rate to publisher per song on record.

How to Contact Submit demo tape by mail. Unsolicited submissions are OK. Prefers CD or VHS videocassette with 3 songs and lead sheets. Does not return material. Responds only if interested.

Music Mostly **country**, **bluegrass** and **classical**; also **instrumentals**. Released "Fiddlestix" (single by Jana Jae); "Mayonnaise" (single by Steve Upfold); and "Flyin' South" (single by Cindy Walker), all recorded by Jana Jae on Lark Records (country). Other artists include Syndi, Hotwire and Matt Greif.

⬛ ⬜ LOCK

Coachhouse, Mansion Farm, Liverton Hill, Sandway, Maidstone, Kent ME172NJ England. E-mail: info@eddielock.com. Website: www.eddielock.co.uk. **Contact:** Eddie Lock, A&R. Record company, music publisher (Lock 'n' S) and record producer (Carpe Diem). Estab. 1988. Staff size: 2. Releases 10 singles/year. Pays negotiable royalty to artists on contract; statutory rate to publisher per song on record.

Distributed by Unique and Essential.

How to Contact Submit demo CD by mail. Unsolicited submissions are OK. Prefers CD. Does not return material.

Music Mostly **dance** and **house**. Released "Quiero Bailar La Salsa" (single by Eddie Lock/Dylan Burns), recorded by Lock & Burns (house); "Work So Hard" (single by Dylan Burns/James Lock), recorded by Yardmen (house), both released 2004 on Lock; and "Situation" (single by Robbie Rivera/Marc Sacheli), recorded by Kings of Tribal (Robbie Rivera) (tribal), released 2003 on Lock.

⬛ LUCIFER RECORDS, INC.

P.O. Box 263, Brigantine NJ 08203-0263. (609)266-2623. Fax: (609)266-4870. **Contact:** Ron Luciano, president. Labels include TVA Records. Record company, music publisher (Ciano Publishing and Legz Music), record producer (Pete Fragale and Tony Vallo), management firm and booking agency (Ron Luciano Music Co. and TVA Productions). "Lucifer Records has offices in South Jersey; Palm Beach, Florida; and Las Vegas, Nevada."

How to Contact *Call or write to arrange personal interview.* Prefers cassette with 4-8 songs. Include SASE. Responds in 3 weeks.

Music Mostly **dance**, **easy listening**, **MOR**, **rock**, **soul** and **top 40/pop**. Released "I Who Have Nothing," (single), by Spit-N-Image (rock); "Lucky" (single), by Legz (rock); and "Love's a Crazy Game" (single), by Voyage (disco/ballad). Other artists include Bobby Fisher, Jerry Denton, FM, Zeke's Choice, Al Caz, Joe Vee and Dana Nicole.

⬛ ⬛ ⬛ MAKOCHE RECORDING COMPANY

208 N. Fourth St., Bismarck ND 58501. (701)223-7316. Fax: (701)255-8287. E-mail: info@makoche. com. Website: www.makoche.com. **Contact:** Lisa Dowhaniuk, A&R assistant. Labels include Makoche and Chairmaker's Rush. Record company and recording studio. Estab. 1995. Staff size: 5. Releases 4 CDs/year. Pays negotiable royalty to artists on contract; statutory rate to publisher per song on record.

Distributed by DNA, Music Design, Four Winds Trading, Zango Music and New Leaf Distribution.

• Makoche is noted for releasing quality music based in the Native American tradition. Recognized by the Grammys, Nammys, New Age Voice Music Awards and C.O.V.R. Music Awards.
How to Contact *Call first and obtain permission to submit.* "Please submit only fiddle and American Indian-influenced music." Include SASE. Responds in 2 months.
Music Mostly **Native American**, **flute** and **fiddle**. Released *Edge of America* (album), written and recorded by Annie Humphrey (folk), released 2004 on Makoche; and *Togo* (album), written and recorded by Andrew Vasquez (Native American flute), released on Makoche 2004; *Way of Life* (album), recorded by Lakota Thunder (drum group), released on Makoche 2004. Other artists include Gary Stroutsos, Bryan Akipa, Keith Bear, Andrew Vasquez, Lakota Thunder, Sissy Goodhouse and Kevin Locke.
Tips "We are a small label with a dedication to quality."

☑ MALACO RECORDS
P.O. Box 9287, Jackson MS 39286-9287. (601)982-4522. E-mail: malaco@malaco.com. Website: www.malaco.com. Executive Director: Jerry Mannery. Record company. Estab. 1986. Releases 20 projects/year. Pays variable royalty to artists on contract; statutory rate to publisher per song.
How to Contact Submit demo tape by mail. Unsolicited submissions are OK. Prefers cassette or CD. Does not return material.
Music Mostly **traditional** and **contemporary gospel**. Artists include Mississippi Mass Choir, The Bonner Brothers, Lou Rawls, Men of Standard, Mississippi Children's Choir, Bryan Wilson, The Pilgrim Jubilees, Lillian Lilly, Dorothy Norwood, The Sensational Nightengales, The Angelic Gospel Singers, Carolyn Traylor, Christopher Brinson and Rudolph Stanfield & New Revelation.

☒ ☑ MCA NASHVILLE
(formerly MCA Records), 60 Music Square E., Nashville TN 37203. (615)244-8944, Fax: (615)880-7447. Website: www.mca-nashville.com. Record company and music publisher (MCA Music).
How to Contact MCA Nashville cannot accept unsolicited submissions.
Music Artists include Tracy Byrd, George Strait, Vince Gill, The Mavericks and Trisha Yearwood.

☒ ☐ MEGAFORCE RECORDS
(formerly Megaforce Worldwide Entertainment), P.O. Box 1955, New York NY 10113. (212)741-8861. Fax: (509)757-8602. E-mail: gregaforce@aol.com. Website: www.megaforcerecords.com. **Contact:** Robert John, President. General Manager: Missi Callazzo. Record company. Estab. 1983. Staff size: 5. Releases 6 CDs/year. Pays various royalties to artists on contract; 3/4 statutory rate to publisher per song on record.
Distributed by Red/Sony Distribution.
How to Contact *Contact first and obtain permission to submit.*
Music Mostly **rock**. Artists include Clutch and S.O.D.

☑ METAL BLADE RECORDS
2828 Cochran St., Suite 302, Simi Valley CA 93065. (805)522-9111. Fax: (805)522-9380. E-mail: metalblade@metalblade.com. Website: www.metalblade.com. Record company. Estab. 1982. Releases 20 LPs, 2 EPs and 20 CDs/year. Pays negotiable royalty to artists on contract.
How to Contact Submit demo CD by mail. Unsolicited submissions are OK. CD with 3 songs. Does not return material. Responds in 3 months.
Music Mostly **heavy metal** and **industrial**; also **hardcore**, **gothic** and **noise**. Released "Gallery of Suicide," recorded by Cannibal Corpse; "Voo Doo," recorded by King Diamond; and "A Pleasant Shade of Gray," recorded by Fates Warning, all on Metal Blade Records. Other artists include As I Lay Dying, The Red Chord, The Black Dahlia Murder, and Unearth.
Tips "Metal Blade is known throughout the underground for quality metal-oriented acts."

☑ MIGHTY RECORDS
150 West End, Suite 6-D, New York NY 10023. Manager: Danny Darrow. Labels include Mighty Sounds & Filmworks. Record company, music publisher (Rockford Music Co./BMI, Stateside Music

Co./BMI and Corporate Music Publishing Co./ASCAP) and record producer (Danny Darrow). Estab. 1958. Releases 1-2 singles, 1-2 12″ singles and 1-2 LPs/year. Pays standard royalty to artists on contract; statutory rate to publisher per song on record.

How to Contact Submit demo tape by mail. Unsolicited submissions are OK. ''No phone calls.'' Prefers cassette or CD with 2 songs and lyric sheet. Does not return material. Responds in 1 month only if interested.

Music Mostly **pop**, **country** and **dance**; also **jazz**. Released ''Carnival Nights'' (single by Vincent C. Delucia and Raymond Squillacote) from *Fallin In Love* (album), recorded by Danny Darrow (country); ''Motherless Child'' (adaptation by Danny Darrow) from *Great Folk Songs* (album), recorded by Danny Darrow (folk); and ''Impulse'' (single by Danny Darrow) from *Love To Dance* (album), recorded by Danny Darrow (Euro jazz), all released 2004 on Mighty Records.

ⓝ ⊘ MINOTAUR RECORDS

P.O. Box 620, Redwood Estates CA 95044. Estab. 1987. (408)353-1006. E-mail: dminotaur@hotmail. com. Website: www.cdbaby.com/ceglio. **Contact:** A&R. Record company. Estab. 1987. Staff size: 2. Releases 2 CDs/year. Pays statutory royalty to publishers per song on record. Distributed by CDbaby.com. Member of BMI, ASCAP, NARAS, TAXI.

How to Contact We only accept material referred to us by a reputable industry source (manager, entertainment attorney, etc.). Does not return submissions. Responds only if interested.

Music Mostly **adult contemporary**, **country**, **dance**. Also **easy rock**, **pop**. Does not want rap, heavy metal, jazz, hip-hop, hard rock and instrumentals. ''Maybe Love'' written by D. Baumgartner and Steven Worthy, from the *Dancing in the Dark* (album), recorded by Andrew Ceglio (pop/dance); ''That Was A Great Affair'' written by Tab Morales and Ron Dean Tomich, from the *This Side of Heaven* (album), recorded by Doug Magpiong (adult contemporary); ''Baby Blue Eyes and Tight Levis'' written by Ron Dean Tomich, from the *This Side of Nashville* (album), recorded by Candy Chase (country).

⊘ MISSILE RECORDS FILM & TV, INC.

P.O. Box 5537, Kreole Station, Moss Point MS 39563-1537. (228)475-0059. ''No collect calls!'' Estab. 1974. **Contact:** Joe F. Mitchell, executive vice president/general manager. First Vice President: Justin F. Mitchell. Second Vice President: Jonita F. Mitchell. Record company and music publisher (Abalorn Music/ASCAP, Bay Ridge Publishing/BMI) and record producer. Releases 28 singles and 10 LPs/year. Pays ''10-16% royalty to new artists on contract, higher rate to established artists''; statutory rate to publisher for each record sold. ''Missile Records has National and International Distribution.''

- Also see the listing for Bay Ridge Publishing and Abalorn Music in the Music Publishers section.

Distributed by Star Sound Music Distributors, Hits Unlimited, Action Music Sales, Inc., Allegro Corp., Big Easy Distributing, Select-O-Hits, Total Music Distributors, Music Network, Impact Music, Universal Record Distributing Corporation, Dixie Rak Records & Tapes, Navaree Corporation, Curtis Wood Distributors, Big Daddy Music Distribution Co., ATM Distributors, HL Distribution, Bayside Distribution, Blue Sky Distribution, Alamo Record Distributors and MDI Distribution.

How to Contact *''Please don't send us anything until you contact us by phone or in writing and receive submission instructions. You must present your songs the correct way to get a reply.* No registered mail—no exceptions!'' Always whenever you write to us, be sure you include a #10 business-size envelope addressed back to you with a first class USA postage stamp on the envelope. We reply back to you from the SASE. All songs sent for review must include sufficient return postage. No reply made back to you without SASE or return of material without sufficient return postage. **Absolutely no reply postcards—only SASE**. If you only write lyrics, do not submit. We only accept completed songs, so you must find a collaborator. We are not interested in reviewing homemade recordings.'' Prefers CD (first choice) or cassette with 3-8 songs and lyrics to songs submitted. Responds in 2 months. A good quality demo recording will always get preference over a poor recording.

Music All types and styles of songs. Released ''Excuse Me Lady'' and ''When She Left Me'' (singles by Rich Wilson); "Everyone Gets A Chance (To Lose In Romance)" and "I'm So Glad We Found Each Other" (singles by Joe F. Mitchell), from *Excuse Me Lady* (album), recorded by Rich Wilson (country/western); "Rose Up On A Stem" (single by Joe F. Mitchell), from *My Kind of Kountry* (album), recorded by Jerry Piper (country); "Southern Born" and "Old Folks Know" (singles by Christian Ramsey); "Innocent Little One" (single by Bob Levy), "Pretty Lady Come Closer" (single by David L. Resler) and "She Was Sittin' Pretty" (single by Jim Hendricks) all from *If It Takes All Night* (album), recorded by Christian Ramsey (modern pop country), all released on Missile Records. Other artists include Moto (reggae), Jackie Lambarella (country pop), Sarah Cooper (pop/R&B), Della Reed (contemporary Christian), Metellica (heavy metal), Coco Hodge (alternative) and Lady Love (rap).

Tips "Our doors are always open to young recording artists who are exceptionally talented and want to make a name for themselves in the music business. Your success is our success. We will work with you to reach your goal. We also are in the business of getting your professionally-recorded album of 10-12 well-produced and well-written, radio-ready songs placed with record companies in the USA and foreign countries for the possibility of record deals. Here is what we have gotten for some artists: $850,000 record deal for Charity (religious singing group) on Big Easy (USA) in 2001; $500,000 record deal for Vance Greek on Dime-A-Dozen (Germany) in 2002; and a $150,000 record deal for Randell Ruthledge (country) on Dime-A-Dozen (Germany) in 2003. Two more artists are under consideration as of 2004, and others may be considered. Missile Records, Abalorn Music (ASCAP) and Bay Ridge Publishing Co. (BMI) are listed in some well-known publications such as the *Billboard International Buyer's Guide*, *Mix Master Directory*, *Industrial Source Book*, *Pollstar*, *Yellow Pages of Rock* and other publications. Some well-known recording artists born and raised in Mississippi include Elvis Presley, Conway Twitty, B.B. King and Faith Hill. The Moss Point, MS area music scene is also home to nationally-known rock group Three Doors Down, who sold more than 10 million of their CD albums and singles. Singers and songwriters thinking about doing professional recording, give us a call before you make that move. We can save you money, time, headaches, heartaches and troubles you may run into. We know what to do and how to do it to benefit you and get the best results."

☐ MODAL MUSIC, INC.℠

P.O. Box 6473, Evanston IL 60204-6473. (847)864-1022. E-mail: info@modalmusic.com. Website: www.modalmusic.com. President: Terran Doehrer. Assistant: J. Distler. Record company and agent. Estab. 1988. Staff size: 2. Releases 1-2 LPs/year. Pays negotiable royalty to artists on contract; negotiable rate to publisher per song on record.

How to Contact Submit demo tape by mail. Unsolicited submissions are OK. Prefers CD or cassette with bio, PR, brochures, any info about artist and music. Does not return material. Responds in 4 months.

Music Mostly **ethnic** and **world**. Released *Dance The Night Away* (album by T. Doehrer), recorded by Balkan Rhythm Band™; *Sid Beckerman's Rumanian (D. Jacobs)* (album), recorded by Jutta & The Hi-Dukes™; and *Hold Whatcha Got* (album), recorded by Razzemetazz™, all on Modal Music Records. Other artists include Ensemble M'chaiya™, Nordland Band™ and Terran's Greek Band™.

Tips "Please note our focus is ethnic. You waste your time and money by sending us any other type of music. If you are unsure of your music fitting our focus, please call us before sending anything. Put your name and contact info on every item you send!"

⚫ ⚫ MONTICANA RECORDS

P.O. Box 702, Snowdon Station, Montreal QC H3X 3X8 Canada. **Contact:** David P. Leonard, general manager. Record company, record producer (Monticana Productions) and music publisher (Montina Music/SOCAN). Estab. 1963. Staff size: 1. Pays negotiable royalty to artists on contract.

How to Contact Submit demo tape by mail. Unsolicited submissions are OK. Prefers CD. Include SASE.

Music Mostly **top 40**, **blues**, **country**, **dance-oriented**, **easy listening**, **folk** and **gospel**; also **jazz**, **MOR**, **progressive**, **R&B**, **rock** and **soul**.

Tips "Be excited and passionate about what you do. Be professional."

NATION RECORDS INC.

6351 W. Montrose 333, Chicago IL 60634. E-mail: philip@nationrecords.com. Website: www.natio nrecords.com. **Contact:** Phil Vaughan, A&R. Record company. Estab. 1996. Releases 5 CDs/year. Pays negotiable royalty to artists on contract; statutory rate to publisher per song on record.

Distributed by Midwest Artist Distribution.

How to Contact *Contact first and obtain permission to submit.* Prefers CD with lyric sheet. Does not return material. Responds in 6 months.

Music All types. Released *American Stories* (album by Bob Young); and *Steve & Johnnie Present Life After Dark* (album), both on Nation Records Inc. Other artists include The Buckinghams, Pete Special and World Class Noise.

NBT RECORDS

228 Morgan Lane, Berkeley Springs WV 25411-3475. (304)258-3656. E-mail: nbtoys@verizon.net. **Contact:** John S. Newbraugh, owner. Record company, music publisher (Newbraugh Brothers Music/BMI, NBT Music/ASCAP). Estab. 1967. Staff size: 1. Releases 4 singles and 52 CDs/year. Pays negotiable royalty to artists on contract; statutory royalty to publishers per song on record.

Distributed by "Distribution depends on the genre of the release. Our biggest distributor is perhaps the artists themselves, for the most part, depending on the genre of the release. We do have product in some stores and on the Internet as well."

How to Contact Submit demo by mail. Unsolicited submissions are OK. Prefers CD or cassette with any amount of songs, lyric sheet and cover letter. Include SASE. Responds in 4-6 weeks.

Music Mostly **rockabilly, hillbilly, folk** and **bluegrass**; also **rock, country** and **gospel**. Does not want any music with vulgar lyrics. "We will accept all genres of music except songs that contain vulgar language." Released "Momma Likes To Boogie" (single by Dale Brooks) from *Hot Rod Daddy* (album), recorded by The Rhythmatics (rockabilly); "Nonstop Holiday" (single by Kurt Christensen) from *Don't Wear Me Out* (album), recorded by The Gyros (rock); and "Clackty Clack" (single by A.V. "Sonny" May/Steven Cooper) from *Ride the Train—Volume Three* (album), recorded by William Ray (country), all released 2004 on NBT Records.

Tips "We are best known for our rockabilly releases. Reviews of our records can be found on both the American and European rockabilly websites. Our 'registered' trademark is a train. From time to time, we put out a CD with various artists featuring original songs that use trains as part of their theme. We use all genres of music for our train releases. We have received train songs from various parts of the world. All submissions on this topic are welcomed."

NERVOUS RECORDS

5 Sussex Crescent, Northolt, Middlesex UB5 4DL England. 44(20)8423 7373. E-mail: nervous@com puserve.com. Website: www.nervous.co.uk. **Contact:** R. Williams, managing director. Record company (Rage Records), record producer and music publisher (Nervous Publishing and Zorch Music). Member: MCPS, PRS, PPL, ASCAP, NCB. Releases 10 CDs/year. Pays 8-12% royalty to artists on contract; statutory rate to publisher per song on records. Royalties paid directly to US songwriters and artists or through US publishing or recording affiliate.

• Nervous Records' publishing company, Nervous Publishing, is listed in the Music Publishers section.

How to Contact Submit demo tape by mail. Unsolicited submissions are OK. Prefers cassette with 4-15 songs and lyric sheet. SAE and IRC. Responds in 3 weeks.

Music Mostly **psychobilly** and **rockabilly**. "No heavy rock, AOR, stadium rock, disco, soul, pop—only wild rockabilly and psychobilly." Released "Extra Chrome," written and recorded by Johnny Black; "It's Still Rock 'N' Roll to Me," written and recorded by The Time. Other artists include Restless Wild and Taggy Tones.

NEURODISC RECORDS, INC.

3801 N. University Dr., Suite 403, Ft. Lauderdale FL 33351. (954)572-0289. Fax: (954)572-2874. E-mail: info@neurodisc.com. Website: www.neurodisc.com. President: Tom O'Keefe. Label Manager: John Wai. Record company and music publisher. Estab. 1990. Releases 3 singles, 10 LPs and

10 CDs/year. Pays negotiable royalty to artists on contract; 75% "to start" to publisher per song on record.

Distributed by Capital Records/EMI.

How to Contact Submit demo CD by mail. Unsolicited submissions are OK. Prefers CD, DAT or VHS videocassette. Include SASE. Responds only if interested.

Music Mostly **electronic**, **dance**, **New Age** and **electro-bass**; also **rap**. Released albums from Peplab, Etro Anime, Tastexperience, Ryan Farish & Amethystium, as well as Bass Lo-Ryders and Bass Crunk. Other artists include Eric Hansen, Bella Sonus and NuSound as well as DJ's Suzy Solar, Vicious Vic, Andy Hughes and Scott Stubbs.

☑ NIGHTMARE RECORDS

7751 Greenwood Dr., St. Paul MN 55112. (763)784-9654. Fax: (763)784-7914. E-mail: info@nightm arerecords.com. Website: www.nightmarerecords.com. **Contact**: Lance King. Record company, distributor and management firm (Jupiter Productions). Estab. 1983. Pays 10-15% royalty to artists on contract.

Distributed by US: Best Buy stores, Sam Goody/Musicland/Media Play/On Cue, Blockbuster Music, Nightmare-Records.com, Dream Disc, Perris Records, Dynasty Music, Two Guys Music, Wildside Imports, Molten Metal, Impulse Music, Alta Mira, Amazon.com, D.S.B. Music, Echo Rider/Music Works, Generations Underground, Lasers Edge, CD Baby, Outer Limites, Moremetal.com, Sentinel Steel, Restless & Wild, CD's and More, Amazingcds.com, Sounds of Metal, Seven Gates, Must Have Music, Oarfin Records & Distribution, Select-O-Hits, Neh Records, Phoenix Records, Metal Mayhem Music, Century Media, The Sounds of Metal, Rasputin Music, Loud Distribution. Foreign: Bertus Distribution (Netherlands), Bee Bee Records/Distribee (Netherlands), Mega Rock Distribution (Sweden), Nordic Metal (Denmark), Scrape Records (Canada), HMV (Canada), Lament Distribution (Mexico), Steel Gallery (Greece), Sleaszy Rider (Greece), Sun Records, Sounds Machine (Italy), Heavencross (Spain), Leyenda (Spain), The Rock Shop (Spain), JPM Music (Chile), Rising Sun (Germany), Lobel Music (GeK), Concrete (Germany), War of Horns Records (Germany), Discos Sun Records (Spain), Rockhouse Records (Holland), Hellion Records (Germany), DSB (Germany), AOR Basement (UK), Diskheaven (Japan), Sheer Records (Czech Republic), Music Hunter (Finland), Heavy Sound Rock Shop (Sweden), Lament Distributions (Mexico). Christian: Holy Rollers, The Crossing (CDHC), Christian Demo Clearing House, M8, Spring Arbor, C.M.P. (Australia), Rugged Cross, Rad Rockers, Bibles Plus, Ultimatum Music, Blast Beats Music, Nordic Mission, Something More Christian Bookstore, ClassicGod.com.

How to Contact Submit demo tape by mail. Unsolicited submissions are OK. Prefers cassette or CD with 3 songs. Include brief bio, photo and press clippings (if available). Does not return material. Responds only if interested.

Music Mostly **hard rock-metal**, with a special interest in **progressive metal**. Released *Untitled* (by King/Barilla), recorded by The Kings Machine (rock); *From Cradle to Grave* (by Petrick/Cassidy), recorded by Malicious (rock); and *Pavlov's Dog's* (by Stevenson/Christensen), recorded by Conditioned Response (rock), all on Nightmare. Current acts include Godhead (Southern fried grunge), Visionary (progressive metal), Balance of Power (progressive metal), Cains Alibi (power metal), Empyria (progressive power metal), Antithesis (progressive thrash metal), USM (Nu-metal) and Sonic Boom (industrial dance).

Tips "Be patient, persistent and positive! We're busy and we know what were looking for, if we like what we hear, we'll call you ASAP."

☑ OGLIO RECORDS

P.O. Box 404, Redondo Beach CA 90277. Fax: (310)791-8670. Record company. Estab. 1992. Releases 20 LPs and 20 CDs/year. Pays negotiable royalty to artist on contract; statutory rate to publisher per song on record.

How to Contact No unsolicited demos.

Music Mostly **alternative rock** and **comedy**. Released *Shine* (album), recorded by Cyndi Lauper (pop); *Live At The Roxy* (album), recorded by Brian Wilson (rock); *Team Leader* (album), recorded by George Lopez (comedy).

□ ONLY NEW AGE MUSIC, INC.

8033 Sunset Blvd. #472, Hollywood CA 90046. (323)851-3355. Fax: (323)851-7981. E-mail: info@ne
wagemusic.com. Website: www.newagemusic.com. or www.newageuniverse.com. **Contact:** Suzanne Doucet, president. Record company, music publisher and consulting firm. Estab. 1987.
How to Contact *Call first and obtain permission to submit.* Does not return material.
Music Mostly **New Age**; also **world music**.
Tips "You should have a marketing strategy and at least a small budget for marketing your product."

◙ OUTSTANDING RECORDS

P.O. Box 2111, Huntington Beach CA 92647. (714)377-7447 or (800)749-8469. Fax: (714)377-7468.
Website: www.outstandingmusic.com. **Contact:** Earl Beecher, owner. Labels include Morrhythm.
Record company, music publisher (Earl Beecher Publishing/BMI and Beecher Music Publishing/
ASCAP) and record producer (Earl Beecher). Estab. 1968. Staff size: 1. Releases 40 CDs/year. Pays
$2/CD royalty to artists on contract; statutory rate to publisher per song on record.
Distributed by Sites on the Internet and "through distribution companies who contact me directly,
especially from overseas."
How to Contact Submit demo by mail. Unsolicited submissions are OK. Prefers CD or videocassette
(VHS) with 3 songs, lyric sheet, photo and cover letter. Include SASE. Responds in 3 weeks.
Music Mostly **jazz**, **rock** and **country**; also **everything else especially Latin**. Does not want music
with negative, anti-social or immoral messages.
Tips "Keep selections short (three to three and a half minutes. Short intros and fade outs, if any).
No dirty language. Do not encourage listeners to use drugs, alcohol or engage in immoral behavior.
I'm especially looking for upbeat, happy, danceable music."

◲ □ P. & N. RECORDS

61 Euphrasia Dr., Toronto ON M6B 3V8 Canada. (416)782-5768. Fax: (416)782-7170. E-mail: panfilo
@sympatico.ca. **Contact:** Panfilo Di Matteo, president, A&R. Record company, record producer
and music publisher (Lilly Music Publishing). Estab. 1993. Staff size: 2. Releases 10 singles, 20 12″
singles, 15 LPs, 20 EPs and 15 CDs/year. Pays 25-35% royalty to artists on contract; statutory rate
to publisher per song on record.
How to Contact Submit demo by mail. Unsolicited submissions are OK. Prefers cassette or videocassette with 3 songs and lyric or lead sheet. Does not return material. Responds in 1 month only if
interested.
Music Mostly **dance**, **ballads** and **rock**. Released *Only This Way* (album), written and recorded by
Angelica Castro; *The End of Us* (album), written and recorded by Putz, both on P. & N. Records
(dance); and "Lovers" (single by Marc Singer), recorded by Silvana (dance), released 2001 on P.
and N. Records.

ℕ ◙ PAINT CHIP RECORDS

P.O. Box 12401, Albany NY 12212. (518)765-4027. E-mail: paintchipr@aol.com. **Contact:** Dominick
Campana, owner/producer. Record/production company. Estab. 1992. Staff size: 1. Releases 2
CDs/year. Pays negotiable royalty to artists on contract; statutory rate to publisher per song on
record.
Distributed by Paint Chip Records.
How to Contact Submit demo tape by mail. Unsolicited submissions are OK. Prefers cassette with
4 songs. Does not return material. Responds in several weeks only if interested.
Music Mostly "**alternative**" **guitar rock** (bands). Released "Hollywood" (single by Pendergast)
from *WEQXclusives* (album), recorded by The Wait (alternative rock), released 2001 on Arms;
Holding on Line One (album by Pendergast/Barnum), recorded by The Wait, released 2001 on
Paint Chip; and *Dear Soul* (album by Pendergast/Barnum), recorded by The Wait, released 2000
on Paint Chip.
Tips "Do not submit music if you haven't heard of any of the artists on this label. Do not submit

music if you are not currently performing. Do not submit music if you don't think your work is absolutely amazing. Do not phone without written permission.''

◑ PICKWICK/MECCA/INTERNATIONAL RECORDS
P.O. Box 725, Daytona Beach FL 32115. (386)252-4849. Fax: (386)252-7402. E-mail: CharlesVickers @aol.com. or KingofKingsCV@aol.com. **Contact:** Clarence Dunklin, president. Record company and music publisher (Pritchett Publications). Estab. 1980. Releases 20 singles, 30 LPs and 30 CDs/ year. Pays 5-10% royalty to artists on contract; negotiable rate to publisher per song on record.
How to Contact Submit demo tape by mail. Unsolicited submissions are OK. Prefers cassette with 12 songs and lyric or lead sheet. Does not return material.
Music Mostly **gospel**, **disco** and **rock/pop**; also **country**, **ballads** and **rap**. Released *Give It To Me Baby* (album by Loris Doby), recorded by Gladys Knight; *Baby I Love You* (album), written and recorded by Joe Simmon; and *I Love Sweetie* (album by Doris Doby), recorded by Bobby Blane.

☑ ◑ PLATEAU MUSIC
P.O. Box 947, White House TN 37188. (615)654-8131. Fax: (615)654-8207. E-mail: nville93@comca st.com. Website: www.plateaumusic.com. **Contact:** Tony Mantor, owner. Record company and record producer. Estab. 1990. Staff size: 1. Pays negotiable royalty to artists on contract; statutory rate to publisher per song on record.
How to Contact Submit demo by mail. Unsolicited submissions are OK. Prefers CD with 4 songs and lyric sheet. Does not return material. Responds only if interested. ''Include an e-mail address and we will respond quicker.''
Music Mostly **country**, **R&B** and **rock/pop**. Released ''On My Way to You'' (single) from *On My Way to You* (album), recorded by Nina Sharp (country), released 2003-2004; ''Child of the City'' (single by Michael Constantino) (rock/pop), released 2004; ''Fly'' (single) from *Did You Miss Me*, recorded by Rani (R&B), released 2004-2005, all on Plateau Music; ''Hero At Home'' from *Hero At Home* (album), recorded by April Taylor (country), released 2005 on Plateau Music. Other artists include Carlynne DeVine, Nina Sharp, Charles Walsh and Jason Lee Ward.
Tips ''Be prepared for hard work. The music business is not easy, if it was everyone would be doing it. Plateau Music develops and manages the client until they are ready to be shopped to potential management and major record labels. We record only a few singles per year. We impress the music industry with the quality of our singers not the quantity of our singers. The focus at Plateau Music is to get the singer radio ready and radio friendly so the singer will have an opportunity for success with their music career. We are honest and straight-forward in our approach with no sugar-coating. We tell you what you need to hear not what you want to hear, so prepare yourself for hard work.''

⊕ ☑ ◑ PLAYBONES RECORDS
Symphony House, Eppendorfer Weg 7, D-20259 Hamburg Germany. (040)22716552 + -53. Fax: (040)22716554. E-mail: mento_music@t-online.de. **Contact:** Arno H. van Vught, managing director. Producer: Anna C. Nova. Labels include Rondo Records. Record company, music publisher (Mento Music Group) and record producer (Arteg Productions). Estab. 1975. Releases 30 CDs/year. Pays 8-16% royalty to artists on contract; statutory rate to publisher per song on record.
How to Contact Submit demo by mail. Unsolicited submissions are OK. Prefers CD-R with 3-4 songs. Put your strongest/best song first. ''Put your name and address on the inlay card of the CD. Tell us in a typed cover letter what you want/what you are looking for.'' Does not return material. Responds in 3 weeks.
Music Mostly **instrumentals**, **country** and **jazz**; also **background music**, **rock** and **gospel**. Released *Paradise* (album), written and recorded by Anna C. Nova (pop); ''Vergessen wir die Mark'' (single by DP/Volker Frank), recorded by Volker Frank (pop); and *Lord of the Dance* (album), written and recorded by Wolfgang Bauer (world music), all released 2003/2004 on Playbones Records. Other artists include Ellen Obier, Volker Frank, Dianna Jean, Bianca 4 Harry.

☑ ◻ PMG RECORDS

P.O. Box 816, Van Buren Township MI 48152. E-mail: prejippie@comcast.net. Website: www.presji ppie.com. **Contact:** Bruce Henderson, president. Record company, music publisher (Prejippie Music Group/BMI) and record producer (PMG Productions, Prejippie Music Group). Estab. 1990. Staff size: 3. Releases 6-12 12″ singles, 2 LPs and 2 EPs/year. Pays 40% royalty to artists on contract; statutory rate to publisher per song on record.

- Publishes *Direct Hitz*, a newsletter "where other independents can learn how to work effectively in the music business today."

Distributed by Dancefloor and Win.

How to Contact Submit demo tape by mail. Unsolicited submissions are OK. Prefers CD or VHS videocassette with 3-4 songs and lyric sheet. "Include photo if possible. No calls please." Include SASE. Responds in 6 weeks.

Music Mostly **funk/rock**, **alternative R&B**, **alternative rock**, **experimental** and **techno/dance**. Released *Tony Webb's Bass Christmas* (album), written and recorded by Tony Webb (alternative jazz) on PMG Records. Other artists include Urban Transit and the Prejippies.

Tips "Be very original in your approach to a song: concentrate on creating an interesting arrangement; concentrate on having at least one good hook; and put some thought into creating interesting lyrical themes."

◙ POP RECORD RESEARCH

10 Glen Ave., Norwalk CT 06850. E-mail: horar@earthlink.net. Director: Gary Theroux. Estab. 1962. Pays statutory rate to publisher per song on record.

- Also see their listing in the Organizations section.

How to Contact Submit demo tape by mail. Unsolicited submissions are OK. Prefers CD, cassette or VHS videocassette. Does not return material.

Music Mostly **pop**, **country** and **R&B**. Released "The Declaration" (single by Theroux-Gilbert), recorded by An American; "Thoughts From a Summer Rain" (single), written and recorded by Bob Gilbert, both on Bob Records; and "Tiger Paws" (single), written and recorded by Bob Gilbert on BAL Records. Other artists include Gary and Joan, The Nightflight Singers and Ruth Zimmerman.

Tips "Help us keep our biographical file on you and your career current by sending us updated bios/press kits, etc. They are most helpful to writers/researchers in search of accurate information on your success."

☑ ◙ PPL ENTERTAINMENT GROUP

P.O. Box 261488, Encino, CA 91426. (818)506-8533. Fax: (818)506-8534. Website: www.pplentertai nmentgroup.com. E-mail: a&r/labels@pplzmi.com. **Contact:** Cisco Crowe, vice president A&R. Vice President A&R: Dakota Kelly. Vice President, A&R: Kaitland Diamond. General Manager: Jim Sellavain. President, Creative: Suzette Cuseo. Labels include Bouvier, Credence and JBK. Record company, music publisher (Pollybyrd Publications), management firm (Sa'mall Management) and distributor (Malibu Trading Company). Estab. 1979. Staff size: 15. Releases 10-30 singles, 12 12″ singles, 6 LPs and 6 CDs/year. Pays 10-15% royalty to artists on contract; statutory rate to publisher per song on record.

Distributed by Sony and The Malibu Trading Company.

How to Contact *E-mail and obtain permission to submit.* Prefers CD, cassette or videocassette with 3 songs. Include SASE. Responds in 6 weeks.

Music Released "The Return of the Players" (album) by Juz-Cuz on PPL2004; "Bigg Leggeded Woman" (single by Buddy Wright) from *Destiny* (album), recorded by Buddy Wright (blues), released 2003 on PPL; *Ghost* (album), recorded by The Band AKA, written and produced by J. James Jarrett; "Step Aside" (single by Gary Johnson) from *Step Aside* (album), recorded by Gary J., released 2003 on PPL/Sony. Other artists include Phuntaine, Condottiere and Gary J.

◙ PRAVDA RECORDS

6311 N. Neenah, Chicago IL 60631. (773)763-7509. Fax: (773)763-3252. E-mail: pravdausa@aol.c om. Website: pravdamusic.com. **Contact:** Mo Goodman, director of A&R. A&R (pop/rock): Matt

Favazza. Labels include Bughouse. Record company. Estab. 1985. Releases 3-6 singles, 1 EP and 5-6 CDs/year. Pays 10-15% royalty to artists on contract; statutory rate to publisher per song on record.
Distributed by Hep Cat, Alliance and Carrot Top.
How to Contact Submit demo tape by mail. Unsolicited submissions are OK. Prefers CD with 3-4 songs. Does not return material. "Will contact only if interested."
Music Mostly **rock**. Released *Variations On A Goddamn Old Man* (album), recorded by Cheer-Accident (alternative), released 2002 on Pravda; *Vodka & Peroxide* (album), recorded by The Civil Tones (R&B), released 2003 on Pravda; and *album title TBA* (album), recorded by The Goldstars (garage), released 2003 on Pravda. Other artists include Tiny Tim, Frantic Flattops, Gringo, Javelin Boot, The Slugs, The New Duncan Imperials and Legendary Stardust Cowboy.
Tips "Be nice! Tour behind your release, don't take yourself too seriously."

ⓝ ◖ PRESENCE RECORDS
67 Candace Lane, Chatham NJ 07928-1115. (201)701-0707. **Contact:** Paul Payton, president. Record company, music publisher (Paytoons/BMI) and record producer (Presence Productions). Estab. 1985. Staff size: 1. Pays 1-2% royalty to artists on contract; statutory rate to publisher per song on record.
Distributed by Clifton Music.
How to Contact Submit demo tape by mail. Unsolicited submissions are OK. "No phone calls." Prefers cassette or CD with 2-4 songs and lyric sheet. Include SASE. Responds in 1 month. "Tapes and CDs not returned without prepaid mailer."
Music Mostly **doo-wop ('50s)**, **rock** and **new wave rock**. "No heavy metal, no 'Christian' or religious rock." Released "Ding Dong Darling," "Bette Blue Moon" and "Davilee/Go On" (singles by Paul Payton/Peter Skolnik), recorded by Fabulous Dudes (doo-wop), all on Presence Records.
Tips "Would you press and distribute it if it was *your* money? Only send it here if the answer is yes."

◖ QUARK RECORDS
P.O. Box 7320, FDR Station, New York NY 10150. (917)687-9988. E-mail: quarkent@aol.com. **Contact:** Curtis Urbina, (pop, dance). A&R: Michelle Harris (alternative). Record company and music publisher (Quarkette Music/BMI and Freedurb Music/ASCAP). Estab. 1984. Releases 3 singles and 3 LPs/year. Pays negotiable royalty to artists on contract; ¾ statutory rate to publisher per song on record.
How to Contact Prefers CD with 2 songs (max). Include SASE. "Must be an absolute 'hit' song!" Responds in 6 weeks.
Music Mostly **dance/pop**. Released "Uncommon Scents" by XENCHAOS in 2005. Coming in 2006, new releases from XENCHAOS, Mark P. Adler and Curtis Urbina.

◖ RADICAL RECORDS
77 Bleecker St., Suite C2-21, New York NY 10012. (212)475-1111. Fax: (212)475-3676. E-mail: info@radicalrecords.com. Website: www.radicalrecords.com. **Contact:** Johnny Chiba, A&R. Record company. "We also do independent retail distribution for punk, hardcore music." Estab. 1986. Staff size: 7. Releases 1 single and 6 CDs/year. Pays 14% royalty to artists on contract; statutory rate to publisher per song on record.
Distributed by City Hall, Revelation, Select-O-Hits, Revolver, Choke.
How to Contact *E-mail first for permission to submit demo.* Prefers cassette or CD. Does not return material. Responds in 1 month.
Music Mostly **punk** and **hardcore**. Released *Too Legit for the Pit—Hardcore Takes the Rap* (album), recorded by various; *Punk's Not Dead—A Tribute to the Exploited* (album), recorded by various; *Fresh Out of Give-a-Fucks* (album), recorded by Submachine; and *East Coast of Oi!* (album), recorded by various. Other artists include The Agents, Social Scare, Blanks 77 and Inspector 7.
Tips "Create the best possible demos you can and show a past of excellent self-promotion."

⊘ RAVE RECORDS, INC.

Attn: Production Dept., 13400 W. Seven Mile Rd., Detroit MI 48235. E-mail: info@raverecords.com. Website: www.raverecords.com. **Contact:** Carolyn and Derrick, production managers. Record company and music publisher (Magic Brain Music/ASCAP). Estab. 1992. Staff size: 2. Releases 2-4 singles and 2 CDs/year. Pays various royalty to artists on contract; statutory rate to publisher per song on record.

Distributed by Action Music Sales.

How to Contact Submit demo CD by mail. Prefers CD with 3 songs, lyric sheet. "Include any bios, fact sheets, and press you may have. We will contact you if we need any further information. Does not return materials.

Music Mostly **alternative rock** and **dance**. Artists include Cyber Cryst, Dorothy, Nicole and Bukimi 3.

⊘ RAZOR & TIE ENTERTAINMENT

214 Sullivan St., Suite 4A, New York NY 10012. (212)473-9173. E-mail: info@razorandtie.com. Website: www.razorandtie.com. Record company.

How to Contact *Does not accept unsolicited material.*

Music Released *The Beauty of the Rain* (album) by Dar Williams; *The Sweetheart Collection* by Frankie & The Knockouts; *Everybody's Normal But Me* by Stuttering John; and *Marigold* (album) by Marty Lloyd, all on Razor & Tie Entertainment. Other artists include Graham Parker, Marshall Crenshaw, Sam Champion and Toshi Reagon.

☑ 🔱 ⊘ RCA RECORDS

1540 Broadway, 36th Floor, New York NY 10036. (212)930-4936. Fax: (212)930-4447. Website: www.rcarecords.com. A&R: Donna Pearce. **Beverly Hills:** 8750 Wilshire Blvd., Beverly Hills CA 90211. (310)358-4105. Fax: (310)358-4127. Senior Vice President of A&R: Jeff Blue. **Nashville:** 1400 18th Ave. S., Nashville TN 37212. A&R Director: Jim Catino. Labels include Loud Records, Deconstruction Records and Judgment/RCA Records. Record company.

Distributed by BMG.

How to Contact *RCA Records does not accept unsolicited submissions.*

Music Artists include The Strokes, Dave Matthews Band, Clay Aiken, Christina Aguilera, and Velvet Revolver.

🄽 ⊕ ◻ RED ADMIRAL RECORDS

The Cedars, Elvington Lane, Folkestone Kent CT18 7AD United Kingdom. Estab. 1979. (01)(303)893-472. Fax: (01)(303)893-833. E-mail: info@redadmiralrecords.com. Website: www.re dadmiralrecords.com. **Contact:** Chris Ashman, CEO. Labels include: Registered members of MCPS, PRS, and PPL. Record company. Music publisher (Cringe Music [PRS]). Estab. 1979.

How to Contact Submit demo tape by mail. Unsolicited submissions are OK. Include CD with unlimited number of songs. Responds in 3 months.

Music Mostly **AOR, MOR**, and **pop**. Also **soul, R&B, reggae/ska**. Artists include Rik Waller's Mighty Soul Band, The Sharpee's and Rhythm of Blues.

⊕ ⊘ RED SKY RECORDS

P.O. Box 27, Stroud, Glos. GL6 0YQ United Kingdom. 01453-836877. Fax: 01453-836877. Website: www.redskyrecords.co.uk. **Contact:** Johnny Coppin, producer. Record company and record producer (Johnny Coppin). Estab. 1985. Staff size: 1. Releases 1 album/year. Pays 8-10% to artists on contract; statutory rate to publisher per song on record.

Distributed by ADA, CM.

How to Contact *Write first and obtain permission to submit.* Does not return material. Responds in 6 months.

Music Mostly **rock/singer-songwriters, modern folk** and **roots music**. Released *The Dolan Brothers* (album), written and recorded by Dolan Brothers (blues); *A Journey* (album), written and recorded by Johnny Coppin (singer/songwriter); and *Dead Lively!* (album), written and recorded by Paul Burgess (folk) on Red Sky Records. Other artists include David Goodland.

☑ ▢ REDEMPTION RECORDS

P.O. Box 10238, Beverly Hills CA 90213. (323)666-0221. E-mail: info@redemption.net. Website: www.redemption.net. A&R Czar: Ryan D. Kuper (indie rock, power pop, rock, etc.). Record company. Estab. 1990. Staff size: varies. Releases 2-3 singles, 2-3 EPs and 2-3 CDs/year. Pays standard royalty to artists on contract; statutory rate to publisher per song on record.

Distributed by Navarre and others.

How to Contact *Does not accept unsolicited material. E-mail to obtain permission to submit.* Submit demo CD by mail or send mp3 link by e-mail. "Include band's or artist's goals." Does not return material. Responds only if interested.

Music Mostly **indie rock** and **power pop**. Artists include Vicious Vicious, The Working Title, Race For Titles, Schatzi, Motion City Soundtrack, Nolan, and the *Redemption Versus Series* featuring indie rock bands from different geographical locations.

Tips "Be prepared to tour to support the release. Make sure the current line-up is secure."

▨ REPRISE RECORDS

3300 Warner Blvd., 4th Floor, Burbank CA 91505. (818)846-9090. Fax: (818)840-2389. Website: www.repriserecords.com. Labels include Duck and Sire. Record company.

Distributed by WEA.

How to Contact *Reprise Records does not accept unsolicited submissions.*

Music Artists include Eric Clapton, Guster, Josh Groban, The Distillers, and Neil Young.

▢ ROAD RECORDS

P.O. Box 2620, Victorville CA 92393. E-mail: staff@askland.net. Website: www.roadrecords.com. **Contact:** Conrad Askland, president. Record company, record producer (Road Records) and music publisher (Askland Publishing). Estab. 1989. Produces 6 singles and 10 albums/year.

How to Contact Prefers at least 3 songs with lyric and lead sheet. Does not return submissions. Responds only if interested. "We accept complete songs, soundtracks and ambient recordings."

Music Mostly **alternative**, **modern country** and **dance**; also **orchestral instrumental**. Does not want jazz. Released "You're the Best Lie" (single by Gailyn Addis and Conrad Askland) from *Gailyn Addis* (album), recorded by Gailyn Addis (pop/AC), released 2001 on Road Records.

Tips "Do not submit what you think we are looking for. A lot of our projects are 'on the edge.' We are looking for people that have a different, original sound. We supply music for dozens of companies worldwide."

☑ ▣ ROBBINS ENTERTAINMENT LLC

159 W. 25th St., 4th Floor, New York NY 10001. (212)675-4321. Fax: (212)675-4441. E-mail: info@r obbinsent.com. Website: www.robbinsent.com. **Contact:** John Parker, vice president, A&R/dance promotion. Record company and music publisher (Rocks, No Salt). Estab. 1996. Staff size: 8. Releases 25 singles and 12-14 CDs/year. Pays negotiable royalty to artists on contract; statutory rate to publisher per song on record.

Distributed by BMG.

How to Contact Accepts unsolicited demos as long as it's dance music. Prefers CD with 2 songs or less. "Make sure everything is labeled with the song title information and our contact information. This is important in case the CD and the jewel case get separated. Do not call us and ask if you can send your package. The answer is yes."

Music Commercial **dance** only. Released top 10 pop smash, "Heaven" (single), recorded by DJ Sammy, as well as Hot 100 records from Rockell, Lasgo, Reina and K5. Other artists include Ian Van Dahl, Andain, Judy Torres, Marly, Dee Dee, Milky, Kreo and many others.

Tips "Do not send your package 'Supreme-Overnight-Before-You-Wake-Up' delivery. Save yourself some money. Do not send material if you are going to state in your letter that, 'If I had more (fill in the blank) it would sound better.' We are interested in hearing your best and only your best."

Do not call us and ask if you can send your package. The answer is yes. We are looking for dance music with crossover potential."

☐ ROLL ON RECORDS®

112 Widmar Pl., Clayton CA 94517. (925)833-4680. E-mail: rollonrecords@aol.com. **Contact:** Edgar J. Brincat, owner. Record company and music publisher (California Country Music). Estab. 1985. Pays 10% royalty to artists on contract; statutory rate to publisher per song on record. Member of Harry Fox Agency.

Distributed by Tower.

How to Contact Submit demo tape by mail. Unsolicited submissions are OK. Do not call or write for permission to submit, if you do you will be rejected. Prefers CD's or cassette with 3 songs and lyric sheet. Include SASE and phone number. Responds in 6 weeks.

Music Mostly **contemporary/country**, **MOR** and **R&B**; also **pop**, **light rock** and **modern gospel**. Released "Broken Record" (single by Horace Linsley/Dianne Baumgartner), recorded by Edee Gordon on Roll On Records; *Maddy* and *For Realities Sake* (albums both by F.L. Pittman/Madonna Weeks), recorded by Ron Banks/L.J. Reynolds on Life Records/Bellmark Records.

Tips "Be patient and prepare to be in it for the long haul. A successful songwriter does not happen overnight. It's rare to write a song today and have a hit tomorrow. If you give us your song and want it back, then don't give it to us to begin with."

☐ ROTTEN RECORDS

Attn: A&R Dept., P.O. Box 56, Upland CA 91786. E-mail: rotten@rottenrecords.com. Website: www .rottenrecords.com. President: Ron Peterson. Promotions/Radio/Video: Andi Jones. Record company. Estab. 1988. Releases 3 LPs, 3 EPs and 3 CDs/year.

Distributed by Shock (Australia), Sonic Rendezvous (UK), DNA, Smash (US) and St. Clair (Canada).

How to Contact Submit demo tape by mail. Unsolicited submissions are OK. Prefers CD. Does not return material.

Music Mostly **rock**, **alternative** and **commercial**; also **punk** and **heavy metal**. Released *Paegan Terrorism* (album), written and recorded by Acid Bath; *Kiss the Clown* (album by K. Donivon), recorded by Kiss the Clown; and *Full Speed Ahead* (album by Cassidy/Brecht), recorded by D.R.T., all on Rotten Records.

Tips "Be patient."

☑ RUSTIC RECORDS

6337 Murray Lane, Brentwood TN 37027. (615)371-0646. Fax: (615)370-0353. E-mail: rusticrecordsi nc@aol.com. Website: www.rusticrecordsinc.com. President: Jack Schneider. Office Manager: Nell Schneider. Traditional country independent music record label and music publisher (Iron Skillet Music/ASCAP, Covered Bridge/BMI, Town Square/SESAC). Estab. 1979. Staff size: 3. Releases 2-3 albums/year. Pays negotiable royalty to artists on contract; statutory royalty to publisher per song on record.

 • Also see the listings for Rustic Records, Inc. Publishers in the Music Publishers section of this book.

Distributed by CDBaby.com, BathtubMusic.com and MusicUtopia.com. "We are also working with CDBaby on digital distribution. Look for us soon on favorite music services like Rhapsody, iTunes and MSN Music."

How to Contact Submit professional demo by mail. Unsolicited submissions are OK. Prefers CD or cassette; no mp3s or e-mails. Include no more than 3-4 songs with corresponding lyric sheets and a cover letter. Include SASE. Responds in 4-5 weeks.

Music Mostly **traditional country, novelty**, and **old-time gospel**. 2005 releases include "Drankin Business" (single from Colte Bradley) and "Mercy" (single from new artist, Beckey Burr).

Tips "Submit a professional demo."

☑ ☐ RUSTRON MUSIC PRODUCTIONS

1156 Park Lane, West Palm Beach FL 33417-5957. (561)686-1354. E-mail: rmp_wmp@bellsouth.n et. **Contact:** Sheelah Adams, office administrator. Executive Director: Rusty Gordon (folk fusions, blues, women's music, adult contemporary, electric, acoustic, New Age instrumentals, children's, cabaret). Director A&R: Ron Caruso. Associate Director of A&R: Kevin Reeves (pop, country, blues, R&B, jazz, folk). Labels include Rustron Records and Whimsong Records. "Rustron administers 20 independent labels for publishing and marketing." Record company, record producer, management firm and music publisher (Whimsong/ASCAP and Rustron Music/BMI). Estab. 1970. Releases 5-10 CDs/year. Pays variable royalty to artists on contract. "Artists with history of product sales get higher percent than those with no sales track record." Pays statutory rate to publisher.

How to Contact *Songwriters may write or call first to discuss your submission.* Submit demo tape or CD by mail. Unsolicited submissions are OK. Prefers CD with up to 15 songs and typed lyric sheets. Cassette is limited to 3 songs. "Include cover letter with complete information regarding your submission with your promo pack. If singer/songwriter has independent product (cassette or CD) produced and sold at gigs—send this product." SASE required for all correspondence, no exceptions. Responds in 4 months.

Music Mostly **mainstream** and **women's music**, **adult contemporary electric acoustic**, pop (**cabaret, blues**) and **blues (R&B, country and folk)**; also **soft rock** (ballads), **New Age fusions** (instrumentals), **modern folk fusions** (environmental, socio-political), **children's music** and **light jazz**. Released "Solstice in The Big Cypress" (single) from *Solstice in The Big Cypress* (album), written and recorded by The Dinner Key Boys (folk-rock blues), released 2005 on Whimsong Records; "Yankee Reggae All The Rave" (single) from *Yankee Reggae All The Rave* (album), written and recorded by Jeremy White & Kalliope (yankee reggae), released 2005 on Whimsong Records; and "A Trimaran on The Gulf of Mexico" (single) from *A Trimaran on The Gulf of Mexico* (album), written and recorded by Song On A Whim (folk fusions), released 2005 on Rustron Records.

Tips "Find your own unique style; write well crafted songs with unpredictable concepts, strong hooks and definitive melody. New Age composers: evolve your themes and add multi-cultural diversity with instruments. Don't be predictable. Don't over produce your demos and don't drown vocals. Send cover letter clearly explaining your reasons for submitting. Carefully craft songs for single-song marketing. Always include a typed lyric sheet for each song sent."

☐ SAFIRE RECORDS

5617 W. Melvina, Milwaukee WI 53216. (414)444-3385. **Contact:** Darnell Ellis, president. A&R Representatives: Darrien Kingston (country, pop); Reggie Rodriqez (world, Latin, Irish). Record company, music publisher (Ellis Island Music/ASCAP), record producer (Darnell Ellis) and management firm (The Ellis International Talent Agency). Estab. 1997. Staff size: 2. Releases 3 singles, 3 LPs, 1 EP and 3 CDs/year. Pays negotiable royalty to artists on contract; statutory rate to publisher per song on record.

   • Also see the listing for The Ellis International Talent Agency in the Managers & Booking Agents section of this book.

How to Contact Submit demo tape by mail. Unsolicited submissions are OK. Prefers cassette or CD with 3-4 songs. Does not return material. Responds in 2 months. "We will respond only if we are interested."

Music Mostly **country**, **pop**, **mainstream pop**, all styles of **rock** and anything else except **rap** or **hip-hop**. Artists include Tracy Beck. Released *Into The Sun* (album), recorded by Tracy Beck (blues, alt. country/acoustic/roots), released 2004 on Safire Records.

Tips "Songwriters need to get back to the basics of songwriting: great hooklines, strong melodies. We would love to hear from artists and songwriters from all over the world. And remember, just because someone passes on a song it doesn't mean that it's a bad song. Maybe it's a song that the label is not able to market or the timing is just bad."

☑ 🔾 ⦰ SAHARA RECORDS AND FILMWORKS ENTERTAINMENT

28 E. Jackson Bldg., 10th Floor #S627, Chicago IL 60604-2263. (773)509-6381. Fax: (312)922-6964. Website: www.edmsahara.com. **Contact:** Edward De Miles, president. Record company, music publisher (EDM Music/BMI, Edward De Miles Music Company) and record producer (Edward De Miles). Estab. 1981. Releases 15-20 CD singles and 5-10 CDs/year. Pays 9½-11% royalty to artists on contract; statutory rate to publishers per song on record.

How to Contact *Does not accept unsolicited submissions.*

Music Mostly **R&B/dance**, **top 40 pop/rock** and **contemporary jazz**; also **TV-film themes**, **musical scores** and **jingles**. Released "Hooked on U," "Dance Wit Me" and "Moments" (singles), written and recorded by Steve Lynn (R&B) on Sahara Records. Other artists include Lost in Wonder, Dvon Edwards and Multiple Choice.

Tips "We're looking for strong mainstream material. Lyrics and melodies with good hooks that grab people's attention."

☑ SALEXO MUSIC

P.O. Box 18093, Charlotte NC 28218-0093. (704)392-2477. E-mail: salexo@bellsouth.net. **Contact:** Samuel Obie, president. Record company. Estab. 1992. Releases 1 CD/year.

How to Contact *Write first and obtain permission to submit.* Prefers cassette with 3 songs and lyric sheet. Include SASE. Responds in 1 month.

Music Mostly **contemporary gospel** and **jazz**. Released *A Joyful Noise* (album), recorded by Samuel Obie with J.H. Walker Unity Choir (gospel), released 2003, Macedonia Baptist Church; and "Favor" (single) from *Favor*, written and recorded by Samuel Obie (contemporary gospel), released 2004 on Salexo Music.

Tips "Make initial investment in the best production."

ℕ ☐ SANDALPHON RECORDS

P.O. Box 29110, Portland OR 97296. (503)957-3929. E-mail: jackrabbit01@sprintpcs.com. **Contact:** Ruth Otey, president. Record company, music publisher (Sandalphon Music/BMI), and management agency (Sandalphon Management). Estab. 2005. Staff size: 2. Pays negotiable royalty to artists on contract; statutory royalty to publisher per song on record.

Distributed by "We are negotiating for a distributor."

How to Contact Submit demo tape by mail. Unsolicited submissions are OK. Include cassette or CD with 1-5 songs with lyric sheet and cover letter. Returns submissions if accompanied by a SASE or SAE and IRC for outside the United States. Responds in 1 month.

Music Mostly **rock**, **country**, and **alternative**; also **pop**, **gospel** and **blues**.

⊕ ☑ ☐ SATELLITE MUSIC

34 Salisbury St., London NW8 8QE United Kingdom. (+44)207-402-9111. Fax: (+44)207-723-3064. E-mail: eliot@amimedia.co.uk. Website: www.amimedia.co.uk. **Contact:** Eliot Cohen, CEO. Director: Ray Dorset. Labels include Saraja and Excalibur. Record company and music publisher. Estab. 1976. Staff size: 10. Releases 5 singles, 3 LPs and 3 CDs/year. Pays negotiable royalty to artists on contract; statutory rate to publisher per song on record.

Distributed by S. Gold & Sons and Total Home Entertainment.

How to Contact Submit demo tape by mail. Unsolicited submissions are OK. Prefers cassette, CD, DAT or VHS videocassette with 4 songs, cover letter and press clippings. SAE and IRC. Responds in 6 weeks.

Music Mostly **dance**, **disco** and **pop**. Does not want blues, jazz or country. Released "In the Snow" (by Ray Dorset), recorded by Mungo Jerry on BME (pop).

☑ SILVER WAVE RECORDS

P.O. Box 7943, Boulder CO 80306. (303)443-5617. Fax: (303)443-0877. E-mail: info@silverwave.com. Website: www.silverwave.com. **Contact:** James Marienthal. Record company. Estab. 1986. Releases 3-4 CDs/year. Pays varying royalty to artists on contract and to publisher per song on record.

How to Contact *Call first and obtain permission to submit.* Prefers CD. Include SASE. Responds only if interested.

Music Mostly **Native American** and **world**.

☑ SIN KLUB ENTERTAINMENT, INC.

P.O. Box 2507, Toledo OH 43606. (419)537-9293. E-mail: esthree@buckeye-express.com. Website: www.sinklub.com. (419)475-1189. President/A&R: Edward Shimborske III. Labels include Sin-Ka-

Bob Records. Record company, music publisher (Morris St. James Publishing) and record producer (ES3). Estab. 1990. Releases 1 single, 1 LP and 5 CDs/year. Pays negotiable royalty to artists on contract; statutory rate to publisher per song on record.
Distributed by Cargo.
How to Contact Submit demo tape by mail. Unsolicited submissions are OK. Prefers cassette or CD with 3 songs and lyric sheet. "Send a good press kit (photos, bio, articles, etc.)." Does not return material. Responds in 1 month.
Music Mostly **harder-edged alternative**, **punk** and **metal/industrial**; also **rap, alternative** and **experimental**. Released *Urban Witchcraft* (album), recorded by Thessalonian Dope Gods (industrial), released 1994; *All Balled Up* (album), recorded by Bunjie Jambo (punk), released 1996, both on Sin Klub. Other artists include Kid Rock, Dan Hicks, Lucky Boys Confusion, Crashdog, The Geminus Sect, Evolotto, Lazy American Workers, The PB Army and The Dead Heroes.

☑ ☑ SMALL STONE RECORDS
P.O. Box 02007, Detroit MI 48202. Fax: (248)541-6536. E-mail: sstone@smallstone.com. Website: www.smallstone.com. **Owner:** Scott Hamilton. Record company. Estab. 1995. Staff size: 1. Releases 2 singles, 2 EPs and 10 CDs/year. Pays negotiable royalty to artists on contract; statutory rate to publisher per song on record.
Distributed by AEC, Allegro/Nail.
How to Contact Submit CD/CDrom by mail. Unsolicited submissions are OK. Does not return material. Responds in 2 months.
Music Mostly **alternative**, **rock** and **blues**; also **funk (not R&B)**. Released *Fat Black Pussy Cat*, written and recorded by Five Horse Johnson (rock/blues); *Wrecked & Remixed*, written and recorded by Morsel (indie rock, electronica); and *Only One Division*, written and recorded by Soul Clique (electronica), all on Small Stone Records. Other artists include Acid King, Perplexa, and Novadriver.
Tips "Looking for esoteric music along the lines of Bill Laswell to Touch & Go/Thrill Jockey records material. Only send along material if it makes sense with what we do. Perhaps owning some of our records would help."

☑ SMITHSONIAN FOLKWAYS RECORDINGS
750 9th St. NW, Suite 4100, Washington DC 20560-0953. (202)275-1144. Fax: (202)275-1164. E-mail: folkways@aol.com. Website: www.folkways.si.edu. **Contact:** Daniel Sheehy, curator/director. Labels include Smithsonian Folkways Recordings, Dyer-Bennet, Cook, Paredon, Folkway, Monitor and Fast Folk. Record company and music publisher. Estab. 1948. Releases 25 CDs/year. Pays negotiable royalty to artists on contract and to publisher per song on record.
Distributed by Koch Entertainment.
How to Contact *Write first and obtain permission to submit or to arrange personal interview.* Prefers CD or DAT. Does not return material. Responds in 6 months.
Music Mostly **traditional US folk music, world music** and **children's music**. Released *We Shall Overcome* (by Pete Seeger), recorded by various artists (folk/Americana), from *Classic Folk Music from Smithsonian Folkways* (album), released 2004; *Goodnight Irene*, written and recorded by Lead Belly (folk/Americana), from *Lead Belly—Where Did You Sleep Last Night* (album), released 1996; *This Land is Your Land*, written and recorded by Woody Guthrie, from *This Land is Your Land* (album), released 1997; all released by Smithsonian Folkways Recordings. "We only are interested in music publishing associated with recordings we are releasing. Do not send demos of songwriting only."
Tips "If you are a touring artist and singer/songwriter, consider carefully the advantages of a non-museum label for your work. We specialize in ethnographic and field recordings from people around the world."

☐ SOLANA RECORDS
2440 Great Highway, #5, San Francisco CA 94116. (415)566-0411. E-mail: info@solanarecords.com. Website: www.solanarecords.com. **Contact:** Eric Friedmann, president. Record company, music

publisher (Neato Bandito Music) and record producer (Eric Friedmann). Estab. 1992. Staff size: 1. Releases 1 single and 2 CDs/year. Pays negotiable royalty to artists on contract; statutory rate to publisher per song on record.

How to Contact Submit demo tape by mail but please e-mail permissions first. Prefers CD with 3-5 songs, photo and cover letter. Include SASE. Responds in 1 month.

Music Mostly any kind of guitar/vocal-based **rock/pop** and **country**. Does not want rap, hip-hop. Released *Spacious* (by Valerie Moorhead), recorded by Enda (alternative rock); *Livin' the High Life* (by James Cook), recorded by The Wags (hardcore); *The Grain* (by Rick Ordin), recorded by The Grain (progressive rock); and *To Hell with the Road*; *Live at the Sandbox*, recorded by Delectric (Skiffle). Other artists include The Detonators, Eric Friedman and the Lucky Rubes, The Mudkats and Doormouse.

Tips "Be honest and genuine. Know how to write a good song, and know how to sing. Don't send my your résumé or life story please. Big bonus points for Telecaster players."

☑ ◯ SONAR RECORDS & PRODUCTION

2342 20th St., Suite A, Santa Monica CA 90405. Fax: (310)392-1973. E-mail: info@sonarproductions .com. Website: www.sonarproductions.com. Artist Development: Ken Moody (Moodini). Vice President Urban Music: William Collins. A&R: Geo Clinton and Shana Holyfield. Labels include Sounds of New Artist Recordings. Record producer (Sonar, Moodini). Estab. 1994. Staff size: 4. Releases 3 singles, 1 LP, and 1 CD/year. Pays 12% royalty to artists on contract; statutory rate to publisher per song on record.

Distributed by WEA.

How to Contact Submit demo tape by mail. Unsolicited submissions are OK. Prefers CD. Does not return material. Responds in 1 month if interested.

Music Mostly **R&B**, **positive rap**, **hip-hop** and **gospel**; also **contemporary gospel.** Artists include Locaine, XL, OX, Peaches and Huzzy, Sons of Abraham and Shank.

Tips "Invest in yourself and others will follow."

ⓝ ☑ ◯ SONIC UNYON RECORDS CANADA

P.O. Box 57347, Jackson Station, Hamilton ON L8P 4X2 Canada. (905)777-1223. Fax: (905)777-1161. E-mail: jerks@sonicunyon.com. Website: www.sonicunyon.com. Co-owners: Tim Potocic; Mark Milne. Record company. Estab. 1992. Releases 2 singles, 2 EPs and 6-10 CDs/year. Pays negotiable royalty to artists on contract; statutory rate to publisher per song on record.

Distributed by Caroline Distribution.

How to Contact *Call first and obtain permission to submit*. Prefers cassette or CD. "Research our company before you send your demo. We are small; don't waste my time and your money." Does not return material. Responds in 4 months.

Music Mostly **rock**, **heavy rock** and **pop rock**. Released *Doberman* (album), written and recorded by Kittens (heavy rock); *What A Life* (album), written and recorded by Smoother; and *New Grand* (album), written and recorded by New Grand on Sonic Unyon Records (pop/rock). Other artists include Tricky Woo, Danko Jones, Crooked Fingers, Frank Black and the Catholics, Jesus Lizard, Chore, Sectorseven, The Dirtmitts, Sianspheric, gorp, Hayden and Poledo.

Tips "Know what we are about. Research us. Know we are a small company. Know signing to us doesn't mean that everything will fall into your lap. We are only the beginning of an artist's career."

⊘ SONY MUSIC

550 Madison Ave., New York NY 10022. Website: www.sonymusic.com.

How to Contact *For specific contact information see the listings in this section for Sony subsidiaries Columbia Records, Epic Records and Sony Nashville.*

⊘ SONY MUSIC NASHVILLE

34 Music Square E., Nashville TN 37203. (615)742-4321. Labels include Columbia, Epic, Lucky Dog Records, Monument.

How to Contact *Sony Music Nashville does not accept unsolicited submissions.*

☑ SOUND GEMS

P.O. Box 801, South Eastern PA 19399. Website: www.soundgems.com. CEO: Frank Fioravanti. A&R Director: Trish Wassel. Record company and music publisher (Melomega Music, Meloman Music). Estab. 1972. Staff size: 3. Pays negotiable royalty to artists on contract; statutory rate to publisher per song on record.

Distributed by EMI, Sony, Warner.

How to Contact Submit demo tape by mail. Unsolicited submissions are OK. Prefers cassette, CD with lyric sheet, cover letter and press clipping. "Do not send registered or certified mail." Does not return material. Responds only if interested.

Music R&B only. Released "Be Thankful" (single by William Devaughn) from *Bones* (soundtrack album), recorded by William DeVaughn (R&B), released 2001 on PRI; and "Limo Dream" (single by Hopkins/Rakes/Fioravanti), recorded by Corey (R&B), released 2001 on Sound Gems; and "Girl I Wanna Take You Home" (single by Rueben Cross), recorded by Corey Wims (R&B/neo-soul), released 2002 on Sound Gems.

Tips "Be sure your style fits our catagory. Submit R&B material only."

☐ SOUTHLAND RECORDS, INC.

P.O. Box 1547, Arlington TX 76004-1547. (817)461-3280. E-mail: SteveReed@SouthlandRecords.com. Website: www.SouthlandRecords.com. **Contact:** Steve Reed, president. Record company and record producer (Steve Reed). Estab. 1980. Releases 12 CDs/year. Pays negotiable royalty to artists on contract; statutory rate to publisher per song on record.

How to Contact Submit demo tape or CD by mail. Unsolicited submissions are OK. Prefers cassette or CD with 4 songs, lyric and lead sheet, cover letter and press clippings. Does not return material. Responds in 3 months.

Music Country only. Artists include Leon Rausch, Rob Dixon, Bob Willis & the Texas Playboys, Ron Gaddis, Tommy Allsup, Jake Hooker, Curtis Potter and Darrell McCall.

☑ SUGAR HILL RECORDS

P.O. Box 55300, Durham NC 27717-5300. E-mail: info@sugarhillrecords.com. Record company. Estab. 1978.

● Welk Music Group acquired Sugar Hill Records in 1998.

How to Contact *No unsolicited submissions.* "If you are interested in having your music heard by Sugar Hill Records or the Welk Music Group, we suggest you establish a relationship with a manager, publisher, or attorney that has an ongoing relationship with our company."

Music Mostly **Americana**, **bluegrass** and **country**. Artists include Nickel Creek, The Duhks, Sonny Landreth, Lonesome River Band, Del McCoury Band, New Grass Revival, Gray Larsen, Marty Stuart, and Psychograss.

Ⓝ ☑ SURESHOT RECORDS

P.O. Box 9117, Truckee CA 96162. (530)587-0111. E-mail: alanred@telis.org. Website: www.alanredstone.com. **Contact:** Alan Redstone, owner. Record company, record producer and music publisher. Estab. 1979. Releases 1 LP/year. Pays statutory rate to publisher per song on record.

How to Contact "Currently not looking for material. Please do not send anything until further notice."

Music Mostly **country**, **comedy**, **novelty** and **blues**.

Tips "Read up and learn to submit properly. Submit like a pro."

☐ TANGENT® RECORDS

P.O. Box 383, Reynoldsburg OH 43068-0383. (614)751-1962. Fax: (614)751-6414. E-mail: info@tangentrecords.com. Website: www.tangentrecords.com. **Contact:** Andrew Batchelor, president. Director of Marketing: Elisa Batchelor. Record company and music publisher (ArcTangent Music/BMI). Estab. 1986. Staff size: 3. Releases 10-12 CDs/year. Pays negotiable royalty to artists on contract; statutory rate to publisher per song on record.

How to Contact Submit demo tape or CD by mail. Unsolicited submissions are OK. Prefers CD, with minimum of 3 songs and lead sheet if available. "Please include a brief biography/history of artist(s) and/or band, including musical training/education, performance experience, recording studio experience, discography and photos (if available)." Does not return material. Responds in 3 months.

Music Mostly **artrock** and **contemporary instrumental/rock instrumental**; also **contemporary classical**, **world beat**, **jazz/rock**, **ambient**, **electronic**, and **New Age**.

Tips "Take the time to pull together a quality CD or cassette demo with package/portfolio, including such relevant information as experience (on stage and in studio, etc.), education/training, biography, career goals, discography, photos, etc. Should be typed. We are *not* interested in generic sounding or 'straight ahead' music. We are seeking music that is innovative, pioneering and eclectic with a fresh, unique sound."

◢ TEXAS MUSIC CAFE

3801 Campus Dr., Waco TX 76705. (254)867-3372. E-mail: info@texasmusiccafe.com. Website: www.texasmusiccafe.com. **Contact:** Paula Unger, booking. Labels include E-Cleff Records Inc. Television show. Estab. 1987. Staff size: 3. Releases 26 CDs/year. Pays negotiable royalty to artists on contract. *ORIGINAL MUSIC ONLY!*

Distributed by PBS, Hastings, Sony.

How to Contact Submit demo by mail. Unsolicited submissions are OK. Prefers CD, videocassette (VHS/DVD) with sample songs. Does not return material. Responds only if interested.

Music Released *Live At the Texas Music Cafe, Vol 1 and 2*, written and recorded by various (eclectic).

Tips "Must be willing to travel to Texas at your expense to be taped."

⚠ ◢ TEXAS ROSE RECORDS

P.O. Box 726, Terrell TX 75160-6765. (972)563-3161. Fax: (972)563-2655. E-mail: txrr1@aol.com. Website: www.texasroserecords.com. **Contact:** Nancy Baxendale, president. Record company, music publisher (Yellow Rose of Texas Publishing) and record producer (Nancy Baxendale). Estab. 1994. Staff size: 3. Releases 3 CDs/year. Pays negotiable royalty to artists on contract; statutory rate to publisher per song on record.

Distributed by Self distribution.

How to Contact *Call, write or e-mail first for permission to submit.* Submit maximum of 2 songs on CD and lyrics. Does not return material. Responds only if interested.

Music Mostly **country**, **soft rock** and **blues**; also **pop** and **gospel**. Does not want hip-hop, rap, heavy metal. Released *Flyin' High Over Texas* (album), recorded by Dust Martin (country); *Time For Time to Pay* (album), recorded by Jeff Elliot (country); and *Pendulum Dream* (album), written and recorded by Maureen Kelly (alternative/americana), and "Cowboy Super Hero" (single) written and recorded by Robert Mauldin.

Tips "We are interested in songs written for today's market with a strong hook. Always use a good vocalist."

⚠ ⚠ ◯ THIRD WAVE PRODUCTIONS LTD.

P.O. Box 563, Gander NL A1V 2E1 Canada. (709)256-8009. Fax: (709)256-7411. Website: www.bud dywasisname.com. Manager: Wayne Pittman. President: Arch Bonnell. Labels include Street Legal Records. Record company, music publisher, distributor and agent. Estab. 1986. Releases 2 singles, 2 LPs and 2 CDs/year. Pays negotiable royalty to artists on contract; statutory rate to publisher per song on record.

How to Contact Submit demo tape by mail. Unsolicited submissions are OK. Prefers cassette, DAT and lyric sheet. Include SASE. Responds in 2 months.

Music Mostly **folk/traditional**, **bluegrass** and **country**; also **pop**, **Irish** and **Christmas**. Released *Salt Beef Junkie* (album), written and recorded by Buddy Wasisname and Other Fellers (folk/traditional); *Newfoundland Bluegrass* (album), written and recorded by Crooked Stovepipe (bluegrass); and *Nobody Never Told Me* (album), written and recorded by The Psychobilly Cadillacs (rockabilly/country), all on Third Wave Productions. Other artists include Lee Vaughn.

Tips "We are not really looking for songs but are always open to take on new artists who are interested in recording/producing an album. We market and distribute as well as produce albums. Not much need for 'songs' per se, except maybe country and rock/pop.''

☑ TOMMY BOY RECORDS
32 W. 18th St., Penthouse, New York NY 10011. (212)388-8300. Fax: (212)388-8400. E-mail: mail@t ommyboy.com. Website: www.tommyboy.com. Record company. Labels include Penalty Recordings, Outcast Records, Timber and Tommy Boy Gospel.
Distributed by WEA.
How to Contact Call to obtain current demo submission policy.
Music Artists include Everlast, Screwball, Amber and Capone-N-Noreaga.

☐ TON RECORDS
4474 Rosewood Ave., Los Angeles CA 90004. (323)656-1749. Fax: (323)467-7737. E-mail: tonmusic @earthlink.net. Website: www.tonrecords.com. Vice President: Jay Vasquez. Labels include 7″ collectors series and Ton Special Projects. Record company and record producer (RJ Vasquez). Estab. 1992. Releases 6-9 LPs, 1-2 EPs and 10-11 CDs/year. Pays negotiable royalty to artists on contract; statutory rate to publisher per song on record.
Distributed by MS, Com Four, Rotz, Subterranean, Revelation, Get Hip, Impact, Page Canada and Disco Dial.
How to Contact Submit demo tape by mail. Unsolicited submissions are OK. Prefers cassette or CD. Include SASE. Responds in 1 month.
Music Mostly **new music**; also **hard new music**. Released *Intoxicated Birthday Lies*, recorded by shoegazer (punk rock); *The Good Times R Killing Me*, recorded by Top Jimmy (blues); and *Beyond Repair*, recorded by Vasoline Tuner (space rock), all on Ton Records. Other artists include Why? things burn, Hungry 5 and the Ramblers.
Tips ''Work as hard as we do.''

🅽 ☑ TOPCAT RECORDS
P.O. Box 670234, Dallas TX 75367. (972)484-4141. Fax: (972)620-8333. E-mail: info@topcatrecords. com. Website: topcatrecords.com. President: Richard Chalk. Record company and record producer. Estab. 1991. Staff size: 3. Releases 4-6 CDs/year. Pays 10-15% royalty to artists on contract; statutory rate to publisher per song on record.
Distributed by City Hall.
How to Contact *Call first and obtain permission to submit.* Prefers CD. Does not return material. Responds in 1 month.
Music Mostly **blues**, **swing** and **R&B**. Released *If You Need Me* (album), written and recorded by Robert Ealey (blues); *Texas Blueswomen* (album by 3 Female Singers), recorded by various (blues/ R&B); and *Jungle Jane* (album), written and recorded by Holland K. Smith (blues/swing), all on Topcat. Released CDs: *Jim Suhler & Alan Haynes—Live*; Bob Kirkpatrick *Drive Across Texas; Rock My Blues to Sleep,* by Johnny Nicholas; *Walking Heart Attack,* by Holland K. Smith; *Dirt Road* (album), recorded by Jim Suhler; *Josh Alan Band* (album), recorded by Josh Alan; *Bust Out* (album), recorded by Robin Sylar. Other artists include Grant Cook, Muddy Waters, Big Mama Thornton, Big Joe Turner, Geo. ''Harmonica'' Smith, J.B. Hutto and Bee Houston.
Tips ''Send me blues (fast, slow, happy, sad, etc.) or good blues oriented R&B. No pop, hip-hop, or rap.''

☑ ☑ TRANSDREAMER RECORDS
P.O. Box 1955, New York NY 10113. (212)741-8861. Fax: (509)757-8602. E-mail: gregaforce@aol.c om. Website: www.transdreamer.com. **Contact:** Greg Caputo. President: Robert John. Marketing Savant: Greg Caputo. Record company. Estab. 2002. Staff size: 5. Released 4 CDs/year. Pays negotiable rate to artists on contract; ¾ statutory rate to publisher per song on record.
• Also see the listing for Megaforce in this section of the book.
Distributed by Red/Sony.
How to Contact *Contact first and obtain permission to submit.*
Music Mostly **alternative/rock**. Artists include Delgados, Dressy Bessy and Wellwaer Conspiracy.

⊘ TVT RECORDS

A&R Dept. 23 E. Fourth St., 3rd Floor, New York NY 10003. (212)979-6410. Website: www.tvtrecord s.com. **Contact:** A&R. Labels include Tee Vee Toons, TVT Soundtrax, 1001 Sundays. Record company and music publisher (TVT Music). Estab. 1986. Releases 25 singles, 20 12″ singles, 40 LPs, 5 EPs and 40 CDs/year. Pays varying royalty to artists on contract; statutory rate to publisher per song on record.

How to Contact Send e-mail to demo-help@tvtrecords.com to receive information on how to submit your demo.

Music Mostly **alternative rock**, **rap** and **techno**; also **jazz/R&B**. Released *Home*, recorded by Sevendust; *Hoopla*, recorded by Speeches; and *Retarder*, recorded by The Unband.

Tips "We look for seminal, ground breaking, genre-defining artists of all types with compelling live presentation. Our quest is not for hit singles but for enduring important artists."

◻ UAR RECORDS (Universal-Athena Records)

P.O. Box 1264, 6020 W. Pottstown Rd., Peoria IL 61654-1264. (309)673-5755. Fax: (309)673-7636. E-mail: uarltd@A5.com. Website: www.unitedcyber.com/uarltd. **Contact:** Jerry Hanlon, A&R director. Record company and music publisher (Jerjoy Music/BMI). Estab. 1978. Staff size: 1. Releases 3 or more CDs/year. Pays standard royalty to artists on contract; statutory rate to publisher for each record sold.

How to Contact Unsolicited submissions are OK. "We *do not* return phone calls." Prefers CD or cassette with 3-5 songs and lyric sheet. Include SASE. "*We do not critique work unless asked.*" Responds in 2 weeks. "Simple demos—vocal plus guitar or keyboard—are acceptable. We *do not* require a major demo production to interpret the value of a song."

Music Mostly **country**. Released "Kingdom I Call Home," "We Could" (country), recorded by Danny Blakey and "Millionaires in Love" and "Since I've Found You" (country and religious), recorded by Micah Spayer; and "For Old Loves Sake" recorded by Melanie Hiatt.

☑ ⊘ VAI DISTRIBUTION

109 Wheeler Ave., Pleasantville NY 10570. 1-800-477-7146 or (914)769-3691. Fax: (914)769-5407. E-mail: inquiries@vaimusic.com. Website: www.vaimusic.com. President: Ernest Gilbert. Record company, video label and distributor. Estab. 1983. Pays negotiable royalty to artists on contract; other amount to publisher per song on record.

How to Contact *Does not accept unsolicited material.*

Music Mostly **opera (classical vocal)**, **classical (orchestral)** and **classical instrumental/piano**. Released *Susannah* (album by Carlisle Floyd), recorded by New Orleans Opera Orchestra and Chorus, on VAI Audio. Other artists include Jon Vickers, Rosalyn Tureck, Evelyn Lear and Thomas Stewart.

☑ ☑ ⊘ THE VERVE MUSIC GROUP

1755 Broadway, 3rd Floor, New York NY 10019. (212)331-2000. Fax: (212)331-2064. Website: www.vervemusicgroup.com. A&R Director: Dahlia Ambach. A&R Coordinator: Heather Buchanan. **Los Angeles:** 100 N. First St., Burbank CA 91502. (818)729-4804. Fax: (818)845-2564. Vice President A&R: Bud Harner. A&R Assistant: Heather Buchanan. Record company. Labels include Verve, GRP, Blue Thumb and Impulse! Records.

  ● Verve's Diana Krall won a 1999 Grammy Award for Best Jazz Vocal Performance; Wayne Shorter won Best Jazz Instrumental Solo; and the Charlie Haden Quartet West won Best Instrumental Arrangement with Vocals.

How to Contact *The Verve Music Group does not accept unsolicited submissions.*

Music Artists include Roy Hargrove, Diana Krall, George Benson, Al Jarreau, John Scofield, Natalie Cole and David Sanborn.

☑ ⊘ VIRGIN RECORDS

5750 Wilshire Blvd., Los Angeles CA 90036. (323)692-1100. Fax: (310)278-6231. Website: www.vir ginrecords.com. New York office: 150 5th Ave., 3rd Floor, New York NY 10016. (212)786-8200.

Fax: (212)786-8343. Labels include Rap-A-Lot Records, Pointblank Records, SoulPower Records, AWOL Records, Astralwerks Records, Cheeba Sounds and Noo Trybe Records. Record company. **Distributed by** EMD.

How to Contact Virgin Records does not accept recorded material or lyrics unless submitted by a reputable industry source. "If your act has received positive press or airplay on prior independent releases, we welcome your written query. Send a letter of introduction accompanied by all pertinent artist information. Do not send a tape until requested. All unsolicited materials will be returned unopened." Artists include Lenny Kravitz, Janet Jackson, Mick Jagger, Nikka Cosla, Ben Harper, Boz Scaggs and Moth.

WARNER BROS. RECORDS

3300 Warner Blvd., 3rd Floor, Burbank CA 91505. (818)846-9090. Fax: (818)953-3423. Website: www.wbr.com. **New York:** 75 Rockefeller Plaza, New York NY 10019. (212)275-4500. Fax: (212)275-4596. A&R: James Dowdall, Karl Rybacki. **Nashville:** 20 Music Square E., Nashville TN 37203. (615)748-8000. Fax: (615)214-1567. Labels include American Recordings, Eternal Records, Imago Records, Mute Records, Giant Records, Malpaso Records and Maverick Records. Record company.

Distributed by WEA.

How to Contact *Warner Bros. Records does not accept unsolicited material.* All unsolicited material will be returned unopened. Those interested in having their tapes heard should establish a relationship with a manager, publisher or attorney that has an ongoing relationship with Warner Bros. Records.

Music Released *Van Halen 3* (album), recorded by Van Halen; *Evita* (soundtrack); and *Dizzy Up the Girl* (album), recorded by Goo Goo Dolls, both on Warner Bros. Records. Other artists include Faith Hill, Tom Petty & the Heartbreakers, Jeff Foxworthy, Porno For Pyros, Travis Tritt, Yellowjackets, Bela Fleck and the Flecktones, Al Jarreau, Joshua Redmond, Little Texas and Curtis Mayfield.

WESTPARK MUSIC—RECORDS, PRODUCTION & PUBLISHING

P.O. Box 260227, Rathenauplatz 4, 50515 Cologne Germany. (49)221 247644. Fax: (49)221 231819. E-mail: westparkmusic@aol.com. Website: www.westparkmusic.com. **Contact:** Ulli Hetscher. Record company and music publisher. Estab. 1986. Staff size: 3. Releases 10-12 CDs/year. Pays 9-18% royalty to artists on contract.

Distributed by Indigo (Germany), Music & Words (Netherlands), Musik Ver Trieb (Switzerland), Ixthucu (Austria), Resistencia (Spain), Mega Musica (Italy), Digelius (UK, Proper Finland).

How to Contact *Write first and obtain permission to submit or submit demo tape by mail.* Unsolicited submissions are OK. Does not return material. Responds in 4 months.

Music "Check website."

Tips "Don't send country, mainstream rock/pop or MOR. Mark cassettes clearly. Save yourself money by sending just the CD and booklet (no box and no tray). Don't include stamps (we cannot use them). Send e-mail with brief description first."

WINCHESTER RECORDS

% McCoy, Route 2, Box 114, Berkeley Springs WV 25411. (304)258-9381. E-mail: mccoytroubadour @aol.com. Website: www.troubadourlounge.com. **Contact:** Jim or Bertha McCoy, owners. Labels include Master Records and Real McCoy Records. Record company, music publisher (Jim McCoy Music, Clear Music, New Edition Music/BMI), record producer (Jim McCoy Productions) and recording studio. Releases 20 singles and 10 LPs/year. Pays standard royalty to artists; statutory rate to publisher for each record sold.

How to Contact *Write first and obtain permission to submit.* Prefers CD with 5-10 songs and lead sheet. Include SASE. Responds in 1 month.

Music Mostly **bluegrass, church/religious, country, folk, gospel, progressive** and **rock.** Released "Runaway Girl" (single by Earl Howard/Jim McCoy) from *Earl Howard Sings His Heart Out* CD, recorded by Earl Howard (country), released 2002 on Winchester; *Jim McCoy and Friends Remember Ernest Tubb* (album), recorded by Jim McCoy (country), released January 2003 on Winchester;

The Best of Winchester Records (album), recorded by RileeGray/J.B. Miller/Jim McCoy/Carroll County (country), released 2002 on Winchester.

□ WORLD BEATNIK RECORDS

20 Amity Lane, Rockwall TX 75087. Fax: (972)771-0853. E-mail: tropikalproductions@juno.com. Website: www.tropikalproductions.com. **Producers:** J. Towry (world beat, reggae, ethnic, jazz); Jembe (reggae, world beat, ethnic); Arik Towry (ska, pop, ragga, rock). Labels include World Beatnik Records. Record company and record producer (Jimi Towry). Estab. 1983. Staff size: 4. Releases 6 singles, 6 LPs, 6 EPs and 6 CDs/year. Pays negotiable royalty to artists on contract; statutory rate to publisher per song on record.

Distributed by Midwest Records, Southwest Wholesale, Reggae OneLove, Ejaness Records, Ernie B's, CD Waterhouse and Borders.

How to Contact Submit demo tape by mail. Unsolicited submissions are OK. Prefers cassette, DAT, mini disk or VHS videocassette with lyric sheet. Include SASE. Responds in 2 weeks.

Music Mostly **world beat, reggae** and **ethnic**; also **jazz, hip-hop/dance** and **pop**. Released *I and I* (album by Abby I/Jimbe), recorded by Abby I (African pop); *Rastafrika* (album by Jimbe/Richard Ono), recorded by Rastafrika (African roots reggae); and *Vibes* (album by Jimbe/Bongo Cartheni), recorded by Wave (worldbeat/jazz), all released 2001/2002 on World Beatnik. Other artists include Ras Richi (Cameroon), Wisdom Ogbor (Nigeria), Joe Lateh (Ghana), Dee Dee Cooper, Ras Lyrix (St. Croix), Ras Kumba (St. Kitts), Gary Mon, Darbo (Gambia), Ricki Malik (Jamaica), Arik Miles, Narte's (Hawaii), Gavin Audagnotti (South Africa) and Bongo (Trinidad).

⊕ □ X.R.L. RECORDS/MUSIC

White House Farm, Shropshire TF9 4HA England. (01630)647374. Fax: (01630)647612. **Contact:** Xavier Lee, International A&R Manager. A&R: Tanya Woof. UK A&R Manager: Cathrine Lee. Labels include Swoop, Zarg Records, Genouille, Pogo and Check Records. Record company, record producer and music publisher (Le Matt Music, Lee Music, R.T.F.M. and Pogo Records). Member MPA, PPL, PRS, MCPS, V.P.L. Estab. 1972. Staff size: 11. Releases 30 12″ singles, 20 LPs and 20 CDs/year. Pays negotiable royalty to artists on contract; negotiable rate to publisher for each record sold. Royalties paid to US songwriters and artists through US publishing or recording affiliate.

Distributed by Lematt Music.

How to Contact Submit demo tape by mail. Unsolicited submissions are OK. Prefers CD, cassette, MD, DVD, or VHS 625 PAL standard videocassette with 1-3 songs and lyric sheet. Include bio and still photos. IRC only. Responds in 6 weeks.

Music Mostly **pop/top 40**; also **bluegrass, blues, country, dance-oriented, easy listening, MOR, progressive, R&B, '50s rock, disco, new wave, rock** and **soul**. Released *Now and Then* (album), written and recorded by Daniel Boone (pop rock), released 2000 on Swoop; *The Creepies* (album), recorded by Nightmare (horror rock), released 2000 on Zarg; and *It's a Very Nice* (album), recorded by Groucho (pop), released 2000 on Swoop. Other artists include Orphan, The Chromatics, Mike Sheriden and the Nightriders, Johnny Moon, Dead Fish, Sight 'N' Sound and Mush.

Tips "Be original."

◪ XEMU RECORDS

19 W. 21st St., Suite 503, New York NY 10010. (212)807-0290. Fax: (212)807-0583. E-mail: xemu@x emu.com. Website: www.xemu.com. **Contact:** Dr. Claw, vice president A&R. Record company. Estab. 1992. Staff size: 4. Releases 4 CDs/year. Pays negotiable royalty to artists on contract; statutory rate to publisher per song on record.

Distributed by Redeye Distribution.

How to Contact *Write first and obtain permission to submit.* Prefers cassette with 3 songs. Does not return material. Responds in 2 months.

Music Mostly **alternative**. Released *Guess What* (album), recorded by Mikki James (alternative rock); *A is for Alpha* (album), recorded by Alpha Bitch (alternative rock); *Hold the Mayo* (album), recorded by Death Sandwich (alternative rock); *Stockholm Syndrom* (album), recorded by Trigger Happy (alternative rock); and *The Evolution of Despair* (album), recorded by The Love Kills Theory (alternative rock), all released on Xemu Records. Other artists include Malvert P. Redd, The Fifth Dementia, and the Neanderthal Spongecake.

⬛ YOUNG COUNTRY RECORDS/PLAIN COUNTRY RECORDS

P.O. Box 5412, Buena Park CA 90620. E-mail: swampbasque@msn.com. **Contact:** Leo J. Eiffert, Jr., owner. Labels include Eiffert Records and Napoleon Country Records. Record company, music publisher (Young Country Music Publishing Co./BMI, Eb-Tide Music/BMI) and record producer (Leo J. Eiffert, Jr). Releases 10 singles and 5 LPs/year. Pays negotiable royalty to artists on contract; negotiable rate to publishers per song on record.

- Also see the listings for Leo J. Eiffert, Jr. in the Record Producers section of this books and Crawfish Productions in the Managers & Booking Agents section.

How to Contact Submit demo tape by mail. Unsolicited submissions are OK. "Please make sure your song or songs are copyrighted." Prefers cassette with 2 songs and lyric sheet. Does not return material. Responds in 1 month.

Music Mostly **country**, **easy rock** and **gospel music**. Released "Time Table" (single by Leo J. Eiffert, Jr./Larry Settle), recorded by Larry Settle, released 2004 on Eiffert Records; "Burn Out" (single by Leo J. Eiffert, Jr./Mary T. Eiffert), recorded by Mary T. Eiffert; "Picture" (single by Leo J. Eiffert, Jr./Tom "Slim" Lattimer/Stephen F. Curry, Jr.), recorded by Pigeons, both released 2004 on Young Country Records. Other artists include the Woodshedders, Brandi Holland, Homemade, Crawfish Band and Larry Settle.

ADDITIONAL RECORD COMPANIES

The following companies are also record companies, but their listings are found in other sections of the book. Read the listings for submission information.

Record Producers

T he independent producer can best be described as a creative coordinator. He's often the one with the most creative control over a recording project and is ultimately responsible for the finished product. Some record companies have in-house producers who work with the acts on that label (although, in more recent years, such producer-label relationships are often non-exclusive). Today, most record companies contract out-of-house, independent record producers on a project-by-project basis.

WHAT RECORD PRODUCERS DO

Producers play a large role in deciding what songs will be recorded for a particular project and are always on the lookout for new songs for their clients. They can be valuable contacts for songwriters because they work so closely with the artists whose records they produce. They usually have a lot more freedom than others in executive positions and are known for having a good ear for potential hit songs. Many producers are songwriters and musicians themselves. Since they wield a great deal of influence, a good song in the hands of the right producer at the right time stands a good chance of being cut. And even if a producer is not working on a specific project, he is well-acquainted with record company executives and artists and can often get material through doors not open to you.

SUBMITTING MATERIAL TO PRODUCERS

It can be difficult to get your tapes to the right producer at the right time. Many producers write their own songs and even if they don't write, they may be involved in their own publishing companies so they have instant access to all the songs in their catalogs. Also, some genres are more dependent on finding outside songs than others. A producer working with a rock group or a singer-songwriter will rarely take outside songs.

It's important to understand the intricacies of the producer/publisher situation. If you pitch your song directly to a producer first, before another publishing company publishes the song, the producer may ask you for the publishing rights (or a percentage thereof) to your song. You must decide whether the producer is really an active publisher who will try to get the song recorded again and again or whether he merely wants the publishing because it means extra income for him from the current recording project. You may be able to work out a co-publishing deal, where you and the producer split the publishing of the song. That means he will still receive his percentage of the publishing income, even if you secure a cover recording of the song by other artists in the future. Even though you would be giving up a little bit initially, you may benefit in the future.

Some producers will offer to sign artists and songwriters to "development deals." These can range from a situation where a producer auditions singers and musicians with the intention of building a group from the ground up, to development deals where a producer signs a band or singer-songwriter to his production company with the intention of developing the act and producing an album to shop to labels (sometimes referred to as a "baby record deal").

You must carefully consider whether such a deal is right for you. In some cases, such a deal can open doors and propel an act to the next level. In other worst-case scenarios, such a deal can result in loss of artistic and career control, with some acts held in contractual bondage for years at a time. Before you consider any such deal, be clear about your goals, the producer's reputation, and the sort of compromises you are willing to make to reach those goals. If you have any reservations whatsoever, don't do it.

The listings that follow outline which aspects of the music industry each producer is involved in, what type of music he is looking for, and what records and artists he's recently produced. Study the listings carefully, noting the artists each producer works with, and consider if any of your songs might fit a particular artist's or producer's style. Then determine whether they are open to your level of experience (see the A Sample Listing Decoded on page 11).

Consult the Category Index on page 383 to find producers who work with the type of music you write, and the Geographic Index at the back of the book to locate producers in your area.

Icons

For more instructional information on the listings in this book, including explanations of symbols (![symbols]), read the article *Songwriter's Market: How Do I Use It?* on page 5.

For More Info

ADDITIONAL RECORD PRODUCERS

There are **more record producers** located in other sections of the book! On page 222 use the list of Additional Record Producers to find listings within other sections who are also record producers.

Record Producers

◨ ✓ ⃠ "A" MAJOR SOUND CORPORATION

RR #1, Kensington PE COB 1MO Canada. (902)836-1051. E-mail: paul.milner@summerside.ca. **Contact:** Paul C. Milner, producer. Record producer and music publisher. Estab. 1989. Produces 8 CDs/year. Fee derived in part from sales royalty when song or artist is recorded, and/or outright fee from recording artist or record company, or investors.

How to Contact Submit demo CD by mail. Unsolicited submissions are OK. Prefers CD with 5 songs and lyric sheet (lead sheet if available). Does not return material. Responds only if interested in 3 months.

Music Mostly **rock, A/C, alternative** and **pop**; also **Christian** and **R&B**. Produced *Great is the Privilege of Achievment* (album, written by David Angelis and Paul Derosa and Phil X), recorded by Supervox (rock), released 2002; *Rock Classics* (album, by various writers), recorded by Phe Cullen with Randy Waldman Trio (jazz), released 2002 on United One Records; *Jazz Standards* (album, by various writers), recorded by Phe Cullen with the Norm Amadio Trio (jazz), to be released in 2003 on United One Records; "Temptation" (single by Verdi, Paul Milner and Patrizia Pomeroy) from *Edge of Emotion* (album), recorded by Patrizia, released 2005 on Nuff Entertainment; and *Fury* (album, adapted from public domain), recorded by Patricia Pomeroy, Paul Milner and Dan Cutrona, released 2003 on B&B/Edel/Nuff Entertainment.

⃠ ABERDEEN PRODUCTIONS

524 Doral Country Dr., Nashville TN 37221. (615)646-9750. **Contact:** Scott Turner, executive producer. Record producer and music publisher (Buried Treasure Music/ASCAP, Captain Kidd/BMI). Estab. 1971. Produces 10 singles, 15-20 12" singles, 8 LPs and 8 CDs/year. Fee derived from outright fee from recording artist.

 • Also see the listing for Buried Treasure Music in the Music Publishers section of this book.

How to Contact Submit demo tape by mail. Unsolicited submissions OK. Prefers cassette with maximum 4 songs and lead sheet. Include SASE. "No SASE, no reply." Responds in 2 weeks. No "lyrics only."

Music Mostly **country, MOR** and **rock**; also **top 40/pop**. Produced "All of the Above" (single by Douglas Bush) from *The Entrance* (album), recorded by Lea Brennan (country/MOR), released 2000. Other artists include Jimmy Clanton.

Tips "Start out on an independent basis because of the heavy waiting period to get on a major label."

⃠ ACR PRODUCTIONS

P.O. Box 5636, Midland TX 79704. (432)687-2702. E-mail: dwaine915@juno.com. **Contact:** Dwaine Thomas, owner. Record producer, music publisher (Joranda Music/BMI) and record company (ACR Records). Estab. 1986. Produces 120 singles, 8-15 12" singles, 25 LPs, 25 EPs and 25 CDs/year. Fee derived from sales royalty when song or artist is recorded. "We charge for in-house recording only. Remainder is derived from royalties."

How to Contact Submit demo tape by mail. Unsolicited submissions are OK. Prefers cassette or VHS videocassette with 5 songs and lyric sheet. Does not return material. Responds in 6 weeks if interested.

Music Mostly **country swing, pop** and **rock**; also **R&B** and **gospel**. Produced *Bottle's Almost Gone* (album) and "Black Gold" (single), written and recorded by Mike Nelson (country), both released 1999 on ACR Records; and *Nashville Series* (album), written and recorded by various (country), released 1998 on ProJam Music.

Tips "Be professional. No living room tapes!"

⃠ AIF MUSIC PRODUCTIONS

P.O. Box 691, Mamaroneck NY 10543. (914)381-3559. E-mail: aif@erols.com. Website: www.robert jackson.net/aif%20records.htm. **Contact:** Robert Jackson, president. Record producer. Estab. 1995. Produces 3 singles and 4 CDs/year. Fee derived from sales royalty when song or artist is recorded or outright fee from recording artist. "We work on a combination of fee basis, plus a percentage after the deal is made."

How to Contact Submit demo by mail. Unsolicited submissions are OK. Prefers CD or cassette. "Don't send photos, lyrics or press. We work on a fee plus percentage basis." Responds in 2-3 weeks.

Music Mostly **rock, hard rock** and **alternative**; also **metal, blues, folk, pop** and **country**. Does not want rap, dance, hip-hop, death/black metal, industrial or house. Produced "Much Better" (single by Nard) from *Highways, Biways* (album), recorded by Liquor Daddies (rock/alternative), released 2002 on PA/AIF; "Found A Way" (single by M. Lough) from *Spankin' America* (album), recorded by Young Spank (rock/alternative), released 2002 on Core; and "Eastern Sands" (single by R. Zucker) from *Time Waltz* (album), recorded by Rob Zucker (rock/instrumental), released 2002 on Grease/AIF. Other artists include First Spawn.

Tips "Contact us. If you like what we say, and we are compatible, we will work with you, period. For producing, you must travel to NY/NJ/CT tri-state area or pay for my transportation. My role in a project is to coach, coordinate and oversee music, lyrics, instrumentation, arrangements, re-structuring of songs (if need be), and selection of studio musicians and facilities for recording, mixing and mastering. If you want a fantastic producer, contact me. I can hear everything, including your out-of-tune instrument."

☑ STUART J. ALLYN

250 Taxter Rd., Irvington NY 10533. (212)486-0856. Fax: (914)591-5617. E-mail: adrstudios@adrinc.org. Website: www.adrinc.org. Associate: Jack Walker. **Contact:** Jack Davis, general manager. President: Stuart J. Allyn. Record producer. Estab. 1972. Produces 6 singles and 3-6 CDs/year. Fee derived from sales royalty and outright fee from recording artist and record company.

How to Contact *Does not accept unsolicited submissions.*

Music Mostly **pop, rock, jazz** and **theatrical**; also **R&B** and **country**. Produced *Thad Jones Legacy* (album), recorded by Vanquard Jazz Orchestra (jazz), released 2000 on New World Records. Other artists include Billy Joel, Aerosmith, Carole Demas, Bob Stewart, The Dixie Peppers, Nora York, Buddy Barnes and various video and film scores.

☑ AUDIO 911

(formerly Steve Wytas Productions), P.O. Box 212, Haddam CT 06438. (860)345-3300. E-mail: info@audio911.com. Website: www.audio911.com. **Contact:** Steven J. Wytas. Record producer. Estab. 1984. Produces 4-8 singles, 3 LPs, 3 EPs and 4 CDs/year. Fee derived from outright fee from recording artist or record company.

How to Contact Submit demo tape by mail. Unsolicited submissions are OK. Prefers CD or VHS videocassette with several songs and lyric or lead sheet. "Include live material if possible." Does not return material. Responds in 3 months.

Music Mostly **rock, pop, top 40** and **country/acoustic**. Produced *Already Home* (album), recorded by Hannah Cranna on Big Deal Records (rock); *Under the Rose* (album), recorded by Under the Rose on Utter Records (rock); and *Sickness & Health* (album), recorded by Legs Akimbo on Joyful Noise Records (rock). Other artists include King Hop!, The Shells, The Gravel Pit, G'nu Fuz, Tuesday Welders and Toxic Field Mice.

⊕ ☑ BIG BEAR

Box 944, Birmingham B16 8UT United Kingdom. 44-121-454-7020. E-mail: jim@bigbearmusic.com. Website: www.bigbearmusic.com. Managing Director: Jim Simpson. Record producer, music publisher (Bearsongs) and record company (Big Bear Records). Produces 10 LPs/year. Fee derived from sales royalty.

- Also see the listings for Bearsongs in the Music Publishers section of this book and Big Bear Records in the Record Companies section of this book.

How to Contact Write first about your interest, then submit demo tape and lyric sheet. Does not return material. Responds in 2 weeks.

Music Blues, **swing** and **jazz**.

◖ CACOPHONY PRODUCTIONS
2400 Vasanta Way, Los Angeles CA 90068. (917)856-8532. Producer: Steven Miller. Record producer and music publisher (In Your Face Music). Estab. 1981. Fee derived from sales royalty when song or artist is recorded, or outright fee from recording artist or record company.
How to Contact *Call first and obtain permission to submit.* Prefers CD with 3 songs and lyric sheet. "Send a cover letter of no more than three paragraphs giving some background on yourself and the music. Also explain specifically what you are looking for Cacophony Productions to do." Does not return material. Responds only if interested.
Music Mostly **progressive pop/rock**, **singer/songwriter** and **progressive country**. Produced Dar Williams, Suzanne Vega, John Gorka, Michael Hedges, Juliana Hatfield, Toad the Wet Sprocket and Medeski-Martin & Wood.

◖ CANDYSPITEFUL PRODUCTIONS
2051 E. Cedar St., #8, Tempe AZ 85281. (480)468-7017. E-mail: mandrakerocks@yahoo.com. Website: www.candyspiteful.com. **Contact:** William Ferraro, president. Record producer, record company (Candyspiteful Productions), music publisher (Candyspiteful Productions). Estab. 2000. Produces 12 singles, 2 albums per year. Fee derived from outright fee from recording artist.
• Also see the listings for Candyspiteful Productions in the Record Companies section of this book and Major Entertainment in the Music Publishers section of this book.
How to Contact Submit demo tape by mail. Unsolicited submissions are OK. Prefers CD/CDR with 3 songs and lyric sheet and cover letter. Does not return material. Responds only if interested.
Music Mostly **progressive rock**, **rock/pop/R&B** and **smooth jazz/rock**. Produced *Cloud Nine* (album written by David Farnsworth), recorded by Thunderhead (hard rock), released 2001 on Candyspiteful Productions.

◻ JAN CELT MUSICAL SERVICES
4015 NE 12th Ave., Portland OR 97212. E-mail: flyheart@teleport.com. Website: http://home.teleport.com/~flyheart. **Contact:** Jan Celt, owner. Record producer, music producer and publisher (Wiosna Nasza Music/BMI) and record company (Flying Heart Records). Estab. 1982. Produces 3-5 CDs/year.
• Also see the listing for Flying Heart Records in the Record Companies section of this book.
How to Contact Submit demo tape by mail. Unsolicited submissions are OK. Prefers high-quality cassette with 1-10 songs and lyric sheet. "SASE required for any response." Does not return materials. Responds in 4 months.
Music Mostly **R&B**, **rock** and **blues**; also **jazz**. Produced "Vexatious Progressions" (single), written and recorded by Eddie Harris (jazz); "Bong Hit" (single by Chris Newman), recorded by Snow Bud & the Flower People (rock); and "She Moved Away" (single by Chris Newman), recorded by Napalm Beach, all on Flying Heart Records. Other artists include The Esquires and Janice Scroggins.

◻ COACHOUSE MUSIC
P.O. Box 1308, Barrington IL 60011. (847)382-7631. Fax: (847)382-7651. E-mail: coachouse1@aol.com. **Contact:** Michael Freeman, president. Record producer. Estab. 1984. Produces 6-8 CDs/year. Fee derived from sales royalty when song or artist is recorded.
How to Contact *Write or e-mail first and obtain permission to submit.* Prefers CD, cassette, with 3-5 songs and lyric sheet. Include SASE. Responds in 6 weeks.
Music Mostly **rock**, **pop** and **blues**; also **alternative rock** and **country/Americana/roots**. Produced *Casque Nu* (album), written and recorded by Charlelie Couture on Chrysalis EMI France (contemporary pop); *Time Will Tell*, recorded by Studebaker John on Blind Pig Records (blues); *Where Blue Begins* (album by various/D. Coleman), recorded by Deborah Coleman on Blind Pig Records (contemporary blues); *A Man Amongst Men* (album), recorded by Bo Diddley (blues); and *Voodoo Menz* (album), recorded by Corey Harris and Henry Butler. Other artists include Echosend, Eleventh Dream Day, Magic Slim, The Tantrums, The Pranks, The Bad Examples, Mississippi Heat and Supermint.
Tips "Be honest, be committed, strive for excellence."

▦ ◯ COAL HARBOR MUSIC

P.O. Box 148027, Nashville TN 37214-8027. (615)883-2020. E-mail: jerry@coalharbormusic.com. Website: www.coalharbormusic.com. **Contact:** Jerry Ray Wells, producer. Record producer, record company (Coal Harbor Music), music publisher (Coal Harbor Music), and radio promotion company. Estab. 1990. Produces 10-15 singles/year and 3-5 albums/year. Fee derived from sales royalty when song or artist is recorded, outright fee from recording artist, outright fee from record company, or from investors (depending on situation/artist/project).

How to Contact Submit a demo tape by mail. Unsolicited submissions are OK with 3-5 songs and cover letter. We do not return submissions. Responds only if interested.

Music Mostly **country, Christian (all forms), bluegrass**; also **pop/AC, jazz/blues, Christmas/ novelty**. Does not want hard rock, heavy metal, or rap. Produced "It Overwhelms Me" (single by Sara Aten/Vicky Schneider) from *The Cross of Christ* (album), recorded by Sara Aten (contemporary Christian), released 2005 on Coal Harbor Music; "You" (single) from *Unraveled* (album), written and recorded by Anne Borgen (contemporary Christian), released 2004 on Coal Harbor Music; and "So Good To Know" (single) from *All I Need* (album), written and recorded by Damon Westfaul (southern gospel), released 2004 on Coal Harbor Music.

Tips "Other artists include Angela Baker Wells, Holly Norman, Don Freeman, and Teri Garrison."

▦ ◪ COLD CREEK RECORDS (CCR)

(formerly Interstate Records), 2479 Murfreesboro Rd. #327, Nashville TN 37217-3554. (615)361-4438. Fax: (615)361-4438. E-mail: coldcreekent@aol.com. CEO: Jack Batey. President of A&R: Jackson Smith. Record producer and record company. Estab. 2001. Produces 10 singles and 2 CDs/year. Pays negotiable royalty to artist on contract; statutory rate to publisher per song on record.

How to Contact Submit demo tape or CD by mail. Unsolicited submissions are OK. Prefers CD or cassette with 3-5 songs and lyric sheet. "In screening artists we ask for original material only. Thus we can listen for originality in vocal delivery and judge the strength of writing capabilities. (Please no cover songs or karaoke voice overs)." Does not return material. Responds in 2 months.

Music Mostly **traditional country, bluegrass, Texas swing** and **cowboy ballads**. Produced "Bad Love" (single), written and recorded by Barbi Presley; and "Us Cowboys Know How to Take a Fall" (by Larry and Rob Matson), recorded by Bart McEntire, all on Ameri-Star.

Tips "Be original in your vocals, lyrics and melodies. Submitting full production demos is not necessary. We prefer a vocal with guitar or piano to accompany."

▦ ◪ COLLECTOR RECORDS

P.O. Box 1200, 3260 AE Oud Beyerland, Holland, The Netherlands. (31)(18)660-4266. Fax: (32)(18)660-4366. E-mail: info@collectorrecords.nl. Web site: www.collectorrecords.nl. **Contact:** Cees Klop, president. Record producer and music publisher (All Rock Music). Produces 25 CDs/year. Fee derived from outright fee from record company.

- Also see the listings for All Rock Music in the Music Publishers section and Collector Records in the Record Companies section of this book.

How to Contact Submit demo tape by mail. Unsolicited submissions are OK. Prefers cassette. SAE and IRC. Responds in 2 months.

Music Mostly **'50s rock, rockabilly** and **country rock**; also **piano boogie woogie**. Produced *When You Rock And Roll* (album), recorded by Marvin Jackson (1950s rockers); *Bobby Crown & The Kapers* (album), recorded by Bobby Crown (1950s rockers); and *Rock, Rock, Rockin' Tonight* (album), recorded by various artists (1950s rockers), all released 2004 on Collector Records.

Tips "Only send the kind of music we produce."

▦ ◪ JOHNNY COPPIN/RED SKY RECORDS

P.O. Box 27, Stroud, Glos. GL6 0YQ United Kingdom. Tel./Fax: (01)(45)383-6877. E-mail: johnny@j ohnnycoppin.co.uk. **Contact:** Johnny Coppin, producer. Record producer, music publisher (PRS) and record company (Red Sky Records). Estab. 1985. Produces 1 album/year. Fee derived from sales royalty when song or artist is recorded.

• Also see the listing for Red Sky Records in the Record Companies section of this book.

How to Contact *Write first and obtain permission to submit.* Does not return material. Responds in 6 months.

Music Mostly **rock**, **modern folk** and **roots music**. Produced "A Country Christmas" and "Keep the Flame" written and recorded by Johnny Coppin; and "Dead Lively!," written and recorded by Paul Burgess, all on Red Sky Records. Other artists include David Goodland.

✪ CHARLIE CRAIG PRODUCTIONS

P.O. Box 1448, Mt. Juliet TN 37121-1448. Website: www.charliecraig.com. **Contact:** Charlie Craig, producer. Record producer and music publisher (Song Machine/BMI, Walker Publishing Co. L.L.C./ASCAP/BMI). Estab. 2001. Produces 5 singles and 5 CDs/year. Fee derived from sales royalty and/or outright fee from recording artist.

• Charlie Craig Productions received a Grammy nomination in 1991 and Song of the Year nominations in 1986 and 1991. Was inducted into the South Carolina Entertainment Hall of Fame in 1998.

How to Contact *Write or call first to arrange personal interview.* For song publishing submissions, prefers CD with 3 songs, lyric sheet and lead sheet. "Include e-mail address for response." Does not return submissions. Responds in 3 weeks via e-mail only.

Music Mostly **traditional country**, **new country** and **country pop**. Co-produced *The Nashville Super Pickers* (album), recorded by The Nashville Super Pickers Band (country), released 1972 on Royal American Records. "First Nashville writer to work with Alan Jackson. Extensively involved in getting a record deal for the Wilkinsons with Giant Records"

Tips "Be prepared to record only the best songs, even if it takes an extended length of time. We won't go into the studio until we have great songs. Vocals should be memorized before going into the studio. You need to express as much emotion as possible. Suggestions are welcome from artists and musicians, but final decisions are made by the Producer. We will make sure the vocals are perfect no matter how many takes are necessary. Be prepared to work."

☑ ✪ CREATIVE SOUL

(formerly Masterscore Music), Nashville TN 37179. (859)492-6403. E-mail: info@creativesoulonline.com. Website: www.creativesoulonline.com. **Contact:** Eric Copeland, producer/writer. Record producer. Produces 5-10 singles and 8-15 albums/year. Fee derived from outright fee from recording artist or company. Other fees include critique/review services.

How to Contact *Contact first by e-mail to obtain permission to submit demo.* Prefers CD with 2-3 songs and lyric sheet and cover sheet. Does not return submissions. Responds only if interested.

Music Mostly **contemporary Christian**, **jazz** and **instrumental**; also **R&B** and **pop/rock**. Does not want country, metal, punk, or hardcore. Produced *Leaving Egypt* (album), recorded by Tom Dolan (Contemporary Christian); *Invitation* (album), recorded by Brett Rush (Worship/Rock); *Out of the Box* (album), recorded by Erin Hutchison (Contemporary Christian), all released 2005 on Creative Soul Records. Other artists include Kristyn Leigh, Eleanor Riley, and Amanda Fessant.

Tips "Contact us first by e-mail, but please do not send mp3s without e-mailing first. We will delete any unsolicited mp3s without listening. E-mail us and let's start talking about your music and ministry!"

▢ DAP ENTERTAINMENT

PMB 364, 7100 Lockwood Blvd., Boardman OH 44512. (330)726-8737. Fax: (330)782-6954. Website: www.dapentertainment.com. **Contact:** Darryl Alexander, producer. Record Producer and music publisher (Alexander Sr. Music, BMI). Estab. 1997. Produces 12 singles and 2-4 CDs/year. Fee derived from sales royalty (producer points) when song or artist is recorded or outright fee from recording artist or record company.

• Also see the listing for Alexander Sr. Music in the Music Publishers section of this book.

How to Contact *Write first and obtain permission to submit.* Prefers CD with 2-4 songs and lyric sheet. Include SASE. Responds in 1 month. "No phone calls or faxes will be accepted."

Music Mostly **contemporary jazz**, **urban contemporary gospel**; also **R&B**. Produced "Plumb

Line'' (single by Herb McMullen/Darryl Alexander) from *Diamond In the Sky* (album); ''Cafe Rio'' and ''Garden of My Heart'' (singles) from *Diamond In the Sky*, written and recorded by Darryl Alexander (contemporary jazz), all released 2004 on DAP Entertainment. Other artists include Kathryn Williams.

◢ ◎ DAVINCI'S NOTEBOOK RECORDS

Niagara Falls, ON L2P 1G6 Canada. (905)359-1616. E-mail: admin@davincismusic.com. Website: www.davincismusic.com. **Owner:** Kevin Richard. Record producer, record company, music publisher, distributor and MIDI recording facility. Estab. 1992. Produces 1 cassette and 1 CD/year. Fee derived from outright fee from artist or commission on sales.

How to Contact E-mail first for postal details then submit demo CD by mail. Unsolicited submissions are OK. Prefers CD and bio. Does not return material. Responds in 6 weeks.

Music Mostly **rock**, **instrumental rock**, **New Age** and **progressive-alternative**; also **R&B**, **pop** and **jazz**. Produced *Windows* (by Kevin Hotte/Andy Smith), recorded by Musicom on DaVinci's Notebook Records (power New Age); *Inventing Fire*, written and recorded by Kevin Richard on DNR/Independent (instrumental rock); and *The Cunninghams*, written and recorded by The Cunninghams on Independent (gospel).

Tips ''DNR is an artist-run label. Local bands and performers will receive priority. Be more interested in getting a-foot-in-the-door exposure as opposed to making a fortune. Be satisfied with conquering the world using 'baby steps.' Indie labels don't have large corporate budgets for artist development. We are more about online distribution than artist development. Being a local act means that you can perform live to promote your releases. For indie artist, selling from the stage is probably going to bring you the biggest volume of sales.''

◢ ◎ EDWARD DE MILES

28 E. Jackson Bldg., 10th Floor #S627, Chicago IL 60604-2263. (773)509-6381. Fax: (312)922-6964. Website: www.edmsahara.com. **Contact:** Edward De Miles, president. Record producer, music publisher (Edward De Miles Music Co./BMI) and record company (Sahara Records and Filmworks Entertainment). Estab. 1981. Produces 5-10 CDs/year. Fee derived from sales royalty when song or artist is recorded.

• Also see the listing for Edward De Miles in the Music Publishers and Managers & Booking Agents sections, as well as Sahara Records and Filmworks Entertainment in the Record Companies section of this book.

How to Contact *Does not accept unsolicited submissions.*

Music Mostly **R&B/dance**, **top 40 pop/rock** and **contemporary jazz**; also **country**, **TV and film themes—songs** and **jingles**. Produced ''Moments'' and ''Dance Wit Me'' (singles) (dance), both written and recorded by Steve Lynn; and ''Games'' (single), written and recorded by D'von Edwards (jazz), all on Sahara Records. Other artists include Multiple Choice.

Tips ''Copyright all material before submitting. Equipment and showmanship a must.''

◢ ◎ AL DELORY AND MUSIC MAKERS

3000 Hillsboro Rd. #11, Nashville TN 37215. Fax: (615)297-6031. E-mail: aldelory@mn.rr.com. Website: www.aldelory.com. **Contact:** Al DeLory, president. Record producer and career consultant (MUSIC MAKERS/ASCAP). Estab. 1987. Fee derived from outright fee from recording artist.

• Al DeLory has won two Grammy Awards and has been nominated five times.

How to Contact *Write or e-mail first and obtain permission to submit or to arrange personal interview.* Prefers CD or cassette. Include SASE. Responds in 1-2 months only if interested.

Music Mostly **pop** and **Latin**. Produced ''Gentle On My Mind'' (single), ''By the Time I Get to Phoenix'' (single) and ''Wichita Lineman'' (single), all recorded by Glen Campbell. Other artists include Lettermen, Wayne Newton, Bobbie Gentry and Anne Murray.

Tips ''Seek advice and council only with professionals with a track record and get the money up front.''

☑ JOEL DIAMOND ENTERTAINMENT

Dept. SM, 3940 Laurel Canyon Blvd., Suite 441, Studio City CA 91604. (818)980-9588. Fax: (818)980-9422. E-mail: jdiamond20@aol.com. Website: www.joeldiamond.com. **Contact:** Joel Diamond. Record producer, music publisher and manager. Fee derived from sales royalty when song is recorded or outright fee from recording artist or record company.

• Also see the listing for Silver Blue Music/Oceans Blue Music in the Music Publishers section of this book.

How to Contact Does not return material. Responds only if interested.

Music Mostly **dance**, **R&B**, **soul** and **top 40/pop**. Produced "One Night In Bangkok" (single by Robey); "I Think I Love You," recorded by Katie Cassidy (daughter of David Cassidy) on Artemis Records; "After the Loving" (single), recorded by E. Humperdinck; "Forever Friends," recorded by Vaneza (featured on Nickelodeon's "The Brothers Garcia"); and "Paradise" (single), recorded by Kaci.

☑ ESQUIRE INTERNATIONAL

P.O. Box 6032, Station B, Miami FL 33101-6032. (305)547-1424. Fax: (305)547-1424. E-mail: stuacr @aol.com. **Contact:** Jeb Stuart, president. Record producer, music publisher (Jeb Stuart Music) and management firm. Produces 6 singles and 2 LPs/year. Fee derived from sales royalty or independent leasing of masters and placing songs.

• Also see the listing for Jeb Stuart Music Co. in the Music Publishers section of this book.

How to Contact Submit demo tape by mail. Unsolicited submissions are OK. Prefers cassette or CD with 2-4 songs and lead sheet. Include SASE. Responds in 1 month.

Music Mostly **blues**, **church/religious**, **country**, **dance**, **gospel**, **jazz**, **rock**, **soul** and **top 40/pop**. Produced "Go to Sleep, Little Baby" (single by Jeb Stuart), recorded by Cafidia and Jeb Stuart; "Guns Guns (No More Guns)" (single) and "No One Should Be Alone on Christmas" (single), both written and recorded by Jeb Stuart; "Mr. Love Jinx" and "Peer Pressure" from *Peer Pressure* (album), recorded by Cafidia Stuart (blues/rock); "Hey Foxy Lady" and "Maxie D" from *Jeb Stuart Collection By Request* (album), recorded by Jeb Stuart. Other artists include Moments Notice and Night Live.

☑ HAILING FREQUENCY MUSIC PRODUCTIONS

7438 Shoshone Ave., Van Nuys CA 91406. (818)881-9888. Fax: (818)881-0555. E-mail: blowinsmok eband@ktb.net. Website: www.blowinsmokeband.com. President: Lawrence Weisberg. Vice President: Larry Knight. Record producer, record company (Blowin' Smoke Records), management firm (Blowin' Smoke Productions) and music publisher (Hailing Frequency Publishing). Estab. 1992. Produces 3 LPs and 3 CDs/year. Fee derived from sales royalty when song or artist is recorded or outright fee from artist.

• Also see the listing for Blowin' Smoke Productions/Records in the Managers & Booking Agents section of this book.

How to Contact *Write or call first and obtain permission to submit.* Prefers cassette or VHS ½″ videocassette. "Write or print legibly with complete contact instructions." Include SASE. Responds in 1 month.

Music Mostly **contemporary R&B**, **blues** and **blues-rock**; also **songs for film**, **jingles for commercials** and **gospel (contemporary)**. Produced "Beyond the Blues Horizon" (single), recorded by Blowin' Smoke Rhythm & Blues Band, released 2004. Other artists include the Fabulous Smokettes.

⃞ ☑ HEART CONSORT MUSIC

410 First St. W., Mt. Vernon IA 52314. E-mail: mail@heartconsortmusic.com. Website: www.heartc onsortmusic.com. **Contact:** Catherine Lawson, manager. Record producer, record company and music publisher. Estab. 1980. Produces 2-3 CDs/year. Fee derived from sales royalty when song or artist is recorded.

How to Contact Submit demo tape by mail. Unsolicited submissions are OK. Prefers cassette or VHS videocassette with 3 songs and 3 lyric sheets. Include SASE. Responds in 3 months.

Music Mostly **jazz**, **New Age** and **contemporary**. Produced *New Faces* (album), written and recorded by James Kennedy on Heart Consort Music (world/jazz).

Tips "We are interested in jazz/New Age artists with quality demos and original ideas. We aim for an international audience."

☑ ⊘ HESFREE PRODUCTIONS & PUBLISHING COMPANY

P.O. Box 1214, Bryan TX 77806-1214. (979)268-3263. Fax: (979)589-2544. E-mail: hesfreeprodandp ubco@yahoo.com. Website: www.hesfreeproductions.com. President/CEO/Owner: Brenda M. Freeman-Heslip. Producer of songwriting: Jamie Heslip. Vice President/Owner: Rochelle Heslip. Record producer, music publisher and management agency. Estab. 2001. Fee derived from sales royalty when song or artist is recorded, outright fee from recording artist and outright fee from record company.

How to Submit *Only accepts material referred to by a reputable industry source (manager, entertainment attorney, etc.).* Include CD/CDR. Does not return submissions. Responds in 6 weeks only if interested.

Music Mostly **R&B**, **gospel**, **rap** and **rock**. Does not want country. "We will ensure that each project is complete with professionalism, with the highest technology methods possible. Additionally, our goal is to publish and record over 200 songs annually." Produced "Texas Boys" (single by Chris Idlebird) from *Texas Boys* (album), recorded by Chris Idlebird and Vicki Diggs (rap), released 2002; "Controversial Crossover" (single by "Mike-Ray" Ray Brooks) from *Controversial Crossover* (album), recorded by "Mike-Ray" Ray Brooks (R&B), released 2002; "Walk through the Rays" (single by Donell Travis), from *Dontray the Ghetto Prophet* (album), recorded by Conett Travis and Ralatraneka Mercer (rap), released 2002; "Feel My Pain" (single by Emmett Wilson), recorded by Li'l Dee (hip-hop); "Body Rock Your Block" (single by Marcus Franklin), recorded by Marky D, both released 2003. Also Donnise Williams; Damion Turner; "Michael-Wayne" Wells.

☐ ☑ HUMAN FACTOR PRODUCTIONS

(formerly HF Productions), P.O. Box 3742, Washington DC 20027. (202)415-7748. E-mail: info@hfp roductions.com. Website: www.hfproductions.com. **Contact:** Blake Althen or Paula Bellenoit, producers/owners. Estab. 2001. Record producer. "Human Factor Productions is a full service music production company featuring the hottest multi-talented producers, engineers, and state-of-the-art studios. We work with labels, seasoned artists, and develop/shop new talent. Services include production, arranging, composition, recording services, mixing, mastering, artist development and artist label shop."

• See the article written by Blake Althen with Paula Bellenoit on pg. 56 about dance remixing songs for the dance market entitled "The Power of the Remix."

How to Contact *Please call or e-mail to get permission to submit.* "Solicited material only."

Music Mostly **adult contemporary**, **pop**, **singer/songwriter**, **rock (all types)**, **world/ethnic**, **techno/electronica**, **rap** and **soundtrack/film score**. Produced "Fall Down," and "Without Light" (by S. Bitz), recorded by Abby Someone (heartland rock). Other artists include Jennifer Cutting's Ocean Orchestra (contemporary folk rock, celtic), Rachel Paney (dance), Pale Beneath the Blue (adult contemporary/singer/songwriter), Tommy Wosyluk (singer/songwriter), Mark Bodino (adult contemporary), Scandelle (adult contemporary/techno/electronica), Gate 22 (rock), and more.

Tip "Get your goals clear in your mind and on paper. What do want a producer to do for you? Know the answer to this question, and it will guide you to the industry professionals who are right for you."

☑ ☐ INTEGRATED ENTERTAINMENT

1815 JFK Blvd., Philadelphia PA 19103. (215)563-7147. E-mail: gelboni@aol.com. **Contact:** Gelboni, president. Record producer. Estab. 1991. Produces 6 EPs and 6 CDs/year. Fee derived from sales royalty when song or artist is recorded or outright fee from recording artist or record company.

How to Contact Submit demo CD by mail. Solicited submissions only. CD only with 3 songs. "Draw a guitar on the outside of envelope so we'll know it's from a songwriter." Responds in 2 months.

Music Mostly **rock** and **pop**. Produced *Gold Record* (album), written and recorded by Dash Rip Rock on Ichiban Records (rock); *Virus* (album), written and recorded by Margin of Error on Treehouse Records (modern rock); and *I Divide* (album), written and recorded by Amy Carr on Evil Twin Records (AAA). Other artists include Land of the Blind, Gatlin, Ash Wednesday, Playing for Audrey, Three Miles Out and others.

Michelangelo

Makes the Future Perfect
with Human Factor

Photo by Ashnell G. Tyson

Pop artist Michelangelo (née Michelangelo Sosnowitz) got an early start in his relationship with music as a pianist. "I just loved playing piano," he says. "I played it the way other kids played Sega." This eventually led to classical piano and composition studies in the New York University film scoring program. He later composed music for HBO, USA, PBS, and Off-Broadway, as well as the Jumbotron at Madison Square Garden with the Harlem Boys Choir.

Michelangelo eventually dropped his soundtrack career to focus on his pop ambitions as both songwriter and performer. He recorded his first album, *In the Beginning* (1999), in his bedroom on a digital 8-track recorder, then put together a band for his second release, *Elements* (2000). His third self-released album, *Future Perfect* (2004), began with a three-track sampler of new songs recorded with Blake Althen and Paula Bellenoit of Human Factor Productions (interviewed in the 2005 *Songwriter's Market*). Here Michelangelo talks about those sessions and the current progression of his career:

Do you feel like Blake and Paula connected with you as producers?
Working with Blake and Paula was great. Blake has ears like no one else. We started with one song. I had the song completed but hadn't fleshed out the arrangement, so we did it right there on his computer. That first song was "Linger," and when you hear the first three chords, the whole thing—the style, the sound, the look, the image, the feel—is laid out in front of you.

Blake told me he will look for the heart of the song by overproducing it, and then bring Paula in to comment and cut back. Is this what they did?
That's exactly what happened. Blake and I recorded a scratch version, and then Paula came in, listened to it, and gave us her gut reaction. Blake is more sonically attuned. He hears stuff that I would never, ever even think to listen for. When doing the songs, I would hear, "Oh, maybe the bass should come out here and start up here." And he's hearing, "Oh, maybe the snare needs to be compressed, and some exciter put on this thing, and this needs . . ." He was hearing sonics. Paula was able to come in and bring out the emotional appeal in the songs. She's also a piano player and so she could connect with my way of writing. They make a great team.

Did you choose Human Factor from Blake's demo reel?
When it came time for me to record, Nira Paliwoda, my manager, went after these producers and got a bunch of CDs. The reason I went with Blake was because his sound was very

clean and very slick. Just a big, shiny sound, and without bringing the entire band to record, his was my favorite.

So you worked with other producers and then had Blake master your full-length?

I got into a songwriting factory and one of the producers, Tony Woodroffen, was really interested in recording my music for a full CD, so we recorded six more songs, and a few more with another producer, Arham Lee, in Queens. It was the six with Tony, one with Aaron, and three with Blake that turned out to be the CD. Then, Blake mastered it to give it all one sheen, and he has the best ears of anyone, so who better?

Would you produce yourself or do you like having that other voice and viewpoint in the studio?

Producing is a passion, and I'd rather leave that to people with a passion for it. I have a passion for writing music and collaborating. There are a lot of composers who engineer and produce and all of that, but I don't really have a passion for it. Although I do hear songs and think, "Oh, you shouldn't do that!" In the studio, if someone's changing a song into a Klingon opera, then it's like, "NOOO!! Bring it back!" But, it is good to have someone there, because you second-guess yourself.

What kind of relationship with Blake and Paula have you had since in terms of helping your career?

I bounce stuff off them to see what they think. We've kept each other updated as we've grown. Blake was one of my first experiences in the pop world, so just off that initial thing we've created a relationship. We stay in touch, and he mastered my full-length album. The only frustrating thing is that he's five hours away, so it's kind of hard to bring my band to him.

What kind of things did you bring back to pop songwriting from your classical training and experience in the film world?

The manifestation of the training was the songs were not generic pop songs. They had an intricacy which appealed to musicians, but which might not always appeal to everyone, so I've actually had to mainstream it out since then. But when I started I was all over the place and very complicated.

Also, in the film world, I have to make the music fit what someone else wants it to be. And it's funny because when I first started my ego took a big hit. I'd be like *It has to be this!* And the director would be like, *No, it has to do this, and change that, and there shouldn't be music here, and there should be music here!* And I have to say, in the end it was always better after the director changed it.

But one thing about film scoring that is really nice is that you can have breadth. You can write something with span and scope. I did one indie film where they wanted an electronic lullabye, one that was all-out classical, one that was kind of punk, and I'm learning in the pop world if something strikes me and I want to go Latin with it, or I want to go reggae, or I want to go ska, or I want to go wherever, you can't stray. They want you to keep to a narrow road. It all has to be within the same style.

Do you start with lyrics first or music first?

Music first. Then lyrics are a whole separate thing. I start singing along with what I'm playing, vowel sounds come out, [*scats some vowels*] and then these turn into actual words. Based on how the vowels go, the words come, and then the story behind it, which might be totally incongruous to the song. The music might pop out and be really happy and upbeat, and then the words are totally depressed.

I'll write pages and pages with stuff x-ed out. I like to edit on the computer now, since you can edit and paste right there. Sometimes in rehearsal, the more I sing with it and the more we live with it, the lyrics change a little bit. Then my background singers hate me because I'll forget the lyrics.

How have your record sales been as an independent?

We've done pretty well considering our main publicity and radio campaign has not launched yet. We were on the college charts for a while, which was the most advertising we got. We've sold CDs in places we haven't played yet, such as Alaska and Oregon, Sweden, and Budapest. So I get excited, and I think for CD sales we're doing fine. We move them at shows, too, which is nice.

Has it mostly been your established fan base, or have online sales been instrumental?

Online, on the CDFreedom website, is where a lot of my CDs have sold. They're also available online at CDBaby.com and Tower.com, and we've made them available for download through iTunes, MSN, etc. We do also sell them at shows, which aren't recorded on SoundScan. But, yeah, online has been great, and it lets us know who has been buying it, so you can see an address and say, "Oh, that's my best friend in L.A." Or you'll see an address and think, "I don't know anyone in Morristown, New Jersey, Palo Alto, California, or Duluth, Minnesota!"

Have you done a radio promotion campaign? If so, how did that work?

We did put money into a promoter, and then they funneled the CD out to the stations, and then follow up. The stations then decide whether they're going to add it to their list, and if they do, whether they're going to add it to heavy, medium, or light rotation. I feel really fortunate that we got so many adds—well over a hundred—and a big bulk in heavy rotation, too. That was very flattering.

Have record labels shown interest?

We have labels that are interested and are watching us. The live show has gotten so much more powerful and energized, which is important. It wasn't until recently that I learned you've got to *put on a show!* And you've got to move around and dance and be a powerhouse full of energy. So, I guess now I'm aware there's a formula to all of that, too, and in the last year I've been writing with a consciousness toward all of that.

What kind of advice do you have for *Songwriter's Market* readers?

I don't mean for this to be negative, but don't always think that listeners know and appreciate music. Even A&R people, label people, music industry people, might not know how to spell a G minor chord. And so you could write Mozart's *Mass Requiem*, and a lot of people wouldbe like, "Well, that was long." So keep that in mind. That, and it doesn't happen overnight, no matter how brilliant you are. I don't know how a genius like Frank Zappa would break through in today's music world. Or Steely Dan for that matter. Also, no one is going to hand you rock stardom. You really have to go out there and prove it. And that unfortunately—this really does sound negative, but this is what I've learned—the music industry is not about music. It seems to be about business. But—and this is an Ayn Rand, *Fountainhead*-sort of point of view—I really hope the music will speak for itself, that the art will speak for itself, no matter who or what is the new hot thing.

—Ian Bessler

ALEXANDER JANOULIS PRODUCTIONS/BIG AL JANO PRODUCTIONS

1957 Kilburn Dr., Atlanta GA 30324. (770)662-6661. E-mail: ajproductions@hottrax.com. **Contact:** Oliver Cooper, vice president of A&R. CEO: Alex Janoulis. Record producer. Produces 6 singles and 2 CDs/year. Fee derived from sales royalty when song or artist is recorded or outright fee from recording artist or record company.

• Also see the listing for Hottrax Records in the Record Companies section of this book.

How to Contact *Write first and obtain permission to submit.* "Letters should be short, requesting submission permission." Prefers CD with 1-3 songs. Does not return material. Responds in 6 months.

Music Mostly **top 40, rock** and **pop**; also **black** and **disco**. Produced *Lady That Digs the Blues* (album), recorded by Big Al Jano's Blues Mafia Show; *Everythang & Mo'* (album), written and recorded by Sammy Blue (blues); and *Blues You Can't Refuse* (album), written and recorded by Big Al (blues), both released 2000 on Hottrax Records. Other artists include Butch Trivette, Little Phil, Bullitthead, Roger Hurricane Wilson, The Bob Page Project, Mike Lorenz and Chesterfield Kings.

JAY JAY PUBLISHING & RECORD CO.

P.O. Box 41-4156, Miami Beach FL 33141. (305)758-0000. Owner: Walter Jagiello. Associate: J. Kozak. Record producer, music publisher (BMI) and record company (Jay Jay Record, Tape and Video Co.). Estab. 1951. Produces 12 singles, 12 LPs and 12 CDs/year. Fee derived from sales royalty when song or artist is recorded.

How to Contact Submit demo by mail. Unsolicited submissions are OK. Prefers CD of cassette or VHS videocassette with 6 songs and lyric and lead sheet. "Quality cassette or reel-to-reel, sheet music and lyrics." Does not return material. Responds in 2 months.

Music Mostly **ballads, love songs, country music** and **comedy**; also **polkas, hymns, gospel** and **waltzes**. Produced seven Christmas albums in English and Polish, recorded by the S.P. Stanislaus Choral Group of Michigan City, IN and the Lucky Harmony Boys Orchestra. Other artists include Eddie & The Slovenes, Johnny Vandal, Wisconsin Dutchmen and Eddie Zima.

JERICHO SOUND LAB

4 River Rd., P.O. Box 407, Jericho VT 05465. (802)899-3787. E-mail: jerichosoundlab@aol.com Website: http://members.aol.com/jerichosoundlab/. **Contact:** Bobby Hackney, owner. Record producer, music publisher (Elect Music/BMI) and record company (LBI Records). Estab. 1988. Produces 5 singles, 2 12" singles and 3 LPs/year. Fee derived from sales royalty when song or artist is recorded.

• Also see the listings for Elect Music Publishing in the Music Publishers section and LBI Records in the Record Companies section of this book.

How to Contact *Write first and obtain permission to submit.* Prefers CD, cassette or VHS videocassette with 3-4 songs and lyric sheet. Include SASE. Responds in 6 weeks.

Music Mostly **reggae, R&B** and **pop**; also **rock** and **jazz-poetry**. Produced "Spotlight on You" (by B. Hackney), and "Sharing and Caring," recorded by Lambsbread (reggae), both on LBI Records.

Tips "Make it plain and simple. Send only your best. Most producers know within 10 to 15 seconds if a song catches their attention."

JUMP PRODUCTIONS

31 Paul Gilsonstraat, 8200 St-Andries Belgium. (050)31-63-80. E-mail: happymelody@skynet.be. **Contact:** Eddy Van Mouffaert, general manager. Record producer and music publisher (Jump Music). Estab. 1976. Produces 25 singles and 2 CDs/year. Fee derived from sales royalty when song or artist is recorded.

• Also see the listing for Happy Melody in the Music Publishers section of this book.

How to Contact Submit demo CD or tape by mail. Unsolicited submissions are OK. Prefers CD. Does not return material. Responds in 2 weeks.

Music Mostly **ballads, up-tempo, easy listening, disco** and **light pop**; also **instrumentals**. Produced "De Club Is Kampioen" (single by H. Spider/E. Govert), recorded by Benny Scott (light pop), released 2005 on Scorpion; *A Christmas of Hope* (album), recorded by Chris Clark (pop), released 2004 on 5 Stars; and *The Best of Le Grand Julot* (album), recorded by Le Grand Julot (accordion), released 2000 on Happy Melody.

🌐 🖉 JUNE PRODUCTIONS LTD.
"Toftrees," Church Rd., Woldingham, Surrey CR3 7JH England. Fax: 44(0)1883 652457. E-mail: david@mackay99.plus.com. **Contact:** David Mackay, producer. Record producer and music producer (Sabre Music). Estab. 1970. Produces 6 singles, 3 LPs and 3 CDs/year. Fee derived from sales royalty.

How to Contact Submit demo tape by mail. Unsolicited submissions are OK. Prefers CD or cassette with 1-2 songs and lyric sheet. SAE and IRC. Responds in 2 months.

Music Mostly **MOR**, **rock** and **top 40/pop**. Produced *Web of Love* (by various), recorded by Sarah Jory on Ritz Records (country rock). Other artists include Bonnie Tyler, Cliff Richard, Frankie Miller, Johnny Hallyday, Dusty Springfield, Charlotte Henry and Barry Humphries.

🌑 KINGSTON RECORDS AND TALENT
15 Exeter Rd., Kingston NH 03848. (603)642-8493. E-mail: kingstonrecords@ttlc.net. Website: www.kingstonrecords.com. **Contact:** Harry Mann, coordinator. Record producer, music publisher (Strawberry Soda Publishing/ASCAP) and record company (Kingston Records). Estab. 1988. Produces 3-4 singles, 2-3 12″ singles, 2-3 LPs and 1-2 CDs/year. Fee derived from sales royalty when song or artist is recorded. Deals primarily with NE and local artists.
   • Also see the listing for Kingston Records in the Record Companies section of this book.

How to Contact *Write first and obtain permission to submit.* Prefers cassette with 1-2 songs and lyric sheet. Does not return material. Responds in 2 months.

Music Mostly **rock**, **country** and **pop**; "no heavy metal." Produced *Count the Stars* (album), written and recorded by award winning singer/songwriter Doug Mitchell; *Time Machine* (album), written and recorded by Gratefull Ted, both released 1999 on Kingston Records. Other artists include Bob Moore, Candy Striper Death Orgy, Pocket Band, Jeff Walker, J. Evans, NTM, Miss Bliss, Ted Solovicus, Armand LeMay, Four On The Floor and Sumx4.

◻ L.A. ENTERTAINMENT, INC.
7095 Hollywood Blvd., #826, Hollywood CA 90028. (323)467-1496. Fax: (323)467-0911. E-mail: info@warriorrecords.com. Website: www.WarriorRecords.com. **Contact:** Jim Ervin, A&R. Record producer, record company (Warrior Records) and music publisher (New Entity Music/ASCAP, New Copyright Music/BMI, New Melody Music/SESAC). Estab. 1988. Fee derived from sales royalty when song or artist is recorded.

How to Contact Submit demo by mail. Unsolicited submissions are OK. Prefers CD and/or videocassette with original songs, lyric and lead sheet if available. "We do not review internet sites. Do not send MP3s, unless requested. All written submitted materials (e.g., lyric sheets, letter, etc.) should be typed." Does not return material unless SASE is included. Responds in 2 months only via e-mail or SASE.

Music All styles. "All genres are utilized with our music supervision company for Film & TV, but our original focus is on **alternative rock** and **urban genres** (e.g., **R&B**, **rap**, **gospel**).

◻ LANDMARK COMMUNICATIONS GROUP
P.O. Box 1444, Hendersonville TN 37077. E-mail: lmarkcom@bellsouth.net. **Contact:** Bill Anderson Jr., producer. Record producer, record company, music publisher (Newcreature Music/BMI) and TV/radio syndication. Produces 6 singles and 6 LPs/year. Fee derived from sales royalty.
   • Also see the listings for Newcreataive Music in the Music Publishers section and Landmark Communications Group in the Record Companies section of this book.

How to Contact *Write first and obtain permission to submit.* Prefers CD, DAT or videocassette with 4-10 songs and lyric sheet. Include SASE.

Music Mostly **country crossover**; also **blues**, **country**, **gospel**, **jazz**, **rock** and **top 40/pop**. Produced *Vernon Oxford* (album), written and recorded by Vernon Oxford (country), released 1999 on Norway; *Cowboy Church* (album), written and recorded by various (Christian country), released 1999 on Landmark; and "Nothin' Else Feels Quite Like It" (single by B. Nash/K. Nash/B. Anderson), recorded on TV Theme Records (country). Other artists include Skeeter Davis, Gail Score and Joanne Cash Yates.

LARK TALENT & ADVERTISING
P.O. Box 35726, Tulsa OK 74153. (918)786-8896. Fax: (918)786-8897. E-mail: janajae@janajae.com. Website: www.janajae.com. **Contact:** Kathleen Pixley, vice president. Owner: Jana Jae. Record producer, music publisher (Jana Jae Music/BMI) and record company (Lark Record Productions, Inc.). Estab. 1980. Fee derived from sales royalty when song or artist is recorded.
- Also see the listings for Jana Jae Music in the Music Publishers section, Lark Record Productions in the Record Companies section, and Jana Jae Enterprises in the Managers & Booking Agents section of this book.

How to Contact Submit demo tape by mail. Unsolicited submissions are OK. Prefers CD or VHS videocassette with 3 songs and lead sheet. Does not return material. Responds in 1 month only if interested.

Music Mostly **country**, **bluegrass** and **classical**; also **instrumentals**. Produced "Bussin' Ditty" (single by Steve Upfold); "Mayonnaise" (single by Steve Upfold); and "Flyin' South" (single by Cindy Walker), all recorded by Jana Jae on Lark Records (country). Other artists include Sydni, Hotwire and Matt Greif.

LAZY BONES PRODUCTIONS/RECORDINGS, INC.
9594 First Ave. NE, Suite 449, Seattle WA 98115-2012. (206)447-0712. Fax: (425)821-5720. E-mail: lbrinc@earthlink.net. Website: www.lazybones.com. **Contact:** Scott Schorr, president. Record producer, record company and music publisher (Lazy Bones Music/BMI, Cat from Guatemala Music/ASCAP). Estab. 1992. Produces 4-6 CDs/year. Fee derived from sales royalty when song or artist is recorded or outright fee from recording artist (if unsigned) or outright fee from record company (if signed) or publishing royalties when co-songwriting with artist.

How to Contact Submit demo tape by mail. Unsolicited submissions are OK. Prefers cassette, DAT or CD with 3 songs (minimum) and lyric sheet. "If you honestly believe you can do better, improve your project to its greatest potential before submitting. With the number of projects received, if the material is not truly special and unique, it will not be taken seriously by a legitimate company." Does not return material. Responds in 1 month only if interested.

Music Mostly **alternative** and **rock**; also **hip-hop**. Produced *No Samples* (album by Da Blasta/Ratboy), recorded by Turntable Bay (hip-hop); and *Headland II* (album by Dave Hadland), recorded by Headland (pop), both on Lazy Bones. Other artists include Blackhead, MFTJ, B. Chestnut and Alan Charing.

Tips "Have outstanding and unique talent!"

LINEAR CYCLE PRODUCTIONS
P.O. Box 2608, Sepulveda CA 91393-2608. E-mail: LCP@wgn.net. Website: www.westworld.com/lcp/. **Contact:** Manny Pandanceski, producer. Record producer. Estab. 1980. Produces 15-25 singles, 6-10 12" singles, 15-20 LPs and 10 CDs/year. Fee derived from sales royalty when song or artist is recorded.

How to Contact Submit demo tape by mail. Unsolicited submissions are OK. Prefers cassette, 7³/₈ ips reel-to-reel or ½" VHS or ¾" videocassette. Include SASE. Responds in 6 months.

Music Mostly **rock/pop**, **R&B/blues** and **country**; also **gospel** and **comedy**. Produced "Lost In a Fog 4U" (single by B. Hitte/N. Nigle/P. Grippe, etc.), recorded by L'il Shette (pop/dance), released 2003 on WIPie; "Noz No Fippos" (single by G. Juan) from his self titled album, recorded by Glax Aleart (alternative), released 2003 on Swip; and "I Wanna F" (single by Washington/"P"/Jaletyme/Supick) from *Bitty & Beans* (album), recorded by Y78H 22A (3W) (rap/hip-hop), released 2004 on Blyacke.

Tips "We only listen to songs and other material recorded on quality tapes and CDs. We will not accept anything that sounds distorted, muffled and just plain bad! If you cannot afford to record demos on quality stock, or in some high aspects, shop somewhere else!"

☑ HAROLD LUICK & COUNTRY MUSIC SHOWCASE INTL. ASSOCIATES

Box #368, Carlisle IA 50047. (515)989-3748. E-mail: haroldl@cmsshowcase.org. Website: www.cms howcase.org. Producer: Harold L. Luick. Record producer, music industry consultant, music print publisher and music publisher. Produces 20 singles and 6 LPs/year. Fee derived from sales royalty, outright fee from artist/songwriter or record company, and from consulting fees for information or services.

- Also see the listing for Country Music Showcase International in the Organizations section of this book.

How to Contact *Write or call first and obtain permission to submit.* Prefers cassette with 3-5 songs and lyric sheet. Include SASE. Responds in 3 weeks.

Music Mostly **traditional country**, **gospel**, **contemporary country** and **MOR**. "Over a 12-year period, Harold Luick has produced and recorded 412 singles and 478 albums, 7 of which charted and some of which have enjoyed independent sales in excess of 30,000 units."

Tips "If you are looking to place a song with us and have it considered for a recording, make sure you have a decent demo, and all legals in order."

☐ MAC-ATTACK PRODUCTIONS

868 NE 81st St., Miami FL 33138. (305)949-1422. E-mail: GoMacster@aol.com. **Contact:** Michael McNamee, engineer/producer. Record producer and music publisher (Mac-Attack Publishing/AS-CAP). Estab. 1986. Fee derived from outright fee from recording artist or record company.

How to Contact Submit demo tape by mail. Unsolicited submissions are OK. Prefers CD or cassette or VHS videocassette with 3-5 songs, lyric sheet and bio. Does not return material. Responds in up to 3 months.

Music Mostly **pop**, **alternative rock** and **dance**. Produced and engineered *Tuscan Tongue* (album by Caution Automatic), recorded by Caution Automatic (rock), released 2005 on C.A. Records; Produced and engineered 'Never Gonna Let You Go' (single by Bruce Jordan/John Link/Michael McNamee), recorded by Bruce Jordan (pop), released 2002 on H.M.S. Records; Produced and engineered 'They Don't Want This' (single by Rip the Mic), recorded by Rip the Mic (hip-hop), released 2002 on Mac-Attack. Other artists include Blowfly, Tally Tal, Nina Llopis, The Lead, Girl Talk, Tyranny of Shaw and Jacobs Ladder.

☑ COOKIE MARENCO

P.O. Box 874, Belmont CA 94002. E-mail: cojema@aol.com. (650)595-8475. Record producer/engi-neer. Estab. 1981. Produces 10 CDs/year. $2,000 per day payable in advance.

How to Contact Contact only if interested in production. Does not accept unsolicited material.

Music Mostly **alternative modern rock**, **country**, **folk**, **rap**, **ethnic** and **avante-garde**; also **classical**, **pop** and **jazz**. *Winter Solstice II* (album), written and recorded by various artists; *Heresay* (album by Paul McCandless); and *Deep At Night* (album by Alex DeGrassi), all on Windham Hill Records (instrumental). Other artists include Tony Furtado Band, Praxis, Oregon, Mary Chapin Carpenter, Max Roach and Charle Haden & Quartet West.

Tips "If you're looking for beat detective and autotune, please call someone else. We still believe in analog recording and great musicianship."

☑ PETE MARTIN/VAAM MUSIC PRODUCTIONS

P.O. Box 29550, Hollywood CA 90029-0550. (323)664-7765. E-mail: vaampubl@aol.com or pmarti3 636@aol.com. **Contact:** Pete Martin, president. Record producer, music publisher (Vaam Music/ BMI and Pete Martin Music/ASCAP) and record company (Blue Gem Records). Estab. 1982.

- Also see the listings for Vaam Music Group in the Music Publishers section of this book and Blue Gem Records in the Record Companies section of this book.

How to Contact Send CD or cassette with 2 songs and a lyric sheet. Send small packages only. Include SASE. Responds in 1 month.

Music Mostly **top 40/pop**, **country** and **R&B**.

Tips "Study the market in the style that you write. Songs must be capable of reaching top 5 on charts."

⚓ ○ SCOTT MATHEWS, D/B/A HIT OR MYTH PRODUCTIONS INC.

246 Almonte Blvd., Mill Valley CA 94941. Fax: (415)389-9682. E-mail: hitormyth@aol.com. Website: www.scottmathews.com. **Contact:** Mary Ezzell, A&R Director. President: Scott Mathews. Assistant: Tom Luekens. Record producer, song doctor, studio owner and music publisher (Hang On to Your Publishing/BMI). Estab. 1990. Produces 6-9 CDs/year. Fee derived from recording artist or record company (with royalty points). *"Beware of these and other imposters using the name 'Scott Mathews.' "*

- Scott Mathews has several gold and platinum awards for sales of over 13 million records. He has worked on several Grammy and Oscar winning releases. In 2005, Scott Mathews-produced a full length album by The Rock and Roll Soldiers released on Atlantic records.

How to Contact *"No phone calls or publishing submissions, please."* Submit demo by mail. Unsolicited submissions are OK. Prefers CD (mp3 and cassette accepted). Include SASE and e-mail address. Responds in 2 months.

Music Mostly **rock/pop**, **alternative** and **singer/songwriters of all styles**. Produced 4 tracks on *Anthology (Best of)*, recorded by John Hiatt (rock/pop), released 2001 on Hip-O. Has produced Elvis Costello, Roy Orbison, Rosanne Cash, John Hiatt and many more. Has recorded platinum records with everyone from Barbra Streisand to John Lee Hooker, including Keith Richards, George Harrison, Mick Jagger, Van Morrison, Elvis Costello, Bonnie Raitt and Eric Clapton to name but a few, plus several Grammy and Oscar-winning projects.

Tips *"Waiting for a major label to come tap you on the shoulder and say, 'It's your turn,' is the last thing a new artist should even be thinking of. In my humble opinion, today's A&R stands for 'Afraid & Running.' Sorry to all my friends in that department, but the cold truth is, huge corporations are interested only in pleasing the shareholders. Most labels are all about the bottom line, not the music. Recently, I had a president of a major label admit to me that he hates his job because he's not allowed to sign and develop what he wants. So, it's our job to develop our careers by making incredible masters on our own. Fair deals are born from artists being in control. Set your goal (EP or LP) and budget, find the right producer, and make a stellar CD that can compete with anything on the radio. Early on, you can do more for yourself than a label can. When you prove yourself, they offer the moon and as an artist, you are able to keep creataive control of your music. Developing new artists that will sustain long careers is my main focus. Let me know if I can help. (Please check www.scottmathews.com for more info, and also check my entry at www.allmusic.com.)"*

⚓ ○ MONTICANA PRODUCTIONS

P.O. Box 702, Snowdon Station, Montreal QC H3X 3X8 Canada. **Contact:** David Leonard, executive producer. Record producer, music publisher (Montina Music) and record company (Monticana Records). Estab. 1963. Fee derived from sales royalty when song or artist is recorded.

- Also see the listings for Monticana Records in the Record Companies section and Montina Music in the Music Publishers section of this book.

How to Contact Submit demo by mail. Unsolicited submissions are OK. Prefers CD with maximum 4 songs. *"Demos should be as tightly produced as a master."* Include SASE.

Music Mostly **top 40**; also **bluegrass**, **blues**, **country**, **dance-oriented**, **easy listening**, **folk**, **gospel**, **jazz**, **MOR**, **progressive**, **R&B**, **rock** and **soul**.

Tips *"Work creatively and believe passionately in what you do and aspire to be. Success comes to those who persevere, have talent, develop their craft and network."*

○ MUSTROCK PRODUCTIONZ WORLDWIDE

167 W. 81st St., Suite 5C, New York NY 10024-7200. (212)799-9268. E-mail: recordmode@hotmail.com. President: Ivan "DOC" Rodriguez. Record producer and recording/mixing/mastering engineer. Estab. 1987. Produces 5 singles, engineers 6 CDs/year. Fee derived from sales royalty when song or artist is recorded. *We do not shop deals.*

How to Contact *E-mail first and obtain permission to submit.* Prefers CD, DVD and lyric sheet. Does not return material. Responds in 2 months.

Music Mostly **hip-hop**, **R&B** and **pop**; also **soul**, **ballads** and **soundtracks**. Produced "Poor Georgie" (by MC Lyte/DJ DOC), recorded by MC Lyte on Atlantic Records (rap). Other artists include

Caron Wheeler, The Hit Squad, The Awesome II, Black Steel Music, Underated Productions, EPMD, Redman, Dr. Dre & Ed-Lover, Das-EFX, Biz Markie, BDP, Eric B & Rakim, The Fugees, The Bush-wackass, Shai and Pudgee, Alisha Keys, 50 cent, Tiro de Garcia, etc.

Tips "Services provided include production (pre/post/co), tracking, mixing, remixing, live show tapes, jingles, etc. Additional info available upon request. Go to www.allmusic.com, type 'Ivan Doc Rodriguez' under 'artist' and enter."

◘ NEU ELECTRO PRODUCTIONS

P.O. Box 1582, Bridgeview IL 60455. (630)257-6289. E-mail: neuelectro@e-mail.com. Website: www.neuelectro.com. **Contact:** Bob Neumann, owner. Record producer and record company. Estab. 1984. Produces 16 singles, 16 12″ singles, 20 LPs and 4 CDs/year. Fee derived from outright fee from record company or recording artist.

How to Contact Submit demo tape by mail. Unsolicited submissions are OK. Prefers cassette or CD with 3 songs and lyric sheet or lead sheet. "Provide accurate contact phone numbers and addresses, promo packages and photos." Include SASE for reply. Responds in 2 weeks. "A production fee estimate will be returned to artist."

Music Mostly **dance, house, techno, rap** and **rock**; also **experimental, New Age** and **top 40**. Produced "Juicy" (single), written and recorded by Juicy Black on Dark Planet International Records (house); "Make Me Smile" (single), written and recorded by Roz Baker (house); *Reactovate-6* (album by Bob Neumann), recorded by Beatbox-D on N.E.P. Records (dance); and *Sands of Time* (album), recorded by Bob Neumann (New Age). Other artists include Skid Marx and The Deviants.

◙ NEW EXPERIENCE RECORDS

P.O. Box 683, Lima OH 45802. E-mail: st_chilling_2002@yahoo.com. **Contact:** A&R Department. Music Publisher: James L. Milligan Jr. Record producer, music publisher (A New Rap Jam Publishing/ASCAP), management firm (Creative Star Management) and record company (New Experience Records, Grand-Slam Records and Pump It Up Records). Estab. 1989. Produces 15-20 12″ singles, 2 LPs, 3 EPs and 2-5 CDs/year. Fee derived from sales royalty when song or artist is recorded or outright fee from record company, "depending on services required."

  • Also see the listings for A New Rap Jam Publishing in the Music Publishers section and Creative Star Management in the Managers & Booking Agents section of this book.

How to Contact *Write first to arrange personal interview.* Address material to A&R Dept. or Talent Coordinator. Prefers CD with a minimum of 3 songs and lyric or lead sheet (if available). "If tapes are to be returned, proper postage should be enclosed and all tapes and letters should have SASE for faster reply." Responds in 6-8 weeks.

Music Mostly **pop, R&B** and **rap**; also **gospel, contemporary gospel** and **rock**. Produced "The Son of God" (single by James Milligan/Anthony Milligan/Melvin Milligan) from *The Final Chapter* (album), recorded by T.M.C. Milligan Conection (R&B, Gospel), released 2002 on New Experience/Pump It Up Records. Other artists include Qutina Milligan, Melvin Milligan and Venesta Compton.

Tips "Do your homework on the music business. Be aware of all the new sampling laws. There are too many sound alikes. Be yourself. I look for what is different, vocal ability, voice range and sound stage presence, etc. Be on the look out for our new blues label Rough Edge Records/Rough Edge Entertainment. Blues material is now being reviewed. Send your best studio recorded material. Also be aware of the new sampling laws and the New Digital downloading laws. People are being jailed and fined for recording music that has not been paid for. Do your homework."

◘ NIGHTWORKS RECORDS

355 W. Potter Dr., Anchorage AK 99518. (907)562-3754. Fax: (907)561-4367. E-mail: kurt@nightworks.com. Website: www.surrealstudios.com. **Contact:** Kurt Riemann, owner. Record producer. Produces 16 CDs/year. Fees derived from sales royalty when song or artist is recorded.

How to Contact Submit demo CD by mail. Unsolicited submissions are OK. Prefers CD with 2-3 songs "produced as fully as possible. Send jingles and songs on separate CDs." Does not return material. Responds in 1 month.

Music Produces a variety of music from **native Alaskan** to **Techno** to **Christmas**.

☐ PANIO BROTHERS LABEL

P.O. Box 99, Montmartre SK S0G 3M0 Canada. (306)424-2258. Fax: (306)424-2269. E-mail: panioja @sk.sympatico.ca. **Contact:** John Panio, Jr., executive director. Record producer. Estab. 1977. Produces 1 single and 1 LP/year. Fee derived from sales royalty or outright fee from artist/songwriter or record company.

How to Contact Submit demo tape by mail. Unsolicited submissions are OK. Prefers cassette with any number of songs and lyric sheet. SAE and IRC. Responds in 1 month.

Music Mostly **country**, **dance**, **easy listening** and **Ukrainian**. Produced *Vlad Panio Sings* (album), written and recorded by Vlad Panio on PB Records.

☑ PATTY PARKER

Comstock Records, Ltd., P.O. Box 19720, Fountain Hills AZ 85269. (480)951-3115. Fax: (480)951-3074. **Contact:** Patty Parker, producer. Record producer, music publisher (White Cat Music) and record company (Comstock Records). Estab. 1978. Produces 6-8 CD singles and 3-4 albums/year. Fee derived from outright fee from recording artist or recording company.

• Also see the listings for White Cat Music in the Music Publishers section and Comstock Records Ltd. in the Record Companies section of this book.

How to Contact Submit demo by mail. Submit CD by postal mail only. We do not accept audio files onlines. Unsolicited submissions are OK. Submit CD only (no cassettes) with 2-4 songs and lyric sheet. Voice up front on demos. Include SASE. Responds in 2 weeks.

Music Mostly **country—traditional** to **crossover**. Produced "Great American Country" (single by Paula Mengarelli/Tom Mengarelli/Jeff Hansel), recorded by Paula Mengarelli (country); "Down to the Wire" (single by Maria Carmi), recorded by Maria Carmi (country); and "Your Daddy Would be Proud" (single by Paul Gibson) from *Reason to Believe* (album), recorded by Derek Carle (country), all released on Comstock Records. Other artists include Jentille, R.J. McClintock, Beth Hogan.

Tips "To catch the ears of radio programmers worldwide, I need good medium to uptempo songs for all the artists coming from Europe, Canada and the U.S. that I produce sessions on in Nashville."

☐ PHILLY BREAKDOWN RECORDING CO.

216 W. Hortter St., Philadelphia PA 19119. (215)848-6725. E-mail: mattcozar@juno.com. **Contact:** Matthew Childs, president. Music Director: Charles Nesbit. Record producer, music publisher (Philly Breakdown/BMI) and record company. Estab. 1974. Produces 3 singles and 2 LPs/year. Fee derived from sales royalty when song or artist is recorded.

How to Contact *Contact first and obtain permission to submit.* Prefers cassette with 4 songs and lead sheet. Does not return material. Responds in 2 months.

Music Mostly **R&B**, **hip-hop** and **pop**; also **jazz**, **gospel** and **ballads**. Produced "Lonely River" (single by Clarence Patterson/M. Childs) from *Lonely River* (album), recorded by Gloria Clark; and *Taps* (album), recorded by H Factor, both released 2001 on Philly Breakdown. Other artists include Leroy Christy, Gloria Clark, Jerry Walker, Nina Bundy, Mark Adam, Emmit King, Betty Carol, The H Factor and Four Buddies.

Tips "If you fail, just learn from your past experience and keep on trying, until you get it done right. Never give up."

☑ JIM PIERCE

Dept. SM, 101 Hurt Rd., Hendersonville TN 37075. (615)824-5900. Fax: (615)824-8800. E-mail: jim@jimpierce.net. Website: www.jimpierce.net. **Contact:** Jim Pierce, president. Record producer, music publisher (Strawboss Music/BMI) and record company (Round Robin Records). Estab. 1974. Fee derived from sales royalty or outright fee from recording artist. "Many artists pay me in advance for my services." Has had over 200 chart records to date.

How to Contact *E-mail first and obtain permission to submit.* Prefers CD with 3 songs and lyric sheet. Will accept cassettes. Does not return material. Responds only if interested. "All submissions should include their contact phone number and/or e-mail address."

Music Mostly **country**, **contemporary**, **country/pop**, **gospel** and **traditional country**. Have produced projects with Tommy Cash, George Jones, Jimmy C. Newman, Margo Smith, Bobby Helms, Sammi Smith, Roy Drusky, Charlie Louvin and Melba Montgomery.

Tips "Industry is seeking good singers who can write songs. Viewing our website is highly recommended."

☐ PREJIPPIE MUSIC GROUP

P.O. Box 216, Van Buren Twp. MI 48152. (734)697-0945. E-mail: prejippie@comcast.net. Website: www.prejippie.com. **Contact:** Bruce Henderson, president. Record producer, music publisher and record company (PMG Records). Estab. 1990. Produces 5 12″ singles, 2 LPs and 2 EPs/year. Fee derived from sales royalty when song or artist is recorded.

• Also see the listings for Prejippie Music Group in the Music Publishers section and PMG Records in the Record Companies section of this book.

How to Contact Submit demo tape by mail. Unsolicited submissions are OK. No phone calls please. Prefers cassette or CD with 3-4 songs and lyric sheet. Include SASE. Responds in 6 weeks.

Music Mostly **alternative R&B**, **experimental**, **alternative rock** and **techno/house**. Produced "Welcome to My World" (single) and "Freaky On You" (single), written and recorded by Bourgeoisie Paper Jam (funk/rock); and "Astral Traveler (Part 1)" (single), written and recorded by Synthetic Living Organism (techno), all released 1999 on PMG Records. Other artists include Tony Webb.

☐ THE PRESCRIPTION CO.

P.O. Box 222249, Great Neck NY 11021. (415)553-8540. Fax: (415)553-8541. E-mail: hasf525@sbcglobal.net. **Contact:** David F. Gasman, president. San Francisco office: 525 Ashbury St., San Francisco CA 94117. (415)553-8540. VP Sales (West Coast warehouse): Bruce Brennan. Record producer and music publisher. Fee derived from sales royalty when artist or song is recorded or outright fee from record company.

• Also see the listing for Prescription Company in the Music Publishers section of this book.

How to Contact *Write or call first about your interest then submit demo.* Prefers cassette with any number of songs and lyric sheet. Include SASE. "Does not return material without SASE and sufficient postage."

Music Mostly **bluegrass**, **blues**, **children's**, **country**, **dance**, **easy listening**, **jazz**, **MOR**, **progressive**, **R&B**, **rock**, **soul** and **top 40/pop**. Produced "The World's Most Dangerous Man," "Here Comes Trouble" and "Automated People" (singles by D.F. Gasman) from *Special EP No. 1* (album), all recorded by Medicine Mike (rock), all released 2003 on Prescription.

☐ REEL ADVENTURES

9 Peggy Lane, Salem NH 03079. (603)898-7097. Website: www.reeladventures1.homestead.com. **Contact:** Rick Asmega, chief engineer/producer. Record producer. Estab. 1972. Produces 100 12″ singles, 200 LPs, 5 EPs and 40 CDs/year. Fee derived from sales royalty when song or artist is recorded, or outright fee from recording artist or record company.

How to Contact Submit demo tape by mail. Unsolicited submissions are OK. Prefers cassette or CD. Include SASE. Responds in 6 weeks.

Music Mostly **pop**, **funk** and **country**; also **blues**, **Christian reggae** and **rock**. Produced *Funky Broadway* (album), recorded by Chris Hicks; *Testafye* (album), recorded by Jay Williams; and "Acoustical Climate" (single by John G.). Other artists include Nicole Hajj, The Bolz, Second Sinni, Larry Sterling, Broken Men, Melvin Crockett, Fred Vigeant, Monster Mash, Carl Armand, Cool Blue Sky, Ransome, Backtrax, Push, Too Cool for Humans and Burn Alley.

⊠ ☐ RN'D DISTRIBUTION, LLC

(formerly RN'D Productions), P.O. Box 540102, Houston TX 77254-0102. (713)521-2616, ext. 10. Fax: (713)529-4914. E-mail: AandR@aol.com. Website: www.rnddistribution.com **Contact:** Caudell Baham, A&R director. National Sales Director: Ramon Smith. Record producer, record company (Albatross Records), distributor (labels distributed include Suavehouse Records, Albatross Records, TDA Music and Ball In' Records) and music publisher (Ryedale Publishing). Estab. 1986. Produces 25 singles, 20 LPs, 4 EPs and 21 CDs/year.

• Also see the listing for Albatross Records in the Record Companies section of this book.
How to Contact Submit demo CD by mail. Unsolicited submissions are OK. Prefers CD with 4 songs and lyric sheet. Does not return material. Responds in 1 month.
Music All types.

☐ ROAD RECORDS

P.O. Box 2620, Victorville CA 92393. E-mail: staff@ roadrecords.com. Website: www.roadrecords.c om. **Contact:** Conrad Askland, president. Record producer, record company (Road Records) and music publisher (Askland Publishing). Estab. 1989. Produces 6 singles and 10 albums/year. Fee derived from sales royalty when song or artist is recorded.
• Also see the listing for Road Records in the Record Companies section of this book.
How to Contact *Write or call first and obtain permission to submit.* Prefers at least 3 songs with lyric and lead sheet. "We are looking for people that have a different, original sound." Does not return submissions. Responds in 3 weeks.
Music Mostly **alternative**, **modern country** and **dance**; also **orchestral instrumental**. Does not want jazz. "We supply music to Grand Ole Opry, United Airlines, Knoxbury Farm and G.T.E."
Tips "Do not submit what you think we are looking for. A lot of our projects are 'on the edge.'"

☐ RUSTRON MUSIC PRODUCTIONS

1156 Park Lane, West Palm Beach FL 33417-5957. (561)686-1354. E-mail: rmp_wmp@bellsouth.n et. **Contact:** Sheelah Adams, office administrator. Executive Director: Rusty Gordon. A&R Director: Ron Caruso. Assistant A&R Director: Kevin Reeves. Record producer, record company, manager and music publisher (Rustron Music Publishers/BMI and Whimsong Publishing/ASCAP). Estab. 1970. Produces 10 CDs/year. Fee derived from sales royalty when song or artist is recorded or outright fee from record company. "This branch office reviews all material submitted for the home office in Connecticut."
• Also see the listings for Rustron Music Publishers in the Music Publishers section and Rustron Music Productions in the Record Companies and Managers & Booking Agents sections of this book.
How to Contact *Write or call to discuss your submission* or submit demo tape or CD by mail. Prefers CD with up to 15 songs that was produced to sell at gigs or cassette with 1-3 songs and typed lyric sheets, 1 sheet per song. Also send cover letter clearly explaining your reason for submitting. "Songs should be 3½ minutes long or less and must be commercially viable for today's market. Exception: New Age fusion compositions 3-10 minutes each, 1 hour maximum. Singer/songwriters and collaborators are preferred." SASE required for all correspondence. No exceptions. Responds in 4 months.
Music Mostly **progressive country**, **pop** (ballads, blues, theatrical, cabaret), **folk/rock**, and **adult contemporary electric acoustic**; also **R&B**, **New Age instrumental fusions**, **children's music**, **reggae**, and **women's music**. Produced "A Trimaran on The Gulf of Mexico" (single) from *A Trimaran on The Gulf of Mexico* (album), written and recorded by Song On A Whim (Folk Fusions), released 2005 on Rustron Records; "Solstice in The Big Cypress" (single) from *Solstice in The Big Cypress* (album), written and recorded by The Dinner Key Boys (folk/rock/blues), released 2005 on Whimsong Records; and "Yankee Reggae All The Rave" (single) from *Yankee Reggae All The Rave* (album), written and recorded by Jeremy White & Kalliope (yankee reggae), released 2005 on Whimsong Records. Other artists include Haze Coates, Star Smiley, Jayne Margo-Reby, Stacie Jubal, Deb Criss, Robin Plitt, Boomslang Swampsinger.
Tips "Be open to developing your own unique style. Write well-crafted songs with unpredictable concepts, strong hooks and definitive melodies. New Age composers: evolve your themes and use multiculturally diverse instruments to embellish your compositions/arrangements. Don't be predictable. Experiment with instrumental fusion with jazz and/or classical themes, pop themes and international styles. Send cover letter clearly explaining your reason for submitting."

☐ STEVE SATKOWSKI RECORDINGS

P.O. Box 3403, Stuart FL 34995. (772)225-3128. Website: www.clearsoulproductions.com/stevesat kowski.html. Engineer/producer: Steven Satkowski. Record producer, recording engineer, management firm and record company. Estab. 1980. Produces 20 CDs/year. Fee derived from outright fee from recording artist or record company.

How to Contact Submit demo tape by mail. Unsolicited submissions are OK. Prefers CD or cassette. Does not return material. Responds in 2 weeks.

Music Mostly **classical**, **jazz** and **big band**. Produced recordings for National Public Radio and affiliates. Engineered recordings for Steve Howe, Patrick Moraz, Kenny G and Michael Bolton.

☑ SEGAL'S PRODUCTIONS

16 Grace Rd., Newton MA 02459. (617)969-6196. Fax: (617)969-6614. Website: www.charlessegal.c om. **Contact:** Charles Segal. Record producer, music publisher (Segal's Publications/BMI and Samro South Africa) and record company (Spin Records). Produces 6 singles and 6 LPs/year. Produced 21 CD's in 2005. Fee derived from sales royalty when song or artist is recorded.

- Also see the listing for Segal's Publications in the Music Publishers section of this book. Also look for *Instant Songwriting with the Piano*, by Charles and colleen Segal, available from Writer's Digest Books in Spring 2006.

How to Contact *Write first and obtain permission to submit or to arrange personal interview.* Prefers cassette, CD or videocassette with 3 songs and lyric sheet or lead sheet of melody, words, chords. "Please record keyboard/voice or guitar/voice if you can't get a group." Does not return material. Do not send originals. Responds in 3 months only if interested.

Music Mostly **rock**, **pop** and **country**; also **R&B** and **comedy**. "You're not alone" (single by Barbera Brilliant), *African Fantasy* (album by Charles Segal), "Animal Concepts" (single by Lindsy Duplesey), *My Way* (LP by Rick Shrider) "Michelle meets Mark" (single), "Reeve's Song" (single), *Steve's Favorites* (album) and *Magical Mystery Man* and *Everyday Things* (albums by Colleen Segal, produced by Collen and Charles Segal). Other artists include Art Heatley, Dan Hill and Melanie. Has also published songbooks which include *Opus Africa* and *Songs of Africa*.

Tips "Make a good and clear production of cassette even if it is only piano rhythm and voice. Also do a lead sheet of music, words and chords."

🅽 ☑ ⬭ SILVER BOW PRODUCTIONS

556 Amess St., New Westminster BC V3L 4A9 Canada. (604)930-9309. Fax: (604)523-9310. E-mail: saddles@telus.net. Website: http://saddlestone.ontheweb.uu. **Contact:** Candice James, Rex Howard, Grant Lucas—A&R. Record producers. Estab. 1986. Produces 16 singles, and 6 CDs/year. Fee derived from outright fee from recording artist.

- Also see the listings for Saddlestone Publishing in the Music Publishers section and Silver Bow Management in the Managers & Booking Agents section of this book.

How to Contact Prefers CD or cassette with 2 songs and lyric sheet. Does not return material. Responds in 6 weeks.

Music Mostly **country**, **pop**, and **rock**; also **gospel**, **blues** and **jazz**. Produced *Fragile-Handle With Care*, recorded by Razzy Bailey on SOA Records (country); *High Society*, written and recorded by Darrell Meyers (country); and *Man I Am*, written and recorded by Stang Giles (country crossover), both released 2000 on Saddlestone Records. Other artists include Rex Howard, Gerry King, Joe Lonsdale, Barb Farrell, Dorrie Alexander, Peter James, Matt Audette and Cordel James.

🅽 ☑ ⊘ SOUL CANDY PRODUCTIONS

176-B Woodridge Crescent, Ottawa ON K2B 7S9 Canada. (613)820-5715. Fax: (613)820-8736. E-mail: jshakka@hotmail.com. Website: www.jonesshakka.com. **Contact:** Jon E. Shakka, co-president. Record producer. Estab. 1988. Produces 1 album/year. Fee derived from sales royalty when song or artist is recorded.

How to Contact *Does not accept unsolicited submissions.*

Music Mostly **funk**, **rap** and **house music**; also **pop**, **ballads** and **funk-rock**. Produced *I'm My Brother's Keeper* (album), recorded by The Jon E. Shakka Project (funk rap), released 2001 on Poku Records. Other artists include Uncut Records, Double F, and LY.

⬛ SOUND ARTS RECORDING STUDIO

8377 Westview Dr., Houston TX 77055. (713)464-GOLD. E-mail: sarsjef@aol.com. Website: sounda rtsrecording.com. **Contact:** Jeff Wells, president. Record producer and music publisher (Earthscream Music). Estab. 1974. Produces 12 singles and 3 LPs/year. Fee derived from sales royalty when song or artist is recorded.

- Also see the listings for Earthscream Music Publishing in the Music Publishers section and Surface Records in the Record Companies section of this book.

How to Contact Submit demo tape by mail. Unsolicited submissions are OK. Prefers cassette with 2-5 songs and lyric sheet. Does not return material. Responds in 6 weeks.

Music Mostly **pop/rock**, **country** and **blues**. Produced *Texas Johnny Brown* (album), written and recorded by Texas Johnny Brown on Quality (blues). Other artists include Tim Nichols, Perfect Strangers, B.B. Watson, Jinkies, Joe "King" Carasco (on Surface Records), Mark May (on Icehouse Records), The Barbara Pennington Band (on Earth Records), Tempest Under the Sun and Atticus Finch.

☑ ◻ SOUND WORKS ENTERTAINMENT PRODUCTIONS INC.

680 Hot Springs Rd., Carson City NV 89706. (775)690-2155. E-mail: mike@musicjones.com. Website: www.musicjones.com. **Contact:** Michael E. Jones, president. Record producer, record company (Sound Works Records) and music publisher (Sound Works Music). Estab. 1989. Produces 16 singles, 2 LPs and 20 CDs/year. Fee derived from sales royalty when song or artist is recorded or outright fee from recording artist or record company.

How to Contact Submit demo tape by mail. Unsolicited submissions are OK. Prefers cassette with 3-6 songs and lyric sheet. "Please include short bio and statement of goals and objectives." Does not return material. Responds in 6 weeks.

Music Mostly **country, folk** and **pop**; also **rock**. Produced "Lonelyville," and "Alabama Slammer" (singles), both written and recorded by Wake Eastman; and "Good Looking Loser" (single), written and recorded by Renee Rubach, all on Sound Works Records (country). Other artists include Matt Dorman, Steve Gilmore, The Tackroom Boys, The Las Vegas Philharmonic and J.C. Clark.

Tips "Put your ego on hold. Don't take criticism personally. Advice is meant to help you grow and improve your skills as an artist/songwriter. Be professional and business-like in all your dealings."

⬛ SPHERE GROUP ONE

921 Dolphin Court, Marco Island FL 34145. (239)398-6800. Fax: (239)597-5611. E-mail: spheregrou pone@att.net. **Contact:** Tony Zarrella, president. Talent Manager: Janice Salvatore. Record producer, artist development and management firm. Produces 5-6 singles and 3 CDs/year. Estab. 1986.

How to Contact Submit CD/video by mail. Unsolicited submissions are OK. Prefers CD or DVD with 3-5 songs and lyric sheets. "Must include: photos, press, résumé, goals and specifics of project submitted, etc." Does not return material.

Music Mostly **pop/rock (mainstream)**, **progressive/rock**, **New Age** and **crossover country/pop**; also **film soundtracks**. Produced song titles: *Rock to the Rescue, Sunset At Night, Double Trouble, Take This Heart, It's Our Love* and *You and I* (albums by T. Zarrella), recorded by 4 of Hearts (pop/rock) on Sphere Records. Other artists include Frontier 9, Myth, Survivor and Wicked Lester/Kiss.

Tips "Take direction and have faith in yourself, producer and manager. Currently seeking artists/groups incorporating various styles into a focused mainstream product. Groups with a following are a plus. Artist development is our expertise and we listen!"

Ⓝ ⬛ STUART AUDIO SERVICES

134 Mosher Rd., Gorham ME 04038. (207)892-0960. E-mail: js@stuartaudio.com. Website: www.st uartaudio.com. **Contact:** John A. Stuart, producer/owner. Record producer and music publisher. Estab. 1979. Produces 5-8 CDs/year. Fee derived from sales royalty when song or artist is recorded, outright fee from recording artist or record company, or demo and consulting fees.

How to Contact *Write or call first and obtain permission to submit or to arrange a personal interview.* Prefers CD with 4 songs and lyric sheet. Include SASE. Responds in 2 months.

Music Mostly **alternative folk-rock**, **rock** and **country**; also **contemporary Christian, children's**

and **unusual**. Produced *One of a Kind* (by various artists), recorded by Elizabeth Boss on Bosco Records (folk); *Toad Motel*, written and recorded by Rick Charrette on Fine Point Records (children's); and *Holiday Portrait*, recorded by USM Chamber Singers on U.S.M. (chorale). Other artists include Noel Paul Stookey, Beavis & Butthead (Mike Judge), Don Campbell, Jim Newton and John Angus.

☐ STUDIO SEVEN

417 N. Virginia, Oklahoma City OK 73106. (405)236-0643. Fax: (405)236-0686. E-mail: cope@okla. net. Website: www.lunacyrecords.com. **Contact:** Dave Copenhaver, producer. Record producer, record company (Lunacy Records) and music publisher (Lunasong Music). Estab. 1990. Produces 10 LPs and CDs/year. Fee is derived from sales royalty when song or artist is recorded or outright fee from recording artist or record company. "All projects are on a customized basis."

How to Contact *Contact first and obtain permission to submit.* Prefers cassette with lyric sheet. Include SASE. Responds in 6 weeks.

Music Mostly **rock**, **jazz-blues** and **world-Native American**; also **country** and **blues**. Produced *"Like A Lifetime* (single) from *Where the Wind Blows* (album), written and recorded by Stephanie Musser (easy listening), released 2004 on Passio Productions; "Wouldn't Be the First Time" (single) from *Picasso's Clouds* (album), written and recorded by Dustin Pittsley (rock), released 2004 on Lunacy Records; and "On My Way" (single) from *On My Way* (album), written and recorded by Joe Merrick (country), all released 2004 on Lunacy Records. Other artists include Harvey Shelton, Steve Pryor and Ken Taylor.

☐ SWIFT RIVER PRODUCTIONS

P.O. Box 231, Gladeville TN 37071. (615)316-9479. E-mail: office@andymay.com. Website: www.s wiftrivermusic.com. **Contact:** Andy May, producer/owner. Record producer and record company. Estab. 1979. Produces 40 singles and 4 CDs/year. Fee paid by artist or artist's management. Works with recording client to come up with budget for individual project.

How to Contact *Write or call first and obtain permission to submit.* "Let us know your background, present goals and reason for contacting us so we can tell if we are able to help you. Demo should be clear and well thought out. Vocal plus guitar or piano is fine." Does not return material. Responds in up to 1 months.

Music Mostly **country**, **singer/songwriters** and **"roots"** (folk, acoustic, bluegrass and rock); also **instrumental**. Produced *Natick, There's Talk About a Fence* and *Look What Thoughts Will Do* (albums), recorded by Rick Lee (folk/Americana); *Second Wind* (album), recorded by Bill Mulroney (contemporary folk/Americana); and *Flyin' Fast* (album), recorded by Brycen Fast (country), released 2003 on Swift River. Other artists include Marinda Flom and Curtis McPeake.

Tips "I'm interested in artists who are accomplished, self-motivated and able to accept direction. I'm looking for music that is intelligent, creative and in some way contributes something positive. We are a production house; we accept song submissions from our production clients only."

☐ ROGER VINCENT TARI

P.O. Box 576, Piscataway NJ 08855. E-mail: rogervtari@earthlink.net. **Contact:** Roger Vincent Tari, president/producer. Vice President: Mike Roze. A&R: Joe Tasi. Booking Department: Mike Bino. Record producer, record company (VT Records), music publisher (Vintari Music/ASCAP) and magazine publisher (*Music of the World for Youth Culture*). Estab. 1979. Produces 6-8 singles/year. Fee derived from sales royalty when song or artist is recorded or outright fee from recording artist.

How to Contact Submit demo tape by mail. Unsolicited submissions are OK. Prefers cassette or VHS videocassette with 3 songs and lyric sheet (videocassette is optional). "The artist should send any relevant literature and a simple black and white picture along with the 3-song cassette and lyric sheet." Include SASE. Responds in 1 month.

Music Mostly **Girl-pop**, **new wave**, **synth-pop** and **punk pop**; also **world pop**, **J-pop**, **80's style hair rock bands** and **avant jazz** . Produced "Bad Apple" (single by Reiko Lai/Chung Ho J Lee), recorded by Flush (indie-pop/rock), released 2002 on VT Music/VR Records; "Notice of Death" (single by Scott Cheng), recorded by Scott Cheng (hard rock), released 2002 on VT Music/VT

Records; and "Rocket Adventure To Jupiter" written and recorded by John Paul Immordino (synth-pop) released 2005 on VT Music/VT Records. Other artists include Neko Zhang, Trippin on Dolls, Fractured Glass, The Subterraneans, 54 Nude Honeys, and GELANTINE.

Tips "We seek Pop artists from around the world. Especially female oriented artists and bands etc. The music should be new and creative regardless of style. VT Records and Music of the World are distributed by Seven Gods/Benten in Tokyo. We are distributor for Benten/Sister Records in the East Coast of the U.S.A. Benten Bentoh Series, Hang On The Box and Peety Booka are all signed to Benten/Sister Records Japan. VT Music is also exclusive distributor/licenser for all Canadian American and Caprice International records and its affiliate labels throughout Asia and rhe Pacific rim. Canadian American artists include; Joey Welz, Noble Gas etc."

☐ TMC PRODUCTIONS

P.O. Box 12353, San Antonio TX 78212. (210)829-1909. Website: www.axbarmusic.com. **Contact:** Joe Scates, producer. Record producer, music publisher (Axbar Productions/BMI, Scates & Blanton/BMI and Axe Handle Music/ASCAP), record company (Axbar, Trophy, Jato, Prince and Charro Records) and record distribution and promotion. Produces 2-3 CDs/year. Fee derived from sales royalty.

How to Contact *Please write or call first and obtain permission to submit.* Prefers CD and accepts cassettes with 1-5 songs and lyric sheet. Does not return material. Responds "as soon as possible, but don't rush us."

Music Mostly **traditional country**; also **blues**, **novelty** and **rock (soft)**. Produced "Chicken Dance" (single) (traditional), recorded by George Chambers and "Hobo Heart" (single), written and recorded by Juni Moon, both on Axbar Records. Other artists include Jim Marshall, Caroll Gilley, Rick Will, Wayne Carter, Kathi Timm, Leon Taylor, Mark Chestnutt, Kenny Dale and Britney Hendrickson.

Tips "We are in the business of making good music."

◙ TRAC RECORD CO.

170 N. Maple, Fresno CA 93702. (559)255-1717. E-mail: tracsell@aol.com. **Contact:** Stan Anderson, Bev Anderson, owners. Record producer, music publisher (Sellwood Publishing/BMI) and record company (TRAC Records). Estab. 1972. Produces 5 12″ singles, 5 LPs and 5 CDs/year. Fee derived from outright fee from recording artist or outside investor.

- Also see the listings for Trac Record Co. in the Record Companies section of this book and Sellwood Publishing in the Music Publishers section of this book.

How to Contact Submit demo by mail. Unsolicited submissions are OK. Prefers cassette or CD with 3 songs and lyric sheet. "Send professional studio demo." Include SASE. Responds in 3 weeks.

Music Mostly **country, all styles** and **southern gospel**. Produced "City Days & Country Nights" (single by Jon Jensen) from *Back to Country* (album); "Sweet Deliverance" (single by H.C. "Chuck" House/Mary Miller) from *Back to Country* (album); and "Headed Right Out The Wrong Door" (single by Johnny Spears) from *Back to Country* (album), all recorded by H.C. "Chuck" House (country), released 2004 on TRAC Records. Also released *The Best Ten Years of Kevin Willard* (12-song CD).

☐ THE TRINITY STUDIO

P.O. Box 1417, Corpus Christi TX 78403. (361)854-SING. E-mail: info@trinitystydio.com. Website: www.trinitystudio.com. **Contact:** Jim Wilken, owner. Record producer and recording studio. Estab. 1988. Fee derived from outright fee from recording artist or record company.

How to Contact Submit demo tape by mail. Unsolicited submissions are OK. Prefers cassette, CD or VHS videocassette. Does not return material. Responds in 1 month.

Music Mostly **Christian-country**. Produced *Miracle Man* (album), written and recorded by Merrill Lane (country Christian) on TC Records; and *Higher Love* (album by Merrill Lane/Becky Redels), recorded by Becky Redels (country Christian). Other artists include Kerry Patton, Patty Walker, Leah Knight, Lofton Kline, Rockports Gospel Force and Jackie Cole.

☑ VALTEC PRODUCTIONS
P.O. Box 6018, Santa Maria CA 93456. (805)928-8559. Website: www.valtec.net. **Contact:** Joe Valenta, producer. Record producer. Estab. 1986. Produces 20 singles and 10 CDs/year. Fee derived from sales royalty when song or artist is recorded.
How to Contact Submit demo tape by mail. Unsolicited submissions are OK. Prefers CD or DVD with 3 songs and lyric or lead sheet. Send photo. Does not return material (kept on file for 2 years). Responds in 6 weeks.
Music Mostly **country, Christian, pop/AC** and **rock**.

☐ THE WEISMAN PRODUCTION GROUP
449 N. Vista St., Los Angeles CA 90036. (323)653-0693. E-mail: parlirec@aol.com. **Contact:** Ben Weisman, owner. Record producer and music publisher (Audio Music Publishers). Estab. 1965. Produces 10 singles/year. Fee derived from sales royalty when song or artist is recorded.
• Also see the listings for Audio Music Publishers and Queen Esther Music Publishers in the Music Publishers section of this book.
How to Contact Submit demo CD or tape by mail. Unsolicited submissions are OK. Prefers CD or cassette with 3-10 songs and lyric sheet. Include SASE. "Mention *Songwriter's Market*. Please make return envelope the same size as the envelopes you send material in, otherwise we cannot send everything back. Just send tape." Responds in 6 weeks.
Music Mostly **R&B, soul, dance, rap** and **top 40/pop**; also **gospel** and **blues**.

☑ WESTWIRES RECORDING
(formerly Westwires Digital USA), 1042 Club Ave., Allentown PA 18109. (610)435-1924. E-mail: info@westwires.com. Website: www.westwires.com. **Contact:** Wayne Becker, owner/producer. Record producer and production company. Fee derived from outright fee from record company or artist retainer.
How to Contact Submit demo tape by mail. Unsolicited submissions are OK. Prefers cassette, CD or VHS videocassette with 3 songs and lyric sheet. Does not return material. Responds in 1 month.
Music Mostly **rock, R&B, dance, alternative, folk** and **eclectic**. Produced *Trap Door* (album), recorded by Trad Door (dance), released on Interstellar. Also engineered *Live & Acoustic* (album), recorded by Zakk Wylde (hard rock), released on Spitfire Records. Other artists include Weston, Anne Le Baron and Gary Hassay.
Tips "We are interested in singer/songwriters and alternative artists living in the mid-Atlantic area. Must be able to perform live and establish a following."

☑ FRANK WILLSON
P.O. Box 2297, Universal City TX 78148. (210)653-3989. E-mail: bswr18@wmconnect.com. **Contact:** Frank Willson, producer. Record producer, management firm (Universal Music Marketing) and record company (BSW Records/Universal Music Records). Estab. 1987. Produces 20-25 albums/year. Fee derived from sales royalty when song or artist is recorded.
• Also see the listings for BSW Records in the Music Publishers and Record Companies sections and Universal Music Marketing in the Managers & Booking Agents section of this book.
How to Contact Submit demo CD by mail. Unsolicited submissions are OK. Prefers cassette with 3-4 songs and lyric sheets. Include SASE. Responds in 1 month.
Music Mostly **country, blues, jazz** and **soft rock**. Produced *Follow the Roses* (album), written and recorded by Larry Butler on BSW Records (country). Other artists include Candee Land, Dan Kimmel, Brad Lee, John Wayne, Sonny Marshall, Bobby Mountain and Crea Beal.

☑ WLM MUSIC/RECORDING
2808 Cammie St., Durham NC 27705-2020. (919)471-3086. Fax: (919)471-4326. E-mail: wlm-musicrecording@nc.rr.com. **Contact:** Watts Lee Mangum, owner. Record producer. Estab. 1980. Fee derived from outright fee from recording artist. "In some cases, an advance payment requested for demo production."

How to Contact Submit demo CD by mail. Unsolicited submissions are OK. Prefers CD with 2-4 songs and lyric or lead sheet (if possible). Include SASE. Responds in 6 months.

Music Mostly **country**, **country/rock** and **blues/rock**; also **pop**, **rock**, **blues**, **gospel** and **blue-grass**. Produced "911," and "Petals of an Orchid" (singles), both written and recorded by Johnny Scoggins (country); and "Renew the Love" (single by Judy Evans), recorded by Bernie Evans (country), all on Independent. Other artists include Southern Breeze Band and Heart Breakers Band.

WORLD RECORDS

5798 Deer Trail Dr., Traverse City MI 49684. E-mail: jack@worldrec.org. Website: www.worldrec.org. **Contact:** Jack Conners, producer. Record producer, engineer/technician and record company (World Records). Estab. 1984. Produces 1 CD/year. Fee derived from outright fee from recording artist.

How to Contact *Write first and obtain permission to submit.* Prefers CD with 1 or 2 songs. Include SASE. Responds in 6 weeks.

Music Mostly **classical**, **folk** and **jazz**. Produced *Have You Heard?* (album by Traverse Symphony Orchestra), (classical), released 2003, and *Music From the Monastery* (album by Nancy Larson), (classical), released 2002. Other artists include The Murphy Brothers and The Camerata Singers.

ADDITIONAL RECORD PRODUCERS

The following companies are also record producers, but their listings are found in other sections of the book. Read the listings for submission information.

N

Naked Jain Records 118

P

P. & N. Records 174
Plateau Music 175
Playbones Records 175
PMG Records 176
Prejippie Music Group 122
Prescription Company 122
Presence Records 177

R

R.T.L. Music 123
Red Sky Records 178
Rockford Music Co. 125
Rustic Records, Inc Publishing 125

S

Sinus Musik Produktion, Ulli Weigel 128
Sound Cellar Music 129
Sound Management Direction 255
Southland Records, Inc. 185
Sphere Group One 255
Starbound Publishing Co. 130
Stuart Music Co., Jeb 130
Succes 130
Supreme Enterprises Int'l Corp. 131
Sureshot Records 185

T

T.C. Productions/Etude Publishing Co. 131
Tiki Enterprises, Inc. 132
Ton Records 187
Topcat Records 187
Tower Music Group 132
Twentieth Century Promotions 257

U

Unknown Source Music 134

V

Vaam Music Group 134

W

Wagner Agency, William F. 258
Warner Productions, Cheryl K. 258
White Cat Music 136
Wilder Artists' Management, Shane 259
Williams Management, Yvonne 259
World Beatnik Records 190

X

X.R.L. Records/Music 190

Z

Young Country Records/Plain Country Records 191

Managers & Booking Agents

Before submitting to a manager or booking agent, be sure you know exactly what you need. If you're looking for someone to help you with performance opportunities, the booking agency is the one to contact. They can help you book shows either in your local area or throughout the country. If you're looking for someone to help guide your career, you need to contact a management firm. Some management firms may also handle booking; however, it may be in your best interest to look for a separate booking agency. A manager should be your manager—not your agent, publisher, lawyer or accountant.

MANAGERS

Of all the music industry players surrounding successful artists, managers are usually the people closest to the artists themselves. The artist manager can be a valuable contact, both for the songwriter trying to get songs to a particular artist and for the songwriter/performer. A manager and his connections can be invaluable in securing the right publishing deal or recording contract if the writer is also an artist. Getting songs to an artist's manager is yet another way to get your songs recorded, since the manager may play a large part in deciding what material his client uses. For the performer seeking management, a successful manager should be thought of as the foundation for a successful career.

The relationship between a manager and his client relies on mutual trust. A manager works as the liaison between you and the rest of the music industry, and he must know exactly what you want out of your career in order to help you achieve your goals. His handling of publicity, promotion and finances, as well as the contacts he has within the industry, can make or break your career. You should never be afraid to ask questions about any aspect of the relationship between you and a prospective manager.

Always remember that a manager works *for the artist*. A good manager is able to communicate his opinions to you without reservation, and should be willing to explain any confusing terminology or discuss plans with you before taking action. A manager needs to be able to communicate successfully with all segments of the music industry in order to get his client the best deals possible. He needs to be able to work with booking agents, publishers, lawyers and record companies.

Keep in mind that you are both working together toward a common goal: success for you and your songs. Talent, originality, professionalism and a drive to succeed are qualities that will attract a manager to an artist—and a songwriter.

BOOKING AGENTS

The function of the booking agent is to find performance venues for their clients. They usually represent many more acts than a manager does, and have less contact with their acts. A booking agent charges a commission for his services, as does a manager. Managers usually ask for a 15-20% commission on an act's earnings; booking agents usually charge around 10%. In the area of managers and booking agents, more successful acts can negotiate lower percentage deals than the ones set forth above.

SUBMITTING MATERIAL TO MANAGERS & BOOKING AGENTS

The firms listed in this section have provided information about the types of music they work with and the types of acts they represent. You'll want to refer to the Category Index on page 383 to find out which companies deal with the type of music you write, and the Geographic Index at the back of the book to help you locate companies near where you live. Then determine whether they are open to your level of experience (see A Sample Listing Decoded on page 11). Each listing also contains submission requirements and information about what items to include in a press kit and will also specify whether the company is a management firm or a booking agency. Remember that your submission represents you as an artist, and should be as organized and professional as possible.

Icons

For More Info

For more instructional information on the listings in this book, including explanations of symbols (![N] ![check] ![Y] ![clover] ![globe] ![circle] ![circle/] ![heart] ![circle/]), read the article *Songwriter's Market: How Do I Use It?* on page 7.

ADDITIONAL MANAGERS & BOOKING AGENTS

There are **more managers & booking agents** located in other sections of the book! On page 261 use the list of Additional Managers & Booking Agents to find listings within other sections who are also managers/booking agents.

Managers & Agents

N ○ A&A MERSIER TRUCKING ENTERTAINMENT
P.O. Box 12024, Fort Wayne IN 46853-0621. (260)348-2883. Fax: (260)747-1688. **Contact:** Leonard Mersir, owner. Management firm. Estab. 2001. Represents local and regional individual artists and groups; currently handles 6 acts. Receives 10-20% commission. Reviews material for acts.
How to Contact Submit demo. Prefers cassette, videocassette or CD/CDR. Press kit should include a demo with at least 3-5 songs, cover lyric sheet and a photo. Does not return material. Responds only if interested.
Music Mostly **R&B, rap** and **gospel**; also **jazz, blues** and **hip-hop**. Does not want heavy metal, rock or country. Works primarily with the Elite Untouchables and Too Real. Other acts include Nathan Johnson (R&B singer), Richard Harris (rap artist) and Melinda Silva (R&B, rap singer.)
Tips "Keep your dreams alive, believe in yourself, know who you are and never give up because we won't let you."

○ AIR TIGHT MANAGEMENT
115 West Rd., P.O. Box 113, Winchester Center CT 06094. (860)738-9139. Fax: (860)738-9135. E-mail: mainoffice@airtightmanagement.com. Website: www.airtightmanagement.com. **Contact:** Jack Forchette, president. A&R: Scott Fairchild. Management firm. Estab. 1969. Represents individual artists, groups or songwriters from anywhere; currently handles 8 acts. Receives 15-20% commission. Reviews material for acts.
How to Contact *Write or e-mail first and obtain permission to submit.* Prefers CD or VHS videocassette. If seeking management, press kit should include photos, bio and recorded material. "Follow up with a fax or e-mail, not a phone call." Does not return material. Responds in 1 month.
Music Mostly **rock, country** and **jazz**. Current acts include P.J. Loughran (singer/songwriter), Johnny Colla (songwriter/producer, and guitarist/songwriter for Huey Lewis and the News), Jason Scheff (lead singer/songwriter for the group "Chicago"), Gary Burr (Nashville songwriter/producer), Nathan East (singer/songwriter/bassist—Eric Clapton, Michael Jackson, Madonna, 4-Play and others), Rocco Prestia (legendary R&B musician, "Tower of Power" bassist), and Steve Oliver (contemporary jazz/pop songwriter/guitarist/vocalist, recording artist).

N ⊠ ○ ALERT MUSIC INC.
41 Britain St., Suite 305, Toronto ON M5A 1R7 Canada. (416)364-4200. Fax: (416)364-8632. E-mail: contact@alertmusic.com. Website: www.alertmusic.com. **Contact:** W. Tom Berry, president. Management firm, record company and recording artist. Represents local and regional individual artists and groups; currently handles 5 acts. Reviews material for acts.
How to Contact *Write first and obtain permission to submit.* Prefers CD. If seeking management, press kit should include finished CD, photo, press clippings and bio. Include SASE.
Music All types. Works primarily with bands and singer/songwriters. Current acts include Holly Cole (jazz vocalist), Kim Mitchell (rock singer/songwriter), Gino Vannelli (singer/songwriter), Crystal Pistol (rock, singer/songwriter), and Roxanne Potvin (blues, singer/songwriter).

☑ ○ ALL STAR MANAGEMENT
3142 Rainier Ave., Columbus OH 43231-3145. (614)794-2102. Fax: (614)794-2103. E-mail: allstarmanage@msn.com. **Contact:** John or Mary Simpson, owners. Management firm. Estab. 1980. Represents individual artists, groups and songwriters from anywhere; currently handles 3 acts. Receives 20% commission. Reviews material for acts.
  • Also see the listing for All Star Record Promotions in the Record Companies section of this book.
How to Contact Submit demo tape by mail. Unsolicited submissions are OK. Prefers cassette or videocassette with 3 songs and lyric or lead sheet. If seeking management, press kit should include CD with 3 songs, bio, 8×10 photo or any information or articles written about yourself or group, and video if you have one. Does not return material. Responds in 2 months.
Music Mostly **country, Christian, adult contemporary, smooth jazz** and **pop rock**. Works primarily with bands and singers/songwriters. Current acts include Debbie Robins (singer/songwriter,

Christian contemporary), Allen Austin (singer/songwriter, country rock) and Leon Seiter (country singer/songwriter).

☑ ALL STAR TALENT AGENCY
P.O. Box 717, White House TN 37188. (615)643-4208. Fax: (615)643-2228. E-mail: kirbyjoy@aol.com. **Contact:** Joyce Kirby, owner/agent. Booking agency. Estab. 1966. Represents professional individuals, groups and songwriters; currently handles 6 acts. Receives 15% commission. Reviews material for acts.

How to Contact Submit demo tape by mail. Unsolicited submissions are OK. Prefers cassette or VHS videocassette with 4 songs (can be cover songs) and lead sheet. If seeking management, press kit should include bios, cover letter, press clippings, demo and photos. Does not return material. Does not return long distance phone calls. Responds in 1 month.

Music Mostly **country**; also **bluegrass**, **gospel**, **MOR**, **rock (country)** and **top 40/pop**. Works primarily with dance, show and bar bands, vocalists, club acts and concerts. Current acts include Chris Hartley (country), Alek Houston (MOR) and Joe Trice (blues).

☑ MICHAEL ALLEN ENTERTAINMENT DEVELOPMENT
P.O. Box 111510, Nashville TN 37222. (615)754-0059. E-mail: michael@michaelallencreates.com. Website: www.michaelallencreates.com. **Contact:** Michael Allen. Management firm and public relations. Represents individual artists, groups and songwriters; currently handles 2 acts. Receives 15-25% commission. Reviews material for acts.

How to Contact Submit demo tape by mail. Unsolicited submissions are OK. Prefers CD or cassette or VHS videocassette with 3 songs and lyric or lead sheets. If seeking management, press kit should include photo, bio, press clippings, letter and tape. Include SASE. Responds in 3 months.

Music Mostly **country** and **pop**; also **rock** and **gospel**. Works primarily with vocalists and bands. Currently doing public relations for Shotgun Red, Ricky Lynn Gregg, Easy Street and Kyle Raines.

☒ ☑ AMERICAN ARTISTS ENTERTAINMENT
1143 Fitzgerald St., Philadelphia PA 19148-3611. E-mail: online@aaeg.com. Website: www.aaeg.com. **Contact:** A&R Department. Management firm, music publisher (David Music, BMI), record company (East Coast Records) and record and motion picture distribution. Represents individual artists, groups, actors and models from anywhere; currently handles 3 acts. Receives 20% commission. Reviews material for acts.

How to Contact Submit demo tape by mail. Unsolicited submissions are OK. Prefers cassette, videocassette or CD with 3 songs. If seeking management, press kit should include bio, press releases, photos, performing, training and background. Include SASE. Responds in 1 month.

Music Mostly **R&B**, **top 40**, **rap** and **country**; also **modern rock** and **motion picture scores**. Current acts include The Blue Notes (R&B), The Trammps (disco), Clarice Rose (country) and Bliss (Top 40).

☒ ☐ AMERICAN BANDS MANAGEMENT
P.O. Box 840607, Houston TX 77284. (713)785-3700. Fax: (713)785-4641. E-mail: johnblomstrom@aol.com. President: John Blomstrom, Sr. Vice President: Cheryl Byrd. Management firm. Estab. 1973. Represents groups from anywhere; currently handles 3 acts. Receives 15-25% commission. Reviews material for acts.

How to Contact Submit demo tape by mail prior to making phone contact. Unsolicited submissions are OK. Prefers cassette or CD. If seeking management, press kit should include cover letter, bio, photo, demo tape/CD, press clippings, video, résumé and professional references with names and numbers. Does not return material. Responds in 1 month.

Music Mostly **rock (all forms)** and **modern country**. Works primarily with bands. Current acts include Captain Pink (Motown), Vince Vance & the Valiants (show band) and Rachel (guitarist/singer/modern folk).

◩ ◪ AMOK ARTISTS AGENCY

Box 12, Fergus ON N1M 2W7 Canada. (519)787-1100. Fax: (519)787-0084. E-mail: amok@sentex.n et. Website: www.amokmusic.com. **Contact:** Hugo Ranpen, owner. Management firm and booking agency. Estab. 1985. Represents groups from anywhere; currently handles 20 acts. Receives 15-20% commission.

How to Contact Submit demo tape by mail. Unsolicited submissions are OK. Prefers VHS videocassette or CD with lyric sheet. If seeking management, press kit should include bio, past performances, photo, cassette, CD or video. "Due to the large amount of submissions we receive we can only respond to successful applicants." Does not return material.

Music Mostly **world beat**, **new roots**, **aboriginal** and **folk**. Works primarily with bands in the world music and new roots field; no mainstream rock/pop. Current acts include Amampondo (world beat, Melt 2000), Mighty Popo (World), Madagascar Slim (world), and Tri-continental (roots).

☑ ◪ ANGEL GOMEZ MUSIC

21742 Nowlin Ave., Dearborn MI 48124. (313)274-7000. Fax: (313)274-9255. E-mail: angelgomezm usic@aol.com. Website: www.angelgomezmusic.com. **Contact:** Angel Gomez, president. Management firm. Estab. 1979. Represents local and international individual artists, groups and songwriters; currently handles 3 acts. Receives 15-20% commission. Reviews material for acts.

How to Contact *Write first and obtain permission to submit.* Prefers CD/CDR or DVD of performance with 3-5 songs. If seeking management, include photo, tape/CD, bio, cover letter, press clippings and itinerary of dates. Does not return material. Responds in 2 months.

Music Mostly **rock**, **pop** and **top 40**; also **funk**. Works primarily with individual artists, groups and songwriters. Current artists include Kat McAllister (pop T-40), The Rev. Right Time and the First Cuzins of Funk (new funk) and Bridge (rock).

▨ ◪ APODACA PROMOTIONS INC.

717 E. Tidwell Rd., Houston TX 77022. (713)691-6677. Fax: (713)692-9298. E-mail: houston@apoda capromotions.com. Website: www.apodacapromotions.com. Manager: Domingo A. Barrera. Management firm, booking agency, music publisher (Huina Publishing, Co. Inc.). Estab. 1991. Represents songwriters and groups from anywhere; currently handles 40 acts. Receives 15% commission. Reviews material for acts.

How to Contact Submit demo tape by mail. Unsolicited submissions are OK. Prefers CD and lyric and lead sheet. Include SASE. Responds in 2 months.

Music Mostly **international** and **Hispanic**; also **rock**. Works primarily with bands and songwriters. Current acts include Bobby Pulido (Tex-Mex music) Kubia Kings, Alicia Billarreal, Atrapado, Jennifer Pena and Ninelconde.

◪ ARTIST REPRESENTATION AND MANAGEMENT

1257 Arcade St., St. Paul MN 55106. (651)483-8754. Fax: (651)776-6338. E-mail: ra@armentertainm ent.com. Website: www.armentertainment.com. **Contact:** Roger Anderson, agent/manager. Management firm and booking agency. Estab. 1983. Represents artists from anywhere; currently handles 10 acts. Receives 15% commission. Reviews material for acts.

How to Contact Submit CD and video by mail. Unsolicited submissions are OK. Please include minimum 3 songs. If seeking management, references, current schedule, bio, photo, press clippings should also be included. "Priority is placed on original artists with product who are currently touring." Does not return material. Responds only if interested within 30 days.

Music Mostly **melodic rock**. Current acts include Knight Crawler (melodic rock), Great White, Warrant, Firehouse and Jesse Lang.

◖ ATCH RECORDS AND PRODUCTIONS

9894 Bissonnet, Suite 906, Houston TX 77036. (713)981-6540. Fax: (713)981-0083. Website: www.a tchrecords.com. Chairman/CEO: Charles Atchison. Management firm, recording studio and record company. Estab. 1989. Represents local, regional and international individual artists, groups and songwriters; currently handles 2 acts. Receives 20% commission. Reviews material for acts.

How to Contact Submit demo by mail. Unsolicited submissions are OK. Prefers CD with 2 songs and lyric sheet. If seeking management, include cover letter, bio, photo, demo and lyrics. Does not return material. Responds in 3 weeks.

Music Mostly **R&B** and **gospel**; also **pop**, **rap** and **hip-hop**. Works primarily with vocalists and groups. Current acts include Prime Flo and Joy (rap).

Tips "Send a good detailed demo with good lyrics. Looking for wonderful love stories, dance music."

☑ BACCHUS GROUP PRODUCTIONS, LTD.

5701 N. Sheridan Rd., Suite 8-U, Chicago IL 60660. (773)334-1532. Fax: (773)334-1531. E-mail: bacchusgrp@uron.cc. Website: www.BacchusGroup.com. **Contact:** D. Maximilian, managing director and executive producer. Director of Marketing: M. Margarida Rainho. Management firm and record producer (D. Maximilian). Estab. 1990. Represents individual artists or groups from anywhere; currently handles 9 acts. Receives 15-25% commission. Reviews material for acts.

How to Contact *Does not accept unsolicited submissions.*

Music Mostly **pop**, **R&B/soul** and **jazz**; also **Latin** and **world beat**. Works primarily with singer/songwriters, composers, arrangers, bands and orchestras. "Visit our website for current acts."

▓ ◯ BACKSTAGE ENTERTAINMENT

26239 Senator Ave., Harbor City CA 90710. (310)325-9997. Fax: (310)325-2560. E-mail: staff@backstageentertainment.net. Website: www.backstageentertainment.net. **Contact:** Paul Loggins. Management and publicity firm. Represents individual artists, groups, and songwriters. Currently handles 5 acts. Receives 20% commission. Reviews material for acts.

How to Contact If seeking management and/or publicity, press kit should include picture, short bio, cover letter, press clippings and CD (preferred). "Mark on the CD which cut you, as the artist, feel is the strongest." Does not return material. Responds in 2 weeks.

Music Mostly **AC/Hot AC**, **top 40**, and **country**; also **urban**, **rap**, **smooth jazz**, **Americana**, and **alternative**.

☑ ◪ BACKSTREET BOOKING

5658 Kirby Ave., Cincinnati OH 45239. (513)542-9544. Fax: (513)542-9545. E-mail: info@backstreetbooking.com. Website: www.backstreetbooking.com. **Contact:** James Sfarnas, president. Booking agency. Estab. 1992. Represents individual artists and groups from anywhere; currently handles 30 acts. Receives 10-15% commission. Reviews material for acts.

How to Contact *Call first and obtain permission to submit.* Accepts only signed acts with product available nationally.

Music Mostly **niche-oriented music** and **rock**. Current acts include Billy Preston, Acumen (progressive rock group), Niacin (fusion), Mike Keneally Band (progressive rock), Cab (jazz fusion) and Spock's Beard (progressive rock).

Tips "Build a base on your own."

▦ ◯ ◪ PAUL BARRETT ROCK 'N' ROLL ENTERPRISES

16 Grove Place, Penarth, Vale of Glamorgan CF64 2ND United Kingdom. 02920-704279. Fax: 02920. E-mail: barrettrocknroll@amserve.com. **Contact:** Paul Barrett, director. Management firm, booking agency, record company (Rock 'n' Roll Records) and record producer (Paul Barrett). Estab. 1969. Represents individual artists and groups from anywhere; currently handles 37 acts. Receives 10% commission. Reviews material for acts.

• This company only represents acts who perform '50s rock 'n' roll.

How to Contact Submit demo tape by mail. Unsolicited submissions are OK. Prefers CD or DAT with picture and bio (for performers). SAE and IRC. Responds in 3 weeks.

Music Mostly **'50s rock 'n' roll**. Works primarily with "performers plus some writers." Current acts include The Jets (trio), Matchbox (rockabilly) and Crazy Caravan & The Rhythm Rockers (rockabilly).

Tips "Paul Barrett Rock 'N' Roll Enterprises is, more than anything else, a specialist booking agency dealing on an international basis on with pre-Beatles rock 'n' rollers. We have no recording plans for the foreseeable future, and we have all the acts we intend to manage."

☑ ◐ BASSLINE ENTERTAINMENT, INC.
P.O. Box 2394, New York NY 10185. E-mail: info@basslineinc.com. Website: www.basslineinc.com. **Contact:** Talent Relations Dept. Management firm. Estab. 1993. Represents local and regional individual artists, groups and songwriters. Receives 20-25% commission. Reviews material for acts.
How to Contact Submit demo tape by mail. Unsolicited submissions are OK. Prefers cassette, CD, DVD, or VHS. If seeking management, press kit should include cover letter, press clippings, bio, demo (cassette, CD or VHS), picture and accurate contact telephone number. Include SASE. Responds in 3 weeks.
Music Mostly **pop**, **R&B**, **club/dance** and **hip-hop/rap**; some **Latin**. Works primarily with singer/songwriters, producers, rappers and bands. Current acts include Iceman (hip-hop) and Daz (rap/R&B).

◐ BIG J PRODUCTIONS
2516 S. Sugar Ridge, Laplace LA 70068. (504)652-2645. **Contact:** Frankie Jay, agent. Booking agency. Estab. 1968. Represents individual artists, groups and songwriters; currently handles over 50 acts. Receives 15-25% commission. Reviews material for acts.
How to Contact *Call first and obtain permission to submit* (office hours Monday-Friday: noon-5 pm). Prefers cassette or VHS videocassette with 3-6 songs and lyric or lead sheet. "It would be best for an artist to lip-sync to a prerecorded track. The object is for someone to see how an artist would perform more than simply assessing song content." Artists seeking management should include pictures, biography, tape or CD and video. Does not return material. Responds in 2 weeks.
Music Mostly **rock**, **pop** and **R&B**. Works primarily with groups with self-contained songwriters. Current acts include Zebra (original rock group), Crowbar (heavy metal) and Kyper (original dance).

◐ BLACK STALLION COUNTRY, INC.
P.O. Box 368, Tujunga CA 91043. (818)487-9803. Fax: (818)487-9803. E-mail: bscmgmt@aol.com. **Contact:** Kenn E. Kingsbury, Jr., president. Management firm, production company and music publisher (Black Stallion Country Publishing/BMI). Estab. 1979. Represents individual artists from anywhere; currently handles 20 acts. Receives 15-20% commission. Reviews material for acts.
How to Contact Submit demo tape by mail. Unsolicited submissions are OK. Prefers cassette with 3 songs and lyric sheet. If seeking management, press kit should include picture/résumé and audio and/or video tape. "I would also like a one-page statement of goals and why you would be an asset to my company or me." Include SASE. Responds in 2 months.
Music Mostly **country**, **jazz** and **A/C**. Works primarily with country acts, variety acts and film/TV pictures/actors. Current acts include Lane Brody (country singer), Thom Bresh (musician), Rebecca Holden (actress/singer).

◐ BLANK & BLANK
1 Belmont Ave., Suite 320, Bala Cynwyd PA 19004-1604. (610)664-8200. Fax: (610)664-8201. **Contact:** E. Robert Blank, manager. Management firm. Represents individual artists and groups. Reviews material for acts.
How to Contact *Contact first and obtain permission to submit.* Prefers videocassette. If seeking management, press kit should include cover letter, demo tape/CD and video. Does not return material.

◐ ◐ BLOWIN' SMOKE PRODUCTIONS/RECORDS
7438 Shoshone Ave., Van Nuys CA 91406-2340. (818)881-9888. Fax: (818)881-0555. E-mail: blowinsmokeband@ktb.net. Website: www.blowinsmokeband.com. **Contact:** Larry Knight, president. Management firm and record producer. Estab. 1990. Represents local and West Coast individual

artists and groups; currently handles 6 acts. Receives 15-20% commission. Reviews material for acts.

- Also see the listing for Hailing Frequency Music Productions in the Record Producers section of this book.

How to Contact *Write or call first and obtain permission to submit.* Prefers cassette or CD. If seeking management, press kit should include cover letter, demo tape/CD, lyric sheets, press clippings, video if available, photo, bios, contact telephone numbers and any info on legal commitments already in place. Include SASE. Responds in 1 month.

Music Mostly **R&B**, **blues** and **blues-rock**. Works primarily with single and group vocalists and a few R&B/blues bands. Current acts include Larry "Fuzzy" Knight (blues singer/songwriter), King Floyd (R&B artist), The Blowin' Smoke Rhythm & Blues Band, The Fabulous Smokettes, and Joyce Lawson.

☑ THE BLUE CAT AGENCY

P.O. Box 4036, San Rafael CA 94913-4036. (415)713-2538. E-mail: bluecat_agency@yahoo.com. Website: www.geocities.com/bluecat_agency. **Contact:** Karen Kindig, owner/agent. Management firm and booking agency. Estab. 1989. Represents individual artists and/or groups from anywhere; currently handles 2 acts. Receives 10-15% commission. Reviews material for acts.

How to Contact *E-mail only for permission to submit.* Prefers cassette or CD. If seeking management, press kit should include demo, CD or tape, bio, press clippings and photo. SASE. Responds in 2 months.

Music Mostly **rock/pop "en espanol"** and **jazz/latin jazz**. Works primarily with bands. Current acts include Kai Eckhardt, Alejandro Santos, Ania Paz, Gabriel Rosati.

☐ BLUE WAVE PRODUCTIONS

3221 Perryville Rd., Baldwinsville NY 13027. (315)638-4286. Fax: (315)635-4757. E-mail: bluewave @localnet.com. Website: www.bluewaverecords.com. **Contact:** Greg Spencer, owner/president. Management firm, music publisher (G.W. Spencer Music/ASCAP), record company (Blue Wave Records) and record producer (Blue Wave Productions). Estab. 1985. Represents individual artists and/or groups and songwriters from anywhere; currently handles 5 acts. Receives 10% commission. Reviews material for acts.

- Also see the listing for Blue Wave in the Record Companies section of this book.

How to Contact Submit demo tape by mail. Unsolicited submissions are OK. Prefers CD or VHS videocassette with 3-6 songs. "Just the music first, reviews and articles are OK. No photos or lyrics until later." If seeking management, press kit should include cover letter and demo tape/CD. Include SASE. Responds in 1 month. No phone calls.

Music Mostly **blues**, **blues/rock** and **roots rock**. Current acts include Kim Lembo (female blues vocalist), Kim Simmonds (blues guitarist and singer/songwriter) and Downchild Bluesband (blues).

Tips "I'm looking for great singers with soul. Not interested in pop/rock commercial material."

☑ BOUQUET-ORCHID ENTERPRISES

P.O. Box 1335, Norcross GA 30091. (770)339-9088. **Contact:** Bill Bohannon, president. Management firm, booking agency, music publisher (Orchid Publishing/BMI) and record company (Bouquet Records). Represents individuals and groups; currently handles 3 acts. Receives 10-15% commission. Reviews material for acts.

- Also see the listing for Orchid Publishing in the Music Publishers section of this book.

How to Contact Submit demo tape by mail. Unsolicited submissions are OK. Prefers cassette, CD or videocassette with 3-5 songs, song list and lyric sheet. Include brief résumé. If seeking management, press kit should include current photograph, 2-3 media clippings, description of act, and background information on act. Include SASE. Responds in 1 month.

Music Mostly **country**, **rock** and **top 40/pop**; also **gospel** and **R&B**. Works primarily with vocalists and groups. Current acts include Susan Spencer, Jamey Wells, Adam Day and the Bandoleers.

☐ BREAD & BUTTER PRODUCTIONS

P.O. Box 1539, Wimberley TX 78676. (512)301-7117. E-mail: sgladson@gmail.com. **Contact:** Steve Gladson, managing partner. Management firm and booking agency. Estab. 1969. Represents individual artists, songwriters and groups from anywhere; currently handles 6 acts. Receives 10-20% commission. Reviews material for acts.

How to Contact Submit demo tape by mail. Unsolicited submissions OK. Prefers cassette, videocassette or CD and lyric sheet. If seeking management, press kit should include cover letter, demo tape/CD, lyric sheets, press clippings, video, résumé, picture and bio. Does not return material. Responds in 1 month.

Music Mostly **alternative rock**, **country** and **R&B**; also **classic rock**, **folk** and **Americana**. Works primarily with singer/songwriters and original bands. Current acts include Lou Cabaza (songwriter/producer/manager), Duck Soup (band) and Gaylan Ladd (songwriter/singer).

Tips "Remember why you are in this biz. The art comes first."

☑ BROTHERS MANAGEMENT ASSOCIATES

141 Dunbar Ave., Fords NJ 08863. (732)738-0880. Fax: (732)738-0970. E-mail: bmaent@yahoo.com. Website: www.bmaent.com. **Contact:** Allen A. Faucera, president. Management firm and booking agency. Estab. 1972. Represents artists, groups and songwriters; currently handles 25 acts. Receives 15-20% commission. Reviews material for acts.

How to Contact *Write first and obtain permission to submit.* Prefers CD or DVD with 3-6 songs and lyric sheets. Include photographs and résumé. If seeking management, include photo, bio, tape and return envelope in press kit. Include SASE. Responds in 2 months.

Music Mostly **pop**, **rock**, **MOR** and **R&B**. Works primarily with vocalists and established groups. Current acts include Nils Lofgren and Danny Federici.

Tips "Submit very commercial material—make demo of high quality."

🌐 ☺ BUXTON WALKER P/L

P.O. Box 2197, St. Kilda West, Vic 3182 Australia. (61)(39)537-7155. Fax: (61)(39)537-7166. E-mail: andrew@buxtonwalker.com. Website: www.buxtonwalker.com. **Contact:** Andrew Walker. Management firm, music publisher (Head Records Publishing) and record company (Head Records). Estab. 1995. Represents individual artists and groups from anywhere; currently handles 5 acts. Management company receives 20% commission.

How to Contact Submit demo by mail. Unsolicited submissions are OK. CD only. If seeking management, press kit should include CD, bio and history. Please ensure submission is accompanied with clear notice detailing reason for submission. "Processing takes time. Contact by fax or e-mail is best as it allows for time differences to be no obstacle." SAE and IRC. Responds in 2 months.

Music Mostly **rock/pop**, **jazz** and **acoustic**; also **reggae**, **blues** and **world**. No maintstream pop. Works primarily with singers/songwriters and bands. Current acts include The Jaynes (rock), Black Sorrows (blues and jazz), The Revelators (blues), Tess McKenna (alt rock) and Jen Anderson (scores).

Tips "We have low need for songs to be supplied to our artists. We are mostly interested in recorded artists/writers looking for distribution/release in Australia/New Zealand."

☑ CIRCUIT RIDER TALENT & MANAGEMENT CO.

123 Walton Ferry Rd., Hendersonville TN 37075. (615)824-1947. Fax: (615)264-0462. E-mail: dotwool@bellsouth.net. **Contact:** Linda S. Dotson, president. Consultation firm, booking agency and music publisher (Channel Music, Cordial Music, Dotson & Dotson Music Publishers, Shalin Music Co.). Represents individual artists, songwriters and actors; currently handles 10 acts. Works with a large number of recording artists, songwriters, actors, producers. (Includes the late multi-Grammy-winning producer/writer Skip Scarborough.) Receives 10-15% commission (union rates). Reviews material for acts (free of charge).

How to Contact *Write or call first and obtain permission to submit.* Prefers cassette or videocassette with 3 songs and lyric sheet. If seeking consultation, press kit should include bio, cover letter, résumé, lyric sheets if original songs, photo and tape with 3 songs. Videocassettes required of artist's submissions. Include SASE. Responds in 2 months.

Music Mostly **Latin blues**, **pop**, **country** and **gospel**; also **R&B** and **comedy**. Works primarily with vocalists, special concerts, movies and TV. Current acts include Razzy Bailey (award winning blues artist/writer), Clint Walker (actor/recording artist) and Ben Calder (comedy/novelty).

Tips ''Artists, have your act together. Have a full press kit, videos and be professional. Attitudes are a big factor in my agreeing to work with you (no egotists). This is a business, and we will be building your career.''

☑ CLASS ACT PRODUCTIONS/MANAGEMENT

P.O. Box 55252, Sherman Oaks CA 91413. (818)980-1039. E-mail: pkimmel@gr8gizmo.com. **Contact:** Peter Kimmel, president. Management firm. Estab. 1985. Currently handles 2 acts. Receives 20% commission. Reviews material for acts.

How to Contact Submit demo CD by mail. Unsolicited submissions are OK. Include cover letter, bio, lyric sheets (essential), CD in press kit. Include SASE. Responds in 1 month.

Music All styles. Current acts include Terpsichore (cyber dance/pop), Karma (high energy bluesy rock).

☑ CLOUSHER PRODUCTIONS

P.O. Box 1191, Mechanicsburg PA 17055. (717)766-7644. Fax: (717)766-1490. E-mail: clousher@we btv.net. Website: www.clousherentertainment.com. **Contact:** Fred Clousher, owner. Booking agency and production company. Estab. 1972. Represents groups from anywhere; currently handles over 100 acts.

How to Contact Submit demo tape by mail. Unsolicited submissions are OK. Prefers VHS videocassette. If seeking management, press kit should include press clippings, testimonials, credits, glossies, video demo tape, references, cover letter, résumé and bio. Does not return material. ''Performer should check back with us!''

Music Mostly **country**, **old rock** and **ethnic** (German, Hawaiian, etc.); also **dance bands** (regional) and **classical musicals**. ''We work mostly with country, old time R&R, regional variety dance bands, tribute acts, and all types of variety acts.'' Current acts include Jasmine Morgan (country/ pop vocalist), Robin Right (country vocalist) and Island Breeze (ethnic Hawaiian group).

Tips ''The songwriters we work with are entertainers themselves, which is the aspect we deal with. They usually have bands or do some sort of show, either with tracks or live music. We engage them for stage shows, dances, strolling, etc. We do not publish music or submit performers to recording companies for contracts. We strictly set up live performances for them.''

Ⓝ ☑ COAL HARBOR MUSIC

P.O. Box 148027, Nashville TN 37214-8027.(615)883-2020. E-mail: info@coalharbormusic.com. Website: www.coalharbormusic.com. **Contact:** Jerry Ray Wells, President/Owner. Management firm, booking agency, music publisher (Coal Harbor Music), record company (Coal Harbor Music), record producer (Jerry Ray Wells), and radio promoter (''We promote clients' single released songs to radio stations.'') Estab. 1990. Represents individual artists, groups. Works with artists from anywhere. Receives 10-20% commission. Reviews material for acts.

How to Contact Write or call first and obtain permission to submit a demo. Prefers CD/CDR with 2-3 songs and cover letter. Include SASE or stampled reply postcard. If seeking management representation send CD, photo, bio, VHS videocassette or DVD (if possible), letters of recommendation, newspaper articles, and/or reviews. Be prepared to furnish extra press kits if interested in booking. Put what you are interested in on outside of submission, for example ''ATTN: Mgmt,'' ''ATTN: Booking,'' ''ATTN: Songs,'' etc. Does not return material.

Music Mostly **country**, **Christian (all forms)** and **bluegrass**; also **Christmas**, **patriotic** and **comedy**. Does not want hard rock, heavy metal, or rap. Works primarily with country and Christian. ''We are a company that strives to seek the best, most profitable business deal for both parties involved, both our clients and ourselves. We are looking for talent that we can market.'' Current acts include Don Freeman (country/Christian singer-songwriter), Anne Borgen (contemporary Christian singer-songwriter), Back On Track (contemporary Christian group).

Tips ''Send us your very best work and state clearly in your cover letter your career goals along with exactly what it is you want us to do with you or your material. We work with a lot of singer-songwriters, but are open to any talent that can be marketed and booked. A career is something you have to build. Don't expect us, or anyone, to make you an overnight sensation!''

CONCEPT 2000 INC.

P.O. Box 2950, Columbus OH 43216-2950. (614)276-2000. Fax: (614)275-0163. E-mail: info2k@con cept2k.com. Website: www.concept2k.com. Florida office: P.O. Box 2070, Largo FL 33779-2070. (727)585-2922. Fax: (727)585-3835. **Contact:** Brian Wallace, president. Management firm and booking agency. Estab. 1981. Represents international individual artists, groups and songwriters; currently handles 4 acts. Receives 20% commission. Reviews material for acts.

How to Contact Submit demo tape by mail. Unsolicited submissions are OK. Prefers cassette with 4 songs. If seeking management, include demo tape, press clips, photo and bio. Does not return material. Responds in 2 weeks.

Music Mostly **country**, **gospel** and **pop**; also **jazz**, **R&B** and **soul**. Current acts include Bryan Hitch (contemporary gospel), Shades of Grey (R&B/soul), Dwight Lenox (show group) and Gene Walker (jazz).

Tips "Send quality songs with lyric sheets. Production quality is not necessary."

CONCERTED EFFORTS, INC./FOGGY DAY MUSIC

P.O. Box 600099, Newtonville MA 02460. (617)969-0810. Fax: (617)969-6761. Website: www.conce rtedefforts.com. **Owner:** Paul Kahn. Management firm, booking agency and music publisher (Foggy Day Music). Represents individual artists, groups and songwriters from anywhere. Commission varies. Reviews material for acts.

How to Contact Submit demo tape by mail. Unsolicited submissions are OK *"but call first!"* Prefers CD, will accept cassette, with lyric sheet. "No management submissions." Does not return material.

Music **Folk**, **country** and **rock**; also **world music**, **zydeco** and **blues**. Current acts include Luther Johnson (blues singer), Holmes Brothers, Roseanne Cash and Orchestra Baobab.

Tips "Simple recorded demo is OK, with lyrics."

CONSCIENCE MUSIC

P.O. Box 617667, Chicago IL 60661. (312)226-4858. E-mail: towrecords@aol.com. **Contact:** Karen M. Smith, consultant/personal manager. Management firm, artist/rehearsal studio and record company (TOW Records). Estab. 1985. Represents individual artists, groups and songwriters from anywhere; currently handles 1 act. Receives 20% commission.

How to Contact *Write first and obtain permission to submit.* Prefers CD with 2-3 songs and lyric sheet. If seeking management, info should include demo CD, lyric sheets, list of performance locations, and letter with band or artist objectives. "Cannot overemphasize the importance of having objectives you are ready to discuss with us." Include SASE. Responds in 4 months.

Music Mostly **rock** and **pop**; also **visual artists**, **writers** and **models**. Works primarily with indie bands in the States and Great Britain. Currently represents Lance Porter (drummer with the Flash Express). "Many clients are on a consulting basis only."

COUNTRYWIDE PRODUCERS

2466 Wildon Dr., York PA 17403. (717)741-2658. E-mail: cwpent@wmconnect.com. **Contact:** Bob Englar, president. Booking agency. Represents individuals and groups; currently handles 8 acts. Receives 15% commission. Reviews material for acts.

How to Contact Query or submit demo tape by mail. Unsolicited submissions are OK. If seeking management, press kit should include photo and demo tape. Include SASE. Responds in 1 week.

Music Bluegrass, **blues**, **classical** and **country**; also **folk**, **gospel**, **polka**, **rock (light)** and **top 40/ pop**. Works primarily with show bands. Current acts include The Walls of Time (bluegrass), The W. Va. Connections (bluegrass), Shilha Ridge (bluegrass) and Iron Ridge (bluegrass).

STEPHEN COX PROMOTIONS & MANAGEMENT

6708 Mammoth Ave., Van Nuys CA 91405. (818)377-4530. Fax: (818)782-5305. E-mail: stephencox @earthlink.net. **Contact:** Stephen Cox, president. Management firm. Estab. 1993. Represents individual artists, groups or songwriters from anywhere; currently handles 5 acts. Receives 15% commission. Reviews material for acts.

How to Contact *Call first and obtain permission to submit.* Prefers CD. If seeking management, press kit should include biographies, performance history and radio play. "Include a clear definition of goals in a thoughtful presentation." Include SASE. Responds in 2 weeks.

Music Mostly **rock**, **New Age/world** and **alternative**; also **blues**, **folk** and **progressive**. Works primarily with bands. Current acts include Joe Sherbanee (jazz), Val Ewell & Pulse (blues rock), Paul Micich & Mitch Espe (New Age/jazz), Covet (metal) and Jill Cohn (folk rock).

Tips "Establish goals based on research, experience and keep learning about the music business. Start the business as though it will always be you as an independent. Establish a foundation before considering alternative commitments. We aim to educate and consult to a level that gives an artist the freedom of choice to choose whether to go to the majors etc., or retain independence. Remember, promote, promote and promote some more. Always be nice to people, treat them as you would wish to be treated."

◙ CRAWFISH PRODUCTIONS

P.O. Box 5412, Buena Park CA 90620. (909)941-8216. E-mail: swampbasque@msn.com. Producer: Leo J. Eiffert, Jr. Management firm, music publisher (Young Country/BMI), record producer (Leo J. Eiffert) and record company (Plain Country Records). Estab. 1968. Represents local and international individual artists and songwriters; currently handles 4 acts. Commission received is open. Reviews material for acts.

- Also see the listings for Young Country Records/Plain Country Records in the Record Companies section of this book and Leo J. Eiffert, Jr. in the Record Producers section of this book.

How to Contact Submit demo tape by mail. Unsolicited submissions are OK. Prefers cassette with 2-3 songs and lyric sheet. Include SASE. Responds in 3 weeks.

Music Mostly **country** and **gospel**. Works primarily with vocalists. Current acts include Pigeons, Southern Spirit and Nashville Snakes.

☑ ◯ CREATIVE STAR MANAGEMENT

720 Deleon Street, Ottawa IL 61350. E-mail: st_chilling_2002@yahoo.com. President/Owner: James Milligan. Vice President: William Roach. Management firm, booking agency, music publisher (Party House Publishing/BMI, A New Rap Jam Publishing/ASCAP), record company (New Experience Records/Grand Slam Records). Estab. 1989. Represents individual artists, groups and songwriters from anywhere; currently handles 6 acts. Receives 15-20% commission. Reviews material for acts.

- Creative Star Management's publishing company, A New Rap Jam Publishing (ASCAP), is listed in the Music Publishers section, and their record label, New Experience Records/Grand Slam Records, is listed in the Record Companies section.

How to Contact *Contact first and obtain permission to submit.* Prefers cassette, VHS, or DVD with 3-5 songs and lyric sheet. If seeking management, press kit should include press clippings, bios, résumé, 8×10 glossy photo, any information that will support material and artist. Include SASE. Responds in 6-8 weeks.

Music Mostly **R&B**, **pop** and **country**; also **rap**, **contemporary gospel** and **soul/funk**. Current acts include T.M.C. (gospel), James Junior (R&B singer) and Dennis Esapa (rap).

Tips "We are seeking '70s and '80s groups looking to re-sign and for management. Please include any releases of recordings and videos in support of all materials. Rap artists—we want clean positive material! Thanks."

⬛ ◙ CROSSFIRE PRODUCTIONS

304 Braeswood, Austin TX 78704-7200. (512)442-5678. Fax: (512)442-1154. E-mail: vicky@crossfir eproductions.net. **Contact:** Vicky Moerbe, president. Management firm. Estab. 1990. Represents local, individual artists and songwriters; currently handles 4 acts. Receives 15% commission. Reviews material for acts.

How to Contact *Write or call first and obtain permission to submit.* Prefers CD with any number of songs and lyric sheet. If seeking management, press kit should include biography, press releases/articles/reviews, photograph/discography and copy of current release or demo.

Music Mostly **blues**, **swing** and **country**; also **soul** and **contemporary rock**. Works primarily with singers and songwriters. Current acts include W.C. Clark (singer/songwriter/touring act; blues/soul), Rusty Weir (songwriter), Roomful of Blues (Grammy-nominated blues act), Michael Klein Band (country/rock writer and performer/touring act) and Haydn Vitera (country/rock singer).
Tips "Please submit only material to be considered for recordings for blues/soul, swing, country or Spanish-language recordings. Our artists are looking for material to be considered for recordings for national releases."

❍ D&R ENTERTAINMENT
308 N. Park, Broken Bow OK 74728. (580)584-9429. **Contact:** Don Walton, president. Management firm. Estab. 1985. Represents individual artists from anywhere; currently handles 2 acts. Receives 15% commission. Reviews material for acts. Also reviews for other country singers.
How to Contact Submit demo tape by mail. Unsolicited submissions are OK. Prefers cassette and videocassette with lyric and lead sheet. If seeking management, press kit should include brief background of artist, videotape of performance, cover letter, résumé, photo, press clippings and cassette or CD. "Indicate whether you have any financial or prospective financial backing." Does not return material. Responds in 3 months.
Music Mostly **contemporary Christian**; also **country** and **pop**. Works primarily with young beginning singers. Current acts include Kristi Reed (positive country) and Thomas Wells (contemporary Christian).
Tips "I need songs (country) that would fit a young singer under 20. In other words no drinking, cheating, marrying songs. A pretty tough choice. Also Christian contemporary songs."

◉ DAS COMMUNICATIONS, LTD.
83 Riverside Dr., New York NY 10024. (212)877-0400. Fax: (212)595-0176. Management firm. Estab. 1975. Represents individual artists, groups and producers from anywhere; currently handles 25 acts. Receives 20% commission.
How to Contact *Call for permission to submit.* Responds only if interested. Prefers demo with 3 songs, lyric sheet and photo. Does not return material.
Music Mostly **rock**, **pop**, **R&B**, **alternative** and **hip-hop**. Current acts include Joan Osborne (rock), Wyclef Jean (hip-hop), Black Eyed Peas (hip-hop), John Legend (R&B), Spin Doctors (rock), The Bacon Brothers (rock).

☑ ◑ DCA PRODUCTIONS
330 W. 38th St., Suite 904, New York NY 10018. (212)245-2063. Fax: (212)245-2367. Website: www.dcaproductions.com. **Contact:** Suzanne Perotta, office manager. President: Daniel Abrahamsen. Vice President: Geraldine Abrahamsen. Management firm. Estab. 1975. Represents individual artists, groups and songwriters from anywhere; currently handles 14 acts.
How to Contact If seeking management, press kit should include cover letter, bio, photo, demo tape/CD and video. Prefers cassette or VHS videocassette with 2 songs. "All materials are reviewed and kept on file for future consideration. Does not return material. We respond only if interested."
Music Mostly **acoustic**, **rock** and **mainstream**; also **cabaret** and **theme**. Works primarily with acoustic singer/songwriters, top 40 or rock bands. Current acts include Gabrielle (singer/songwriter), Sean Altman (singer/songwriter) and 1910 Fruitgum Company (oldies band). Visit our website for a current roster of acts.
Tips "Please do not call for a review of material."

◉ THE EDWARD DE MILES COMPANY
28 E. Jackson Bldg., 10th Floor, #S627, Chicago IL 60604-2263. (773)509-6381. Fax: (312)922-6964. Website: www.edmsahara.com. **Contact:** Edward de Miles, president. Management firm, booking agency, entertainment/sports promoter and TV/radio broadcast producer. Estab. 1984. Represents film, television, radio and musical artists; currently handles 15 acts. Receives 10-20% commission. Reviews material for acts. Regional operations in Chicago, Dallas, Houston and Nashville through marketing representatives. Licensed A.F. of M. booking agent.

• Also see listings for Edward De Miles in the Music Publishers and Record Producers sections, and Sahara Records and Filmworks Entertainment in the Record Companies section of this book.

How to Contact *Does not accept unsolicited materials.* Prefers cassette with 3-5 songs, 8×10 b&w photo, bio and lyric sheet. "Copyright all material before submitting." If seeking management, include cover letter, bio, demo cassette with 3-5 songs, 8×10 b&w photo, lyric sheet, press clippings and video if available in press kit. Include SASE. Does not return material. Responds in 1 month.

Music Mostly **country**, **dance**, **R&B/soul**, **rock**, **top 40/pop** and **urban contemporary**; also looking for material for television, radio and film productions. Works primarily with dance bands and vocalists. Current acts include Steve Lynn (R&B/dance), Multiple Choice (rap) and D'von Edwards (jazz).

Tips "Performers need to be well prepared with their presentations (equipment, showmanship a must)."

ℕ ☐ BILL DETKO MANAGEMENT

378 Palomares Ave., Ventura CA 93003. (805)644-0447. Fax: (805)644-0469. **Contact:** Bill Detko, president. Management firm. Estab. 1984. Represents individual artists, groups and songwriters from anywhere; currently handles 4 acts. Receives 15% commission. Reviews material for acts.

How to Contact *Contact first and obtain permission to submit.* Prefers CD with 3 songs and lyric sheet. If seeking management, press kit should include bio, cover letter, résumé, photo, plus above items and any press or radio action. Does not return material. "Artist must call back."

Music All styles of rock.

ℕ ☒ ☑ DIVINE INDUSTRIES

(formerly Gangland Artists), Unit 191, 101-1001 W. Broadway, Vancouver BC V6H 4E4 Canada. Fax: (604)737-3602. E-mail: divine@divineindustries.com. Website: www.divineindustries.com. **Contact:** Allen Moy. Management firm, production house and music publisher. Estab. 1985. Represents artists and songwriters; currently handles 5 acts. Reviews material for acts.

How to Contact *Write first and obtain permission to submit.* Prefers CD or MP3 with lyric sheet. "Videos are not entirely necessary for our company. It is certainly a nice touch. If you feel your audiocassette is strong—send the video upon later request. Something wildly creative and individual will grab our attention." Does not return material. Responds in 2 months.

Music **Rock**, **pop** and **R&B**. Works primarily with "original rock/left of center" show bands. Current acts include 54-40 (rock/pop), Tom Wilson (folk rock), Chin (R&B).

ℕ ☑ COL. BUSTER DOSS PRESENTS

341 Billy Goat Hill Rd., Winchester TN 37398. (931)649-2577. Fax: (615)649-2732. **Contact:** Col. Buster Doss, producer. Management firm, booking agency, record company (Stardust Records), record producer and music publisher (Buster Doss Music/BMI). Estab. 1959. Represents individual artists, groups, songwriters and shows; currently handles 14 acts. Receives 15% commission. Reviews material for acts.

• Also see the listings for Col. Buster Doss in the Music Publishers and Record Producers sections and Stardust in the Record Companies section of this book.

How to Contact *Write first and obtain permission to submit.* Prefers cassette with 2-4 songs and lyric sheet. If seeking management, press kit should include demo, photos, video if available and bio. Include SASE. Responds back on day received.

Music Mostly **country**, **gospel** and **progressive**. Works primarily with show and dance bands, single acts and package shows. Current acts include "Rooster" Quantrell, Linda Wunder, The Border Raiders, "Bronco" Buck Cody, Jerri Arnold, Bob Norman, Cindy Lee, John Hamilton, Brant Miller, Troy Cooker, Mark Brumfield and Tennessee Bill Foster.

☒ ☑ EAO MUSIC CORPORATION OF CANADA

P.O. Box 1240, Station "M," Calgary AB T2P 2L2 Canada. (403)228-9388. Fax: (403)229-3598. E-mail: eao@telusplanet.net. Website: www.oliverio.ca. **Contact:** Edmund A. Oliverio, president. Management firm and record company. Estab. 1985. Represents individual artists, groups and songwriters from western Canada (aboriginal artists); currently handles 52 acts. Receives 15-20% commission. Reviews material for acts.

How to Contact Submit demo tape by mail. Unsolicited submissions are OK. Prefers cassette with 3 songs and lyric and lead sheets. If seeking management, press kit should include cover letter, résumé, b&w glossy photo, cassette tape, bio, media clippings and list of venues and festivals performed. SAE and IRC. Responds in 2 weeks.

Music Mostly **folk** and **native (aboriginal)**; also **rock**. Works primarily with singer/songwriters. Current acts include Activate (funky reggae), Feeding Like Butterflies (folk rock/Celtic), Katrina (country/folk) and Gloria K. MacRae (adult contemporary).

Tips "Be upfront and honest. Establish your long term goals and short term goals. Have you joined your music associations (i.e., CMA, etc.)? Recent demand for cowboy artists rather than country."

☐ THE ELLIS INTERNATIONAL TALENT AGENCY

5617 W. Melvina, Milwaukee WI 53216. (414)444-3385. **Contact:** Darnell Ellis, CEO/president. Management firm, booking agency, music publisher (Ellis Island Music/ASCAP) record company (Safire Records) and record producer (Darnell Ellis). Estab. 1997. Represents individual artists, groups and songwriters from anywhere; currently handles 2 acts. Receives 15-20% commission. Reviews material for acts.

• Also see the listing for Safire Records in the Record Companies section of this book.

How to Contact Submit demo tape by mail. Unsolicited submissions are OK. Prefers cassette or videocassette with 4-6 songs and press kit. If seeking management, press kit should include cassette tape or CD with 4-6 songs (demo), 8×10 photo, video tape and reviews. Does not return material. Responds in 6 weeks. "We will respond only if we are interested."

Music Mostly **country**, **pop**, **mainstream pop**, **rock** (all styles) and anything else except rap and hip-hop. Works primarily with singers, singer/songwriters, songwriters and bands. Current acts include Tracy Beck (acoustic, roots, blues, alt country, pop, swing) and Sheri Roloff (pop/rock).

☐ SCOTT EVANS PRODUCTIONS

P.O. Box 814028, Hollywood FL 33081-4028. (954)963-4449. E-mail: evansprod@aol.com. Website: www.theentertainmentmall.com. **Contact:** Ted Jones, new artists. Management firm and booking agency. Estab. 1979. Represents local, regional or international individual artists, groups, songwriters, comedians, novelty acts and dancers; currently handles over 200 acts. Receives 10-50% commission. Reviews material for acts.

How to Contact New artists can make submissions through the "auditions" link located on the website. Unsolicited submissions are OK. "Please be sure that all submissions are copyrighted and not your original copy as we do not return material."

Music Mostly **pop**, **R&B** and **Broadway**. Deals with "all types of entertainers; no limitations." Current acts include Scott Evans and Company (variety song and dance), Dorit Zinger (female vocalist), Jeff Geist, Actors Repertory Theatre, Entertainment Express, Perfect Parties, Joy Deco (dance act), Flashback 2000 Revue (musical song and dance), Everybody Salsa (Latin song and dance) and Around the World (international song and dance).

Tips "Submit a neat, well put together, organized press kit."

☐ EXCLESISA BOOKING AGENCY

716 Windward Rd., Jackson MS 39206. Phone/fax: (601)366-0220. E-mail: exclesis@bellsouth.net. Website: www.exclesisabooking.com. **Contact:** Roy and Esther Wooten, booking managers/owners. Booking agency. Estab. 1989. Represents groups from anywhere; currently handles 8 acts. Receives 15% commission. Reviews material for acts.

How to Contact *Call first and obtain permission to submit.* Submit demo tape by mail. Unsolicited submissions are OK. Prefers CD or videocassette. If seeking management, press kit should include CD or cassette, videocassette, pictures, address and telephone contact and bio. Does not return material. Responds in 2 months.

Music Gospel only. Current acts include Slim & The Supreme Angels, The Pilgrim Jubilees, Spencer

Taylor & the Highway QC's, Evangelist Bertha Jackson, The Annointed Jackson Singers, The Southern Sons and David R. Curry, Jr.
Tips "Make sure your demo is clear with a good sound so the agent can make a good judgement."

⚡ ▢ ◪ S.L. FELDMAN & ASSOCIATES
1505 W. Second Ave. #200, Vancouver BC V6H 3Y4 Canada. (604)734-5945. Fax: (604)732-0922.
E-mail: feldman@slfa.com. Website: www.slfa.com. Booking agency and artist management firm.
Estab. 1970. Agency represents mostly Canadian artists and groups; currently handles over 200 acts.
How to Contact *Write or call first to obtain permission to submit a demo.* Prefers CD, photo and bio. If seeking management, contact Watchdog for consideration and include video in press kit. SAE and IRC. Responds in 2 months.
Music Current acts include Avril Lavigne, Elvis Costello, Hot Hot Heat, Bryan Adams, The Chieftains, Joni Mitchell, Anne Murray, Sarah McLachlan, Diana Krall, Martina McBride, Barenaked Ladies, Norah Jones, Swollen Members and Nelly Furtado.

◪ FRED T. FENCHEL ENTERTAINMENT AGENCY
2104 S. Jefferson Avenue, Mason City IA 50401. (641)423-4177. Fax: (641)423-8662. **Contact:** Fred T. Fenchel, president. Booking agency. Estab. 1964. Represents local and international individual artists and groups; currently handles up to 10 acts. Receives 20% commission.
How to Contact Submit demo tape by mail. Unsolicited submissions are OK. Prefers cassette or videocassette. Does not return material. Responds in 3 weeks.
Music Mostly **country**, **pop** and some **gospel**. Works primarily with dance bands and show groups; "artists we can use on club dates, fairs, etc." Current acts include New Odyssey (comedy & music), Nerness Family (family, variety music) and The Buck Hollow Band (duo, huge variety of music). "We deal primarily with established name acts with recording contracts, or those with a label and starting into popularity."
Tips "Be honest. Don't submit unless your act is exceptional rather than just starting out, amateurish and with lyrics that are written under the pretense of coming from qualified writers."

⚡ ◪ B.C. FIEDLER MANAGEMENT
53 Seton Park Rd., Toronto ON M3C 3Z8 Canada. (416)421-4421. Fax: (416)421-0442. E-mail: info@bcfiedler.com. **Contact:** B.C. Fiedler/Alysha Main. Management firm, music publisher (B.C. Fiedler Publishing) and record company (Sleeping Giant Music Inc.). Estab. 1964. Represents individual artists, groups and songwriters from anywhere; currently handles 3 acts. Receives 20-25% or consultant fees. Reviews material for acts.
How to Contact *Call first and obtain permission to submit.* Prefers CD or VHS videocassette with 3 songs and lyric sheet. If seeking management, press kit should include bio, list of concerts performed in past 2 years including name of venue, repertoire, reviews and photos. Does not return material. Responds in 2 months.
Music Mostly **classical/crossover**, **voice** and **pop**. Works primarily with classical/crossover ensembles, instrumental soloists, operatic voice and pop singer/songwriters. Current acts include Liona Boyd (classical guitar) and Pavlo (instrumental).
Tips "Invest in demo production using best quality voice and instrumentalists. If you write songs, hire the vocal talent to best represent your work. Submit CD and lyrics. Artists should follow up 6-8 weeks after submission."

▦ ◪ FIRST TIME MANAGEMENT
Sovereign House, 12 Trewartha Rd., Praa Sands-Penzance, Cornwall TR20 9ST England (01736)762826. Fax: (01736)763328. E-mail: panamus@aol.com. Website: www.songwriters-guild .co.uk. **Contact:** Roderick G. Jones, managing director. Management firm, record company (First Time Records) and music publisher (First Time Music). Estab. 1986. Represents local, regional and international individual aritsts, groups, composers and songwriters. Receives 15-25% commission. Reviews material for acts.

• Also see the listings for First Time Music (Publishing) in the Music Publishers section and First Time Records in the Record Companies section of this book.

How to Contact Submit demo tape by mail. Unsolicited submissions are OK. Prefers CD with 3 songs and lyric sheets. If seeking management, press kit should include cover letter, bio, photo, demo tape/CD, press clippings and anything relevant to make an impression. Does not return material. Responds in 1 month.

Music Mostly **all styles**. Works primarily with songwriters, composers, vocalists, groups and choirs. Current acts include Willow (pop), Animal Cruelty (indie/heavy thrash), Bram Stoker (gothic rock group), Kevin Kendle (New Age) and Peter Arnold (folk/roots).

Tips "Become a member of the Guild of International Songwriters and Composers. Keep everything as professional as possible. Be patient and dedicated to your aims and objectives."

☑ ERIC GODTLAND MANAGEMENT, INC.

18352 160th Pl. SE, Renton WA 98058. Fax: (415)522-5293. **Contact:** Wayne Ledbetter, manager. Management firm. Estab. 1995. Represents individual artists, groups or songwriters from anywhere; currently handles 8 acts. Receives 20% commission. Reviews material for acts.

How to Contact Submit CD by mail. Unsolicited submissions are OK. Prefers CD. If seeking management, press kit should include brief information on how to reach you. Does not return material.

Music Mostly **pop**, **rock** and **hip-hop**. Works primarily with bands, producers and songwriters. Current acts include Third Eye Blind (pop, rock), Retrograde (pop, rock), Honestly (pop rock) and Dakona (pop, rock).

☐ GUESTSTAR ENTERTAINMENT AGENCY

17321 Ritchie Ave. NE, Sand Lake MI 49343-9475. (616)636-5068. Fax: (775)743-4169. E-mail: gueststarww@wingsisp.com. Website: www.mountainmanww.com. **Contact:** Raymond G. Dietz, Sr., president. Management firm, booking agency, music publisher (Sandlake Music/BMI), record company (Gueststar Records, Inc.), record producer and record distributor (Gueststar Music Distributors). Represents individual artists, groups, songwriters and bands from anywhere; currently handles 3 acts. Receives 20% commission. Reviews material for acts.

• Also see the listing for Gueststar Records in the Record Companies section of this book. Mr. Dietz is also the editor of several music books, including *Everything You Should Know Before You Get into the Music Business.*

How to Contact Submit demo tape by mail "and include your contact information." Unsolicited submissions are OK. Prefers CD, cassette or VHS videocassette with unlimited songs, but send your best with lyric or lead sheet. If seeking management, press kit should include shoulder shot photo, demo tape, bio, music résumé and VHS videocassette (live on stage) if possible and press clippings. Returns material after 1 year if SASE and correct postage are included. Responds in 6 months.

Music Mostly **traditional country**. Current acts include DJ & The Dawgs (country band, traditional), Ikinoram (2 country singers, new country) and Dee Dee "D" (country singer, country rock).

☑ ☑ GURLEY & CO.

P.O. Box 150657, Nashville TN 37215. (615)269-0474. Fax: (615)297-8755. E-mail: cathy@gurleybiz .com. Website: www.gurleybiz.com. President: Cathy Gurley. Vice President: Meagan Gurley. Management firm and public relations/marketing. Estab. 1985. Represents individual artists, groups and songwriters from anywhere; currently handles 8 acts. Receives 15% commission. Reviews material for acts.

How to Contact *No longer accepting unsolicited submissions.*

☑ BILL HALL ENTERTAINMENT & EVENTS

138 Frog Hollow Rd., Churchville PA 18966-1031. (215)357-5189. Fax: (215)357-0320. E-mail: Billha llevents@verizon.net. **Contact:** William B. Hall III, owner/president. Booking agency and production company. Represents individuals and groups; currently handles 20-25 acts. Receives 15% commission. Reviews material for acts.

How to Contact Submit demo tape by mail. Unsolicited submissions are OK. Prefers cassette or videocassette of performance with 2-3 songs "and photos, promo material and record or tape. We need quality material, preferably before a 'live' audience." Does not return material. Responds only if interested.

Music **Marching band**, **circus** and **novelty**. Works primarily with "unusual or novelty attractions in musical line, preferably those that appeal to family groups." Current acts include Fralinger and Polish-American Philadelphia Championship Mummers String Bands (marching and concert group), "Mr. Polynesian" Show Band and Hawaiian Revue (ethnic group), the "Phillies Whiz Kids Band" of Philadelphia Phillies Baseball team, Paul Richardson (Phillies' organist/entertainer), Mummermania Musical Quartet, Philadelphia German Brass Band (concert band), Vogelgesang Circus Calliope, Kromer's Carousel Band Organ, Reilly Raiders Drum & Bugle Corps, Hoebel Steam Calliope, Caesar Rodney Brass Band, Rohe Calliope, Philadelphia Police & Fire Pipes Band, Larry Rothbard's Circus Band and Tim Laushey Pep & Dance Band.

Tips "Please send whatever helps us to most effectively market the attraction and/or artist. Provide something that gives you a clear edge over others in your field!"

HANSEN ENTERPRISES, LTD.
855 E. Twain #123411, Las Vegas NV 89109. (702)896-8115. Fax: (702)792-1363. **Contact:** J. Malcom Baird. Management firm. Estab. 1971. Represents individual artists, groups and songwriters from anywhere; currently handles 3 acts. Receives 15-25% commission "or contracted fee arrangement." Reviews material for acts.

How to Contact Submit demo tape by mail. Unsolicited submissions are OK. Prefers cassette. Include SASE. Responds in 3 weeks. We are looking for potential *hit songs* only: top 40, pop and Spanish. From time to time we need music for TV shows, commercials and films. Send SASE for requirements, which change from time to time depending upon the project(s).

Music Mostly '50s & '60s rock and **Spanish adult contemporary**. Current acts include The Ronettes, Pilita Corrales (top selling female Spanish recording star), Mandrake and Carmen Soriano.

HARDISON INTERNATIONAL ENTERTAINMENT CORPORATION
P.O. Box 1732, Knoxville TN 37901-1732. (865)688-8680. Fax: (865)219-8094. E-mail: dennishardinson@bellsouth.net. Website: www.iuma/bands/dynamo.com. **Contact:** Dennis K. Hardison, CEO/founder. Management firm, booking agency, music publisher (Denlatrin Music), record company (Denlatrin Records) and record producer. Estab. 1984. Represents individual artists from anywhere; currently handles 3 acts. Receives 20% commission. Reviews material for acts.

• This company has promoted acts including New Edition, Freddie Jackson, M.C. Lyte and Kool Moe Dee.

How to Contact Submit demo tape by mail. Unsolicited submissions are OK. Prefers cassette or CD with 3 songs. If seeking management, press kit should include bio, promo picture and CD. Does not return material. Responds in 6 weeks to the best material.

Music Mostly **R&B**, **hip-hop** and **rap**. Current acts include Dynamo (hip-hop), Shorti (R&B singer) and Triniti (record producer, Public Enemy).

Tips "We have an in-house production staff to critique your music."

M. HARRELL & ASSOCIATES
5444 Carolina, Merrillville IN 46410. (219)887-8814. Fax: (480)345-2255. E-mail: mhmkbmgs95@hotmail.com. **Contact:** Mary Harrell, owner. Management firm and booking agency. Estab. 1984. Represents individual artists, groups, songwriters, all talents—fashion, dancers, etc.; currently handles 30-40 acts. Receives 10-20% commission. Reviews material for acts.

How to Contact *Call first and obtain permission to submit.* Submit demo tape by mail. Prefers cassette or videocassette with 2-3 songs. Send résumé, bio, photo, demo tape/CD and press clippings. "Keep it brief and current." Does not return material. Responds in 1 month.

Music All types, **country**, **R&B**, **jazz**, **gospel**, **Big Band**, **light rock** and **reggae**. Current acts include Many B (showact), Michael Essany (celebrity talk show host), Bill Shelton & 11th Avenue ('50s rock & roll), Bang (R&B/jazz) and Retroactive.

Tips "The bands listed can and do tour in the U.S. and Europe (variety, mostly R&B, jazz and top

40) as well as the Chicagoland area. They get steady work and repeat business, because they are good and beat their competition. We also manage showbands.''

☑ ⊘ HESFREE PRODUCTIONS & PUBLISHING COMPANY

P.O. Box 1214, Bryan TX 77806-1214. (979)268-3263. Fax: (979)589-2544. E-mail: hesfreeprodandp ubco@yahoo.com. Website: www.hesfreeproductions.com. CEO/Owner: Brenda M. Freeman-Heslip. Producer of songwriting: Jamie Heslip. VP/Director of A&R/Owner: Rochelle Heslip. Management agency, record producer and music publisher. Estab. 2001. Represents individual artists, groups, songwriters. Works with individual artists, regional artists in the Bryan, TX and Brazos Valley Area. Currently handles 1 act. Receives 40% commission.

- Also see the listings for Hesfree Production & Publishing Company in the Music Publishers and Record Producers sections of this book.

How to Submit *We only accept material referred to us by a reputable industry source (manager, entertainment attorney, etc.)* Include CD/CDR with 10 songs and lyric sheet, lead sheet and cover letter. Send résumé and updated application for a management firm. Does not return submissions. Responds in 6 weeks only if interested. ''Make sure you are serious about your career choice. Only serious clients need to contact us.''

Music Mostly **gospel** and **R&B**, some **rap** and **rock**. Does not want country. ''We strive to make our professional performing artists the most successful artists possible.'' We represent the Individualistics who consist of: Ralatraneka Mercer (R&B and Gospel singer), Monica Gibbs (R&B and rap singer) and Erica Hardy (R&B and rap singer).

☐ HORIZON MANAGEMENT INC.

P.O. Box 8770, Endwell NY 13762. (607)785-9120. Fax: (607)785-4516. E-mail: hmi67@aol.com. **Contact:** New Talent Department. Management firm, booking agency and concert promotion. Estab. 1967. Represents regional, national and international artists, groups and songwriters; currently handles over 1,500 acts. Receives 20% commission. Reviews material for acts.

How to Contact *Call first and obtain permission to submit.* Prefers CD, cassette or VHS videocassette with 1-4 songs and lead sheet. Send cover letter, résumé, lead sheets, photo, bio, lyric sheets, equipment list, demo tape/CD, video, press clippings, reviews, etc. Does not return material. Responds in 1 week.

Music **All styles**, originals or covers. Current acts include Pete Best Band (The Beatles original drummer), Queen Makedah (reggae from Africa) and Mafalda Nogueira (Bralian music/jazz).

☐ HOT STEAMING COFFEE FILMS

7522 Ave. T, #1, Brooklyn NY 11234. E-mail: enigpublus@aol.com. **Contact:** David K., personal manager. Management firm. Estab. 1997. Represents individual artists, groups and (rarely) songwriters; currently does not represent any act. Receives 12-25% commission.

How to Contact ''E-mail for permission to submit, include a description of the type of material you have. Do not submit anything via mail or e-mail without written permission via e-mail. When approved for submission mail a CD with original songs and include lyrics sheet. Press kit should include cover letter, bio, photo, all lyrics with songs, a CD of original songs and the ages of the artists. All submissions must include lyric sheets or material will not be heard.'' **Does not return material.** Responds in 1 month. ''We will contact artist if interested.'' Include e-mail address for reply. **No MP3 files!** Songs must be copyrighted to submit!

Music **Commercial rock** (all kinds), **pop** and **alternative acoustic** only. Absolutely no rap, R&B, hip-hop, metal, or hard modern rock. ''Limp Bizkit is *not* what I want. I am a small company. I do not handle anyone presently. I am looking for a *great* artist to work with exclusively. I am patient. I can wait until I find who I am looking for; so expect to be turned down.'' Works with original, solo artists and groups.

Tips ''I am dedicated to artists I believe in. I act strictly as a personal manager for an artist which means I help them choose songs, submit songs, find a publisher, and/or a record company. Prefer artists who write and perform their own songs. I am currently seeking material. CDs, CDRs and CDRWs accepted. Young artists mainly considered for development (ages 16-25). Be original! I charge no upfront fees. HINT: I like poetic melodic rock (Bob Dylan, Jewel, etc.)—'singer-songwriters' so to speak—with artistic top 40 potential, but writes from the heart (not the wallet in mind). No 'American Idol' types. Not looking for singers, but artists who can develop a long career as a singer/songwriter and plays an instrument!''

⊘ INTERNATIONAL ENTERTAINMENT BUREAU
3612 N. Washington Blvd., Indianapolis IN 46205-3592. (317)926-7566. E-mail: ieb@prodigy.net. Booking agency. Estab. 1972. Represents individual artists and groups from anywhere; currently handles 157 acts. Receives 20% commission.
How to Contact *No unsolicited submissions.*
Music Mostly **rock**, **country** and **A/C**; also **jazz**, **nostalgia** and **ethnic**. Works primarily with bands, comedians and speakers. Current acts include Five Easy Pieces (A/C), Scott Greeson (country), and Cool City Swing Band (variety).

◙ J & V MANAGEMENT
143 W. Elmwood, Caro MI 48723. (989)673-2889. Manager/Publisher: John Timko. Management firm, booking agency and music publisher. Represents local, regional or international individual artists, groups and songwriters. Receives 10% commission. Reviews material for acts.
How to Contact *Write first and obtain permission to submit.* Prefers CD or cassette with 3 songs maximum and lyric sheet. If seeking management, include short reference bio, cover letter and résumé in press kit. Include SASE. Responds in 2 months.
Music Mostly **country**. Works primarily with songwriters/vocalists and dance bands. Current acts include John Patrick (country) and Brandi Ewald (country).

◙ JANA JAE ENTERPRISES
P.O. Box 35726, Tulsa OK 74153. (918)786-8896. Fax: (918)786-8897. E-mail: janajae@janajae.com. Website: www.janajae.com. **Contact:** Kathleen Pixley, agent. Booking agency, music publisher (Jana Jae Publishing/BMI) and record company (Lark Record Productions, Inc.). Estab. 1979. Represents individual artists and songwriters; currently handles 12 acts. Receives 15% commission. Reviews material for acts.
  • Also see the listings for Jana Jae Music in the Music Publishers section, Lark Record Productions in the Record Companies section and Lark Talent & Advertising in the Record Producers section of this book.
How to Contact Submit demo tape by mail. Unsolicited submissions are OK. Prefers CD or videocassette of performance. If seeking management, press kit should include cover letter, bio, photo, demo tape/CD, lyric sheets and press clippings. Does not return material.
Music Mostly **country**, **classical** and **jazz instrumentals**; also **pop**. Works with vocalists, show and concert bands, solo instrumentalists. Represents Jana Jae (country singer/fiddle player), Matt Greif (classical guitarist), Sydni (solo singer) and Hotwire (country show band).

Ⓝ ⊕ ◙ ROGER JAMES MANAGEMENT
The Return, 10A Margaret Rd., Barnet Herts EN4 9NP England. 020 844 9788. **Contact:** Susana Boyle, professional manager. Management firm and music publisher (R.J. Music/PRS). Estab. 1977. Represents songwriters. Receives 50% commission (negotiable). Reviews material for acts.
  • Also see the listing for R.J. Music in the Music Publishers section of this book.
How to Contact Submit demo tape by mail. Unsolicited submissions are OK. Prefers cassette with 3 songs and lyric sheet. Does not return material.
Music Mostly **pop**, **country** and ''any good song.''

✣ ◙ SHELDON KAGAN INTERNATIONAL
35 McConnell, Dorval QC H9S 5L9 Canada. (514)631-2160. Fax: (514)631-4430. E-mail: sheldon@sheldonkagan.com. Website: www.sheldonkagan.com. **Contact:** Sheldon Kagan, president. Booking agency. Estab. 1965. Represents local individual artists and groups; currently handles 6 acts. Receives 10-20% commission. Reviews materials for acts.

How to Contact Submit demo tape by mail. Unsolicited submissions are OK. Prefers DVD, CD or VHS videocassette with 6 songs. Include SASE. Responds in 5 weeks.

Music Mostly **top 40**. Works primarily with vocalists and bands. Current acts include Quazz (jazz trio), City Lights (top 40 band), Jeux de Cordes (violin and guitar duo), The Soulmates (top 40) and Travelin' Band (top 40).

🌐 ◯ KICKSTART MUSIC LTD.

12 Port House, Square Rigger Row, Plantation Wharf, London SW11 3TY England. (020)7223 8666. Fax: (020)7223 8777. E-mail: info@kickstart.uk.net. **Contact:** Frank Clark, director. Management/ publishing company. Estab. 1994. Represents individual artists, groups or songwriters from any- where; currently handles 7 acts. Receives 20-40% commission, "depends on contract." Reviews material for acts.

How to Contact Submit demo by mail. Unsolicited submissions are OK. Prefers CD, cassette or DAT with 3 songs and lyric and lead sheet. If seeking management, press kit should include photo- graph and bio. SAE and IRC. Responds in 2 weeks.

Music All genres including **pop**, **dance**, **rock**, **country** and **blues**. Works primarily with bands who perform a live set of original music and talented singer/songwriters who can cross over to all types of music. Current acts include Pal Joey (rock band), Simon Fox (songwriter) and The Electric Blues Anthology (blues band).

Tips "We prefer songwriters whose songs can cross over to all types of music, those who do not write in one style only."

◯ KUPER PERSONAL MANAGEMENT/RECOVERY RECORDINGS

P.O. Box 66274, Houston TX 77266. (713)520-5791. Fax: (713)520-5791. E-mail: recovery@wt.net. Website: www.recoveryrecordings.com. **Contact:** Ivan "Koop" Kuper, owner. Management firm, music publisher (Kuper-Lam Music/BMI and Uvula Music/BMI) and record label (Recovery Record- ings). Estab. 1979/2002. Represents individual artists, groups and songwriters from Texas; currently handles 5 acts. Receives 20% commission. Reviews material for acts.

How to Contact Submit demo tape by mail. Unsolicited submissions are OK. Prefers CD-R. If seeking management, press kit should include cover letter, press clippings, photo, bio (1 page) tearsheets (reviews, etc.) and demo tape/CD. Does not return material. Responds in 2 months.

Music Mostly **singer/songwriters**, **triple AAA**, **roots rock** and **Americana**. Works primarily with self-contained and self-produced artists. Current acts include Philip Rodriguez (singer/songwriter), David Rodriguez (singer/songwriter), U.S. Representative for The Watchman (Dutch singer/song- writer) and The Very Girls (Dutch vocal duo).

Tips "Create a market value for yourself, produce your own master tapes, create a cost-effective situation."

◪ LARI-JON PROMOTIONS

P.O. Box 216, Rising City NE 68658. (402)542-2336. **Contact:** Larry Good, owner. Management firm, music publisher (Lari-Jon Publishing Co./BMI) and record company (Lari-Jon Records). Represents individual artists, groups and songwriters; currently handles 3 acts. Receives 15% commission. Reviews material for acts.

How to Contact Submit demo tape by mail. Unsolicited submissions are OK. Prefers CD with 5 songs and lyric sheet. If seeking management, press kit should include 8×10 photos, cassette, videocassette and bio sheet. Include SASE. Responds in 2 months.

Music Mostly **country**, **gospel** and **'50s rock**. Works primarily with dance and show bands. Repre- sents Kent Thompson (singer), Nebraskaland 'Opry (family type country show) and Brenda Allen (singer and comedienne).

Ⓝ ◪ RAY LAWRENCE, LTD.

P.O. Box 1987, Studio City CA 91614. (818)508-9022. Fax: (818)508-5672. **Contact:** Ray Lawrence, president. Management firm, booking agency and music publisher (Boha Music/BMI). Estab. 1963. Represents individual artists from anywhere; currently handles 15 acts. Receives 10-15% commis- sion.

How to Contact Submit demo tape by mail. Unsolicited submissions are OK. Prefers VHS videocassette. If seeking management, press kit should include 8×10 professional photographs and bio. Does not return material. Responds in 2 weeks.

Music All types. Works primarily with musical and variety acts. Current acts include Trini Lopez (recording artist), Wayland Pickard (recording artist) and Glenn Ash (recording artist).

LEVINSON ENTERTAINMENT VENTURES INTERNATIONAL, INC.

1440 Veteran Ave., Suite 650, Los Angeles CA 90024. (323)663-6940. E-mail: leviinc@aol.com. President: Bob Levinson. **Contact:** Jed Leland, Jr. Management firm. Estab. 1978. Represents national individual artists, groups and songwriters; currently handles 4 acts. Receives 15-25% commission. Reviews material for acts.

How to Contact *Write first and obtain permission to submit.* Prefers cassette or VHS videocassette with 6 songs and lead sheet. If seeking management, press kit should include bio, pictures and press clips. Include SASE. Responds in 1 month.

Music Mostly **rock**, **MOR**, **R&B** and **country**. Works primarily with rock bands and vocalists.

Tips "Should be a working band, self-contained and, preferably, performing original material."

RICK LEVY MANAGEMENT

4250 A1AS, D-11, St. Augustine FL 32080. (904)460-1225. Fax: (904)460-1226. E-mail: rick@ricklevy.com. Website: www.ricklevy.com. **Contact:** Rick Levy, president. Management firm, music publisher (Flying Governor Music/BMI) and record company (Luxury Records). Estab. 1985. Represents local, regional or international individual artists and groups; currently handles 5 acts. Receives 15-20% commission. Reviews material for acts.

How to Contact *Write or call first and obtain permission to submit.* Prefers CD or videocassette with 3 songs and lyric sheet. If seeking management, press kit should include cover letter, bio, demo tape/CD, VHS video, photo and press clippings. Include SASE. Responds in 2 weeks.

Music Mostly **R&B** (no rap), **pop**, **country** and **oldies**; also **children's** and **educational videos** for schools. Current acts include Jay & the Techniques ('60s hit group), The Original Box Tops ('60s), The Limits (pop), Freddy Cannon ('60s), The Fallin Bones (blues/rock).

Tips "If you don't have 200% passion and committment, don't bother."

LIVE-WIRE MANAGEMENT

P.O. Box 653, Morgan Hill, CA 95038. (408)778-3526. Fax: (408)778-3567. E-mail: bruceh@l-wm.com. Website: www.L-WM.com. **Contact:** Bruce Hollibaugh, president. Management firm. Estab. 1990. Represents individual artists and groups from anywhere; currently handles 2 acts. Receives 15-25% commission. Reviews material for acts.

How to Contact Submit demo tape by mail. Unsolicited submissions are OK. Prefers CD or cassette with 3-6 songs and lyric sheet. If seeking management, press kit should include what region you are currently performing in; how often you are doing live shows; any reviews; photos. Does not return material. Responds in 1 month.

Music Mostly **pop**, **acoustic pop** and **New Age**; also **jazz**, **R&B** and **country**. Works primarily with bands and singer/songwriters. Current acts include Tommy Elskes (singer/songwriter) and Janny Choi (jazz).

LIVING EYE PRODUCTIONS LTD.

P.O. Box 12956, Rochester NY 14612. (585)425-3640. E-mail: c.kings@att.net. Website: www.chesterfieldkings.com. Secretaries: Monica or Carol. **Contact:** Andy Babiuk, president. Vice President: Greg Prevost. Management firm, music publisher (Pussy Galore Publishing/BMI) and record producers (Andy Babiuk and Greg Prevost). Estab. 1982. Represents individual artists, groups and songwriters from anywhere; currently handles 3 acts. Receives 20% commission. Reviews material for acts.

How to Contact Submit demo tape by mail. Unsolicited submissions are OK. Prefers CD and "what the artist feels necessary." If seeking management, press kit should include cover letter, bio, photo, demo tape/CD, lyric sheet, press clippings, video and résumé. Does not return material. Responds in 2 weeks.

Music Mostly **'60s rock**, **'50s rock** and **blues**; also **folk rock** and **surf**. Works primarily with bands that can tour to promote record releases. Current acts include The Chesterfield Kings (rock), The Mean Red Spiders (rock) and the Moviees ('60s rock).

Tips "We don't like trendy new stuff. Don't follow fads, create your own music by having good rock-n-roll influences."

☐ LOGGINS PROMOTION

26239 Senator Ave., Harbor City CA 90710. (310)325-2800. Fax: (310)325-2560. E-mail: promo@log ginspromotion.com. Website: www.logginspromotion.com. **Contact:** Paul Loggins, CEO. Management firm and radio promotion. Represents individual artists, groups and songwriters from anywhere; currently handles 6 acts. Receives 20% commission. Reviews material for acts.

How to Contact If seeking management, press kit should include picture, short bio, cover letter, press clippings and CD (preferred). "Mark on CD which cut you, as the artist, feel is the strongest." Does not return material. Responds in 2 weeks.

Music Mostly **adult**, **top 40** and **AAA**; also **urban**, **rap**, **alternative**, **college**, **smooth jazz** and **Americana**. Works primarily with bands and solo artists.

☑ ☐ ◙ MANAGEMENT BY JAFFE

68 Ridgewood Ave., Glen Ridge, NJ 07028. (973)743-1075. Fax: (973)743-1075. E-mail: jerjaf@aol.c om. President: Jerry Jaffe. Management firm. Estab. 1987. Represents individual artists and groups from anywhere; currently handles 2 acts. Receives 20% commission. Reviews material for acts "rarely." Reviews for representation "sometimes."

How to Contact *Write or call first to arrange personal interview.* Prefers CD or cassette and videocassette with 3-4 songs and lyric sheet. Does not return material. Responds in 2 months.

Music Mostly **rock/alternative**, **pop** and **Hot AC**. Works primarily with groups and singers/songwriters. Current acts include Joe McIntrye (pop) and others.

Tips "Create some kind of 'buzz' first."

◙ MANAGEMENT PLUS

1617 E. Commerce #4104, San Antonio TX 78205. (210)226-8450, ext. 205. Fax: (210)223-3251. E-mail: bill@bookyourevent.com. Website: www.bookyourevent.com. **Contact:** Bill Angelini, owner. Management firm and booking agency. Estab. 1980. Represents individual artists and groups from anywhere; currently handles 6 acts. Receives 10-15% commission. Reviews material for acts.

How to Contact Submit demo tape by mail. Unsolicited submissions are OK. Prefers CD, VHS videocassette and bio. If seeking management, press kit should include pictures, bio, résumé and discography. Does not return material. Responds in 1 month.

Music Mostly **Latin American**, **Tejano** and **international**; also **Norteno** and **country**. Current acts include Jay Perez (Tejano), Ram Herrera (Tejano), Rodeo (Tejano) and Grupo Vida (Tejano).

☒ ◙ THE MANAGEMENT TRUST LTD.

411 Queen St. W, 3rd Floor, Toronto ON M5V 2A5 Canada. (416)979-7070. Fax: (416)979-0505. E-mail: mail@mgmtrust.ca. Website: www.mgmtrust.ca. President: Jake Gold. General Manager: Shelley Stertz. Management firm. Estab. 1986. Represents individual artists and/or groups; currently handles 7 acts.

How to Contact Submit demo tape by mail (Attn: A&R Dept.). Unsolicited submissions are OK. If seeking management, press kit should include CD or tape, bio, cover letter, photo and press clippings. Does not return material. Responds in 2 months.

Music All types. Current acts include Gord Downie (alternative rock), Doctor (rock band), Sass Jordan (rock), Brian Dyrne (folk rock), and The Populars (rock).

☑ ☐ RICK MARTIN PRODUCTIONS/EASYWAY MUSIC

125 Fieldpoint Road, Greenwich CT 06830. E-mail: rick@easywaysystems.com. **Contact:** Rick Martin, president. Personal manager, music publisher, and independent producer. Held the Office of

Secretary of the National Conference of Personal Managers for 22 years. Represents vocalists, songwriters, and actresses; currently produces pop music artists in private project studio. Receives 15% commission as a personal manager and/or customary production and publishing distributions.

How to Contact E-mail for initial contract and/or submit 2-3 songs and picture.

Music Top 40 and dance.

Tips "Your demo does not have to be professionally produced to submit to producers, publishers, or managers. In other words, save your money. It's really not important what you've done. It's what you can do now that counts."

☐ ☑ PHIL MAYO & COMPANY

P.O. Box 304, Bomoseen VT 05732. (802)468-2554. Fax: (802)468-2554. E-mail: pmcamgphil@aol.com. **Contact:** Phil Mayo, president. Management firm and record company (AMG Records). Estab. 1981. Represents individual artists, groups and songwriters from anywhere; currently handles 4 acts. Receives 15-20% commission. Reviews material for acts.

How to Contact *Contact first and obtain permission to submit.* Prefers CD with 3 songs (professionally recorded) and lyric or lead sheet. If seeking management, include bio, photo and lyric sheet in press kit. Does not return material. Responds in 2 months.

Music Mostly **contemporary Christian pop**. Current and past acts have included John Hall, Guy Burlage, Jonell Mosser, Pam Buckland, Orleans, Gary Nicholson and Jon Pousette-Dart.

☑ MAZUR ENTERTAINMENT/MAZUR PUBLIC RELATIONS

P.O. Box 2425, Trenton NJ 08607. (609)890-4550. Fax: (609)890-4556. E-mail: michael@mazurpr.com. Website: www.mazurpr.com. **Contact:** Michael Mazur. Management and PR firm. Estab. 1994. Represents groups from anywhere; currently handles 30 acts. Commission varies. Reviews material for acts.

How to Contact Submit demo tape by mail. Unsolicited submissions are OK. Prefers CD with 2 songs. If seeking management, send music and press kit. Include SASE. "We try to reply." Responds in 1 month.

Music **All types**. Current acts include international and national artists. See website.

☑ MEDIA MANAGEMENT

P.O. Box 3773, San Rafael CA 94912-3773. (415)457-0700. Fax: (415)457-0964. E-mail: mediamanagement9@aol.com. **Contact:** Eugene, proprietor. Management firm. Estab. 1990. Represents local, regional or international individual artists, groups and songwriters; currently handles 5 acts. Receives 15% commission. Reviews material for acts.

How to Contact Submit demo by mail. Unsolicited submissions are OK. Prefers CD or DVD with lyric sheet. If seeking management, include lyric sheets, demo tape, photo and bio. Does not return material.

Music Mostly **rock**, **blues** and **pop**; also **R&B**. Works primarily with songwriting performers/bands. Current acts include Zakiya Hooker (R&B/blues/singer/songwriter), Greg Anton/Greggs Eggs (rock songwriter/group), John Lee Hooker Estate (blues) and Ollan Christopher Bell (producer).

Tips "Write great *radio-friendly* songs with great musical and lyrical hooks."

🅽 ☑ MEGA MUSIC PRODUCTIONS

16950 North Bay Road, Suite 1706, Sunny Isle, FL 33160. (305)956-5525. E-mail: marco@megamusicevents.com. Website: www.MegaMusicEvents.com. **Contact:** Marco Vinicio Carvajal, general manager. Management firm, booking agency and record producer. Represents individual artists and groups from anywhere; currently handles 10 acts. Receives 25-35% commission. Reviews material for acts.

How to Contact Submit demo CD, DVD and pictures by mail. Unsolicited submissions are OK. Prefers CD, DVD or VHS videocassette with 4 songs and lyric sheet. If seeking management, press kit should include cover letter, demo tape/CD, video, photos and bio. Does not return material. Responds in 1 month.

Music Mostly **rock, techno-dance** and **Latin rock**; also **Latin** and **pop**. Works primarily with bands and singers.
Tips "Send us compact information and describe your goals."

☑ ⬚ METRO TALENT GROUP, INC.
83 Walton St., 3rd Floor, Atlanta GA 30303. (404)954-6620. Fax: (404)954-6681. E-mail: mail@metr otalentgroup.com. Website: www.metrotalentgroup.com. **Contact:** Tanner Smith. Booking agency. Represents individual artists and groups; currently handles 12-15 acts. Receives 10-15% commission. Reviews material for acts.
How to Contact *Write or call first and obtain permission to submit.* "We prefer to be contacted via e-mail." Prefers CD or DVD. Include clubs/venues played, guarantees for each show and who you've opened for. Does not return material. Responds in 2 weeks.
Music Mostly **rock/alternative, blues** and **jazz**; also **acoustic**. Visit website for full roster of current acts.

⬚ MIDCOAST, INC.
1002 Jones Rd., Hendersonville TN 37075. (615)400-4664. E-mail: mid-co@ix.netcom.com. **Contact:** Bruce Andrew Bossert, managing director. Management firm and music publisher (MidCoast, Inc./BMI). Estab. 1984. Represents individual artists, groups and songwriters; currently handles 2 acts. Reviews material for acts.
How to Contact Submit demo tape by mail. Unsolicited submissions are OK. Prefers CD, cassette, VHS videocassette or DAT with 2-4 songs and lyric sheet. If seeking management, press kit should include cover letter, "short" bio, tape, video, photo, press clippings and announcements of any performances in Nashville area. Does not return material. Responds in 6 weeks if interested.
Music Mostly **rock, pop** and **country**. Works primarily with original rock and country bands and artists. Current acts include Room 101 (alternative rock).

⬚⬚ MONTEREY ARTISTS, INC.
124 12th Ave. S., Suite 410, Nashville TN 37203. (615)251-4400. Fax: (615)251-4401. Booking agency. Represents individual artists, groups from anywhere; currently handles 37 acts. Receives 10% commission. Reviews material for acts.
How to Contact *Write or call first to arrange personal interview.*
Music Mostly **country**. Current acts include Lyle Lovett, Ricky Skaggs, Sawyer Brown, Junior Brown, Toby Keith, Travis Tritt, Montgomery Gentry, The Del McCoury Band, Grand Funk Railroad, Kasey Chambers, Night Ranger, Robert Earl Keen, Shooter Jennings and Uncle Kracker.

⬚ ☑ ⬚ MUSIC MARKETING & PROMOTIONS
Post Office Kendenup 6323, South Perth 6951 Australia. (61)(89)851-4311. Fax: (61)(89)851-4225. E-mail: mmp@global.net.au. Website: www.global.net.au/~mmp/. **Contact:** Eddie Robertson. Booking agency. Estab. 1991. Represents individual artists and/or groups; currently handles 50 acts. Receives 20% commission. Reviews material for acts.
How to Contact *Write first and obtain permission to submit.* Unsolicited submissions are OK. Prefers cassette or videocassette with photo, information on style and bio. If seeking management, press kit should include photos, bio, cover letter, résumé, press clippings, video, demo, lyric sheets and any other useful information. Does not return material. Responds in 1 month.
Music Mostly **top 40/pop, jazz** and **'60s-'90s**; also **reggae** and **blues**. Works primarily with show bands and solo performers. Current acts include Faces (dance band), N.R.G. (show band) and C.J. & the Thorns (soul).
Tips "Send as much information as possible. If you do not receive a call after four to five weeks, follow up with letter or phone call."

⬚ NIK ENTERTAINMENT CO.
274 N. Goodman St., Rochester NY 14607. (585)244-0331. Fax: (585)244-0356. E-mail: nikniceguy @aol.com. Website: www.nikentertainment.com. **Contact:** Gary Webb, general manager/presi-

dent. Management firm and booking agency. Estab. 1988. Represents groups from anywhere; currently handles 10 acts. Reviews material for acts.

How to Contact Submit demo tape by mail. Unsolicited submissions are OK. Prefers cassette, VHS or CD with lyric or lead sheet. If seeking management, press kit should include photo, bio and demo tape. Does not return material.

Music Mostly **mainstream rock** and **pop**. Works primarily with bands. Current acts include Nik and the Nice Guys (pop show band), The Shag-adelics ('60s meets '90s), Fever—The Wrath of Polyester ('70s retro), Alpha Delta Nik (the world's only tribute to *Animal House*), The Blues Family (R&B review), Jazz Nik (basic jazz trio and more), The Bugzappers (swing band), Shamalama (oldies with an edge) and the Rochester Rat Pack (the cocktail culture revival).

☑ NOTEWORTHY PRODUCTIONS

124½ Archwood Ave., Annapolis MD 21401. (410)268-8232. Fax: (410)268-2167. E-mail: mcshane @mcnote.com. Website: www.mcnote.com. **Contact:** McShane Glover, president. Management firm and booking agency. Estab. 1985. Represents individual artists, groups and songwriters from everywhere; currently handles 6 acts. Receives 15-20% commission. Reviews material for acts.

How to Contact *Write first and obtain permission to submit.* Prefers CD/CDR with lyric sheet. If seeking management, press kit should include cassette or CD, photo, bio, venues played and press clippings (preferably reviews). "Follow up with a phone call 3-5 weeks after submission." Does not return material. Responds in 2 months.

Music Mostly **Americana**, **folk**, and **Celtic**. Works primarily with performing singer/songwriters. Current acts include Seamus Kennedy (Celtic/contemporary), Dave's True Story (jazz) and the McKrells (Celtic/bluegrass).

☑ ☐ ON THE LEVEL MUSIC!

P.O. Box 508, Owego NY 13827. (607)222-4151. E-mail: fredny2020@yahoo.com. **Contact:** Fred Gage, CEO/president. Management firm, booking agency and music publisher (On The Level Music! Publishing). Estab. 1970. Represents individual artists, groups and songwriters from anywhere; currently handles 30 acts. Receives 15% commission. Reviews material for acts.

How to Contact Submit demo tape by mail. Unsolicited submissions are OK. Prefers CDs, DAT or VHS videocassette with 4 songs and lyric or lead sheet. If seeking management, press kit should include cover letter, bio, demo tape/CD, lyric sheets, press clippings, 8 × 10 photo and video. Does not return material. Responds in 1 month.

Music Mostly **rock**, **alternative** and **jazz**; also **blues**. Current acts include Ice River Blues and Summer Jam 2004.

⊕ ☑ GORDON POOLE AGENCY LIMITED

The Limes, Brockley, Bristol BS48 3BB England. (440)(127)546-3222. Fax: (440)(127)546-2252. E-mail: agents@gordonpoole.com. Website: www.gordonpoole.com. **Contact:** Gordon Poole, managing director. Booking agency. Estab. 1963. Represents individual artists and groups from anywhere; currently handles 100 acts. Receives 20% commission. Reviews material for acts.

How to Contact Submit demo tape by mail. Unsolicited submissions are OK. Prefers cassette or videocassette and lyric sheet. If seeking management, press kit should include cv, tape/CD, cover letter, bio, photo, press clippings and video. SAE and IRC. Responds in 1 month.

Music Mostly **MOR**. Works primarily with bands.

☐ PRECISION MANAGEMENT

110 Coliseum Crossing, #158, Hampton VA 23666-5902. (800)275-5336, ext. 0381042. E-mail: precisionmanagement@netzero.com. Website: www.pmmusicgroup.com. **Contact:** Cappriccieo Scates, operations director. Management firm and music publisher (Mytrell/BMI). Estab. 1990. Represents individual artists and/or groups and songwriters from anywhere; currently handles 3 acts. Receives 20% commission. Reviews material for acts.

How to Contact Submit demo tape by mail. Unsolicited submissions are OK. Prefers cassette or VHS videocassette with 3-4 songs and lyric sheet. If seeking management, press kit should include photo, bio, demo tape/CD, lyric sheets, press clippings and all relevant press information. Include SASE. Responds in 6 weeks.

Music Mostly **R&B**, **rap** and **gospel**; also **all types**. Current acts include Nastacia "Nazz" Kendall (DreamWorks), Darius Brooks (Grammy, Stellar, and Dove Award Winner) and David Broom (MTV Real World).

✓ ◐ PRIME TIME ENTERTAINMENT

125 Ryan Industrial Court, Suite 310, San Ramon CA 94583. (408)289-9333. Fax: (415)532-2501. E-mail: artistmanager@aol.com. **Contact:** Jim Douglas, owner. Management firm and booking agency. Estab. 1988. Represents individual artists, groups and songwriters from anywhere. Receives 10-20% commission. Reviews material for acts.

How to Contact Submit demo tape by mail. Unsolicited submissions are OK. Prefers cassette with 3-5 songs. If seeking management, press kit should include 8×10 photo, reviews and CDs/tapes. Include SASE. Responds in 1 month.

Music Mostly **jazz**, **country** and **alternative**; also **ethnic**. Artists include Michel Lington (jazz), Craig Chaquico (jazz), Jeff Berlin (fusion, rock), Ronnie Montrose (rock) and Dick Dale (surf).

Tips "A quality package states a commitment to the project at the outset."

◐ PRO TALENT CONSULTANTS

P.O. Box 233, Nice CA 95464. (707)349-1809. E-mail: pro_talent_artists@yahoo.com. **Contact:** John Eckert, coordinator. Management firm and booking agency. Estab. 1979. Represents individual artists and groups; currently handles 12 acts. Receives 15% commission. Reviews material for acts.

How to Contact Submit demo tape by mail. Unsolicited submissions are OK. Prefers cassette or VHS videocassette with at least 4 songs and lyric sheet. "We prefer audiocassette (4 songs). Submit videocassette with live performance only." If seeking management, press kit should include an 8×10 photo, a cassette or CD of at least 4-6 songs, a bio on group/artist, references, cover letter, press clippings, video and business card or a phone number with address. Does not return material. Responds in 5 weeks.

Music Mostly **country**, **country/pop** and **rock**. Works primarily with vocalists, show bands, dance bands and bar bands. Current acts include Ronny and the Daytonas (pop/rock-top 40 band), Jimmy Torres (country singer) and Stephen Bishop (pop/easy listening vocalist).

◐ RAINBOW TALENT AGENCY

146 Round Pond Lane, Rochester NY 14626. (585)723-3334. Fax: (585)720-6172. E-mail: rtalent@frontiernet.net. **Contact:** Carl Labate, president. Management firm and booking agency. Represents artists and groups; currently handles 6 acts. Receives 15-20% commission.

How to Contact Submit demo tape by mail. Unsolicited submissions are OK. Prefers CD/CDR with minimum 3 songs. May send DVD if available; "a still photo and bio of the act; if you are a performer, it would be advantageous to show yourself or the group performing live. Theme videos are not helpful." If seeking management, include photos, bio, markets established, CD/DVD. Does not return material. Responds in 1 month.

Music Blues, **rock** and **R&B**. Works primarily with touring bands and recording artists. Current acts include Nancy Kelley (jazz singer); The Grifters (new funk rock); Rockin Blues Revue (R&B); Hannah (original rock); The Buddhahood (jammin world beat) and Spanky Haschmann Swing Orchestra (high energy swing).

Tips "My main interest is with groups or performers that are currently touring and have some product. And are at least 50% percent original. Strictly songwriters should apply elsewhere."

✓ ◐ RASPBERRY JAM MUSIC

(formerly Endangered Species Artist Management), 4 Berachah Ave., South Nyack NY 10960-4202. (845)353-4001. Fax: (845)353-4332. E-mail: muzik@jerizon.net. Website: www.musicandamerica.com. President: Fred Porter. Vice President: Suzanne Buckley. Management firm. Estab. 1979. Represents individual artists, groups and songwriters from anywhere; currently handles 3 acts. Receives 20% commission. Reviews material for acts.

How to Contact *Call first and obtain permission to submit.* Prefers CD with 3 or more songs and lyric sheet. "Please include a demo of your music, a clear, recent photograph as well as any current press, if any. A cover letter indicating at what stage in your career you are and expectations for your future. Please label the cassette and/or CD with your name and address as well as the song titles." If seeking management, press kit should include cover letter, bio, photo, demo/CD, lyric sheet and press clippings. Include SASE. Responds in 6 weeks.

Music Mostly **pop**, **rock** and **world**; also **Latin/heavy metal**, **R&B**, **jazz** and **instrumental**. Current acts include Jason Wilson & Tabarruk (pop/reggae, nominated for Juno award 2001), and Anna (teen singer).

Tips "Listen to everything, classical to country, old to contemporary, to develop an understanding of many writing styles. Write with many other partners to keep the creativity fresh. Don't feel your style will be ruined by taking a class or a writing seminar. We all process moods and images differently. This leads to uniqueness in the music."

☑ DIANE RICHARDS WORLD MANAGEMENT, INC.

E-mail: drworldmgm@aol.com. **Contact:** Diane Richards, president. Management firm. Estab. 1994. Represents individual artists, groups, songwriters and producers from anywhere; currently handles 8 acts. Receives 20% commission. Reviews material for acts.

How to Contact *Write first (via e-mail) and obtain permission to submit.* If seeking management, press kit should include cover letter, photograph, biography, cassette tape, telephone number and address. Does not return material. Responds in 1 month.

Music Mostly **dance**, **pop** and **rap**; also **New Age**, **A/C** and **jazz**. Works primarily with pop and dance acts, and songwriters who also are recording artists. Current acts include Sappho (songwriter/artist), Menace (songwriter/producer/artist) and Babygirl (R&B/rap artist).

☑ RIOHCAT MUSIC

P.O. Box 764, Hendersonville TN 37077-0764. (615)824-9313. Fax: (615)824-0797. E-mail: tachoir@ bellsouth.net. Website: www.tachoir.com. **Contact:** Robert Kayne, manager. Management firm, booking agency, record company (Avita Records) and music publisher. Estab. 1975. Represents individual artists and groups; currently handles 4 acts. Receives 15-20% commission.

• Also see the listing for Avita Records in the Record Companies section of this book.

How to Contact *Contact first and obtain permission to submit.* Prefers cassette and lead sheet. If seeking management, press kit should include cover letter, bio, photo, demo tape/CD and press clippings. Does not return material. Responds in 6 weeks.

Music Mostly **contemporary jazz** and **fusion**. Works primarily with jazz ensembles. Current acts include Group Tachoir (jazz), Tachoir/Manakas Duo (jazz) and Jerry Tachoir (jazz vibraphone artist).

☑ A.F. RISAVY, INC.

1312 Vandalia, Collinsville IL 62234. (618)345-6700. Fax: (618)345-2004. E-mail: swingcitymusic@ ameritech.net. Website: www.swingcitymusic.com. **Contact:** Art Risavy, president. Management firm and booking agency. Divisions include Artco Enterprises, Golden Eagle Records, Swing City Music and Swing City Sound. Estab. 1960. Represents artists, groups and songwriters; currently handles 35 acts. Receives 10% commission. Reviews material for acts.

How to Contact Submit demo tape by mail. Unsolicited submissions are OK. Prefers CD/CDR, cassette or VHS videocassette with 2-6 songs and lyric sheet. If seeking management, press kit should include pictures, bio and VHS videocassette. Include SASE. Responds in 3 weeks.

Music Mostly **rock**, **country**, **MOR** and **top 40**.

☐ ROCK OF AGES PRODUCTIONS

1001 W. Jasmine Dr., Suite K, Lake Park FL 33403-2119. (561)848-1500. Fax: (561)848-2400. E-mail: rock_of_agesproduc@bellsouth.net. **Contact:** Joseph E. Larson, president/agency director. Booking agent, literary agency and publisher. Estab. 1980. Represents individual artists and groups from anywhere; currently handles 500 acts. Receives 15-25% commission. Reviews material for acts.

How to Contact Submit demo tape by mail. Unsolicited submissions are OK. Prefers CD, cassette or VHS videocassette with 3 or more songs and lead sheet. If seeking management, press kit should include videocassette and/or audiocassette, lyric sheets, relevant press, bio, cover letter, résumé and recent photo. Include SASE. Responds in 3 months.

Music Mostly **top 40**, **country/western** and **rock**; also **gospel** and **opera**. Works primarily with bands, singers, singer/songwriters. Current acts include Adonis (solo Caribbean act), Johnny Violin (renowned violinist) and Barracuda (6-piece energy variety band).

N ☑ CHARLES R. ROTHSCHILD PRODUCTIONS INC.

330 E. 48th St., New York NY 10017. (212)421-0592. **Contact:** Charles R. Rothschild, president. Booking agency. Estab. 1971. Represents individual artists, groups and songwriters from anywhere; currently handles 25 acts. Receives 25% commission. Reviews material for acts.

How to Contact *Call first and obtain permission to submit.* Prefers cassette, CD or VHS videocassette with 1 song and lyric and lead sheet. If seeking management, include cassette, photo, bio and reviews. Include SASE. Responds in 6 weeks.

Music Mostly **rock**, **pop**, **family** and **folk**; also **country** and **jazz**. Current acts include Richie Havens (folk singer), Leo Kottke (guitarist/composer), Emmylou Harris (country songwriter), Tom Chapin (kids' performer and folksinger) and John Forster (satirist).

☐ RUSTRON MUSIC PRODUCTIONS

Send all artist song submissions to: 1156 Park Lane, West Palm Beach FL 33417-5957. (561)686-1354. E-mail: RMP_WMP@bellsouth.net. **Contact:** Sheelah Adams, office administrator. Main Office in Connecticut. ("Main office does not review artist submissions—only South Florida Branch office does.") Executive Director: Rusty Gordon. Artist Consultants: Rusty Gordon and Davilyn Whims. Composition Management: Ron Caruso. Management firm, booking agency, music publisher (Rustron Music Publishers/BMI and Whimsong Publishing/ASCAP), record company and record producer. Estab. 1970. Represents individuals, groups and songwriters; currently handles 20 acts. Receives 10-30% commission. Reviews material for acts.

   • Also see listings for Rustron Music in the Music Publishers, Record Companies and Record Producers sections of this book.

How to Contact *Call to discuss submission.* Send CD or cassette with 10-15 songs (CD produced to sell at gigs with up to 15 songs preferred). Provide typed lyric sheets for every song in the submission. If seeking management, send press kit including: cover letter, bio, CD demo, typed lyric sheets and press clippings. "SASE required for all correspondence." Responds in 4 months.

Music Mostly **adult contemporary**, **electric acoustic**, **blues** (**country folk/urban**, **Southern**), **country** (**rock**, **blues**, **progressive**), **easy listening**, **Cabaret**, **soft rock** (**ballads**), **women's music**, **R&B**, **folk/rock**; also **New Age instrumentals** and **New Age folk fusion**. Current acts include Jayne Margo-Reby (folk rock), Star Smiley (country), Robin Plitt (historical folk), Lisa Cohen (Cabaret/pop/acapella), Song on A Whim (folk/world music), Jeremy White (yankee reggae), Haze Coates (ACGA) and Boomslang Swampsinger (Florida folk).

Tips "Carefully mix demo, don't drown the vocals, 10-15 songs in a submission. Prefer a for-sale CD made to sell at gigs with up to 15 songs. Send photo if artist is seeking marketing and/or production assistance. Very strong hooks, definitive melody, evolved concepts, unique and unpredictable themes. Flesh out a performing sound unique to the artist. Stage presence a must!"

☑ SAFFYRE MANAGEMENT

23401 Park Sorrento, #38, Calabasas CA 91302. (818)842-4368. E-mail: ebsaffyre@yahoo.com. **Contact:** Esta G. Bernstein, president. Management firm. Estab. 1990. Represents individual artists, groups and songwriters from anywhere; currently handles 2 acts. Receives 15% commission.

How to Contact *Call first and obtain permission to submit.* If seeking management, press kit should include cover letter, bio, photo, cassette with 3-4 songs and lyric sheets. Does not return material. Responds in 2 weeks only if interested.

Music **Alternative/modern rock** and **top 40**. "We work only with bands and solo artists who write their own material; our main objective is to obtain recording deals and contracts, while advising our artists on their careers and business relationships."

□ ST. JOHN ARTISTS

P.O. Box 619, Neenah WI 54957-0619. (920)722-2222. Fax: (920)725-2405. Website: www.stjohn-artists.com/. E-mail: jon@stjohn-artists.com. **Contact:** Jon St. John and Gary Coquoz, agents. Booking agency. Estab. 1968. Represents local and regional individual artists and groups; currently handles 20 acts. Receives 15-20% commission. Reviews material for acts.

How to Contact *Call first and obtain permission to submit.* Prefers CD or VHS videocassette. If seeking management, press kit should include cover letter, bio, photo, demo tape/CD, video and résumé. Include SASE.

Music Mostly **rock** and **MOR**. Current acts include Tribute (variety/pop/country), Boogie & the Yo-Yo's ('60s to 2000s), Vic Ferrari (Top 40 '80s-2000's), The Competition (variety '50s-2000's), Center Stage Variety Show Band (variety '60s-2000's) and Da Yoopers (musical comedy/novelty).

☑ ☑ SA'MALL MANAGEMENT

P.O. Box 261488, Encino CA 91426. (310)317-0322. Fax: (818)506-8534. E-mail: samusa@aol.com. Website: www.pplentertainmentgroup.com. **Contact:** Ted Steele, vice president of talent. Management firm, music publisher (Pollybyrd Publications) and record company (PPL Entertainment Group). Estab. 1990. Represents individual artists, groups and songwriters worldwide; currently handles 10 acts. Receives 10-25% commission. Reviews material for acts.

• Also see the listings for Pollybyrd Publications Limited and Zettitalia Music International in the Music Publishers section and PPL Entertainment Group in the Record Companies section of this book.

How to Contact *E-mail first and obtain permission to submit.* Prefers CD or cassette. If seeking management, press kit should include picture, bio and tape. Include SASE. Responds in 2 months.

Music All types. Current acts include Riki Hendrix (rock), Buddy Wright (blues), Fhyne, Suzette Cuseo, The Band AKA, LeJenz, B.D. Fuoco, Juz-cuz and Donato.

☒ □ SANDALPHON MANAGEMENT

P.O. Box 29110, Portland OR 97296. (503)957-3929. E-mail: jackrabbit01@sprintpcs.com. **Contact:** Ruth Otey, president. Management firm, music publisher (Sandalphon Music Publishing/BMI), and record company (Sandalphon Records). Estab. 2005. Represents individual artists, groups, songwriters; works with individual artists and groups from anywhere. Currently handles 0 acts. Receives negotiable commission. Reviews material for acts.

How to Contact Submit demo by mail. Unsolicited submissions are OK. Prefers cassette or CD with 1-5 songs and lyric sheet, cover letter. "Include name, address, and contact information." Include SASE or SAE and IRC for outside the United States. Responds in 1 month.

Music Mostly **rock, country** and **alternative**; also **pop, gospel** and **blues**. "We are looking for singers, bands, and singer/songwriters who are original but would be current in today's music markets. We help singers, bands, and singer-songwriters achieve their personal career goals."

Tips "Submit material you feel best represents you, your voice, your songs, or your band. Fresh and original songs and style are a plus. We are a West Coast management company looking for singers, bands, and singer-songwriters who are ready for the next level. We are looking for those with talent who are capable of being national and international contenders."

☑ SENDYK, LEONARD & CO. INC.

532 Colorado Ave., Santa Monica CA 90401. (310)458-8860. Fax: (310)458-8862. **Contact:** Gerri Leonard, partner. Business management. Represents individual artists, groups and songwriters from anywhere; currently handles 25 acts. Receives 5% commission.

How to Contact "We do not solicit any songwriters for works to be submitted to artists, but are certainly interested in representing songwriters with respect to their financial affairs. We can also monitor their royalties; we have an extensive royalty administration department."

Music Current acts include Marilyn Manson (hard rock), Jonathon Butler (jazz/urban) and The Cranberries (alternative).

⚑ ☻ SERGE ENTERTAINMENT GROUP

P.O. Box 2760, Acworth GA 30102. (678)445-0006. Fax: (678)494-9289. E-mail: sergeent@aol.com. Website: www.serge.org. **Contact:** Sandy Serge, president. Management and PR firm and song publishers. Estab. 1987. Represents individual artists, groups, songwriters from anywhere; currently handles 20 acts. Receives 20% commission for management. Monthly fee required for PR acts.

How to Contact *E-mail first for permission to submit.* Submit demo tape or CD by mail. Unsolicited submissions are OK. Prefers cassette or CD with 4 songs and lyric sheet. If seeking management, press kit should include 8×10 photo, bio, cover letter, lyric sheets, max of 4 press clips, VHS videocassette, performance schedule and CD. "All information submitted must include name, address and phone number on each item." Does not return material. Responds in 6 weeks if interested.

Music Mostly **rock**, **pop** and **country**; also **New Age**. Works primarily with singer/songwriters and bands. Current acts include Kelly Keeling (rock), Moossa (jam band) and Sonya Heller (folk/pop/singer/songwriter).

☑ ☐ SIDDONS & ASSOCIATES

14727 Ventura Blvd., Penthouse Floor, Sherman Oaks CA 91403. (818)986-8040. Fax: (818)986-8041. E-mail: bill@coreentertainment.biz. **Contact:** Bill Siddons, president. Management firm. Estab. 1972. Represents individual artists and groups from anywhere; currently handles 4 acts. Receives 15-20% commission. Reviews material for acts.

How to Contact *Write first and obtain permission to submit.* Prefers CD or VHS videocassette with 3 songs and lyric sheet. If seeking management, press kit should include cassette of 3 songs, lyric sheet, VHS videocassette if available, biography, past credits and discography. Does not return material. Responds in 3 months.

Music All styles. Current acts include Elayne Boosler (comedian), Jerry Cantrell (rock), D-SiSive (rapper/songwriter) and BSG (formerly Little River Band).

☒ ☐ SIEGEL ENTERTAINMENT LTD.

1736 W. 2nd Ave., Vancouver BC V6J 1H6 Canada. (604)736-3896. Fax: (604)736-3464. E-mail: siegelent@telus.net. **Contact:** Robert Siegel, president. Management firm and booking agency. Estab. 1975. Represents individual artists, groups and songwriters from anywhere; currently handles more than 100 acts (for bookings). Receives 15-20% commission. Reviews material for acts.

How to Contact Submit demo CD, photo, songlist and bio by mail or e-mail. Unsolicited submissions are OK. Prefers CD, DVD or VHS videocassette. Does not return material. Responds in 1 month.

Music Mostly **rock**, **pop** and **country**; also **specialty** and **children's**. Current acts include Johnny Ferreira & The Swing Machine, Lee Aaron, Kenny Blues Boss Wayne (boogie) and Tim Brecht (pop/children's).

☒ ☐ SILVER BOW MANAGEMENT

556 Amess St., New Westminster BC V3L 4A9 Canada. (604)523-9309. Fax: (604)523-9310. E-mail: saddles@telus.net. Website: http://saddlestone.ontheweb.nu. President: Grant Lucas. CEO: Candice James. Management firm, music publisher (Saddlestone Publishing, Silver Bow Publishing), record company (Saddlestone Records) and record producer (Silver Bow Productions, Krazy Cat Productions). Estab. 1988. Represents individual artists, groups, songwriters from anywhere; currently handles 8 acts. Receives standard commission. Reviews material for acts.

- Also see the listings for Saddlestone Publishing in the Music Publishers section and Silver Bow Productions in the Record Producers section of this book.

How to Contact Submit demo tape by mail. Unsolicited submissions are OK. Prefers cassette with 3 songs and lyric sheet. If seeking management, press kit should include 8×10 photo, bio, cover letter, demo tape or CD with lyric sheets, press clippings, video, résumé and current itinerary. "Visuals are everything—submit accordingly." Does not return material. Responds in 2 months.

Music Mostly **country**, **pop** and **rock**; also **R&B**, **Christian** and **alternative**. Works primarily with bands, vocalists and singer/songwriters. Current acts include Darrell Meyers (country singer/songwriter), Nite Moves (variety band), Mark Vance (country/pop) and Stan Giles (country).

☑ T. SKORMAN PRODUCTIONS, INC.

5156 S. Orange Ave., Orlando FL 32809. (407)895-3000. Fax: (407)895-1422. E-mail: ted@talentage ncy.com. Website: www.talentagency.com. **Contact:** Ted Skorman, president. Management firm and booking agency. Estab. 1983. Represents groups; currently handles 40 acts. Receives 10-25% commission. Reviews material for acts.

How to Contact *E-mail first for permission to submit.* Prefers CD with 2 songs, or videocassette of no more than 6 minutes. "Live performance—no trick shots or editing tricks. We want to be able to view act as if we were there for a live show." If seeking management, press kit should include cover letter, bio, photo and demo CD or video. Does not return material. Responds only if interested.

Music Mostly **top 40, dance, pop** and **country**. Works primarily with high-energy dance acts, recording acts, and top 40 bands. Current acts include Steph Carse (pop).

Tips "We have many pop recording acts and are looking for commercial material for their next albums."

☐ GARY SMELTZER PRODUCTIONS

603 W. 13th #2A, Austin TX 78701. (512)478-6020. Fax: (512)478-8979. E-mail: gsptalent@aol.com. **Contact:** Gary Smeltzer, president. Management firm and booking agency. Estab. 1967. Represents individual artists and groups from anywhere; currently handles 20 acts. "We book about 100 different bands each year—none are exclusive." Receives 20% commission. Reviews material for acts.

How to Contact Submit demo tape by mail. Unsolicited submissions are OK. Prefers cassette, videocassette or CD. If seeking management, press kit should include cover letter, résumé, cassette or CD, bio, picture, lyric sheets, press clippings and video. Does not return material. Responds in 1 month.

Music Mostly **alternative**, **R&B** and **country**. Current acts include Ro Tel & the Hot Tomatoes (nostalgic '60s showband).

Tips "We prefer performing songwriters who can gig their music as a solo or group."

Ⓝ ☐ ☑ SOUND MANAGEMENT DIRECTION

10343 Jennifer Court, Seminole FL 33778. (718)969-0166. Fax: (718)969-8914. E-mail: sounddirectio n@aol.com. **Contact:** Bob Currie, president. Management firm, consultant, music publisher (Sun Face Music/ASCAP, Shaman Drum/BMI) and record producer. Estab. 1986. Former music publisher, A&R with experience in US and UK. Representation for recording artists, songwriters and producers from anywhere. Payment options include fee-based, retainer or commission .

How to Contact Submit CD by mail. Unsolicited submissions are OK. Prefers CD or Internet link with 2 songs and lyric sheet. If seeking management, press kit should include demo, photo and contact information including phone numbers. "If you want material returned, include SASE." Responds in 3 weeks.

Music Seeking commercial, contemporary and radio-oriented **rock**, **dance**, **jazz** and **urban**.

Tips "We only want your best, and be specific with style. Quality, not quantity."

Ⓝ ☐ SPHERE GROUP ONE

795 Waterside Drive, Marco Island FL 34145. (239)398-6800. Fax: (239)394-9881. E-mail: spheregro upone@att.net. President: Tony Zarrella. Talent Manager: Jon Zarrella. Management firm and record producer. Estab. 1987. Represents individual artists and groups from anywhere; currently handles 5 acts. Receives commission.

How to Contact Submit demo tape by mail or e-mail. Unsolicited submissions are OK. Prefers CD or video with 3-5 songs. All submissions must include cover letter, lyric sheets, tape/CD, photo, bio and all press. "Due to large number of submissions we can only respond to those artists which we may consider working with." Does not return material

Music Mostly **pop/rock**, **pop/country** and **New Age**; also **R&B**. Works primarily with bands and solo singer/songwriters. Current acts include 4 of Hearts (pop/rock), Frontier 9 (pop/rock), Viewpoint (experimental) and Bombay Green (hybrid pop).

Tips "Develop and create your own style, focus on goals and work as a team and maintain good chemistry with all artists and business relationships."

STAIRCASE PROMOTION

P.O. Box 211, East Prairie MO 63845. (573)649-2211. **Contact:** Tommy Loomas, president. Vice President: Joe Silver. Management firm, music publisher (Lineage Publishing) and record company (Capstan Record Production). Estab. 1975. Represents individual artists and groups from anywhere; currently handles 6 acts. Receives 25% commission. Reviews material for acts.

- Also see the listings for Lineage Publishing Co. in the Music Publishers section and Capstan Record Production in the Record Companies section of this book.

How to Contact Submit demo tape by mail. Unsolicited submissions are OK. Prefers cassette with 3 songs and lyric sheet. If seeking management, press kit should include bio, photo, audiocassette and/or video and press reviews, if any. "Be as professional as you can." Include SASE. Responds in 2 months.

Music Mostly **country**, **pop** and **easy listening**; also **rock**, **gospel** and **alternative**. Current acts include Skidrow Joe (country comedian, on Capstan Records), Vicarie Arcoleo (pop singer, on Treasure Coast Records) and Scarlett Britoni (pop singer on Octagon Records).

STARKRAVIN' MANAGEMENT

20501 Ventura Blvd., 217, Woodland Hills CA 91364. (818)587-6801. Fax: (818)587-6802. E-mail: bcmclane@aol.com. **Contact:** B.C. McLane, Esq. Management and law firm. Estab. 1994. Represents individual artists, groups and songwriters. Receives 20% commission (management); $200/ hour as attorney.

How to Contact Submit demo tape by mail. Unsolicited submissions are OK. Does not return material. Responds in 1 month if interested.

Music Mostly **rock**, **pop** and **R&B**. Works primarily with bands.

☑ OBI STEINMAN MANAGEMENT

5627 Sepulveda Blvd., #230, Van Nuys CA 91411. (818)787-4065. Fax: (818)787-4194. E-mail: jhfp @aol.com. Website: www.stcent.com. **Contact:** Obi Steinman, manager. Management firm. Represents individual artists and groups from anywhere; currently handles 13 acts. Receives 15-20% commission.

How to Contact Submit demo tape by mail. Unsolicited submissions are OK. Prefers CD with 4 songs and lyric sheet. If seeking management, press kit should include 8 × 10 picture, press clippings and bio. "Concentrate more on the material enclosed than the flashy package." Include SASE. Responds in 5 weeks.

Music Mostly **pop**, **R&B**, **pop rock**, **alternative** and **hard rock**. Works primarily with bands and self-contained artists (write own material, have own backing band). Current acts include Warrant (hard rock), L.A. Guns (hard rock), Great White (hard rock), Veruca Salt (pop alternative) and Red Letter Print (pop).

Tips "We are street level. We are looking for new acts."

☑ STRICTLY FORBIDDEN ARTISTS

320 Avenue Rd., Suite 144, Toronto ON M4V 2H3 Canada. Fax: (416)926-0811. E-mail: creative_age ncy@yahoo.com. **Contact:** Brad Bartley, director of A&R. Management firm, booking agency and record company. Estab. 1986. Represents individual artists and groups from anywhere; currently handles 8 acts. Receives 20-30% commission. Reviews material for acts.

How to Contact Submit demo CD by mail. Unsolicited submissions are OK. Prefers CD and lyric sheet. If seeking management, press kit should include biography, press clippings, 8 × 10, photo and demo tape/CD. "Once you've sent material, don't call us, we'll call you." Does not return material. Responds in 6 weeks.

Music Mostly **alternative rock**, **art rock** and **grindcore**; also **electronic**, **hip-hop** and **experimental**. Works primarily with performing bands, studio acts and performance artists. Current acts include Sickos (experimental/art-rock), Lazer (coldwave/electronica) and Andy Warhead (punk rock/noise).

Tips "As long as you have faith in your music, we'll have faith in promoting you and your career."

◢ T.L.C. BOOKING AGENCY

37311 N. Valley Rd., Chattaroy WA 99003. (509)292-2201. Fax: (509)292-2205. E-mail: tlcagent@ix.netcom.com. Website: www.tlcagency.com. **Contact:** Tom or Carrie Lapsansky, agent/owners. Booking agency. Estab. 1970. Represents individual artists and groups from anywhere; currently handles 17 acts. Receives 10-15% commission. Reviews material for acts.

How to Contact *Call first and obtain permission to submit.* Prefers CD with 3-4 songs. Does not return material. Responds in 3 weeks.

Music Mostly **rock**, **country** and **variety**; also **comedians** and **magicians**. Works primarily with bands, singles and duos. Current acts include Nobody Famous (variety), Menagerie (variety-duo) and Soul Patrol (variety/top 40).

◢ TAS MUSIC CO./DAVE TASSE ENTERTAINMENT

N2467 Knollwood Dr., Lake Geneva WI 53147-9731. E-mail: david@baybreezerecords.com. Website: www.baybreezerecords.com. **Contact:** David Tasse. Booking agency, record company and music publisher. Represents artists, groups and songwriters; currently handles 21 acts. Receives 10-20% commission. Reviews material for acts.

How to Contact Submit demo tape by mail. Unsolicited submissions are OK. Prefers cassette with 2-4 songs and lyric sheet. Include performance videocassette if available. If seeking management, press kit should include tape, bio and photo. Does not return material. Responds in 3 weeks.

Music Mostly **pop** and **jazz**; also **dance**, **MOR**, **rock**, **soul** and **top 40**. Works primarily with show and dance bands. Current acts include Max Kelly (philosophic rock) and L.J. Young (rap).

◢ TRIANGLE TALENT, INC.

10424 Watterson, Louisville KY 40299. (502)267-5466. Fax: (502)267-8244. Website: www.trianglet alent.com. **Contact:** David II. Snowden, president. Booking agency. Represents artists and groups; currently handles 85 acts. Receives 10-20% commission. Reviews material for acts.

How to Contact Submit demo tape by mail. Unsolicited submissions are OK. Prefers CD, cassette or VHS videocassette with 2-4 songs and lyric sheet. If seeking management, press kit should include photo, cassette of at least 3 songs, and video if possible. Does not return material. Responds in 1 month.

Music Mostly **rock/top 40** and **country**. Current acts include Lee Bradley (contemporary country), Karen Kraft (country) and Four Kinsmen (Australian group).

[N] ◢ TWENTIETH CENTURY PROMOTIONS

155 Park Ave., Cranston RI 02905. (401)467-1832. Fax: (401)467-1833. **Contact:** Gil Morse, president. Management firm, booking agency and record producer (20th Century). Estab. 1972. Represents individual artists and groups from anywhere; currently handles 9 acts. Receives 15% commission. Reviews material for acts.

How to Contact *Call first and obtain permission to submit or to arrange personal interview.* Prefers CD or cassette. If seeking management, press kit should include photo and bio. Does not return material. Responds in 3 weeks.

Music Mostly **country** and **blues**. Works primarily with individuals and groups. Current acts include Robbin Lynn, Charlie Brown's Costars and Bobby Buris Pickett (Monster Mash).

Tips ''Don't give up.''

◢ UMPIRE ENTERTAINMENT ENTERPRIZES

1507 Scenic Dr., Longview TX 75604. (903)759-0300. Fax: (903)234-2944. **Contact:** Jerry Haymes, owner/president. Management firm, music publisher (Golden Guitar, Umpire Music) and record company (Enterprize Records). Estab. 1974. Represents individual artists, groups, songwriters and rodeo specialty acts; currently handles 4 acts. Receives 15% commission. Reviews material for acts.

• Also see the listing for Enterprize Records-Tapes in the Record Companies section of this book.

How to Contact *Contact first and obtain permission to submit.* Prefers cassette with lyric and lead sheets. If seeking management, press kit should include cover letter, bio, picture, lyric sheets, video and any recordings. Does not return material. "Submissions become part of files for two years, then disposed of." Responds in 1 month.

Music Mostly **country, pop** and **gospel**. Artists include Johnny Patterson (instrumentalist), Larry McGuire (instrumentalist) and three vocal acts.

☑ ○ UNIVERSAL MUSIC MARKETING

P.O. Box 2297, Universal City TX 78148. (210)653-3989. E-mail: bswrl8@wmconnect.net. **Contact:** Frank Willson, president. Management firm, record company (BSW Records), booking agency, music publisher and record producer (Frank Wilson). Estab. 1987. Represents individual artists and groups from anywhere; currently handles 12 acts. Receives 15% commission. Reviews material for acts.

- Also see the listings for BSW Records in the Music Publishers and Record Companies sections and Frank Wilson in the Record Producers section of this book.

How to Contact Submit demo tape by mail. Unsolicited submissions are OK. Prefers CD or ¾" videocassette with 3 songs and lyric sheet. If seeking management, include tape/CD, bio, photo and current activities. Include SASE. Responds in 6 weeks.

Music Mostly **country** and **light rock**; also **blues** and **jazz**. Works primarily with vocalists, singer/songwriters and bands. Current acts include Candee Land, Darlene Austin, Larry Butler, John Wayne, Sonny Marshall, Bobby Mountain, Crea Beal and Butch Martin (country).

⊕ ☑ ◑ HANS VAN POL MANAGEMENT

Utrechtseweg 39B, 1381 GS Weesp, Netherlands (0)294-413-633. Fax: (0)294-480-844. E-mail: hansvanpol@yahoo.com. Managing Director: Hans Van Pol. A&R/Producer: Jochem Fluitsma. Management firm, consultant (Hans Van Pol Music Consultancy), record company (J.E.A.H.! Records) and music publisher (Blue & White Music). Estab. 1984. Represents regional (Holland/Belgium) individual artists and groups, currently handles 7 acts. Receives 20% commission. Reviews material for acts.

How to Contact Submit demo tape by mail. Unsolicited submissions are OK. Prefers CD/DVD with 3 songs and lyric sheets. If seeking management, press kit should include demo, possible DVD, bio, press clippings, photo and release information. SAE and IRC. Responds in 1 month.

Music Mostly **MOR, dance: rap/swing beat/hip house/R&B/soul/c.a.r.** Current acts include Fluitsma & Van Tyn (production, commercials, MOR), Tony Scott (rap) and MC Miker "G" (rap/R&B).

◐ WILLIAM F. WAGNER AGENCY

14343 Addison St. #221, Sherman Oaks CA 91423. (818)905-1033. **Contact:** Bill Wagner, owner. Management firm and record producer (Bill Wagner). Estab. 1957. Represents individual artists and groups from anywhere; currently handles 2 acts. Receives 15% commission. Reviews materials for acts.

How to Contact Submit demo tape or CD by mail. Unsolicited submissions are OK. Prefers cassette or CD with 5 songs and lead sheet. If seeking management, press kit should include cover letter, bio, picture, tape or CD with 5 songs. "If SASE and/or return postage are included, I will reply in 30 days."

Music Mostly **jazz, contemporary pop** and **contemporary country**; also **classical, MOR** and **film and TV background**. Works primarily with singers, with or without band, big bands and smaller instrumental groups. Current acts include Page Cavanaugh (jazz/pop/contemporary/pianist), Sandy Graham (jazz singer), and Spellbox (contemporary rock-folk duo).

Tips "Indicate in first submission what artists you are writing for, by name if possible. Don't send material blindly. Be sure all material is properly copyrighted. Be sure package shows 'all material herein copyrighted' on outside."

◐ CHERYL K. WARNER PRODUCTIONS

P.O. Box 2127, Pearland TX 77588-2127. Phone: (615)429-7849. E-mail: cherylkwarner@sbcglobal.net. Website: www.cherylkwarner.com. **Contact:** Cheryl K. Warner and associates. Recording and stage production, music consulting, music publisher. Estab. 1988. Currently works with 2 acts. Reviews material for acts.

How to Contact Submit demo CD/DVD by mail. Unsolicited submissions are OK. Prefers CD or DVD, but will accept cassette with 3 best songs, lyric or lead sheet, bio and picture. Press kit should include CD, DVD, video/audiocassette with up-to-date bio, cover letter, lyric sheets, press clippings, and picture. Does not return material. Responds in 6 weeks if interested.

Music Mostly **country/traditional and contemporary**, **Christian/gospel** and **A/C/pop**. Works primarily with singer/songwriters and bands with original and versatile style. Current acts include Cheryl K. Warner (recording artist/entertainer) and Cheryl K. Warner Band (support/studio alt).

☑ WEMUS ENTERTAINMENT

2006 Seaboard, Suite 400, Midland TX 79705. (432)689-3687. Fax: (432)687-0930. E-mail: wemus@ aol.com. Website: www.wemus.com. **Contact:** Dennis Grubb, president. Management firm, booking agency and music publisher (Wemus Music, Inc.). Estab. 1983. Represents local and regional individual artists and groups; currently handles 4 acts. Receives 15-25% commission. Reviews material for acts.

How to Contact Submit demo tape by mail. Unsolicited submissions are OK. Prefers cassette, CD, DVD or VHS videocassette with 3-5 songs and lyric sheet. If seeking management, press kit should include glossy head and full body shots and extensive biography. "Make sure address, phone number and possible fax number is included in the packet, or a business card." Does not return material. Responds in 1 month if interested.

Music Mostly **country**. Current acts include The Image (variety), The Big Time (variety), The Pictures (variety) and Pryce Conner.

Tips "We preview and try to place good songs with national artists who are in need of good materials. We have a very tough qualification process and are very selective in forwarding materials to artists and their management."

☐ SHANE WILDER ARTISTS' MANAGEMENT

P.O. Box 335687, North Las Vegas NV 89033-0012. (702)395-5624. **Contact:** Shane Wilder, president. General Manager: Aaron Wilder. Management firm, music publisher (Shane Wilder Music/ BMI) and record producer (Shane Wilder Productions). Represents artists and groups; currently handles 4 acts. Receives 10% commission. Reviews material for acts.

How to Contact Submit demo tape by mail. Unsolicited submissions are OK. Prefers cassette or videocassette of performance with 4-10 songs and lyric sheet. If seeking management, send cover letter, bio, lyric sheets, cassette with 4-10 songs, photos of individuals or groups, video if possible and any press releases. "Submissions should be highly commercial." Include SASE. Responds in 2 weeks.

Music Country. Works primarily with single artists and groups. Current acts include Isabel Marie (country), Darren Collier (rock), Ann Lee (country) and Judy Kanyo (country).

Ⓝ ☑ YVONNE WILLIAMS MANAGEMENT

6433 Topanga Blvd. #142, Canoga Park CA 91303. (818)366-0510. Fax: (818)366-0520. E-mail: rawspitt@aol.com. **Contact:** Yvonne Williams, president. Management firm, music publisher (Jerry Williams Music), record company (S.D.E.G.) and record producer (Jerry Williams). Estab. 1978. Represents individual artists and songwriters from anywhere; currently handles 12 acts. Receives 10-20% commission. Reviews material for acts.

How to Contact Submit CD by mail. Unsolicited submissions are OK. Prefers CD/CDR only with any number of songs and lyric sheet. If seeking management, press kit should include cover letter, bio, photo, CD, press clippings, video and résumé. Include SASE, name, phone and any background in songs placed. Responds in 2 months.

Music Mostly **rap**, **R&B**, **rock** and **country**; also **gospel** and **blues**. Works primarily with singer/ songwriters and singers. Current acts include Swamp Dogg (R&B, rock, soca), Wilson Williams (blues), Cold Blue (rap) and Charlie Whitehead (blues).

Tips "Make a good clean demo, with a simple pilot vocal that is understandable."

▨ ☐ WINTERLAND ENTERTAINMENT MANAGEMENT & PUBLISHING

P.O. Box 969, Rossland BC VOG 1YO Canada. (250)362-7795. E-mail: winterland@netidea.com. **Contact:** Tom Jones, owner. Management firm, booking agency and music publisher. Estab. 1976. Represents individual artists, groups and songwriters from anywhere; currently handles 6 acts. Receives 15% commission. Reviews material for acts.

How to Contact Submit demo tape by mail. Unsolicited submissions are OK. Prefers CD, cassette or videocassette with 3 songs. If seeking management, include demo tape or CD, picture, cover letter and bio in press kit. Does not return material. Responds in 1 month.
Music Mostly **MOR, crossover, rock, pop** and **country**. Works primarily with vocalists, show bands, dance bands and bar bands. Current acts include Kirk Orr (folk/country), Mike Hamilton (rock/blues) and Larry Hayton (rock/blues).

○ RICHARD WOOD ARTIST MANAGEMENT
69 North Randall Ave., Staten Island NY 10301. (718)981-0641. Fax: (718)273-0797. **Contact:** Richard Wood. Management firm. Estab. 1974. Represents musical groups; currently handles 3 acts. Receives 20% commission. Reviews material for acts.
How to Contact Submit demo tape by mail. Unsolicited submissions are OK. Prefers cassette and lead sheet. If seeking management, press kit should include demo tape, photo, cover letter and résumé. Include SASE. Responds in 1 month.
Music Mostly **dance, R&B** and **top 40/pop**; also **MOR**. Works primarily with "high energy" show bands, bar bands and dance bands.

☑ ○ WORLDSOUND, LLC
17837 1st Ave. South Suite 3, Seattle WA 98148. (206)444-0300. Fax: (206)244-0066. E-mail: wmw @wyattworld.com. Website: www.worldsound.com. **Contact:** Warren Wyatt, A&R manager. Management firm. Estab. 1976. Represents individual artists, groups and songwriters from anywhere; currently handles 8 acts. Receives 20% commission. Reviews material for acts.
How to Contact Submit demo tape by mail. Unsolicited submissions are OK. Prefers CD or VHS videocassette with 2-10 songs and lyric sheet. If seeking management, press kit should include band biography, photos, video, members' history, press and demo reviews. Include SASE. Responds in 1 month.
Music Mostly **rock, pop** and **world**; also **heavy metal, hard rock** and **top 40**. Works primarily with pop/rock groups. Current acts include Carmine Appice (rock), Makana (world music) and Carbon 9 (tribal rock/industrial pop metal).
Tips "Always submit new songs/material, even if you have sent material that was previously rejected; the music biz is always changing."

○ ZANE MANAGEMENT, INC.
1650 Market St., One Liberty Place, 21st Floor, Philadelphia PA 19103. (215)575-3803. Fax: (215)575-3801. E-mail: lzr@braverlaw.com. Website: www.zanemanagement.com. **Contact:** Lloyd Z. Remick, Esq., president. Entertainment/sports consultants and managers. Represents artists, songwriters, producers and athletes; currently handles 7 acts. Receives 10-15% commission.
How to Contact Submit demo tape by mail. Unsolicited submissions are OK. Prefers CD and lyric sheet. If seeking management, press kit should include cover letter, bio, photo, demo tape and video. Does not return material. Responds in 3 weeks.
Music Mostly **dance, easy listening, folk, jazz** (fusion), **MOR, rock** (hard and country), **soul** and **top 40/pop**. Current acts include Bunny Sigler (disco/funk), Peter Nero and Philly Pops (conductor), Cast in Bronze (rock group), Pieces of a Dream (jazz/crossover), Don't Look Down (rock/pop) and Christian Josi (pop-swing).

○ D. ZIRILLI MANAGEMENT
P.O. Box 255, Cupertino CA 95015-0255. (408)257-2533. Fax: (408)252-8938. E-mail: donzirilli@aol.c om. Website: www.zirilli.com. **Owner:** Don Zirilli. Management firm. Estab. 1965. Represents groups from anywhere; currently handles 1 act. Receives 20% commission. Reviews material for acts.
How to Contact Submit demo tape by mail. Unsolicited submissions are OK. Prefers CD, DAT, videocassette or DVD. If seeking management, press kit should include video. Does not return material. Responds in 2 weeks.
Music Mostly **rock, surf** and **MOR**. Current acts include Papa Doo Run Run (band).
Tips "Less is more."

ADDITIONAL MANAGERS & BOOKING AGENTS

The following companies are also managers/booking agents, but their listings are found in other sections of the book. Read the listings for submission information.

Music Firms

Advertising, Audiovisual & Commercial

I t's happened a million times—you hear a jingle on the radio or television and can't get it out of your head. That's the work of a successful jingle writer, writing songs to catch your attention and make you aware of the product being advertised. But the field of commercial music consists of more than just memorable jingles. It also includes background music that many companies use in videos for corporate and educational presentations, as well as films and TV shows.

SUBMITTING MATERIAL

More than any other market listed in this book, the commercial music market expects composers to have made an investment in the recording of their material before submitting. A sparse, piano/vocal demo won't work here; when dealing with commercial music firms, especially audiovisual firms and music libraries, high quality production is important. Your demo may be kept on file at one of these companies until a need for it arises, and it may be used or sold as you sent it. Therefore, your demo tape or reel must be as fully produced as possible.

The presentation package that goes along with your demo must be just as professional. A list of your credits should be a part of your submission, to give the company an idea of your experience in this field. If you have no experience, look to local television and radio stations to get your start. Don't expect to be paid for many of your first jobs in the commercial music field; it's more important to get the credits and exposure that can lead to higher-paying jobs.

Commercial music and jingle writing can be a lucrative field for the composer/songwriter with a gift for writing catchy melodies and the ability to write in many different music styles. It's a very competitive field, so it pays to have a professional presentation package that makes your work stand out.

Three different segments of the commercial music world are listed here: advertising agencies, audiovisual firms and commercial music houses/music libraries. Each looks for a different type of music, so read these descriptions carefully to see where the music you write fits in.

ADVERTISING AGENCIES

Ad agencies work on assignment as their clients' needs arise. Through consultation and input from the creative staff, ad agencies seek jingles and music to stimulate the consumer to identify with a product or service.

When contacting ad agencies, keep in mind they are searching for music that can capture and then hold an audience's attention. Most jingles are short, with a strong, memorable hook. When an ad agency listens to a demo, it is not necessarily looking for a finished product so much as for an indication of creativity and diversity. Many composers put together a reel of excerpts of work from previous projects, or short pieces of music that show they can write in a variety of styles.

AUDIOVISUAL FIRMS

Audiovisual firms create a variety of products, from film and video shows for sales meetings, corporate gatherings and educational markets, to motion pictures and TV shows. With the increase of home video use, how-to videos are a big market for audiovisual firms, as are spoken word educational videos. All of these products need music to accompany them. For your quick reference, companies working to place music in movies and TV shows (excluding commercials) have a ▣ preceding their listing (also see the Film & TV Index on page 419 for a complete list of these companies).

Like ad agencies, audiovisual firms look for versatile, well-rounded songwriters. When submitting demos to these firms, you need to demonstrate your versatility in writing specialized background music and themes. Listings for companies will tell what facet(s) of the audiovisual field they are involved in and what types of clients they serve. Your demo tape should also be as professional and fully produced as possible; audiovisual firms often seek demo tapes that can be put on file for future use when the need arises.

COMMERCIAL MUSIC HOUSES & MUSIC LIBRARIES

Commercial music houses are companies contracted (either by an ad agency or the advertiser) to compose custom jingles. Since they are neither an ad agency nor an audiovisual firm, their main concern is music. They use a lot of it, too—some composed by in-house songwriters and some contributed by outside, freelance writers.

Music libraries are different in that their music is not custom composed for a specific client. Their job is to provide a collection of instrumental music in many different styles that, for an annual fee or on a per-use basis, the customer can use however he chooses.

In the following listings, commercial music houses and music libraries, which are usually the most open to works by new composers, are identified as such by **bold** typeface.

The commercial music market is similar to most other businesses in one aspect: experience is important. Until you develop a list of credits, pay for your work may not be high. Don't pass up opportunities if a job is non- or low-paying. These assignments will add to your list of credits, make you contacts in the field, and improve your marketability.

Money and rights

Many of the companies listed in this section pay by the job, but there may be some situations where the company asks you to sign a contract that will specify royalty payments. If this happens, research the contract thoroughly, and know exactly what is expected of you and how much you'll be paid.

Depending on the particular job and the company, you may be asked to sell one-time rights or all rights. One-time rights involve using your material for one presentation only. All rights means the buyer can use your work any way he chooses, as many times as he likes. Be sure you know exactly what you're giving up, and how the company may use your music in the future.

In the commercial world, many of the big advertising agencies have their own publishing companies where writers assign their compositions. In these situations, writers sign contracts whereby they do receive performance and mechanical royalties when applicable.

ADDITIONAL LISTINGS

For additional names and addresses of ad agencies that may use jingles and/or commercial music, refer to the *Standard Directory of Advertising Agencies* (National Register Publishing).

Commercial Music Firms

For a list of audiovisual firms, check out the latest edition of *AV Marketplace* (R.R. Bowker). Both these books may be found at your local library. To contact companies in your area, see the Geographic Index at the back of this book.

ADVERTEL, INC.

P.O. Box 18053, Pittsburgh PA 15236-0053. (412)344-4700. Fax: (412)344-4712. E-mail: pberan@ad vertel.com. Website: www.advertel.com. **Contact:** Paul Beran, president/CEO. Telephonic/Internet production company. Clients include small and multi-national companies. Estab. 1983. Uses the services of music houses and independent songwriters/composers for scoring of instrumentals (all varieties) and telephonic production. Commissions 3-4 composers/year. Pay varies. Buys all rights and phone exclusive rights.

How to Contact Submit demo of previous work. Prefers CD. "Most compositions are 2 minutes strung together in 6, 12, 18 minute length productions." Does not return material; prefers to keep on file. Responds "right away if submission fills an immediate need."

Music Uses all varieties, including unusual; mostly subdued music beds. Radio-type production used exclusively in telephone and Internet applications.

Tips "Go for volume. We have continuous need for all varieties of music in two minute lengths."

☑ BRG MUSIC WORKS

200 Eagle Road, Suite 2, Wayne PA 19087. (610)971-9490. Fax: (610)971-9630. E-mail: lnapier@brg musicworks.com. Website: www.brgmusicworks.com. Creative Director: Doug Reed. **Contact:** Lee Napier. **Jingle producers/music library producers**. Uses independent composers and music houses for background music for radio, TV and commercials and jingles for radio and TV. Commissions 20 songwriters/year. Pays per job. Buys all rights.

How to Contact Submit demo tape of previous work. Prefers cassette. "We are looking for quality jingle tracks already produced, as well as instrumental pieces between 2 and 3 minutes in length for use in AV music library." Include SASE. Responds in 2 weeks.

Music All types.

Tips "Send your best and put your strongest work at the front of your demo tape."

☒ CANTRAX RECORDERS

Dept. SM, 2119 Fidler Ave., Long Beach CA 90815. (562)498-4593. Fax: (562)498-4852. E-mail: cantrax@earthlink.net. **Contact:** Richard Cannata, owner. Recording studio. Clients include anyone needing recording services (i.e., industrial, radio, commercial). Estab. 1980. Uses the services of independent songwriters/composers and lyricists for scoring of independent features and films and background music for radio, industrials and promotions, commercials for radio and TV and jingles for radio. Commissions 10 composers/year. Pays fees set by the artist. "We take 15%."

How to Contact *"No phone calls, please."* Query with résumé of credits or submit demo CD of previous work. Prefers CD—no cassettes. Does not return material. Responds in 2 weeks if SASE is provided.

Music Uses jazz, New Age, rock, easy listening and classical for slide shows, jingles and soundtracks.

Tips "You must have a serious, professional attitude."

CEDAR CREST STUDIO

P.O. Box 28, Mountain Home AR 72653. (870)488-5777. Fax: (253)681-8194. E-mail: cedarcrest@sp ringfield.net. Website: www.oznet.com/cedarcrest. **Contact:** Bob Ketchum, owner. Audiovisual firm and **jingle/commercial music production house**. Clients include corporate, industrial, sales, music publishing, training, educational, legal, medical, music and Internet. Estab. 1973. Sometimes uses the services of independent songwriters/composers for background music for video productions, jingles for TV spots and commercials for radio and TV. Pays by the job or by royalties. Buys all rights or one-time rights.

How to Contact Query with résumé of credits or submit demo tape of previous work. Prefers CD, cassette, DAT, 7.5 or 15 IPS reel-to-reel or videocassette. Does not return material. "We keep it on file for future reference." Responds in 2 months.

Music Uses up-tempo pop (not too "rocky"), unobtrusive—no solos for commercials and background music for video presentations.

Tips "Hang, hang, hang. Be open to suggestions. Improvise, adapt, overcome."

CINEVUE/STEVE POSTAL PRODUCTIONS

108 Carraway St., Palatka FL 32177-1150. (386)328-6656. E-mail: birdshum@aol.com. Website: www.hometown.aol.com/cinemapostal/myhomepage/movies.html. **Contact:** Steve Postal, director/producer. Motion picture production company. Estab. 1955. Serves all types of film distributors. Uses the services of music houses, independent songwriters, composers and lyricists for scoring and background music for films and nature documentaries. Commissions 10 composers and 5 lyricists/year. Pays by the job. Buys all rights.

How to Contact Query with résumé of credits or submit demo tape of previous work ("good tape only!"). Submit manuscript showing music scoring skills. Prefers cassette or CD with 10 pieces and lyric or lead sheet. Only returns material if accompanied by SASE with sufficient postage for return of all materials. "Send good audiocassette, then call me in a week." Responds in 2 weeks.

Music Uses all styles of music for features (educational films and slide presentations). "Need horror film music on traditional instruments—no electronic music."

Tips "Be flexible, fast—do first job free to ingratiate yourself and demonstrate your style. Follow up with two phone calls."

COMMUNICATIONS FOR LEARNING

395 Massachusetts Ave., Arlington MA 02474. (781)641-2350. E-mail: comlearn@thecia.net. Website: www.communicationsforlearning.com. **Contact:** Jonathan L. Barkan, executive producer/director. Video, multimedia, exhibit and graphic design firm. Clients include multi-nationals, industry, government, institutions, local, national and international nonprofits. Uses services of music houses and independent songwriters/composers as theme and background music for videos and multimedia. Commissions 1-2 composers/year. Pays $2,000-5,000/job and one-time fees. Rights purchased varies.

How to Contact Submit demo of previous work. Prefers CD. Does not return material; prefers to keep on file. "For each job we consider our entire collection." Responds in 3 months.

Music Uses all styles of music for all sorts of assignments.

Tips "Please don't call. Just send good material and when we're interested, we'll be in touch. Make certain your name and phone number are on all submitted work itself, not only on the cover letter."

DBF A MEDIA COMPANY

P.O. Box 2458, Waldorf MD 20604. (301)843-7110. Fax: (301)843-7148. E-mail: info@dbfmedia.com. Website: www.dbfmedia.com. **Contact:** Randy Runyon, general manager. Advertising agency, audiovisual and media firm and audio and video production company. Clients include business and industry. Estab. 1981. Uses the services of music houses, independent songwriters/composers and lyricists for background music for industrial, training, educational and promo videos, jingles and commercials for radio and TV. Commissions 5-12 composers and 5-12 lyricists/year. Pays by the job. Buys all rights.

How to Contact Submit demo tape of previous work. Prefers cassette or CD or VHS videocassette with 5-8 songs and lead sheet. Include SASE, but prefers to keep material on file. Responds in 6 months.

Music Uses up-tempo contemporary for industrial videos, slide presentations and commercials.

Tips "We're looking for commercial music, primarily A/C."

DISK PRODUCTIONS

1100 Perkins Rd., Baton Rouge LA 70802. Fax: (225)343-0210. E-mail: disk_productions@yahoo.com. **Contact:** Joey Decker, director. **Jingle/production house.** Clients include advertising agencies, slide production houses and film companies. Estab. 1982. Uses the services of music houses, independent songwriters/composers and lyricists for scoring and background music for TV spots, films and jingles for radio and TV. Commissions 7 songwriters/composers and 7 lyricists/year. Pays by the job. Buys all rights.

How to Contact Submit demo tape of previous work. Prefers CD, cassette or DAT (or ½″ videocassette). Does not return material. Responds in 2 weeks.

Music Needs all types of music for jingles, music beds or background music for TV and radio, etc.

Tips "Advertising techniques change with time. Don't be locked in a certain style of writing. Give me music that I can't get from pay needle-drop."

ENTERTAINMENT PRODUCTIONS, INC.

2118 Wilshire Blvd., PMB 744, Santa Monica CA 90403. (310)456-3143. Fax: (310)456-8950. **Contact:** Anne Bell, music director. Producer: Edward Coe. Motion picture and television production company. Clients include motion picture and TV distributors. Estab. 1972. Uses the services of music houses and songwriters for scores, production numbers, background and theme music for films and TV and jingles for promotion of films. Commissions/year vary. Pays by the job or by royalty. Buys motion picture, video and allied rights.

How to Contact Query with résumé of credits. Demo should show flexibility of composition skills. "Demo records/tapes sent at own risk—returned if SASE included." Responds by letter within 1 month, "but only if SASE is included."

Tips "Have résumé on file. Develop self-contained capability."

GOLD & ASSOCIATES, INC.

6000 Sawgrass Village Circle #C, Ponte Vedra Beach FL 32082. Fax: (904)285-1579. E-mail: gold@str ikegold.com. Website: www.strikegold.com. **Contact:** Keith Gold, creative director. Marketing, design and advertising firm. Clients include DeBeers, Harcourt, GEICO, The State of Florida and Time Warner. Estab. 1988. Uses the services primarily of music houses, but also independent songwriters/composers. Agency develops its own lyrics for scoring background music for presentations, websites, radio and TV commercials, special events and CDs. Commissions 5-10 music projects/year. "We pay 2-3 firms $1,500-2,500 for demos. For the final production, we pay between $5,000 and $35,000. We normally buy all rights. However, sometimes one time rights, for a year or specific markets."

- Gold & Associates, Inc. has won over 850, national and international awards, including honors from the Clio Awards, New York Advertising Awards, London International Advertising Awards, Global Awards and The Telly Awards.

How to Contact Submit CD of previous work. Will keep submitted material on file. "Agency contacts writers and music houses only when we are ready to have music developed."

Music Uses every style.

Tips "Send demos once a year."

HODGES ASSOCIATES, INC.

912 Hay St., Fayetteville NC 28305. (910)483-8489. Fax: (910)483-7197. E-mail: anna@hodgesassoc .com. Website: www.hodgesassoc.com. **Contact:** Anna Smith, president, or Eileen Moore, production manager. Advertising agency. Clients include industrial, retail and consumer. ("We handle a full array of clientele.") Estab. 1974. Uses the services of music houses and independent songwriters/composers for background music for industrial films and slide presentations, and commercials for radio and TV. Commissions 1-2 composers/year. Pays by the job. Buys all rights.

How to Contact Submit demo tape of previous work. Prefers cassette or CD. Does not return material; prefers to keep on file. Responds in 3 months.

Music Uses all styles for industrial videos, slide presentations and TV commercials.

K&R'S RECORDING STUDIOS

28533 Greenfield, Southfield MI 48076. (248)557-8276. E-mail: recordav@knr.net. Website: www.k nr.net. **Contact:** Ken Glaza. Scoring service and **jingle/commercial music production house**. Clients include commercial and industrial firms. Services include sound for pictures (music, dialogue).

Uses the services of independent songwriters/composers and lyricists for scoring of film and video, commercials and industrials and jingles and commercials for radio and TV. Commissions 1 composer/month. Pays by the job. Buys all rights.

How to Contact Submit demo tape of previous work. Prefers CD or VHS videocassette with 5-7 short pieces. "We rack your tape for client to judge." Does not return material.

Tips "Keep samples short. Show me what you can do in five minutes. Go to knr.net 'free samples' and listen to the sensitivity expressed in emotional music." Current projects: Proof and D12 soundtracks.

KEN-DEL PRODUCTIONS INC.

First State Production Center, 1500 First State Blvd., Wilmington DE 19804-3596. (302)999-1111. Estab. 1950. **Contact:** Edwin Kennedy, A&R manager. Clients include publishers, industrial firms and advertising agencies, how-to's and radio/TV. Uses services of songwriters for radio/TV commercials, jingles and multimedia. Pays by the job. Buys all rights.

How to Contact "Submit all inquiries and demos in any format to general manager." Does not return material. Will keep on file for 3 years. Generally responds in 1 month or less.

☑ LAPRIORE VIDEOGRAPHY

67 Millbrook St. Suite 114, Worcester MA 01606. (508)755-9010. E-mail: peter@lapriorevideo.com. Website: www.lapriorevideo.com. **Contact:** Peter Lapriore, owner. Video production company. Clients include corporations, retail stores, educational and sports. Estab. 1985. Uses the services of music houses, independent songwriters/composers for background music for marketing, training, educational videos and TV commercials and for scoring video. "We also own several music libraries." Commissions 2 composers/year. Pays $150-1,000/job. Buys all or one-time rights.

How to Contact Submit demo tape of previous work. Prefers cassette, CD, or VHS videocassette with 5 songs and lyric sheet. Does not return material; prefers to keep on file. Responds in 3 weeks.

Music Uses slow, medium, up-tempo, jazz and classical for marketing, educational films and commercials.

Tips "Be very creative and willing to work on all size budgets."

MALLOF, ABRUZINO & NASH MARKETING

765 Kimberly Dr., Carol Stream IL 60188. (630)929-5200. Fax: (630)752-9288. E-mail: emallof@man marketing.com. Website: www.manmarketing.com. **Contact:** Edward G. Mallof, president. Advertising agency. Works primarily with auto dealer jingles. Estab. 1980. Uses music houses for jingles for retail clients and auto dealers, and commercials for radio and TV. Commissions 5-6 songwriters/ year. Pays $600-2,000/job. Buys all rights.

How to Contact Submit demo tape of previous work. Prefers cassette with 4-12 songs. Include SASE. Does not return material. Responds if interested.

Tips "Send us produced jingles we could re-lyric for our customers' needs."

⬛ PATRICK MOORE COMPOSITIONS

84 Harris Ave., Oshawa ON L1J 5K7 Canada. (905)576-9039. Website: www.patrickmoore.ca. **Contact:** Patrick Moore, owner/president. Scoring service and **jingle/commercial music production house**. Clients include producers of documentaries/films (educational). Estab. 1988. Uses the services of orchestrators for scoring of orchestral scores.

How to Contact Write first to arrange personal interview. Prefers cassette. Does not return material. Prefers to keep submitted material on file. Responds in 1 month.

Music "I specialize in combining ethnic music with current music for educational films/documentaries."

Tips "My needs are very specific and must meet the requirements of the producer and music editor on each project. It is not unusual for me to work with film producers and music writers from all over the world. I do a great deal of work by mailing video tapes, cassette tapes and CDs of rough drafts to producers and other professionals involved in a film or video production."

☑ MUSIC LIBRARY: EDITORS CHOICE MUSIC LIBRARY

208 W. 30th St., Suite 1006, New York NY 10001. (212)643-0404. E-mail: ecmlibrary@aol.com. Website: www.editorschoicemusic.com. **Contact:** Gary Fitzgerald, composer/producer. **Commercial music production house**. "We service the advertising, film and television community." Estab. 1987. Uses the music of independent composers in library to be placed on TV, radio and industrials, background music for film and television, and jingles and commercials for radio and TV.

How to Contact Call first to obtain permission to submit demo tape. Will not open unsolicited submissions. Prefers CD. Include SASE, but prefers to keep on file. "A follow-up call must follow submission."

Music Uses all styles of music.

Tips "Complete knowledge of how music is used on TV and in the film business is essential."

☑ NORTON RUBBLE & MERTZ, INC. ADVERTISING

One Tower Lane, Suite 3120, Oakbrook Terrance IL 60181. (630)954-0500. E-mail: mmiller@nrmad v.com. Website: www.nrmadv.com. **Contact:** Mark Miller. Advertising agency. Clients include consumer products, retail, business to business. Estab. 1987. Uses the services of music houses and independent songwriters/composers for jingles and background music for radio/TV commercials. Commissions 2 composers/year. Pays by the job.

How to Contact Submit tape of previous work; query with résumé of credits. Prefers cassette or CD. Does not return materials; prefers to keep on file. "Please do not call."

Music Uses up-tempo and pop for commercials.

OMNI COMMUNICATIONS

Dept. SM, P.O. Box 302, Carmel IN 46032-0302. (317)574-6664. E-mail: omni@omniproductions.c om. Website: www.omniproductions.com. President: W.H. Long. Creative Director: S.M. Long. Production Manager: Jim Mullet. Television production and audiovisual firm. Estab. 1978. Serves industrial, commercial and educational clients. Uses the services of music houses and songwriters for scoring of films and television productions, CD-ROMs and Internet streams; background music for voice overs; lyricists for original music and themes. Pays by the job. Buys all rights.

How to Contact Submit demo tape of previous work. Prefers CD or DVD. Does not return material. Responds in 2 weeks.

Music Varies with each and every project; from classical, contemporary to commercial industrial.

Tips "Submit good demo tape with examples of your range to command the attention of our producers."

RH POWER AND ASSOCIATES, INC.

320 Osuna NE, Bldg. B, Albuquerque NM 87107. (505)761-3150. Fax: (505)761-3153. E-mail: info@ rhpower.com. Website: www.rhpower.com. **Contact:** Creative Director. Advertising agency. Clients include RV, boat and automotive dealers and manufacturers. Estab. 1988. Uses the services of music houses and independent songwriters/composers for background music, and jingles and commercials for radio and TV. Pay varies per job. Buys all rights.

How to Contact Query with résumé or circular of credits by mail, e-mail or fax only. Write first to arrange personal interview. "No need to include a submission package unless contacted from initial résumé or letter contact."

Music Uses contemporary, jazz and up-tempo for jingles, TV and radio, commercials and music-on-hold.

☑ QUALLY & COMPANY INC.

2 E. Oak, Suite 2903, Chicago IL 60611. (312)280-1898. **Contact:** Robert Qually, creative director. Advertising agency. Uses the services of music houses, independent songwriters/composers and lyricists for scoring, background music and jingles for radio and TV commercials. Commissions 2-4 composers and 2-4 lyricists/year. Pays by the job. Buys various rights depending on deal.

How to Contact Submit demo tape of previous work or query with résumé of credits. Prefers CD. Include SASE, but prefers to keep material on file. Responds in 2 weeks.

Music Uses all kinds of music for commercials.

RAMPION VISUAL PRODUCTIONS

125 Walnut St., Watertown MA 02472. (617)972-1777. Fax: (617)972-9157. E-mail: info@rampion.com. Website: www.rampion.com. **Contact:** Steven V. Tringali, producer/director/managing partner. Full service producing agency. Clients include educational, independent producers, corporate clients and TV producers. Estab. 1981. Uses the services of independent songwriters/composers for jingles, background music and scoring to longer form programming. Commissions 1-2 composers/year. Pays by the job. Buys all rights.

How to Contact Submit demo tape of previous work or query with résumé of credits. Prefers CD with variety of pieces. Does not return material; prefers to keep on file.

Music Uses all styles for corporate, educational and original programming.

Tips "Submit a varied demo reel showing style and client base."

RODEO VIDEO, INC.

412 S. Main St., Snowflake AZ 85937-0412. Fax: (928)536-7120. E-mail: info@rodeovideo.com. Website: www.rodeovideo.com. Video and TV production company. Clients include rodeo contestants and fans. Estab. 1982. Uses the services of music houses, independent songwriters/composers and lyricists for background music for rodeo blooper videos and rodeo documentaries. Commissions 2 composers and 2 lyricists/year. Pay varies. Buys all rights or one-time rights.

How to Contact Submit demo tape of previous work. Prefers cassette or DAT with any number of songs. Mainly interested in country/western with rodeo theme. Does not return material. Responds only if interested.

Music Uses country/western for video backgrounds.

Tips "Looking for up-tempo songs with rodeo theme—country/western or rock."

SOTER ASSOCIATES INC.

209 N. 400 W., Provo UT 84601. (801)375-6200. Fax: (801)375-6280. E-mail: sherrie@soter.net. Website: www.soter.net. President: N. Gregory Soter. Creative Director: Sherrie Hall Everett. Advertising agency. Clients include financial, health care, municipal, computer hardware and software. Estab. 1970. Uses services of music houses, independent songwriters/composers and lyricists for background music for audiovisual presentations and jingles for radio and TV commercials. Commissions 1 composer, 1 lyricist/year. Pays by the job. Buys all rights.

How to Contact Submit tape demonstrating previous work and composition skills. Prefers cassette or VHS videocassette. Does not return submissions; prefers to keep materials on file.

▣ TRF PRODUCTION MUSIC LIBRARIES

Dept. SM, 747 Chestnut Ridge Rd., Chestnut Ridge NY 10977. (845)356-0800. Fax: (845)356-0895. E-mail: info@trfmusic.com. Website: www.trfmusic.com. **Contact:** Anne Marie Russo. **Music/sound effect libraries.** Estab. 1931. Uses the services of independent composers for all categories of production music for television, film and other media. Pays 50% royalty.

• Also see the listing for Alpha Music Inc. in the Music Publishers section of this book.

How to Contact Submit demo CD of new compositions. Prefers CD with 3-7 pieces. Can send audiocassette, DAT or CD with up to 12 tracks. Submissions are not returnable. Responds in 2 to 3 months after receipt.

Music Primarily interested in **acoustic instrumental** music suitable for use as production music, which is theme and background music for TV, film and AV/multimedia.

☑ ▣ UTOPIAN EMPIRE CREATIVEWORKS

P.O. Box 9, Traverse City MI 49685 or P.O. Box 499, Kapa'a (Kaua'i) HI 96746. (231)943-5050. E-mail: creativeworks@utopianempire.com. Website: www.UtopianEmpire.com. **Contact:** Ms. M'Lynn Hartwell, president. Web design, multimedia firm and motion picture/video production company. Serves commercial, industrial and nonprofit clients. We provide the following services: advertising, marketing, design/packaging, distribution and booking. Uses services of music houses, independent songwriters/composers for jingles and scoring of and background music for multi-image/multimedia, film and video. Negotiates pay. Buys all or one-time rights.

How to Contact Submit CD of previous work, demonstrating composition skills or query with résumé of credits. Prefers CD or good quality cassette. Does not return material; prefers to keep on file. Responds only if interested.

Music Uses mostly industrial/commercial themes.

VIDEO I-D, INC.

Dept. SM, 105 Muller Rd., Washington IL 61571. (309)444-4323. Fax: (309)444-4333. E-mail: videoi d@videoid.com. Website: www.VideoID.com. **Contact:** Gwen Wagner, manager, operations. Post production/teleproductions. Clients include law enforcement, industrial and business. Estab. 1977. Uses the services of music houses and independent songwriters/composers for background music for video productions. Pays per job. Buys one-time rights.

How to Contact Submit demo tape of previous work. Prefers CD or VHS videocassette with 5 songs and lyric sheet. Does not return material. Responds in 1 month.

VIS/AID MARKETING/ASSOCIATES

P.O. Box 4502, Inglewood CA 90309-4502. (310)399-0696. **Contact:** Lee Clapp, manager. Advertising agency. Clients include "companies in 23 SIC codes (workable)." Estab. 1965. Uses the services of music houses, independent songwriters/composers and lyricists for background music for films, and commercials, TV jingles for radio/TV and scoring new material. Commissions 1-2 composers and 1-2 lyricists/year. Pay is negotiable. Buys all or one-time rights.

How to Contact Query with résumé of credits. Call first to arrange personal interview or submit demo tape of previous work. Prefers cassette with 1-2 songs and lyric and lead sheet. "Do not send original material that if misplaced/lost cannot be duplicated." Does not return material. Responds in 2 weeks.

Music Uses up-tempo, pop, jazz and classical for educational films, slide presentations and commercials.

Play Producers & Publishers

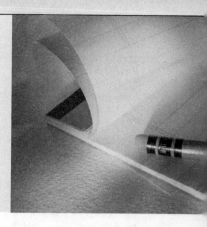

Finding a theater company willing to invest in a new production can be frustrating for an unknown playwright. But whether you write the plays, compose the music or pen the lyrics, it is important to remember not only where to start but how to start. Theater in the U.S. is a hierarchy, with Broadway, Off Broadway and Off Off Broadway being pretty much off limits to all but the Stephen Sondheims of the world.

Aspiring theater writers would do best to train their sights on nonprofit regional and community theaters to get started. The encouraging news is there is a great number of local theater companies throughout the U.S. with experimental artistic directors who are looking for new works to produce, and many are included in this section. This section covers two segments of the industry: theater companies and dinner theaters are listed under Play Producers (beginning on this page), and publishers of musical theater works are listed under the Play Publishers heading (beginning on page 287). All these markets are actively seeking new works of all types for their stages or publications.

BREAKING IN

Starting locally will allow you to research each company carefully and learn about their past performances, the type of musicals they present, and the kinds of material they're looking for. When you find theaters you think may be interested in your work, attend as many performances as possible, so you know exactly what type of material each theater presents. Or volunteer to work at a theater, whether it be moving sets or selling tickets. This will give you valuable insight into the day-to-day workings of a theater and the creation of a new show. On a national level, you will find prestigious organizations offering workshops and apprenticeships covering every subject from arts administration to directing to costuming. But it could be more helpful to look into professional internships at theaters and attend theater workshops in your area. The more knowledgeable you are about the workings of a particular company or theater, the easier it will be to tailor your work to fit its style and the more responsive they will be to you and your work. (See the Workshops & Conferences section on page 346 for more information.) As a composer for the stage, you need to know as much as possible about a theater and how it works, its history and the different roles played by the people involved in it. Flexibility is the key to successful productions, and knowing how a theater works will only help you in cooperating and collaborating with the director, producer, technical people and actors.

If you're a playwright looking to have his play published in book form or in theater publications, see the listings under the Play Publishers section (page 287). To find play producers and publishers in your area, consult the Geographic Index at the back of this book.

PLAY PRODUCERS

ALLIANCE THEATRE

1280 Peachtree St., Atlanta GA 30309.(404)733-4650. Fax: (404)733-4625. Website: www.allianceth eatre.org. **Contact:** Freddie Ashley, literary associate. Artistic Director: Susan V. Booth. Play producer. Estab. 1969. Produces 9-10 plays and 1 new musical/year. Audience is diverse, regional and young. Two performing spaces: 800-seat proscenium and a 200-seat flexible black box. Pays negotiable amount per performance.

How to Contact Query with synopsis, character breakdown and set description. Include SASE. Responds in 6 months.

Musical Theater They are primarily interested in new musicals, but also will consider works for children's theatre. Musicals for young audiences must be no longer than 1 hour in length and have a cast of 8 or fewer.

Productions *The Color Purple*, by Marsha Norman Brenda Russell, Allee Willis, and Stephen Bay (adaptation of Alice Walker novel); *Elaborate Lives: The Legend of Aida*, by Elton John and Tim Rice (musical theatre update of legend); and *Soul Possessed*, by Debbie Allen/James Ingram/Arturo Sandoval (musical dance drama set in bayous of Louisiana).

☑ AMAS MUSICAL THEATRE, INC.

115 MacDougal Street, Suite 2B, New York NY 10012. (212)563-2565. Fax: (212)239-8332. E-mail: amas@amasmusical.org. Website: www.amasmusical.org. Producing Director: Donna Trinkoff. Play producer. Estab. 1968. Produces 2 musicals/year and musical development series (Amas Six O'clock Musical Theatre Lab) produces 5-6 concert versions of new musicals. "We seek to reach a wide and diverse audience by presenting musicals that speak to different cultures." Performance space is on Off-off Broadway theater with 76-99 seats. Payment is standard agreement.

How to Contact Submit complete manuscript, score and tape of songs. Include SASE. Responds in 6 months.

Musical Theater Seeks "innovative, well-written, good music. We seek musicals that lend themselves to multiracial casting."

Productions *Little Ham: A Harlem Jazzical*, by Dan Owens/Richard Engquist/Judd Woldin (the Harlem community in the '30s); *Starmites*, by Stuart Ross/Barry Keating (a sci-fi, pop-rock adventure); and *4 Guys Named Jose*, by Dolores Prida, concieved by David Coffman (a Latino review).

Tips "Submit works that speak to and about racial and cultural themes using a fresh, new, fun style."

AMERICAN MUSICAL THEATRE OF SAN JOSE

1717 Technology Dr., San Jose CA 95110-1305. (408)453-7100. Fax: (408)453-7123. E-mail: mjacobs @amtsj.org. Website: www.amtsj.org. **Contact:** Marc Jacobs, director of new works. Play producer. Estab. 1935. Produces 4 mainstage musicals/year. "Our season subscribers are generally upper-middle class families. Our main season is in the 2,600-seat San Jose Center for the Performing Arts." Pays variable royalty.

How to Contact Submit synopsis and tape of songs. Include SASE. Responds in 3-4 months.

Musical Theater "We are not looking for children's musicals, Christmas shows or puppet shows. We are looking for high quality (professional caliber) musicals to develop for our 2,600-seat main stage theatre, an 800-seat 2nd stage a national tour or possible Broadway production. Submissions from composers and writers with some previous track record only, please. The first thing we look for is quality and originality in the music and lyrics. Next we look for librettos that offer exciting staging possibilities. If writing original music to a pre-existing play please be sure all rights have been cleared."

Tips "We are a company with a $12 million per season operating budget and one of the largest subscription audiences in the country. We are looking for shows we can develop for possible main stage, 2nd stage, or Broadway productions. Therefore it is advisable that any composers or writers have professional production history before submitting to us."

ARDEN THEATRE COMPANY
40 N. Second St., Philadelphia PA 19106. (215)922-8900. E-mail: info@ardentheatre.org. Website: www.ardentheatre.org. **Contact:** Amy Dugas Brown, associate artistic director. Play producer. Estab. 1988. Produces 3-4 plays and 1-2 musicals/year. Adult audience—diverse. Mainstage: 350+ seats, flexible. Studio: 175+ seats, flexible. Pay is negotiable.
How to Contact Query with synopsis, character breakdown and set description. Include SASE. Responds in 1 year.
Musical Theater Full length plays and musicals. The Arden Theatre Company is dedicated to bringing to life the greatest stories by the greatest storytellers of all time. We draw from any source that is inherently dramatic and theatrical—fiction, nonfiction, poetry, music and drama. Especially interested in literary adaptations. Also interested in musicals for children. Will consider original music for use in developing or pre-existing play. Composers should send samples of music on cassette.
Productions *Baby Case*, by Michael Ogborn (Lindbergh baby kidnapping/trial of Bruno Richard Hauptman); *James Joyce's The Dead*, by Richard Nelson (adaptation of Joyce's short story); and *Pacific Overtures*, by Sondheim (musical about Westernization of Japan).

☑ ARKANSAS REPERTORY THEATRE
601 Main, P.O. Box 110, Little Rock AR 72203. (501)378-0405. Fax: (501)378-0012. Website: www.therep.org. **Contact:** Brad Mooy. Play producer. Estab. 1976. Produces 6-10 plays and musicals/year. "We perform in a 354-seat house and also have a 99-seat 2nd stage." Pays 5-10% royalty or $75-150 per performance.
How to Contact Query with synopsis, character breakdown and set description. Include SASE. Responds in 6 months.
Musical Theater "Small casts are preferred, comedy or drama and prefer shows to run 1:45 to 2 hours maximum. Simple is better; small is better, but we do produce complex shows. We aren't interested in children's pieces, puppet shows or mime. We always like to receive a tape of the music with the book."
Productions *Radio Gals*, by Mike Craver/Mark Hardwick; and *Always . . . Patsy Cline*, by Ted Swindley (bio-musical).
Tips "Include a *good* cassette of your music, *sung well*, with the script."

☑ ASOLO THEATRE COMPANY
Dept. SM, 5555 N. Tamiami Trail, Sarasota FL 34243. (941)351-9010. E-mail: corinne_gabrielson@asolo.org. Website: www.asolo.org. Associate Artistic Director: Corinne Gabrielson. Play producer. Produces 7-8 plays (1 musical)/year. Plays are performed at the Asolo Mainstage (500-seat proscenium house). Pays negotiated royalty.
How to Contact Query with synopsis, character breakdown, set description and one page of dialogue. Include SASE. Responds in 6 months.
Musical Theater "We want small to mid-size non-chorus musicals only. They should be full-length, any subject. There are no restrictions on production demands; however, musicals with excessive scenic requirements or very large casts may be difficult to consider."
Productions *Oh What A Lovely War*, by Joan Littlewood (WWI); and *Jane Eyre*, by Ted Davis/David Clark.

☑ BAILIWICK REPERTORY
Bailiwick Arts Center, 1229 W. Belmont, Chicago IL 60657. (773)883-1090. Fax: (773)883-2017. E-mail: david@bailiwick.org. Website: www.bailiwick.org. Director: David Zak. Producer: Rusty Hernandez. Play producer. Estab. 1982. Produces 5 mainstage, 5 one-act plays and 1-2 new musicals/year. "We do Chicago productions of new works on adaptations that are politically or thematically intriguing and relevant. We also do an annual director's festival which produces 50-75 new short works each year." Pays 5-8% royalty.
How to Contact "Review our manuscript submission guidelines or the professional page of our website." Responds in 6 months.

Musical Theater "We want innovative, dangerous, exciting material."
Productions *The Christmas Schooner*, by John Reeger and Julie Shannon (holiday musical); *Bonnie and Clyde*, by Pomerantz/Eickmann/Herron/Ritchie (Roaring 20s).
Tips "Be creative. Be patient. Be persistent. Make me believe in your dream."

☑ BARTER THEATRE
P.O. Box 867, Abingdon VA 24212. (276)628-3991. Fax: (276)619-3335. E-mail: barterinfo@barterth eatre.com. Website: www.bartertheatre.com. **Contact:** Evalyn Baron, associate artistic director. Play producer. Estab. 1933. Produces 15 plays and 5-6 musicals (1 new musical)/year. Audience "varies; middle American, middle age, tourist and local mix." 500-seat proscenium stage, 140-seat thrust stage. Pays 5% royalty.
How to Contact Query with synopsis, character breakdown, set description, and CD/cassette of the songs. "Make sure cassettes and CDs will play back properly." Include SASE. Responds in 1 year.
Musical Theater "We investigate all types. We are not looking for any particular standard. Prefer sellable titles with unique use of music. Prefer small cast musicals, although have done large scale projects with marketable titles or subject matter. We use original music in almost all of our plays." Does not wish to see "political or very urban material, or material with very strong language."
Productions *Something's Afoot*, by James McDonald, David Vos and Robert Girlach; *Oklahoma*, by Rodgers & Hammerstein; *South Pacific*, Rodgers & Hammerstein; and *Sundown*, Peter Link and Joe Bravaco.
Tips "Be patient. Be talented. Don't be obnoxious. Be original and make sure subject matter fits our audience. And make sure your CD or cassette will play before you send it in."

BIRMINGHAM CHILDREN'S THEATRE
P.O. Box 1362, Birmingham AL 35201-1362. (205)458-8899. Fax: (205)458-8895. E-mail: pat@bct12 3.org. Website: www.bct123.org. **Contact:** Pat Anderson-Flowers, artistic director. Play producer. Estab. 1947. Produces 9 plays and 1-4 new musicals/year; "typically, original adaptations of classic children's stories for pre-school through grade 1, K-6, and junior and senior high school." "Wee Folks" Series: preschool through grade 1; Children's Series: K-6; Young Adult Series: junior and senior high. Performs in 1,072-seat flexible thrust mainstage theater, 250 seat black box theater and a 200 seat studio theater (touring venues vary). Pay is negotiable.
How to Contact Query with synopsis, character breakdown and set description. Include SASE. Responds in 3 months.
Musical Theater " 'Wee Folks' productions should be 40-45 minutes; Children's Series 55-60 minutes; Young Adult Series 85-95 minutes. 'Wee Folks' shows should be interactive; all others presentational. Most productions tour, so sets must be lightweight, simple and portable. 'Wee Folks' shows prefer cast of four. Touring Children's Series shows prefer cast of six. All others prefer cast of 12 or less. BCT traditionally ultilizes a great deal of music for underscoring, transitions, etc. We welcome submissions from prospective sound designers."
Productions "The Elves and the Shoemaker" book and lyrics by Jean Pierce and Betty Pewitt, music by Jay Trumminello; "The Princess and the Pea" adapted by Paul Laurakas; "Ferdinand the Bull" adapted by Deborah Wicks, music by Deborah Wicks LaPuma; "The Best Christmas Pageant Ever" by Barbara Robinson.

THE BLOWING ROCK STAGE COMPANY
P.O. Box 2170, Blowing Rock NC 28605. (828)295-9168. Fax: (828)295-9104. E-mail: ken@blowingr ockstage.com. Website: www.blowingrockstage.com. **Contact:** Kenneth Kay, producing director. Play producer. Estab. 1986. Produces 4 shows/year. "Blowing Rock Stage Company provides a professional summer theatre experience for the residents and the high volume of summer tourists." Performances take place in a 240-seat proscenium summer theater in the Blue Ridge Mountains. Pays flat fee/performance or 5-7% royalty.
How to Contact Query with synopsis, character breakdown, set description and music CD. Include SASE. Responds in up to 6 months.

Musical Theater "Casts of ten or less are preferred, with ideal show running time of two hours, intermission included. Limit set changes to three or less; or unit concept. Some comic relief, please. Not producing stark adult themes."

Productions *The Christmas Bus*, by Robert Inman (world premiere Christmas show 2003); *A Dash of Rosemary*, by Douglas Kampsen (SE Premiere of New Revue of Rosemary Clooney); and *Italian 101*, by John D'Aquino (1 man play about growing up Italian).

Tips "We're looking for inspiration. We enjoy supporting projects which are soulful and uplifting. We want light-hearted musicals with some comic relief."

BRISTOL RIVERSIDE THEATRE

Dept. SM, P.O. Box 1250, Bristol PA 19007. (215)785-6664. Website: www.brtstage.org. Producing Director: Susan D. Atkinson. Artistic Director: Edward Keith Baker. Play producer. Estab. 1986. Produces 5 plays and 2 musicals/year (1 new musical every 2 years) and summer concert series. "302-seat proscenium Equity theater with audience of all ages from small towns and metropolitan area." Pays 6-8% royalty.

How to Contact Submit complete manuscript, score and tape of songs. Include SASE. Responds in 18 months.

Musical Theater "No strictly children's musicals. All other types with small to medium casts and within reasonable artistic tastes. Prefer one-set; limited funds restrict. Do not wish to see anything catering to prurient interests."

Productions *Sally Blane, World's Greatest Girl Detective*, by David Levy/Leslie Eberhard (spoof of teen detective genre); *Moby Dick*, by Mark St. Germain, music by Doug Katsarous; and *Texas Flyer*, by Larry Gatlin.

Tips "You should be willing to work with small staff, open to artistic suggestion, and aware of the limitations of newly developing theaters."

CIRCA '21 DINNER PLAYHOUSE

Dept. SM, P.O. Box 3784, Rock Island IL 61204-3784. (309)786-2667, ext. 303. Fax: (309)786-4119. E-mail: dpjh@circa21.com. Website: www.circa21.com. **Contact:** Dennis Hitchcock, producer. Play producer. Estab. 1977. Produces 1-2 plays and 4-5 musicals (1 new musical)/year. Plays produced for a general audience. Three children's works/year, concurrent with major productions. Payment is negotiable.

How to Contact Query with synopsis, character breakdown and set description or submit complete manuscript, score and tape of songs. Include SASE. Responds in 3 months.

Musical Theater "We produce both full length and one act children's musicals. Folk or fairy tale themes. Works that do not condescend to a young audience yet are appropriate for entire family. We're also seeking full-length, small cast musicals suitable for a broad audience." Would also consider original music for use in a play being developed.

Productions *A Closer Walk with Patsy Cline*, *Swingtime Canteen*, *Forever Plaid* and *Lost Highway*.

Tips "Small, upbeat, tourable musicals (like *Pump Boys*) and bright musically-sharp children's productions (like those produced by Prince Street Players) work best. Keep an open mind. Stretch to encompass a musical variety—different keys, rhythms, musical ideas and textures."

N CREEDE REPERTORY THEATRE

124 N. Main St., P.O. Box 269, Creede CO 81130. (719)658-2540. Fax: (719)658-2343. E-mail: crt@creederep.com. Website: www.creederep.org. **Contact:** Maurice Lamee, producing/artistic director. Play producer. Estab. 1966. Produces 6 plays and 1 musical/year. Performs in 243-seat proscenium theatre; audience is ½ local support and ½ tourist base from Texas, Oklahoma, New Mexico and Colorado. Pays 7% royalty.

How to Contact Query first. Include SASE. Responds in 1 year.

Musical Theater "We prefer historical Western material with cast no larger than 11. Staging must be flexible as space is limited."

Productions *Baby Doe Tabor*, by Kenton Kersting (Colorado history); *A Frog in His Throat*, by

Feydeau, adapted by Eric Conger (French farce); and *Tommyknockers*, by Eric Engdahl, Mark Houston and Chris Thompson (mining).

Tips "Songwriter must have the ability to accept criticism and must be flexible."

☑ ENSEMBLE THEATRE

1127 Vine St., Cincinnati OH 45202. (513)421-3555. Fax: (513)562-4104. E-mail: etcin@aol.com. Website: www.cincyetc.com. **Contact:** D. Lynn Meyers, producing artistic director. Play producer. Estab. 1986. Produces 10 plays and at least 1 musical (1 new musical)/year. Audience is multi-generational and multi-cultural. 191 seats, ¾ stage. Pays 5-8% royalty (negotiable).

How to Contact Query with synopsis, character breakdown and set description or full script. Include SASE. Responds in 6 months.

Musical Theater "All types of musicals are acceptable. Cast not over ten; minimum set, please."

Productions *Hedwig & the Angry Inch*, by John Cameron Mitchel (rock star/transgender/love story); *Alice in Wonderland*, by David Kisor and Joe McDonough (update of the classic tale); and *Frog Princess*, by Joe McDonough and David Kisor (family retelling of classic tale).

Tips Looking for "creative, inventive, contemporary subjects or classic tales. Send materials as complete as possible."

☑ THE GASLIGHT THEATRE

7010 E. Broadway, Tucson AZ 85710. (520)886-9428. Fax: (520)722-6232. E-mail: gaslighttheatre@ gci-net.com. Website: www.gaslighttheatre.info. **Contact:** Bonnie Rexroat, general manager. Play producer. Estab. 1977. Produces 5 musical melodramas (2-3 new musicals)/year. "We cater to family audiences. Our musical melodramas are always fun. Ages from toddlers to senior citizens come to our shows." Performance space is 20'×15' (not including the apron). Pays for outright purchase.

How to Contact Query with synopsis, character breakdown, set description. Submit complete ms and score. Include SASE. Responds in 2 months.

Musical Theater Prefers musical melodramas of 1 hour and 30 minutes; with an olio of 18-20 minutes. "Our shows always have a hero and villain." Cast size is usually 3 women and 5-6 men. Does not wish to see anything violent or sad. "Family entertainment only." Looking for slapstick comedy. "We always use fun sets, i.e., rolling rocks, underwater adventure, camels that move, horses, etc. Our musical melodrama is followed by a themed olio (song and dance show with jokes). Include lots of music to accompany the show."

Productions *The Belle of Tombstone* (western with "Belle" [a woman] trying to battle the bad guys to save her mine); *Prince Valiant or Surely You Joust* (medieval—knight-prince valiant wooing the fair maiden and overcoming the black knight); and *Space Rangers 2025, The Battle for the Galaxy* (Rich Rocket travels in space to save the world from the evil queen Spiderella), all by Peter Van Slyke.

Tips "Think fun and comedy! Our productions always have a villian and a hero. In the conflict the hero always wins. Always fun and family entertainment. Lots of music."

☑ THE WILL GEER THEATRICUM BOTANICUM

P.O. Box 1222, Topanga CA 90290. (310)455-2322. Fax: (310)455-3724. E-mail: info@theatricum.c om. Website: www.theatricum.com. **Contact:** Ellen Geer, artistic director. Literary Director: Isreal Baran. Produces 4 plays, 1 new musical/year. Plays are performed in "large outdoor amphitheater with 60'×25' wooden stage. Rustic setting." Pays negotiable royalty.

How to Contact Query with synopsis, tape of songs and character breakdown. Include SASE. Responds as soon as can be read.

Musical Theater Seeking social or biographical works, and full length musicals with cast of up to 10 equity actors (the rest non-equity). Requires "low budget set and costumes. Union contract." Would also consider original music for use in a play being developed. Does not wish to see "anything promoting avarice, greed, violence or apathy."

Productions *Three Penny Opera*, by Brecht; *Robber Bridegroom*, by VHRY/Waldman (country folktale);

and *Pie in the Sky*, by Alsop (nuclear/3 Mile Island); *Dory, a Musical Portrait*, adapted by Dory Previn and Ellen Greer; *Animal Farm*, adapted by Peter Hall/Richard Peaslee/Adrian Mitchell, etc.

HORIZON THEATRE CO.

P.O. Box 5376, Atlanta GA 31107. (404)523-1477. Fax: (404)584-8815. E-mail: horizonco@mindspring.com. Website: www.horizontheatre.com. **Contact:** Lisa and Jeff Adler, artistic directors. Play producer. Estab. 1983. Produces 4 plays and 1 musical/year. "Our audience is comprised mostly of young professionals looking for contemporary comedy with some social commentary. Our theater features a 185-seat facility with flexible stage." Pays 6-8% royalty.

How to Contact Query with synopsis, character breakdown and set description. Include SASE. Responds in 3 months (to query).

Musical Theater "We prefer musicals that have a significant book and a lot of wit (particularly satire). Our casts are restricted to 10 actors. We prefer plays with equal number of male and female roles, or more female than male roles. We have a limited number of musicians available. No musical revues and no dinner theater fluff. We generally contract with a musician or sound designer to provide sound for each play we produce. If interested send résumé, synopsis, references, tape with music or sound design samples."

Productions *Angry Housewives*, by A.M. Collins/Chad Henry; *A . . . My Name Is Still Alice*, conceived by Julianne Boyd/Joan Micklin Silver; and *The Good Times Are Killing Me*, by Lynda Barry.

Tips "Have patience and use subtle persistence. Work with other theater artists to get a good grasp of the form."

LA JOLLA PLAYHOUSE

P.O. Box 12039, La Jolla CA 92039. (858)550-1070. Fax: (858)550-1075. E-mail: ljp@ucsd.edu. Website: www.lajollaplayhouse.com. **Contact:** Allison Horsley, literary manager. Play producer. Estab. 1947. Produces 5 plays and 1 musical (1-2 new musicals)/year. Audience is University of California students to senior citizens. Performance spaces include a large proscenium theatre with 480 seats and a black box with 450 seats.

How to Contact Query with synopsis, character breakdown. Include SASE. Responds in 9-12 months.

Musical Theater "We prefer contemporary music but not necessarily a story set in contemporary times. Retellings of classic stories can enlighten us about the times we live in. For budgetary reasons, we'd prefer a smaller cast size."

Productions *Dracula, The Musical*, book and lyrics by Don Black and Christopher Hampton, music by Frank Wildhorn (adaptation of Bram Stoker's novel); *Thoroughly Modern Millie*, book by Richard Morris and Dick Scanlan, new music by Jeanine Tesori, new lyrics by Dick Scanlan (based on the 1967 movie); and *Jane Eyre*, book and additional lyrics by John Cairo, music and lyrics by Paul Gordon (adaptation of Charlotte Bronte's novel).

☐ MAGIC THEATRE

Ft. Mason Center, Bldg. D, San Francisco CA 94123. (415)441-8001. Fax: (415)771-5505. E-mail: markr@magictheatre.org. Website: www.magictheatre.org. **Contact:** Mark Routhier, literary manager. Play producer. Estab. 1968. Produces 5-6 plays/year. Audience is educated/intelligent, willing to take risks. Two performance spaces: 155-seat modified thrust and 155-seat proscenium. Pays negotiable royalty.

How to Contact Query with synopsis, character breakdown and set description. "We prefer a smaller cast size, and nothing larger than 7 or 8." Include SASE. Responds in 2 months.

Musical Theater Plays are innovative in form and structure. Chamber musicals are best. Cast size of 6-8. "We have only recently decided to start producing musicals. We are interested in stories with a strong book as well as music." Considers original music for use in a play being developed or for use in a pre-existing play.

Productions *Hillary and Soon Yi Shop for Ties*, by Michelle Carter; *Schrodinger's Girlfriend*, by Matthew Wells; and *First Love*, by Charles Mee, Jr.

MANHATTAN THEATRE CLUB

311 W. 43rd St., 8th Floor, New York NY 10036. (212)399-3030. E-mail: questions@mtc-nyc.org. Website: www.mtc-nyc.org. **Contact:** Clifford Lee Johnson III, director of musical theater program. Associate Artistic Director: Michael Bush. Artistic Director: Lynne Meadow. Play producer. Estab. 1971. Produces 8 plays and sometimes 1 musical/year. Plays are performed at the Manhattan Theatre Club before varied audiences. Pays negotiated fee.

How to Contact Query first. Include SASE. Responds in 4 months.

Musical Theater "Original work."

Productions *A Class Act*, by Ed Kleban/Lonny Price/Linda Kline; *The Wild Party*, by Andrew Lippa; and *Newyorkers*, by Stephen Weiner/Glenn Slater.

Tips "Make sure your script is tightly and securely bound."

MIXED BLOOD THEATRE CO.

1501 S. Fourth St., Minneapolis MN 55454. (612)338-0937. E-mail: czar@mixedblood.com. Website: www.mixedblood.com. **Contact:** David Kunz, script czar. Play producer. Estab. 1976. Produces 4-5 plays/year and perhaps 1 new musical every 2 years. "We have a 200-seat theater in a converted firehouse. The audience spans the socio-economic spectrum." Pays royalty or per performance.

How to Contact Query first (1-page cover letter, 1-page synopsis). Include SASE. Responds on queries in 2 months.

Musical Theater "We want full-length, non-children's works with a message. Always query first. Never send unsolicited script or tape."

Productions *Black Belts II*, musical revue (black female vocalists and their music); *Birth of the Boom* (do-wop/hip-hop extravaganza); and *Vices* (musical sketch revue).

Tips "Always query first. The direct approach is best. Be concise. Make it interesting. Surprise us. Contemporary comedies, politically-edged material and sports-oriented shows are usually of interest."

☑ NEW REPERTORY THEATRE

200 Dexter Ave., Watertown MA 02472. (617)332-1646. Fax: (617)527-5217. E-mail: info@newrep.org. Website: www.NewRep.org. **Contact:** Rick Lombardo, producing artistic director. Play producer. Estab. 1984. Produces 5 plays and 1 musical/year. Audience is Metro-Boston based. Performance space is a state of the art 339 seat proscenium venue in the Arsenal Center for Arts in Watertown, MA (metro-Boston). Pays negotiable royalty.

How to Contact Query with synopsis, character breakdown, CD and set description. Include SASE. Responds in 9 months.

Musical Theater Seeks innovative, dramatic musical material. Unusual stories, small orchestra. Full-length with adult themes. Does not wish to see standard musical comedies.

Productions Musicals: *Sweeney Todd; The Threepenny Opera; Into the Woods; Gifts of The Magi;* and *Moby Dick.*

Tips "Be very clever in theatricality and style. Be unconventional."

NEW YORK STATE THEATRE INSTITUTE

37 First St., Troy NY 12180. (518)274-3200. E-mail: pbs@capital.net. Website: www.nysti.org. **Contact:** Patricia Di Benedetto Snyder, producing artistic director. Play producer. Produces 5 plays (1 new musical)/year. Plays performed for student audiences grades K-12, family audiences and adult audiences. Theater seats 900 with full stage. Pay negotiable.

How to Contact Query with synopsis, character breakdown, set description and tape of songs. Include SASE. *Do not send ms unless invited.* Responds in 6 weeks for synopsis, 4 months for ms.

Musical Theater Looking for "intelligent and well-written book with substance, a score that enhances and supplements the book and is musically well-crafted and theatrical." Length: up to 2 hours. Could be play with music, musical comedy, musical drama. Excellence and substance in material is essential. Cast could be up to 20; orchestra size up to 8.

Productions *A Tale of Cinderella*, by W.A. Frankonis/Will Severin/George David Weiss (adaptation of fairy tale); *The Silver Skates*, by Lanie Robertson/Byron Janis/George David Weiss (adaptation of book); *The Snow Queen,* by Adrian Mitchell/Richard Peaslee (adaptation of fairy tale); and *Magna Carta,* by Ed Lange/Will Severin/George David Weiss (new musical drama).

Tips "There is a great need for musicals that are well-written with intelligence and substance which are suitable for family audiences."

NEW YORK THEATRE WORKSHOP

83 E. Fourth St., New York NY 10003. (212)780-9037. Fax: (212)460-8996. E-mail: info@nytw.org. Website: www.nytw.org. **Contact:** James C. Nicola, artistic director. Play producer. Produces 4-6 mainstage plays and approximately 50 readings/year. "Plays are performed in our theater on East Fourth St. Audiences include: subscription/single ticket buyers from New York area, theater professionals, and special interest groups." Pays by negotiable royalty.

How to Contact Query with synopsis, character breakdown and set description. Include SASE. Responds in 5 months.

Musical Theater "As with our nonmusicals, we seek musicals of intelligence and social consciousness that challenge our perceptions of the world and the events which shape our lives. We favor plays that possess a strong voice, distinctive and innovative use of language and visual imagery. Integration of text and music is particularly of interest. Musicals which require full orchestrations would generally be too big for us. We prefer 'musical theater pieces' rather than straightforward 'musicals' per-se. We often use original music for straight plays that we produce. This music may be employed as pre-show, post-show or interlude music. If the existing piece lends itself, music may also be incorporated within the play itself. Large casts (12 or more) are generally prohibitive and require soliciting of additional funds. Design elements for our productions are of the highest quality possible with our limited funds."

Productions *The Waves,* adapted from Virginia Woolf's novel, music and lyrics by David Bucknam and text and direction by Lisa Peterson; *My Children! My Africa,* by Athol Fugard; and *Rent,* by Jonathan Larson.

Tips "Submit ten pages of the script and a one page synopsis which captures the heart of your piece; inject your piece with a strong voice and intent and try to surprise and excite us."

✓ NORTH SHORE MUSIC THEATRE

P.O. Box 62, Beverly MA 01915. (978)232-7200. Fax: (978)921-6351. Website: www.nsmt.org. **Contact:** John La Rock, associate producer. Play producer. Estab. 1955. Produces 1 Shakespearian play and 6 musicals (2 new musicals)/year. General audiences. Performance space is an 1800-seat arena theatre, 120-seat workshop. Pays royalty (all done via individual commission agreements).

How to Contact Submit synopsis and CD of songs. Include SASE. Responds within 6 months.

Musical Theater Prefers full-length adult pieces not necessarily arena-theatre oriented. Cast sizes from 1-30; orchestra's from 1-16.

Productions *Tom Jones,* by Paul Leigh, George Stiles; *I Sent A Letter to My Love,* by Melissa Manchester and Jeffrey Sweet; *Just So,* by Anthony Drewe & George Stiles (musical based on Rudyard Kipling's fables); *Letters from 'Nam,* by Paris Barclay (Vietnam War experience as told through letters from GI's); and *Friendship of the Sea,* by Michael Wartofsky & Kathleen Cahill (New England maritime adventure musical).

Tips "Keep at it!"

✓ ODYSSEY THEATRE ENSEMBLE

P.O. Box 1315, Gilroy CA 95021. (310)477-2055. Fax: (310)444-0455. E-mail: info@odysseytheatre. org. Website: www.odysseytheatre.org. **Contact:** Sally Essex-Lopresti, director of literary programs. Play producer. Estab. 1969. Produces 9 plays and 1 musical (1-2 new musicals)/year. Pays negotiable royalty.

How to Contact Query with synopsis, character breakdown, 8-10 pages of libretto, cassette of music and set description. Query should include résumé(s) of artist(s) and tape of music. Include SASE. "Unsolicited material is not read or screened at all." Responds to query in 2 weeks; ms in 6 months.

Musical Theater "We want nontraditional forms and provocative, unusual, challenging subject matter. We are not looking for Broadway-style musicals. Comedies should be highly stylized or highly farcical. Works should be full-length only and not requiring a complete orchestra (small band preferred). Political material and satire are great for us. We're seeking interesting musical concepts and approaches. The more traditional Broadway-style musicals will generally not be done by the Odyssey. If we have a work in development that needs music, original music will often be used. In such a case, the writer and composer would work together during the development phase. In the case of a pre-existing play, the concept would originate with the director who would select the composer.''

☑ THE OPEN EYE THEATER
P.O. Box 959, 1000 Main St., Margaretville NY 12455. E-mail: openeye@catskill.net. Website: www. theopeneye.org. **Contact:** Amie Brockway, producing artistic director. Play producer. Estab. 1972. Produces approximately 3 full length or 3 new plays for multi-generational audiences. Pays on a fee basis.

How to Contact Query first. "A manuscript will be accepted and read only if it is a play for all ages and is: 1) Submitted by a recognized literary agent; 2) Requested or recommended by a staff or company member; or 3) Recommended by a professional colleague with whose work we are familiar. Playwrights may submit a one-page letter of inquiry including a very brief plot synopsis. Please enclose a self-addressed (but not stamped) envelope. We will reply only if we want you to submit the script (within several months).''

Musical Theater "The Open Eye Theater is a not-for-profit professional company working in a community context. Through the development, production and performance of plays for all ages, artists and audiences are challenged and given the opportunity to grow in the arts. In residence, on tour, and in the classroom, The Open Eye Theater strives to stimulate, educate, entertain, inspire and serve as a creative resource.''

Productions *Twelfth Night or What You Will*, by William Shakespeare, music by Michael Anthony Worden; *The Wide Awake Princess*, adapted by David Paterson from the novel by Katherine Paterson, with music and lyrics by Steve Liebman; and *Pixies, Kings and Magical Things*, by Hans Christian Anderson, adapted by Ric Aver (four children's tales).

PLAYWRIGHTS' ARENA
514 S. Spring St., Los Angeles CA 90013. (213)485-1631. E-mail: jrivera@juno.com. Website: www. playwrightsarena.org. **Contact:** Jon Lawrence Rivera, artistic director. Play producer. Estab. 1992. Produces 3 plays and 1 musical (1 new musical)/year. Audience is in their early 20s to 50s. Performance space is 26' deep × 30' wide proscenium stage with fly system. Pays 6% royalty.

How to Contact Submit complete manuscript, score and tape of songs. Include SASE. Responds in 6 months.

Musical Theater Seeking new musicals like *Rent*. Does not want old fashioned musicals.

Productions *Red Hat and Tales*, by Nick Salamone; *Palm Fever*, by Jean Colonomos; *The Orange Grove*, by Tom Jacobson.

☑ PLAYWRIGHTS HORIZONS
416 W. 42nd St., New York NY 10036. (212)564-1235. Fax: (212)594-0296. E-mail: literary@playwri ghtshorizons.org. Website: www.playwrightshorizons.org. **Contact:** Christie Evangelista, assistant literary manager. Artistic Director: Tim Sanford. Musical Theatre. Play producer. Estab. 1971. Produces about 5 plays and 1 new musical/year. "Adventurous New York City theater-going audience.'' Pays general Off-Broadway contract.

How to Contact Submit complete manuscript and tape or CD of songs. Attn: Musical Theater Program. Include SASE. Responds in 8 months.

Musical Theater American writers. "No revivals, one-acts or children's shows; otherwise we're flexible. We have a particular interest in scores with a distinctively contemporary and American flavor. We generally develop work from scratch; we're open to proposals for shows and scripts in early stages of development.''

Productions *My Life with Albertine*, by Richard Nelson, Ricky Ian Gordon (adapted from Proust's "In Search of Lost Time"); *Wilder*, by Erin Cressida Wilson, Mike Craver, Jack Herrick (growing up in the Depression); and *The Spitfire Grill*, by James Valcq/Fred Alley (adapted from the movie).

PRIMARY STAGES

131 W. 45th St., 2nd Floor, New York NY 10036. (212)840-9705. Fax: (212)840-9725. E-mail: info@primarystages.com. Website: www.primarystages.com. **Contact:** Tyler Marchant, associate artistic director. Play producer. Estab. 1984. Produces 4-5 plays/year. "New York theater-going audience representing a broad cross-section, in terms of age, ethnicity, and economic backgrounds. 99-seat, Off-Broadway theater."

How to Contact Query first with synopsis, character breakdown, set description and tape. "No unsolicited scripts accepted. Submissions by agents only." Include SASE. Responds in up to 8 months.

Musical Theater "We are looking for work of heightened theatricality, that challenges realism—musical plays that go beyond film and televisions standard fare. We are looking for small cast shows under 6 characters total, with limited sets. We are interested in original works, that have not been produced in New York."

Productions *I Sent a Letter to My Love*, by Melissa Manchester/Jeffrey Sweet; and *Nightmare Alley*, by Jonathan Brielle.

THE REPERTORY THEATRE OF ST. LOUIS

P.O. Box 191730, 130 Edgar Road, St. Louis MO 63119. (314)968-7340. E-mail: mail@repstl.org. Website: www.repstl.org/. **Contact:** Susan Gregg, associate artistic director. Play producer. Estab. 1966. Produces 9 plays and 1 or 2 musicals/year. "Conservative regional theater audience. We produce all our work at the Loretto Hilton Theatre." Pays by royalty.

How to Contact Query with synopsis, character breakdown and set description. Does not return material. Responds in 2 years.

Musical Theater "We want plays with a small cast and simple setting. No children's shows or foul language. After a letter of inquiry we would prefer script and demo tape."

Productions *Almost September* and *Esmeralda*, by David Schechter and Steve Lutvak; *Jack*, by Barbara Field and Hiram Titus; and *Young Rube*, by John Pielmeier and Nattie Selman.

☑ SHAKESPEARE SANTA CRUZ

Theater Arts Center, U.C.S.C., 1156 High Street, Santa Cruz CA 95064. (831)459-2121. Fax: (831)459-3316. E-mail: iago@cats.ucsc.edu. Website: www.shakespearesantacruz.org. **Contact:** Paul Whitworth, artistic director. Play producer. Estab. 1982. Produces 4 plays/year. Performance spaces are an outdoor redwood grove; and an indoor 540-seat thrust. Pay is negotiable.

How to Contact Query first. Include SASE. Responds in 2 months.

Musical Theater "Shakespeare Santa Cruz produces musicals in its Winter Holiday Season (Oct-Dec). We are also interested in composers' original music for pre-existing plays—including songs, for example, for Shakespeare's plays."

Productions *Cinderella*, by Kate Hawley (book and lyrics) and Gregg Coffin (composer); and *Gretel and Hansel*, by Kate Hawley (book and lyrics) and composer Craig Bohmler (both are British pantomime treatment of fairy tale).

Tips "Always contact us before sending material."

☑ ◻ SHENANDOAH INTERNATIONAL PLAYWRIGHTS

10169 Woodlawn Dr., Portage MI 49002. (269)492-8182. E-mail: sip@ntelos.net. **Contact:** Robert G. Small, artistic director. Play producer. Estab. 1976. Develops 10-12 plays/year for family audience.

How to Contact Submit 2 copies complete manuscript, score and tape of songs. Include SASE and bio/résumé. Responds in 4 months.

Tips "Submit full materials by February 1."

STAGE ONE

501 W. Main St., Louisville KY 40202. (502)562-0100. Fax: (502)562-0750. E-mail: stageone@stageone.org. Website: www.stageone.org. **Contact:** J. Daniel Herring, artistic director. Play producer. Estab. 1946. Produces 7-8 plays and 0-2 new plays or musicals/year. "Audience is mainly young people ages 5-18, teachers and families." Pays 5-7% royalty.

How to Contact Submit letter with new play/musical idea and short treament/synopsis to the artistic director.

Musical Theater "We seek stageworthy and respectful dramatizations of the classic tales of childhood, both ancient and modern as well as original works about the human condition. Ideally, the plays are relevant to young people and their families, as well as related to school curriculum. Cast is rarely more than 12."

Productions *Come Sing Jimmy*, by David Paterson/Mark J. Thompson (bluegrass musical); *Trials: The Life of Joan of Arc*, by James DeVita (classic w/modern twist); and *Miss Nelson is Missing*, by Joan Cushing (modern musical).

Tips "Stage One does not accept unsolicited manuscripts. We commission one or two new works each season that meet our artistic objectives. Cast size is not a factor, although, in practice, Stage One rarely employs casts of over 12."

STAGES REPERTORY THEATRE

3201 Allen Parkway, Houston TX 77019. (713)527-0220. Fax: (713)527-8669. E-mail: rbundy@stage stheatre.com. Website: www.stagestheatre.com. **Contact:** Rob Bundy, artistic director. Play producer. Estab. 1979. Produces 6 plays and 1 musical/year. Performance space includes 170-seat thrust and 230-arena theatre. Pays negotiable royalty.

How to Contact Query with synopsis, character breakdown and set description. Include SASE. Responds in 7 months.

Musical Theatre Prefers edgy, theatrical, non-realistic stories, with a maximum cast size of 10, and single unit set with multiple locations.

Productions *Nixon's Nixon*, by Russell Lees; *Funny Girl*, by Jules Styne; and *The Pitchfork Disney*, by Philip Ridley.

SWINE PALACE PRODUCTIONS

The Reilly Theatre, Tower Dr.—LSU, Baton Rouge LA 70803. (225)578-3533. Fax: (225)578-9279. E-mail: info@swinepalace.org. Website: www.swinepalace.com. **Contact:** Kristin Sosnowsky, managing director. Play producer. Estab. 1991. Produces 3 productions/year. "Swine's audience is made up of the community of Louisiana which ranges from the upper-lower classes. Many college and high school students. Not for the blue-haired group. The brand new Reilly theatre is a traverse stage with an earth floor converted from an old livestock judging/viewing pavillion (hence "Swine" Palace). Audience sits across from each other a la stadium seating. 488 seats and one of the largest performing stages in North America. Truly unique, bold and original." Pay negotiated with the artistic staff.

How to Contact Submit complete ms, score and tape of songs. Include SASE. Responds in 6 months if interested.

Musical Theater "Swine Palace's commitment is to new work reflects the Deep South experience. Work must contain substance. No light musical comedies based on trite gimmicks. The Reilly theatre is an epic space and lends itself to large cast productions (i.e., operas are perfectly acceptable). Large casts are acceptable." Does not want works that are in no way related to the Deep South experience. Interested in musicals "that are new and rock. 5-7 piece instrumentation is best. Innovative, original and possibly dangerous material."

Productions *A Midsummer Night's Dream*, by Shakespeare; *Gumbo Ya-Ya*, by Swine Palace Company (adaptation with music of book from 1940s Federal writer's project); *Four Joans and a Fire-Eater*, by Elizabeth Dewberry (reexamination of folk-lore, 3 women and 1 drag queen in New Orleans discover that they were all Joan of Arc in a former life—new play premiered at Swine); and *Jesus Christ Superstar*, by Andrew Lloyd Weber (fall 2000).

Tips "Love the art in yourself not yourself in the art. Don't be afraid of work. Take the work seriously but not yourself. André du Broc, music director for Swine Palace has been composing scores for Swine since 1993. His work focuses on use of music as the supporting cast member in the productions. Live music is almost always an essential part in all of Swine Palace's work whether it be Shakespeare or Beckett. Songs and original scoring are always included in our season and audiences expect excellence in our musical support. Intelligent music based on support of the text that has been worked in through the production process is a must. Composers do not 'phone in' our scores but work alongside the design team during the production process."

✅ TADA!

150 W. 28th St., 3rd Floor, New York NY 10001. (212)252-1619. Fax: (212)252-8763. E-mail: info@tadatheater.com. Website: www.tadatheater.com. **Contact:** Janine Nina Trevens, artistic director. Play producer. Estab. 1984. Produces 4 staged readings and 2-4 new musicals/year. "TADA! is a company producing works performed by children ages 8-18 for family audiences in New York City. Performances run approximately 45 to an hour. Pays varying royalty.

- Also see the listing for Free Staged Reading Series Playwriting Competition in the Contests and Awards section.

How to Contact Submit complete manuscript with synopsis, character breakdown, score and tape of songs. Include SASE. Responds in 1 year.

Musical Theater "We do not produce plays as full productions. At this point, we do staged readings of plays. We produce original commissioned musicals written specifically for the company."

Productions *The History Mystery*, by Janine Nina Trevens (kids time traveling through history); *New York New Year*, by Gary Bagley (a young midwestern girl discovers New York and herself); and *Golly Gee Whiz*, by Erick Rockwell (based on the "Mickey & Judy" film classics).

Tips "Musical playwrights should concentrate on themes and plots meaningful to children and their families as well as consider our young actors' abilities and talents as well. Vocal ranges of children 7-17 should be strongly considered when writing the score."

THE TEN-MINUTE MUSICALS PROJECT

P.O. Box 461194, West Hollywood CA 90046. E-mail: info@tenminutemusicals.org. Website: www.tenminutemusicals.org. **Contact:** Michael Koppy, producer. Play producer. Estab. 1987. All pieces are new musicals. Pays $250 advance.

How to Contact Submit complete manuscript, score and tape of songs. Include SASE. Responds in 3 months.

Musical Theater Seeks complete short stage musicals of 8-15 minutes in length. Maximum cast: 9. "No parodies—original music only."

Productions *Away to Pago Pago*, by Jack Feldman/Barry Manilow/John PiRoman/Bruce Sussman; *The Bottle Imp*, by Kenneth Vega (from the story of the same title by Robert Louis Stevenson); and *The Furnished Room*, by Saragail Katzman (from the story of the same title by O. Henry).

Tips "Start with a *solid* story—either an adaptation or an original idea—but with a solid beginning, middle and end (probably with a plot twist at the climax). We caution that it will surely take much time and effort to create a quality work. (Occasionally a clearly talented and capable writer and composer seem to have almost 'dashed' something off, under the misperception that inspiration can carry the day in this format. Works selected in previous rounds all clearly evince that considerable deliberation and craft were invested.) We're seeking short contemporary musical theater material, in the style of what might be found on Broadway, Off-Broadway or the West End. Think of shows like *Candide* or *Little Shop of Horrors*, pop operas like *Sweeney Todd* or *Chess*, or chamber musicals like *Once on this Island* or *Falsettos*. (Even small accessible operas like *The Telephone* or *Trouble in Tahiti* are possible models.) All have solid plots, and all rely on sung material to advance them. Of primary importance is to start with a strong story, even if it means postponing work on music and lyrics until the dramatic foundation is complete."

✅ THEATRE THREE, INC.

2800 Routh St., Suite 168, Dallas TX 75201. (214)871-3300. Fax: (214)871-3139. E-mail: admin@theatre3dallas.com. Website: www.theatre3dallas.com. **Contact:** Terry Dobson, musical director. Artistic Director: Jac Alder. Play producer. Estab. 1961. Produces 10-12 plays and 3-4 musicals (1 or 2 new musicals)/year. "Subscription audience of 4,500 enjoys adventurous, sophisticated musicals." Performance space is an "arena stage (modified). Seats 250 per performance. Quite an intimate space." Pays varying royalty.

How to Contact *Submit through agent only*. Include SASE. Responds in 2 months.

Musical Theater "Off the wall topics. We have, in the past, produced *Little Shop of Horrors, Angry Housewives, Sweeney Todd, Groucho, A Life in Revue, The Middle of Nowhere* (a Randy Newman revue) and *A . . . My Name Is Alice*. We prefer small cast shows, but have done shows with a cast as large as 15. Orchestrations can be problematic. We usually do keyboards and percussion or some variation. Some shows can be a design problem; we cannot do 'spectacle.' Our audiences generally like good, intelligent musical properties. Very contemporary language is about the only thing that sometimes causes 'angst' among our subscribers. We appreciate honesty and forthrightness . . . and good material done in an original and creative manner."

Productions *A Class Act*, by Ed Kleban, Lonny Price & Linda Klein; *Beguiled Again*, the songs of Rodgers & Hart; *Bat Boy, The Musical*, by Farley, Flemming & O'Keefe.

✅ THEATRE WEST VIRGINIA

P.O. Box 1205, Beckley WV 25802. (800)666-9142. E-mail: contact@theaterwestvirginia.com. Website: www.theatrewestvirginia.com. **Contact:** Marina Honley, artistic director. Play producer. Estab. 1955. Produces 5 plays and 2 musicals/year. "Audience varies from mainstream summer stock to educational tours (ages K-high school)." Pays 3-6% royalty, negotiable.

How to Contact Query with synopsis, character breakdown and set description; should include cassette tape. Include SASE. Responds in 3 months.

Musical Theater "Theatre West Virginia is a year-round performing arts organization that presents a variety of productions including community performances and statewide educational programs on primary, elementary and secondary levels. This is in addition to our summer, outdoor dramas of *Hatfields & McCoys* and *Honey in the Rock*, now in their 43rd year." Anything suitable for school tours. No more than 6 in cast. Play should be able to be accompanied by piano/synthesizer.

Productions *The Apple Tree*, by Sheldon Harnick and Jerry Bock (used for educational tour grades 7th-12th); *The Tinderbox*, by Mark LaPierre (musical adaptation, used for educational tour grades K-6th); and *The Sound of Music*, by Rodgers & Hammerstein.

THEATREWORKS/USA

151 W. 26th St., 7th Floor, New York NY 10001. (212)647-1100. Fax: (212)924-5377. Website: www.theatreworksusa.org. Literary Manager: Michael Alltop. Play producer. Produces 10-13 plays, most are musicals (3-4 are new musicals)/year. Audience consists of children and families. Pays 6% royalty and aggregate of $1,500 commission-advance against future royalties.

How to Contact Query with synopsis, character breakdown and sample scene and song. Include SASE. Responds in 6 months.

Musical Theater "One hour long, 5-6 adult actors, highly portable, good musical theater structure; adaptations of children's literature, historical or biographical musicals, issues, fairy tales—all must have something to say. We demand a certain level of literary sophistication. No kiddy shows, no camp, no fractured fables, no shows written for school or camp groups to perform. Approach your material, not as a writer writing for kids, but as a writer addressing any universal audience. You have one hour to entertain, say something, make them care—don't preach, condescend. Don't forget an antagonist. Don't waste the audience's time. We always use original music—but most of the time a project team comes complete with a composer in tow."

Productions *Island of the Blue Dolphins*, book/lyrics by Beth Blatt, music by Jennifer Giering (literary adaptation); *The Mystery of King Tut*, book/lyrics by Mindi Dickstein, music by Dan Messe (original historical); *Gold Rush!*, book by David Armstrong, music by Dick Gallagher, lyrics by Mark Waldrop (original historical); and *Sarah, Plain and Tall*, book by Julia Jordan, music by Larry O'Keefe, and lyrics by Nell Benjamin.

Tips "Write a good show! Make sure the topic is something we can market! Come see our work to find out our style."

✅ VIRGINIA STAGE COMPANY

P.O. Box 3770, Norfolk VA 23514. (757)627-1234. Fax: (757)628-5958. E-mail: channa@vastage.com. Website: www.vastage.com. **Contact:** Chris Hanna, artistic director. Play producer. Estab. 1978. Produces 7-10 plays and 1-2 musicals (0-1 new musical)/year. "We have a diverse audience.

As home to a large, well-traveled population from NATO and the U.S. Navy, we serve many sophisticated theatregoers as well as those for whom theatre is not yet a habit. Located in Southeastern Virginia, we also play to a number of people from Southern backgrounds.'' Performance space is a 670-seat, Beaux-Arts proscenium theatre built in 1913—a national historic landmark. This hemp house features a proscenium opening 36' wide and 28' high with a stage depth of 28'. Pay is negotiable.

How to Contact Query with synopsis, character breakdown and set description. Include SASE. Responds in 6 months.

Musical Theater "We have produced the world premieres of *The Secret Garden* and *Snapshots* (with music by Stephen Schwartz). Our tastes are eclectic and have covered a number of styles. We have recently expanded our programming for young audiences.'' At this time, shows with less than 20 in the cast have a better chance of production. They have commissioned original music and adaptations for plays including *Hamlet, Twelfth Night, Terra Nova* and *A Christmas Carol.*

Productions *Appalachian Strings*, by Randal Myler/Dan Wheetman (social history of the Appalachian region); *Snapshots*, by David Stern/Michael Scheman, music by Stephen Schwartz (a middle-aged couple trying to save their marriage); *Twelfth Night*, by Shakespeare (set in 18th century Ireland with live musicians playing Celtic music); and *Blues in the Night*, by Sheldon Epps.

Tips "Be patient. We review material as quickly as possible. It also takes time to establish the relationships and resources needed to lead us into full, top-quality productions.''

WALNUT STREET THEATRE

825 Walnut St., Philadelphia PA 19107. (215)574-3550, ext. 515. Fax: (215)574-3598. E-mail: wstpc @wstonline.org. Website: www.wstonline.org. **Contact:** Literary Office. Play producer. Estab. 1809. Produces 7 plays and 3 musicals/year. Plays produced on a mainstage with seating for 1,078; and in studio theaters with seating for 90. Pays by royalty or outright purchase.

How to Contact *Unsolicited scripts accepted with professional reference/recommendation only.*

Musical Theater "We seek musicals with lyrical non-operatic scores and a solid book. We are looking for a small musical for springtime and one for a family audience at Christmas time. We remain open on structure and subject matter and would expect a tape with the script. Cast size: around 20 equity members (10 for smaller musical); preferably one set with variations." Would consider original music for incidental music and/or underscore. This would be at each director's discretion.

Productions *She Loves Me*, Jerry Bock, music/Sheldon Harnick (musical); *The Sound of Music*, Richard Rodgers, music/Oscar Hammerstein II, lyrics (musical); *Evita* (scheduled for Spring 2003), Andrew Lloyd Webber, music/Tim Rice, lyrics (musical).

WEST COAST ENSEMBLE

P.O. Box 38728, Los Angeles CA 90038. (323)876-9337. E-mail: WCEmusicalstairs@aol.com. Website: www.wcensemble.org. **Contact:** Les Hanson, artistic director. Play producer. Estab. 1982. Produces 4-8 plays and 1 new musical/year. "Our audience is a wide variety of Southern Californians. Plays will be produced in our theater in Hollywood." Pays $35-50 per performance.

 • See the listing for West Coast Ensemble—Musical Stairs in the Contests & Awards section of this book.

How to Contact Submit complete manuscript, score and tape of songs. Include SASE. Responds in 8 months.

Musical Theater "There are no limitations on subject matter or style. Cast size should be no more than 12 and sets should be simple. If music is required we would commission a composer; music would be used as a bridge between scenes or to underscore certain scenes in the play.''

Productions *Cabaret, Merrily We Roll Along* and *A New Brain.*

Tips "Submit work in good form and be patient. We look for musicals with a strong book and an engaging score with a variety of styles.''

WEST END ARTISTS

18034 Ventura Blvd. #291, Encino CA 91316. (818)623-0040. Fax: (818)623-0202. E-mail: egaynes@ aol.com. **Contact:** Pamela Hall, associate artistic director. Artistic Director: Edmund Gaynes. Play

producer. Estab. 1983. Produces 5 plays and 3 new musicals/year. Audience "covers a broad spectrum, from general public to heavy theater/film/TV industry crowds. Pays 6% royalty.
How to Contact Submit complete manuscript, score and tape of songs. Include SASE. Responds in 3 months.
Musical Theater "Prefer small-cast musicals and revues. Full length preferred. Interested in children's shows also." Cast size: "Maximum 12; exceptional material with larger casts will be considered."
Productions *The Taffetas*, by Rick Lewis ('50s nostalgia, received 3 Ovation Award nominations); *Songs the Girls Sang*, by Alan Palmer (songs written for women now sung by men, received 1 Ovation Award nomination); *Crazy Words, Crazy Tunes* (played 2 years to Los Angeles and nationwide).
Tips "If you feel every word or note you have written is sacred and chiseled in stone and are unwilling to work collaboratively with a professional director, don't bother to submit."

☑ WESTBETH THEATRE CENTER
111 W. 17th St., 3rd Floor, New York NY 10011. (212)691-2272. Fax: (212)924-7185. E-mail: general @westbethent.com. Website: www.westbethent.com. **Contact:** Jill Beckman, executive assistant. Producing Director: Arnold Engleman. Play producer. Estab. 1977. Produces 1-2 musicals/year. Audience consists of artists, New York professionals and downtown theater goers. "We have five performance spaces, including a music hall and cafe theater." Pay varies. Uses usual New York showcase contract.
How to Contact Query with résumé, one page project proposal—or one page synopsis with cast and production requirements for scripted plays and any relevant audiovisual material. Include SASE. Does not return material from outside the US. Responds in 3 months. "Artists must reside in NYC or surrounding areas and be desirous of extensive development and intense collaboration."
Musical Theater "The New Works Program has expanded its focus to include performance proposals from a range of various disciplines including dancers, playwrights, musicians, and other performance artists. Proposals should be sharp, urban, and contemporary—period pieces or plays set in rural/regional locales will not be considered.
Productions *20th Century Man*, by Ray Davies (bio of rock group The Kinks); *Almost Famous*, by Bruce Vilanch; and *Exactly Like You*, by Cy Coleman/E. Hutchner (musical comedy).
Tips "Be open to the collaborative effort. We are a professional theater company, competing in the competitive world of Broadway and off-Broadway, so the work we present must reach for the highest standard of excellence."

THE WILMA THEATER
265 S. Broad St., Philadelphia PA 19107. (215)893-9456. Fax: (215)893-0895. E-mail: info@wilmath eater.org. Website: www.wilmatheater.org. **Contact:** Walter Bilderback, literary manager. Play producer. Produces 4 shows/year. Performance space is a 300-seat, state of the art proscenium theater, with full fly system and large backstage area. Pays royalty negotiated between managing director and agent.
How to Contact Submit through agent only. Include SASE. Responds in 6 months.
Musical Theater "We seek to produce the most adventurous work possible. Because this is a director-driven theater, the full-length projects must pose creative challenges that engage the imaginations of our two artistic directors. The eclectic tastes of the artistic directors make it almost impossible to identify specific styles or topics. We look for work that is original, bold, challenging and stimulating."
Productions *Bed and Sofa*, by Polly Pen/Laurence Klavan; *Tin Pan Alley Rag*, by Mark Saltzman; and *Threepenny Opera*, by Brecht/Weill.
Tips "Please be familiar with the Wilma's production history before submitting your material."

WINGS THEATRE CO.
154 Christopher St., New York NY 10014. (212)627-2960. Fax: (212)462-0024. E-mail: jcorrick@win gstheatre.com. Website: www.wingstheatre.com. **Contact:** Tricia Gilbert, literary manager. Artistic

Director: Jeffrey Corrick. Play producer. Estab. 1987. Produces 3-5 plays and 3-5 musicals/year. Performance space is a 74-seat O.O.B. proscenium; repertoire includes a New Musicals Series, a gay-play series—we produce musicals in both series. Pays $100 for limited rights to produce against 6% of gross box office receipts.

How to Contact Submit complete manuscript, score and tape of songs (score is not essential). Include SASE. Responds in 1 year.

Musical Theater "Eclectic. Entertaining. Enlightening. This is an O.O.B. theater. Funds are limited." Does not wish to see "movies posing as plays. Television theater."

Productions *Scott & Zelda*, by Dave Bates (The Fitzgeralds); *Cowboys*, by Clint Jefferies (gay western spoof); and *The Three Musketeers*, by Clint Jefferies (musical adaptation).

Tips "Book needs to have a well-developed plot line and interesting, fully-realized characters. We place emphasis on well-written scripts, as opposed to shows which rely exclusively on the quality of the music to carry the show. Also be patient—we often hold onto plays for a full year before making a final decision."

WOOLLY MAMMOTH THEATRE
641D. St. NW, Washington DC 20004. (202)312-5270. E-mail: mary@woollymammoth.net. Website: www.woollymammoth.net. **Contact:** Mary Resing, literary manager. Play producer. Estab. 1978. Produces 5 plays/year. Royalties vary.

How to Contact *Submit through agent only.* We do not accept unsolicited manuscripts. Include SASE. Responds in 6 months.

Musical Theater "We do unusual works, including musicals and plays with music. We do not wish to see one-acts."

Productions *The Dark Kalamazoo*, by Oni Faida Lampley (coming of age/trip to Sierra Leone with African-based music); *Wanted*, by All Carmines (musical comedy about the FBI's golden years under J. Edgar Hoover); *The Rocky Horror Picture Show*.

Tips "Know what we do. Read or see our plays."

PLAY PUBLISHERS

ARAN PRESS
1036 S. Fifth St., Louisville KY 40203. (502)568-6622. Fax: (502)561-1124. E-mail: aranpres@aye.net. Website: http://members.aye.net/ ~ aranpres. **Contact:** Tom Eagan, editor/publisher. Play publisher. Estab. 1983. Publishes 5-10 plays and 1-2 musicals/year. Professional, college/university, community, summer stock and dinner theater audience. Pays 50% production royalty or 10% book royalty.

How to Contact Submit manuscript, score and tape of songs. Include SASE. Responds in 2 weeks.

Musical Theater "The musical should include a small cast, simple set for professional, community, college, university, summer stock and dinner theater production."

Publications *Whiskey & Wheaties*, by Bruce Feld; *Who Says Life is Fair*, by Mike Willis; and *Burning Bridges*, by Stephen Avery.

BAKER'S PLAYS
P.O. Box 699222, Quincy MA 02269-9222. (617)745-0805. Fax: (617)745-9891. E-mail: info@bakersplays.com. Website: www.bakersplays.com. **Contact:** Associate Editor. Play publisher. Estab. 1845. Publishes 15-22 plays and 0-3 new musicals/year. Plays are used by children's theaters, junior and senior high schools, colleges and community theaters. Pays negotiated book and production royalty.

• See the listing for Baker's Plays High School Playwriting Contest in the Contests & Awards section.

How to Contact Submit complete manuscript, score and cassette tape of songs. Include SASE. Responds in 4 months.

Musical Theater "Seeking musicals for teen production and children's theater production. We prefer large cast, contemporary musicals which are easy to stage and produce. Plot your shows strongly, keep your scenery and staging simple, your musical numbers and choreography easily explained and blocked out. Music must be camera-ready.'' Would consider original music for use in a play being developed or in a pre-existing play.

Productions *Oedipus/A New Magical Comedy*, by Bob Johnson.

Tips ''As we publish musicals that can be produced by high school theater departments with high school talent, the writer should know if their play can be done on the high school stage. I recommend that the writer go to performances of original high school musicals whenever possible.''

CONTEMPORARY DRAMA SERVICE

885 Elkton Dr., Colorado Springs CO 80907. (719)594-4422. E-mail: merpcds@aol.com. Website: www.contemporarydrama.com. **Contact:** Arthur Zapel, associate editor. Play publisher. Estab. 1979. Publishes 40-50 plays and 4-6 new musicals/year. ''We publish for young children and teens in mainstream Christian churches and for teens and college level in the secular market. Our musicals are performed in churches, schools and colleges.'' Pays 10-50% book and performance royalty.

How to Contact *Query first* then submit complete manuscript, score and tape of songs. Include SASE. Responds in 1 month.

Musical Theater ''For churches we publish musical programs for children and teens to perform at Easter, Christmas or some special occasion. Our school musicals are for teens to perform as class plays or special entertainments. Cast size may vary from 15-25 depending on use. We prefer more parts for girls than boys. Music must be written in the vocal range of teens. Staging should be relatively simple but may vary as needed. We are not interested in elementary school material. Elementary level is OK for church music but not public school elementary. Music must have full piano accompaniment and be professionally scored for camera-ready publication.''

Publications *Lucky, Lucky Hudson and the 12th Street Gang*, by Tim Kelly, book, and Bill Francoeur, music and lyrics (spoof of old time gangster movies); *Is There A Doctor in the House?*, by Tim Kelly, book, and Bill Francoeur, music and lyrics (adapted from Moliere comedy); and *Jitterbug Juliet*, by Mark Dissette, book, and Bill Francoeur, music and lyrics (spoof of *Romeo and Juliet*).

Tips ''Familiarize yourself with our market. Send $1 postage for catalog. Try to determine what would fit in, yet still be unique.''

THE DRAMATIC PUBLISHING COMPANY

311 Washington St., Woodstock IL 60098. (815)338-7170. E-mail: plays@dramaticpublishing.com. Website: dramaticpublishing.com. **Contact:** Linda Habjan, acquisitions editor. Play publisher. Publishes 35 plays and 3-5 musicals/year. Estab. 1885. Plays used by professional and community theaters, schools and colleges. Pays negotiable royalty.

How to Contact Submit complete manuscript, score and tape of songs. Include SASE. Responds in 3 months.

Musical Theater Seeking ''children's musicals not over $1\frac{1}{4}$ hours, and adult musicals with 2 act format. No adaptations for which the rights to use the original work have not been cleared. If directed toward high school market, large casts with many female roles are preferred. For professional, stock and community theater small casts are better. Cost of producing a play is always a factor to consider in regard to costumes, scenery and special effects.'' Would also consider original music for use in a pre-existing play, ''if we or the composer hold the rights to the non-musical work.''

Publications *The Little Prince*, by Rick Cummins/John Scoullar; *Hans Brinker*, by Gayle Hudson/Bobbe Bramson; and *Bubbe Meises, Bubbe Stories*, by Ellen Gould/Holly Gewandter (all are full-length family musicals).

Tips ''A complete score, ready to go is highly recommended. Tuneful songs which stand on their own are a must. Good subject matter which has wide appeal is always best but not required.''

ELDRIDGE PUBLISHING CO., INC.

P.O. Box 14367, Tallahassee FL 32317. (800)HI-STAGE. E-mail: info@histage.com. Website: www.histage.com. **Contact:** Susan Shore, musical editor. Play publisher. Estab. 1906. Publishes 50 plays and 1-2 musicals/year. Seeking ''large cast musicals which appeal to students. We like variety and originality in the music, easy staging and costuming. Also looking for children's theater musicals which have smaller casts and are easy to tour. We serve the school market (6th grade through 12th); and church market (Christmas musicals)." Pays 50% royalty and 10% copy sales in school market.

How to Contact Submit manuscript, score or lead sheets and CD of songs. Include SASE. Responds in 1 month.

Publications *The Bard is Back*, by Stephen Murray ("a high school's production of Romeo & Juliet is a disaster!"); and *Boogie-Woogie Bugle Girls*, book by Craig Sodaro, music and lyrics by Stephen Murray (WWII themed musical).

Tips "We're always looking for talented composers but not through individual songs. We're only interested in complete school or church musicals. Lead sheets, CDs tape and script are best way to submit. Let us see your work!"

THE FREELANCE PRESS

P.O. Box 548, Dover MA 02030. (508)785-8250. E-mail: info@freelancepress.org. Website: www.freelancepress.org. Managing Editor: Narcissa Campion. Play publisher. Estab. 1979. Publishes up to 3 new musicals/year. "Pieces are primarily to be acted by elementary/middle school to high school students (9th and 10th grades); large casts (approximately 30); plays are produced by schools and children's theaters." Pays 10% of purchase price of script or score, 50% of collected royalty.

How to Contact Query first. Include SASE. Responds in 6 months.

Musical Theater "We publish previously produced musicals and plays to be acted by children in the primary grades through high school. Plays are for large casts (approximately 30 actors and speaking parts) and run between 45 minutes to 1 hour and 15 minutes. Subject matter should be contemporary issues (sibling rivalry, friendship, etc.) or adaptations of classic literature for children (*Syrano de Bergerac, Rip Van Winkle, Pied Piper, Treasure Island*, etc.). We do not accept any plays written for adults to perform for children."

Publications *Tortoise vs. Hare*, by Stephen Murray (modern version of classic); *Tumbleweed*, by Sebastian Stuart (sleepy time western town turned upside down); and *Mything Links*, by Sam Abel (interweaving of Greek myths with a great pop score).

Tips "We enjoy receiving material that does not condescend to children. They are capable of understanding many current issues, playing complex characters, handling unconventional material, and singing difficult music."

SAMUEL FRENCH, INC.

45 W. 25th St., New York NY 10010. (212)206-8990. Fax: (212)206-1429. Website: www.samuelfrench.com. Hollywood office: 7623 Sunset Blvd., Hollywood CA 90046. (323)876-0570. Fax: (323)876-6822. President: Charles R. Van Nostrand. **Contact**: Lawrence Harbinson, editor. Play publisher. Estab. 1830. Publishes 40-50 plays and 2-4 new musicals/year. Amateur and professional theaters.

How to Contact Query first. Include SASE. Responds in 10 weeks.

Musical Theater "We publish primarily successful musicals from the NYC, London and regional stage."

Publications *Prince And The Pauper*, by Neil Berg, Bernie Garzia, Ray Roderick and John Glaudini; *Elegies: A Song Cycle*, by William Finn; *Golf: The Musical*, by Michael Roberts; and *Jewish Girlz*, by Elizabeth Swados.

☑ HEUER PUBLISHING CO.

211 First Ave., SE Suite 200, Cedar Rapids IA 52401. (319)364-6311. E-mail: editor@hitplays.com. Website: www.hitplays.com. Publisher: C. Emmett McMullen. Play publisher. Estab. 1928. Publishes plays, musicals, operas/operettas and guides (choreography, costume, production/staging) for amateur and professional markets, including junior and senior high schools, college/university and community theatres. Focus includes comedy, drama, fantasy, mystery and holiday. Pays by percentage royalty or outright purchase. Pays by outright purchase or percentage royalty.

How to Contact Query with musical CD/tape or submit complete manuscript and score. Include SASE. Responds in 2 months.

Musical Theater "We prefer one, two or three act comedies or mystery-comedies with a large number of characters."

Publications *Happily Ever After*, by Allen Koepke (musical fairytale); *Brave Buckaroo*, by Renee J. Clark (musical melodrama); and *Pirate Island*, by Martin Follose (musical comedy).

Tips "We are willing to review single-song submissions as cornerstone piece for commissioned works. Special interest focus in multicultural, historic, classic literature, teen issues, and biographies."

PIONEER DRAMA SERVICE

P.O. Box 4267, Englewood CO 80155. (303)779-4035. Fax: (303)779-4315. E-mail: playwrights@pioneerdrama.com. Website: www.pioneerdrama.com. **Contact:** Lori Conary, assistant editor. Play publisher. Estab. 1963. "Plays are performed by junior high and high school drama departments, church youth groups, college and university theaters, semi-professional and professional children's theaters, parks and recreation departments." Playwrights paid 50% royalty (10% sales).

How to Contact Query with character breakdown, synopsis and set description. Include SASE. Responds in 6 months.

Musical Theater "We seek full length children's musicals, high school musicals and one act children's musicals to be performed by children, secondary school students, and/or adults. We want musicals easy to perform, simple sets, many female roles and very few solos. Must be appropriate for educational market. We are not interested in profanity, themes with exclusively adult interest, sex, drinking, smoking, etc. Several of our full-length plays are being converted to musicals. We edit them, then contract with someone to write the music and lyrics."

Publications *The Stories of Scheherazade*, book by Susan Pargmon, music and lyrics by Bill Francoeur (musical *Arabian Nights*); *Hubba Hubba: The 1940s Hollywood Movie Musical*, by Gene Casey and Jan Casey (tribute to the 1940s Hollywood movie musical); and *Cinderella's Glass Slipper*, book by Vera Morris, music and lyrics by Bill Francoeur (musical fairy tale).

Tips "Research and learn about our company. Our website and catalog provide an incredible amount of information."

PLAYERS PRESS, INC.

P.O. Box 1132, Studio City CA 91614. (818)789-4980. Associate Editor: Karen Flathers. Vice President: Robert W. Gordon. Play publisher, music book publisher, educational publisher. Estab. 1965. Publishes 20-70 plays and 1-3 new musicals/year. Plays are used primarily by general audience and children. Pays variable royalty and variable amount/performance.

How to Contact Query first. Include SASE. Responds in 3-6 months (3 weeks on queries).

Musical Theater "We will consider all submitted works. Presently musicals for adults and high schools are in demand. When cast size can be flexible (describe how it can be done in your work) it sells better."

Publications *Jack and The Beanstalk*, by William-Alan Landes (family musical); *Tall Betsy and The Crackerbarrel Tales*, by Jacque Wheeler (family musical); and *Shenker Made Simple*, by Steve Porter (How to music book).

Tips "For plays and musicals, have your work produced at least twice. Be present for rehearsals and work with competent people. Then submit material asked for in good clear copy with good audio tapes."

Classical Performing Arts

Finding an audience is critical to the composer of orchestral music. Fortunately, baby boomers are swelling the ranks of classical music audiences and bringing with them a taste for fresh, innovative music. So the climate is fair for composers seeking their first performance.

Finding a performance venue is particularly important because once a composer has his work performed for an audience and establishes himself as a talented newcomer, it can lead to more performances and commissions for new works.

BEFORE YOU SUBMIT

Be aware that most classical music organizations are nonprofit groups, and don't have a large budget for acquiring new works. It takes a lot of time and money to put together an orchestral performance of a new composition, therefore these groups are quite selective when choosing new works to perform. Don't be disappointed if the payment offered by these groups is small or even non-existent. What you gain is the chance to have your music performed for an appreciative audience. Also realize that many classical groups are understaffed, so it may take longer than expected to hear back on your submission. It pays to be patient, and employ diplomacy, tact and timing in your follow-up.

In this section you will find listings for classical performing arts organizations throughout the U.S. But if you have no prior performances to your credit, it's a good idea to begin with a small chamber orchestra, for example. Smaller symphony and chamber orchestras are usually more inclined to experiment with new works. A local university or conservatory of music, where you may already have contacts, is a great place to start.

All of the groups listed in this section are interested in hearing new works from contemporary classical composers. Pay close attention to the music needs of each group, and when you find one you feel might be interested in your music, follow submission guidelines carefully. To locate classical performing arts groups in your area, consult the Geographic Index at the back of this book.

N ACADIANA SYMPHONY ORCHESTRA

P.O. Box 53632, Lafayette LA 70505. (337)232-4277. Fax: (337)237-4712. E-mail: information@acad ianasymphony.org. Website: www.acadianasymphony.org. **Contact:** Geraldine Hubbel, executive director. Symphony orchestra. Estab. 1984. Members are amateurs and professionals. Performs 20 concerts/year, including 1 new work. Commissions 1 new work/year. Performs in 2,230-seat hall with "wonderful acoustics." Pays "according to the type of composition."

How to Contact Call first. Does not return material. Responds in 2 months.

Music Full orchestra: 10 minutes at most. Reduced orchestra, educational pieces: short, up to 5 minutes.

Performances Quincy Hilliard's *Universal Covenant* (orchestral suite); James Hanna's *In Memoriam* (strings/elegy); and Gregory Danner's *A New Beginning* (full orchestra fanfare).

THE AMERICAN BOYCHOIR

19 Lambert Dr., Princeton NJ 08540. (609)924-5858. Fax: (609)924-5812. E-mail: jkaltenbach@ame ricanboychoir.org. Website: www.americanboychoir.org. General Manager: Janet B. Kaltenbach. Music Director: Vincent Metallo. Professional boychoir. Estab. 1937. Members are musically talented boys in grades 5-8. Performs 200 concerts/year, including 10-25 new works. Commissions 1 new work approximately every 3 years. Actively seeks high quality arrangements. Performs national and international tours, orchestral engagements, church services, workshops, school programs, local concerts, and at corporate and social functions.

How to Contact Submit complete score. Include SASE. Responds in 1 year.

Music Choral works in unison, SA, SSA, SSAA or SATB division; unaccompanied and with piano or organ; occasional chamber orchestra or brass ensemble. Works are usually sung by 28 to 60 boys. Composers must know boychoir sonority.

Performances *Four Seasons*, by Michael Torke (orchestral-choral); *Garden of Light*, by Aaron Kernis (orchestral-choral); *Reasons for Loving the Harmonica*, by Libby Larsen (piano); and *Songs Eternity*, by Steven Paulus (piano).

AMHERST SAXOPHONE QUARTET

64 Roycroft Blvd., Amherst NY 14226. (716)839-9716. E-mail: steve@caramaxstudio.com. Website: www.amherstsaxophonequartet.buffalo.edu. **Contact:** Steve Rosenthal, director. Chamber music ensemble. Estab. 1978. Performs 80 concerts/year including 10-20 new works. Commissions 1-2 composers or new works/year. "We are a touring ensemble." Payment varies.

How to Contact Query first. Include SASE. Responds in 1 month.

Music "Music for soprano, alto, tenor and baritone (low A) saxophone. We are interested in great music of many styles. Level of difficulty is commensurate with full-time touring ensembles."

Performances Lukas Foss's *Saxophone Quartet* (new music); David Stock's *Sax Appeal* (new music); and Chan Ka Nin's *Saxophone Quartet* (new music).

Tips "Professionally copied parts help! Write what you truly want to write."

ARCADY

P.O. Box 955, Simcoe ON N3Y 5B3 Canada. (519)428-3185. E-mail: info@arcady.ca. Website: www. arcady.ca. **Contact:** Ronald Beckett, director. Semi-professional chorus and orchestra. Members are professionals, university music majors and recent graduates from throughout Ontario. "Arcady forms the bridge between the student and the professional performing career." Performs 12 concerts/year including 1-2 new works. Commissions 1 composer or new work/year. Pay negotiable.

How to Contact Submit complete score and tape of piece(s). Does not return material. Responds in 3 months.

Music "Compositions appropriate for ensemble accustomed to performance of chamber works, accompanied or unaccompanied, with independence of parts. Specialize in repertoire of 17th, 18th and 20th centuries. Number of singers does not exceed 30. Orchestra is limited to strings, supported by a professional quartet. No popular, commercial or show music."

Performances Ronald Beckett's *I Am* (opera); Ronald Beckett's *John* (opera); and David Lenson's *Prologue to Dido and Aeneas* (masque).
Tips "Arcady is a touring ensemble experienced with both concert and stage performance."

N ATLANTA POPS ORCHESTRA
P.O. Box 15037, Atlanta GA 30333. (404)636-0020. E-mail: ladkmusic@aol.com. Website: www.atl antapops.com. **Contact:** Leonard Altieri, general manager. Pops orchestra. Estab. 1945. Members are professionals. Performs 5-10 concerts/year. Concerts are performed for audiences of 5,000-10,000, "all ages, all types." Composers are not paid; concerts are free to the public.
How to Contact Call to request permission to submit. Then send cassette, and score or music, if requested. Include SASE. Responds "as soon as possible."
Performances Vincent Montana, Jr.'s *Magic Bird of Fire*; Louis Alter's *Manhattan Serenade*; and Nelson Riddle's *It's Alright With Me*.
Tips "My concerts are pops concerts—no deep classics."

THE ATLANTA YOUNG SINGERS OF CALLANWOLDE
980 Briarcliff Rd. N.E., Atlanta GA 30306. (404)873-3365. Fax: (404)873-0756. E-mail: info@aysc.o rg. Website: www.aysc.org. **Contact:** Paige F. Mathis, music director. Community children's chorus. Estab. 1975. Members are amateurs. Performs 45 concerts/year including new works. Audience consists of community churches, retirement homes, schools. Performs most often at churches. Pay is negotiable.
How to Contact Submit complete score and tape of piece(s). Include SASE. Responds in accordance with request.
Music "Subjects and styles appealing to 3rd-12th grade boys and girls. Contemporary concerns of the world of interest. Unusual sacred, folk, classic style. Internationally and ethnically bonding. Medium difficulty preferred, with or without keyboard accompaniment."
Tips "Our mission is to promote service and growth through singing."

BILLINGS SYMPHONY
201 N. Broadway., Suite 350, Billings MT 59101-1936. (406)252-3610. Fax: (406)252-3353. E-mail: symphony@billingssymphony.org. Website: www.billingssymphony.org. **Contact:** Dr. Uri Barnea, music director. Symphony orchestra, orchestra and chorale. Estab. 1950. Members are professionals and amateurs. Performs 12-15 concerts/year, including 6-7 new works. Traditional audience. Performs at Alberta Bair Theater (capacity 1,416). Pays by outright purchase (or rental).
How to Contact Query first. Include SASE. Responds in 2 weeks.
Music Any style. Traditional notation preferred.
Performances Jim Cockey's *Symphony No. 2 (Parmly's Dream)* (symphony orchestra with chorus and soloists); Ilse-Mari Lee's *Cello Concerto* (concerto for cello solo and orchestra); and Jim Beckel's *Christmas Fanfare* (brass and percussion).
Tips "Write what you feel (be honest) and sharpen your compositional and craftsmanship skills."

BIRMINGHAM-BLOOMFIELD SYMPHONY ORCHESTRA
1592 Buckingham, Birmingham MI 48009. (248)645-2276. Fax: (248)645-2276, *51. Website: www. bbso.org. **Contact:** Charles Greenwell, music director and conductor. Felix Resnick, Conductor Laureate. President and Executive Director: Carla Lamphere. Symphony orchestra. Estab. 1975. Members are professionals. Performs 5 concerts including 1 new work/year. Commissions 1 composer or new work/year "with grants." Performs for middle-to-upper class audience at Temple Beth El's Sanctuary. Pays per performance "depending upon grant received."
How to Contact Query first. Does not return material. Responds in 6 months.
Music "We are a symphony orchestra but also play pops. Usually 3 works on program (2 hrs.) Orchestra size 65-75. If pianist is involved, they must rent piano."
Performances Brian Belanger's *Tuskegee Airmen Suite* (symphonic full orchestra); and Larry Nazer & Friend's *Music from "Warm" CD* (jazz with full orchestra).

☑ THE BOSTON PHILHARMONIC

295 Huntington Ave., #210, Boston MA 02115. (617)236-0999. Fax: (617)236-8613. E-mail: office@ bostonphil.org. Website: www.bostonphil.org. Music Director: Benjamin Zander. Symphony orchestra. Estab. 1979. Members are professionals, amateurs and students. Performs 2 concerts/year. Audience is ages 30-70. Performs at New England Conservatory's Jordan Hall, Boston's Symphony Hall and Sanders Theatre in Cambridge. Both Jordan Hall and Sanders Theatre are small (approximately 1,100 seats) and very intimate.

How to Contact *Does not accept new music at this time.*

Music Full orchestra only.

Performances Dutilleuxs' *Tout un monde lointain* for cello and orchestra (symphonic); Bernstein's *Fancy Free* (symphonic/jazzy); Copland's *El Salon Mexico* (symphonic); Gershwin's *Rhapsody in Blue*; Shostakovitch's *Symphony No. 10*; Harbison's *Concerto for Oboe*; Holst's *The Planet Suite*; Schwantner's *New Morning for the World*; Berg's *Seven Early Songs*; and Ive's *The Unanswered Question*.

BRAVO! L.A.

16823 Liggett St., North Hills CA 91343. (818)892-8737. Fax: (818)892-1227. E-mail: info@bravo-la.com. Website: www.bravo-la.com. **Contact:** Dr. Janice Foy, director. An umbrella organization of recording/touring musicians, formed in 1994. Includes the following musical ensembles: Celllissimo! L.A. (cello ensemble); Interstellar Strings (expandable string group with optional piano); Mesto Chamber Players; the New American Quartet (string quartet); The Ascending Wave (harp, soprano, cello or harp/cello duo); Cellissimo! L.A. (cello ensemble); Musical Combustion (harp, flute, cello); I Musicanti (singer, piano and cello); and the Sierra Chamber Players (piano with strings or mixed ensemble). Performs 4 concerts/year, including 1 new work. ''We take care of PR. There is also grant money the composer can apply for.''

How to Contact Submit complete score and tape of piece(s). Include SASE. Responds in a few months.

Music ''Classical, Romantic, Baroque, Popular (including new arrangements done by Shelly Cohen, from the 'Tonight Show Band'), ethnic (including gypsy) and contemporary works (commissioned as well). The New American Quartet has a recording project which features music of Mozart's *Eine Kleine Nachtmusik*, Borodin's *Nocturne*, a Puccini Opera Suite (S. Cohen), Strauss' *Blue Danube Waltz*, *Trepak* of Tschaikovsky, *'El Choclo'* (Argentinian tango), *Csardas!* and arrangements of Cole Porter, Broadway show tunes and popular classics.''

Performances Joe Giarrusso's *Rhapsody for Cello and Piano* (concert piece modern romantic); Joe Giarrusso's *Cello Sonata* (concert piece); and Dan Bogley's *Foybles* (contemporary solo cello).

Tips ''Please be open to criticism/suggestions about your music and try to appeal to mixed audiences. We also look for innovative techniques, mixed styles or entertaining approaches, such as classical jazz or Bach and pop, or ethnic mixes. There are four CD's currently available for purchase online for $20 each. There are also sound clips on the website.''

⚄ ☑ CALGARY BOYS CHOIR

B4 - Building Currie Barracks, 2452 Battleford Avenue SW, Calgary AB T3E 7K9 Canada. (403)217-7790. Fax: (403)217-7796. E-mail: manager@calgaryboyschoir.ab.ca. Website: www.calgaryboysc hoir.ab.ca. **Contact:** Jenny Haldeman, office administrator. Artistic Director: Arlie Langager. Boys choir. Estab. 1973. Members are amateurs age 6 and up. Performs 50-70 concerts/year including 1-2 new works. Pay negotiable.

How to Contact Query first. Submit complete score and tape of piece(s). Include SASE. Responds in 6 weeks. Does not return material.

Music ''Style fitting for boys choir. Lengths depending on project. Orchestration preferable a cappella/for piano/sometimes orchestra.''

Performances Dr. William Jordan's *City of Peace* (world premiere Wednesday September 11, 2002); Lydia Adam's arrangement of *Mi'kmaq Honour Song* (May 26, 2002); and Bruce Sled's *Jing-ga-lye-ya* (May 12, 2002).

☑ ☑ CANADIAN OPERA COMPANY

227 Front St. E., Toronto ON M5A 1E8 Canada. (416)363-6671. Fax: (416)363-5584. E-mail: ensembl e@coc.ca. Website: www.coc.ca. **Contact:** Sandra J. Gavinchuk, music administrator. Opera company. Estab. 1950. Members are professionals. 50-55 performances, including a minimum of 1 new work/year. Pays by contract.

How to Contact Submit complete score and tapes of vocal and/or operatic works. "Vocal works please." Include SASE. Responds in 5 weeks.

Music Vocal works, operatic in nature. "Do not submit works which are not for voice. Ask for requirements for the Composers-In-Residence program."

Performances Dean Burry's *Brothers Grimm* (children's opera, 50 minutes long); Paul Ruders' *Handmaid's Tale* (full length opera, 2 acts, epilogue); Benjamin Britten's *Albert Herring* (opera in 3 acts, full length).

Tips "We have a Composers-In-Residence program which is open to Canadian composers or landed immigrants."

☑ CARSON CITY SYMPHONY

P.O. Box 2001, 191 Heidi Circle, Carson City NV 89701-6532, Carson City NV 89702-2001. (775)883-4154. Fax: (775)883-4371. E-mail: dcbugli@aol.com. Website: www.ccsymphony.com. **Contact:** David C. Bugli, music director/conductor. Amateur community orchestra. Estab. 1984. Members are amateurs. Performs 5 concerts, including 2 new works/year. Audience is largely Carson City/ Reno area residents, many of them retirees. "Most concerts are performed in the Carson City Community Center Auditorium, which seats 800." Pay varies for outright purchase.

How to Contact Submit complete score and tape or CD of works. Does not return material. Responds in 2 months.

Music "We want classical, pop orchestrations, orchestrations of early music for modern orchestras, concertos for violin or piano, holiday music for chorus and orchestra (children's choirs and handbell ensemble available), music by women, music for brass choir. Most performers are amateurs, but there are a few professionals who perform with us. Available winds and percussion: 2 flutes and flute/piccolo, 2 oboes (E.H. double sometimes), 2 clarinets, 1 bass clarinet, 2 bassoons, 4 horns, 3 trumpets, 3 trombones, 1 tuba, timpani, and percussion. Harp and piano. Strings: 8-8-5-6-3 (or fewer). Avoid music that lacks melodic appeal. Composers should contact us first. Each concert has a different emphasis. Note: Associated choral group, Carson Chamber Singers, performs several times a year with the orchestra and independently."

Performances Thomas Svoboda's *Overture of the Season* (minimalist overture); Gwyneth Walker's *A Concerto of Hymns and Spirituals for Trumpet and Orchestra*; and Jim Cockey's *A Land of Sage and Sun.*

Tips "It is better to write several short movements well than to write long, unimaginative pieces, especially when starting out. Be willing to revise after submitting the work, even if it was premiered elsewhere."

☑ CHARLOTTE PHILHARMONIC ORCHESTRA

P.O. Box 470987, Charlotte NC 28247-0987. (704)846-2788. Fax: (704)847-6043. E-mail: info@charl ottephilharmonic.org. Website: www.charlottephilharmonic.org. **Contact:** Albert Moehring, music director. Symphony orchestra. Estab. 1991. Members are professionals. Performs 12 concerts/year including 2-4 new works. Audience consists of music lovers, educated and uneducated. "We regularly perform Broadway/movie soundtracks, also standard classical repertoire." Performance spaces are up to 2,500 seats. Pay is negotiable.

• The Charlotte Philharmonic Orchestra was voted Charlotte's Best Entertainment in 1998.

How to Contact Submit complete score and tape of piece(s). Does not return material. Responds in 6 weeks.

Music Seeks full orchestrations, lush strings always popular. Maximum 8-10 minutes. Would review classical styles, but also interested in Boston Pops type selections. Require lyrical music with interesting melodies and good rhythms. "We are not interested in atonal, dissonant styled music. We will neither perform it, nor bother to review it. Our audiences do not like it." Players are professional. Limited rehearsals. String passages playable in limited time. Full orchestra sound—excellent brass players. 75 piece orchestra. Always interested in fine Broadway styled arrangements. Look for strong, smooth transpositions/modulations.

Performances Davis Brown's *Battle of the Fire Ants* (part of a suite); Robert Kerr's *Irish Legend* (medley of Celtic style melodies).

Tips "With a new composer, we recommend pieces under 10 minutes, lyrical basis with definite melodies. Full use of 75 piece orchestra. Lush strings without exceedingly difficult passages for limited rehearsals. Variety of materials welcomed. Enjoy standard classics, bib band, ballroom dance-type music, ballet style. Also enjoy operatic arrangements. Use our own Philharmonic Chorus as well as regular vocalists. Good choral arrangements with full orchestra always of interest. Appreciate a tape when possible. If a composer submits during a really busy period of performances, please be patient. If there is no response in 4-6 weeks, they may contact us again."

☑ CHATTANOOGA GIRLS CHOIR

P.O. Box 6036, Suite 612 Maclellan Building, Chattanooga TN 37401. (423)266-9422. E-mail: office @chattanoogagirlschoir.com. Website: http://chattanoogagirlschoir.com. **Contact:** LuAnne Holdenl, artistic director. Vocal ensemble. Estab. 1986. Members are amateurs. Performs 2 concerts/year including at least 1 new work. Audience consists of cultural and civic organizations and national and international tours. Performance space includes concert halls and churches. Pays for outright purchase or per performance.

How to Contact Query first. Include SASE. Responds in 6 weeks.

Music Seeks renaissance, baroque, classical, romantic, twentieth century, folk and musical theatre for young voices of up to 8 minutes. Performers include 5 treble choices: 4th grade (2 pts.); 5th grade (2 pts.) (SA); grades 6-9 (3 pts.) (SSA); grades 10-12 (3-4 pts.) (SSAA); and a combined choir: grades 6-12 (3-4 pts.) (SSAA). Medium level of difficulty. "Avoid extremely high Tessitura Sop I and extremely low Tessitura Alto II."

Performances Jan Swafford's *Iphigenia Book: Meagher* (choral drama); Penny Tullock's *How Can I Keep from Singing* (Shaker hymn).

Ⓝ CHEYENNE SYMPHONY ORCHESTRA

P.O. Box 851, Cheyenne WY 82003. (307)778-8561. Fax: (307)634-7512. E-mail: director@cheyenn esymphony.org. Website: www.cheyennesymphony.org. **Contact:** Chloe Illoway, executive director. Symphony orchestra. Estab. 1955. Members are professionals. Performs 6 concerts/year including 1-3 new works. "Orchestra performs for a conservative, mid-to-upper income audience of 1,200 season members." Pay varies.

How to Contact Query first. Does not return material. Responds in 2 months.

Performances Bill Hill's *Seven Abstract Miniatures* (orchestral).

COMMONWEALTH OPERA INC.

140 Pine St., Florence MA 01062. (413)586-5026. Fax: (413)587-0380. E-mail: info@commonwealth opera.org. Website: www.commonwealthopera.org. **Contact:** Richard R. Rescia, artistic director. Opera company. Estab. 1977. Members are professionals and amateurs. Performs 4 concerts/year. "We perform at the Calvin Theatre Northampton in an 1,200-seat opera house. Depending on opera, audience could be family oriented or adult." Pays royalty.

How to Contact Query first. Does not return material. Response will take months.

Music "We are open to all styles of opera. We have the limitations of a regional opera company with local chorus. Principals come from a wide area. We look only at opera scores."

Performances Arnold Black's *The Phantom Tollbooth* (children's opera); *Diefledermaus*, and *The Magic Flute*.

Tips "We're looking for opera that is accessible to the general public and performable by a standard opera orchestra."

☑ CONNECTICUT CHORAL ARTISTS/CONCORA

52 Main St., New Britain CT 06051. (860)224-7500. Website: www.concora.org. **Contact:** Jane Penfield, executive director. Richard Coffey, artistic director. Professional concert choir, also an

18-voice ensemble dedicated to contemporary a cappella works. Estab. 1974. Members are professionals. Performs 15 concerts/year, including 3-5 new works. "Mixed audience in terms of age and background; performs in various halls and churches in the region." Payment "depends upon underwriting we can obtain for the project."

How to Contact Query first. "No unsolicited submissions accepted." Include SASE. Responds in 1 year.

Music Seeking "works for mixed chorus of 36 singers; unaccompanied or with keyboard and/or small instrumental ensemble; text sacred or secular/any language; prefers suites or cyclical works, total time not exceeding 15 minutes. Performance spaces and budgets prohibit large instrumental ensembles. Works suited for 750-seat halls are preferable. Substantial organ or piano parts acceptable. Scores should be very legible in every way."

Performances Wm. Schuman's *Carols of Death* (choral SATB); Robert Cohen's *Peter Quince as the Clavier* (choral, a cappella); Chen Yi's *The Flowing Station* (choral, a cappella); Charles Ives' *Psalm 90* (choral SATB); and Frank Martin's *Mass for Double Chorus* (regional premiere).

Tips "Use conventional notation and be sure manuscript is legible in every way. Recognize and respect the vocal range of each vocal part. Work should have an identifiable *rhythmic* structure."

N DESERT CHORALE
811 St. Michael's Dr. Suite 208, Santa Fe NM 87504. (505)988-2282. Fax: (505)988-7522. E-mail: info@desertchorale.org. Website: www.desertchorale.org. Music Director: Dennis Shrock. Executive Director: Jillian Sandrock. Business Manager: Jay Reep. Box Office Manager: Natalia Chavez. Vocal ensemble. Members are professionals. Performs 35 concerts/year including 2 new works. Commissions 1 new composer or new work/year. "Highly sophisticated audiences who are eager for interesting musical experiences. We pay $5,000 to $2,000 for premieres, often as part of consortium."

How to Contact Query first. Submit complete score and tape *after* query. Does not return material. Responds in 2 years.

Music "Challenging chamber choir works 6 to 20 minutes in length. Accompanied works are sometimes limited by space—normally no more than 5 or 6 players. "We sing both a cappella and with chamber orchestra; size of choir varies accordingly (20-32). No short church anthem-type pieces."

Performances Edwin London's *Jove's Nectar* (choral with 5 instruments); Lanham Deal's *Minituras de Sor Juana* (unaccompanied); and Steven Sametz's *Desert Voices* (choral with 4 instruments).

Tips "Call me or see me and I'll be happy to tell you what I need and I will also put you in touch with other conductors in the growing professional choir movement."

⊕ ✓ EUROPEAN UNION CHAMBER ORCHESTRA
Hollick, Yarnscombe EX31 3LQ United Kingdom. (44)1271 858249. Fax: (44)1271 858375. E-mail: eucorchl@aol.com. Website: www.etd.gb.com. **Contact:** Ambrose Miller, general manager. Chamber orchestra. Members are professionals. Performs 70 concerts/year, including 6 new works. Commissions 2 composers or new works/year. Performs regular tours of Europe, Americas and Asia, including major venues. Pays per performance or for outright purchase, depending on work.

How to Contact Query first. Does not return material. Responds in 6 weeks.

Music Seeking compositions for strings, 2 oboes and 2 horns with a duration of about 8 minutes.

Performances S. Gardner's *More Pricks Than Kicks* (strings); F. Festa's *Pegasus* (flute, strings); and T. Agerfeldt's *Ground* (strings).

Tips "Keep the work to less than 15 minutes in duration, it should be sufficiently 'modern' to be interesting but not too difficult as this could take up rehearsal time. It should be possible to perform without a conductor."

GREATER GRAND FORKS SYMPHONY ORCHESTRA
P.O. Box 7084, Grand Forks ND 58202-7084. (701)777-3359. Fax: (701)777-3320. E-mail: ggfso@un d.nodak.edu. Website: www.und.nodak.edu/org/ggfso. **Contact:** Timm Rolek, music director. Symphony orchestra. Estab. 1908. Members are professionals and/or amateurs. Performs 6 concerts/year. "New works are presented in 2-4 of our programs." Audience is "a mix of ages and

musical experience. In 1997-98 we moved into a renovated, 420-seat theater.'' Pay is negotiable, depending on licensing agreements.

How to Contact Submit complete score or complete score and tape of pieces. Include SASE. Responds in 6 months.

Music ''Style is open, instrumentation the limiting factor. Music can be scored for an ensemble up to but not exceeding: 3,2,3,2/4,3,3,1/3 perc./strings. Rehearsal time limited to 3 hours for new works.''

Performances Michael Harwood's *Amusement Park Suite* (orchestra); Randall Davidson's *Mexico Bolivar Tango* (chamber orchestra); and John Corigliano's *Voyage* (flute and orchestra); Linda Tutas Haugen's *Fable of Old Turtle* (saxophone concerto).

HEARTLAND MEN'S CHORUS

P.O. Box 32374, Kansas City MO 64171-5374. (816)931-3338. Fax: (816)531-1367. E-mail: hmc@hmckc.org. Website: www.hmckc.org. **Contact:** Joseph Nadeau, artistic director. Men's chorus. Estab. 1986. Members are professionals and amateurs. Performs 3 concerts/year; 9-10 are new works. Commissions 1 composer or new works/year. Performs for a diverse audience at the Folly Theater (1,100 seats). Pay is negotiable.

How to Contact Query first. Include SASE. Responds in 2 months.

Music ''Interested in works for male chorus (ttbb). Must be suitable for performance by a gay male chorus. We will consider any orchestration, or a cappella.''

Performances Mark Hayes' ''Two Flutes Playing'' (commissioned song cycle); Alan Shorter's ''Country Angel Christmas'' (commissioned chidren's musical); Kevin Robinson's ''Life is a Cabaret: The Music of Kander and Ebb'' (commissioned musical).

Tips ''Find a text that relates to the contemporary gay experience, something that will touch peoples' lives.''

N HELENA SYMPHONY

P.O. Box 1073, Helena MT 59624. (406)442-1860. E-mail: info@helenasymphony.org. Website: www.helenasymphony.org. **Contact:** Allan R. Scott, music director and conductor. Symphony orchestra. Estab. 1955. Members are professionals and amateurs. Performs 7-10 concerts/year including new works. Performance space is an 1,800 seat concert hall. Payment varies.

How to Contact Query first. Include SASE. Responds in 3 months.

Music ''Imaginative, collaborative, not too atonal. We want to appeal to an audience of all ages. We don't have a huge string complement. Medium to difficult okay—at frontiers of professional ability we cannot do.''

Performances Eric Funk's *A Christmas Overture* (orchestra); Donald O. Johnston's *A Christmas Processional* (orchestra/chorale); and Elizabeth Sellers' *Prairie* (orchestra/short ballet piece).

Tips ''Try to balance tension and repose in your works. New instrument combinations are appealing.''

N HENDERSONVILLE SYMPHONY ORCHESTRA

P.O. Box 1811, Hendersonville NC 28793. (828)697-5884. Fax: (828)697-5765. E-mail: hso@brinet.com. Website: www.hendersonvillesymphony.org. **Contact:** Sandie Salvaggio-Walker, general manager. Symphony orchestra. Estab. 1971. Members are professionals and amateurs. Performs 6 concerts/year. ''We would welcome a new work per year.'' Audience is a cross-section of retirees, professionals and some children. Performance space is a 857-seat high school auditorium.

How to Contact Query first. Include SASE. Responds in 1 month.

Music ''We use a broad spectrum of music (classical concerts and pops).''

Performances Nelson's *Jubilee* (personal expression in a traditional method); Britten's ''The Courtly Dances'' from Glorina (time-tested); and Chip Davis' arrangement for Mannheim Steamroller's *Deck the Halls* (modern adaptation of traditional melody).

Tips ''Submit your work even though we are a community orchestra. We like to be challenged. We have the most heavily patronized fine arts group in the county. Our emphasis is on education.''

☑ HERMANN SONS GERMAN BAND

P.O. Box 162, Medina TX 78055. (830)589-2268. E-mail: herbert@festmusik.com. Website: www.fe stmusik.com. **Contact:** Herbert Bilhartz, music director. Community band with German instrumentation. Estab. 1990. Members are both professionals and amateurs. Performs 12 concerts/year including 6 new works. Commissions no new composers or new works/year. Performs for "mostly older people who like German polkas, waltzes and marches. We normally play only published arrangements from Germany."

How to Contact Query first; then submit full set of parts and score, condensed or full. Include SASE. Responds in 6 weeks.

Music "We like European-style polkas or waltzes (Viennese or Missouri tempo), either original or arrangements of public domain tunes. Arrangements of traditional American folk tunes in this genre would be especially welcome. Also, polkas or waltzes featuring one or two solo instruments (from instrumentation below) would be great. OK for solo parts to be technically demanding. Although we have no funds to commission works, we will provide you with a cassette recording of our performance. Also, we would assist composers in submitting works to band music publishers in Germany for possible publication. Polkas and waltzes generally follow this format: Intro; 1st strain repeated; 2nd strain repeated; DS to 1 strain; Trio: Intro; 32 bar strain; 'break-up' strain; Trio DS. Much like military march form. Instrumentation: Fl/Picc, 3 clars in Bb, 2 Fluegelhorns in Bb; 3 Tpts in Bb, 2 or 4 Hns in F or Eb, 2 Baritones (melody/countermelody parts; 1 in Bb TC, 1 in BC), 2 Baritones in Bb TC (rhythm parts), 3 Trombones, 2 Tubas (in octaves, mostly), Drum set, Timpani optional. We don't use saxes, but a German publisher would want 4-5 sax parts. Parts should be medium to medium difficult. All brass parts should be considered one player to the part; woodwinds, two to the part. No concert type pieces; no modern popular or rock styles. However, a 'theme and variations' form with contrasting jazz, rock, country, modern variations would be clever, and our fans might go for such a piece (as might a German publisher)."

Performances Darryl Lyman's *American Folk Music Waltz* medley and *American Folk Music Polka* medley; and David Lorrien's *Cotton-Eyed Joe* arrangement.

Tips "German town bands love to play American tunes. There are many thousands of these bands over there and competition among band music publishers in Germany is keen. Few Americans are aware of this potential market, so few American arrangers get published over there. Simple harmony is best for this style, but good counterpoint helps a lot. Make use of the dark quality of the Fluegelhorns and the bright, fanfare quality of the trumpets. Give the two baritones (one in TC and one in BC) plenty of exposed melodic material. Keep them in harmony with each other (3rds and 6ths), unlike American band arrangements, which have only one Baritone line. If you want to write a piece in this style, give me a call, and I will send you some sample scores to give you a better idea."

HUDSON VALLEY PHILHARMONIC

35 Market St., 1st Floor, Poughkeepise NY 12601. (845)473-5288. Fax: (845)473-4259. E-mail: slama rca@bardavon.org. Website: www.bardavon.org. **Contact:** Stephen LaMarca, production manager. Symphony orchestra. Estab. 1969. Members are professionals. Performs 20 concerts/year including 1 new work. "Classical subscription concerts for all ages; Pops concerts for all ages; New Wave concerts—crossover projects with a rock 'n' roll artist performing with an orchestra. HVP performs in three main theatres which are concert auditoriums with stages and professional lighting and sound." Pay is negotiable.

How to Contact Query first. Include SASE. Responds in 8 months.

Music "HVP is open to serious classical music, pop music and rock 'n' roll crossover projects. Desired length of work between 10-20 minutes. Orchestrations can be varied by should always include strings. There is no limit to difficulty since our musicians are professional. The ideal number of musicians to write for would include up to a Brahms-size orchestra 2222, 4231, T, 2P, piano, harp, strings."

Performances Joan Tower's *Island Rhythms* (serious classical work); Bill Vanaver's *P'nai El* (symphony work with dance); and Joseph Bertolozzi's *Serenade* (light classical, pop work).

Tips "Don't get locked into doing very traditional orchestrations or styles. Our music director is interested in fresh, creative formats. He is an orchestrator as well and can offer good advice on what works well. Songwriters who are into crossover projects should definitely submit works. Over the past four years, HVP has done concerts featuring the works of Natalie Merchant, John Cale, Sterling Morrison, Richie Havens and R. Carlos Naka (Native American flute player), all reorchestrated by our music director for small orchestra with the artist."

N KENTUCKY OPERA

101 S. Eighth St. at Main, Louisville KY 40202. (502)584-4500. Fax: (502)584-7484. E-mail: info@ky opera.org. Website: www.kyopera.org. **Contact:** Kimcherie Lloyd, director of music. Opera. Estab. 1952. Members are professionals. Performs 3 main stage/year. Performs at Whitney Hall, The Kentucky Center for the Arts, seating is 2,400; Bomhard Theatre, The Kentucky Center for the Arts, 620; Macauley Theatre, 1,400. Pays by royalty, outright purchase or per performance.

How to Contact *Write or call first before submitting. No unsolicited submissions.* Submit complete score. Include SASE. Responds in 6 months.

Music Seeks opera—1 to 3 acts with orchestrations. No limitations.

Performances *Turandot*; *Susannah!*; and *Rigaletto*.

N LIMA SYMPHONY ORCHESTRA

67 Town Square, P.O. Box 1651, Lima OH 45802. (419)222-5701. Fax: (419)222-6587. Website: www.limasymphony.com. **Contact:** Crafton Beck, music conductor. Symphony orchestra. Estab. 1953. Members are professionals. Performs 17-18 concerts including at least 1 new work/year. Commissions at least 1 composer or new work/year. Middle to older audience; also Young People's Series. Mixture for stage and summer productions. Performs in Veterans' Memorial Civic & Convention Center, a beautiful hall seating 1,670; various temporary shells for summer outdoors events; churches; museums and libraries. Pays $2,500 for outright purchase (Anniversary commission) or grants $1,500-5,000.

How to Contact Submit complete score if not performed; otherwise submit complete score and tape of piece(s). Include SASE. Responds in 3 months.

Music "Good balance of incisive rhythm, lyricism, dynamic contrast and pacing. Chamber orchestra to full (85-member) symphony orchestra." Does not wish to see "excessive odd meter changes."

Performances Frank Proto's *American Overture* (some original music and fantasy); Werner Tharichen's *Concerto for Timpani and Orchestra*; and James Oliverio's *Pilgrimage—Concerto for Brass* (interesting, dynamic writing for brass and the orchestra).

Tips "Know your instruments, be willing to experiment with unconventional textures, be available for in depth analysis with conductor, be at more than one rehearsal. Be sure that individual parts are correctly matching the score and done in good, neat calligraphy."

LITHOPOLIS AREA FINE ARTS ASSOCIATION

3825 Cedar Hill Rd., Canal Winchester OH 43110-8929. (614)837-8925. Website: www.cwda.net/LAFAA/. **Contact:** Virginia E. Heffner, series director. Performing Arts Series. Estab. 1973. Members are professionals and amateurs. Performs 6-7 concerts/year including 2-3 new works. "Our audience consists of couples and families 30-80 in age. Their tastes run from classical, folk, ethnic, big band, pop and jazz. Our hall is acoustically excellent and seats 400. It was designed as a lecture-recital hall in 1925." Composers "may apply for Ohio Arts Council Grant under the New Works category." Pays straight fee to ASCAP.

How to Contact Query first. Include SASE. Responds in 3 weeks.

Music "We prefer that a composer is also the performer and works in conjunction with another artist, so they could be one of the performers on our series. Piece should be musically pleasant and not too dissonant. It should be scored for small vocal or instrumental ensemble. Dance ensembles have difficulty with 15' high 15' deep and 27' wide stage. We do not want avant-garde or obscene dance routines. No ballet (space problem). We're interested in something historical—national or Ohio emphasis would be nice. Small ensembles or solo format is fine."

Performances Patsy Ford Simms' *Holiday Gloria* (Christmas SSA vocal); Andrew Carter's *A Maiden Most Gentle* (Christmas SSA vocal); and Luigi Zaninelli's *Alleluia, Silent Night* (Christmas SSA vocal).

Tips "Call in December of 2005 or January 2006 for queries about our 2006-2007 season. We do a varied program. We don't commission artists. Contemporary music is used by some of our artist or groups. By contacting these artists, you could offer your work for inclusion in their program."

LYRIC OPERA OF CHICAGO

20 N. Wacker Dr., Chicago IL 60606. (312)322-2244. Fax: (312)419-8345. E-mail: jgriffin@lyricopera.org. Website: www.lyricopera.org. **Contact:** Julie Griffin-Meadors, music administrator. Opera company. Estab. 1953. Members are professionals. Performs 80 operas/year including 1 new work in some years. Commissions 1 new work every 4 or 5 years. "Performances are held in a 3,563 seat house for a sophisticated opera audience, predominantly 30 + years old." Payment varies.
How to Contact Query first. Does not return material. Responds in 6 months.
Music "Full-length opera suitable for a large house with full orchestra. No musical comedy or Broadway musical style. We rarely perform one-act operas. We are only interested in works by composers and librettists with extensive theatrical experience. We have few openings for new works, so candidates must be of the highest quality. Do not send score or other materials without a prior contact."
Performances William Bolcom's *View from the Bridge*; John Corigliano's *Ghosts of Versailles*; and Leonard Bernstein's *Candide*.
Tips "Have extensive credentials and an international reputation."

☑ ☑ HENRY MANCINI INSTITUTE ORCHESTRA

(formerly American Jazz Philharmonic), 10811 Washington Blvd., Suite 250, Culver City CA 90232. (310)HMI-1903. Website: www.manciniinstitute.org. **Contact:** Patrick Williams, artistic director. Symphonic jazz orchestra (72 piece). Estab. 1979. Members are professionals. Performs 8 concerts/year, including 10 new works. Commissions 2-5 composers or new works/year. Performs in major concert halls nationwide: Avery Fisher (New York), Karen & Richard Carpenter Performing Arts Center (Long Beach), Royce Hall (Los Angeles), Pick-Staiger (Chicago). Pays $2,500-5,000 for commission.
How to Contact Query first then submit complete score and tape of piece(s) with résumé. Include SASE. "Newly commissioned composers are chosen each July. Submissions should be sent by June 15th, returned by August 15th."
Music "The AJP commissions 1-2 new symphonic jazz works annually. Decisions to commission are based on composer's previous work in the symphonic jazz genre. The AJP is a 72-piece symphonic jazz ensemble that includes a rhythm section and woodwinds who double on saxophones, plus traditional symphonic orchestra."
Performances John Clayton's *Three Shades of Blue* (solo tenor sax and orchestra); Lennie Niehaus' *Tribute to Bird* (solo alto sax and orchestra); and Eddie Karam's *Stay 'N See* (symphonic jazz overture).
Tips "The AJP has been a recipient of a Reader's Digest/Meet the Composer grant and has received awards from ASCAP and the American Symphony Orchestra League for its programming. The ensemble has also received a Grammy Award nomination for its debut album on GRP Records featuring Ray Brown and Phil Woods. The AJP has recently established the Henry Mancini Institute—a four week summer educational music program for talented young musicians and composer/arrangers chosen from auditions held nationally. Participants study and perform with the principal players of the AJP and guest artists and composers/conductors. Program includes private lessons, ensemble rehearsals, panel discussions/clinics, master classes, soloist opportunities and performances in orchestra, big band, chamber ensembles and combos."

MASTER CHORALE OF WASHINGTON

1200 29th St. NW, Suite LL2, Washington DC 20007. (202)471-4050. Fax: (202)471-4051. E-mail: singing@masterchorale.org. Website: www.masterchorale.org. **Contact:** Donald McCullough, music director. Vocal ensemble. Estab. 1967. Members are professionals and amateurs. Performs 8 concerts/year including 1-3 new works. Commissions one new composer or work every 2 years. "Audience covers a wide range of ages and economic levels drawn from the greater Washington

DC metropolitan area. Kennedy Center Concert Hall seats 2,400." Pays by outright purchase.
How to Contact Submit complete score and tape of piece(s). Include SASE. Responds in 9 months.
Music Seeks new works for: 1) large chorus with or without symphony orchestras; 2) chamber choir and small ensemble.
Performances Stephen Paulus' *Mass*; Joonas Kokkonen's *Requiem* (symphonic choral with orchestra); Morten Lauridsen's *Lux Aeterna*; Donald McCullough's *Let My People Go!: A Spiritual Journey*; and Daniel E. Gawthorp's *In Quiet Resting Places*.

☑ MILWAUKEE YOUTH SYMPHONY ORCHESTRA

325 West Walnut St., Milwaukee WI 53212. (414)267-2950. Fax: (414)267-2960. E-mail: general@myso.org. Website: www.myso.org. **Contact:** Frances Richman, executive director. Multiple youth orchestras and other instrumental ensembles. Estab. 1956. Members are students. Performs 12-15 concerts/year including 1-2 new works. "Our groups perform in Uihlein Hall at the Marcus Center for the Performing Arts in Milwaukee plus area sites. The audiences usually consist of parents, music teachers and other interested community members, with periodic reviews in the *Milwaukee Journal Sentinel*." Payment varies.
How to Contact Query first. Include SASE. Does not return material. Responds in 1 month.
Performances James Woodward's *Tuba Concerto*.
Tips "Be sure you realize you are working with *students* (albeit many of the best in southeastern Wisconsin) and not professional musicians. The music needs to be on a technical level students can handle. Our students are 8-18 years of age, in 2 full symphony orchestras, a wind ensemble and 2 string orchestras, plus two flute choirs, advanced chamber orchestra and 15-20 small chamber ensembles."

☑ MOORES OPERA CENTER

Moores School of Music, University of Houston, 120 School of Music Building, Houston TX 77204-4201. (713)743-3009. E-mail: bross@www.orpheus.music.uh.edu. Website: www.uh.edu/music/Mooresopera/. Director of Opera: Buck Ross. Opera/music theater program. Members are professionals, amateurs and students. Performs 12-14 concerts/year including 1 new work. Performs in a proscenium theater which seats 800. Pit seats approximately up to 75 players. Audience covers wide spectrum, from first time opera-goers to very sophisticated. Pays per performance.
How to Contact Submit complete score and tapes of piece(s). Include SASE. Responds in 6 months.
Music "We seek music that is feasible for high graduate level student singers. Chamber orchestras are very useful. No more than two and a half hours. No children's operas."
Performances John Corigliano's *The Ghosts of Versailles*; Carlisle Floyd's *Bilby's Doll*; Robert Nelson's *A Room With a View*; Conrad Susa's *The Dangerous Liaisons*; and Dominick Argento's *Casanova's Homecoming*.

☑ OPERA MEMPHIS

6745 Wolf River Parkway, Memphis TN 38120. (901)257-3100. Fax: (901)257-3109. E-mail: david@operamemphis.org. Website: www.operamemphis.org. **Contact:** Michael Ching, artistic director. Opera company. Estab. 1955. Members are professionals. Performs 8-12 concerts/year including new works. Occasionally commissions composers. Audience consists of older, wealthier patrons, along with many students and young professionals. Pay is negotiable.
How to Contact Query first. Include SASE. Responds in 1 year or less.
Music Accessible practical pieces for educational or second stage programs. Educational pieces should not exceed 90 minutes or 4-6 performers. We encourage songwriters to contact us with proposals or work samples for theatrical works. We are very interested in crossover work.
Performances Mike Reid's *Different Fields* (one act opera); David Olney's *Light in August* (folk opera); and Sid Selvidge's *Riversongs* (one act blues opera).
Tips "Spend many hours thinking about the synopsis (plot outline)."

☑ ORCHESTRA SEATTLE/SEATTLE CHAMBER SINGERS

P.O. Box 15825, Seattle WA 98115. (206)682-5208. E-mail: osscs@osscs.org. Website: www.osscs.org. **Contact:** Andrew Danilchik, librarian. Symphony orchestra, chamber music ensemble and community chorus. Estab. 1969. Members are amateurs and professionals. Performs 8 concerts/year including 2-3 new works. Commissions 1-2 composers or new works/year. "Our audience is made up of both experienced and novice classical music patrons. The median age is 45 with an equal number of males and females in the upper income range. Most concerts now held in Benaroya Hall."

How to Contact Query first. Include SASE. Responds in 1 year.

Performances Robert Kechley's *Trumpet Concerto* (classical concerto); Carol Sams's *Earthmakers* (oratorio); and Murl Allen Sanders's *Accordion Concerto* (classical concerto).

ℕ OREGON SYMPHONY

921 SW Washington St., Suite 200, Portland OR 97205. (503)228-4294. E-mail: symphony@orsymp hony.org. Website: www.orsymphony.org. **Contact:** Susan Nielson, concert director. Symphony orchestra. Estab. 1896. Members are professionals. Performs 110 concerts/year including 5-10 new works. Commissions 1 composer or new work/every other year. "Classical concerts are attended predominantly by 35-60 year olds. Hall seats 2,776—renovated vaudeville house." Pay varies for outright purchase.

How to Contact Query first. Does not return material. Responds in 1 month.

Music "Classical 10-20 min.: 3333-5331 3 perc, 1 tmp, 1 harp, 1 keyboard, strings: 16-14-12-10-8; pops, jazz: same, except strings 12-10-8-6-4. No country. Send a list of other orchestras with whom you have performed."

Performances John Adam's *Violin Concerto* (classical); Aaron Vernis' *New Era Dance* (classical); and George Rochberg's *Oboe Concerto* (classical).

ℕ PALMETTO MASTERSINGERS

P.O. Box 7441, Columbia SC 29202. (803)765-0777. Fax: (928)441-6083. E-mail: info@palmettomas tersingers.org. Website: www.palmettomastersingers.org. **Contact:** Walter Cuttino, music director. 80 voice male chorus. Estab. 1981 by the late Dr. Arpad Darasz. Members are professionals and amateurs. Performs 8-10 concerts/year. Commissions 1 composer of new works every other year (on average). Audience is generally older adults, "but it's a wide mix." Performance space for the season series is the Koger Center (approximately 2,000 seats) in Columbia, SC. More intimate venues also available. Fee is negotiable for outright purchase.

How to Contact Query first. Include SASE. Or e-mail to info@palmettomastersingers.org.

Music Seeking music of 10-15 minutes in length, "not too far out tonally. Orchestration is negotiable, but chamber size (10-15 players) is normal. We rehearse once a week and probably will not have more than 8-10 rehearsals. These rehearsals (2 hours each) are spent learning a 1½-hour program. Only 1-2 rehearsals (max) are with the orchestra. Piano accompaniments need not be simplified, as our accompanist is exceptional."

Performances Randal Alan Bass' *Te Deum* (12-minute, brass and percussion); Dick Goodwin's *Mark Twain Remarks* (40 minute, full symphony); and Randol Alan Bass' *A Simple Prayer* (a capella 6 minute).

Tips "Contact us as early as possible, given that programs are planned by July. Although this is an amateur chorus, we have performed concert tours of Europe, performed at Carnegie Hall, The National Cathedral and the White House in Washington, DC. We are skilled amateurs."

PRINCETON SYMPHONY ORCHESTRA

P.O. Box 250, Princeton NJ 08542. E-mail: info@princetonsymphony.org. Website: www.princeton symphony.org. **Contact:** Mark Laycock, music director. Symphony orchestra. Estab. 1980. Members are professionals. Performs 6-10 concerts/year including some new works. Commissions 1 composer or new work/year. Performs in a "beautiful, intimate 800-seat hall with amazing sound." Pays by arrangement.

How to Contact Submit through agent only. Include SASE. Responds in 6 months.

Music "Orchestra usually numbers 40-60 individuals."

⛶ PRISM SAXOPHONE QUARTET

257 Harvey St., Philadelphia PA 19144. (215)438-5282. E-mail: info@prismquartet.com. Website: www.prismquartet.com. President, New Sounds Music Inc. Prism Quartet: Matthew Levy. Chamber music ensemble. Estab. 1984. Members are professionals. Performs 80 concerts/year including 10-15 new works. Commissions 4 composers or new works/year. "Ours are primarily traditional chamber music audiences." Pays royalty per performance from BMI or ASCAP or commission range from $100 to $15,000.

How to Contact Submit complete score (with parts) and tape of piece(s). Does not return material. Responds in 3 months.

Music "Orchestration—sax quartet, SATB. Lengths—5-25 minutes. Styles—contemporary, classical, jazz, crossover, ethnic, gospel, avant-garde. No limitations on level of difficulty. No more than 4 performers (SATB sax quartet). No transcriptions. The Prism Quartet places special emphasis on crossover works which integrate a variety of musical styles."

Performances David Liebman's *The Gray Convoy* (jazz); Bradford Ellis's *Tooka-Ood Zasch* (ethnic-world music); and William Albright's *Fantasy Etudes* (contemporary classical).

⛶ RIDGEWOOD SYMPHONY ORCHESTRA

P.O. Box 176, Ridgewood NJ 07451. (201)612-0118. Fax: (201)529-4343. E-mail: info@ridgewoodsymphony.org. Website: www.ridgewoodsymphony.org. **Contact:** Gary S. Fagin, music director and conductor. Symphony orchestra. Estab. 1939. Members (95 plus) are professionals and amateurs. Performs 4-6 concerts/year and 3-5 children's concerts including 1-2 new works. Commissions possibly 1 new work/year. Audience is "sophisticated." Performance space is 744-seat school auditorium. Pays commission fee.

How to Contact Submit complete score and tape of piece(s). Include SASE. Responds in 3 months ("it depends on how busy we are").

Music "Symphonic works of various lengths and types which can be performed by a nonprofessional orchestra. We are flexible but would like to involve all of our players; very restrictive instrumentations do not suit our needs."

Performances Shostakovich's *Festive Overture*; Gerschwin's *Piano Concerto in F*; Gerschwin's *American in Paris* (rhapsody); Dvorak's *Symphony No. 7 in d Minor*; Mussorgsky's *Pictures at an Exhibition*; Schumann's *Symphony No. 2 in C Major*; Berlioz's *Symphonie Fantastique*; and Elgar's *Enigma Variations*.

Tips "Please lay out rehearsal numbers/letters and rests according to phrases and other logical musical divisions rather than in groups of ten measures, etc., which is very unmusical, wastes time and causes a surprising number of problems. Also, please *do not* send a score written in concert pitch; use the usual transpositions so that the conductor sees what the players see. Rehearsal is much more effective this way. Cross cue all important solos; this helps in rehearsal where instruments may be missing."

⛶ SACRAMENTO MASTER SINGERS

P.O. Box 417997, Sacramento CA 95841. (916)971-3159. Fax: (916)788-7464. E-mail: smscbarb@aol.com. Website: www.mastersingers.org. **Contact:** Ralph Hughes, conductor/artistic director. Vocal ensemble. Estab. 1984. Members are professionals and amateurs. Performs 9 concerts/year including 5-6 new works. Commissions 2 new works/year. Audience is made up of mainly college age and older patrons. Performs mostly in churches with 500-900 seating capacity. Pays $200 for outright purchase.

How to Contact Submit complete score and tape of piece(s). Include SASE. Responds in 5 weeks.

Music "A cappella works; works with small orchestras or few instruments; works based on classical styles with a 'modern' twist; multi-cultural music; shorter works probably preferable, but this is not a requirement. We usually have 38-45 singers capable of a high level of difficulty, but find that often simple works are very pleasing."

Performances Joe Jennings' *An Old Black Woman, Homeless and Indistinct* (SATB, oboe, strings, dramatic).

Tips "Keep in mind we are a chamber ensemble, not a 100-voice choir."

✓ 🗓 SAN FRANCISCO GIRLS CHORUS

44 Page Street, Suite 200, San Francisco CA 94102. (415)863-1752. E-mail: info@sfgirlschorus.org. Website: www.sfgirlschorus.org. **Contact:** Susan McMane, artistic director. Vocal ensemble. Estab. 1978. Volunteer chorus with a core of paid professionals. Performs 8-10 concerts/year including 3-4 new works. Commissions 2-3 composers or new works/year. Concerts are performed for "choral/classical music lovers, plus family audiences and audiences interested in international repertoire. Season concerts are performed in a 900-seat church with excellent acoustics and in San Francisco's Davies Symphony Hall, a 2,800-seat state-of-the-art auditorium." Pay negotiable for outright purchase.

- The San Francisco Girls Chorus was a featured guest performer on the San Francisco Symphony's recording of Stravinsky's *Persephone*, which won a 2000 Grammy Award for Best Classical Album and Best Orchestral Performance.

How to Contact Submit complete score. Does not return material. Responds in 6 months.

Music "Music for treble voices (SSAA); a cappella, piano accompaniment, or small orchestration; 3-10 minutes in length. Wide variety of styles; 45 singers; challenging music is encouraged."

Performances Lisa Bielawa's *Letter to Anna (1998)* (a cappella); Jake Heggie's *Patterns* (piano, mezzo-soprano soloist, chorus); and Chen Yi's *Chinese Poems* (a cappella).

Tips "Choose excellent texts and write challenging and beautiful music. The San Francisco Girls Chorus has pioneered in establishing girls choral music as an art form in the United States. The Girls Chorus is praised for its 'stunning musical standard' (*San Francisco Chronicle*) in performances in the San Francisco Bay Area and on tour. SFGC's annual concert season showcases the organization's concert/touring ensembles, Chorissima and Virtuose, in performances of choral masterworks from around the world, commissioned works by contemporary composers, and 18th-century music from the Venetian Ospedali and Mexican Baroque which SFGC has brought out of the archives and onto the concert stage. Chorissima and Virtuose tour through California with partial support provided by the California Arts Council Touring Program and have represented the U.S. and the City of San Francisco nationally and abroad. The choruses provide ensemble and solo singers for performances and recordings with the San Francisco Symphony and San Francisco Opera, Women's Philharmonic, and many other music ensembles. SFGC's discography includes four CD recordings, *I Never Saw Another Butterfly* (20th Century music); *A San Francisco Christmas;* Benjamin Britten's *A Ceremony of Carols* and other holiday music; a 1998 release, *Music from the Venetian Ospedali* (18th-century works for girls chorus) (called "fresh" by *The New Yorker*); and a 2000 release, *Crossroads* (a collection of international music)."

Ⓝ SINGING BOYS OF PENNSYLVANIA

P.O. Box 206, Wind Gap PA 18091. (610)759-6002. Fax: (727)526-6197. **Contact:** K. Bernard Schade, Ed. D., director. Vocal ensemble. Estab. 1970. Members are professional children. Performs 100 concerts/year including 3-5 new works. "We attract general audiences: family, senior citizens, churches, concert associations, university concert series and schools." Pays $300-3,000 for outright purchase.

How to Contact Query first. Does not return material. Responds in 3 weeks.

Music "We want music for commercials, voices in the SSA or SSAA ranges, sacred works or arrangements of American folk music with accompaniment. Our range of voices are from G below middle C to A (13th above middle C). Reading ability of choir is good but works which require a lot of work with little possibility of more than one performance are of little value. We sing very few popular songs except for special events. We perform music by composers who are well-known and works by living composers who are writing in traditional choral forms. Works which have a full orchestral score are of interest. The orchestration should be fairly light, so as not to cover the voices. Works for Christmas have more value than some other, since we perform with orchestras on an annual basis."

Performances Don Locklair's *The Columbus Madrigals* (opera).

Tips "It must be appropriate music and words for children. We do not deal in pop music. Folk music, classics and sacred are acceptable."

SOLI DEO GLORIA CANTORUM

3402 Woolworth Ave., Omaha NE 68105. (402)341-4111. E-mail: cantorum@berkey.com. Website: www.berkey.com. **Contact:** Almeda Berkey, music director. Professional choir. Estab. 1988. Members are professionals. Performs 5-7 concerts/year; several are new works. Commissions 1-2 new works/year. Performance space: "cathedral, symphony hall, smaller intimate recital halls as well." Payment is "dependent upon composition and composer."

How to Contact Submit complete score and tape of piece(s). Include SASE. Responds in 2 months.

Music "Chamber music mixed with topical programming (e.g., all Celtic or all Hispanic programs, etc.). Generally a cappella compositions from very short to extended range (6-18 minutes) or multi-movements. Concerts are of a formal length (approx. 75 minutes) with 5 rehearsals. Difficulty must be balanced within program in order to adequately prepare in a limited rehearsal time. 28 singers. Not seeking orchestral pieces, due to limited budget."

Performances Jackson Berkey's *Native Am Ambience* (eclectic/classical); John Rutter's *Hymn to the Creator of Light* (classical); and Arvo Part's *Te Deum* (multi-choir/chant-based classical).

N SOUTHERN ARIZONA SYMPHONY ORCHESTRA

P.O. Box 43131, Tucson AZ 85733-3131. (520)323-7166. Fax: (480)585-4485. E-mail: info@sasomusic.org. Website: www.sasomusic.org. **Contact:** Warren Cohen, musical director. Symphony orchestra. Estab. 1979. Members are amateurs. Performs 9 concerts/year at least 2 new works every year. Commissions 1 composer or new work/year. Audience is a cross-section of Tucson as well as retirees. Perfoms in the 400-seat Berger Performing Arts Center and the 700-seat Saddlebrooke Arts Center. Pay varies. "We arrange each case differently, usually pay per performance."

How to Contact Submit complete score and tape of piece(s). Include SASE. Responds in 4 months "or longer."

Music Seeking works for a full symphony or chamber orchestra. Open to all styles of music, and will consider works of any length under 30 minutes. "Concertos are harder to program, as are works with chorus, but we will consider them. We have an amateur orchestra, but we have played a good deal of fairly difficult music. We could not, however, do Bruckner or Mahler symphonies. Most contemporary music has been fairly conservative in style, but we are open to things that are different, as long as it's not extremely difficult. Please keep orchestration fairly standard; no bass oboes or theremins."

Performances 1999-2000 season included world premiere of James Barnes' *Autumn Soliloquy*. Other performances include Richard Arnell's *Symphony No. 6*, and Malcolm Arnold's *Clarinet Concerto No. 2*.

Tips "Send a nice clean score. Don't get discouraged as we only have limited performance options. We appreciate knowing if you have orchestral parts available. We are especially excited by the possibility of discovering talented, unknown composers who have not had the opportunities available to those who are well-connected."

N SPACE COAST POPS, INC.

P.O. Box 3344, 2150 Lake Dr., Cocoa FL 32926, Cocoa FL 32924. (321)632-7445. Fax: (321)632-1611. E-mail: popsorch@aol.com. Website: www.spacecoastpops.com. **Contact:** Robert Coleman, music director and conductor. Pops orchestra and chamber music ensemble. Estab. 1986. Members are professionals. Performs 7 concerts/year, including 1-2 new works. Concerts are performed for "average audience—they like familiar works and pops. Concert halls up to 2,000 seats."

How to Contact Query first. Include SASE. Responds in 6 months.

Music Seeks "pops and serious music for full symphony orchestra, but not an overly large orchestra with unusual instrumentation. We use about 60 musicians because of hall limitations. Works should be medium difficulty—not too easy and not too difficult—and not more than ten minutes long." Does not wish to see avant-garde music.

Performances Dussich's *First March* (march).

Tips "If we would commission a work it would be to feature the space theme in our area."

N ST. LOUIS CHAMBER CHORUS

P.O. Box 11558, Clayton MO 63105. (636)458-4343. E-mail: maltworm@inlink.com. Website: www .chamberchorus.org. **Contact:** Philip Barnes, artistic director. Vocal ensemble, chamber music ensemble. Estab. 1956. Members are professionals and amateurs. Performs 6 concerts/year including 5-10 new works. Commissions 1-2 new works/year. Audience is "diverse and interested in unaccompanied choral work and outstanding architectural/acoustic venues." Performances take place at various auditoria noted for their excellent acoustics—churches, synagogues, schools and university halls. Pays by arrangement.

How to Contact Query first. Does not return material. "Panel of 'readers' submit report to Artistic Director. Responds in 3 months. 'General Advice' leaflet available on request."

Music *"Only a cappella* writing; no contemporary 'popular' works; historical editions welcomed. No improvisatory works. Our programs are tailored for specific acoustics—composers should indicate their preference."

Performances Sir Richard Rodney Bennett's *A Contemplation Upon Flowers* (a cappella madrigal); Stuart McIntosh's *Can Thou Lov'st Me, Lady?* (a cappella glee for men's voices); and Sasha Johnson Manning's *Dies Irae* (a cappella motet).

Tips "We only consider a cappella works which can be produced in five rehearsals. Therefore pieces of great complexity or duration are discouraged."

SUSQUEHANNA SYMPHONY ORCHESTRA

P.O. Box 485, Forest Hill MD 21050. (410)838-6465. E-mail: sheldon.bair@ssorchestra.org. Website: www.ssorchestra.org. **Contact:** Sheldon Bair, music director. Symphony orchestra. Estab. 1978. Members are amateurs. Performs 6 concerts/year including 1-2 new works. Composers paid depending on the circumstances. "We perform in 1 hall, 600 seats with fine acoustics. Our audience encompasses all ages."

How to Contact Query first. Include SASE. Responds in 3 or more months.

Music "We desire works for large orchestra, any length, in a 'conservative 20th and 21st century' style. Seek fine music for large orchestra. We are a community orchestra, so the music must be within our grasp. Violin I to 7th position by step only; Violin II—stay within 5th position; English horn and harp are OK. Full orchestra pieces preferred."

Performances Derek Bourgeois' *Trombone Concerto*; Gwyneth Walker's *The Magic Oboe*; and Johan de Meij's *Symphony No. 1 "Lord of the Rings."*

◘ TORONTO MENDELSSOHN CHOIR

60 Simcoe St., Toronto ON M5J 2H5 Canada. (416)598-0422. Fax: (416)598-2992. E-mail: manager @tmchoir.org. Website: www.tmchoir.org. **Contact:** Eileen Keown, executive director. Vocal ensemble. Members are professionals and amateurs. Performs 25 concerts/year including 1-3 new works. "Most performances take place in Roy Thomson Hall. The audience is reasonably sophisticated, musically knowledgeable but with moderately conservative tastes." Pays by commission and ASCAP/SOCAN.

How to Contact Query first or submit complete score and tapes of pieces. Include SASE. Responds in 6 months.

Music All works must suit a large choir (180 voices) and standard orchestral forces or with some other not-too-exotic accompaniment. Length should be restricted to no longer than ½ of a nocturnal concert. The choir sings at a very professional level and can sight-read almost anything. "Works should fit naturally with the repertoire of a large choir which performs the standard choral orchestral repertoire."

Performances Holman's *Jezebel*; Orff's *Catulli Carmina*; and Lambert's *Rio Grande*.

N TOURING CONCERT OPERA CO. INC.

228 E. 80th, New York NY 10021. (212)988-2542. Fax: (518)851-6778. E-mail: tcoc@mhonline.net. **Contact:** Anne DeFigols, director. Opera company. Estab. 1971. Members are professionals. Performs 30 concerts/year including 1 new work. Payment varies.

How to Contact Submit complete score and tape of piece(s). Does not return material. Response time varies.

Music "Operas or similar with small casts."

Tips "We are a touring company which travels all over the world. Therefore, operas with casts that are not large and simple but effective sets are the most practical."

N TULSA OPERA INC.

1610 S. Boulder, Tulsa OK 74119-4479. (918)582-4035. Fax: (918)592-0380. E-mail: tulsaopera@tul saopera.com. Website: www.tulsaopera.com. **Contact:** Carol I. Crawford, general director. Opera company. Estab. 1948. Members are professionals. Performs 3 concerts/year including 1 new work. Commissions 1 composer or new work/year. "We have a contract with the Performing Arts Center. It holds approximately 2,300." Pays for outright purchase or by royalty (negotiable).

How to Contact Query first. Include SASE. Responds in 2 months.

Music "At the present time we are looking for new material for student operas. They need to be approximately 45-50 minutes in length, with piano accompaniment. For our main stage productions we use the Philharmonic Orchestra and our Artistic Director auditions our singers. Our student performances are sometimes done by young artists. The student materials need to be adapted for four-five singers. These young artists are usually just beginning their careers therefore they are limited in difficulty of the music. Our main stage artists are adept in doing more difficult roles and roles of the classic operas."

Performances Seymour Barab's *Little Red Riding Hood* (children's 1-act opera).

Tips "Our Artistic Director is very open to ideas and materials. She is interested in new works to present for our opera season."

⊠ VANCOUVER CHAMBER CHOIR

1254 W. Seventh Ave., Vancouver BC V6H 1B6 Canada. E-mail: info@vancouverchamberchoir.c om. Website: www.vancouverchamberchoir.com. **Contact:** Jon Washburn, artistic director. Vocal ensemble. Members are professionals. Performs 40 concerts/year including 5-8 new works. Commissions 2-4 composers or new works/year. Pays SOCAN royalty or negotiated fee for commissions.

How to Contact Submit complete score and tape of piece(s). Does not return material. Responds in 6 months if possible.

Music Seeks "choral works of all types for small chorus, with or without accompaniment and/or soloists. Concert music only. Choir made up of 20 singers. Large or unusual instrumental accompaniments are less likely to be appropriate. No pop music."

Performances The VCC has commissioned and premiered over 180 new works by Canadian and international composers, including Alice Parker's *That Sturdy Vine* (cantata for chorus, soloists and orchestra); R. Murray Schafer's *Magic Songs* (SATB a cappella); and Jon Washburn's *A Stephen Foster Medley* (SSAATTBB/piano).

Tips "We are looking for choral music that is performable yet innovative, and which has the potential to become 'standard repertoire.' Although we perform much new music, only a small portion of the many scores which are submitted can be utilized."

N VIRGINIA OPERA

P.O. Box 2580, Norfolk VA 23501. (757)627-9545. E-mail: info@vaopera.com. Website: www.vaop era.org. Director of Education: Jeff Corrirean. Artistic Director: Peter Mark. Opera company. Estab. 1974. Members are professionals. Performs more than 560 concerts/year. Commissions vary on number of composers or new works/year. Concerts are performed for school children throughout Virginia, grades K-5, 6-8 and 9-12 at the Harrison Opera House in Norfolk, and at public/private schools in Virginia. Pays on commission.

How to Contact Query first. Include SASE. Response time varies.

Music "Audience accessible style approximately 45 minutes in length. Limit cast list to three vocal artists of any combination. Accompanied by piano and/or keyboard. Works are performed before school children of all ages. Pieces must be age appropriate both aurally and dramatically. Musical styles are encouraged to be diverse, contemporary as well as traditional. Works are produced and presented with sets, costumes, etc." Limitations: "Three vocal performers (any combination). One keyboardist. Medium to difficult acceptable, but prefer easy to medium. Seeking only pieces which are suitable for presentation as part of an opera education program for Virginia Opera's education and outreach department. Subject matter must meet strict guidelines relative to Learning Objectives, etc. Musical idiom must be representative of current trends in opera, musical theater. Extreme dissonance, row systems not applicable to this environment.''

Performances Seymour Barab's *Cinderella*; John David Earnest's *The Legend of Sleepy Hollow*; and Seymour Barab's *The Pied Piper of Hamelin*.

Tips ''Theatricality is very important. New works should stimulate interest in musical theater as a legitimate art form for school children with no prior exposure to live theatrical entertainment. Composer should be willing to create a product which will find success within the educational system.''

Contests & Awards

Participating in contests is a great way to gain exposure for your music. Prizes vary from contest to contest, from cash to musical merchandise to studio time, and even publishing and recording deals. For musical theater and classical composers, the prize may be a performance of your work. Even if you don't win, valuable contacts can be made through contests. Many times, contests are judged by music publishers and other industry professionals, so your music may find its way into the hands of key industry people who can help further your career.

HOW TO SELECT A CONTEST

It's important to remember when entering any contest to do proper research before signing anything or sending any money. We have confidence in the contests listed in *Songwriter's Market*, but it pays to read the fine print. First, be sure you understand the contest rules and stipulations once you receive the entry forms and guidelines. Then you need to weigh what you will gain against what they're asking you to give up. If a publishing or recording contract is the only prize a contest is offering, you may want to think twice before entering. Basically, the company sponsoring the contest is asking you to pay a fee for them to listen to your song under the guise of a contest, something a legitimate publisher or record company would not do. For those contests offering studio time, musical equipment or cash prizes, you need to decide if the entry fee you're paying is worth the chance to win such prizes.

Be wary of exorbitant entry fees, and if you have any doubts whatsoever as to the legitimacy of a contest, it's best to stay away. Songwriters need to approach a contest, award or grant in the same manner as they would a record or publishing company. Make your submission as professional as possible; follow directions and submit material exactly as stated on the entry form.

Contests in this section encompass all types of music and levels of competition. Read each listing carefully and contact them if the contest interests you. Many contests now have websites that offer additional information and even entry forms you can print. Be sure to read the rules carefully and be sure you understand exactly what a contest is offering before entering.

AGO/ECS PUBLISHING AWARD IN CHORAL COMPOSITION

American Guild of Organists, 475 Riverside Dr., Suite 1260, New York NY 10115. (212)870-2310. Fax: (212)870-2163. E-mail: info@agohq.org. Website: www.agohq.org. **Contact:** Harold Calhoun, competitions coordinator. Biannual award.

Requirements Composers are invited to submit a work for SATB choir and organ in which the organ plays a significant and independent role. Work submitted must be unpublished and approximately 3.5 to 5 minutes in length. There is no age restriction. Deadline: TBA, "but usually late fall in even numbered years." Application information on the website.

Awards $2,000 cash prize, publication by ECS Publishing and premier performance at the AGO National Convention.

ALEA III INTERNATIONAL COMPOSITION PRIZE

855 Commonwealth Ave., Boston MA 02215. (617)353-3340. E-mail: kalogeras@earthlink.com. Website: www.aleaiii.com. For composers. Annual award.

Purpose To promote and encourage young composers in the composition of new music.

Requirements Composers born after January 1, 1966 may participate; 1 composition per composer. Works may be for solo voice or instrument or for chamber ensemble up to 15 members lasting between 6 and 15 minutes. Available instruments are: one flute (doubling piccolo or alto), one oboe (doubling English horn), one clarinet (doubling bass clarinet), one bassoon, one horn, one trumpet, one trombone, one tuba, two percussion players, one harp, one keyboard player, one guitar, two violins, one viola, one cello, one bass, tape and one voice. All works must be unpublished and must not have been publicly performed or broadcast, in whole or in part or in any other version before the announcement of the prize in late September or early October of 2006. Works that have won other awards are not eligible. Deadline: March 15 2006. Send for application. Submitted work required with application. "Real name should not appear on score; a nom de plume should be signed instead. Sealed envelope with entry form should be attached to each score."

Awards ALEA III International Composition Prize: $2,500. Awarded once annually. Between 6-8 finalists are chosen and their works are performed in a competition concert by the ALEA III contemporary music ensemble. At the end of the concert, one piece will beselected to receive the prize. One grand prize winner is selected by a panel of judges.

Tips "Emphasis placed on works written in 20th century compositional idioms."

AMERICAN SONGWRITER LYRIC CONTEST

50 Music Sq. West Suite 604, Nashville TN 37203. (615)321-6096. Fax: (615)321-6097. E-mail: info@americansongwriter.com. Website: www.americansongwriter.com. **Contact:** Office Administrator. Estab. 1984. For songwriters and composers. Award for each bimonthly issue of *American Songwriter* magazine, plus grand prize at year-end.

Purpose To promote the art of songwriting.

Requirements Lyrics must be typed and a check for $10 (per entry) must be enclosed. Deadlines: January 21, March 21, May 23, July 19, September 17, November 13. Call for required official form or get it from our website. Lyrics only, no cassettes.

Awards A Martin guitar to each contest winner. Awards airfare to Nashville and a demo session for yearly winner; certificates to all winners; and top 5 winning lyrics reprinted in each magazine. Lyrics judged by 6-7 industry people—songwriters, publishers, journalists.

Tips "You do not have to be a subscriber to enter or win. You may submit as many entries as you like."

N ANNUAL ONE-ACT PLAYWRIGHTING COMPETITION

15 W. 28th St., 3rd Floor, New York NY 10001. (212)252-1619. Fax: (212)252-8763. E-mail: info@ta datheater.com. Website: www.tadatheater.com. **Contact:** Playwrighting Contest. Estab. 1984. For musical playwrights of any age, both professionals and students are encouraged to apply.

 • Also see the listing for Tada! in the Play Producers section of this book.

Purpose "The series was initiated to encourage playwrights, composers, and lyricists to create theatrical works which address issues important to teens."

Requirements "Script must be original, unproduced and unpublished one-act plays primarily for teen actors and teen audiences. Scripts submitted must handle issues that are relevant to teens and the teen experience. Plays do not have to be contemporary. Cast must be made up primarily of teenagers ages 13 to 18; children do not play adults—adult actors will be hired. Limit 1-2 adults per cast. Musicals are not accepted for this series but can be submitted to TADA! separately. Plays with animals and non-human characters are highly discouraged. Submit a completed entry form, résumé, short bio and three copies of the play in standard format. Scripts must be typed; include character breakdown, set and costume descriptions. A self-addressed stamped envelope is required if you want your script returned."

Tips "In a staged reading, actors read their lines from scripts that they carry as they move around the stage. There are no sets, costumes, or props. Instead, the emphasis is on the text and the message it sends to the audience. Following each performance, the audience participates in an open discussion with the playwright, actors, and director. Past Staged Reading plays have focused on topics ranging from teenage crushes, friendship, and peer pressure to date rape, alcoholism, AIDS, divorce, and war."

BAKER'S PLAYS HIGH SCHOOL PLAYWRITING CONTEST

Baker's Plays, P.O. Box 699222, Quincy MA 02269-9222. (617)745-0805. Fax: (617)745-9891. E-mail: info@bakersplay.com. Website: www.bakersplays.com. **Contact:** Contest Director. Estab. 1990. For high school students. Annual award.

Requirements Plays should be about the "high school experience," but may also be about any subject and of any length, so long as the play can be reasonably produced on the high school stage. Plays must be accompanied by the signature of a sponsoring high school drama or English teacher, and it is recommended that the play receive a production or a public reading prior to the submission. Multiple submissions and co-authored scripts are welcome. Teachers may not submit a student's work. The manuscript must be firmly bound, typed and come with a SASE. Include enough postage to cover the return of the manuscript. Scripts that do not come with an SASE will not be returned. Do not send originals; copies only. Deadline: January 30. Send for guidelines.

Awards 1st Place: $500 and the play will be published by Baker's Plays; 2nd Place: $250 and an Honorable Mention; 3rd Place: $100 and an Honorable Mention.

BILLBOARD SONG CONTEST

P.O. Box 470306, Tulsa OK 74147. (918)624-2100. Fax: (918)477-7252. E-mail: david@jimhalsey.com. Website: www.billboard.com/songcontest. **Contact:** David Kindred, Director. Estab. 1988. For songwriters, composers and performing artists. Annual international contest.

Purpose "To reward deserving songwriters and performers for their talent."

Requirements Entry fee: $30.

Awards To be announced. For entry forms and additional information send SASE to the above address or visit website.

Tips "Participants should understand popular music structure."

BUSH ARTIST FELLOWS PROGRAM

E-900 First National Bank Bldg., 332 Minnesota St., St. Paul MN 55101. (651)227-5222. E-mail: kpolley@bushfound.org. Website: www.bushfoundation.org. **Contact:** Kathi Polley, program assistant. Estab. 1976. For songwriters, composers and musical playwrights. Applications in music composition are accepted in even-numbered years.

Purpose "To provide artists with significant financial support that enables them to further their work and their contribution to their communities."

Requirements Applicant must be a Minnesota, North Dakota, South Dakota or western Wisconsin resident for 12 of preceeding 36 months, 25 years or older, not a student. Deadline: late October. Send for application. Audio work samples required with application. "Music composition applications will not be taken again until the fall of 2006. Applications will be taken in the fall of 2006 in the following areas: music composition, scriptworks (screenwriting and playwriting), literature (creative non-fiction, fiction, poetry) and film/video.

Awards Fellowships: $44,000 stipend for a period of 12-24 months. "Five years after completion of preceeding fellowship, one may apply again." Applications are judged by peer review panels.

THE CLW MUSIC AWARD/LIAISON
Beverly Hills CA 90209. (310)775-1238. E-mail: bej@india.com. Website: www.clwma.5u.com. **Contact:** Holly Nigelson, Brenda Jackson or Jeremiah Lyles, owners/partners (for information and an application). Estab. 2002. For Songwriters and Composers.
Purpose "To aid or further the careers of independent musicians, eligible enrolled music students and certain Native/African/Asian/American Organizations musically."
Requirements "Each song entered must be an original work. The songs may have multiple writers, but only one name need be on the application. The performer or performers must be the writers of the material submitted and must be the same individuals who are attend the awards. Division of the prizes to any co-writers shall be the responsibility of the person named on the entry form as the leader of the band or group. No song previously recorded and released through national or any other type of distribution in any country will be eligible to win. Each entry must consist of: 1) A CD or audiocassette containing 1 song, which shall be 5 minutes in length or less. The side with the entry shall be cued to the beginning of the song and it shall be named or marked so. Failure to maintain this regulation shall result in disqualification; 2) The entry form must be signed in ink, in any color, no roller balls, felt tips, Magic Markers, or anything similar shall be accepted. Any non-legible entry forms shall be disqualified. All signatures must be the originals, and shall be verified; 3) If there are any lyrics included with a song, a lyric sheet must be typed or laser printed, no hand written or ink jet printed lyric sheets shall be accepted. Lyrics must have an English translation lyric sheet also, if applicable. Instrumental music shall not require either; 4) The entry fee of $30, payable by money order, personal or business check or credit card. Entry fees are not refundable. No solo entries or a-cappella entries shall be accepted *Employees family, friends, affiliates and associates of this contest are not eligible to win the contest. Do not send cash and if you use a major credit card, an additional $1.50 will be charged to your account!* There are 5 preliminary rounds of Judging and the contest final rounds. 1 Finalist from each category will be selected as a finalist and 5 finalists with the highest point totals from the rest of the field will be chosen as finalists also. After judging, the 15 finalists shall be notified by mail and will be sent the proper affidavits, which must be returned not more than 40 business days after the date on the congratulatory letter each shall receive. Any fraudulent or inaccurate information shall result in disqualification and an alternate winner shall be selected. Any printed or recorded submissions shall not be returned. Each contestant must be age 15 or older. Any winners under the age of 21 shall require a parent or guardian present for the administering of prizes. In the instances where any entrants are younger than age 21, the parent or guardian must also sign the entry form. Winners shall be determined 3 months after the close of submissions for the current contest. The odds for winning the overall CLW Music Award are, at maximum, 12,000 to 1 based upon a person making 1 entry, of the 12,000 required to start the Judging round. The format of this contest does not allow these odds to be greater. If a person enters more than 1 recording, the odds for winning increase accordingly, if the entries are in the same contest. A person can enter more than once in any category but a separate fee is required for each entry. If a contestant does not make the finals they may enter a future contest if they choose to. If a contestant finishes in third place or lower and finishes no higher by replacing any finalists that may be disqualified by some means, that contestant may enter a future contest if they choose to. The CLW Music Award and Aubusson Music Publishing are not responsible for any late, lost, damaged or mishandled entries. The contest is open to all Amateur persons in the world who have not earned more than $5,000 from music royalties in the last 2 years. This rule shall apply to an individual or all members of a group or band collectively. If it is found that an entrant violates these requirements, the entrant shall be prosecuted for fraud, and in addition, any amount of winnings shall be returned and the contestant will be disqualified, with another winner being selected in place of the fraudulent one. 15 finalists will perform their entry song, or songs at the finals and be Judged. Those entrants who finish 3rd place or lower and no higher, are eligible to enter again in the next contest. There are a total of 15 rounds of judging and the results remain unknown to everyone until the presentations. The Awards ceremony will be taped for broadcast at a later date.

Awards Prizes: 1 CLW Music Award Winner, who will receive $30,000 cash and a Publishing Award; 1 Grand Prize Winner, who will receive $15,000 in cash and a Publishing Award; 1 First Prize Winner, who will receive $7,500 cash and a Publishing Award; 1 Second Prize Winner, who will receive $5,000 cash and a Publishing Award; 1 Third Prize Winner, who will receive $2,500 in cash only; 1 Fourth Prize Winner, who will receive $1,500 cash; 1 Honorary Native American Music Award; 1 Honorary Asian American Music Award; and 1 Honorary African-American Music Award. There will also be 5 runners up with the runners up each receiving $1,000 cash. No substitutions for any prizes can, or will be, made.

Tips "DO NOT PHOTOCOPY YOUR ENTRY FORM FOR SOMEONE ELSE, they must have their own contestant serial number on their application. Photocopies are only for you in other categories. Make sure you read the rules and prepare your recording properly. Judging has been configured so that all types of music DO have the same chance of winning this contest. Make sure that you can perform your song live and be prepared to come to do so."

COLUMBIA ENTERTAINMENT COMPANY'S JACKIE WHITE MEMORIAL PLAYWRITING CONTEST

309 Parkade Blvd., Columbia MO 65202. (573)874-5628. **Contact:** Betsy Phillips, director, CEC contest. For musical playwrights. Annual award.

Purpose "We are looking for top-notch scripts suitable for family audiences with 7 or more fully-developed roles."

Requirements "May be adaptations or plays with original story lines and cannot have been previously published. Please write or call for complete rules." Send SASE for application; then send scripts to address above. Full-length play, neatly typed. No name on title page, but name, address and name of play on a 3×5 index card and lead sheets, as well as tape of musical numbers. $10 entry fee.

Awards $500 1st Prize. Play may or may not be produced at discretion of CEC. "The judging committee is taken from members of Columbia Entertainment Company's Executive and Advisory boards, and from theater school parents. Readings by up to eight members, with at least three readings of all entries, and winning entries being read by entire committee. All plays will receive a written evaluation."

Tips "We especially like plays that deal with current day problems and concerns. However, if the play is good enough, any suitable subject matter is fine."

CRS NATIONAL COMPOSERS COMPETITION

724 Winchester Rd., Broomall PA 19008. (610)544-5920. E-mail: crsnews@verizon.net. Website: http://mysite.verizon.net/crsnews. **Contact:** Caroline Hunt, administrative assistant. Senior Representative: Jack Shusterman. Estab. 1981. For songwriters, composers and performing artists. College faculty. Annual award.

Requirements For composers, songwriters, performing artists and ensembles. The work submitted must be non-published (prior to acceptance) and not commercially recorded on any label. The work submitted must not exceed nine performers. Each composer may submit one work for each application submitted. (Taped performances are additionally encouraged.) Composition must not exceed twenty-five minutes in length. CRS reserves the right not to accept a First Prize Winner. Write with SASE for application or visit website. Add $3.50 for postage and handling. Deadline: February 28. Send a detailed résumé with application form. Samples of work required with application. Send score and parts on cassette or DAT. Application fee: $50.

Awards 1st Prize: Commercial recording grant. Applications are judged by panel of judges determined each year.

CUNNINGHAM COMMISSION FOR YOUTH THEATRE

(formerly Cunningham Prize for Playwriting), The Theatre School, DePaul University, 2135 N. Kenmore Ave., Chicago IL 60614. (773)325-7938. Fax: (773)325-7920. E-mail: lgoetsch@depaul.edu. Website: www.theatreschool.depaul.edu. **Contact:** Lara Goetsch, director of marketing/public relations. Estab. 1990. For playwrights. Annual award.

Purpose "The purpose of the Commission is to encourage the writing of dramatic works for young audiences that affirm the centrality of religion, broadly defined, and the human quest for meaning, truth, and community. The Theatre School intends to produce the plays created through this commission in its award-winning Chicago Playworks for Families and Young Audiences series at the historic Merle Reskin Theatre. Each year Chicago Playworks productions are seen by 35,000 students and families from throughout the Chicago area."

Requirements "Candidates for the commission must be writers whose residence is in the Chicago area, defined as within 100 miles of the Loop. Playwrights who have won the award within the last five years are not eligible. Deadline: annually by October 1. Candidates should submit a résumé, a 20 page sample of their work, and a brief statement about their interest in the commission. The submission should not include a proposal for a project the playwright would complete if awarded the commission. The writing sample may be from a play of any genre for any audience."

Awards $5,000. "Winners will be notified by May 1. The Selection Committee is chaired by the Dean of The Theatre School and is composed of members of the Cunningham Commission advisory committee and faculty of The Theatre School."

HARVEY GAUL COMPOSITION CONTEST

The Pittsburgh New Music Ensemble, Inc., P.O. Box 99476, Pittsburgh PA 15233. E-mail: pnme@pnme.org. Website: www.pnme.org. **Contact:** Jeffrey Nyfah, DMA, managing director. For composers. Biennial.

Purpose Objective is to encourage composition of new music. Winning piece to be premiered by the PNME.

Requirements "Must be citizen of the US. New works scored for 6 to 16 instruments drawn from the following: flute, oboe, 2 clarinets, bassoon, horn, trumpet, trombone, tuba, 2 violins, cello, bass, 2 percussion, piano, harp, electronic tape." Deadline: September 30, 2004. Send SASE for application or download from www.pnme.org. Samples of work are required with application. Entry fee: $20.

Awards Harvey Gaul Composition Contest: $6,000.

☑ GRASSY HILL KERRVILLE NEW FOLK COMPETITION

(formerly New Folk Concerts For Emerging Songwriters), P.O. Box 291466, Kerrville TX 78029. (830)257-3600. Fax: (830)257-8680. E-mail: info@kerrville-music.com. Website: www.kerrvillefolkfestival.com. **Contact:** Dalis Allen, producer. For songwriters. Annual award.

- Also see the listing for Kerrville Folk Festival in the Workshops section of this book.

Purpose "To provide an opportunity for unknown songwriters to be heard and rewarded for excellence."

Requirements Songwriter enters 2 original previously unrecorded songs on same side of rewound cassette tape with entry fee; no more than one tape may be entered; 6-8 minutes total for 2 songs. No written application necessary; no lyric sheets or press material needed. Submissions accepted between December 1-March 15 or first 600 entries received prior to that date. Call or e-mail to request rules. Entry fee: $20.

Awards New Folk Award Winner. 32 semi-finalists invited to sing the 2 songs entered during The Kerrville Folk Festival in May. 6 writers are chosen as award winners. Each of the 6 receives a cash award of $450 or more and performs at a winner's concert during the Kerrville Folk Festival in June. Initial round of entries judged by the Festival Producer. 32 finalists judged by panel of 3 performer/songwriters.

Tips "Make certain cassette is rewound and ready to play. Do not allow instrumental accompaniment to drown out lyric content. Don't enter without complete copy of the rules. Former winners and finalists include Lyle Lovett, Nanci Griffith, Hal Ketchum, John Gorka, David Wilcox, Lucinda Williams and Robert Earl Keen, Tish Hinojosa, Carrie Newcomer, Jimmy Lafave, etc."

GREAT AMERICAN SONG CONTEST

PMB 135, 6327-C SW Capitol Hill Hwy., Portland OR 97239-1937. E-mail: info@GreatAmericanSong.com. Website: www.GreatAmericanSong.com. **Contact:** Carla Starrett, event coordinator. Estab. 1998. For songwriters, composers and lyricists. Annual award.

- Also see the listing for Songwriters Resource Network in the Organizations section of this book.

Purpose To help songwriters get their songs heard by music-industry professionals; to generate educational and networking opportunities for participating songwriters; to help songwriters open doors in the music business.

Requirements Entry fee: $25. "Annual deadline. Check our website for details or send SASE along with your mailed request for information."

Awards Winners receive a mix of cash awards and prizes. The focus of the contest is on networking and educational opportunities. (All participants receive detailed evaluations of their songs by industry professionals.) Songs are judged by knowledgeable music-industry professionals, including prominent hit songwriters, producers and publishers.

Tips "Focus should be on the song. The quality of the demo isn't important. Judges will be looking for good songwriting talent. They will base their evaluations on the song—not the quality of the recording or the voice performance."

HENRICO THEATRE COMPANY ONE-ACT PLAYWRITING COMPETITION

P.O. Box 27032, Richmond VA 23273. (804)501-5115. Fax: (804)501-5284. E-mail: per22@co.henric o.va.us. **Contact:** Amy A. Perdue, cultural arts coordinator. Cultural Arts Assistant: Elaome Payne. For musical playwrights, songwriters, composers and performing artists. Annual award.

Purpose Original one-act musicals for a community theater organization.

Requirements "Only one-act plays or musicals will be considered. The manuscript should be a one-act original (not an adaptation), unpublished, and unproduced, free of royalty and copyright restrictions. Scripts with smaller casts and simpler sets may be given preference. Controversial themes and excessive language should be avoided. Standard play script form should be used. All plays will be judged anonymously; therefore, there should be two title pages; the first must contain the play's title and the author's complete address and telephone number. The second title page must contain only the play's title. The playwright must submit two excellent quality copies. Receipt of all scripts will be acknowledged by mail. Scripts will be returned if SASE is included. No scripts will be returned until after the winner is announced. The HTC does not assume responsibility for loss, damage or return of scripts. All reasonable care will be taken." Deadline: July 1st. Send for application first.

Awards 1st Prize $300; 2nd Prize $200; 3rd Prize $200.

HOLTKAMP-AGO AWARD IN ORGAN COMPOSITION

American Guild of Organists, 475 Riverside Dr., Suite 1260, New York NY 10115. (212)870-2310. Fax: (212)870-2163. E-mail: info@agohq.org. Website: www.agohq.org. **Contact:** Harold Calhoun, competitions coordinator. For composers and performing artists. Biennial award.

Requirements Organ solo, no longer than 8 minutes in duration. Specifics vary from year to year. Deadline: TBA, but usually early spring of odd-numbered year. Go to the website for application.

Award $2,000 provided by the Holtkamp Organ Company; publication by Hinshaw Music Inc.; performance at the biennial National Convention of the American Guild of Organists.

INDIANA OPERA THEATRE/MACALLISTER AWARDS FOR OPERA SINGERS

P.O. Box 1941, Indianapolis IN 46206. (317)202-0634. E-mail: opera@iquest.net. Website: www.in dianaoperatheatre.com/macallister.html. Artister/General Director: E. Bookwalter. Estab. 1980. For college and professional opera singers.

Requirements For professional and amateurs. Entry fee: $25 professional, free for college students. Send for application or visit website. Auditions are held throughout the year; check the website.

Awards "The Final Awards Program dates are August 23-25."

JEROME COMPOSERS COMMISSIONING PROGRAM

(formerly Composers Commissioning Program), ACF, 332 Minnesota St., E-145, St. Paul MN 55101. (651)251-2824. Fax: (651)291-7978. E-mail: wcollins@composersforum.org. Website: www.compo

sersforum.org. **Contact:** Wendy Collins, program director. Estab. 1979. For songwriters, musical playwrights, composers and performers. Annual award.

Purpose "CCP provides grants to support the commissioning of new works by emerging composers."

Requirements Not for students. Deadline: end of July. Application available on website. Samples of work are required with application. Send score/tape.

Awards 18-22 commissioning grants of $1,500-8,000; each grant good for 5 years. Applications are judged by peer review panel (anonymous).

Tips "Composers pair up with performers: one party must be based in Minnesota or New York City."

THE JOHN LENNON SONGWRITING CONTEST

Fax: (212)579-4320. E-mail: info@jlsc.com. Website: www.jlsc.com. **Contact:** Chris DeCo, assistant director. Estab. 1996. For songwriters. Open year-round.

Purpose "The purpose of the John Lennon Songwriting Contest is to promote the art of songwriting by assisting in the discovery of new talent as well as providing more established songwriters with an opportunity to advance their careers."

Requirements Each entry must consist of the following: completed and signed application; audio-cassette, CD or mp3 containing one song only, 5 minutes or less in length; lyric sheet typed or printed legibly (English translation is required when applicable); $30 entry fee. Applications can be found in various music-oriented magazines and on our website. Prospective entrants can send for an application or contact the contest via e-mail at info@jlsc.com.

Awards Entries are accepted in the following 12 categories: rock, country, jazz, pop, world, gospel/inspirational, R&B, hip-hop, Latin, electronic, folk and children's music. Winners will receive EMI Publishing Contracts, Studio Equipment from Brian Moore Guitars, Roland, Edirol and Audio Technica, 1,000 CDs in full color with premium 6-panel Digipaks courtesy of Discmakers, and gift certificates from Musiciansfriend.com. One entrant wil be chosen to TOUR and PERFORM for one week on Warped Tour '06. One Lennon Award winning song will be named "Maxell Song of the Year" and take home an additional $20,000 in cash courtesy of the Maxell Corporation.

MAXIM MAZUMDAR NEW PLAY COMPETITION

One Curtain Up Alley, Buffalo NY 14202-1911. (716)852-2600. Fax: (716)852-2266. E-mail: newplays@alleyway.com. Website: www.alleyway.com. **Contact:** Literary Manager. For musical playwrights. Annual award.

Purpose Alleyway Theatre is dedicated to the development and production of new works. Winners of the competition will receive production and royalties.

Requirements Unproduced full-length work not less than 90 minutes long with cast limit of 10 and unit or simple set, or unproduced one-act work less than 15 minutes long with cast limit of 6 and simple set; prefers work with unconventional setting that explores the boundaries of theatricality; limit of 1 submission in each category; guidelines available, no entry form. $25 playwright entry fee. Script, résumé, SASE optional. Cassette mandatory. Deadline: July 1.

Awards Production for full-length play or musical with royalty and travel and housing determined on a yearly basis; and production for one-act play or musical.

Tips "Entries may be of any style, but preference will be given to those scripts which take place in unconventional settings and explore the boundaries of theatricality. No more than ten performers is a definite, unchangeable requirement."

N MCKNIGHT VISITING COMPOSER PROGRAM

ACF, 332 Minnesota St., #E-145, St. Paul MN 55101. (651)228-1407. Fax: (651)291-7978. E-mail: pblackburn@composersforum.org. Website: www.composersforum.org. **Contact:** Philip Blackburn, program director. Estab. 1994. For songwriters, musical playwrights and composers. Annual award.

Purpose "Up to 2 annual awards for non-Minnesota composers to come to Minnesota for a self-designed residency of at least 2 months."

Requirements Not for Minnesota residents or students. Deadline: March. Send for application. Samples of work are required with application. Send score/tape.

Awards McKnight Visiting Composer $14,000 stipend. Each award good for 1 year. Applications are judged by peer review panel.

Tips "Find committed partners in Minnesota with whom to work, and explore diverse communities."

MID-ATLANTIC SONG CONTEST

Songwriters' Association of Washington, PMB 106-137, 4200 Wisconsin Ave., NW, Washington DC 20016. (301)654-8434. E-mail: masc@saw.org. Website: www.saw.org. For songwriters and composers. Estab. 1982. Annual award.

   • Also see the listing for Songwriters Association of Washington in the Organizations section, as well as the Insider Report in this section on the Mid-Atlantic Contest 2002 Awards Ceremony.

Purpose This is one of the longest-running contests in the nation; SAW has organized twenty contests since 1982. The competition is designed to afford rising songwriters in a wide variety of genres the opportunity to receive awards and exposure in an environment of peer competition.

Requirements Amateur status is important. Applicants should request a brochure/application using the contact information above. Rules and procedures are clearly explained in that brochure. Cassette or CD and 3 copies of the lyrics are to be submitted with an application form and fee for each entry. Beginning this year, online enteries will also be accepted. Reduced entry fees are offered to members of Songwriters' Association of Washington; membership can be arranged simultaneously with entering. Multi-song discounts are also offered. Applications are mailed out and posted on their website around June 1; the submission deadline is usually sometime in mid-August; awards are typically announced late in the fall.

Awards The two best songs in each of ten categories win prize packages donated by the contest's corporate sponsors: Writer's Digest Books, BMI, Oasis CD Manufacturing, Omega Recording Studios, TAXI, Mary Cliff and Sonic Bids. Winning songwriters are invited to perform in Washington, DC at the Awards Ceremony Gala, and the twenty winning songs are included on a compilation CD. The best song in each category is eligible for three grand cash prizes. Certificates are awarded to other entries meriting honorable mention.

Tips "Enter the song in the most appropriate category. Make the sound recording the best it can be (even though judges are asked to focus on melody and lyric and not on production.) Avoid clichés, extended introductions, and long instrumental solos."

NACUSA YOUNG COMPOSERS' COMPETITION

Box 49256 Barrington Station, Los Angeles CA 90049. (310)838-4465. E-mail: nacusa@music-usa.org. Website: www.music-usa.org/nacusa. **Contact:** Deon Price, president, NACUSA. Estab. 1978. For composers. Annual award.

   • Also see the National Association of Composers/USA (NACUSA) listing in the Organization section.

Purpose To encourage the composition of new American concert hall music.

Requirements Entry fee: $20 (membership fee). Deadline: October 30. Send for application. Samples are not required.

Awards 1st Prize: $400; 2nd Prize: $100; and possible Los Angeles performances. Applications are judged by a committee of experienced NACUSA composer members.

☑ NSAI/CMT ANNUAL SONG CONTEST

1710 Roy Acuff Place, Nashville TN 37203. (615)256-3354. Fax: (615)256-0034. E-mail: songcontest @nashvillesongwriters.com. Website: www.nashvillesongwriters.com. **Contact:** Deanie Williams, director. Annual award for songwriters.

Purpose "A chance for aspiring songwriters to be heard by music industry decision makers. Winners are flown to Nashville for a recording session and an appointment with Music Row executives."

Requirements Entry fee: $35 for one entry; $50 for 2. In order to be eligible contestants must not

be receiving income from any work submitted—original material only. Submissions must include both lyrics and melody. Deadline is different each year; check website or send for application. Samples are required with application in the format of cassette or CD.
Awards Varies from year to year; check website.

PLAYHOUSE ON THE SQUARE NEW PLAY COMPETITION

51 S. Cooper, Memphis TN 38104. (901)725-0776. **Contact:** Jackie Nichols, executive director. For musical playwrights. Annual award. Estab. 1983.
Requirements Send script, tape and SASE. "Playwrights from the South will be given preference." Open to full-length, unproduced plays. Musicals must be fully arranged for piano when received. Deadline: April 1.
Awards Grants may be renewed. Applications judged by 3 readers.

PULITZER PRIZE IN MUSIC

709 Journalism Building, Columbia University, New York NY 10027. (212)854-3841. Fax: (212)854-3342. E-mail: pulitzer@www.pulitzer.org. Website: www.pulitzer.org. **Contact:** Music Secretary. For composers and musical playwrights. Annual award.
Requirements "For distinguished musical composition by an American that has had its first perfomance or recording in the United States during the year." Entries should reflect current creative activity. Works that receive their American premiere between January 16, 2005 and January 15, 2006 are eligible. A public performance or the public release of a recording shall constitute a premiere. Deadline: January 15. Samples of work are required with application, biography and photograph of composer, date and place of performance, score or manuscript and recording of the work, entry form and $50 entry fee.
Awards "One award: $10,000. Applications are judged first by a nominating jury, then by the Pulitzer Prize Board."

ROCKY MOUNTAIN FOLKS FESTIVAL SONGWRITER SHOWCASE

P.O. Box 769, Lyons CO 80540. (800)624-2422 or (303)823-0848. Fax: (303)823-0849. E-mail: emily @bluegrass.com. Website: www.bluegrass.com. **Contact:** Steve Szymanski, director. Estab. 1993. For songwriters, composers and performers. Annual award.
Purpose Award based on having the best song and performance.
Requirements Deadline: July 1. Finalists notified by July 15. Rules available on website. Samples of work are required with application. Send CD or cassette with $10 entry fee. Can now submit online, www.sonicbids.com/rockymountainfolk05.
Awards 1st Place is a custom Hayes Guitar, Festival Main Stage and $100; 2nd: $500 and Taylor Big Baby guitar; 3rd: $400 and Taylor Big Baby guitar; 4th: $300 and Taylor Big Baby guitar; 5th: $200 and Taylor Big Baby guitar; 6th-10th: $100. Applications judged by panel of judges.

RICHARD RODGERS AWARDS

American Academy of Arts and Letters, 633 W. 155th St., New York NY 10032. (212)368-5900. **Contact:** Lydia Kaim, coordinator. Estab. 1978. Deadline: November 1, 2005. "The Richard Rodgers Awards subsidize staged reading, studio productions, and full productions by nonprofit theaters in New York City of works by composers and writers who are not already established in the field of musical theater. The awards are only for musicals—songs by themselves are not eligible. The authors must be citizens or permanent residents of the United States." Guidelines for this award may be obtained by sending a SASE to above address.

ROME PRIZE COMPETITION FELLOWSHIP

American Academy in Rome, 7 E. 60th St., New York NY 10022-1001. (212)751-7200. Fax: (212)751-7220. E-mail: info@aarome.org. Website: www.aarome.org. **Contact:** Programs Department. For composers. Annual award.
Purpose "Rome Prize Competition winners pursue independent projects."
Requirements "Applicants for 11-month fellowships must hold a bachelor's degree in music, musi-

cal composition or its equivalent." Deadline: November 1. Entry fee: $25. Application guidelines are available to download through the Academy's website.

Awards "Up to two fellowships are awarded annually. Fellowship stipend is $21,000 for 11-months, and includes room and board, and a study or studio at Academy facilities in Rome. In all cases, excellence is the primary criterion for selection, based on the quality of the materials submitted. Winners are announced in mid-April."

TELLURIDE TROUBADOUR CONTEST

P.O. Box 769, Lyons CO 80540. (303)823-0848 or (800)624-2422. Fax: (303)823-0849. E-mail: emily @bluegrass.com. Website: www.bluegrass.com. **Contact:** Steve Szymanski, director. Estab. 1991. For songwriters, composers and performers. Annual award.

Purpose Award based on having best song and performance.

Requirements Deadline: must be postmarked by April 25; notified May 9, if selected. Rules available on website. Send cassette or CD and $10 entry fee. Can now submit music online, www.sonicbids.com/telluride2005.

Awards 1st: custom Shanti Guitar, $100 and Festival Main Stage Set; 2nd: $400 and Taylor Big Baby guitar; 3rd: $300 and Taylor Big Baby guitar; 4th: $200 and Martin Backpacker guitar; 5th: $100 and Martin Backpacker guitar. Applications judged by panel of judges.

THE TEN-MINUTE MUSICALS PROJECT

P.O. Box 461194, West Hollywood CA 90046. Website: www.tenminutemusicals.org. **Contact:** Michael Koppy, producer. For songwriters, composers and musical playwrights. Annual award.

Purpose "We are building a full-length stage musical comprised of complete short musicals, each of which play for between 8-14 minutes. Award is $250 for each work chosen for development towards inclusion in the project, plus a share of royalties when produced."

Requirements Deadline: August 31. Write for guidelines. Final submission should include script, cassette and lead sheets.

Awards $250 for each work selected. "Works should have complete stories, with a definite beginning, middle and end."

U.S.-JAPAN CREATIVE ARTISTS EXCHANGE FELLOWSHIP PROGRAM

Japan-U.S. Friendship Commission, 1201 15th St. NW, Suite 330, Washington DC 20005. (202)653-9800. Fax: (202)653-9802. E-mail: jusfc@jusfc.gov. Website: www.jusfc.gov. **Contact:** Sylvia Dandridge, executive. Estab. 1980. For all creative artists. Annual award.

Purpose "For artists to go as seekers, as cultural visionaries, and as living liaisons to the traditional and contemporary life of Japan."

Requirements "Artists' works must exemplify the best in U.S. arts." Deadline: June. Send for application and guidelines. Applications available via Internet. Samples of work are required with application. Requires 2 pieces on cassette or CD, cued to the 3-5 minute section to be reviewed.

Awards Five artists are awarded a six-month residency anywhere in Japan. Awards monthly stipend for living expenses, housing and professional support services; up to $6,000 for pre-departure costs, including such items as language training and economy class roundtrip airfare. Residency is good for 1 year. Applications are judged by a panel of previous recipients of the awards, as well as other arts professionals with expertise in Japanese culture.

Tips "Applicants should anticipate a highly rigorous review of their artistry and should have compelling reasons for wanting to work in Japan."

U.S.-MEXICO FUND FOR CULTURE

Berline 18, 5th Floor, Colonia Juarez, C.P. 06600, Mexico D.F., Mexico (52) (55)5535-6735 or (52) (55)5592-5386. Fax: (52) (55)5566-8071. E-mail: contacto@contacocultural.org. Website: www.fid emexusa.org.mx. **Contact:** Viviana Aguirre, grant coordinator. Estab. 1991. For composers, choreographers, musical playwrights and performers. Annual award.

Purpose "The U.S.-Mexico Fund for Culture, an independent body created through a joint initiative of the Bancomer Cultural Foundation, The Rockefeller Foundation and Mexico's National Fund for

Culture and the Arts, provides financial support for the development of cultural binational projects in music, theater, dance, visual arts, cultural studies, literary and cultural publications, media arts and libraries."

Requirements Deadline: April 16, 2001 (postmarked). Send for application with SASE ($8^1/_2 \times 11$ envelope) or contact us at our website. Samples of work are required with application in duplicate.
Awards Range from $2,000-25,000. Award is good for 1 year. Judged by binational panel of experts in each of the disciplines, one from Mexico and one from the USA.
Tips "Proposals must be binational in character and have a close and active collaboration with artists from Mexico. The creation of new works is highly recommendable."

U.S.A. SONGWRITING COMPETITION

4331 N. Federal Hwy., Suite 403A, Ft. Lauderdale FL 33308. (954)776-1577. Fax: (954)776-1132. E-mail: info@songwriting.net. Website: www.songwriting.net. **Contact:** Contest Manager. Estab. 1994. For songwriters, composers, performing artists and lyricists. Annual award.
Purpose "To honor good songwriters/composers all over the world, especially the unknown ones."
Requirements Open to professional and beginner songwriters. No limit on entries. Each entry must include an entry fee, a cassette tape of song(s) and lyric sheet(s). Judged by music industry representatives. Past judges have included record label representatives and publishers from Arista Records, EMI and Warner/Chappell. Deadline: To be announced. Entry fee: To be announced. Send SASE with request or e-mail for entry forms at any time. Samples of work are not required.
Awards Prizes include cash and merchandise in 15 different categories: pop, rock, country, Latin, R&B, gospel, folk, jazz, "lyrics only" category, instrumental and many others.
Tips "Judging is based on lyrics, originality, melody and overall composition. CD quality production is great but not a consideration in judging."

UNISONG INTERNATIONAL SONG CONTEST

5198 Arlington Ave., PMB 513, Riverside CA 92504. (213)673-4067. E-mail: entry@unisong.com. Website: www.unisong.com. Founders: Alan Roy Scott and David Stark. London office: P.O. Box 13383, London NW3 5ZR United Kingdom. (44)(0208)387-9293. Estab. 1997. For songwriters, composers and lyricists. Annual songwriting contest.
Purpose "Unisong was created by songwriters for songwriters."
Requirements Send for an entry form or request one by phone or e-mail. Download entry form from website or enter online. Send cassette or CD only. No DATs. Entries also accepted via MP3.
Awards Over $50,000 in cash and prizes. Grand Prize winner to write with professional writers and artists through Music Bridges Around The World. Songs judged on song quality only, not demo.
Tips "Please make sure your song is professionally presented. Make sure lyrics are typed or printed clearly. Print your personal information clearly. Enter your song in the most appropriate categories."

WEST COAST ENSEMBLE; MUSICAL STAIRS

P.O. Box 38728, Los Angeles CA 90038. (323)876-9337. Website: www.wcensemble.org. **Contact:** Les Hanson, artistic director. For composers and musical playwrights. Annual award.
  • Also see the listing for West Coast Ensemble in the Play Producers section of this book.
Purpose To provide an arena and encouragement for the development of new musicals for the theater.
Requirements No entry fee. Submit book and a cassette or CD of the score to the above address.
Awards The West Coast Ensemble Musical Stairs Competition Award includes a production of the selected musical and $500 prize. Panel of judges reads script and listen to cassette or CD. Final selection is made by Artistic Director.
Tips "Submit libretto in standard playscript format along with professional sounding cassette or CD of songs."

YOUNG COMPOSERS AWARDS

% NGCSA and the Hartt School, University of Hartford, 200 Bloomfield Ave., West Hartford CT 06117. (860)768-7768, ext. 8558. E-mail: youngcomp@hartford.edu. Website: www.nationalguild.

org. **Contact:** Carissa Reddick, director. For composers. Open to students age 13-18. Annual award. **Purpose** "To encourage young students to write music, so that the art of composition—with no restrictions as to the category of music in which the works are written—will once again occupy the place in the center of music education where it belongs. It takes tons of ore to extract one ounce of gold: by focusing on the inventiveness of many students, the Awards may lead to the discovery of genuine creative talents—that is the eventual goal." Young Composers Awards was established by the late Dr. Herbert Zipperin in 1985 with the initial support of the Rockefeller Foundation. Since 1985, awards in the amount of $42,500 have been granted to 67 young composers.

Requirements "Applicants must be enrolled in a public or private secondary school, in a recognized musical institution, or be engaged in the private study of music with an established teacher. No compositions will be considered without certification by the applicant's teacher. Student composers must not be enrolled in an undergraduate program when they apply. This competition is open to residents of the United States and Canada. Each applicant may submit only one work. Check website for exact date. Send for application. Samples of work are required with application. Four photocopies of the work must be submitted. All manuscripts must be in legible form and may be submitted on usual score paper or reduced under a generally accepted process. The composer's name must not appear on the composition submitted. The composition must be marked with a pseudonym on the manuscript. Copies must be submitted with a check in the amount of $5 made payable to the Hartt School. One copy of score will be returned if entrant sends SASE with application. Entrants must be certain postage purchased has no expiration date. Composers retain full and all legal rights to their submitted composition. Students who have previously won this award are not eligible to reapply."

Awards Herbert Zipper Prizes: 2 separate categories—age group 13-15 (Junior) and 16-18 (Senior). 2 prizes are awarded in each of the Senior and Junior categories—Senior: 1st Place: $1,000; 2nd Place: $500. Junior: 1st Place: $500; 2nd Place: $250. "Announcement of the Awards are made no later than mid-June each year. In the event that no entry is found to be worthy of the $1,000 Prize, the jury may award one or both of the other prizes or none at all. NGCSA appoints an independent jury to review all entries submitted. The jury consists of not less than three qualified judges. Prizes shall be awarded at the discretion of the jury. The decision of the judges is final."

Tips "Paramount would be neatness and legibility of the manuscript submitted. The application must be complete in all respects."

Organizations

One of the first places a beginning songwriter should look for guidance and support is a songwriting organization. Offering encouragement, instruction, contacts and feedback, these groups of professional and amateur songwriters can help an aspiring songwriter hone the skills needed to compete in the ever-changing music industry.

The type of organization you choose to join depends on what you want to get out of it. Local groups can offer a friendly, supportive environment where you can work on your songs and have them critiqued in a constructive way by other songwriters. They're also great places to meet collaborators. Larger, national organizations can give you access to music business professionals and other songwriters across the country.

Most of the organizations listed in this book are non-profit groups with membership open to specific groups of people—songwriters, musicians, classical composers, etc. They can be local groups with a membership of less than 100 people, or large national organizations with thousands of members from all over the country. In addition to regular meetings, most organizations occasionally sponsor events such as seminars and workshops to which music industry personnel are invited to talk about the business, and perhaps listen to and critique demo tapes.

Check the following listings, bulletin boards at local music stores and your local newspapers for area organizations. If you are unable to locate an organization within an easy distance of your home, you may want to consider joining one of the national groups. These groups, based in New York, Los Angeles and Nashville, keep their members involved and informed through newsletters, regional workshops and large yearly conferences. They can help a writer who feels isolated in his hometown get his music heard by professionals in the major music centers.

In the following listings, organizations describe their purpose and activities, as well as how much it costs to join. Before joining any organization, consider what they have to offer and how becoming a member will benefit you. To locate organizations close to home, see the Geographic Index at the back of this book.

ACADEMY OF COUNTRY MUSIC

4100 W. Alameda Ave., Suite 208, Burbank CA 91505. (818)842-8400. Fax: (818)842-8535. E-mail: info@acmcountry.com. Website: www.acmcountry.com. **Contact:** Bob Romeo, executive director. Estab. 1964. Serves country music industry professionals. Eligibility for professional members is limited to those individuals who derive some portion of their income directly from country music. Each member is classified by one of the following categories: artist/entertainer, club/venue operator, musician, on-air personality, manager, talent agent, composer, music publisher, public relations, publications, radio, TV/motion picture, record company, talent buyer or affiliated (general). The purpose of ACM is to promote and enhance the image of country music. The Academy is involved year-round in activities important to the country music community. Some of these activities include charity fund-raisers, participation in country music seminars, talent contests, artist showcases, assistance to producers in placing country music on television and in motion pictures and backing legislation that benefits the interests of the country music community. The ACM is governed by directors and run by officers elected annually. Applications are accepted throughout the year. Membership is $75/year.

ALL SONGWRITERS NETWORK (ASN)

(formerly American Songwriters Network), Dept A95, Box 23912, Ft. Lauderdale FL 33307. (954)537-3463. E-mail: asn@tiac.net. Website: http://home.tiac.net/~asn. **Contact:** Network Manager. Estab. 1995. Serves "professional level songwriters/composers with monthly music industry leads tipsheet. The tipsheet includes the most current listing of producers, A&R managers, record labels, entertainment attorneys, agents and publishing companies looking for specific material for their projects/albums. Any songwriter from any part of the country or world can be a member of this organization. The purpose of this organization is to foster a better professional community by helping members to place their songs." Membership fee: $140/year.

Tips "Please send SASE or e-mail for application form."

☐ AMERICAN COMPOSERS FORUM

332 Minnesota St., Suite East 145, St. Paul MN 55101. (651)228-1407. Fax: (651)291-7978. Website: www.composersforum.org. **Contact:** Wendy Collins, member services manager. Estab. 1973. "The American Composers Forum links communities with composers and performers, encouraging the making, playing and enjoyment of new music. Building two-way relationships between artists and the public, the Forum develops programs that educate today's and tomorrow's audiences, energize composers' and performers' careers, stimulate entrepreneurship and collaboration, promote musical creativity, and serve as models of effective support for the arts. Programs include residencies, fellowships, commissions, producing and performance opportunities, a recording assistance program and a widely-distributed recording label. The Forum's members, more than 1,200 strong, live in 49 states and 16 countries; membership is open to all." Membership dues: Regular (U.S.): $50; Student/Senior (U.S.): $35; Regular (Outside U.S.): $60; Student/Senior (Outside U.S.): $45.

AMERICAN MUSIC CENTER, INC.

30 W. 26th St., Suite 1001, New York NY 10010-2011. (212)366-5260. Fax: (212)366-5265. E-mail: center@amc.net. Website: www.amc.net. **Contact:** Membership Department. The American Music Center, founded by a consortium led by Aaron Copland in 1939, is the first-ever national service and information center for new classical music and jazz by American composers. The Center has a variety of innovative new programs and services, including a montly Internet magazine (www.newmusicbox.org) for new American music, an online catalog of new music for educators specifically targeted to young audiences, a series of professional development workshops, and an online listening library (www.newmusicjukebox.org). Each month, AMC provides its over 2,500 members with a listing of opportunities including calls for scores, competitions, and other new music performance information. Each year, AMC's Information Services Department fields thousands of requests concerning composers, performers, data, funding, and support programs. The AMC Collection presently includes over 60,000 scores and recordings, many unavailable elsewhere. "AMC also contin-

ues to administer several grant programs: the Aaron Copland Fund for Music; the Henry Cowell Performance Incentive Fund; and its own programs Live Music for Dance and the Composer Assistance Program.'' Members also receive a link their websites on www.amc.net. The American Music Center is not-for-profit and has an annual membership fee.

AMERICAN SOCIETY OF COMPOSERS, AUTHORS AND PUBLISHERS (ASCAP)

One Lincoln Plaza, New York NY 10023. (212)621-6000 (administration); (212)621-6240 (membership). E-mail: info@ascap.com. Website: www.ascap.com. President and Chairman of the Board: Marilyn Bergman. CEO: John LoFrumento. Executive Vice President/Membership: Todd Brabec. **Contact:** Member Services at (800)95-ASCAP. **Regional offices: West Coast:** 7920 Sunset Blvd., 3rd Floor, Los Angeles CA 90046, (323)883-1000; **Nashville:** 2 Music Square W., Nashville TN 37203, (615)742-5000; **Chicago:** 1608 N. Milwaukee Ave., Suite 1007, Chicago IL 60647, (773)394-4286; **Atlanta:** PMB 400-541 10th St. NW, Atlanta GA 30318, (404)351-1252; **Florida:** 420 Lincoln Rd., Suite 385, Miami Beach FL 33139, (305)673-3446; **United Kingdom:** 8 Cork St., London WIX 1PB England, 011-44-202-439-0909; **Puerto Rico:** 654 Ave. Munoz Rivera, IBM Plaza Suite 1101 Boz, Hato Rey, Puerto Rico 00918, (787)281-0782. ASCAP is a membership association of over 200,000 composers, lyricists, songwriters, and music publishers, whose function is to protect the rights of its members by licensing and collecting royalties for the nondramatic public performance of their copyrighted works. ASCAP licensees include radio, television, cable, live concert promoters, bars, restaurants, symphony orchestras, new media, and other users of music. ASCAP is the leading performing rights society in the world. All revenues, less operating expenses, are distributed to members (about 86 cents of each dollar). ASCAP was the first US performing rights organization to distribute royalties from the Internet. Founded in 1914, ASCAP is the only society created and owned by writers and publishers. The ASCAP Board of Directors consists of 12 writers and 12 publishers, elected by the membership. ASCAP's Member Card provides exclusive benefits geared towards working music professionals. Among the benefits are health, musical instrument and equipment, tour and studio liability, term life and long term care insurance, discounts on musical instruments, equipment and supplies, access to a credit union, and much more. ASCAP hosts a wide array of showcases and workshops throughout the year, and offers grants, special awards, and networking opportunities in a variety of genres. Visit their website listed above for more information.

ARIZONA SONGWRITERS ASSOCIATION

P.O. Box 678, Phoenix AZ 85001-0678. (602)973-1988. azsongwriters@cox.net **Contact:**John Iger, membership director. Estab. 1977. Members are all ages with wide variety of interests; beginners and those who make money from their songs. Most members are residents of Arizona. Purpose is to educate about the craft and business of songwriting and to facilitate networking with business professionals and other local songwriters. Offers instruction, newsletter, lectures, workshops and performance opportunities. Applications accepted year-round. Membership fee: $25/year.

◼ ASSOCIATION DES PROFESSIONNELS DE LA CHANSON ET DE LA MUSIQUE

292 Montreal Rd, Suite 200, ON K1L 6B7 Canada. (613)745-5642. Fax: (613)745-9715. E-mail: info-apcm@rogers.com. Website: www.apcm.ca. **Contact:** Jean-Emmanuel Simiand, agent de communication. Director: Laurent de Crombrugghe. Estab. 1989. Members are French Canadian singers and musicians. Members must be French singing and may have a CD to be distributed. Purpose is to gather French speaking artists (outside of Quebec, mainly in Ontario) to distribute their material, other workshops, instructions, lectures, etc. Offers instruction, newsletter, lectures, workshops, and distribution. Applications accepted year-round. Membership fee: $50 (Canadian).

ASSOCIATION OF INDEPENDENT MUSIC PUBLISHERS

Los Angeles Chapter: P.O. Box 69473, Los Angeles CA 90069. (818)771-7301. Fax: (212)582-8273. E-mail: LAinfo@aimp.org or NYinfo@aimp.org. Website: www.aimp.org. Estab. 1977. Purpose is to educate members on new developments in the music publishing industry and to provide networking opportunities. Offers lectures, workshops and evaluation services. Applications accepted year-round. Membership fee: NY: $75/year; LA: $65/year.

BALTIMORE SONGWRITERS ASSOCIATION

P.O. Box 22496, Baltimore MD 21203. (410)813-4039. E-mail: baltimoresongwriters@yahoo.com. Website: www.baltimoresongwriters.org. **Contact:** Kryn Oliver, president. Estab. 1997. "The BSA is an inclusive organization with all ages, skill levels and genres of music welcome." Offers instruction, newsletter, lectures, workshops, performance opportunities, music publishing. Applications accepted year-round; membership not limited to location or musical status. Membership fee: $20. **Tips** "We are trying to build a musical community that is more supportive and less competitive We are dedicated to helping songwriters grow and become better in their craft."

THE BLACK ROCK COALITION

P.O. Box 1054, Cooper Station, New York NY 10276. (212)713-5097. E-mail: ldavise@blackrockcoal ition.org. Website: www.blackrockcoalition.org. **Contact:** LaRonda Davis, president. Estab. 1985. Serves musicians, songwriters—male and female ages 18-40 (average). Also engineers, entertainment attorneys and producers. Looking for members who are "mature and serious about music as an artist or activist willing to help fellow musicians. The BRC independently produces, promotes and distributes Black alternative music acts as a collective and supportive voice for such musicians within the music and record business. The main purpose of this organization is to produce, promote and distribute the full spectrum of black music along with educating the public on what black music is. The BRC is now soliciting recorded music by bands and individuals for Black Rock Coalition Records. Please send copyrighted and original material only." Offers instruction, newsletter, lectures, free seminars and workshops, monthly membership meeting, quarterly magazine, performing opportunities, evaluation services, business advice, full roster of all members. Applications accepted year-round. Bands must submit a tape, bio with picture and a self-addressed, stamped envelope before sending their membership fee. Membership fee: $25 per individual/$100 per band.

☑ BROADCAST MUSIC, INC. (BMI)

320 W. 57th St., New York NY 10019. (212)586-2000. E-mail: newyork@bmi.com;. Website: www. bmi.com;. **Los Angeles:** 8730 Sunset Blvd., Los Angeles CA 90069, (310)659-9109. E-mail: losangele s@bmi.com; **Nashville:** 10 Music Square East, Nashville TN 37203, (615)401-2000. E-mail: nashvill e@bmi.com; **Miami:** 5201 Blue Lagoon Dr., Suite 310, Miami FL 33126, (305)266-3636. E-mail: miami@bmi.com; **Atlanta:** Tower Place 100, 3340 Peachtree Rd., NE, Suite 570, Atlanta GA 30326. (404)261-5151. E-mail: atlanta@bmi.com; **Puerto Rico:** BankTrust Plaza, Suite A-262/East Wing, 255 Ponce De Leon Ave., San Juan PR 00917. (787)754-5490; **United Kingdom:** 54 Harley House, Marylebone Rd., London NW1 5HN, United Kingdom. 011-44-207-486-2036 london@bmi.com; President and CEO: Del R. Bryant. President Emeritus: Frances W. Preston. Senior Vice Presidents, New York: Phillip Graham, Writer/Publisher Relations; Alison Smith, Performing Rights. Vice President, New York: Charlie Feldman. Vice Presidents, Los Angeles: Barbara Cane and Doreen Ringer Ross; Vice President, Nashville: Paul Corbin. Assistant Vice President, Miami: Diane J. Almodovar: Assistant Vice President, Atlanta: Catherine Brewton. Senior Executive, London: Brandon Bakshi. BMI is a performing rights organization representing approximately 300,000 songwriters, composers and music publishers in all genres of music, including pop, rock, country, R&B, rap, jazz, Latin, gospel and contemporary classical. "Applicants must have written a musical composition, alone or in collaboration with other writers, which is commercially published, recorded or otherwise likely to be performed." Purpose: BMI acts on behalf of its songwriters, composers and music publishers by insuring payment for performance of their works through the collection of licensing fees from radio stations, Internet outlets, broadcast and cable TV stations, hotels, nightclubs, aerobics centers and other users of music. This income is distributed to the writers and publishers in the form of royalty payments, based on how the music is used. BMI also undertakes intensive lobbying efforts in Washington D.C. on behalf of its affiliates, seeking to protect their performing rights through the enactment of new legislation and enforcement of current copyright law. In addition, BMI helps aspiring songwriters develop their skills through various workshops, seminars and competitions it sponsors throughout the country. Applications accepted year-round. There is no membership fee for songwriters; a one-time fee of $150 is required to affiliate an individually-owned publishing company; $250 for partnerships, corporations and limited-liability companies. "Visit our website for specific contacts, e-mail addresses and additional membership information."

CALIFORNIA LAWYERS FOR THE ARTS

Fort Mason Center, C-255, San Francisco CA 94123. (415)775-7200. Fax: (415)775-1143. E-mail: cla@calawyersforthearts.org. Website: www.calawyersforthearts.org. **Southern California:** 1641 18th St., Santa Monica CA 90404. (310)998-5590 Fax:(310)998-5594. E-mail: usercla@aol.com. **Sacramento Office:** 926 J St., Suite 811, Sacramento CA 95814. (916)442-6210 Fax:(916)442-6281. E-mail: clasacto@aol.com. **Oakland Office:** 1212 Broadway St., Oakland CA 94612. (510)444-6351 Fax:(510)444-6352. E-mail: oakcla@there.net. **Contact:** Alma Robinson, executive director. Systems Coordinator: Josie Porter. Estab. 1974. "For artists of all disciplines, skill levels, and ages, supporting individuals and organizations, and arts organizations. Artists of all disciplines are welcome, whether professionals or amateurs. We also welcome groups and individuals who support the arts. We work most closely with the California arts community. Our mission is to establish a bridge between the legal and arts communities so that artists and art groups may handle their creative activities with greater business and legal competence; the legal profession will be more aware of issues affecting the arts community; and the law will become more responsive to the arts community." Offers newsletter, lectures, library, workshops, mediation service, attorney referral service, housing referrals, publications and advocacy. Membership fee: $20 for senior citizens and full-time students; $25 for working artists; $40 for general individual; $60 for panel attorney; $100 to $1,000 for patrons. Organizations: $50 for small organizations (budget under $100,000); $90 for large organizations (budget of $100,000 or more); $100 to $1,000 for corporate sponsors.

CANADIAN ACADEMY OF RECORDING ARTS & SCIENCES (CARAS)

355 King St. W, Suite 501, Toronto ON M5V 1J6 Canada. (416)485-3135. Fax: (416)485-4978. E-mail: info@carasonline.ca. Website: www.juno-awards.ca. **Contact:** Brenna Knought, project coordinator, President: Melanie Berry. Manager, Awards and Events: Leisa Peacock. Manager, Marketing and Communications: Tammy Watson. Membership is open to all employees (including support staff) in broadcasting and record companies, as well as producers, personal managers, recording artists, recording engineers, arrangers, composers, music publishers, album designers, promoters, talent and booking agents, record retailers, rack jobbers, distributors, recording studios and other music industry related professions (on approval). Applicants must be affiliated with the Canadian recording industry. Offers newsletter, nomination and voting privileges for Juno Awards and discount tickets to Juno awards show. "CARAS strives to foster the development of the Canadian music and recording industries and to contribute toward higher artistic standards." Applications accepted year-round. Membership fee is $50/year (Canadian) + GST=$53.50. Applications accepted from individuals only, not from companies or organizations.

CANADIAN COUNTRY MUSIC ASSOCIATION (CCMA)

626 King Street West, Suite 203, Toronto ON MV5 1M7 Canada. (416)947-1331. Fax: (416)947- 5924. E-mail: country@ccma.org. Website: www.ccma.org. **Contact:** Amanda Power, communications manager. Estab. 1976. Members are artists, songwriters, musicians, producers, radio station personnel, managers, booking agents and others. Offers newsletter, workshops, performance opportunities and the CCMA awards every September. "Through our newsletters and conventions we offer a means of meeting and associating with artists and others in the industry. The CCMA is a federally chartered, nonprofit organization, dedicated to the promotion and development of Canadian country music throughout Canada and the world and to providing a unity of purpose for the Canadian country music industry." See website for membership information.

CANADIAN MUSICAL REPRODUCTION RIGHTS AGENCY LTD.

56 Wellesley St. W, #320, Toronto ON M5S 2S3 Canada. (416)926-1966. Fax: (416)926-7521. E-mail: inquiries@cmrra.ca. Website: www.cmrra.ca. **Contact:** Michael Mackie, membership services. Estab. 1975. Members are music copyright owners, music publishers, sub-publishers and administrators. Representation by CMRRA is open to any person, firm or corporation anywhere in the world, which owns and/or administers one or more copyrighted musical works. CMRRA is a music licensing agency—Canada's largest—which represents music copyright owners, publishers and administrators for the purpose of mechanical and synchronization licensing in Canada. Offers mechanical and synchronization licensing. Applications accepted year-round.

CENTER FOR THE PROMOTION OF CONTEMPORARY COMPOSERS

P.O. Box 631043, Nacogdoches TX 75963.E-mail: cpcc@under.org. Website: www.under.org/cpcc.

CHICAGO DANCE AND MUSIC ALLIANCE

(formerly Chicago Music Alliance), 410 S. Michigan Ave., Suite 819, Chicago IL 60605. (312)987-9296. Fax: (312)987-1127. E-mail: info@chicagoperformances.org. Website: www.chicagoperform ances.org. Executive Director: Matthew Brockmeier. Estab. 1984. "Chicago Dance and Music Alliance provides direct services to members engaged in all genres of dance and music in the Chicago area, acts as an advocate on their behalf, and disseminates information about their activities to the general public. The alliance includes administrators, composers, choreographers, performers, students, performers, educators and others, as well as groups from the smallest ensemble to full symphony orchestras and major dance companies. Members generally have a direct connection to Chicago, with most organizational members based in the Chicago metropolitan area. As a service organization the Alliance is committed to meeting the needs of members. Services for individual members include ticket and merchandise discounts, credit union membership and résumé/career counseling. The Alliance also publishes a monthly Newsletter, and offers occasional workshops or topical meetings. The Newsletter includes audition and employment notices. The website includes a searchable performance directory and a teaching directory. The teaching directory is available to members as well as to for-profit schools. Applications accepted year-round. All memberships expire December 31. Individual dues are $40 per year. Fees for ensembles vary by budget size.

THE COLLEGE MUSIC SOCIETY

312 E. Pine St., Missoula MT 59802. (406)721-9616. Fax: (406)721-9419. E-mail: cms@music.org. Website: www.music.org. Estab. 1959. Serves college, university and conservatory professors, as well as independent musicians. "The College Music Society is a consortium of college, conservatory, university and independent musicians and scholars interested in all disciplines of music. Its mission is to promote music teaching and learning, musical creativity and expression, research and dialogue, and diversity and interdisciplinary interaction." Offers journal, newsletter, lectures, workshops, performance opportunities, job listing service, databases of organizations and institutions, music faculty and mailing lists. Applications accepted year-round. Membership fee: $60 (regular dues), $30 (student dues).

COLORADO MUSIC ASSOCIATION

8 E. First Ave., #107, Denver CO 80203. (720)570-2280. Website: http://coloradomusic.org. **Contact:** David Barber, president. Estab. 1999. Members are musicians of all ages and skill levels, songwriters, recording studios, music business merchants, teachers, performers, attorneys, agents, managers, publicists, promoters, venue owners and operators, and others connected to local music communities. Purpose is to support the local music community and encourage the development of skills, creativity and production. Offers instruction, lectures, workshops, performance and showcase opportunities, evaluation services, music directory, and free UPC (barcode) numbers for CD and other music products. Applications accepted year-round. Membership fee: $35/individual; $60/band; $115/business.

Tips "We meet monthly in Denver and present speakers on topics of interest to the group. Our Internet site is being expanded to provide extensive educational features relative to the music biz.

CONNECTICUT SONGWRITERS ASSOCIATION

P.O. Box 511, Mystic CT 06355. (860)945-1272. E-mail: info@ctsongs.com. Website: www.ctsongs.com. **Contact:** Bill Pere, executive director. Vice President: Robert Williams. "We are an educational, nonprofit organization dedicated to improving the art and craft of original music. Founded in 1979, CSA had almost 2,000 active members and has become one of the best known and respected songwriters' associations in the country. Membership in the CSA admits you to 12-18 seminars/workshops/song critique sessions per year at 3-5 locations in Connecticut. Out-of-state members may mail in songs for free critiques at our meetings. Noted professionals deal with all aspects of the craft and business of music including lyric writing, music theory, music technology, arrangement and production, legal and business aspects, performance techniques, song analysis and recording techniques. CSA offers song screening sessions for members (songs which are voted on by the panel). Songs that 'pass' are then eligible for inclusion on the CSA sampler anthology CD series. Thirteen compilation recordings have been released so far are for sale at local retail outlets and are given to speakers and prospective buyers. CSA also offers showcases and concerts which are open to the public and designed to give artists a venue for performing their original material for an attentive, listening audience. CSA benefits help local soup kitchens, group homes, hospice, world hunger, libraries, nature centers, community centers and more. CSA shows encompass ballads to bluegrass and Bach to rock. Our monthly newsletter, *Connecticut Songsmith* , offers free classified advertising for members, and has been edited and published by Bill Pere since 1980. In addition, CSA offers members free web pages on their website. Annual dues: $40; senior citizen and full time students $30; organizations $80. Memberships are tax-deductible as business expenses or as charitable contributions to the extent allowed by law.''

COUNTRY LEGENDS ASSOCIATION
Corporate Offices, P.O. Box 136592, Fort Worth TX 76136. (218)626-9044. Fax: (218)626-2796. E-mail: cla@clalonestar.com. Website: www.clalonestar.com. **Contact:** Frank Dell, president. Estab. 1997. Members are professional/nonprofessional industry people, fans of classic country music. Members must be active in the country music industry (country music)—artists, songwriters, promoters, record companies, merchandisers, musicians, country radio station disc jockeys and fans of country music. Purpose is to promote classic country music, educate, establish the country classic legends Hall of Fame in Fort Worth, Texas, help new talent, hold annual conventions and award shows. Offers competitions, instruction, newsletter, lectures, workshops, performance opportunities and evaluation services. Applications accepted year-round. Membership fee: $100/industry; $50/artist, musician, songwriters; $25/fans; $20 senior citizens.

DALLAS SONGWRITERS ASSOCIATION
Sammons Center for the Arts, 3630 Harry Hines, Box 20, Dallas TX 75219. (214)750-0916. Fax: (214)692-1392. E-mail: info@dallassongwriters.org. Website: www.dallassongwriters.org. **Contact:** Alex Townes, membership director. President: Mark Hughey. Founding President Emeritis: Barbara McMillen. Estab. 1986. Serves songwriters and lyricists of Dallas/Ft. Worth metroplex. Members are adults ages 18-65, Dallas/Ft. Worth area songwriters/lyricists who are or aspire to be professionals. Purpose is to provide songwriters an opportunity to meet other songwriters, share information, find co-writers and support each other through group discussions at monthly meetings; to provide songwriters an opportunity to have their songs heard and critiqued by peers and professionals by playing cassettes and providing an open mike at monthly meetings and by offering contests judged by publishers; to provide songwriters opportunities to meet other music business professionals by inviting guest speakers to monthly meetings and the Dallas Songwriters Seminar; and to provide songwriters opportunities to learn more about the craft of songwriting and the business of music by presenting mini-workshops at each monthly meeting. ''We offer a chance for the songwriter to learn from peers and industry professionals and an opportunity to belong to a supportive group environment to encourage the individual to continue his/her songwriting endeavors.'' Offers competitions (including the Annual Song Contest with over $5,000 in prizes, and the Quarterly Lyric Contest), field trips, instruction, lectures, newsletter, performance opportunities, social outings, workshops and seminars. ''Our members are eligible for discounts at several local music stores and seminars.'' Applications accepted year-round. Membership fee: $45. ''When inquiring by phone, please leave complete mailing address and phone number where you can be reached day and night.''

THE DRAMATISTS GUILD OF AMERICA, INC.
(formerly The Dramatists Guild, Inc.), 1501 Broadway, Suite 701, New York NY 10036. (212)398-9366. Fax: (212)944-0420. E-mail: membership@dramaguild.com. Website: www.dramatistsguild.com. **Contact:** Tom Epstein, membership director. ''For over three-quarters of a century, The Dramatists Guild has been the professional association of playwrights, composers and lyricists, with

more than 6,000 members across the country. All theater writers, whether produced or not, are eligible for Associate membership ($95/year); those who are engaged in a drama-related field but are not a playwright are eligible for Subscribing membership ($25/year); students enrolled in writing degree programs at colleges or universities are eligible for Student membership ($35/year); writers who have been produced on Broadway, Off-Broadway or on the main stage of a LORT theater are eligible for Active membership ($150/year). The Guild offers its members the following activities and services: use of the Guild's contracts (including the Approved Production Contract for Broadway, the Off-Broadway contract, the LORT contract, the collaboration agreements for both musicals and drama, the 99 Seat Theatre Plan contract, the Small Theatre contract, commissioning agreements, and the Underlying Rights Agreements contract; advice on all theatrical contracts including Broadway, Off-Broadway, regional, showcase, Equity-waiver, dinner theater and collaboration contracts); a nationwide toll-free number for all members with business or contract questions or problems; advice and information on a wide spectrum of issues affecting writers; free and/or discounted ticket service; symposia led by experienced professionals in major cities nationwide; access to a health insurance programs and a group term life insurance plan; and a spacious meeting room which can accommodate up to 50 people for readings and auditions on a rental basis. The Guild's publications are: *The Dramatist*, a bimonthly journal containing articles on all aspects of the theater (which includes *The Dramatists Guild Newsletter*, with announcements of all Guild activities and current information of interest to dramatists); and an annual resource directory with up-to-date information on agents, grants, producers, playwriting contests, conferences and workshops.

THE FIELD

161 Sixth Ave., New York NY 10013. (212)691-6969. Fax: (212)255-2053. E-mail: info@thefield.org. Website: www.thefield.org. **Contact:** Program Manager, programs & outreach. Estab. 1986. "The Field gives independent performing artists the tools to develop and sustain their creative and professional lives, while allowing the public to have immediate, direct access to a remarkable range of contemporary artwork. The organization was started by eight emerging artists who shared common roots in contemporary dance and theater. Meeting regularly, these artists created a structure to help each other improve their artwork, and counter the isolation that often comes with the territory of an artistic career. The Field offers a comprehensive program structure similar to an urban artists' residency or graduate program. Participants select from a broad array of programs and services including art development workshops, performance opportunities, career management training and development, fundraising consultations, fiscal sponsorship, informational publications, and artist residencies. The Field's goal is to help artists develop their best artwork by deepening the artistic process and finding effective ways to bring that art into the marketplace. Most Field programs cost under $100, and tickets to our performance events are $10. In addition, since 1992, The Field has coordinated a network of satellite sites in Atlanta, Chicago, Houston, Miami, North Adams (MA), Philadelphia, Plainfield (MA), Phoenix, Rochester (NY), Salt Lake City, San Francisco, Seattle, Tucson, Richmond (VA), Washington, DC and Tokyo, Japan. The Field is the only organization in New York that provides comprehensive programming for independent performing artists on a completely non-exclusive basis. Programs are open to artists from all disciplines, aesthetic viewpoints, and levels of development." Offers workshops and performance opportunities on a seasonal basis. Applications accepted year-round. Membership fee: $100/year.

Tips "There are two new additions to the field: IPARC (Independent Artists Resource Center) and GoTour. Located at The Field's office, IPARC offers fund-raising resources and hands-on assistance, including databases such as the Foundation Directory Online, computer workstations, and a library of books, journals, and information directories. One-on-one assistance and consultations are also available to guide users through grant writing and other fund-raising endeavors. GoTour (www.gotour.org) is a free website offering independent artists the resources they need to take their show on the road. Visitors log on for free and access a national arts network where they can search for venues, network with artists nationwide, find media contacts, read advice from other artists and arts professionals, add information on their local arts community, post tour anecdotes, and list concert informaton and classified ads."

☑ FILM MUSIC NETWORK

13101 Washington Blvd. Suite 466, Los Angeles CA 90066. 1-800-774-3700. E-mail: info@filmmusic .net. Website: www.filmmusicworld.com or www.filmmusic.net. President/Founder: Mark Northam. NY Chapter Manager: Beth Krakower.

THE FOLK ALLIANCE (North American Folk Music and Dance Alliance)

962 Wayne Ave., Suite 902, Silver Springs MD 20910-4480. (301)588-8185. Fax: (301)588-8186. E-mail: fa@folk.org. Website: www.folk.org. **Contact:** Tony Ziselberger, member services director. Executive Director: Phyllis Barney. Estab. 1989.

• Also see the listing for Folk Alliance Annual Conference in the Workshops section of this book. Members are organizations and individuals involved in traditional and contemporary folk music and dance in the US and Canada (in any genre—blues, bluegrass, Celtic, Latino, old-time, singer/ songwriter, etc.). The Folk Alliance hosts its annual conference (which includes performance showcases) in late February at different locations throughout US and Canada. The conferences include workshops, panel discussions, the largest all folk exhibit hall and showcases. The Folk Alliance also serves members with their newsletter and through education, advocacy and field development. Memberships accepted year-round. Membership fee: $70 ($90 Canadian)/year for individual (voting); $150-505 ($230-700 Canadian)/year for organizational. "We do not offer songwriting contests, but do host performance showcases."

GOSPEL MUSIC ASSOCIATION

1205 Division St., Nashville TN 37203. (615)242-0303. E-mail: joy@gospelmusic.org. Website: www.gospelmusic.org. **Contact:** Joy T. Fletcher, vice president of events and programming. Estab. 1964. Serves songwriters, musicians and anyone directly involved in or who supports gospel music. Professional members include advertising agencies, musicians, agents/managers, composers, retailers, music publishers, print and broadcast media, and other members of the recording industry. Associate members include supporters of gospel music and those whose involvement in the industry does not provide them with income. The primary purpose of the GMA is to expose, promote, and celebrate the Gospel through music. A GMA membership offers a music library, newsletters, performance experiences and workshops, as well as networking opportunities. Applications accepted year-round. Membership fee: $85/year (professional); $60/year (associate); and $25/year (college student).

GOSPEL/CHRISTIAN SONGWRITERS GROUP

1518 Bennett St., Raleigh NC 27604. (919)264-8963. Fax: (919)834-6838. E-mail: dee.u13@ivillage.c om. Website: www.angelfire.com/music/ncgcsg. **Contact:** Deborah E. Ulmer, founder. Estab. 1999. GCSG welcomes all songwriters, lyricists, musicians, singers, poets, music expressionists and industry executives. Our members vary in all styles of Christian music. GCSG is open to all ages, from professional to Church to hobby; in any area of music and the industry. We invite anyone who is in the triangle area to attend our meetings and events. Those who are too far away may join GCSG On The Go, our chapter starting out of town membership. The main purpose of GCSG is to glorify God by ministering to people through music. We want everyone to be able to share their knowledge, learn and work with one another. Offers instruction, newsletter, lectures, workshops, performance opportunities, evaluation services and community events. Applications accepted year-round.

⊕ THE GUILD OF INTERNATIONAL SONGWRITERS & COMPOSERS

Sovereign House, 12 Trewartha Rd., Praa Sands, Penzance, Cornwall TR20 9ST England. (01736)762826. Fax: (01736)763328. E-mail: songmag@aol.com. Website: www.songwriters-guild. com. **Contact:** C.A. Jones, secretary. Serves songwriters, musicians, record companies, music publishers, etc. "Our members are amateur and professional songwriters and composers, musicians, publishers, studio owners and producers. Membership is open to all persons throughout the world of any age and ability. The Guild gives advice and services relating to the music industry. A free magazine is available upon request with an SAE or 3 IRCs or visit our website. We provide contact information for artists, record companies, music publishers, industry organizations; free copyright service; *Songwriting & Composing Magazine*; and many additional free services." Applications accepted year-round. Annual dues: £45 in the U.K.; £50 in E.E.C. countries; 50 overseas (subscriptions in pounds sterling only).

HAWAI'I SONGWRITERS ASSOCIATION

P.O. Box 10248, Honolulu HI 96816. (808)988-6878. Fax: (808)988-6236. E-mail: stanrubens@aol.com. Website: www.stanrubens.com. **Contact:** Stan Rubens, secretary. Estab. 1972. "We have two classes of membership: Professional (must have had at least one song commercially published and for sale to general public) and Regular (any one who wants to join and share in our activities). Both classes can vote equally, but only Professional members can hold office. Must be 18 years old to join. Our members include musicians, entertainers and record producers. Membership is world-wide and open to all varieties of music, not just ethnic Hawaiian. President, Stan Rubens, has published 4 albums." Offers competitions, instruction, monthly newsletter, lectures, workshops, performance opportunities and evaluation services. Applications accepted year-round. Membership fee: $24. Stan Rubens teaches Songwriting at McKinley High, Adult education.

INTERNATIONAL BLUEGRASS MUSIC ASSOCIATION (IBMA)

2 Music Circle South, Suite 100, Nashville TN 37203. 1(888)GET-IBMA. Fax: (615)256-0450. E-mail: info@ibma.org. Website: www.ibma.org. Member Services: Jill Snider. Estab. 1985. Serves songwriters, musicians and professionals in bluegrass music. "IBMA is a trade association composed of people and organizations involved professionally and semi-professionally in the bluegrass music industry, including performers, agents, songwriters, music publishers, promoters, print and broadcast media, local associations, recording manufacturers and distributors. Voting members must be currently or formerly involved in the bluegrass industry as full or part-time professionals. A songwriter attempting to become professionally involved in our field would be eligible. Our mission statement reads: "IBMA: Working together for high standards of professionalism, a greater appreciation for our music, and the success of the world-wide bluegrass music community." IBMA publishes a bimonthly *International Bluegrass*, holds an annual trade show/convention with a songwriters showcase in the fall, represents our field outside the bluegrass music community, and compiles and disseminates databases of bluegrass related resources and organizations. Market research on the bluegrass consumer is available and we offer Bluegrass in the Schools information and matching grants. The primary value in this organization for a songwriter is having current information about the bluegrass music field and contacts with other songwriters, publishers, musicians and record companies." Offers workshops, liability insurance, rental car discounts, consultation and databases of record companies, radio stations, press, organizations and gigs. Applications accepted year-round. Membership fee: for a non-voting patron $40/year; for an individual voting professional $65/year; for an organizational voting professional $150/year.

☑ ⊕ INTERNATIONAL SONGWRITERS ASSOCIATION LTD.

P.O. Box 46, Limerick City, Ireland. E-mail: jliddane@songwriter.iol.ie. Website: www.songwriter.co.uk. **Contact:** Anna M. Sinden, membership department. Serves songwriters and music publishers. "The ISA headquarters is in Limerick City, Ireland, and from there it provides its members with assessment services, copyright services, legal and other advisory services and an investigations service, plus a magazine for one yearly fee. Our members are songwriters in more than 50 countries worldwide, of all ages. There are no qualifications, but applicants under 18 are not accepted. We provide information and assistance to professional or semi-professional songwriters. Our publication, *Songwriter*, which was founded in 1967, features detailed exclusive interviews with songwriters and music publishers, as well as directory information of value to writers." Offers competitions, instruction, library, newsletter and a weekly e-mail newsletter *Songwriter Newswire*. Applications accepted year-round. Membership fee for European writers is £19.95; for non-European writers, US $30.

⊕ IRISH MUSIC RIGHTS ORGANISATION

Copyright House, Pembroke Row, Dublin 2 Ireland. +353 1 6614844. Fax: +353 1 6613789. E-mail: info@imro.ie. Website: www.imro.ie. Membership Department: Justin Dowling. Estab. 1988.

"For songwriters, composers and publishers who must have one work which has been recorded and released for sale, or broadcast on radio or television in the past two years, or who have had their works performed at a live performance." The main purpose of this organization is "the collection and distribution of royalties for the public performance of copyright music." Offers newsletter and workshops. Applications accepted year-round.

JUST PLAIN FOLKS MUSIC ORGANIZATION

(www.jpfolks.com), 1315 N. Butler, Indianapolis IN 46219. (317)513-6557. E-mail: info@jpfolks.com. Website: www.jpfolks.com. **Contact:** Brian Austin Whitney(brian@jpfolks.com), founder or Linda Berger (linda@jpfolks.com), projects director. Estab. 1998. "Just Plain Folks is among the world's largest Music Organizations. Our members cover nearly every musical style and professional field, from songwriters, artists, publishers, producers, record labels, entertainment attorneys, publicists and PR experts, performing rights organization staffers, live and recording engineers, educators, music students, musical instrument manufacturers, TV, Radio and Print Media and almost every major Internet Music entity. Representing all 50 US States and over 90 countries worldwide, we have members of all ages, musical styles and levels of success, including winners and nominees of every major music industry award, as well as those just starting out. A complete demographics listing of our group is available on our website. Whether you are a #1 hit songwriter or artist, or the newest kid on the block, you are welcome to join. Membership does require an active e-mail account." The purpose of this organization is "to share wisdom, ideas and experiences with others who have been there, and to help educate those who have yet to make the journey. Just Plain Folks provides its members with a friendly networking and support community that uses the power of the Internet and combines it with good old-fashioned human interaction. We help promote our members ready for success and educate those still learning." Offers special programs to members, including:

- *Just Plain Notes Newsletter:* Members receive our frequent e-mail newsletters full of expert info on how to succeed in the music business, profiles of members successes and advice, opportunities to develop your career and tons of first-person networking contacts to help you along the way. (Note: we send this out 2-3 times/month via e-mail only.)
- *Just Plain Mentors:* We have some of the friendliest expert educators, writers, artists and industry folks in the business who volunteer their time as part of our Mentor Staff. Included are John and JoAnn Braheny, Jason Blume, Harriet Schock, Pat and Pete Luboff, Derek Sivers, Jodi Krangle, Steve Seskin, Alan O'Day, Walter Egan, Sara Light, Danny Arena, Barbara Cloyd, Michael Laskow, Anne Leighton, Mark Keefner, Valerie DeLaCruz, Karen Angela Moore, Ben McLane, Jack Perricone, Pat Pattison, Mark Baxter, Harold Payne, Joey Arreguin, John Beland, Susan Gibson, Art Twain, Diane Rapaport, Nancy Moran, Fett, Mike Dunbar, R. Chris Murphy, Bobby Borg, Paul Reisler, and many others.
- *JPFolks.com Website:* Our home page serves as your pathway to the resources and members of the group worldwide. With message boards, lyric feedback forums, featured members music, member profiles, member contact listings, member links pages, chapter homepages, demographics information, our Internet radio station and all the back issues of our newsletter, "Just Plain Notes."
- *Roadtrips:* We regularly tour the US and Canada, hosting showcases, workshops and friendly member gatherings in each city we visit. We provide opportunities for all our members, at all levels and welcome everyone to our events. Most events are free of charge.
- *Chapters:* Just Plain Folks has over 100 active local chapters around the world run by local member volunteer coordinators. Each chapter is unique but many host monthly networking gatherings, showcases, educational workshops and community service events. To join a chapter, or start one in your city, please visit the chapter section of the jpfolks.com website for a current list of chapters and guidelines.
- *Music Awards:* Just Plain Folks has one of the largest and most diverse Member Music Awards programs in the world. The most recent awards involved over 10,000 albums and 140,000 songs in over 50 genres. Music Award nominees and winners receive featured performance slots at showcases around the world throughout the year. Current submission instructions can be found on the website in the Awards section.

Membership requests are accepted year-round. "To become a member, simply send an e-mail to join@jpfolks.com with the words 'I Want To Join Just Plain Folks.' In the e-mail, include your name, address, website (if applicable) and phone number for our files." There are currently no membership fees.

Tips "Our motto is 'We're All In This Together!'"

THE LAS VEGAS SONGWRITERS ASSOCIATION

P.O. Box 42683, Las Vegas NV 89116-0683. (702)223-7255. E-mail: Betty_Miller@McGraw-Hill.com. Website: www.lasvegassongwriters.com. **Contact:** Betty Kay Miller, president. Secretary: Barbara Jean Smith. Estab. 1980. "We are an educational, nonprofit organization dedicated to improving the art and craft of the songwriter. We want members who are serious about their craft. We want our members to respect their craft and to treat it as a business. Members must be at least 18 years of age. We offer quarterly newsletters, monthly information meetings, workshops three times a month and quarterly seminars with professionals in the music business. We provide support and encouragement to both new and more experienced songwriters. We critique each song or lyric that's presented during workshops, we make suggestions on changes—if needed. We help turn amateur writers into professionals. Several of our songwriters have had their songs recorded on both independent and major labels." Dues: $30/year.

LOS ANGELES MUSIC NETWORK

P.O. Box 2446, Toluca Lake CA 91610-2446. (818)769-7007. E-mail: info@lamn.com. Website: www.lamn.com. **Contact:** Tess Taylor, president. Membership Director: Roslynn Cobarrubias. Estab. 1988. "Connections. Facts. Career advancement. All that is available with your membership in the Los Angeles Music Network (LAMN). Our emphasis is on sharing knowledge and information, giving you access to top professionals and promoting career development. LAMN an association of music industry professionals, i.e., artists, singers, songwriters, and people who work in various aspects of the music industry with an emphasis on the creative. Members are ambitious and interested in advancing their careers. LAMN promotes career advancement, communication and continuing education among music industry professionals and top executives. LAMN sponsors industry events and educational panels held bi-monthly at venues in the Los Angeles area, and now in other major music hubs around the country (New York, Las Vegas, Chicago)." Offers instruction, newsletter, lectures, seminars, music industry job listings, career counseling, résumé publishing, mentor network, résumé resource guide and many professional networking opportunities. See our website for current job listings and a calendar of upcoming events. Applications accepted year-round. Annual membership fee is $110 (subject to change without notice).

LOUISIANA SONGWRITERS ASSOCIATION

P.O. Box 80425, Baton Rouge LA 70898-0425. (504)443-5390. E-mail: zimshah@aol.com. Website: www.lasongwriters.org. **Contact:** Connie Zimmerman, membership coordinator. Serves songwriters. "LSA was organized to educate songwriters in all areas of their trade, and promote the art of songwriting in Louisiana. LSA is honored to have a growing number of songwriters from other states join LSA and fellowship with us. LSA membership is open to people interested in songwriting, regardless of age, musical ability, musical preference, ethnic background, etc. "This year marks our 20th anniversary and also a new direction for our organization. Our group is now driven by special projects (short term), which are coordinated and implemented by our membership. This arms our members with the knowledge and experience necessary to succeed within the industry." LSA offers competitions, lectures, library, newsletter, directory, marketing, performance opportunities, workshops, discounts on various music-related books and magazines, discounts on studio time, and we are developing a service manual that will contain information on music related topics, such as copyrighting, licensing, etc." Also offers regular showcases in Baton Rouge and New Orleans. General membership dues: $25/year, 45/2 years.

⬛ MANITOBA AUDIO RECORDING INDUSTRY ASSOCIATION (MARIA)

1-376 Donald St., Winnipeg MB R3B 2J2 Canada. (204)942-8650. Fax: (204)942-6083. E-mail: info@manitobamusic.com. Website: www.manitobamusic.com. **Contact:** Rachel Stone, associate coordinator. Estab. 1987. Organization consists of "songwriters, producers, agents, musicians, managers, retailers, publicists, radio, talent buyers, media, record labels, etc. (no age limit, no skill level minimum). Must have interest in the future of Manitoba's sound recording industry." The main purpose of MARIA is to foster growth in all areas of the Manitoba music industry primarily through education, promotion and lobbying. Offers newsletter, lectures, directory of Manitoba's music industry, workshops and performance opportunities; also presents demo critiquing sessions and comprehensive member discount program featuring a host of participating Manitoba businesses. MARIA is also involved with the Prairie Music Weekend festival, conference and awards show. Applications accepted year-round. Membership fee: $50 (Canadian funds).

MEET THE COMPOSER
75 Ninth Ave, 3R Suite C, New York NY 10011. (212)645-6949. Fax: (212)645-9669. E-mail: mtc@meetthecomposer.org. Website: www.meetthecomposer.org. Estab. 1974. "Meet The Composer serves composers working in all styles of music, at every career stage, through a variety of grant programs and information resources. A nonprofit organization, Meet The Composer raises money from foundations, corporations, individual patrons and government sources and designs programs that support all genres of music—from folk, ethnic, jazz, electronic, symphonic, and chamber to choral, music theater, opera and dance. Meet The Composer awards grants for composer fees to non-profit organizations that perform, present, or commission original works. This is not a membership organization; all composers are eligible for support. Meet The Composer was founded in 1974 to increase artistic and financial opportunities for composers by fostering the creation, performance, dissemination, and appreciation of their music." Offers grant programs and information services. Deadlines vary for each grant program.

☑ MEMPHIS SONGWRITERS' ASSOCIATION
4746 Spottswood, #191, Memphis TN 38117-4815. E-mail: admin@memphissongwriters.org Website: www.memphissongwriters.org. **Contact:** Jon Dillard, president. Estab. 1973. "MSA is a nonprofit songwriters organization serving songwriters nationally. Our mission is to dedicate our services to promote, advance, and help songwriters in the composition of music, lyrics and songs; to work for better conditions in our profession; and to secure and protect the rights of MSA songwriters. We also supply copyright forms. We offer critique sessions for writers at our monthly meetings. We also have monthly open mic songwriters night to encourage creativity, networking and co-writing. We host an annual songwriter's seminar and an annual songwriter's showcase, as well as a bi-monthly guest speaker series, which provide education, competition and entertainment for the songwriter. In addition, our members receive a bimonthly newsletter to keep them informed of MSA activities, demo services and opportunities in the songwriting field." Annual fee: $50; Student/Senior: $35.

MINNESOTA ASSOCIATION OF SONGWRITERS
P.O. Box 333, Chicago City MN 55013. (651)254-9779. E-mail: info@mnsongwriters.org. Website: www.mnsongwriters.org. "Includes a wide variety of members, ranging in age from 18 to 80; type of music is very diverse ranging from alternative rock to contemporary Christian; skill levels range from beginning songwriters to writers with recorded and published material. Main requirement is an interest in songwriting. Although most members come from the Minneapolis-St. Paul area, others come in from surrounding cities, nearby Wisconsin, and other parts of the country. Some members are fulltime musicians, but most represent a wide variety of occupations. MAS is a nonprofit community of songwriters which informs, educates, inspires and assists its members in the art and business of songwriting." Offers instruction, newsletter, lectures, workshops, performance opportunities and evaluation services. Applications accepted year-round. Membership fee: Individual: $25; Business: $65.
Tips "Members are kept current on resources and opportunities. Original works are played at meetings and are critiqued by involved members. Through this process, writers hone their skills and gain experience and confidence in submitting their works to others."

NASHVILLE SONGWRITERS ASSOCIATION INTERNATIONAL (NSAI)

1710 Roy Acuff Place, Nashville TN 37203. (615)256-3354 or (800)321-6008. Fax: (615)256-0034.
E-mail: nsai@nashvillesongwriters.com. Website: www.nashvillesongwriters.com. Executive Director: Barton Herbison. Purpose: a not-for-profit service organization for both aspiring and professional songwriters in all fields of music. Membership: Spans the United States and several foreign countries. Songwriters may apply in one of four annual categories: Active ($150 U.S / $100 International—for songwriters who have at least one song contractually signed to a publisher affiliated with ASCAP, BMI or SESAC); Associate ($150 U.S / $100 International—for songwriters who are not yet published or for anyone wishing to support songwriters); Student ($100 U.S / $100 International—for full-time college students or for students of an accredited senior high school); Professional ($100—for songwriters who derive their primary source of income from songwriting or who are generally recognized as such by the professional songwriting community). Membership benefits: music industry information and advice, song evaluations by mail, quarterly newsletter, access to industry professionals through weekly Nashville workshop and several annual events, regional workshops, use of office facilities, discounts on books and discounts on NSAI's three annual events. There are also "branch" workshops of NSAI. Workshops must meet certain standards and are accountable to NSAI. Interested coordinators may apply to NSAI.

- Also see the listing for NSAI Songwriters Symposium (formerly NSAI Spring Symposium) in the Workshops section of this book.

THE NATIONAL ASSOCIATION OF COMPOSERS/USA (NACUSA)

P.O. Box 49256, Barrington Station, Los Angeles CA 90049. E-mail: nacusa@music-usa.org. Website: www.music-usa.org/nacusa. **Contact:** Deon Nielsen Price, president. Estab. 1932. Serves songwriters, musicians and classical composers. "We are of most value to the concert hall composer. Members are serious music composers of all ages and from all parts of the country, who have a real interest in composing, performing, and listening to modern concert hall music. The main purpose of our organization is to perform, publish, broadcast and write news about composers of serious concert hall music—mostly chamber and solo pieces. Composers may achieve national notice of their work through our newsletter and concerts, and the fairly rare feeling of supporting a non-commercial music enterprise dedicated to raising the musical and social position of the serious composer." Offers competitions, lectures, performance opportunities, library and newsletter. Applications accepted year-round. Membership fee: National (regular): $25; National (students/seniors): $15.

- Also see the listing for NACUSA Young Composers' Competition in the Contests section of this book.

Tips "99% of the money earned in music is earned, or so it seems, by popular songwriters who might feel they owe the art of music something, and this is one way they might help support that art. It's a chance to foster fraternal solidarity with their less prosperous, but wonderfully interesting classical colleagues at a time when the very existence of serious art seems to be questioned by the general populace."

NATIONAL SOCIETY OF MEN AND WOMEN OF THE MUSIC BUSINESS (WOMB)

P.O. Box 5170, Beverly Hills CA 90209-5170. (323)210-1515. Fax: (323)467-8468. Website: www.YuleJam.org. **Contact:** Director. Estab. 1996. "WOMB is a non-profit organization of top music industry professionals keeping music education and dreams alive for kids who attend inner-city high schools and community organizations around the U.S. Music industry professionals are encouraged to participate and make a difference in a child's life!" Programs include "WOMB's School Music Network": top music industry professionals volunteer 2-3 hours to visit inner-city high schools; "WOMB's Music for Music": organizes music instrument and material donation drives for schools through corporate sponsorships and events; Yule Jam, a charity concert and music instrument drive with proceeds going to local school music departments. Offers corporate sponsorships, events, performance opportunities and an e-mail newsletter. Future programs include afterschool music programs, college scholarships and special events. Volunteers, music instrument, material donations and corporate sponsorships accepted year-round.

NORTH FLORIDA CHRISTIAN MUSIC WRITERS ASSOCIATION

P.O. Box 61113, Jacksonville FL 32236. (904)786-2372. E-mail: justsongs@aol.com. Website: www.christiansongwriter.com. **Contact:** Jackie Hand, president. Estab. 1974. "Members are people from all walks of life who promote Christian music—not just composers or performers, but anyone who wants to share today's message in song with the world. No age limit. Anyone interested in promoting Christian music is invited to join. If you are talented in several areas you might be asked to conduct a training session or workshop. Your expertise is wanted and needed by our group. The group's purpose is to serve God by using our God-given talents and abilities and to assist our fellow songwriters, getting their music in the best possible form to be ready for whatever door God chooses to open for them concerning their music. Members' works are included in songbooks published by our organization—also biographies." Offers competitions, performance opportunities, field trips, instruction, newsletter, workshops and critiques. This year we offer a new website featuring song clips by members as well as a short bio. Also featured is a special "Memorial Members" list honoring deceased members by keeping their music alive. The one time fee of $100 to place loved ones on the list includes a song clip on our website and entry privileges in our songwriting contest. Applications accepted year-round. Membership fee: $25/year ($35 for outside US), $35 for husband/wife team ($45 for outside US). "The 25th Anniversary Edition songbook of our members music (plus our 25 years as a songwriting organization) is $10 plus $3.00 S&H. White Tee Shirt with black graphic and message, "North Florida Christian Music Writers Association" and a graphic of a beautiful piano and other instruments on front is also $10 plus $3.00 S&H." Make checks payable to Jackie Hand.

Tips "If you are serious about your craft, you need fellowship with others who feel the same. A Christian songwriting organization is where you belong if you write Christian songs."

OPERA AMERICA

1156 15th St., NW, Suite 810, Washington DC 20005-1704. (202)293-4466. Fax: (202)393-0735. E-mail: frontdesk@operaamerica.org. Website: www.operaamerica.org. **Contact:** Rebecca Ackerman, membership operations coordinator. Estab. 1970. Members are composers, librettists, musicians, singers, and opera/music theater producers. "OPERA America maintains an extensive library of reference books and domestic and foreign music periodicals, and the most comprehensive operatic archive in the United States. OPERA America draws on these unique resources to supply information to its members." Offers conferences. Publishes online database of opera/music theater companies in the US and Canada, online directory of opera and musical performances world-wide and US, and an online directory of new works created and being developed by current-day composers and librettists, to encourage the performance of new works. Applications accepted year-round. Publishes 40-page magazine 10 times/year. Membership fee is on a sliding scale by membership level.

OUTMUSIC

P.O. Box 376, Old Chelsea Station, New York NY 10113-0376. (212)330-9197. E-mail: info@outmusic.com. Website: www.outmusic.com. **Contact:** Ed Mannix, communications director. Estab. 1990. "OUTMUSIC is comprised of gay men, lesbians, bisexuals and transgenders. They represent all different musical styles from rock to classical. Many are writers of original material. We are open to all levels of accomplishment—professional, amateur, and interested industry people. The only requirement for membership is an interest in the growth and visibility of music and lyrics created by the LGBT community. We supply our members with support and networking opportunities. In addition, we help to encourage artists to bring their work 'OUT' into the world." Offers newsletter, lectures, workshops, performance opportunities, networking, industry leads and monthly open mics. Sponsors Outmusic Awards. Applications accepted year-round. For membership information go to www.outmusic.com.

Tips "OUTMUSIC has spawned *The Gay Music Guide*, The Gay and Lesbian American Music Awards (GLAMA), several compilation albums and many independent recording projects."

PACIFIC MUSIC INDUSTRY ASSOCIATION

#501-425 Carrall St., Vancouver BC V6B 6E3 Canada. (604)873-1914. Fax: (604)873-9686. E-mail: info@musicbc.org. Website: www.pmia.org. Estab. 1990. Music BC is a non-profit society that supports and promotes the spirit, development, and growth of the BC music community provincially, nationally, and internationally. Music BC provides education, resources, advocacy, funding opportunities, and a forum for communication. Applications accepted year-round. E-mail for info about the different levels of Memberships.

PITTSBURGH SONGWRITERS ASSOCIATION

523 Scenery Dr., Elizabeth PA 15037. (412)751-9584. E-mail: vstragand@aol.com. Website: www.p ittsburghsongwritersassociation.com. **Contact:** Van Stragand, president. Estab. 1983. "We are a non-profit organization dedicated to helping its members develop and market their songs. Writers of any age and experience level welcome. Current members are from 20s to 50s. All musical styles and interests are welcome. Our organization wants to serve as a source of quality material for publishers and other industry professionals. We assist members in developing their songs and their professional approach. We provide meetings, showcases, collaboration opportunities, instruction, industry guests, library and social outings. Annual dues: $25. We have no initiation fee. Prospective members are invited to attend two free meetings. Interested parties please call Van Stragand at (412)751-9584."

POP RECORD RESEARCH

10 Glen Ave., Norwalk CT 06850. E-mail: horar@earthlink.net. **Director:** Gary Theroux. Estab. 1962. Serves songwriters, musicians, writers, researchers and media. "We maintain archives of materials relating to music, TV and film, with special emphasis on recorded music (the hits and hitmakers 1877-present): bios, photos, reviews, interviews, discographies, chart data, clippings, films, videos, etc." Offers library and clearinghouse for accurate promotion/publicity to biographers, writers, reviewers, the media. Offers programming, annotation and photo source for reissues or retrospective album collections on any artist (singers, songwriters, musicians, etc.), also music consultation services for film or television projects. "There is no charge to include publicity, promotional or biographical materials in our archives. Artists, writers, composers, performers, producers, labels and publicists are always invited to add or keep us on their publicity/promotion mailing list with career data, updates, new releases and reissues of recorded performances, etc. Fees are assessed only for reference use by researchers, writers, biographers, reviewers, etc. Songwriters and composers (or their publicists) should keep or put us on their publicity mailing lists to ensure that the information we supply others on their careers, accomplishments, etc. is accurate and up-to-date."

RHODE ISLAND SONGWRITERS' ASSOCIATION (RISA)

P.O. Box 367, Harmony RI 02829. (401)949-0747. E-mail: risa@risongwriters.com or hearingri@ids. net. Website: www.risongwriters.com. **Co-Chairs:** John Fuzekand Bill Furney. Estab. 1993. "Membership consists of novice and professional songwriters. RISA provides opportunities to the aspiring writer or performer as well as the established regional artists who have recordings, are published and perform regularly. The only eligibility requirement is an interest in the group and the group's goals. Non-writers are welcome as well." The main purpose is to "encourage, foster and conduct the art and craft of original musical and/or lyrical composition through education, information, collaboration and performance." Offers instruction, newsletter, lectures, workshops, performance opportunities and evaluation services. Applications accepted year-round. Membership fee: $25/ year. "The group holds twice monthly critique sessions; twice monthly performer showcases (one performer featured) at a local coffeehouse; songwriter showcases (usually 6-8 performers); weekly open mikes; and a yearly songwriter festival called 'Hear In Rhode Island,' featuring approximately 50 Rhode Island acts, over two days."

SAN FRANCISCO FOLK MUSIC CLUB

885 Clayton, San Francisco CA 94117. (415)661-2217. E-mail: sffolk@aol.com. Website: www.sffm c.org. **Contact:** Membership Coordinator. Serves songwriters, musicians and anyone who enjoys

folk music. "Our members range from ages 2 to 80. The only requirement is that members enjoy, appreciate and be interested in sharing folk music. As a focal point for the San Francisco Bay Area folk music community, the SFFMC provides opportunities for people to get together to share folk music, and the newsletter *The Folknik* disseminates information. We publish two songs an issue (six times a year) in our newsletter, our meetings provide an opportunity to share new songs, and at our camp-outs there are almost always songwriter workshops." Offers library, newsletter, informal performance opportunities, annual free folk festival, social outings and workshops. Applications accepted year-round. Membership fee: $10/year.

SESAC INC.
152 W. 57th St., 57th Floor, New York NY 10019. (212)586-3450. Fax: (212)489-5699. Website: www.sesac.com. **Nashville:** 55 Music Square East, Nashville TN 37203. (615)320-0055. Fax: (615)329-9627; **Los Angeles:** 501 Santa Monica Blvd., Suite 450, Santa Monica CA 90401. (310)393-9671. Fax: (310)393-6497; **London:** 67 Upper Berkeley St., London WIH 7QX United Kingdom. (020)76169284. **Contact:** Tim Fink, associate vice president writer/publisher relations. Chief Operating Officer: Pat Collins. Coordinator-Writer/Publisher Relations: Mandy Reilly. SESAC is a selective organization taking pride in having a repertory based on quality rather than quantity. Serves writers and publishers in all types of music who have their works performed by radio, television, nightclubs, cable TV, etc. Purpose of organization is to collect and distribute performance royalties to all active affiliates. As a SESAC affiliate, the individual may obtain equipment insurance at competitive rates. Tapes are reviewed upon invitation by the Writer/Publisher Relations dept.

SOCIETY OF COMPOSERS, INC.
Old Chelsea Station Box 450, New York NY 10113-0450. E-mail: secretary@societyofcomposers.org. Website: www.societyofcomposers.org. **Contact:** Gerald Warfield, General Manager, SCI National Office. Offers promotion of composition, performance opportunities and instruction for composers and performers both inside and out of academia. Applications accepted year-round. Membership fee: $50/year.

SOCIETY OF COMPOSERS & LYRICISTS
400 S. Beverly Dr., Suite 214, Beverly Hills CA 90212. (310)281-2812. Fax: (310)284-4861. E-mail: execdir@thescl.com. Website: www.thescl.com. The professional nonprofit trade organization for members actively engaged in writing music/lyrics for films, TV, and/or video games, or are students of film composition or songwriting for film. Primary mission is to advance the interests of the film and TV music community. Offers an award-winning quarterly publication, educational seminars, screenings, special member-only events, and other member benefits. Applications accepted year-round. Membership fee: $135 Full Membership (composers, lyricists, songwriters—film/TV music credits must be submitted); $85 Associate/Student Membership for composers, lyricists, songwriters without credits only; $135 Sponsor/Special Friend Membership (music editors, music supervisors, music attorneys, agents, etc.).

◪ SOCIETY OF COMPOSERS, AUTHORS AND MUSIC PUBLISHERS OF CANADA/SOCIETE CANADIENNE DES AUTEURS, COMPOSITEURS ET EDITEURS DE MUSIQUE (SOCAN)
Head Office: 41 Valleybrook Dr., Toronto ON M3B 2S6 Canada. (800)55-SOCAN. Fax: (416)445-7108. Website: www.socan.ca. CEO: Andre LeBel. Vice President, Quebec & Atlantic Division and National Licensing: France Lafleur. Vice President, West Coast Division and National Member Services: Kent Sturgeon. The Society licenses public performance of music and distributes performance royalties to composers, lyricists, authors and music publishers. ASCAP, BMI and SESAC license the public performance of SOCAN's repertoire in the US.

◪ SODRAC INC.
759 Victoria Square, Suite 420, Montreal QC H2Y 2J7 Canada. (514)845-3268. Fax: (514)845-3401. E-mail: sodrac@sodrac.com. Website: www.sodrac.com. **Contact:** Chantal Beaudoin, membership department (author, composer and publisher) or Diane Lamarre, membership department (visual

artist and rights owner). Estab. 1985. "Sodrac was founded in 1985 on the initiative of songwriters and composers in order to manage the reproduction rights of authors, composers and publishers of musical repertoire of about 83 countries and more than 5,000 Canadian members, as well as over 25,000 national and international visual artists. SODRAC is the only Reproduction Rights Society in Canada where both songwriters and music publishers are represented, equally and directly." Serves those with an interest in songwriting and music publishing no matter what their age or skill level is. "Members must have written or published at least one musical work that has been reproduced on an audio (CD, cassettte, LP) or audiovisual support (TV, DVD, video). The new member will benefit of a society working to secure his reproduction rights (mechanicals) and broadcast mechanicals." Applications accepted year-round.

SONGWRITERS AND POETS CRITIQUE

P.O. Box 21065, Columbus OH 43221. E-mail: LPretzman@SongwritersCritique.com. Website: www.songwriterscritique.com. **Contact:** LeeAnn Pretzman, secretary. Estab. 1985. Serves songwriters, musicians, poets, lyricists and performers. Meets second and fourth Friday of every month to discuss club events and critique one another's work. Offers seminars and workshops with professionals in the music industry. "We critique mail-in submissions from long-distance members. Our goal is to provide support and opportunity to anyone interested in creating songs or poetry." Applications are accepted year-round. Annual dues: $30.

SONGWRITERS ASSOCIATION OF WASHINGTON

PMB 106-137, 4200 Wisconsin Ave. NW, Washington DC 20016. (301)654-8434. E-mail: membership@SAW.org. Website: www.SAW.org. Estab. 1979. "SAW is a nonprofit organization operated by a volunteer board of directors. It is committed to providing its members opportunities to learn more about the art of songwriting, to learn more about the music business, to perform in public, and to connect with fellow songwriters. SAW sponsors various events to achieve these goals: workshops, open mics, songwriter exchanges, and showcases. In addition, SAW organizes the Mid-Atlantic Song Contest open to entrants nationwide each year; "the competition in 2003 was the twentieth contest SAW has adjudicated since 1982." (Contest information masc@saw.org). As well as maintaining a website, SAW publishes *SAW Notes*, a bimonthly newsletter for members containing information on upcoming local events, member news, contest information, and articles of interest. Joint introductory membership with the Washington Area Music Association is available at a savings. Use the contact information above for membership inquiries.

THE SONGWRITERS GUILD OF AMERICA (SGA)

1560 Broadway, Suite #1306, New York NY 10036. (212)768-7902. Fax: (212)768-9048. E-mail: ny@songwritersguild.com. Website: www.songwritersguild.com. **New York Office:** 1560 Broadway, Suite #408, New York NY 10036; **Los Angeles Office:** 6430 Sunset Blvd., Suite 705, Hollywood CA 90028, (323)462-1108. Fax: (323)462-5430. E-mail: la@songwritersguild.com. **Nashville Office:** 209 10th Ave. S., Suite 534, Nashville TN 37203, (615)742-9945. Fax: (615)742-9948. E-mail: nash@songwritersguild.com. **SGA Administration:** 1500 Harbor Blvd., Wechawken NJ 07086. (201)867-7603. Fax:(201)867-7535. E-mail: corporate@songwritersguild.com.

> • Also see the listings for The Songwriters Guild Foundation in the Workshops & Conferences section.

President: Rick Carnes. Executive Director: Lewis M. Bachman. East Coast Project Manager: Mark Saxon. West Coast Project Manager: Aaron Lynn. Central Project Manager: Evan Shoemke. Estab. 1931. "The Songwriters Guild of America (SGA) is a voluntary songwriter association run by and for songwriters. It is devoted exclusively to providing songwriters with the services and activities they need to succeed in the business of music. The preamble to the SGA constitution charges the board to take such lawful actions as will advance, promote and benefit the profession. Services of SGA cover every aspect of songwriting including the creative, administrative and financial." A full member must be a published songwriter. An associate member is any unpublished songwriter with a desire to learn more about the business and craft of songwriting. The third class of membership comprises estates of deceased writers. The Guild contract is considered to be the best available in the industry, having the greatest number of built-in protections for the songwriter. The Guild's Royalty Collection Plan makes certain that prompt and accurate payments are made to writers. The ongoing Audit Program makes periodic checks of publishers' books. For the self-publisher, the Catalogue Administration Program (CAP) relieves a writer of the paperwork of publishing for a fee lower than the prevailing industry rates. The Copyright Renewal Service informs members a year in advance of a song's renewal date. Other services include workshops in New York and Los Angeles, free Ask-A-Pro sessions with industry pros, critique sessions, collaborator service and newsletters. In addition, the Guild reviews your songwriter contract on request (Guild or otherwise); fights to strengthen songwriters' rights and to increase writers' royalties by supporting legislation which directly affects copyright; offers a group medical and life insurance plan; issues news bulletins with essential information for songwriters; provides a songwriter collaboration service for younger writers; financially evaluates catalogues of copyrights in connection with possible sale and estate planning; operates an estates administration service; and maintains a nonprofit educational foundation (The Songwriters Guild Foundation)."

SONGWRITERS OF OKLAHOMA
P.O. Box 4121, Edmond OK 73083-4121. E-mail: furrowmusic@sbcglobal.net. **Contact:** Harvey Derrick, president. Offers information on the music industry: reviews publishing/artist contracts, where and how to get demo tapes produced, presentation of material to publishers or record companies, royalties and copyrights. Also offers information on the craft of songwriting: co-writers, local songwriting organizations, a written critique of lyrics, songs and compositions on tapes/CDs as long as a SASE is provided for return of critique. No more than 1 song per tape and 3 per cd. All of these services are free to current members. Membership dues: $25/year. A SASE must be included with all submissions/inquiries.

SONGWRITERS OF WISCONSIN INTERNATIONAL
P.O. Box 1027, Neenah WI 54957-1027. (920)725-5129. E-mail: sowi@new.rr.com. Website: www.sowi.cjb.net. **Contact:** Tony Ansems, president. Workshops Coordinator: Mike Heath. Estab. 1983. Serves songwriters. "Membership is open to songwriters writing all styles of music. Residency in Wisconsin is recommended but not required. Members are encouraged to bring tapes and lyric sheets of their songs to the meetings, but it is not required. We are striving to improve the craft of songwriting in Wisconsin. Living in Wisconsin, a songwriter would be close to any of the workshops and showcases offered each month at different towns. The primary value of membership for a songwriter is in sharing ideas with other songwriters, being critiqued and helping other songwriters." Offers competitions (contest entry deadline: May 15), field trips, instruction, lectures, newsletter, performance opportunities, social outings, workshops and critique sessions. Applications accepted year-round. Membership dues: $30/year.
Tips "Critique meetings every last Thursday of each month, January through October, 7 p.m.-10 p.m. at The Hampton Inn, 350 N. Fox River Dr., Appleton WI."

SOUTHEAST TEXAS BLUEGRASS MUSIC ASSOCIATION
130 Willow Run, Lumberton TX 77657-9210. (409)755-0622. E-mail: PickNBow@aol.com. **Contact:** Edy Mathews, editor. Estab. 1976. Members are musicians and listeners of all ages. Purpose is to promote bluegrass, gospel and old time music. Offers newsletter and monthly shows which are free. Applications accepted year-round. Membership fee: $12/year.

SOUTHEASTERN COMPOSERS LEAGUE
4810 Cedarline Dr., Greensboro NC 27409. Website: www.runet.edu/ ~ scl-web. **Contact:** Greg Carroll, vice president. Estab. 1950. Offers performance opporunities, workshops, evaluation services and a newsletter. Applications accepted year-round. Membership fee: $30/year.

SOUTHERN SONGWRITERS GUILD, INC.
P.O. Box 52656, Shreveport LA 71136-2656. E-mail: songguild@aol.com. Website: http://members.aol.com/songguild. **Contact:** Cathy Williams, president. Estab. 1984. "The purpose of the Southern

Songwriters Guild is to promote the art and craft of songwriting through all available educational and charitable means and to endeavor to uphold its objectives in harmony with society. SSG hosts an annual Awards Banquet that features winners of our 'Song of the Year' contest that provides cash prizes; and to induct new members into 'SSG Songwriters Hall of Fame', who may have local or regional roots in either heritage or career development. SSG has monthly Board and General Membership meetings aimed toward education. Fundraiser benefits are occasionally conducted for specific needs. A small educational scholarship program is infrequently available for those who meet certain criteria for need and purpose. SSG offers an opportunity to network or collaborate with other songwriters and songwriter organizations and encourages dual or multi-memberships with other organizations whose purposes are consistent with those of SSG. A newsletter is distributed to the membership and to non-member related entities. Performance opportunities, open mic sessions, songwriting workshops, clinics, annual family picnic, Christmas party and song critiques are additional functions. Please send SASE for membership application or other information." Applications accepted year-round. Membership fee: $30/year, $25 for each additional family member, $100 for organization or institution.

☑ SOUTHWEST CELTIC MUSIC ASSOCIATION
833 Exposition Ave., Suite 101, Dallas TX 75226-2490. Website: www.scmatx.org. **Contact:** John Hebley, president. Estab. 1983. Persons interested in promotion and preservation of Celtic music. Musicians and Celtic music lovers are members (not necessary to be a musician to join). No eligibility requirements, although membership is primarily in Texas and surrounding states. Purpose is to promote, preserve and provide education about Celtic music, dance and culture in Texas and the Southwest region of the US. Offers instruction, newsletter, lectures, workshops, performance opportunities and sponsorships and scholarships. Applications accepted year-round. Membership fee: $15/family; $25/organization; $50/friendship; $100/sponsor; $300/lifetime member.
Tips "We are the producers of the second largest Irish Festival in the U.S."

☑ SOUTHWEST VIRGINIA SONGWRITERS ASSOCIATION
P.O. Box 698, Salem VA 24153. Website: www.svsa.info.com **Contact:** Britt Mistele. Estab. 1981. 80 members of all ages and skill all levels, mainly country, folk, gospel, contemporary and rock but other musical interests too. "The purpose of SVSA is to increase, broaden and expand the knowledge of each member and to support, better and further the progress and success of each member in songwriting and related fields of endeavor." Offers performance opportunities, evaluation services, instruction, newsletter, workshops, monthly meetings and monthly newsletter. Application accepted year-round. Membership fee: $18/year.

☑ SPARS (Society of Professional Audio Recording Services)
9 Music Square South, Suite 222, Nashville TN 37203. 1-800-771-7727. Fax: (615)296-0386. E-mail: spars@spars.com. Website: www.spars.com. **Contact:** Larry Lipman, executive director. Estab. 1979. Members are recording studios, manufacturers of audio recording equipment, individual project studio owners, mastering engineers, regular audio engineers, providers of services to the audio recording industry. Call for application/brochure describing membership. Non-profit professional organization focused on the business issues of multimedia facility ownership; management and operations; and educational networking and communion. Offers newsletter, publications, workshops, evaluation services and SPARS test. Applications accepted year-round. Call or write for information.

⊕ SPNM—PROMOTING NEW MUSIC
(formerly Society for the Promotion of New Music [SPNM]), St. Margarets House, 4th Floor, 18-20 Southwark St., London SE1 1TJ United Kingdom. 020 7407 1640. Fax: 020 7403 7652. E-mail: spnm@spnm.org.uk. Website: www.spnm.org.uk. Executive Director: Abigail Pogson. Administrator: Tina Speed. Estab. 1943. "All ages and backgrounds are welcome, with a common interest in the innovative and unexplored. We enable new composers to hear their works performed by top-class professionals in quality venues." Offers newsletter, lectures, workshops, special offers and

concerts. Annual selection procedure, deadline September 30. "From contemporary jazz, classical and popular music to that written for film, dance and other creative media, spnm is one of the main advocates of new music in Britain today. Through its eclectic program of concerts, workshops, education projects and collaborations and through its publications, *new notes* , spnm brings new music in all guises to many, many people." Other calls for specific events throughout year. Membership fee: Ordinary: £25; Concessions: £10; Friend: £35.

Tips "Most calls for pieces are restricted to those living and/or studying in UK/Ireland, or to British composers living overseas."

☑ THE TENNESSEE SONGWRITERS INTERNATIONAL

P.O. Box 2664, Hendersonville TN 370772664. (615)969-5967. E-mail: asktsai@aol.com. Website: www.clubnashville.com/tsai.htm. **Contact:** Margie Reeves, membership director. Executive Director: Jim Sylvis. Serves songwriters. "Our membership is open to all ages and consists of both novice and experienced professional songwriters. The only requirement for membership is a serious interest in the craft and business of songwriting. Our main purpose and function is to educate and assist the songwriter, both in the art/craft of songwriting and in the business of songwriting. In addition to education, we also provide an opportunity for camaraderie, support and encouragement, as well a chance to meet co-writers. We also critique each others' material and offer suggestions for improvement, if needed. We offer the following to our members: Informative monthly newsletters; 'Pro-Rap'—once a month a key person from the music industry addresses our membership on their field of specialty. They may be writers, publishers, producers and sometimes even the recording artists themselves; 'Pitch-A-Pro'—we schedule a publisher, producer or artist who is currently looking for material to come to our meeting and listen to songs pitched by our members; 'Legends Night'—several times a year, a 'legend' in the music business will be our guest speaker. Annual Awards Dinner—honoring the most accomplished of our TSAI membership during the past year; Tips—letting our members know who is recording and how to get their songs to the right people. Workshops are held at Belmont University, Wedgewood Ave., Nashville TN in the Massey Business Center Building, Room 200-B on Wednesday evenings from 7-9 p.m." Applications accepted year-round. Membership runs for one year from the date you join. Membership fee is $50/year in the U.S. and $65 in all foreign countries.

TEXAS ACCOUNTANTS & LAWYERS FOR THE ARTS

1540 Sul Ross, Houston TX 77006-4730. (713)526-4876 ext. 201 or (800)526-TALA ext. 201. Fax: (713)526-1299. E-mail: info@talarts.org. Website: www.talarts.org. **Contact:** Trena Denley, Esq., executive director. Estab. 1979. TALA's members include accountants, attorneys, museums, theatre groups, dance groups, actors, artists, musicians and filmmakers. Our members are of all age groups and represent all facets of their respective fields. TALA is a nonprofit organization that provides pro bono legal and accounting services to income-eligible artists from all disciplines and to nonprofit arts organizations. TALA also provides mediation services for resolving disputes as a low cost-nonadversarial alternative to litigation. Offers newsletter, lectures, library and workshops. Applications accepted year-round. Membership fee for artists: $30; bands: $75.

Tips TALA's speakers program presents low-cost seminars on topics such as The Music Business, Copyright and Trademark, and The Business of Writing. These seminars are held annually at a location in Houston. TALA's speaker's program also provides speakers for seminars by other organizations.

TEXAS MUSIC OFFICE

P.O. Box 13246, Austin TX 78711. (512)463-6666. Fax: (512)463-4114. E-mail: music@governor.state.tx.us. Website: www.governor.state.tx.us/music. **Contact:** Casey Monahan, director. Estab. 1990. "The main purpose of the Texas Music Office is to promote the Texas music industry and Texas music, and to assist music professionals around the world with information about the Texas market. The Texas Music Office serves as a clearinghouse for Texas music industry information using their seven databases: Texas Music Industry (5,800 Texas music businesses in 94 music business categories); Texas Music Events (700 Texas music events); Texas Talent Register (900

Texas recording artists); Texas Radio Stations (733 Texas stations); U.S. Record Labels; Classical Texas (detailed information for all classical music organizations in Texas); and International (450 foreign businesses interested in Texas music). Provides referrals to Texas music businesses, talent and events in order to attract new business to Texas and/or to encourage Texas businesses and individuals to keep music business in-state. Serves as a liaison between music businesses and other government offices and agencies. Publicizes significant developments within the Texas music industry." Publishes the *Texas Music Industry Directory* (see the Publications of Interest section for more information).

TORONTO MUSICIANS' ASSOCIATION

15 Gervais Dr., Suite 500, Toronto ON M3C 1Y8 Canada. (416)421-1020. Fax: (416)421-7011. E-mail: info@torontomusicians.org. Website: www.torontomusicians.org. Executive Director: Bill Skolnick. Estab. 1887. Serves musicians—*All* musical styles, background, areas of the industry. "Must be a Canadian citizen, show proof of immigration status, or have a valid work permit for an extended period of time." The purpose of this organization is "to unite musicians into one organization, in order that they may, individually and collectively, secure, maintain and profit from improved economic, working and artistic conditions." Offers newsletter. Applications accepted year-round. Joining fee is $235.

VICTORY MUSIC

P.O. Box 2254, Tacoma WA 98401. (253)428-0832. E-mail: victory@nwlink.com. Website: www.victorymusic.org. **Contact:** Deb Seymour, coordinator. Estab. 1969. All-volunteer organization serves songwriters, audiences and local acoustic musicians of all music styles. Victory Music provides places to play, showcases, opportunities to read about the business and other songwriters, referrals and seminars. Produced 6 albums of NW songwriters. Offers library, magazine (including previews of members' concerts), newsletter, performance opportunities, business workshops, music business books and a musician referral service. Applications accepted year-round. Membership fee: $30/year single; $80/year business; $40/family; $250 lifetime.

VOLUNTEER LAWYERS FOR THE ARTS

1 E. 53rd St., 6th Floor, New York NY 10022. (212)319-ARTS (2787), ext. 1 (Monday-Friday 9:30-12 and 1-4 EST). Fax: (212)752-6575. E-mail: vlany@vlany.org. Website: www.vlany.org. **Contact:** Elena M. Paul, esq., executive director. Estab. 1969. Serves songwriters, musicians and all performing, visual, literary and fine arts artists and groups. Offers legal assistance and representation to eligible individual artists and arts organizations who cannot afford private counsel and a mediation service. VLA sells publications on arts-related issues and offers educational conferences, lectures, seminars and workshops. In addition, there are affiliates nationwide who assist local arts organizations and artists. Call for information.
Tips "VLA now offers a monthly copyright seminar, 'Copyright Basics,' for songwriters and musicians as well as artists in other creative fields."

WASHINGTON AREA MUSIC ASSOCIATION

6263 Occoquan Forest Drive, Manassas VA 20112. (202)338-1134. Fax: (703)393-1028. E-mail: dcmusic@wamadc.com. Website: www.wamadc.com. **Contact:** Mike Schreibman, president. Estab. 1985. Serves songwriters, musicians and performers, managers, club owners and entertainment lawyers; "all those with an interest in the Washington music scene." The organization is designed to promote the Washington music scene and increase its visibility. Its primary value to members is its seminars and networking opportunities. Offers lectures, newsletter, performance opportunities and workshops. WAMA sponsors the annual Washington Music Awards (The Wammies) and The Crosstown Jam or annual showcase of more than 300 artists at 60 venues in the DC area. Applications accepted year-round. Annual dues: $30.

WEST COAST SONGWRITERS

(formerly Northern California Songwriters Association), 1724 Laurel St., Suite 120, San Carlos CA 94070. (650)654-3966. E-mail: ian@westcoastsongwriters.org. Website: www.westcoastsongwriter

s.org. **Contact:** Ian Crombie, executive director. Serves songwriters and musicians. Estab. 1979. "Our 1,200 members are lyricists and composers from ages 16-80, from beginners to professional songwriters. No eligibility requirements. Our purpose is to provide the education and opportunities that will support our writers in creating and marketing outstanding songs. WCS provides support and direction through local networking and input from Los Angeles and Nashville music industry leaders, as well as valuable marketing opportunities. Most songwriters need some form of collaboration, and by being a member they are exposed to other writers, ideas, critiquing, etc." Offers annual West Coast Songwriters Conference, "the largest event of its kind in northern California. This 2-day event held the second hand in September features 16 seminars, 50 screening sessions (over 1,200 songs listened to by industry professionals) and a sunset concert with hit songwriters performing their songs." Also offers monthly visits from major publishers, songwriting classes, competitions, seminars conducted by hit songwriters ("we sell audio tapes of our seminars—list of tapes available on request"), mail-in song-screening service for members who cannot attend due to time or location, a monthly e-newsletter, monthly performance opportunities and workshops. Applications accepted year-round. Dues: $40/year, student; $75/year, regular membership; $150/year, pro-membership; $250/year, contributing membership.

Tips "WCS's functions draw local talent and nationally recognized names together. This is of a tremendous value to writers outside a major music center. We are developing a strong songwriting community in Northern and Southern California. We serve the San Jose, Monterey Bay, East Bay, San Francisco, Los Angeles, and Sacramento areas and we have the support of some outstanding writers and publishers from both Los Angeles and Nashville. They provide us with invaluable direction and inspiration."

WISCONSIN ALLIANCE FOR COMPOSERS

653 Charles Lane, Madison WI 53711. Website: www.wiscomposers.org. **Contact:** David Drexler. Estab. 1993. Offers performance opportunities for new music compositions. Applications accepted year-round. Membership fee: $20/year.

☑ WOMEN IN MUSIC

P.O. Box 1215, Chelsea Station, New York NY 10113. (212)459-4580. E-mail: wim@womeninmusic.org. Website: www.womeninmusic.org. Estab. 1985. Members are professionals in the business and creative areas: record company executives, managers, songwriters, musicians, vocalists, attorneys, recording engineers, agents, publicists, studio owners, music publishers and more. Purpose is to support, encourage and educate as well as provide networking opportunities. Offers newsletter, lectures, workshops, performance opportunities and business discounts. Presents annual "Touchstone Award" luncheon helping to raise money to support other organizations and individuals through WIM donations and scholarships. Applications accepted year-round. Membership fee: Professional: $75; Student: $25.

Workshops &
Conferences

F or a songwriter just starting out, conferences and workshops can provide valuable learning opportunities. At conferences, songwriters can have their songs evaluated, hear suggestions for further improvement and receive feedback from music business experts. They are also excellent places to make valuable industry contacts. Workshops can help a songwriter improve his craft and learn more about the business of songwriting. They may involve classes on songwriting and the business, as well as lectures and seminars by industry professionals.

Each year, hundreds of workshops and conferences take place all over the country. Songwriters can choose from small regional workshops held in someone's living room to large national conferences such as South by Southwest in Austin, Texas, which hosts more than 6,000 industry people, songwriters and performers. Many songwriting organizations—national and local—host workshops that offer instruction on just about every songwriting topic imaginable, from lyric writing and marketing strategy to contract negotiation. Conferences provide songwriters the chance to meet one on one with publishing and record company professionals and give performers the chance to showcase their work for a live audience (usually consisting of industry people) during the conference. There are conferences and workshops that address almost every type of music, offering programs for songwriters, performers, musical playwrights and much more.

This section includes national and local workshops and conferences with a brief description of what they offer, when they are held and how much they cost to attend. Write or call any that interest you for further information. To find out what workshops or conferences take place in specific parts of the country, see the Geographic Index at the end of this book.

Get the Most From a Conference

BEFORE YOU GO:
- **Save money.** Sign up early for a conference and take advantage of the early registration fee. Don't put off making hotel reservations either—the conference will usually have a block of rooms reserved at a discounted price.

- **Become familiar with all the pre-conference literature.** Study the maps of the area, especially the locations of the rooms in which your meetings/events are scheduled.

- **Make a list of three to five objectives you'd like to obtain,** e.g., what you want to learn more about, what you want to improve on, how many new contacts you want to make.

AT THE CONFERENCE:
- **Budget your time.** Label a map so you know where, when and how to get to each session. Note what you want to do most. Then, schedule time for demo critiques if they are offered.

- **Don't be afraid to explore new areas.** You are there to learn. Pick one or two sessions you wouldn't typically attend. Keep your mind open to new ideas and advice.

- **Allow time for mingling.** Some of the best information is given after the sessions. Find out "frank truths" and inside scoops. Asking people what they've learned at the conference will trigger a conversation that may branch into areas you want to know more about, but won't hear from the speakers.

- **Attend panels.** Panels consist of a group of industry professionals who have the capability to further your career. If you're new to the business you can learn so much straight from the horse's mouth. Even if you're a veteran, you can brush up on your knowledge or even learn something new. Whatever your experience, the panelist's presence is an open invitation to approach him with a question during the panel or with a handshake afterwards.

- **Collect everything:** especially informational materials and business cards. Make notes about the personalities of the people you meet to later remind you who to contact and who to avoid.

AFTER THE CONFERENCE:
- **Evaluate.** Write down the answers to these questions: Would I attend again? What were the pluses and minuses, e.g., speakers, location, food, topics, cost, lodging? What do I want to remember for next year? What should I try to do next time? Who would I like to meet?

- **Write a thank-you letter** to someone who has been particularly helpful. They'll remember you when you later solicit a submission.

APPEL FARM ARTS AND MUSIC FESTIVAL

P.O. Box 888, Elmer NJ 08318. (856)358-2472. Fax: (856)358-6513. E-mail: appelarts@aol.com. Website: www.appelfarm.org. **Contact:** Sean Timmons, artistic director. Estab Festival: 1989; Series: 1970. "Our annual open air festival is the highlight of our year-round Performing Arts Series which was established to bring high quality arts programs to the people of South Jersey. Festival includes acoustic and folk music, blues, etc." Past performers have included Indigo Girls, John Prine, Ani DiFranco, Randy Newman, Jackson Browne, Mary Chapin Carpenter, David Gray, Nanci Griffith and Shawn Colvin. In addition, our Country Music concerts have featured Toby Keith, Joe Diffie, Ricky Van Shelton, Doug Stone and others. Programs for songwriters and musicians include performance opportunities as part of Festival and Performing Arts Series. Programs for musical playwrights also include performance opportunities as part of Performing Arts Series. Festival is a one-day event held in June, and Performing Arts Series is held year-round. Both are held at the Appel Farm Arts and Music Center, a 176-acre farm in Southern New Jersey. Up to 20 songwriters/musicians participate in each event. Participants are songwriters, individual vocalists, bands, ensembles, vocal groups, composers, individual instrumentalists and dance/mime/movement. Participants are selected by CD submissions. Applicants should send a press packet, CD and biographical information. Application materials accepted year round. Faculty opportunities are available as part of residential Summer Arts Program for children, July/August.

ARCADY MUSIC FESTIVAL

P.O. Box 780, Bar Harbor ME 04609. E-mail: arcady@arcady.org. Website: www.arcady.org. **Contact:** Dean Stein, artistic executive director. Estab. 1980. Promotes classical chamber music, and other musical events, including master classes, fiddle festival and a youth competition in Maine. Offers programs for performers. In-school programs and workshops take place year-round in several towns in Eastern Maine. 30-50 professional, individual instrumentalists participate each year. Performers selected by invitation. "Sometimes we premiere new music by songwriters but usually at request of visiting musician."

ASCAP MUSICAL THEATRE WORKSHOP

1 Lincoln Plaza, New York NY 10023. (212)621-6234. Fax: (212)621-6558. E-mail: mkerker@ascap.com. Website: www.ascap.com. **Contact:** Michael A. Kerker, director of musical theatre. Estab. 1981. Workshop is for musical theatre composers and lyricists only. Its purpose is to nurture and develop new musicals for the theatre. Offers programs for songwriters. Offers programs annually, usually April through May. Event took place in New York City. Four musical works are selected. Others are invited to audit the workshop. Participants are amateur and professional songwriters, composers and musical playwrights. Participants are selected by demo tape submission. Send for application. Deadline: mid-March. Also available: the annual ASCAP/Disney Musical Theatre Workshop in Los Angeles. It takes place in January and February. Deadline is late November. Details similar to New York workshop as above.

ASCAP WEST COAST/LESTER SILL SONGWRITER'S WORKSHOP

7920 Sunset Blvd., 3rd Floor, Los Angeles CA 90046. (323)883-1000. Fax: (323)883-1049. E-mail: chard@ascap.com. Website: www.ascap.com. Estab. 1963. Offers programs for songwriters. Offers programs annually. Event takes place mid-January through mid-February. 14 songwriters/musicians participate in each event. Participants are amateur and professional songwriters. Participants are selected by demo tape submission or by invitation. "Send in two songs with lyrics, bio and brief explanation why you'd like to participate." Deadline: November 10.

BMI-LEHMAN ENGEL MUSICAL THEATRE WORKSHOP

320 W. 57th St., New York NY 10036. (212)830-2508. Fax: (212)262-2824. E-mail: theatreworkshop @bmi.com and jbanks@bmi.com. Website: www.bmi.com. **Contact:** Jean Banks, senior director of musical theatre. Estab. 1961. "BMI is a music licensing company which collects royalties for affiliated writers. We have departments to help writers in jazz, concert, Latin, pop and musical theater writing." Offers programs "to musical theater composers, lyricists and librettists. The BMI-

Lehman Engel Musical Theatre Workshops were formed in an effort to refresh and stimulate professional writers, as well as to encourage and develop new creative talent for the musical theater." Each workshop meets 1 afternoon a week for 2 hours at BMI, New York. Participants are professional songwriters, composers and playwrights. "BMI-Lehman Engel Musical Theatre Workshop Showcase presents the best of the workshop to producers, agents, record and publishing company execs, press and directors for possible option and production." Call for application. Tape and lyrics of 3 compositions required with application. "BMI also sponsors a jazz composers workshop. For more information call David Sanjek at (212)586-2000."

☑ BONK FESTIVAL OF NEW MUSIC
% Bonk Inc., 407 W. Frances Ave., Tampa FL 33602. E-mail: bonk@music.org. Website: www.bonkfest.org. **Contact:** Festival Director. Estab. 1994. Offers programs for composers and performers. Offers programs annually. Event takes place in March. Participants are amateur and professional composers and instrumentalists. Participants are selected by demo tape audition. Demo tape criteria available on Web site. Include SASE. Deadline: September 30.

☑ CANADIAN MUSIC WEEK
P.O. Box 42232, 128 St. S, Mississauga ON L5M 4Z0. Canada. E-mail: festival@cmw.net. Website: www.cmw.net. **Contact:** Phil Klygo, festival coordinator. Estab. 1985. Offers annual programs for songwriters, composers and performers. Event takes place mid-March in Toronto. 100,000 public, 300 bands and 1,200 delegates participate in each event. Participants are amateur and professional songwriters, vocalists, composers, bands and instrumentalists. Participants are selected by submitting demonstration tape. Send for application and more information. Concerts take place in 25 clubs and 5 concert halls, and 3 days of seminars and exhibits are provided. Fee: $375 (Canadian).

CMJ MUSIC MARATHON, MUSICFEST & FILMFEST
151 W. 25th St., 12th Floor, New York NY 10001. (917)606-1908. Fax: (917)606-1914. Website: www.cmj.com/Marathon. **Contact:** Operations Manager. Estab. 1981. Premier annual alternative music gathering of more than 9,000 music business and film professionals. Fall, NYC. Features 4 days and nights of more than 50 panels and workshops focusing on every facet of the industry; exclusive film screenings; keynote speeches by the world's most intriguing and controversial voices; exhibition area featuring live performance stage; over 1,000 of music's brightest and most visionary talents (from the unsigned to the legendary) performing over 4 evenings at more than 50 of NYC's most important music venues. Participants are selected by submitting demonstration tape. Go to website for application.

CUTTING EDGE MUSIC BUSINESS CONFERENCE
1524 N. Claiborne Ave., New Orleans LA 70116. (504)945-1800. Fax: (504)945-1873. E-mail: cut_edge@bellsouth.net. Website: www.jass.com/cuttingedge. Executive Producer: Eric L. Cager. Showcase Producer: Nathaniel Franklin. Estab. 1993. "The conference is a five-day international conference which covers the business and educational aspects of the music industry. As part of the conference, the New Works showcase features over 200 bands and artists from around the country and Canada in showcases of original music. All music genres are represented." Offers programs for songwriters and performers. "Bands and artists should submit material for consideration of entry into the New Works showcase." Event takes place during August in New Orleans. 1,000 songwriters/musicians participate in each event. Participants are songwriters, vocalists and bands. Send for application. Deadline: June 1. "The Music Business Institute offers a month-long series of free educational workshops for those involved in the music industry. The workshops take place each October. Further information is available via our website."

PETER DAVIDSON'S WRITER'S SEMINAR
P.O. Box 497, Arnolds Park IA 51331. (712)332-9329. E-mail: peterdavidson@mchsi.com. **Contact:** Peter Davidson, seminar presenter. Estab. 1985. "Peter Davidson's Writer's Seminar is for persons interested in writing all sorts of materials, including songs. Emphasis is placed on developing salable

ideas, locating potential markets for your work, copyrighting, etc. The seminar is not specifically for writers of songs, but is very valuable to them, nevertheless." Offers programs year-round. One-day seminar, 9:00 a.m.-4:00 p.m. Event takes place on various college campuses. In even-numbered years offers seminars in Minnesota, Iowa, Nebraska, South Dakota, Kansas, Colorado and Wyoming. In odd-numbered years offers seminars in Minnesota, Iowa, Nebraska, South Dakota, Missouri, Illinois, Arkansas and Tennessee. Anyone can participate. Send SASE for schedule. Deadline: day of the seminar. Fee: $45 to $59. "All seminars are held on college campuses in college facilities—various colleges sponsor and promote the seminars."

FILM & TV MUSIC CONFERENCE
%The Hollywood Reporter, 5055 Wilshire Blvd., Los Angeles CA 90036-4396. (323)525-2000. E-mail: kpeppers@billboard.com. Website: www.billboardevents.com/billboardevents/filmtv. **Contact:** Special Events Coordinator. Estab. 1995. Promotes all music for film and television. Offers programs for songwriters and composers. Offers programs annually in April. Held at the Directors Guild of America. More than 350 songwriters/musicians participate in each event. Participants are professional songwriters, composers, plus producers, directors, etc. Conference panelists are selected by invitation. For registration information, call the Special Events Dept. at Hollywood Reporter. Fee: $425/person.

FOLK ALLIANCE ANNUAL CONFERENCE
962 Wayne Ave., Suite 902, Silver Spring MD 20910. (301)588-8185. Fax: (301)588-8186. E-mail: fa@folk.org. Website: www.folk.org. **Contact:** Tony Ziselberger, membership services director. Estab. 1989. Conference/workshop topics change each year. Conference takes place mid-February and lasts 4 days at a different location each year. 2,000 attendees include artists, agents, arts administrators, print/broadcast media, folklorists, folk societies, merchandisers, presenters, festivals, recording companies, etc. Artists wishing to showcase should contact the office for a showcase application form. Closing date for application is May 31. Application fee is $20 for 2005 conference. Additional costs vary from year to year. Housing is separate for the event, scheduled for Feb. 16-19, 2006 in Austin, TX.
- Also see the listing for The Folk Alliance in the Organizations section of this book.

I WRITE THE SONGS
PMB 208, 2250 Justin Rd., Suite 108, Highland Village TX 75077-7164. (972)317-2760. Fax: (972)317-4737. E-mail: info@iwritethesongs.com. Website: www.iwritethesongs.com. **Contact:** Sarah Marshall, administrative director. Estab. 1996. "I Write the Songs is an on-the-air songwriting seminar. It is a syndicated radio talk show available both on the radio and on the Internet. A detailed description of the program and its hosts, Mary Dawson and Sharon Braxton, can be found on the website. The website address will also link you to the Internet broadcasts and list the radio stations that carry the program. You can also hear current and archived shows covering INSTRUCTION on the craft and business of songwriting; INTERVIEWS with famous and 'soon-to-be-famous' songwriters; and CRITIQUES of original songs submitted by our listeners. I Write the Songs has been created to inspire and instruct aspiring songwriters of all genres of music." Offers programs, including weekly programs on radio and the Internet, for songwriters, composers and performers. "We hold regular contests and competitions. All aspiring songwriters earning less than $5,000 annually from song royalties are eligible." I Write the Songs features "Critique Shows" every 4-6 weeks. Songwriters can submit demos on cassette or CD with typed lyric sheet. Does not return material. Featured songs are selected at random. Writers whose songs are selected for a show will receive a taped copy of the program on which their song is critiqued. Mary Dawson conducts songwriting seminars across the country and internationally. For a list of upcoming seminars, check the website.

INDEPENDENT MUSIC CONFERENCE
(formerly Philadelphia Music Conference), 304 Main Ave., PMB 287, Norwalk CT 06851. (203)606-4649. Fax: (215)587-9552. E-mail: info@gopmc.com. Website: www.gopmc.com. Executive Direc-

tor: Noel Ramos. Estab. 1992. "The purpose of the IMC is to bring together rock, hip-hop and acoustic music for of panels and showcases. Offers programs for songwriters, composers and performers. 250 showcases at 20 clubs around the city. Also offer a DJ cutting contest." Held annually at the Sheraton Society Hill Hotel in Philadelphia in September. 3,000 amateur and professional songwriters, composers, individual vocalists, bands, individual instrumentalists, attorneys, managers, agents, publishers, A&R, promotions, club owners, etc. participate each year. Send for application.

KERRVILLE FOLK FESTIVAL
Kerrville Festivals, Inc., P.O. Box 291466, Kerrville TX 78029. (830)257-3600. E-mail: info@kerrville-music.com. Website: www.kerrvillefolkfestival.com. **Contact:** Dalis Allen, producer. Estab. 1972. Hosts 3-day songwriters' school, a 4-day music business school and New Folk concert competition sponsored by *Performing Songwriter* magazine. Festival produced in late spring and late summer. Spring festival lasts 18 days and is held outdoors at Quiet Valley Ranch. 110 or more songwriters participate. Performers are professional songwriters and bands. Participants selected by submitting demo, by invitation only. Send cassette, or CD, promotional material and list of upcoming appearances. "Songwriter and music schools include lunch, experienced professional instructors, camping on ranch and concerts. Rustic facilities. Food available at reasonable cost. Audition materials accepted at above address. These three-day and four-day seminars include noon meals, handouts and camping on the ranch. Usually held during Kerrville Folk Festival, first and second week in June. Write or check the website for contest rules, schools and seminars information, and festival schedules. Also establishing a Phoenix Fund to provide assistance to ill or injured singer/songwriters who find themselves in distress."
- Also see the listing for New Folk Concerts For Emerging Songwriters in the Contests & Awards section of this book.

LAMB'S RETREAT FOR SONGWRITERS
presented by SPRINGFED ARTS, a nonprofit organization, P.O. Box 304, Royal Oak MI 48068-0304. (248)589-1594. Fax: (248)589-3913. E-mail: johndlamb@ameritech.net. Website: www.springfed.org. **Contact:** John D. Lamb, director. Estab. 1995. Offers programs for songwriters on annual basis; November 3-6, 2005 and November 10-13 at The Birchwood Inn, Harbor Springs MI. 60 songwriters/musicians participate in each event. Participants are amateur and professional songwriters. Anyone can participate. Send for application or e-mail. Deadline: two weeks before event begins. Fee: $275-495, includes all meals. Facilities are single/double occupancy lodging with private baths; 2 conference rooms and hospitality lodge. Offers song assignments, songwriting workshops, song swaps, open mic and one-on-one mentoring. Faculty are noted songwriters, such as Michael Smith and Bob Franke. Partial scholarships may be available by writing: Blissfest Music Organization, % Jim Gillespie, P.O. Box 441, Harbor Springs MI 49740. Deadline: 2 weeks before event.

MANCHESTER MUSIC FESTIVAL
P.O. Box 33, Manchester VT 05254. (802)362-1956 or (800)639-5868. Fax: (802)362-0711. E-mail: info@ManchesterMusicFestival.org. Website: www.mmfvt.org. **Contact:** Robyn Madison, managing director. Estab. 1974. Offers classical music education and performances. Summer program for young professional musicians offered in tandem with a professional concert series in the mountains of Manchester, VT. Up to 23 young professionals, age 18 and up, are selected by audition for the Young Artists Program, which provides instruction, performance and teaching opportunities, with full scholarship for all participants. Printable application available on website. Application fee: $40. Commissioning opportunities for new music, and performance opportunities for professional chamber ensembles and soloists for both summer and fall/winter concert series. "Celebrating 28 years of fine music."

MUSIC BUSINESS SOLUTIONS/CAREER BUILDING WORKSHOPS
P.O. Box 230266, Boston MA 02123-0266. (888)655-8335. E-mail: peter@mbsolutions.com. Website: www.mbsolutions.com. **Contact:** Peter Spellman, director. Estab. 1991. Workshop titles in-

clude "Discovering Your Music Career Niche," "How to Release an Independent Record" and "Promoting and Marketing Music in the 21st Century." Offers programs for music entrepreneurs, songwriters, musical playwrights, composers and performers. Offers programs year-round, annually and bi-annually. Event takes place at various colleges, recording studios, hotels, conferences. 10-100 songwriters/musicians participate in each event. Participants are both amateur and professional songwriters, vocalists, music business professionals, composers, bands, musical playwrights and instrumentalists. Anyone can participate. Fee: varies. "Music Business Solutions offers a number of other services and programs for both songwriters and musicians including: private music career counseling, business plan development and internet marketing; publication of *Music Biz Insight: Power Reading for Busy Music Professionals*, a bimonthly e-zine chock full of music management and marketing tips and resources. Free subscription with e-mail address."

NASHVILLE MUSIC FESTIVAL
P.O. Box 291827, Nashville TN 37229-1827. (615)252-8202. Fax: (615)321-0384. E-mail: c4promo@aol.com. Website: www.radiocountry.org. (festivals). **Contact:** Ambassador Charlie Ray, director. Estab. 2000. Offers 100 booth spaces for makers of instruments, craftspeople, independent record companies, and unsigned artists; seminars by successful music industry professionals; contests; and stages on which to perform. "Nashville record companies big and small are looking for new talent. A lot of them will have talent scouts at the festival. If they see you on stage and like what they see, you could be signed to a recording contract. There will also be a songwriter's stage each year. This is an annual event. It takes place Memorial Day weekend each year. It has been expanded to 4 days. It always starts on Friday and ends about 10 p.m. the last Monday in May. Complete directions to festival location will be mailed with your tickets and posted on our webpage."

☑ NEMO MUSIC SHOWCASE & CONFERENCE
312 Stuart St. 4th Floor, Boston MA 02116. (617)348-2899. E-mail: info@nemoboston.com. Website: www.nemoboston.com. **Contact:** Kristin Bredimus, showcase director. Estab. 1996. Music showcase and conference, featuring the Boston Music Awards and 3 days/nights of a conference with trade show and more than 200 nightly showcases in Boston. Offers showcases for songwriters. Offers programs annually. Event takes place in October. 1,500 songwriters/musicians participate at conference; 3,000 at awards show; 20,000 at showcases. Participants are professional songwriters, vocalists, composers, bands and instrumentalists. Participants are selected by invitation. Send for application or visit website.

THE NEW HARMONY PROJECT
P.O. Box 441062, Indianapolis IN 46244-1062. (317)464-1103. E-mail: newharmony@newharmonyproject.org. Website: www.newharmonyproject.org. **Contact:** Joel Grynheim, conference director. Estab. 1986. Selected scripts receive various levels of development with rehearsals and readings, both public and private. "Our mission is to nurture writers and their life-affirming scripts. This includes plays, screenplays, musicals and TV scripts." Offers programs for musical playwrights. Event takes place in May/June in southwest Indiana. Participants are amateur and professional writers and media professionals. Send for application.

☷ NEW MUSIC WEST
1062 Homer St., #301, Vancouver BC V6B 2W9 Canada. (604)684-9338. Fax: (604)688-7155. E-mail: info@newmusicwest.com. Website: www.newmusicwest.com. Producer: Frank Weipert. Estab. 1990. A four day music festival and conference held May each year in Vancouver, BC. The conference offers songwriter intensive workshops; demo critique sessions with A&R and publishers; information on the business of publishing; master producer workshops: "We invite established hit record producers to conduct three-hour intensive hands-on workshops with 30 young producers/musicians in studio environments." The festival offers songwriters in the round and 250 original music showcases. Largest music industry event in the North Pacific Rim. Entry fee: Full Pass: $150; Student: $50; Registered Artists (not selected for showcase): $70. Check website for most recent festival dates.

NORFOLK CHAMBER MUSIC FESTIVAL

September-May address: 165 Elm St., Suite 101, Box 208246, New Haven CT 06520. (203)432-1966. Fax: (203)432-2136. E-mail: norfolk@yale.edu. Website: www.yale.edu/norfolk. June-August address: Ellen Battell, Stoeckel Estate, Box 545, Norfolk CT 06058. (860)542-3000. Fax: (860)542-3004. **Contact:** Deanne E. Chin, operations manager. Estab. 1941. Festival season of chamber music. Offers programs for composers and performers. Offers programs summer only. Approximately 45 fellows participate. Participants are up-and-coming composers and instrumentalists. Participants are selected by following a screening round. Auditions are held in New Haven, CT. Send for application. Deadline: January 16. Fee: $50. Held at the Ellen Battell Stoeckel Estate, the Festival offers a magnificent Music Shed with seating for 1,000, practice facilities, music library, dining hall, laundry and art gallery. Nearby are hiking, bicycling and swimming.

◪ NORTH BY NORTHEAST MUSIC FESTIVAL AND CONFERENCE (NXNE)

189 Church St., Lower Level, Toronto ON M5B 1Y7. Canada. (416)863-6963. Fax: (416)863-0828. E-mail: info@nxne.com. Website: www.nxne.com. **Contact:** Travis Bird, festival manager or Gillian Zulauf, conference registrar. Estab. 1995. "Our festival takes place mid-June at over 30 venues across downtown Toronto, drawing over 2,000 conference delegates, 400 bands and 50,000 music fans. Musical genres include everything from folk to funk, roots to rock, polka to punk and all points in between, bringing exceptional new talent, media front-runners, music business heavies and music fans from all over the world to Toronto." Participants include emerging and established songwriters, vocalists, composers, bands and instrumentalists. Festival performers are selected by submitting a CD or tape and accompanying press kit. Application forms are available by website or by calling the office. Submission period each year is from November 1 to the third weekend in January. Submissions fee: $20. Conference registration fee: $120-200 (US), $145-250 (Canadian). "Our conference is held at the deluxe Holiday Inn King and the program includes mentor sessions—15-minute one-on-one opportunities for songwriters and composers to ask questions of industry experts, roundtables, panel discussions, keynote speakers, etc. North By Northeast 2005 will be held June 9-10."

☑ NSAI SONG CAMPS

1710 Roy Acuff Place, Nashville TN 37023. 1-800-321-6008 or (615)256-3354. Fax: (615)256-0034. E-mail: songcamps@nashvillesongwriters.com. Website: www.nashvillesongwriters.com. **Contact:** Alicia Jones, director of song camps. Estab. 1992. Offers programs strictly for songwriters. Event held 4 times/year in Nashville. "We provide most meals and lodging is available. We also present an amazing evening of music presented by the faculty." Camps are 3 days long, with 36-112 participants, depending on the camp. "There are different levels of camps, some having preferred prerequisites. Each camp varies. Please call, e-mail or refer to website. It really isn't about the genre of music, but the quality of the song itself. Song Camp strives to strengthen the writer's vision and skills, therefore producing the better song. Song Camp is known as 'boot camp' for songwriters. It is guaranteed to catapult you forward in your writing! Participants are all aspiring songwriters led by a pro faculty. We do accept lyricists only and composers only with the hopes of expanding their scope." Participants are selected through submission of 2 songs with lyric sheet. Song Camp is open to NSAI members, although anyone can apply and upon acceptance join the organization. There is no formal application form. See website for membership and event information.

● Also see the listing for Nashville Songwriters Association International (NSAI) in the Organizations section of this book.

NSAI SONGWRITERS SYMPOSIUM

1710 Roy Acuff Place, Nashville TN 37203. (615)256-3354. Fax: (615)256-0034. E-mail: membership @NashvilleSongwriters.com. Website: www.nashvillesongwriters.com. Covers "all types of music. Participants take part in publisher evaluations, as well as large group sessions with different guest speakers." Offers annual programs for songwriters. Event takes place in April in downtown Nashville. 300 amateur songwriters/musicians participate in each event. Send for application.

⚏ ORFORD FESTIVAL

Orford Arts Centre, 3165 Chemim DuParc, Orford QC J1X 7A2 Canada. (819)843-9871 or 1-800-567-6155. Fax: (819)843-7274. E-mail: centre@arts-orford.org. Website: www.arts-orford.org. **Contact:** Judith Munger, registrar/information manager. Artistic Director: Agnes Grossmann. Estab. 1951. "Each year, the Orford Arts Centre produces up to 35 concerts in the context of its Music Festival. It receives artists from all over the world in classical and chamber music." Offers master classes for music students, young professional classical musicians and chamber music ensembles. New offerings include master classes for all instruments, voice, and opera. Master classes last 2 months and take place at Orford Arts Centre from the end of June to the middle of August. 350 students participate each year. Participants are selected by demo tape submissions. Send for application. Closing date for application is mid to late March. Check our website for specific dates and deadlines. Scholarships for qualified students.

⚏ THE SONGWRITERS GUILD FOUNDATION

6430 Sunset Blvd., Suite 705, Hollywood CA 90028. (323)462-1108. Fax: (323)462-5430. E-mail: la@songwritersguild.com. Website: www.songwritersguild.com. West Coast Regional Director: B. Aaron Meza. Assistant West Coast Regional Director: Eric Moromisato. Nashville office: 1222 16th Ave., S, Nashville TN 37212. (615)329-1782. Fax: (615)329-2623. Southern Regional Director: Rundi Ream. Assistant Southern Regional Director: Evan Shoemake. E-mail: sganash@aol.com. New York office: 200 W. 72nd Street, New York NY 10023. (212)768-7902. Fax: (212)768-9048. National Projects Director: George Wurzbach. Offers a series of workshops with discounts to members. "There is a charge for each songwriting class. Charges vary depending on the class. SGA members receive discounts! Also, the Re-write workshop and Ask-A-Pro/Song Critique are free!"

• Also see the Songwriters Guild of America listing in the Organizations section.

Ask-a-Pro/Song Critique (Hollywood and Nashville offices) SGA members are given the opportunity to present their songs and receive constructive feedback from industry professionals. A great chance to meet industry people, make contacts, ask questions and get your song heard! Free to SGA members. Reservations required. Call for schedule. Free.

Phil Swan Song Styles/Songwriting Workshops (Hollywood and Nashville offices) This 8-week workshop taught by Phil Swann, Dreamworks SKG staff writer is perfect for those writers who want to become better songwriters in the country, pop, and rock genres as well as more savvy the changing marketplaces. Fee.

Special Seminars and Workshops Other special seminars have been presented by such industry professionals as Dale Kawashima, John Braheny and Dr. George Gamez. Fee.

Building a Songwriting Career A 3-day workshop for songwriters, musicians and recording artists, etc. to help them discover how they can establish a career in the exciting world of songwriting. Features SGA professional songwriters and music business executives in panel discussions about intellectual property, creativity, the craft and business of songwriting and more. Fee.

Re-Write Workshop (Hollywood Office) Conducted by Michael Allen. Songwriters will have the chance to have their songs critiqued by their peers with an occasional guest critique. Free.

Harriet Schock Songwriting Workshop (Hollywood office) A 10-week course consisting of nine lessons which help create a solid foundation for writing songs effortlessly. Fee.

Jai Josefs Writing Music for Hit Songs (Hollywood office) This 10-week course will show songwriters how to integrate the latest chord progressions, melodies, and grooves from all styles of music into their writing.

Song Critique New York's oldest ongoing song critique. Guild songwriters are invited to either perform their song live or present a cassette demo for feedback. A Guild moderator is on hand to direct comments. Nonmembers may attend and offer comments. Free.

Street Smarts (New York office) Street Smarts is a 3-hour orientation session for new SGA members. It introduces the basics in areas such as: contracts, copyrights, royalties, song marketing and more. The session is free to members and is scheduled whenever there is a minimum of 8 participants.

Pro-Shop For each of 6 sessions an active publisher, producer or A&R person is invited to personally screen material from professional Guild writers. Participation is limited to 10 writers, and audit of

1 session. Audition of material is required. Coordinator is producer/musician/award winning singer, Ann Johns Ruckert. Fee; $75 (SGA members only).

SGA Week Held in spring/summer of each year, this is a week of scheduled events and seminars of interest to songwriters at each of SGA's regional offices. Events include workshops, seminars and showcases. For schedule and details contact the SGA office beginning several weeks prior to SGA Week.

SOUTH BY SOUTHWEST MUSIC CONFERENCE (SXSW)

SXSW Headquarters, P.O. Box 4999, Austin TX 78765. (512)467-7979. Fax: (512)451-0754. E-mail: sxsw@sxsw.com. Website: www.sxsw.com. **Contact:** Conference Organizer. **Europe:** Cill Ruan, 7 Ard na Croise, Thurles, Co. Tipperary, Ireland. Phone: 353-504-26488. Fax: 353-504-26787. E-mail: una@sxsw.com. **Contact:** Una Johnston. **Asia:** Meijidori Bldg. 403, 2-3-21 Kabuki-cho Shinjuku-ku, Tokyo 160-0021, Japan. Phone: +82 3-5292-5551. Fax: +82 3-5292-5552. E-mail: info@sxsw-asia.com. **Contact:** Hiroshi Asada. **Australia/New Zealand/Hawaii:** 20 Hordern St., Newtown NSW 2042, Australia. Phone: 61-2-9557-7766. Fax: 61-2-9557-7788. E-mail: tripp@sxsw.om. **Contact:** Phil Tripp. Estab. 1987. South by Southwest (SXSW) is a private company based in Austin, Texas, with a year-round staff of professionals dedicated to building and delivering conference and festival events for entertainment and related media industry professionals. Since 1987, SXSW has produced the internationally-recognized music and media conference and festival (SXSW). As the entertainment business adjusted to issues of future growth and development, in 1993, SXSW added conferences and festivals for the film industry (SXSW Film) as well as for the blossoming interactive media (SXSW Interactive Festival). Now three industry events converge in Austin during a Texas-sized week, mirroring the ever increasing convergence of entertainment/media outlets. The next SXSW Music Conference and Festival will be held March 15-19, 2006 at the Austin Convention Center in Austin TX. Offers panel discussions, "Crash Course" educational seminars and nighttime showcases. The 2005 Keynote speaker was Robert Plant. SXSW Music seeks out speakers who have developed unique ways to create and sell music. With our Wednesday Crash Courses and introductory panels, the basics will be covered in plain English. From Thursday through Saturday, the conference includes over fifty sessions including a panel of label heads discussing strategy, interviews with notable artists, topical discussions, demo listening sessions and the mentor program. And when the sun goes down, a multitude of performances by musicians and songwriters from across the country and around the world populate the SXSW Music Festival, held in venues in central Austin." Write, e-mail or visit website for dates and registration instructions.

Tips "Go to the website in early-September to apply for showcase consideraton. SXSW is also involved in North by Northeast (NXNE), held in Toronto, Canada in late Spring."

THE SWANNANOA GATHERING—CONTEMPORARY FOLK WEEK

Warren Wilson College, P.O. Box 9000, Asheville NC 28815-9000. E-mail: gathering@warren-wilson.edu. Website: www.swangathering.com. Director: Jim Magill. "For anyone who ever wanted to make music for an audience, we offer a comprehensive week in artist development, divided into four major subject areas: Songwriting, Performance, Sound & Recording and Vocal Coaching, along with daily panel discussions of other business matters such as promotion, agents and managers, logistics of touring, etc." 2005 staff includes James Keelaghan, Erica Wheeler, Bill Staines, Annie Gallup, David Roth, Amy Fradon, Cindy Novelo, Rachel Cross, Greg Trafidlo, Mae Robertson, Siobhan Quinn, Ray Chesna, and Doc & Jean Russell. For a brochure or other info contact Jim Magill, Director, The Swannanoa Gathering, at the phone number/address above. Tuition: $395. Takes place last week in July. Housing (including all meals): $295. Annual program of The Swannanoa Gathering Folk Arts Workshops.

THE TEN-MINUTE MUSICALS PROJECT

P.O. Box 461194, West Hollywood CA 90046. E-mail: info@tenminutemusicals.org Website: www.tenminutemusicals.org. **Contact:** Michael Koppy, producer. Estab. 1986. Promotes short complete stage musicals. Offers programs for songwriters, composers and musical playwrights. "Works selected are generally included in full-length 'anthology musical'—11 of the first 16 selected works are now in the show *Stories 1.0*, for instance." Awards a $250 royalty advance for each work selected. Participants are amateur and professional songwriters, composers and musical playwrights. Participants are selected by demonstration tape, script, lead sheets. Send for application. Deadline: August 31st annually.

■ UNDERCURRENTS

P.O. Box 94040, Cleveland OH 44101-6040. (440)331-0700. E-mail: music@undercurrents.com. Website: www.undercurrents.com. **Contact:** John Latimer, president. Estab. 1989. A yearly music industry expo with online exposure featuring seminars, trade show, media center and showcases of rock, alternative, metal, folk, jazz and blues music. Offers programs for songwriters, composers, music industry professionals and performers. Contact for dates and deadlines. Participants are selected by demo tape, biography and 8×10 photo audition. Send for application. Fee: $25 for 3-day event.

WEST COAST SONGWRITERS CONFERENCE

(formerly Northern California Songwriters Association Conference), 1724 Laurel St., Suite 120, San Carlos CA 94070. (650)654-3966 or (800)FOR-SONG. Fax: (650)654-2156. E-mail: info@westcoasts ongwriters.org. Website: www.westcoastsongwriters.org. **Contact:** Ian Crombie, executive director. Estab. 1980. "Conference offers opportunity and education. 16 seminars, 50 song screening sessions (1,500 songs reviewed), performance showcases, one on one sessions and concerts." Offers programs for lyricists, songwriters, composers and performers. "During the year we have competitive open mics. Winners go into the playoffs. Winners of the playoffs perform at the sunset concert at the conference." Event takes place second weekend in September at Foothill College, Los Altos Hills CA. Over 500 songwriters/musicians participate in this event. Participants are songwriters, composers, musical playwrights, vocalists, bands, instrumentalists and those interested in a career in the music business. Send for application. Deadline: September 1. Fee: $110-315. "See our listing in the Organizations section."

WESTERN WIND WORKSHOP IN ENSEMBLE SINGING

263 W. 86 St., New York NY 10024. (212)873-2848 or (800)788-2187. Fax: (212)873-2849. E-mail: workshops@westernwind.org. Website: www.westernwind.org. **Contact:** William Zukoff, executive producer. Estab. 1981. Participants learn the art of ensemble singing—no conductor, one on-a-part. Workshop focuses on blend, diction, phrasing and production. Offers programs for performers. Limited talent-based scholarship available. Offers programs annually. Takes place June, July and August in the music department at Smith College, Northampton MA. 70-80 songwriters/musicians participate in each event. Participants are amateur and professional vocalists. Anyone can participate. Send for application or register at their website. Workshop takes place in the Smith College music department. Arrangers' works are frequently studied and performed. Also offers additional workshops President's Day weekend in Brattleboro VT and Columbus Day weekend in Woodstock VT.

WINTER MUSIC CONFERENCE INC.

3450 NE 12 Terrace, Ft. Lauderdale FL 33334. (954)563-4444. Fax: (954)563-1599. E-mail: info@win termusicconference.com. Website: www.wintermusicconference.com. President: Margo Possenti. Estab. 1985. Features educational seminars and showcases for dance, hip-hop, alternative and rap. Offers programs for songwriters and performers. Offers programs annually. Event takes place March of each year in Miami FL. 3,000 songwriters/musicians participate in each event. Participants are amateur and professional songwriters, composers, musical playwrights, vocalists, bands and instrumentalists. Participants are selected by submitting demo tape. Send SASE, visit website or call for application. Deadline: February. Event held at either nightclubs or hotel with complete staging, lights and sound.

Retreats & Colonies

This section provides information on retreats and artists' colonies. These are places for creatives, including songwriters, to find solitude and spend concentrated time focusing on their work. While a residency at a colony may offer participation in seminars, critiques or performances, the atmosphere of a colony or retreat is much more relaxed than that of a conference or workshop. Also, a songwriter's stay at a colony is typically anywhere from one to twelve weeks (sometimes longer), while time spent at a conference may only run from one to fourteen days.

Like conferences and workshops, however, artists' colonies and retreats span a wide range. Yaddo, perhaps the most well-known colony, limits its residencies to artists "working at a professional level in their field, as determined by a judging panel of professionals in the field." The Brevard Music Center offers residencies only to those involved in classical music. Despite different focuses, all artists' colonies and retreats have one thing in common: They are places where you may work undisturbed, usually in nature-oriented, secluded settings.

SELECTING A COLONY OR RETREAT

When selecting a colony or retreat, the primary consideration for many songwriters is cost, and you'll discover that arrangements vary greatly. Some colonies provide residencies as well as stipends for personal expenses. Some suggest donations of a certain amount. Still others offer residencies for substantial sums but have financial assistance available.

When investigating the various options, consider meal and housing arrangements and your family obligations. Some colonies provide meals for residents, while others require residents to pay for meals. Some colonies house artists in one main building; others provide separate cottages. A few have provisions for spouses and families. Others prohibit families altogether.

Overall, residencies at colonies and retreats are competitive. Since only a handful of spots are available at each place, you often must apply months in advance for the time period you desire. A number of locations are open year-round, and you may find planning to go during the "off-season" lessens your competition. Other colonies, however, are only available during certain months. In any case, be prepared to include a sample of your best work with your application. Also, know what project you'll work on while in residence and have alternative projects in mind in case the first one doesn't work out once you're there.

Each listing in this section details fee requirements, meal and housing arrangements, and space and time availability, as well as the retreat's surroundings, facilities and special activities. Of course, before making a final decision, send a SASE to the colonies or retreats that interest you to receive their most up-to-date details. Costs, application requirements and deadlines are particularly subject to change.

MUSICIAN'S RESOURCE

For other listings of songwriter-friendly colonies, see *Musician's Resource* (available from Watson-Guptill Publications, 770 Broadway, New York NY 10003, 1-800-278-8477, info@watsonguptill.com), which not only provides information about conferences, workshops and academic programs but also residencies and retreats. Also check the Publications of Interest section in this book for newsletters and other periodicals providing this information.

BREVARD MUSIC CENTER

P.O. Box 312, 349 Andante Ln., Brevard NC 28712. (828)862-2140. Fax: (828)884-2036. E-mail: bmc@brevardmusic.org. Website: www.brevardmusic.org. **Contact:** Dorothy Knowles, admissions coordinator. Estab. 1936. Offers 6-week residencies from June through the first week of August. Open to professional and student composers, pianists, vocalists, collaborative pianists and instrumentalists of classical music. A 2-week jazz workshop is offered in June. Accommodates 400 at one time. Personal living quarters include cabins. Offers rehearsal, teaching and practice cabins.
Costs $4,100 for tuition, room and board. Scholarships are available.
Requirements Call for application forms and guidelines. $50 application fee. Participants are selected by audition or demonstration tape and then by invitation. There are 80 different audition sites throughout the US.

BYRDCLIFFE ARTS COLONY

34 Tinker St., Woodstock NY 12498. (845)679-2079. Fax: (845)679-4529. E-mail: wguild@ulster.net. Website: www.woodstockguild.org. **Contact:** Carla T. Smith, executive director. Estab. 1991. Offers 1-month residencies June-September. Open to composers, writers and visual artists. Accommodates 10 at one time. Personal living quarters include single rooms, shared baths and kitchen facilities. Offers separate private studio space. Composers must provide their own keyboard with headphone. Activities include open studio, readings, followed by pot luck dinner once a month. The Woodstock Guild, parent organization, offers music and dance performances, gallery exhibits and book signings.
Costs $600/month. Residents are responsible for own meals and transportation.
Requirements Send SASE for application forms and guidelines. Accepts inquiries via fax or e-mail. $5 application fee. Submit a score of at least 10 minutes with 2 references, résumé and application.

DORSET COLONY HOUSE

P.O. Box 510, Dorset VT 05251-0510. (802)867-2223. Fax: (802)867-0144. E-mail: dorsetcolony@hotmail.com. Website: www.dorsetcolony.org. **Contact:** John Nassivera, executive director. Estab. 1980. Offers up to 1-month residencies September-November and April-May. Open to writers, composers, directors, designers and collaborators of the theatre. Accommodates 9 at one time. Personal living quarters include single rooms with desks with shared bath and shared kitchen facilities.
Costs $200/week. Meals not included. Transportation is residents' responsibility.
Requirements Send SASE for application forms and guidelines. Accepts inquiries via fax or e-mail. Submit letter with requested dates, description of project and résumé of productions.

⊞ THE TYRONE GUTHRIE CENTRE

Annaghmakerrig, Newbliss, County Monaghan, Ireland. (353)(047)54003. Fax: (353)(047)54380. E-mail: info@tyroneguthrie.ie. Website: www.tyroneguthrie.ie. **Contact:** Program Director. Estab. 1981. Offers year-round residencies. Artists may stay for anything from 1 week to 3 months in the Big House, or for up to 6 months at a time in one of the 5 self-catering houses in the old farmyard. Open to artists of all disciplines. Accommodates 15 at one time. Personal living quarters include bedroom with bathroom en suite. Offers a variety of workspaces. There is a music room for composers and musicians, a photographic darkroom and a number of studios for visual artists. At certain times of the year it is possible, by special arrangement, to accommodate groups of artists, symposiums, master classes, workshops and other collaborations.
Costs Artists who are not Irish residents must pay £600 per week, all found, for a residency in the Big House and £300 per week for one of the self-catering farmyard houses. To qualify for a residency,

it is necessary to show evidence of a significant level of achievement in the relevant field.
Requirements Send SAE and IRC for application forms and guidelines. Accepts inquiries via fax or e-mail. Fill in application form with cv to be reviewed by the board members at regular meetings.

THE HAMBIDGE CENTER

P.O. Box 339, Rabun Gap GA 30568. (706)746-5718. Fax: (706)746-9933. E-mail: center@hambidge. org. Website: www.hambidge.org. **Contact:** Fran Lanier, residency director. Estab. 1934 (Center); 1988 (residency). Offers 2-week to 2-month residencies year round. Open to all artists. Accommodates 8 at one time. Personal living quarters include a private cottage with kitchen, bath, and living/studio space. Offers composer/musical studio equipped with piano. Activities include communal dinners February through December and nightly or periodic sharing of works-in-progress.
Costs $150/week.
Requirements Send SASE for application forms and guidelines, or available on website. Accepts inquiries via fax and e-mail. Application fee: $30. Deadlines: January 15, May 15 and September 15.

ISLE ROYALE NATIONAL PARK ARTIST-IN-RESIDENCE PROGRAM

800 E. Lakeshore Dr., Houghton MI 49931. (906)482-0984. Fax: (906)482-8753. E-mail: ISRO_Parkin fo@nps.gov. Website: www.nps.gov/ISRO/. **Contact:** Greg Blust, coordinator. Estab. 1991. Offers 2-3 week residencies from mid-June to mid-September. Open to all art forms. Accommodates 1 artist with 1 companion at one time. Personal living quarters include cabin with shared outhouse. A canoe is provided for transportation. Offers a guest house at the site that can be used as a workroom. The artist is asked to contribute a piece of work representative of their stay at Isle Royale, to be used by the park in an appropriate manner. During their residency, artists will be asked to share their experience (1 presentation per week of residency, about 1 hour/week) with the public by demonstration, talk, or other means.
Requirements Send for application forms and guidelines. Accepts inquiries via fax or e-mail. A panel of professionals from various disciplines, and park representatives will choose the finalists. The selection is based on artistic integrity, ability to reside in a wilderness environment, a willingness to donate a finished piece of work inspired on the island, and the artist's ability to relate and interpret the park through their work.

KALANI OCEANSIDE RETREAT

RR 2 Box 4500, Pahoa-Beach Road HI 96778-9724. (808)965-7828. Fax: (808)965-0527. E-mail: kalani@kalani.com. Website: www.kalani.com. **Contact:** Richard Koob, director. Estab. 1980. Offers 2-week to 2-month residencies. Open to all artists who can verify professional accomplishments. Accommodates 120 at one time. Personal living quarters include private cottage or lodge room with private or shared bath. Full (3 meals/day) dining service. Offers shared studio/library spaces. Activities include opportunity to share works in progress, ongoing yoga, hula and other classes; beach, thermal springs, Volcanos National Park nearby; olympic pool/spa on 113-acre facility.
Cost $55-120/night lodging with 50% stipend. Meals separate at $43/day. Transportation by rental car from $25/day, Kalani service $50/trip, or taxi $70/trip. 50% discount (''stipend'') on lodging only.
Requirements Send SASE for application forms and guidelines. Accepts inquiries via fax or e-mail. $10 application fee.

THE MACDOWELL COLONY

100 High St., Peterborough NH 03458. (603)924-3886. Fax: (603)924-9142. E-mail: admissions@ma cdowellcolony.org. Website: www.macdowellcolony.org. **Contact:** Admissions Coordinator. Estab. 1907. Offers year-round residencies of up to 2 months (average length is 6 weeks). Open to writers, composers, film/video makers, visual artists, architects and interdisciplinary artists. Personal living quarters include single rooms. Offers private studios on 450-acre grounds.
Cost None (contributions accepted).

Resources

Requirements Send SASE or visit website for application forms and guidelines. Composers should send 2 clearly reproduced scores, one of which was completed in the last 5 years, along with audiocassette (1 piece per cassette) or both works on 1 CD. Application deadline: January 15, April 15 and September 15.

NORTHWOOD UNIVERSITY ALDEN B. DOW CREATIVITY CENTER

4000 Whiting Dr., Midland MI 48640. (989)837-4478. E-mail: creativity@northwood.edu. Website: www.northwood.edu/abd. **Contact:** Director. Estab. 1979. Offers 10-week summer residencies (mid-June through mid-August). Fellowship Residency is open to individuals in all fields (the arts, humanities or sciences) who have innovative, creative projects to pursue. Accommodates 4 at one time. Each Fellow is given a furnished apartment on campus, complete with 2 bedrooms, kitchen, bath and large living room. Fellows' apartments serve as their work space as well as their living quarters unless special needs are requested.
Cost $10 application fee. Room and board is provided plus a $750 stipend to be used toward project costs or personal needs. "We look for projects which are innovative, creative, unique. We ask the applicant to set accomplishable goals for the 10-week residency."
Requirements Send for application information and guidelines. Accepts inquiries via fax or e-mail. Applicants submit 2-page typed description of their project; cover page with name, address, phone numbers plus summary (30 words or less) of project; support materials such as tapes, CDs; personal résumé; facilities or equipment needed; and $10 application fee. Application deadline: December 31 (postmarked).

SITKA CENTER FOR ART & ECOLOGY

P.O. Box 65, Otis OR 97368-0065. (541)994-5485. Fax: (541)994-8024. E-mail: info@sitkacenter.org. Website: www.sitkacenter.org. **Contact:** Randall Koch, executive director. Estab. 1971. Offers 4-month residencies in October through January or February through May; shorter residencies are available upon arrangement. Open to artists or naturalists who have earned a BA, BS, BFA and/or MA, MS, MFA, PhD degree, or equivalent professional experience. Personal living quarters include 3 living quarters, each self-contained with a sleeping area, kitchen and bathroom. Offers 4 studios. Workshops or presentations are encouraged; an exhibition/presentation to share residents' works is held in January and May.
Cost The resident is encouraged to hold an open studio or community outreach program at Sitka one day per month during the residency, exceptions by arrangements with the director. The resident is asked to provide some form of community service on behalf of Sitka.
Requirements Send SASE for application forms and guidelines. Accepts inquiries via fax. Send completed application with résumé, 2 letters of recommendation, work samples and SASE.

VIRGINIA CENTER FOR THE CREATIVE ARTS

154 San Angelo Dr., Amherst VA 24521. (434)946-7236. Fax: (434)946-7239. E-mail: vcca@vcca.com. Website: www.vcca.com. **Contact:** Sheila Gulley Pleasants, director of artists' services. Estab. 1971. Offers residencies year-round, typical residency lasts 2 weeks to 1 month. Open to originating artists: composers, writers and visual artists. Accommodates 22 at one time. Personal living quarters include 20 single rooms, 2 double rooms, bathrooms shared with one other person. All meals are served. Kitchens for fellows' use available at studios and residence. Activities include trips in the VCCA van twice a week into town. Fellows share their work regularly. Three studios have pianos.
Cost No transportation costs are covered. Artists are accepted at the VCCA without consideration for their financial situation. The actual cost of a residency at the Virginia Center is $120 per day per Fellow. "We ask Fellows to contribute according to their ability."
Requirements Send SASE for application forms and guidelines or call the above number. Applications are reviewed by a panel of judges. Application fee: $25. Deadline: May 15 for October-January residency; September 15 for February-May residency; January 15 for June-September residency.

State & Provincial Grants

Arts councils in the United States and Canada provide assistance to artists (including poets) in the form of fellowships or grants. These grants can be substantial and confer prestige upon recipients; however, **only state or province residents are eligible.** Because deadlines and available support vary annually, query first (with a SASE).

UNITED STATES ARTS AGENCIES

Alabama State Council on the Arts, 201 Monroe St., Montgomery AL 36130-1800. (334)242-4076. E-mail: staff@arts.state.al.us. Website: www.arts.state.al.us.

Alaska State Council on the Arts, 411 W. Fourth Ave., Suite 1-E, Anchorage AK 99501-2343. (907)269-6610 or (888)278-7424. E-mail: aksca_info@eed.state.ak.us. Website: www.educ.state.ak.us/aksca.

Arizona Commission on the Arts, 417 W. Roosevelt, Phoenix AZ 85003-1326. (602)255-5882. E-mail: general@arizonaarts.org. Website: www.arizonaarts.org.

Arkansas Arts Council, 1500 Tower Bldg., 323 Center St., Little Rock AR 72201. (501)324-9766. E-mail: info@arkansasarts.com. Website: www.arkansasarts.com.

California Arts Council, 1300 I St., Suite 930, Sacramento CA 95814. (916)322-6555 or (800)201-6201. E-mail: cac@cwo.com. Website: www.cac.ca.gov.

Colorado Council on the Arts, 1380 Lawrence St., Suite 1200, Denver CO 80204. (303)866-2723. E-mail: coloarts@state.co.us. Website: www.coloarts.state.co.us.

Connecticut Commission on the Arts, 755 Main St., 1 Financial Plaza, Hartford CT 06103. (860)566-4770. E-mail: artsinfo@ctarts.org. Website: www.ctarts.org.

Delaware Division of the Arts, Carvel State Office Building, 820 N. French St., Wilmington DE 19801. (302)577-8278. E-mail: delarts@state.de.us. Website: www.artsdel.org.

District of Columbia Commission on the Arts & Humanities, 410 Eighth St. NW, 5th Floor, Washington DC 20004. (202)724-5613. E-mail: dcarts@dc.gov. Website: http://dcarts.dc.gov.

Florida Arts Council, Division of Cultural Affairs, Florida Dept. of State, 1001 DeSoto Park Dr., Tallahassee FL 32301. (850)245-6470. Website: www.florida-arts.org.

Georgia Council for the Arts, 260 14th St. NW, Suite 401, Atlanta GA 30318-5793. (404)685-2787. E-mail: goarts@gaarts.org. Website: www.gaarts.org.

Hawaii State Foundation on Culture & Arts, 250 S. Hotel St., 2nd Floor, Honolulu HI 96813. (808)586-0300. E-mail: ken.hamilton@hawaii.gov/sfca. Website: www.state.hi.us/sfca.

Idaho Commission on the Arts, 2410 North Old Penitentiary Rd., Boise ID 83712. (208)334-2119 or (800)278-3863. E-mail: mestrada@ica.state.id.us. Website: www2.state.id.us/arts.

Illinois Arts Council, 100 W. Randolph, Suite 10-500, Chicago IL 60601. (312)814-6750. E-mail: info@arts.state.il.us. Website: www.state.il.us/agency/iac.

Indiana Arts Commission, 402 W. Washington St., Indianapolis IN 46204-2243. (317)232-1268. E-mail: arts@state.in.us. Website: www.state.in.us/iac.

Iowa Arts Council, 600 E. Locust, Capitol Complex, Des Moines IA 50319-0290. (515)281-6412. E-mail: linda.lee@iowa.gov. Website: www.iowaartscouncil.org.

Kansas Arts Commission, 700 SW Jackson, Suite 1004, Topeka KS 66603. (785)296-3335. E-mail: KAC@arts.state.ks.us. Website: http://arts.state.ks.us.

Kentucky Arts Council, Old Capital Annex, 300 W. Broadway, Frankfort KY 40601-1980. (502)564-3757. E-mail: kyarts@ky.gov. Website: www.kyarts.org.

Louisiana State Arts Council, P.O. Box 44247, Baton Rouge LA 70804-4247. (225)342-8180. E-mail: arts@crt.state.la.us. Website: www.crt.state.la.us/arts.

Maine Arts Commission, 193 State St., 25 State House Station, Augusta ME 04333-0025. (207)287-2724. E-mail: mainearts.info@maine.gov. Website: www.mainearts.com.

Maryland State Arts Council, 175 West Ostend Street, Suite E, Baltimore MD 21230. (410)767-6555. E-mail: msac@msac.org. Website: www.msac.org.

Massachusetts Cultural Council, 10 St. James Ave., 3rd Floor, Boston MA 02116-3803. (617)727-3668. E-mail: web@art.state.ma.us. Website: www.massculturalcouncil.org.

Michigan Council for Arts & Cultural Affairs, 722 West Kalamazoo Street, P.O. Box 30159, Lansing, MI 48909. (517)373-1820. E-mail: artsinfo@cis.state.mi.us. Website: www.michigan.gov/hal/.

Minnesota State Arts Board, Park Square Court, 400 Sibley St., Suite 200, St. Paul MN 55101-1928. (651)215-1600. E-mail: msab@state.mn.us. Website: www.arts.state.mn.us.

Mississippi Arts Commission, 239 N. Lamar St., Suite 207, Jackson MS 39201. (601)359-6030. E-mail: hedgepet@arts.state.ms.us. Website: www.arts.state.ms.us.

Missouri Arts Council, 111 N. Seventh St., Suite 105, St. Louis MO 63101-2188. (314)340-6845. E-mail: moarts@ded.mo.gov. Website: www.missouriartscouncil.org.

Montana Arts Council, P.O. Box 202201, Helena MT 59620-2201. (406)444-6430. E-mail: mac@state.mt.us. Website: www.art.state.mt.us.

National Endowment for the Arts, 1100 Pennsylvania Ave. NW, Washington DC 20506. (202)682-5400. E-mail: webmgr@arts.endow.gov. Website: www.arts.endow.gov.

Nebraska Arts Council, 3838 Davenport St., Omaha NE 68131-2329. (402)595-2122. E-mail: khardin@nebraskaartscouncil.org. Website: www.nebraskaartscouncil.org.

Nevada State Council on the Arts, 716 N. Curry St., Carson City NV 89701. (775)687-6680. E-mail: kjodonne@clan.lib.nv.us. Website: www.dmla.clan.lib.nv.us/docs/arts/

New Hampshire State Council on the Arts, 2½ Beacon St., 2nd Floor, Concord NH 03301-

4974. (603)271-2789. E-mail: mdurkee@nharts.state.nh.us. Website: www.state.nh.us/nharts.

New Jersey State Council on the Arts, P.O. Box 306, 225 W. State St., Trenton NJ 08625. (609)292-6130. E-mail: njsca@arts.sos.state.nj.us. Website: www.njartscouncil.org.

New Mexico Arts Division, P.O. Box 1450, Santa Fe NM 87504. (505)827-6490. E-mail: vcastell@oca.state.nm.us. Website: www.nmarts.org.

New York State Council on the Arts, 175 Varick St., 3rd Floor, New York NY 10014. (212)627-4455. E-mail: msc@nysca.org. Website: www.nysca.org.

North Carolina Arts Council, Department of Cultural Resources and Service Center, Raleigh NC 27699-4632. (919)733-2111. E-mail: ncarts@ncmail.net. Website: www.ncarts.org.

North Dakota Council on the Arts, 1600 East Century Avenue, Suite 6, Bismarck ND 58503. (701)328-7579. E-mail: comserv@state.nd.us. Website: www.state.nd.us/arts.

Ohio Arts Council, 727 E. Main St., Columbus OH 43205-1796. (614)466-2613. E-mail: shannon.ford@oac.state.oh.us. Website: www.oac.state.oh.us.

Oklahoma Arts Council, P.O. Box 52001-2001, Oklahoma City OK 73152-2001. (405)521-2931. E-mail: okarts@arts.state.ok.us. Website: www.state.ok.us/~arts.

Oregon Arts Commission, 775 Summer St. NE, Suite 200, Salem OR 97301-1284. (503)986-0082. E-mail: oregon.artscomm@state.or.us. Website: www.oregonartscommission.org.

Pennsylvania Council on the Arts, Room 216, Finance Bldg., Harrisburg PA 17120. (717)787-6883. E-mail: ngriffiths@state.pa.us. Website: www.artsnet.org/pca.

Institute of Puerto Rican Culture, P.O. Box 9024184, San Juan PR 00902-4184. (787)725-5137. E-mail: IPRAC@aspira.org. Website: http://iprac.aspira.org.

Rhode Island State Council on the Arts, One Capitol Hill, 3rd Floor, Providence RI 02908. (401)222-3880. E-mail: info@risca.state.ri.us. Website: www.risca.state.ri.us.

South Carolina Arts Commission, 1800 Gervais St., Columbia SC 29201. (803)734-8696. E-mail: burnette@arts.state.sc.us. Website: www.state.sc.us/arts.

South Dakota Arts Council, 800 Governors Dr., Pierre SD 57501-2294. (605)773-3131. E-mail: sdac@stlib.state.sd.us. Website: www.state.sd.us/deca/sdarts.

Tennessee Arts Commission, 401 Charlotte Ave., Nashville TN 37243-0780. (615)741-1701. Website: www.arts.state.tn.us.

Texas Commission on the Arts, P.O. Box 13406, Austin TX 78711-3406. (512)463-5535. E-mail: front.desk@arts.state.tx.us. Website: www.arts.state.tx.us.

Utah Arts Council, 617 E. South Temple, Salt Lake City UT 84102-1177. (801)236-7555. E-mail: swaddingham@utah.gov. Website: http://arts.utah.gov/.

Vermont Arts Council, 136 State St., Drawer 33, Montpelier VT 05633-6001. (802)828-3291. E-mail: info@vermontartscouncil.org. Website: www.vermontartscouncil.org.

Virgin Islands Council on the Arts, 41-42 Norre Gada, P.O. Box 103, St. Thomas VI 00802. (340)774-5984. E-mail: adagio@islands.vi. Website: www.vicouncilonarts.org/.html.

Virginia Commission for the Arts, Lewis House, 2nd Floor, 223 Governor St., Richmond VA 23219-2010. (804)225-3132. E-mail: arts@state.va.us. Website: www.arts.state.va.us/.

Resources

Washington State Arts Commission, P.O. Box 42675, Olympia WA 98504-2675. (360)753-3860. E-mail: markg@arts.wa.gov. Website: www.arts.wa.gov.

West Virginia Arts Commission, Cultural Center, 1900 Kanawha Blvd. E., Charleston WV 25305-0300. (304)558-0220. E-mail: barbie.anderson@wvculture.org. Website: www.wvculture.org.

Wisconsin Arts Board, 101 E. Wilson St., 1st Floor, Madison WI 53702. (608)266-0190. E-mail: artsboard@arts.state.wi.us. Website: www.arts.state.wi.us.

Wyoming Arts Council, 2320 Capitol Ave., Cheyenne WY 82002. (307)777-7742. E-mail: ebratt@state.wy.us. Website: http://wyoarts.state.wy.us.

CANADIAN PROVINCES ARTS AGENCIES

Alberta Foundation for the Arts, 901 Standard Life Centre, 10405 Jasper Ave., Edmonton, Alberta T5J 4R7. (780)427-6315. E-mail: afa@mcd.gov.ab.ca. Website: www.cd.gov.ab.ca/affta.

British Columbia Arts Council, P.O. Box 9819, Stn Prov Govt, Victoria, British Columbia V8W 9W3. (250)356-1718. E-mail: bcartscouncil@gems2.gov.bc.ca. Website: www.bcartscouncil.ca.

Manitoba Arts Council, 525 - 93 Lombard Ave., Winnipeg, Manitoba R3B 3B1. (204)945-2237. E-mail: info@artscouncil.mb.ca. Website: www.artscouncil.mb.ca.

New Brunswick Department of Economic Development, Tourism & Culture, Arts Branch, P.O. Box 6000, Fredericton, New Brunswick E3B 5H1. (506)453-3984. E-mail: www@gnb.ca. Website: www.gnb.ca.

Newfoundland & Labrador Arts Council, P.O. Box 98, St. John's, Newfoundland A1C 5H5. (709)726-2212. E-mail: nlacmail@newcomm.net. Website: www.nlac.nf.ca.

Nova Scotia Arts Council, (902)424-1593. Website: www.novascotiaartscouncil.ns.ca.

The Canada Council, 350 Albert St., P.O. Box 1047, Ottawa, Ontario K1P 5V8. (613)566-4414. Website: www.canadacouncil.ca.

Ontario Arts Council, 151 Bloor St. W., 5th Floor, Toronto, Ontario M5S 1T6. (416)961-1660. E-mail: info@arts.on.ca. Website: www.arts.on.ca/.

Prince Edward Island Council of the Arts, 115 Richmond, Charlottetown, Prince Edward Island C1E 1H7. (902)368-4410. E-mail: peiarts@peiartscouncil.com. Website: www.peiartscouncil.com.

Saskatchewan Arts Board, 2135 Broad St., Regina, Saskatchewan S4P 3V7. (306)787-4056. E-mail: sab@artsboard.sk.ca. Website: ww.artsboard.sk.ca.

Yukon Arts Branch, Box 2703, Whitehorse, Yukon Y1A 2C6. (867)667-5036. E-mail: arts@gov.yk.ca. Website: www.btc.gov.yk.ca/cultural/arts.

Publications of Interest

Knowledge about the music industry is essential for both creative and business success. Staying informed requires keeping up with constantly changing information. Updates on the evolving trends in the music business are available to you in the form of music magazines, music trade papers and books. There is a publication aimed at almost every type of musician, songwriter and music fan, from the most technical knowledge of amplification systems to gossip about your favorite singer. These publications can enlighten and inspire you and provide information vital in helping you become a more well-rounded, educated, and, ultimately, successful musical artist.

This section lists all types of magazines and books you may find interesting. From songwriters' newsletters and glossy music magazines to tip sheets and how-to books, there should be something listed here that you'll enjoy and benefit from.

PERIODICALS

The Album Network, 110 West Spazier, Burbank CA 91502. (818)842-2600. Website: www. musicbiz.com. *Weekly music industry trade magazine.*

American Songwriter Magazine, 50 Music Square W., Suite 604, Nashville TN 37203-3227. (615)321-6096. E-mail: info@americansongwriter.com. Website: www.americansongwrit er.com. *Bimonthly publication for and about songwriters.*

Back Stage East, 770 Broadway, 4th Floor, New York NY 10003. (646)654-5700.

Back Stage West, 5055 Wilshire Blvd., Los Angeles CA 90036. (323)525-2358 or (800)745-8922. Website: www.backstage.com. *Weekly East and West Coast performing artist trade papers.*

Bass Player, P.O. Box 57324, Boulder CO 80323-7324. (800)234-1831. E-mail: bassplayer@n eodata.com. Website: www.bassplayer.com. *Monthly magazine for bass players with lessons, interviews, articles, and transcriptions.*

Billboard, 1515 Broadway, New York NY 10036. (800)745-8922. E-mail: bbstore@billboard.c om. Website: www.billboard.com. *Weekly industry trade magazine.*

Canadian Musician, 23 Hannover Dr., Suite 7, St. Catharines, Ontario L2W 1A3 Canada. (877)746-4692. Website: www.canadianmusician.com. *Bimonthly publication for amateur and professional Canadian musicians.*

Chart, 200-41 Britain St., Toronto, Ontario M5A 1R7 Canada. (416)363-3101. E-mail: chart@c
hartnet.com. Website: www.chartattack.com. *Monthly magazine covering the Canadian
and international music scenes.*

CMJ New Music Report, 151 W. 25th St., 12 Floor, New York NY 10001. (917)606-1908.
E-mail: subscriptions@cmj.com. Website: www.cmjmusic.com. *Weekly college radio and
alternative music tip sheet.*

Country Line Magazine, 16150 S. IH-35, Buda TX 78610. (512)295-8400. E-mail: editor@cou
ntrylinemagazine.com. Website: http://countrylinemagazine.com. *Monthly Texas-only
country music cowboy and lifestyle magazine.*

Daily Variety, 5700 Wilshire Blvd., Suite 120, Los Angeles CA 90036. (323)857-6600. Website: www.variety.com. *Daily entertainment trade newspaper.*

Dramalogue, 1456 N. Gordon, Hollywood CA 90028. Website: www.dramalogue.com. *L.A.-
based entertainment newspaper with an emphasis on theatre and cabaret.*

The Dramatist, 1501 Broadway, Suite 701, New York NY 10036. (212)398-9366. Fax:
(212)944-0420. Website: www.dramaguild.com. *The quarterly journal of the Dramatists
Guild, the professional association of playwrights, composers and lyricists.*

Entertainment Law & Finance, New York Law Publishing Co., 345 Park Ave. S., 8th Floor,
New York NY 10010. (212)545-6174. E-mail: leader@ljextra.com. *Monthly newsletter covering music industry contracts, lawsuit filings, court rulings and legislation.*

Exclaim!, 7-B Pleasant Blvd., Suite 966, Toronto, Ontario M4T 1K2 Canada. (416)535-9735.
E-mail: exclaim@exclaim.ca. Website: http://exclaim.ca. *Canadian music monthly covering all genres of non-mainstream music.*

Fast Forward, Disc Makers, 7905 N. Rt. 130, Pennsauken NJ 08110-1402. (800)468-9353.
Website: www.discmakers.com/music/ffwd. *Quarterly newsletter featuring companies
and products for performing and recording artists in the independent music industry.*

Guitar Player, 1601 W. 23rd St., Suite 200, Lawrence KS 60046-0127. (800)289-9839. Website: www.guitarplayer.com. Monthly guitar magazine with transcriptions, columns, and
interviews, including occasional articles on songwriting.

Hits Magazine, 14958 Ventura Blvd., Sherman Oaks CA 91403. (818)501-7900. Website:
www.hitsmagazine.com. *Weekly music industry trade publication.*

Jazztimes, 8737 Colesville Rd., 9th Floor, Silver Spring MD 20910-3921. (301)588-4114. Website: http://jazztimes.com. 10 issues/year magazine covering the American jazz scene.

The Leads Sheet, Allegheny Music Works, 1611 Menoher Blvd., Johnstown PA 15905.
(814)255-4007. Website: www.alleghenymusicworks.com. Monthly tip sheet.

Lyricist Review, 4535 W. Sahara Ave., Suite 100A-638, Las Vegas NV 89102. 1-888-732-
1176. E-mail: info@virtualstudiosystems.com. Website: www.virtualstudiosystems.com.
Quarterly commentaries on song lyrics and previously unpublished lyrics available to
performing musicians.

Music Books Plus, P.O. Box 670, 240 Portage Rd., Lewiston NY 14092. (800)265-8481. E-
mail: mail@nor.com. Website: www.musicbooksplus.com.

Music Business International Magazine, 460 Park Ave., S. of 9th, New York NY 10116.
(212)378-0406. *Bimonthly magazine for senior executives in the music industry.*

Music Connection Magazine, 16130 Ventura Blvd., Suite 540, Encino CA 91436. (818)795-0101. E-mail: contactMC@musicconnection.com. Website: www.musicconnection.com. *Biweekly music industry trade publication.*

Music Morsels, P.O. Box 2760, Acworth GA 30102. (678)445-0006. Fax: (678)494-9269. E-mail: SergeEnt@aol.com. Website: www.serge.org/musicmorsels.htm. *Monthly songwriting publication.*

Music Row Magazine, 1231 17th Ave. S, Nashville TN 37212. (615)321-3617. E-mail: info@musicrow.com. Website: www.musicrow.com. *Biweekly Nashville industry publication.*

Offbeat Magazine, OffBeat Publications, 421 Frenchman St., Suite 200, New Orleans LA 70116. (504)944-4300. E-mail: offbeat@offbeat.com. Website: www.offbeat.com. *Monthly magazine covering Louisiana music and artists.*

Performance Magazine, 1203 Lake St., Suite 200, Fort Worth TX 76102-4504. (817)338-9444. E-mail: sales@performancemagazine.com. Website: www.performancemagazine.com. *Weekly publication on touring itineraries, artist availability, upcoming tours, and production and venue news.*

The Performing Songwriter, P.O. Box 40931, Nashville TN 37204. (800)883-7664. E-mail: order@performingsongwriter.com. Website: www.performingsongwriter.com. *Bimonthly songwriters' magazine.*

Producer Report, 415 S. Topanga Canyon Blvd., Suite 114, Topanga CA 90290. (310)455-0888. Fax: (310)455-0894. E-mail: encyclopedia@mojavemusic.com. Website: www.mojavemusic.com. *Semimonthly newsletter covering which producers are working on which acts, and upcoming, current and recently completed projects.*

Public Domain Report, P.O. Box 3102, Margate NJ 08402. (609)822-9401. Website: www.pubdomain.com. *Monthly guide to significant titles entering the public domain.*

Radio and Records, 2049 Century Park East, 41st Floor, Los Angeles CA 90067. (310)553-4330. Fax: (310)203-9763. E-mail: subscribe@radioandrecords.com. Website: www.radioandrecords.com. *Weekly newspaper covering the radio and record industries.*

Radir, Radio Mall, 2412 Unity Ave. N., Dept. WEB, Minneapolis MN 55422. (800)759-4561. E-mail: info@bbhsoftware.com. Website: www.bbhsoftware.com. *Quarterly radio station database on disk.*

Sing Out!, P.O. Box 5460, Bethlehem PA 18015. (888)SING-OUT. Fax: (610)865-5129. E-mail: info@singout.org. Website: www.singout.org. *Quarterly folk music magazine.*

Songcasting, 15445 Ventura Blvd. #260, Sherman Oaks CA 91403. (818)377-4084. *Monthly tip sheet.*

Songlink International, 23 Belsize Crescent, London NW3 5QY England. Website: www.songlink.com. *10 issues/year newsletter including details of recording artists looking for songs; contact details for industry sources; also news and features on the music business.*

Variety, 5700 Wilshire Blvd., Suite 120, Los Angeles CA 90036. (323)857-6600. Fax: (323)857-0494. Website: www.variety.com. *Weekly entertainment trade newspaper.*

Words and Music, 41 Valleybrook Dr., Don Mills, Ontario M3B 2S6 Canada. (416)445-8700. Website: www.socan.ca. *Monthly songwriters' magazine.*

Resources

BOOKS & DIRECTORIES

88 Songwriting Wrongs & How to Right Them, by Pat & Pete Luboff, Writer's Digest Books, 4700 E. Galbraith Rd., Cincinnati OH 45236. (800)448-0915. Website: www.writers digest.com.

The A&R Registry, by Ritch Esra, SRS Publishing, 7510 Sunset Blvd. #1041, Los Angeles CA 90046-3418. (800)377-7411 or (800)552-7411. E-mail: musicregistry@compuserve.com.

Attention: A&R, by Teri Muench and Susan Pomerantz, Alfred Publishing Co. Inc., P.O. Box 10003, Van Nuys CA 91410-0003. (818)892-2452. Website: www.alfredpub.com.

The Billboard Guide to Music Publicity, revised edition, by Jim Pettigrew, Jr., Billboard Books, 1695 Oak St., Lakewood NJ 08701. (800)344-7119.

Breakin' Into Nashville, by Jennifer Ember Pierce, Madison Books, University Press of America, 4501 Forbes Rd., Suite 200, Lanham MD 20706. (800)462-6420.

CMJ Directory, 151 W. 25th St., 12th Floor, New York NY 10001. (917)606-1908. Website: www.cmj.com.

Contracts for the Music industry, P.O. Box 952063, Lake Mary FL 32795-2063. (407)834-8555. E-mail: info@songwriterproducts.com. Website: www.songwriterproducts.com. *Book and computer software of a variety of music contracts.*

The Craft and Business of Songwriting, by John Braheny, Writer's Digest Books, 4700 E. Galbraith Rd., Cincinnati OH 45236. (800)448-0915. Website: www.writersdigest.com.

The Craft of Lyric Writing, by Sheila Davis, Writer's Digest Books, 4700 E. Galbraith Rd., Cincinnati OH 45236. (800)448-0915. Website: www.writersdigest.com.

Creating Melodies, by Dick Weissman, Writer's Digest Books, 4700 E. Galbraith Rd., Cincinnati OH 45236. (800)448-0915. Website: www.writersdigest.com.

Directory of Independent Music Distributors, by Jason Ojalvo, Disc Makers, 7905 N. Rt. 130, Pennsauken NJ 08110. (800)468-9353. E-mail: discman@discmakers.com. Website: www.discmakers.com.

Easy Tools for Composing, by Charles Segal, Segal's Publications, 16 Grace Rd., Newton MA 02159. (617)969-6196.

FILM/TV MUSIC GUIDE, by Ritch Esra, SRS Publishing, 7510 Sunset Blvd. #1041, Los Angeles CA 90046-3418. (800)552-7411. E-mail: musicregistry@compuserve.com or srspu bl@aol.com. Website: www.musicregistry.com.

Finding Fans & Selling CDs, by Veronique Berry and Jason Ojalvo, Disk Makers, 7905 N. Rt. 130, Pennsauken NJ 08110-1402. (800)468-9353. E-mail: discman@diskmakers.com. Website: www.discmakers.com.

Guide to Independent Music Publicity, by Veronique Berry, Disc Makers, 7905 N. Rt. 130, Pennsauken NJ 08110-1402. (800)468-9353. E-mail: discman@discmakers.com.

Guide to Master Tape Preparation, by Dave Moyssiadis, Disk Makers, 7905 N. Rt. 130, Pennsauken NJ 08110-1402. (800)468-9353. E-mail: discman@discmakers.com.

Hollywood Creative Directory, 3000 W. Olympic Blvd. #2525, Santa Monica CA 90404. (800)815-0503. Website: www.hcdonline.com. *Lists producers in film and TV.*

The Hollywood Reporter Blu-Book Production Directory, 5055 Wilshire Blvd., Los Angeles CA 90036. (323)525-2150. Website: www.hollywoodreporter.com.

Hot Tips for the Home Recording Studio, by Hank Linderman, Writer's Digest Books, 4700 E. Galbraith Rd., Cincinnati OH 45236. (800)448-0915. Website: www.writersdigest.com.

How to Promote Your Music Successfully on the Internet, by David Nevue, Midnight Rain Productions, P.O. Box 21831, Eugene OR 97402. Website: www.rainmusic.com.

How to Write Songs on Guitar: A Guitar-Playing and Songwriting Course, by Rikky Rooksby, Backbeat Books, 600 Harrison St., San Francisco CA 94107. (415)947-6615. E-mail: books@musicplayer.com. Website: www.backbeatbooks.com.

How You Can Break Into the Music Business, by Marty Garrett, Lonesome Wind Corporation, P.O. Box 2143, Broken Arrow OK 74013-2143. (800)210-4416.

Louisiana Music Directory, OffBeat, Inc., 421 Frenchmen St., Suite 200, New Orleans LA 70116. (504)944-4300. Website: www.offbeat.com.

Melody in Songwriting, by Jack Perricone, Berklee Press, 1140 Boylston St., Boston MA 02215. (617)747-2146. E-mail: info@berkleepress.com. Website: www.berkleepress.com.

Melody: How to Write Great Tunes, by Rikky Rooksby, Backbeat Books, 600 Harrison St., San Francisco CA 94107. (415)947-6115. E-mail: books@musicplayer.com. Website: www.backbeatbooks.com.

Music Attorney Legal & Business Affairs Registry, by Ritch Esra and Steve Trumbull, SRS Publishing, 7510 Sunset Blvd. #1041, Los Angeles CA 90046-3418. (800)552-7411. E-mail: musicregistry@compuserve.com or srspubl@aol.com.

Music Directory Canada, seventh edition, Norris-Whitney Communications Inc., 23 Hannover Dr., Suite 7, St. Catherines, Ontario L2W 1A3 Canada. (877)RING-NWC. E-mail: mail@nor.com. Website: http://nor.com.

Music Law: How to Run Your Band's Business, by Richard Stin, Nolo Press, 950 Parker St., Berkeley CA 94710-9867. (510)549-1976. Website: www.nolo.com.

Music, Money and Success: The Insider's Guide to the Music Industry, by Jeffrey Brabec and Todd Brabec, Schirmer Books, 1633 Broadway, New York NY 10019.

The Music Publisher Registry, by Ritch Esra, SRS Publishing, 7510 Sunset Blvd. #1041, Los Angeles CA 90046-3418. (800)552-7411. E-mail: musicregistry@compuserve.com or srspubl@aol.com.

Music Publishing: A Songwriter's Guide, revised edition, by Randy Poe, Writer's Digest Books, 4700 E. Galbraith Rd., Cincinnati OH 45236. (800)448-0915. Website: www.writersdigest.com.

The Musician's Guide to Making & Selling Your Own CDs & Cassettes, by Jana Stanfield, Writer's Digest Books, 4700 E. Galbraith Rd., Cincinnati OH 45236. (800)448-0915. Website: www.writersdigest.com.

Musicians' Phone Book, The Los Angeles Music Industry Directory, Get Yourself Some Publishing, 28336 Simsalido Ave., Canyon Country CA 91351. (805)299-2405. E-mail: mpb@earthlink.net. Website: www.musiciansphonebook.com.

Nashville Music Business Directory, by Mark Dreyer, NMBD Publishing, 9 Music Square S., Suite 210, Nashville TN 37203. (615)826-4141. E-mail: nmbd@nashvilleconnection.com. Website: www.nashvilleconnection.com.

Resources

Nashville's Unwritten Rules: Inside the Business of the Country Music Machine, by Dan Daley, Overlook Press, One Overlook Dr., Woodstock NY 12498. (845)679-6838. E-mail: overlook@netstep.net.

National Directory of Independent Record Distributors, P.O. Box 452063, Lake Mary FL 32795-2063. (407)834-8555. E-mail: info@songwriterproducts.com. Website: www.song writerproducts.com.

The Official Country Music Directory, ICMA Music Directory, P.O. Box 271238, Nashville TN 37227.

Radio Stations of America: A National Directory, P.O. Box 452063, Lake Mary FL 32795-2063. (407)834-8555. E-mail: info@songwriterproducts.com. Website: www.songwriterpr oducts.com.

The Real Deal—How to Get Signed to a Record Label from A to Z, by Daylle Deanna Schwartz, Billboard Books, 1695 Oak St., Lakewood NJ 08701. (800)344-7119.

Recording Industry Sourcebook, Music Books Plus, P.O. Box 670, 240 Portage Rd., Lewiston NY 14092. (800)265-8481. Website: www.musicbooksplus.com.

Reharmonization Techniques, by Randy Felts, Berklee Press, 1140 Boylston St., Boston MA 02215. (617)747-2146. E-mail: info@berkleepress.com. Website: www.berkleepress.com.

The Songwriters Idea Book, by Sheila Davis, Writer's Digest Books, 4700 E. Galbraith Rd., Cincinnati OH 45236. (800)448-0915. Website: www.writersdigest.com.

Songwriter's Market Guide to Song & Demo Submission Formats, Writer's Digest Books, 4700 E. Galbraith Rd., Cincinnati OH 45236. (800)448-0915. Website: www.writersdigest.com.

Songwriter's Playground—Innovative Exercises in Creative Songwriting, by Barbara L. Jordan, Creative Music Marketing, 1085 Commonwealth Ave., Suite 323, Boston MA 02215. (617)926-8766.

The Songwriter's Workshop: Harmony, by Jimmy Kachulis, Berklee Press, 1140 Boylston St., Boston MA 02215. (617)747-2146. E-mail: info@berkleepress.com. Website: www.ber kleepress.com.

The Songwriter's Workshop: Melody, by Jimmy Kachulis, Berklee Press, 1140 Boylston St., Boston MA 02215. (617)747-2146. E-mail: info@berkleepress.com. Website: www.ber kleepress.com.

Songwriting and the Creative Process, by Steve Gillette, Sing Out! Publications, P.O. Box 5640, Bethlehem PA 18015-0253. (888)SING-OUT. E-mail: singout@libertynet.org. Website: www.singout.org/sopubs.html.

Songwriting: Essential Guide to Lyric Form and Structure, by Pat Pattison, Berklee Press, 1140 Boylston St., Boston MA 02215. (617)747-2146. E-mail: info@berkleepress.com. Website: www.www.berkleepress.com.

Songwriting: Essential Guide to Rhyming, by Pat Pattison, Berklee Press, 1140 Boylston St., Boston MA 02215. (617)747-2146. E-mail: info@berkleepress.com. Website: www.w ww.berkleepress.com.

The Songwriting Sourcebook: How to Turn Chords Into Great Songs, by Rikky Rooksby, Backbeat Books, 600 Harrison St., San Francisco CA 94107. (415)947-6615. E-mail: books @musicplayer.com. Website: www.backbeatbooks.com.

The Soul of the Writer, by Susan Tucker with Linda Lee Strother, Journey Publishing, P.O. Box 92411, Nashville TN 37209. (615)952-4894. Website: www.journeypublishing.com.

Successful Lyric Writing, by Sheila Davis, Writer's Digest Books, 4700 E. Galbraith Rd., Cincinnati OH 45236. (800)448-0915. Website: www.writersdigest.com.

This Business of Music Marketing and Promotion, by Tad Lathrop and Jim Pettigrew, Jr., Billboard Books, Watson-Guptill Publications, 770 Broadway, New York NY 10003. E-mail: info@watsonguptill.com.

Tim Sweeney's Guide to Releasing Independent Records, by Tim Sweeney, TSA Books, 31805 Highway 79 S., Temecula CA 92592. (909)303-9506. E-mail: info@tsamusic.com. Website: www.tsamusic.com.

Tim Sweeney's Guide to Succeeding at Music Conventions, by Tim Sweeney, TSA Books, 31805 Highway 79 S., Temecula CA 92592. (909)303-9506. Website: www.tsamusic.com.

Texas Music Industry Directory, Texas Music Office, Office of the Governor, P.O. Box 13246, Austin TX 78711. (512)463-6666. E-mail: music@governor.state.tx.us. Website: www.governor.state.tx.us/music.

Tunesmith: Inside the Art of Songwriting, by Jimmy Webb, Hyperion, 77 W. 66th St., 11th Floor, New York NY 10023. (800)759-0190.

Volunteer Lawyers for the Arts Guide to Copyright for Musicians and Composers, One E. 53rd St., 6th Floor, New York NY 10022. (212)319-2787.

Writing Better Lyrics, by Pat Pattison, Writer's Digest Books, 4700 E. Galbraith Rd., Cincinnati OH 45236. (800)448-0915. Website: www.writersdigest.com.

Writing Music for Hit Songs, by Jai Josefs, Schirmer Trade Books, 257 Park Ave. S., New York NY 10010. (212)254-2100.

The Yellow Pages of Rock, The Album Network, 120 N. Victory Blvd., Burbank CA 91502. (800)222-4382. Fax: (818)955-9048. E-mail: ypinfo@yprock.com.

RESOURCES

Websites of Interest

The Internet provides a wealth of information for songwriters and performers, and the number of sites devoted to music grows each day. Below is a list of some websites that can offer you information, links to other music sites, contact with other songwriters and places to showcase your songs. Since the online world is changing and expanding at such a rapid pace, this is hardly a comprehensive list. But it gives you a place to start on your journey through the Internet to search for opportunities to get your music heard.

About.com Musicians' Exchange: http://musicians.miningco.com
Site featuring headlines and articles of interest to independent musicians, as well as numerous links.

American Music Center: www.amc.net
Classical/jazz archives, includes a list of composer organizations and contacts.

American Society of Composers, Authors and Publishers (ASCAP) www.ascap.com
Database of performed works in ASCAP's repertoire. Also includes songwriter, performer and publisher information, ASCAP membership information and industry news.

Ampcast.com: www.ampcast.com
Online musicians community and music hosting site.

Backstage Commerce: www.backstagecommerce.com
Offers secure online ordering support to artist websites for a commission.

The Bandit A&R Newsletter: www.banditnewsletter.com
Offers newsletter to help musicians target demos and press kits to labels, publishers, managers and production companies actively looking for new talent.

Bandname.com: www.bandname.com
Online band name registry and archive, as well as digital storefront services and classifieds.

Bandstand: www.bandstand.com
Music news and links.

Berklee School of Music: www.berkleemusic.com
Offers online instruction, including a certificate program in songwriting.

The Bard's Crier: http://thebards.net/crier/
A free guerilla music marketing e-zine.

Billboard.com: www.billboard.com
Music industry news and searchable online database of music companies by subscription.

The Blues Foundation: www.blues.org
Information on the foundation, its membership and events.

John Braheny Homepage: www.johnbraheny.com
John Braheny is the author of *The Craft and Business of Songwriting*, and his site features articles, interviews, and a blog with commentary on business and creative issues.

Broadcast Music, Inc. (BMI): www.bmi.com
Offers lists of song titles, songwriters and publishers of the BMI repertoire. Also includes BMI membership information, and general information on songwriting and licensing.

The Buzz Factor: www.thebuzzfactor.com
Offers press kit evaluation, press release writing, guerrilla music marketing, tips and weekly newsletter.

CDBABY: www.cdbaby.com
An online CD store dedicated solely to independent music.

CDFreedom: www.cdfreedom.com
Online CD store for independent musicians.

Chorus America: www.chorusamerica.org
The website of Chorus America, a national service organization for professional and volunteer choruses, including job listings and professional development information.

CPCC: www.under.org/cpcc
Website for the Center for the Promotion of Contemporary Composers.

Creative Musicians Coalition (CMC): www.aimcmc.com
Website of the CMC, an international organization dedicated to the advancement of independent musicians, links to artists, and tips and techniques for musicians.

Ensemble 21: www.ensemble21.com/e21.html
Website of the New York contemporary music performance group dedicated to promotion and performance of new orchestral compositions.

Film Music Network: www.filmmusicworld.com
Offers new about the fim music world, as well as educational and networking opportunities and an e-mail newsletter.

Fourfront Media and Music: www.knab.com
This site by music industry consultant Christopher Knab offers in-depth information on product development, promotion, publicity and performance.

Garageband.com: www.garageband.com
Online music hosting site where bands can post music and profiles, and then be critiqued by online listeners and industry insiders.

Getsigned.com: www.getsigned.com
Interviews with industry executives, how-to business information and more.

Government Liaison Services: www.trademarkinfo.com
An intellectual property research firm. Offers an online trademark search.

Resources

Guitar Nine Records: www.guitar9.com
Offers articles by music professionals and insiders.

Harry Fox Agency: www.harryfox.com
Offers a comprehensive FAQ about licensing songs for use in recording, performance and film.

Independent Artists' Services: www.idiom.com/~upend/
Full of information including searchable databases of bands and booking/touring information and other resources.

Independent Distribution Network: www.idnmusic.com/
Website of independent bands distributing their music, with advice on everything from starting a band to finding labels.

Independent Songwriter Web Magazine: www.independentsongwriter.com
Independent music reviews, classifieds, message board and chat sessions.

Indie-Music.com: http://indie-music.com
Full of how-to articles, record label directory, radio links and venue listing.

Internet Underground Music Archive (IUMA): www.iuma.com
Online musicians community and music hosting site.

Jazz Composers Collective: www.jazzcollective.com
Industry information on composers, projects, recordings, concerts and events.

Jazz Corner: www.jazzcorner.com
Website for musicians and organizations featuring links to 70 websites for jazz musicians and organizations and the Speakeasy, an interactive conference area.

Just Plain Folks: www.jpfolks.com
Online songwriting organization featuring messageboards, lyric feedback forums, member profiles, featured members' music, contact listings, chapter homepages, and an Internet radio station. (See the Just Plain Folks listing in the Organizations section).

Kathode Ray Music: www.kathoderaymusic.com
Specializes in marketing and promotion consultation and offers a business forum, e-newsletter and a free classified ads board.

Li'l Hank's Guide for Songwriters in L.A.: www.halsguide.com
Website for songwriters with information on clubs, publishers, books, etc. as well as links to other songwriting sites.

Los Angeles Goes Underground: http://lagu.somaweb.org
Website dedicated to underground rock bands from Los Angeles and Hollywood.

Lyrical Line: www.lyricalline.com
Offers places to market your songs, critique service, industry news and more.

Lyricist.com: www.lyricist.com
Jeff Mallet's songwriter site offering contests, tips and job opportunities in the music industry.

MI2N (THE MUSIC INDUSTRY NEWS NETWORK): www.mi2n.com
Offers news on happenings in the music industry and career postings.

The Muse's Muse: www.musesmuse.com
Classifieds, catalog of lyric samples, songwriting articles, organizations and chat room.

Music & Audio Connection: www.musicandaudio.com
Guide to Canadian artists, associations and other resources from Norris-Whitney Communications, Inc.

Music Publishers Association: http://host.mpa.org
Provides a copyright resource center, directory of member publishers and information on the organization.

Music Yellow Pages: www.musicyellowpages.com
Phone book listings of music-related businesses.

Musicians Assistance Site (MAS): www.musicianassist.com
Features site reviews and databases of venues, contacts, promoters, manufacturers and record labels. Also includes an archive of music business articles, columns, and pre-made contracts and agreements.

The Musicians Guide Through the Legal Jungle: www.legaljungleguide.com/resource.htm
Offers articles on copyright law, music publishing and talent agents.

National Association of Composers USA (NACUSA): www.music-usa.org/nacusa
Website of the organization dedicated to promotion and performance of new music by Americans, featuring a young composers' competition, concert schedule, job opportunities and more.

National Music Publishers Association: www.nmpa.org
The organization's online site with information about copyright, legislation and other concerns of the music publishing world.

Online Rock: www.onlinerock.com
Offers e-mail, marketing and free webpage services. Also features articles, chat rooms, links, etc.

Opera America: www.operaam.org
Website of Opera America, featuring information on advocacy and awareness programs, publications, conference schedules and more.

Outersound: www.outersound.com
Information on finding a recording studio, educating yourself in the music industry, and a list of music magazines to advertise in or get reviewed by.

PerformerMag: www.performermag.com
Offers articles, music industry news, classifieds, and reviews.

Public Domain Music: www.pdinfo.com
Articles on public domain works and copyright, including public domain song lists, research resources, tips and a FAQ.

PUMP AUDIO: www.pumpaudio.com
License music for film and TV on a non-exclusive basis. (See the Insider Report with singer/songwriter Bibi Farber on page 160.)

Rhythm Net: www.rhythmnet.com
Online CD store for independent musicians.

Resources

SESAC Inc.: www.sesac.com
Includes SESAC performing rights organization information, songwriter profiles, organization news, licensing information and links to other sites.

Song Shark: www.geocities.com/songshark
Website of information on known song sharks.

Songcatalog.com: www.songcatalog.com
Online song catalog database for licensing.

Songlink: www.songlink.com
Offers opportunities to pitch songs to music publishers for specific recording projects, also industry news.

Songscope.com: www.songscope.com
Online song catalog database for pitching and licensing.

Songwriter Products Ideas & Necessities (SPIN): www.songwriterproducts.com
Offer songwriting tips, tools and accessories, including tapes, CDs, duplication products and music business career packages.

Songwriter's Guild of America (SGA): www.songwritersguilt.com
Offers industry news, member services information, newsletters, contract reviews and more.

Songwriter's Resource Network: www.songwritersresourcenetwork.com
Online information and services designed especially for songwriters.

The Songwriting Education Resource: www.craftofsongwriting.com
An educational site for Nashville songwriters offering discussion boards, articles and links.

SongU.com: www.songu.com
Offers online songwriting courses, networking opportunities, e-mail newsletter, and opportunities to pitch songs to industry professionals.

Sonic Bids: www.sonicbids.com
Features an online press kit template with photos, bio, music samples, and a date calendar.

StarPolish: www.starpolish.com
Features articles and interviews on the music industry, as well as the Velvet Rope Forum.

TAXI: www.taxi.com
Independent A&R vehicle that shops tapes to A&R professionals.

United States Copyright Office: http://www.copyright.gov
The homepage for the U.S. copyright office, offering information on registering songs.

Yahoo!: www.yahoo.com/Entertainment/Music/
Use this search engine to retrieve over 20,000 music listings.

Glossary

A cappella. Choral singing without accompaniment.

AAA form. A song form in which every verse has the same melody; often used for songs that tell a story.

AABA, ABAB. A commonly used song pattern consisting of two verses, a bridge and a verse, or a repeated pattern of verse and bridge, where the verses are musically the same.

A&R Director. Record company executive in charge of the Artists and Repertoire Department who is responsible for finding and developing new artists and matching songs with artists.

A/C. Adult contemporary music.

Advance. Money paid to the songwriter or recording artist, which is then recouped before regular royalty payment begins. Sometimes called "up front" money, advances are deducted from royalties.

AFIM. Association for Independent Music (formerly NAIRD). Organization for independent record companies, distributors, retailers, manufacturers, etc.

AFM. American Federation of Musicians. A union for musicians and arrangers.

AFTRA. American Federation of Television and Radio Artists. A union for performers.

AIMP. Association of Independent Music Publishers.

Airplay. The radio broadcast of a recording.

AOR. Album-Oriented Rock. A radio format that primarily plays selections from rock albums as opposed to hit singles.

Arrangement. An adaptation of a composition for a recording or performance, with consideration for the melody, harmony, instrumentation, tempo, style, etc.

ASCAP. American Society of Composers, Authors and Publishers. A performing rights society. (See the Organizations section.)

Assignment. Transfer of rights of a song from writer to publisher.

Audio Visual Index (AVI). A database containing title and production information for cue sheets which are available from a performing rights organization. Currently, BMI, ASCAP, SOCAN, PRS, APRA and SACEM contribute their cue sheet listings to the AVI.

Audiovisual. Refers to presentations that use audio backup for visual material.

Background music. Music used that creates mood and supports the spoken dialogue of a radio program or visual action of an audiovisual work. Not feature or theme music.

b&w. Black and white.

Bed. Prerecorded music used as background material in commercials. In rap music, often refers to the sampled and looped drums and music over which the rapper performs.

Black box. Theater without fixed stage or seating arrangements, capable of a variety of formations. Usually a small space, often attached to a major theater complex, used for workshops or experimental works calling for small casts and limited sets.

BMI. Broadcast Music, Inc. A performing rights society. (See the Organizations section.)

Booking agent. Person who schedules performances for entertainers.

Bootlegging. Unauthorized recording and selling of a song.

Business manager. Person who handles the financial aspects of artistic careers.

Buzz. Attention an act generates through the media and word of mouth.

b/w. Backed with. Usually refers to the B-side of a single.

C&W. Country and western.

Catalog. The collected songs of one writer, or all songs handled by one publisher.

CD. Compact Disc (see below).

CD-R. A recordable CD.

CD-ROM. Compact Disc-Read Only Memory. A computer information storage medium capable of holding enormous amounts of data. Information on a CD-ROM cannot be deleted. A computer user must have a CD-ROM drive to access a CD-ROM.

Chamber music. Any music suitable for performance in a small audience area or chamber.

Chamber orchestra. A miniature orchestra usually containing one instrument per part.

Chart. The written arrangement of a song.

Charts. The trade magazines' lists of the best-selling records.

CHR. Comtemporary Hit Radio. Top 40 pop music.

Collaboration. Two or more artists, writers, etc., working together on a single project; for instance, a playwright and a songwriter creating a musical together.

Compact disc. A small disc (about 4.7 inches in diameter) holding digitally encoded music that is read by a laser beam in a CD player.

Composers. The men and women who create musical compositions for motion pictures and other audio visual works, or the creators of classical music composition.

Co-publish. Two or more parties own publishing rights to the same song.

Copyright. The exclusive legal right giving the creator of a work the power to control the publishing, reproduction and selling of the work. Although a song is technically copyrighted at the time it is written, the best legal protection of that copyright comes through registering the copyright with the Library of Congress.

Copyright infringement. Unauthorized use of a copyrighted song or portions thereof.

Cover recording. A new version of a previously recorded song.

Crossover. A song that becomes popular in two or more musical categories (e.g., country and pop).

Cut. Any finished recording; a selection from a LP. Also to record.

DAT. Digital Audio Tape. A professional and consumer audio cassette format for recording and playing back digitally-encoded material. DAT cassettes are approximately one-third smaller than conventional audio cassettes.

DCC. Digital Compact Cassette. A consumer audio cassette format for recording and playing back digitally-encoded tape. DCC tapes are the same size as analog cassettes.

Demo. A recording of a song submitted as a demonstration of a writer's or artist's skills.

Derivative work. A work derived from another work, such as a translation, musical arrangement, sound recording, or motion picture version.

Distributor. Wholesale marketing agent responsible for getting records from manufacturers to retailers.

Donut. A jingle with singing at the beginning and end and instrumental background in the middle. Ad copy is recorded over the middle section.

E-mail. Electronic mail. Computer address where a company or individual can be reached via modem.

Engineer. A specially-trained individual who operates recording studio equipment.

Enhanced CD. General term for an audio CD that also contains multimedia computer information. It is playable in both standard CD players and CD-ROM drives.

EP. Extended play record or cassette containing more selections than a standard single, but fewer than a standard album.

Exploit. To seek legitimate uses of a song for income.

Final mix. The art of combining all the various sounds that take place during the recording session into a two-track stereo or mono tape. Reflects the total product and all of the energies and talents the artist, producer and engineer have put into the project.

Fly space. The area above a stage from which set pieces are lowered and raised during a performance.

Folio. A softcover collection of printed music prepared for sale.

Following. A fan base committed to going to gigs and buying albums.

Foreign rights societies. Performing rights societies other than domestic which have reciprocal agreements with ASCAP and BMI for the collection of royalties accrued by foreign radio and television airplay and other public performance of the writer members of the above groups.

Harry Fox Agency. Organization that collects mechanical royalties.

Grammy. Music industry awards presented by the National Academy of Recording Arts and Sciences.

Hip-hop. A dance oriented musical style derived from a combination of disco, rap and R&B.

Hit. A song or record that achieves top 40 status.

Hook. A memorable "catch" phrase or melody line that is repeated in a song.

House. Dance music created by remixing samples from other songs.

Hypertext. Words or groups of words in an electronic document that are linked to other text, such as a definition or a related document. Hypertext can also be linked to illustrations.

Indie. An independent record label, music publisher or producer.

Infringement. A violation of the exclusive rights granted by the copyright law to a copyright owner.

Internet. A worldwide network of computers that offers access to a wide variety of electronic resources.

ips. Inches per second; a speed designation for tape recording.

IRC. International reply coupon, necessary for the return of materials sent out of the country. Available at most post offices.

Jingle. Usually a short verse set to music designed as a commercial message.

Lead sheet. Written version (melody, chord symbols and lyric) of a song.

Leader. Plastic (non-recordable) tape at the beginning and between songs for ease in selection.

Libretto. The text of an opera or any long choral work. The booklet containing such text.

Listing. Block of information in this book about a specific company.

LP. Designation for long-playing record played at 33⅓ rpm.

Lyric sheet. A typed or written copy of a song's lyrics.

Market. A potential song or music buyer; also a demographic division of the record-buying public.

Master. Edited and mixed tape used in the production of records; the best or original copy of a recording from which copies are made.

MD. MiniDisc. A 2.5 inch disk for recording and playing back digitally-encoded music.

Mechanical right. The right to profit from the physical reproduction of a song.

Mechanical royalty. Money earned from record, tape and CD sales.

MIDI. Musical instrument digital interface. Universal standard interface that allows musical instruments to communicate with each other and computers.

Mini Disc. (See **MD** above.)

Mix. To blend a multi-track recording into the desired balance of sound, usually to a 2-track stereo master.

Modem. MOdulator/DEModulator. A computer device used to send data from one computer to another via telephone line.

MOR. Middle of the road. Easy-listening popular music.

MP3. File format of a relatively small size that stores audio files on a computer. Music saved in a MP3 format can be played only with a MP3 player (which can be downloaded onto a computer).

Ms. Manuscript.

Multimedia. Computers and software capable of integrating text, sound, photographic-quality images, animation and video.

Music bed. (See **Bed** above.)

Music jobber. A wholesale distributor of printed music.

Music library. A business that purchases canned music, which can then be bought by producers of radio and TV commercials, films, videos and audiovisual productions to use however they wish.

Music publisher. A company that evaluates songs for commercial potential, finds artists to record them, finds other uses (such as TV or film) for the songs, collects income generated by the songs and protects copyrights from infringement.

Music Row. An area of Nashville, TN, encompassing Sixteenth, Seventeeth and Eighteenth avenues where most of the major publishing houses, recording studios, mastering labs, songwriters, singers, promoters, etc. practice their trade.

NARAS. National Academy of Recording Arts and Sciences.

The National Academy of Songwriters (NAS). The largest U.S. songwriters' association. (See the Organizations section.)

Needle-drop. Refers to a type of music library. A needledrop music library is a licensed library that allows producers to borrow music on a rate schedule. The price depends on how the music will be used.

Network. A group of computers electronically linked to share information and resources.

NMPA. National Music Publishers Association.

One-off. A deal between songwriter and publisher which includes only one song or project at a time. No future involvement is implicated. Many times a single song contract accompanies a one-off deal.

One-stop. A wholesale distributor of who sells small quantities of records to "mom and pop" record stores, retailers and jukebox operators.

Operetta. Light, humorous, satiric plot or poem, set to cheerful light music with occasional spoken dialogue.

Overdub. To record an additional part (vocal or instrumental) onto a basic multi-track recording.

Parody. A satirical imitation of a literary or musical work. Permission from the owner of the copyright is generally required before commercial exploitation of a parody.

Payola. Dishonest payment to broadcasters in exchange for airplay.

Performing rights. A specific right granted by U.S. copyright law protecting a composition from being publicly performed without the owner's permission.

Performing rights organization. An organization that collects income from the public performance of songs written by its members and then proportionally distributes this income to the individual copyright holder based on the number of performances of each song.

Personal manager. A person who represents artists to develop and enhance their careers. Personal managers may negotiate contracts, hire and dismiss other agencies and personnel relating to the artist's career, review material, help with artist promotions and perform many services.

Piracy. The unauthorized reproduction and selling of printed or recorded music.

Pitch. To attempt to solicit interest for a song by audition.

Playlist. List of songs a radio station will play.

Points. A negotiable percentage paid to producers and artists for records sold.

Producer. Person who supervises every aspect of a recording project.

Production company. Company specializing in producing jingle packages for advertising agencies. May also refer to companies specializing in audiovisual programs.

Professional manager. Member of a music publisher's staff who screens submitted material and tries to get the company's catalog of songs recorded.

Proscenium. Permanent architectural arch in a theater that separates the stage from the audience.

Public domain. Any composition with an expired, lapsed or invalid copyright, and therefore belonging to everyone.

Purchase license. Fee paid for music used from a stock music library.

Query. A letter of inquiry to an industry professional soliciting his interest.

R&B. Rhythm and blues.

Rack Jobber. Distributors who lease floor space from department stores and put in racks of albums.

Rate. The percentage of royalty as specified by contract.

Release. Any record issued by a record company.

Residuals. In advertising or television, payments to singers and musicians for use of a performance.

RIAA. Recording Industry Association of America.

Royalty. Percentage of money earned from the sale of records or use of a song.

RPM. Revolutions per minute. Refers to phonograph turntable speed.

SAE. Self-addressed envelope (with no postage attached).

SASE. Self-addressed stamped envelope.

SATB. The abbreviation for parts in choral music, meaning Soprano, Alto, Tenor and Bass.

Score. A complete arrangement of all the notes and parts of a composition (vocal or instrumental) written out on staves. A full score, or orchestral score, depicts every orchestral part on a separate staff and is used by a conductor.

Self-contained. A band or recording act that writes all their own material.

SESAC. A performing rights organization, originally the Society of European Stage Authors and Composers. (See the Organizations section.)

SFX. Sound effects.

Shop. To pitch songs to a number of companies or publishers.

Single. 45 rpm record with only one song per side. A 12″ single refers to a long version of one song on a 12″ disc, usually used for dance music.

Ska. Fast tempo dance music influenced primarily by reggae and punk, usually featuring horns, saxophone and bass.

SOCAN. Society of Composers, Authors and Music Publishers of Canada. A Canadian performing rights organization. (See the Organizations section.)

Solicited. Songs or materials that have been requested.

Song plugger. A songwriter representative whose main responsibility is promoting uncut songs to music publishers, record companies, artists and producers.

Song shark. Person who deals with songwriters deceptively for his own profit.

SoundScan. A company that collates the register tapes of reporting stores to track the actual number of albums sold at the retail level.

Resources

Soundtrack. The audio, including music and narration, of a film, videotape or audiovisual program.

Space stage. Open stage that features lighting and, perhaps, projected scenery.

Split publishing. To divide publishing rights between two or more publishers.

Staff songwriter. A songwriter who has an exclusive agreement with a publisher.

Statutory royalty rate. The maximum payment for mechanical rights guaranteed by law that a record company may pay the songwriter and his publisher for each record or tape sold.

Subpublishing. Certain rights granted by a U.S. publisher to a foreign publisher in exchange for promoting the U.S. catalog in his territory.

Synchronization. Technique of timing a musical soundtrack to action on film or video.

Take. Either an attempt to record a vocal or instrument part, or an acceptable recording of a performance.

Tejano. A musical form begun in the late 1970s by regional bands in south Texas, its style reflects a blended Mexican-American culture. Incorporates elements of rock, country, R&B and jazz, and often features accordion and 12-string guitar.

Thrust stage. Stage with audience on three sides and a stagehouse or wall on the fourth side.

Top 40. The first 40 songs on the pop music charts at any given time. Also refers to a style of music which emulates that heard on the current top 40.

Track. Divisions of a recording tape (e.g., 24-track tape) that can be individually recorded in the studio, then mixed into a finished master.

Trades. Publications covering the music industry.

12″ Single. A 12-inch record containing one or more remixes of a song, originally intended for dance club play.

Unsolicited. Songs or materials that were not requested and are not expected.

VHS. ½″ videocassette format.

Vocal score. An arrangement of vocal music detailing all vocal parts, and condensing all accompanying instrumental music into one piano part.

Website. An address on the World Wide Web that can be accessed·by computer modem. It may contain text, graphics and sound.

Wing space. The offstage area surrounding the playing stage in a theater, unseen by the audience, where sets and props are hidden, actors wait for cues, and stagehands prepare to chance sets.

World music. A general music category which includes most musical forms originating outside the U.S. and Europe, including reggae and calypso. World music finds its roots primarily in the Caribbean, Latin America, Africa and the south Pacific.

World Wide Web (WWW). An Internet resource that utilizes hypertext to access information. It also supports formatted text, illustrations and sounds, depending on the user's computer capabilities.

Category Indexes

The Category Indexes are a good place to begin searching for a markets. They break down the listings by section (music publishers, record companies, etc.) and by the type of music they are interested in. For example, if you write country songs, and are looking for a publisher to pitch them, go to the Music Publishers heading and then check the companies listed under the Country subheading. The music categories cover a wide range of variations within each genre, so be sure to read each listing thoroughly to make sure your own unique take on that genre is a good match. Some listings do not appear in these indexes because they did not cite a specific preference. Listings that were very specific, or whose music descriptions don't quite fit into these categories also do not appear. (Category listings for **Music Publishers** begin on this page, **Record Companies** on page 392, **Record Producers** on page 398 and **Managers & Booking Agents** begin on page 403.)

MUSIC PUBLISHERS

Adult Contemporary (also easy listening, middle of the road, AAA, ballads, etc.)

Category Index

Category Index

World Music (also reggae, ethnic, calypso, international, world beat, etc.)

Latin (also Spanish, salsa, Cuban, conga, Brazilian, cumbja, rancheras, Mexican, merengue, Tejano, Tex Mex, etc.)

Americatone Records International USA 146
Avitor Music 148
BMX Entertainment 151
Discmedia 159
Discos Fuentes/Miami Records & Edimusica USA 159
Hacienda Records & Recording Studio 164
Outstanding Records 174

Metal (also thrash, grindcore, heavy metal, etc.)

Avitor Music 148
Cellar Records 153
Dwell Records 160
Metal Blade Records 169
Missile Records Film & TV, Inc. 170
Nightmare Records 173
Rotten Records 180
Sin Klub Entertainment, Inc. 182

New Age (also ambient)

Avitor Music 148
BMX Entertainment 151
CAPP Records 152
Dale Productions, Alan 158
Missile Records Film & TV, Inc. 170
Neurodisc Records, Inc. 172
Only New Age Music, Inc. 174
Rustron Music Productions 180
Tangent® Records 185

Novelty (also comedy, humor, etc.)

Avitor Music 148
Oglio Records 173
Rustic Records 180
Sureshot Records 185

Pop (also top 40, top 100, popular, chart hits, etc.)

A.A.M.I. Music Group 145
ABL Records 145
Allegheny Music Works 145
Arkadia Entertainment Corp. 147
Avitor Music 148
Awal.com 149
Aware Records 149
Blue Gem Records 150
BMX Entertainment 151
Candyspiteful Productions 152
CAPP Records 152
Capstan Record Production 153
Case Entertainment Group/C.E.G. Records, Inc. 153
Cellar Records 153
Coal Harbor Music 155
CPA Records 156
Crank! A Record Company 157
Deep South Entertainment 158
Dental Records 159
Discmedia 159
Enterprize Records-Tapes 160
Generic Records, Inc. 162
Gotham Records 163
Hacienda Records & Recording Studio 164
Heads Up Int., Ltd. 164
Heart Music, Inc. 164
Hi-Bias Records Inc. 165
Hottrax Records 165
Idol Records Publishing 166
Jupiter Records 167
Kaupp Records 167
Kingston Records 167
Lucifer Records, Inc. 168
Minotaur Records 170
Mighty Records 169
Missile Records Film & TV, Inc. 170
Monticana Records 171
Nation Records Inc. 172
Pickwick/Mecca/International Records 175
Plateau Music 175
Pop Record Research 176

Rock (also rockabilly, AOR, rock 'n' roll, etc.)

RECORD PRODUCERS

Rock (also rockabilly, AOR, rock 'n' roll, etc.)

World Music (also reggae, ethnic, calypso, international, world beat, etc.)

R&B (also soul, black, urban, etc.)

World Music (also reggae, ethnic, calypso, international, world beat, etc.)

Openness to Submissions Index

Use this index to find companies open to your level of experience. It is recommended to use this index in conjunction with the Category Indexes found on page 383. Once you have compiled a list of companies open to your experience and music, read the information in these listings, paying close attention to the **How to Contact** subhead. (Also see A Sample Listing Decoded on page 11.)

◯ OPEN TO BEGINNERS

Music Publishers

Managers & Booking Agents

◑ PREFERS EXPERIENCED, BUT OPEN TO BEGINNERS

Music Publishers

Openness Index

Film & TV Index

This index lists companies who place music in motion pictures and TV shows (excluding commercials). To learn more about their film/TV experience, read the information under **Film & TV** in their listings. It is recommended to use this index in conjunction with the Openness to Submissions Index beginning on page 411.

Geographic Index

This Geographic Index will help you locate companies by state, as well as those in countries outside of the U.S. It is recommended to use this index in conjunction with the Openness to Submissions Index on page 411. Once you find the names of companies in this index you are interested in, check the listings within each section for addresses, phone numbers, contact names and submission details.

Writer's Digest

WRITE BETTER
GET PUBLISHED

DISCOVER A WORLD OF WRITING SUCCESS!

Are you ready to be praised, published, and paid for your writing? It's time to invest in your future with *Writer's Digest!* Beginners and experienced writers alike have been relying on *Writer's Digest*, the world's leading magazine for writers, for more than 80 years — and it keeps getting better! Each issue is brimming with:

Get **2 FREE ISSUES** of *Writer's Digest!*

- Technique articles geared toward specific genres, including fiction, nonfiction, business writing and more

- Business information specifically for writers, such as organizational advice, tax tips, and setting fees

- Tips and tricks for rekindling your creative fire

- The latest and greatest markets for print, online and e-publishing

- And much more!

That's a lot to look forward to every month. Let *Writer's Digest* put you on the road to writing success!

NO RISK!
Send No Money Now!

☐ **Yes!** Please rush me my 2 FREE issues of *Writer's Digest* — the world's leading magazine for writers. If I like what I read, I'll get a full year's subscription (12 issues, including the 2 free issues) for only $19.96. That's 72% off the newsstand rate! If I'm not completely satisfied, I'll write "cancel" on your invoice, return it and owe nothing. The 2 FREE issues are mine to keep, no matter what!

Name _____

Address_____

City _____

State_____ZIP _____

E-mail _____

☐ You may contact me about my subscription via e-mail.
  (We won't use your address for any other purpose.)

Subscribers in Canada will be charged an additional US$10 (includes GST/HST) and invoiced. Outside the U.S. and Canada, add US$10 and remit payment in U.S. funds with this order. Annual newsstand rate: $71.88. Please allow 4-6 weeks for first-issue delivery.

Writer's Digest   www.writersdigest.com

J5FSMK

Get 2 FREE TRIAL ISSUES of

Writer's Digest
WRITE BETTER
GET PUBLISHED

Packed with creative inspiration, advice, and tips to guide you on the road to success, *Writer's Digest* offers everything you need to take your writing to the next level! You'll discover how to:

- Create dynamic characters and page-turning plots
- Submit query letters that publishers won't be able to refuse
- Find the right agent or editor
- Make it out of the slush-pile and into the hands of publishers
- Write award-winning contest entries
- And more!

See for yourself — order your 2 FREE trial issues today!

Geographic Index

NORTH DAKOTA
Record Companies
Makoche Recording Company 168

Classical Performing Arts
Greater Grand Forks Symphony Orchestra 297

OHIO
Music Publishers
Alexander Sr. Music 88
Barkin' Foe the Master's Bone 91
Marvin Publishing, John Weller 115
New Rap Jam Publishing, A 118

Record Companies
Deary Me Records 158
Heads Up Int., Ltd. 164
Sin Klub Entertainment, Inc. 182
Tangent® Records 185

Record Producers
DAP Entertainment 200
New Experience Records 212

Managers & Booking Agents
All Star Management 226
Backstreet Booking 229
Concept 2000 Inc. 234
Creative Star Management 235

Play Producers & Publishers
Ensemble Theatre 276

Classical Performing Arts
Lima Symphony Orchestra 300
Lithopolis Area Fine Arts Association 300

Organizations
Songwriters and Poets Critique 340

Workshops & Conferences
Undercurrents 356

OKLAHOMA
Music Publishers
Furrow Music 105
Jae Music, Jana 109
Old Slowpoke Music 120
SME Publishing Group 129

Record Companies
Cherry Street Records 154
Garrett Entertainment, Marty 162
Lark Record Productions, Inc. 168

Record Producers
Lark Talent & Advertising 209
Studio Seven 218

Managers & Booking Agents
D&R Entertainment 236
Jae Enterprises, Jana 243

Classical Performing Arts
Tulsa Opera Inc. 308

Contests & Awards
Billboard Song Contest 312

Organizations
Songwriters of Oklahoma 341

OREGON
Music Publishers
Earitating Music Publishing 102
High-Minded Moma Publishing & Productions 108
Moon June Music 117
Sandalphon Music Publishing 127

Record Companies
Flying Heart Records 161
Sandalphon Records 182

General Index

Use this index to locate specific markets and resources. Also, we list companies that appeared in the 2005 edition of *Songwriter's Market*, but do not appear this year. Instead of page numbers beside these markets you will find two-letter codes in parentheses that explain why these markets no longer appear. The codes are (**ED**)—Editorial Decision, (**NS**)—Not Accepting Submissions, (**NR**)No (or late) Response to Listing Request, (**OB**)—Out of Business, (**RR**)—Removed by Listing's Request, (**UC**)—Unable to Contact.

General Index

Songwriter's Market
Feedback

If you have a suggestion for improving *Songwriter's Market*, or would like to take part in a reader survey we conduct from time to time, please make a photocopy of this form (or cut it out of the book), fill it out, and return it to:

Songwriter's Market Feedback
4700 East Galbraith Road
Cincinnati, OH 45236
Fax: (513) 531-2686

◯ **Yes!** I'm willing to fill out a short survey by mail or online to provide feedback on *Songwriter's Market* or other books on songwriting.

◯ **Yes!** I have a suggestion to improve *Songwriter's Market* (attach a second sheet if more room is necessary):

_____

_____

_____

_____

_____

_____

_____

_____

Name: _____

Address: _____

City: _____ State: _____ Zip: _____

Phone: _____ Fax: _____

E-mail: _____ Website: _____

I am a

◯ songwriter
◯ performing songwriter
◯ musician
◯ other: _____